THE WORLD TRANSFORMED:

Swedenborg *and the* Last Judgment

THE WORLD TRANSFORMED:

Swedenborg *and the* Last Judgment

Dan A. Synnestvedt, General Editor

Bryn Athyn College Press
Bryn Athyn, Pennsylvania
2011

Copyright © 2011 by Bryn Athyn College Press
All rights reserved. Published 2011
General Editor, Dan A. Synnestvedt
Typeset by Lisa Childs
Dust jacket by Caroline Kline
Printed in the United States of America

ISBN-13: 978-0-910557-81-8 (HARDBACK)

Library of Congress Cataloging-in-Publication Data

Last Judgment Conference (2007 : Bryn Athyn, Pa.)
 The world transformed : Swedenborg and the Last Judgment / edited by Dan A.
Synnestvedt.
    p. cm.
 Includes bibliographical references and index.
 ISBN 978-0-910557-81-8 (hardback)
 1. Judgment Day--Congresses. 2. Swedenborg, Emanuel, 1688-1772--Congresses.
 3. New Jerusalem Church--Doctrines--Congresses. I. Synnestvedt, Dan A., 1964-
 II. Title.
 BX8729.L3L37 2007
 236'.9--dc22

                              2011010346

Printed in the United States of America

www.brynathyn.edu

Contents

Foreword

The book of Revelation is filled with dramatic events and images that captivate the mind: four six-winged creatures full of eyes along with twenty-four crowned elders worship Him who sits on the throne; a great red dragon with seven crowns on its heads attempts to devour a male baby born of a woman clothed with the sun; a blood-splattered lamb opens seven seals on a scroll, thereby unleashing conflict, scarcity, death, cosmic darkness, and earthquakes; an angel clothed with a rainbow, fire, and the sun hands John a little book which he eats; seated upon a white horse, Christ leads armies of heaven against the beast and the false prophet who are thrown into a lake of fire in defeat; then a fortified, square, shining, bejeweled city, the New Jerusalem, brings its light, a river of life, and a tree of life to heal the nations.

This letter of John's is also full of dramatic sounds: angels cry, martyrs cry, and the woman clothed with the sun cries out from her labor pains; seven trumpets sound; locusts with wings beating like the sound of chariots with many horses swarm out of the smoke; the kings and merchants who lived luxuriously with Babylon the Great cry out with weeping and wailing at her desolation; angels speak with trumpet-like voices; John hears great noises and thunderings, as well as the voice of a great multitude like the sound of many waters and thunderings saying, "Alleluia!" There are also ominous silences: the sound of harpists, musicians, flutists, trumpeters, craftsmen, and millstones will no longer be heard in the city of Babylon.

With such amazing sights and sounds, it is no wonder that John's Apocalypse is often viewed through a cataclysmic lens. After all, he recounts water turning into blood, and men being scorched with heat and getting malignant sores; he recounts earthquakes, hailstorms, and floods; he recounts several wars, and the destruction of a third of the sun, moon, and stars. So today we find books with titles such as *Apocalypse Burning: The Earth's Last Days*, and *Edge of the Apocalypse: The End Series*. Yet there is a positively-toned phase of apocalypticism too. The concluding vision of the New Jerusalem includes no curse, death, sorrow, pain, nor crying in a city that is full of light, life, healing, and peace. Accordingly, Barbara Rossing subtitled her book: *The Message of Hope in the Book of Revelation*. The reader of the present work will find that its contributors take this more hopeful approach to the future.

What are we to make of such an exciting prophetic letter? Some have made of it "everything," while others, like the Christian man who found it "bizarre and tangential" to a maturing faith, have made of it "nothing." Certainly the world is transformed through this dramatic revealing, but what sort of transformation is it? There is a very long tradition of reading and interpreting the book of Revelation, one that begins with theologians of the early Christian church. It is thought that John wrote his letter sometime between AD 49 and 95 while he was exiled from Rome and living on the island of Patmos near the coast of modern day Turkey. From AD 130, when Bishop Papias of Hierapolis flourished, down to our own day, theologians and others have struggled to comprehend the meaning of this letter. Evidence of a variety of interpretations of Revelation is found in the book *Dialogue with the Jew Tryphon* by Justin Martyr, who lived between 100 and 165 AD. Indeed, each era in the history of western civilization contains debates over the meaning of Revelation. For example, the great physicist Isaac Newton complained of the private, non-methodical interpretations prevalent in the seventeenth century and spent quite a bit of time searching for the right hermeneutical method. After Newton's death, his nephew Benjamin Smith published his famous uncle's *Observations upon the Prophecies of Daniel, and the Apocalypse of St. John* in 1733. It sold very well. The scientist, inventor, philosopher, and theologian Emanuel Swedenborg (1688-1772) states, in the preface to his *Apocalypse Revealed* of 1766, that "There are many who have labored in the explanation of the *Apocalypse*. . . ." After searching for a book that compared some major credible approaches to Revelation and not finding one, a twentieth century American Christian teacher, Steve Gregg, wrote *Revelation: Four Views, a Parallel Commentary* in 1997. While Gregg's book does not contain all possible approaches to Revelation, we will summarize his four views in order to provide context for Swedenborg's interpretation, which is the one that is used in the present volume.

Gregg describes the following four views: historicist, preterist, futurist, and idealist. We will begin with the historicist view.

The historicist approach assumes that the book of Revelation predicts the events that will befall the Christian church. For example, the breaking of the seven seals represents the barbarian invasions of the western Roman empire and church. The scorpion-like locusts from the smoke of the bottomless pit represent the Arab hordes attacking the eastern Roman empire and church. This approach also uses the "year-for-a-day" principle when dealing with designations of time, so that 1,260 days (Rev.11.3) = 1,260 years. One firm idea in classic Protestant historicist exposition is that the Antichrist represents the papacy.

When it comes to the second view, preterism, Gregg uses a conservative early-date version. This approach assumes that the prophecies in Revelation were fulfilled with the fall of Jerusalem in AD 70 and the fall of the Roman empire. "Preter" means in the past; bygone; past action or state. From this viewpoint many of the prophecies were fulfilled centuries ago. One strength of this approach is that John's letter is relevant to the original readers, as it promises deliverance from persecutions of the second century AD. Another is that it does not require an alternative meaning to the literal sense of passages such as Revelation 1.1 and 22.10, which state that the events predicted "must shortly take place" and that "the time is at hand".

The third view, futurism, holds that the book refers to events which are to occur in the future. This is the position taken by a majority of the most popular evangelical writers. Based upon the statement in Revelation 1.19, the book is divided into three sections: the first, having to do with the things that John has seen, is chapter one. The second, having to do with the things "which are," is chapters two and three. The third, having to do with "the things which will take place after this," is chapters four to the end. Futurists apply everything after chapter four to a relatively brief period before the return of Christ. Of the four views, futurists are the most likely to take a literal approach. Gregg observes that "every generation of futuristic interpreters for the past 150 years or longer has been able to find in Revelation a description of their own times" and that this approach has been referred to as "newspaper exegesis" (42).

The idealist view, which Gregg calls the spiritual approach, is also known as the non-literal, allegorical, symbolic, or poetic view. Into the idealist category he places all approaches "that do not look for individual or specific fulfillments of the prophecies in Revelation in the natural sense, but which believe only that spiritual lessons and principles (which may find recurrent expression in history) are depicted symbolically in the visions" (43). There is no single fulfillment of the prophecies. The book is a great drama involving transcendent truths, such as the conflict between good and evil, or Christ and Satan, that can be applied to Christians in any age. Thus the battles in Apocalypse are about spiritual warfare and principles of human conduct, and the great harlot is the compromised church in any era and how the divine moral government operates with such a worldly institution.

Here are two examples from *Revelation: Four Views* that clearly illustrate each approach. First, in Revelation chapters eight through ten, seven angels blow seven trumpets that produce a variety of results, ranging from hail and fire mingled with blood that burns up a third of the trees and all of the grass, to the releasing of the four angels bound at the Euphrates river, to John himself being given a book to eat. According to Gregg, this is the interpretation of these chapters given by each of the four approaches:

The historicist thinks that the trumpets

speak of a series of invasions against the Roman Empire (Vandals, Huns, Saracens, and Turks). The sixth trumpet brings the fall of Constantinople to the Turks (1453). The little book represents the Bible being made available to the masses of Europe after the invention of the printing press (143).

The preterist holds that the

first four trumpets correspond to disasters inflicted by the Romans on the Jews in the Jewish war (A.D. 66-70). The fifth trumpet probably depicts the demonic spirits rendering the besieged Jews irrational and self-destructive. The sixth trumpet refers to the Roman armies, who destroyed Jerusalem and slaughtered or deported all the Jews (143).

The futurist believes that

either literally or symbolically, the trumpets represent calamities that will be endured by the unrepentant inhabitants of earth during the coming seven year Tribulation. These may be supernatural judgments direct from the hand of God or merely the disastrous effects of man's improper stewardship of the earth and his abuse of technology (e.g., nuclear weapons) (143).

Lastly, the idealist maintains that

catastrophes reminiscent of the plagues of Egypt befall sinful humanity many times in history, demonstrating God's displeasure and, like trumpet blasts, warning of worse things to come upon the unrepentant. Sinful humanity typically absorbs these injuries with defiance, refusing to repent (143).

Our second example is from Revelation chapters fourteen through sixteen. Here, while an angel announces that Babylon is fallen, other angels use a sickle to reap the harvest of earth, and then one of the four living creatures gives to the seven angels seven golden bowls full of the wrath of God, and the angels pour them out upon the earth with cataclysmic effects.

According to Gregg, the historicist believes, in general, that

the seven bowls of wrath find fulfillment in the judgment upon the papacy (Babylon), beginning with the French Revolution and the Napoleonic Wars and concluding yet in the future (309).

The preterist holds that

the judgments of these bowls are largely against Jerusalem, culminating in its fall in A.D. 70, though the fifth bowl touches the Roman Empire as well—probably referring to the chaotic state of affairs that prevailed after Nero's suicide. Alternatively, this section says nothing about the fall of Jerusalem and refers strictly to the judgment of God upon pagan Rome. (309)

The futurist believes that

the bowls represent future, global judgments that, in their devastating effect, are unparalleled in history. These occur at the very end of the Tribulation period, culminating in World War III, or the Battle of Armageddon. This war is the last battle to be fought by mankind, and it will be ended by the personal appearing of Christ as He comes to establish His millennial kingdom. (309)

Lastly, the idealist maintains that

there is a relationship between the bowl judgments and the trumpet judgments. The former may be a recapitulation of the latter. The principal distinction between the trumpets and the bowls is that the former are partial in their effects and serve to warn the wicked of their spiritual danger, whereas the latter are complete and represent final judgment upon the unrepentant. The same event in history may serve as a trumpet judgment for one person (a mere warning) and as a bowl judgment for another (a final judgment, resulting in death). The disasters described recur in history repeatedly. (309)

As distinct in their interpretation of Revelation as they are, these four views are not mutually exclusive. As Gregg observes, though evangelical commentators commonly reject the idealist view as a liberal alternative, they employ its methods in their books. Indeed, they often mix futurism, preterism, and idealism. I found that each approach uses, even if it does not acknowledge, a symbolic hermeneutic. While not much of a departure from the literal sense, even the historicist principle of "year-for-a-day" still takes the word "day" to stand for something different from one twenty-four hour period. The question is, which, if any, of these four views does Swedenborg hold? Let us explore the answer to this question.

Swedenborg's approach is historicist in the sense that the book of Revelation does make predictions about the spiritual, and thence the natural, future of the church. In this sense, John's letter is about the ages of the church, including its birth, maturity, decline, death, and eventual re-birth as a new Christianity. Swedenborg takes historical events and links them to verses in Revelation, but the events are not Roman, barbarian, Turkish or Arab invasions. Instead, they are events (usually innovations in doctrine and life) within the Christian church primarily, and secondarily among all people on earth who were either genuinely religious or pseudo-religious.

As for preterism, I find no similarities between this approach and Swedenborg's. The same is mostly true of futurism. Except for the continuing descent of the Holy City New Jerusalem, all of the events in Revelation are *not* still in the future from a New Church or Swedenborgian point of view. The events of Revelation are in the past (hence the commemoration of the 250th anniversary of the Last Judgment), and they were in the *present* from Swedenborg's standpoint. Even so, there is no evidence of "newspaper exegesis" in his *Apocalypse Revealed*. Significantly for his hermeneutic, there is also an overwhelming rejection of the literalism that accompanies futurism.

Of the four approaches, the one with which Swedenborg has the most in common is the last, the idealist. His interpretation is in agreement with the claim that there are transcendental principles and recurrent themes in Revelation and its meaning. This is due to the transcendent and eternal nature of God, who is the ultimate author of the Word, the transcendent and immortal nature of human beings, and the use of correspondential writing. The other terms used for this view—symbolic and spiritual—also apply to Swedenborg's approach. Swedenborg shows that the writers of the Old Testament and the Gospels use a set of symbols consistently to convey the message of God to humans throughout history. He is also emphatic that the events of the Apocalypse take place in the spiritual world, which is linked to the spiritual sense of John's letter and the rest of the Bible, for the sake of the spiritual salvation of each individual human being as part of the spiritual renewal of the church and the spiritual development of humanity across the universe. Revelation did have meaning for those alive at the time it was written, at least for those who knew something of correspondences, but it also had meaning for the angels and spirits in the spiritual world, both then and now.

However, there is one caveat to the similarity between Swedenborg's approach and that of the idealist. His approach contradicts the idealist assertion that there was no single fulfillment of the prophecies, and this is based upon Swedenborg's witnessing the prophesied events themselves. For Swedenborg, there was indeed a single fulfillment of the prophecies, primarily in the spiritual world and secondarily in the natural world through his writing and publication of several theological works revealing the inner meaning of the Bible and the nature of true Christianity.

Another phrase used to describe the fourth view, the philosophy of history approach, is also applicable to the Swedenborgian or New Church perspective. Like other philosophers of history, the authors of this book engage in making sense out of the past by using a set of assumptions to interpret events. The following contributors especially use a New Church framework that sees natural effects caused by a spiritual event 250 years ago: Michael Hogan, Jeremy Simons, Erik E. Sandstrom, Christopher Bown, Jane Williams Hogan, Sonia Werner, Brian Henderson, Forrest Dristy, and Dan Synnestvedt. The chapters by Walter Orthwein and the final contribution by Michael Hogan give us a perspective not on the past, but a glimpse into the future.

Steve Gregg provided a useful book to those who wish to use their reason in freedom to understand John's letter and then choose the interpretation of it that makes the most sense to them. We are in his debt for helping to further the spiritual enlightenment and increase the choices of clergy and laity alike. Such a book is entirely within the spirit of a New Church understanding of the effects of the Last Judgment and the Second Advent of the Lord. The New Church scholars who have contributed to this book also intend to further the spiritual enlightenment of humanity while offering a new interpretation of the Last Judgment. It is my hope that this foreword has whetted the reader's appetite to explore not only the current volume, whose individual essays or sections may be read independently of one another, but also Swedenborg's explanations of the Last Judgment and Second Coming contained in his theological works. As John wrote, "And the Spirit and the bride say, 'Come!' And let him who thirsts come. And whoever desires, let him take the water of life freely" (Rev. 22.17).

Dan A. Synnestvedt
January, 2011
Bryn Athyn, Pennsylvania, USA

Preface

H "The Last Judgment Conference was the best conference I have attended, and I hope there will be many more of the same high quality. The [New] Church would need that as an injection again and again."

Testimony of Rev. Erik Sandstrom, Sr., age 98

New Church scholarship in Last Judgment studies is absolutely unique. It derives its premises and problematic from the inspired Writings of Emanuel Swedenborg. An essential element of the Writings is that the Last Judgment has already taken place. It was a judgment on the Christian Church which occurred in the spiritual world in the year 1757. Unlike contemporary Christian views of that judgment, the New Church does not believe that it will bring about the end of the natural world. Instead, the Writings state that this event was a spiritual judgment and had no immediate physical impact on the natural world. This judgment ended the Christian Church as a spiritual organization while setting the stage for the founding of the New Christian Church in 1770. This was done for the spiritual salvation of mankind.

To say that this judgment had no immediate impact on nature is not to say that it had no impact whatsoever. The impact, in fact, was real and far-reaching. It was, however, a mediated impact. The Last Judgment removed spiritual impediments from the human pursuit of truth and good. It quickened and enlivened the spiritual and intellectual capacities of the natural man by restoring his spiritual freedom and permitting him to enter "intellectually" into the mysteries of faith. Thus, we would expect to see increased intellectual and cultural activity in its wake. Given the fact that humans remain in spiritual freedom, there is no guarantee that only good would flow from this increased power. In fact, as we know, great evils have been committed in our time. The essential point to keep in mind is that the Last Judgment permitted vast amounts of energy to animate the human mind, and through it to penetrate into nature. In addition, since this influx was from the Lord, there was another dimension to it. The Lord is both good itself and truth itself. Thus, increased influx from Him contains both of these qualities. Mixed with the power of truth we see a desire for the good of use. This desire to do good to and for the neighbor was also quickened during this time: we find reform societies and improvement movements of every description being founded and increasing well into the nineteenth century. But as we know, great evils have been committed by perverted "good" as well as by false "truth." The power of the unregenerate can be a very dangerous thing. To contain and direct this power we have been given a new revelation and the New Church. We must use this revelation to understand the origins of our age and construct ways to bring the Lord's Word to it.

These were the purposes behind the conference held in Bryn Athyn, Pennsylvania on October 5th and 6th, 2007. Its formal title was: *The World Transformed: The Impact of the Last Judgment on Human Knowledge and Values.* It was sponsored by the Cole Foundation for Renewing the Culture and supported by Bryn Athyn College of the New Church. The conference participants are extremely grateful for the constant support provided by these two institutions. The papers given at the conference are presented in these Proceedings. They are grouped by topic and are given here in full text, whereas the conference presentations were altered to meet time constraints. Following each set of three papers there is an analytical discussion of them by a senior New Church scholar. These are also full text versions of the comments made by these reviewers at the conference. The first paper in this volume is an introduction provided by the conference chair. The last paper is a retrospective on the conference and a call for ongoing work in this area. The conference format and brief biographical sketches of the participants are included.

We find ourselves in the post-Last Judgment world. This modern age is dominated by the naturalism of the Enlightenment. The papers in this volume attempt to shed a New Church light on the nature of this world. This light is sorely needed today since the temper of our times shuns any form of spiritual analysis. However, the widespread persistence of religion in the face of the triumph of modern rationalism suggests that there are many, even at the very end of the Christian Church, who would welcome a deepened spiritual life. These are the "simple" whom the established churches dominated for the sake of secular power. It was for the salvation of these people, and for the billions of others around the world, both born and unborn, that the Lord brought the Last Judgment on the Christian Church. It was for this end that Swedenborg was chosen to receive the new revelation for the New Church. This revelation is the Second Coming of the Lord Jesus Christ whose heavenly purposes we seek to glorify and serve. ⚜

Michael H. Hogan
Conference Chair

The Cole Foundation and Bryn Athyn College Present

The World Transformed:
The Impact of the Last Judgment
on Human Knowledge and Values

Friday, October 5th and Saturday, October 6th, 2007

Schedule of Presentations: Each presentation/discussion is between 30–40 min.
The papers are delivered consecutively.

Friday, Oct. 5—(morning session 9:00 a.m.-noon)
Introduction and Welcoming Remarks—Michael H. Hogan, Conference Chair
African Spirituality—Rev. Jeremy Simons, Ekow Eshun, Brian Smith (assist)
Islam and the Last Judgment—Rev. Dr. Erik Sandstrom, Abigail Echols (assist)

Break—15 min.
The Last Judgment and the Ancient Word in China—
    Rev. Christopher Bown
Discussant—Rev. Eric Carswell
Open discussion and questions
Afternoon Session (1:00 p.m.–4:00 p.m.)
The Child and Songs of Innocence—Dr. Jane Williams-Hogan,
    Kendra Knight (assist)
The Last Judgment's Profound Effect on Women—
    Dr. Sonia Soneson Werner, Megan Malone (assist)
Break—15 min.
Swedenborg and Abolition—Dean Brian Henderson,
    Wystan Carswell (assist)
Discussant—Rev. Göran Appelgren
Open discussion and questions

Evening (7:30 p.m.)
Film: *Amazing Grace*—Open to Bryn Athyn community, high school
    age & older.
    Host: Dean Brian Henderson

Saturday, Oct. 6 (morning session 9:00 a.m.–noon)
Swedenborg's New Scientific Paradigm—Dr. Reuben Bell
The Liberation of Mathematics—Prof. Forrest Dristy
Break—15 min.
Ideas for Swedenborgian Mathematical Illustration—
    Dr. Neil Simonetti, Robert Cooper (assist)
Discussant—Dr. Gregory Baker
Open discussion and questions

Afternoon Session (1:00 p.m.–4:00 p.m.)
Swedenborg and Locke—Rev. Andrew Dibb, Christopher Barber
    (assist)
The Last Judgment, Cosmology and Theological Interpretation—
    Dr. Allen Bedford

Break—15 mins.

The Prominence of Naturalism after the Last Judgment—

Dr. Dan Synnestvedt, Malcolm Smith (assist)

Discussant—Rev. Stephen Cole

Open discussion and questions

Evening (7:00 p.m.)

Banquet at Glencairn—Keynote address—Rev. Walter Orthwein

CONFERENCE SPEAKERS AND DISCUSSANTS

Rev. Göran Appelgren. Pastor of the Stockholm Society since 1994. Regional Pastor for Europe. Ordained in 1992. Visiting minister to Copenhagen from 1992-1996. Traveling to different countries in Europe, including the Ukraine, Georgia, and Russia. Married to Josephine Turner from England, 3 children who are 14, 12, and 9 (in 2007). Email: 1.6.1770@telia.com

Dr. Gregory Baker is Professor Emeritus of Physics and Mathematics at Bryn Athyn College. He is the author of more than sixty publications and the author or co-author of three books, *Chaotic dynamics: an introduction* (Cambridge Univ. Press, 1990, 1996), *Religion and Science: from Swedenborg to chaotic dynamics* (Solomon Press, 1992), and *The Pendulum: a case study in physics* (Oxford Univ. Press, 2005). Email: gregmarg@msn.com

Dr. Allen Bedford is Associate Professor of Chemistry at Bryn Athyn College and was Chair of the Mathematics and Science Division. He has been heavily involved in developing the College's Core curriculum. His New Church research interests are in building a framework for academic inquiry that balances information from revelation and experience. Over the past few years he has been developing and testing this framework in the context of the plurality of worlds question. Email: allen.bedford@brynathyn.edu

Dr. Reuben P. Bell. B.S. and M.S. in Zoology from the Univ. of Tulsa, graduated from Oklahoma State Univ. College of Osteopathic Medicine in 1979. Board certified in Family Medicine. M.Div. from Bryn Athyn College of the New Church Theological School in 1997. Associate Professor of Biology at Bryn Athyn College. Associate Professor of Family Medicine and Director of Medical Humanities at the Univ. of New England College of Osteopathic Medicine (2003). His academic interests include the philosophy of osteopathy, and the science and metaphysics of Emanuel Swedenborg.
Email: reubenpbell@gmail.comnpbell@gmail.com

Rev. Christopher Bown was pastor for the New Church Buccleauch in Johannesburg, South Africa. Chris Bown has explored the questions about the Ancient Word in China since he was a college student. During the past 10 years he has traveled to China three times in search of the Ancient Word.
Email: chrisbown@mweb.co.za@mweb.co.za

Rev. Eric H. Carswell. Vice Chancellor of the Bryn Athyn College of the New Church. B.A., Pennsylvania State Univ., M.Ed., Lehigh Univ., M.Div., BAC Theological School.
Email: eric.carswell@ancts.orgeric.carswell@ancts.org

Rev. Stephen Cole is an Assistant Professor of Philosophy and Religion and Head of the Religion and Sacred Language Division at Bryn Athyn College of the New Church.
Email: stephen.cole@brynathyn.edu

Rev. Andrew Dibb. Head of the Academy of the New Church Theological School, B.A., Bryn Athyn College, M.Div., ANC Theological School, B.Th., M.Th., D.Th., Univ. of South Africa.
Email: andrew.dibb@ancts.org

Professor Forrest Dristy obtained a Ph.D. from Florida State Univ. in 1962. From 1968-1993 he was Professor of Mathematics at the State

Univ. of New York at Oswego. He now is a migratory retiree who lives with his wife Peggy in Delray Beach, Florida and Oswego, New York.

Email: fdristy@hotmail.com

Dean Brian Henderson is Assistant Professor of History and the Dean of Student Affairs at Bryn Athyn College. He has also collaborated with Ed Gyllenhaal as co-creators and co-editors of www.newchurch-history.org, a website dedicated to scholarship related to the influence of the theological works of Emanuel Swedenborg and the history of the New Church from the eighteenth century to the present.

Email: brian.henderson@brynathyn.edu

Mr. Michael H. Hogan is an Assistant Librarian at the Swedenborg Library of Bryn Athyn College. He has a B.A. from Fordham College and a M.A. from the Univ. of Pennsylvania.

Email: michael.hogan@brynathyn.edu

Rev. Walter O. Orthwein was Assistant Professor of Religion, Bryn Athyn College Theological School. B.A. Univ. of Missouri, M.Div., Andover-Newton Theological School.

Email: walter.orthwein@ancts.org

Rev. Dr. Erik Sandstrom was editor of *New Church Life* and is Curator of Swedenborgiana at the Swedenborg Library. He has been teaching at Bryn Athyn College since 1993 and introduced the first courses on Islam. In 2002 he served as Head of the Religion and Sacred Languages Division. In 2005 he received a Ph.D. in Religious Thought from Temple Univ.

Email: erik.sandstrom@brynathyn.edu

Dr. Neil Simonetti. Associate Professor of Computer Science and Mathematics, Bryn Athyn College (10 years). B.S., Virginia Polytechnic Inst., M.S., Ph.D., Carnegie Mellon Univ. His research centers around a dynamic programming algorithm for the Traveling Salesman

Problem, a classic problem in the field of combinatorial optimization, with applications ranging from scheduling to vehicle routing.
Email: neil.simonetti@brynathyn.edu

Rev. Jeremy Simons is Pastor of the Bryn Athyn Church, has a degree in economics from the Univ. of Pennsylvania, a Masters and Principal's Certificate in Ed. from Lehigh Univ., as well as an M.Div. from BAC Theological School. 1976-78 he was a Peace Corps volunteer working in agricultural education in Togo, West Africa, and has traveled widely in Africa, visiting Ghana and Togo most recently in 1999.
Email: jeremy.simons@bacs-gc.org

Dr. Sonia Soneson Werner studied at Bryn Athyn College, Western Connecticut State and Univ., Iowa State Univ. She has taught at Bryn Athyn College for eleven years. She holds a Ph.D. in developmental psychology, with focus on moral development of children. Teaching psychology courses in educational psych., social psych. psych. at the workplace, introductory psych., and leadership.
Email: soni.werner@brynathyn.edu

Dr. Dan Synnestvedt is an Associate Professor of Philosophy at Bryn Athyn College of the New Church where he has taught philosophy for twenty-two years. He lives in Bryn Athyn with his wife, Lisa, and their two children.
Email: dan.synnestvedt@brynathyn.edu

Professor Jane Williams-Hogan Ph.D. has taught sociology and history at Bryn Athyn College since 1975. She has written articles on Swedenborg and Swedenborgianism for a variety of publications. She is currently writing a biography of Swedenborg to be published in 2010 entitled: *The Making of a Modern Visionary, Emanuel Swedenborg: Eyewitness to the Apocalypse*. Married to Michael H. Hogan, together they have six children and ten grandchildren!
Email: janewh@dwave.com

Acknowledgments

As one can see from the table of contents, this book is the result of many minds. Without New Church scholars' willingness to participate in the 2007 conference dedicated to marking the 250th anniversary of the Last Judgment, the book you hold would not exist. The idea for the conference came from the creative minds of Jane and Michael Hogan, two scholars whose eagerness to promote New Church research and education is seemingly tireless. Along with Michael's consistent communication with all the parties involved and Jane's encouragement, Erik Odhner's coordination with The Cole Foundation ensured a successful conclusion to the event and these proceedings. The "creative space" made possible by The Cole Foundation and its financial support were essential in launching this endeavor. We have also benefited mightily from the minds of two English majors. Skye Kerr and Chara Odhner substantially improved the quality of our discourse and clarified the prose for our readers. This general editor is very, very thankful for their detailed editorial work. Dr. Erland Brock's relationship with the ANC publication committee and his knowledge of the printing of books is, once again, invaluable. Appreciation must also be expressed for the ANC publication committee; its members have enthusiastically supported the project.

This book is also the result of many hands, but none more so than Lisa B. Childs'. Through the seasons, house renovations, editorial revisions, and in sickness and in health, Lisa has patiently formatted this volume. She is a master of software, organization, and detail. I am deeply grateful for the faithful application of her skills to this project and her consistent dedication to the work.

Dan A. Synnestvedt
January, 2011
Bryn Athyn, Pennsylvania, USA

A Note On Citations

The essays in this book refer to works of the Heavenly Doctrine of the New Jerusalem (commonly known as "the Writings" in Swedenborgian circles) by means of a style that is often used when the works of a single author play a major part in a book. For example, the reader will find this quotation in the first essay of this book: "Spiritual equilibrium is a state of freedom for us and for spirits." This is followed by a parenthetical citation: (HH 590). This citation refers to the work published by Emanuel Swedenborg in 1758 entitled *De Caelo et Ejus Mirabilibus et de Inferno, Ex Auditis et Visis.* This title is translated as *Heaven and Its Wonder and Hell, from Things Heard and Seen* which is abbreviated HH, for *Heaven and Hell.* Since Swedenborg himself numbered paragraphs in the originals and the pagination of different editions varies, with good reason it has become common practice to refer to ideas in, or statements from, the theological and philosophical works of Swedenborg using an abbreviation of the title followed by a paragraph number. Thus, in our example, a reader can turn to any edition or translation of *De Caelo et Ejus Mirabilibus et de Inferno* that contains paragraph numbers, find number 590, and read that spiritual equilibrium is a state of freedom for us and for spirits. As stated above, this citation style is not unusual in the humanities. Books on Immanuel Kant's philosophy, for example, frequently use this style. (See *Kant's Philosophy of Religion Reconsidered*, edited by Philip J. Rossi and Michael Wreen, Bloomington, IN: Indiana University Press, 1991, xxi–xxiii, where Kant's *Critique of Pure Reason* is referred to as CPR followed by a number.) What follows is a list of the works of the Heavenly Doctrines (also referred to as the Writings) in English that are cited by the authors of the essays in this volume, preceded by the abbreviation that is used.

Abom—*Abomination of Desolation*

AC—*Arcana Coelestia*, E. Swedenborg. (1748-1756) (see SH)

Adv—*Adversaria*

AE—*Apocalypse Explained*, E. Swedenborg. (written 1758-1759*)

AR—*Apocalypse Revealed*, E. Swedenborg. (1766)

Ath—*Athanasian Creed*

BE—*Brief Exposition*, E. Swedenborg (1768-1769)

Calvin—*Conversations with Calvin**

Canons—*Canons of the New Church*, E. Swedenborg. (written 1769*)

Charity—*Doctrine of Charity*, E. Swedenborg. (written 1766*)

CL—*Delights of Wisdom concerning Conjugial Love*, E. Swedenborg. (see also ML)

CLJ—*Continuation concerning the Last Judgment*, E. Swedenborg (1763) see also *Supplements*

Conv—*Conversation with Angels*, E. Swedenborg. (written 1766*)

Coro—*Coronis or Appendix to the True Christian Religion*, E. Swedenborg. (written 1771*)

De Verbo—de Verbo (or *Concerning the Sacred Scripture or the Word of the Lord from Experience*), E. Swedenborg. (written 1762*)

DLW— *Angelic Wisdom concerning the Divine Love and Wisdom*, E. Swedenborg. (1763)

DP—*Angelic Wisdom concerning the Divine Providence*, E. Swedenborg. (1764)

D.Wis—*Concerning Divine Wisdom*, E. Swedenborg. (written 1763*)

EU—*Earths in the Universe*, E. Swedenborg. (1756-1758) (see OP)

Faith—*Doctrine of the New Jerusalem concerning Faith*, E. Swedenborg. (1763)

HH—*Heaven and its wonders and Hell*, E. Swedenborg. (1758)

Inf—*The Infinite and the Final Cause of Creation*, E. Swedenborg. (1734)

Inv—*Invitation to the New Church*, E. Swedenborg. (written 1771*) (abbreviation also seen as "I")

ISB—*Interaction of the Soul and Body* (also *Intercourse between the Soul and Body*) (1769)

Life—*Doctrine of Life for the New Jerusalem*, E. Swedenborg. (1763)

LJ—*Last Judgment*, E. Swedenborg.

LJ post—*Last Judgment Posthumous*, E. Swedenborg. (written 1762*)

Lord—*Doctrine of the New Jerusalem concerning the Lord*, E. Swedenborg. (1763)

ML—*Married Love*, Delights of Wisdom concerning Conjugial Love, E. Swedenborg. (1768) (see also CL)

MTW—*Miscellaneous Theological Works*, E. Swedenborg.

NewSearch—a computer program that enables a person to search Swedenborg's theological Writings and other related documents. Available at www.Heavenlydoctrines.org. Can be purchased as "NewSearch CD" from New Church Bookstore online.

NCE—New Century Edition of the theological works of Swedenborg

NIV—*New International Version (Bible)*

NJHD—*New Jerusalem and Its Heavenly Doctrine*, E. Swedenborg. (1758)

OP—*Other Planets* (NCE), E. Swedenborg. (1756-1758) (see EU)

PP—*Summaries of the Internal Sense of the Prophets and the Psalms*, E. Swedenborg. (written 1759-1760*)

SD—*The Soul's Domain* (*Dynamics of the Soul's Domain*), E. Swedenborg. (1744-1745)

SE—*Spiritual Experiences*, published first under English title, *Spiritual Diary*, E. Swedenborg. (written 1747-1765*)

SEm—*Spiritual Experiences Minor*, repeated passages 4545-4792 in Swedenborg's diary *Spiritual Experiences*

SH—*Secrets of Heaven (NCE)*, E. Swedenborg.(1748-1756) (see also AC)

SS—*Doctrine of the New Jerusalem concerning the Sacred Scripture*, E. Swedenborg. (1763)

SPL—*Supplements (NCE)*, E. Swedenborg. (1763) (see CLJ)

TC—*True Christianity (NCE)*, E. Swedenborg. (1771) (see TCR)

TCR—*True Christian Religion*, E. Swedenborg. (1771) (see TC)

WH—*White Horse*, E. Swedenborg. (1758)

* published posthumously

For a complete list of Swedenborg's published and unpublished works see "Annotated Bibliography of Swedenborg's Writings" by Jonathan S. Rose in *Scribe of Heaven: Swedenborg's Life, Work, and Impact*, edited by Jonathan S. Rose, Stuart Shotwell, and Mary Lou Bertucci (West Chester, PA: Swedenborg Foundation, 2005).

The Last Judgment and Its Challenge To New Church Scholarship

MICHAEL H. HOGAN[1]

INTRODUCTION

The first version of this paper was produced in September 2005 for the Cole Foundation for Renewing the Culture. Its purpose was to provide a rationale for a conference of New Church scholars to commemorate the 250th anniversary of the Last Judgment. This conference was held in 2007 and the papers which were presented there have been collected in this volume of Proceedings. This revised version of the paper provides an introduction to these collected papers and provides the theological and intellectual groundwork for them.

The following essay will describe the spiritual context of the Last Judgment, how and where it took place, and its implications for the human race on earth. I will structure this discussion around various relevant passages from the Writings (denoted by Roman numerals) and develop appropriate implications from them as the essay progresses.

I. There is constant balance between heaven and hell. An effort to do evil is constantly emanating up from hell, and an effort to do good is constantly emanating down from heaven. The world of spirits is in this equilibrium (its location is halfway between heaven and hell). The reason the world of spirits is in this equilibrium is that after death we first enter the world of spirits and are kept in the same state in which we were in the world. This could not happen unless there were a perfect balance there. This allows everyone to be examined

1. The author wishes to acknowledge the assistance of Kendra Knight in the preparation of the draft of this essay.

there as to quality, since we keep the same kind of freedom we had in the world. Spiritual equilibrium is a state of freedom for us and for spirits. (HH 590)

The spiritual world is arranged so that human freedom can be maintained within the balance of competing forces, and unless the Lord Himself maintained this balance we would be overwhelmed. This balance permits us, in freedom, to choose the life of heaven or of hell since without human freedom there can be no judgment. The hells are very powerful and can be kept in check only by constant, intricate effort on the Lord's part (HH 593). In fact, the hells are so powerful that they are permitted no direct contact with humans on earth or in the world of spirits.

The inhabitants of hell—demons—are so consumed with self-love that they cannot now be saved. They are implacably hostile to heaven and constantly try to strike against it. They hate anything that is not of service to themselves. It is almost impossible to describe their fury. It is also quite frightening to realize that this intense self-love exists within all of us as well. This profound self-love is called the "proprium" because it is the most defining, the most appropriate passion of all natural life. If we were not held in balance by the Lord, we would choose to be in hell; a demon is nothing more than a human being who has rejected the Lord's call to love Him and the neighbor. Although such an individual takes many of his human characteristics with him to hell—speech, symbolic thought, guile, planning skills, and the talent of coordinated action—this state of rejection makes him "viler than the beasts" because these human attributes make him more dangerous. He can imagine creative ways to achieve his will, justify himself through his perverted intellect, and carry out despicable acts with imaginative brutality. We are no match for his formidable malice. The Lord's action alone enables us the free space, externally and internally, to choose heaven.

Just as the Lord's Providence does not permit direct contact between demons and people, neither does it permit contact between people and the angels of the highest heaven since contact with these angels would also violate human freedom. Humans would be overwhelmed by the Divine love present with these angels to such an extent that they could not choose good or evil through their own free will but would be immediately swept into heaven without the internal reformation necessary to have acted voluntarily. Only the choice to be led by the Lord made in true freedom permits entry into heaven. The Lord never compels anyone to be saved.

So the question arises: if the highest heaven and the lowest hell, powerful as they are, are not permitted direct contact with us, how are the choices of good and evil effectively provided for us without our freedom being compromised? Swedenborg addresses this issue in the following passages:

> II. So that we can be in freedom for the sake of our reformation, we are united in spirit with heaven and with hell. With each of us there are spirits from hell and angels from heaven. By means of the spirits from hell we encounter our evil, and by means of angels from heaven we encounter the good we have from the Lord. As a result, we are in a spiritual equilibrium—that is, in freedom. We need to be aware that our union with heaven and with hell is not directly with them but is mediated by spirits who are in the world of spirits. These spirits are with us, more from hell itself or from heaven itself. We are united to hell through evil spirits in the world of spirits, and with heaven through the good spirits there. Because of this arrangement, the world of spirits is halfway between heaven and hell and is at the point of balance. We can see from this where we get our freedom. (HH 599–600)

The world of spirits thus provides a medium of contact between heaven, hell, and the human race. The good spirits there are in love to the neighbor and the bad spirits are in love to the world. These spirits entered the spiritual world after death and remained there until they freely chose the life of heaven (love to the Lord) or that of hell (love of self). It should be noted that love to the neighbor is a form of love to the Lord that has yet to be fully developed and its inner essence made manifest. The same can be said of love of the world, which is clearly a form of self-love still differentiated from it only because it still accommodates itself to other persons and objects. It is not yet so obsessed that it must satisfy itself at every moment, in every circumstance. Thus love of the world uses honor, reputation, and gain to achieve the fruits of self-love. It seduces rather than rapes, swindles rather than robs, flatters rather than coerces, and commands rather than destroys. As Swedenborg tells us, a life of this kind eventually confirms itself in us until we become impatient, dispense with the forms and niceties of worldly social order, and seize objects of our desire directly. At this point we acknowledge no external restraints and become frank predators. The Lord then allows us to be removed into hell, which is the true goal of our love. There we act out our evils with similar demons in a never-ending cycle of obsession and victimization.

A parallel reality with an opposite outcome unfolds among those spirits in love to the neighbor. Here the continuing effort to act charitably for the good of another produces both control of the self and a genuine desire to learn what real good is. Since the ultimate of charity consists of doing the highest good for the neighbor, the spirit is constantly driven to seek the greatest good. Over time this striving after the essence of good leads the spirit to the conclusion that the Lord Himself is the highest good. Thus, love to the Lord is discovered to be the true end of charity. At this point the Lord allows the spirit to enter heaven and live out eternity with the other angels.

It must be stressed that the world of spirits exists for the salvation of mankind. Spirits from there, both good and bad, visit humans in the natural world in order that humans may be presented with the means for making spiritual choices. Temptations, hardships, inspiration, humiliation, and triumph are all part of the spiritual drama that is the legacy of every human. The passage through the natural world is the context within which we make eternal spiritual choices. With us at every step of the way are spirits who wish us good or ill. They provide charitable explanation for adversity, or they fan our resentment even as we receive high honors. They enflame our jealousies as well as justify our lusts. They help us marvel at the innocence of newborns, and they encourage us to unsolicited acts of kindness. In the face of grievous temptation some of them give us strength; others of them will undermine our resolve. All of this is done so that we may be aware of the spiritual implications of even the least things of our natural life.

All of this is permitted by the Lord's Providence for the sake of our salvation.

The question may rightfully be asked: why are these spirits chosen for this task instead of the angels and demons already in their place in heaven or in hell? The answer is that these spirits can approach humans without destroying their freedom because they are still in a state of working out their own deepest spiritual choices and so, while they have definite tendencies toward good or evil, these tendencies have not yet been fully confirmed. This similarity to humans still on earth permits their contact with them. As this contact appears to be somewhat mutual, perhaps the Lord intends for spirits to confront the destructive ends of the choices they made and are making by having them once more in contact with the natural world. In any case, no angel or demon is permitted contact with humans because the power of their confirmed state is too great and would therefore destroy rather than enhance human freedom.[2]

As the state of the Christian Church on earth degenerated until it was no longer spiritual, an increasing number of evil spirits entered

---

2. At this point it is appropriate to clarify what is meant by the "power of hell" to overwhelm human freedom. Strictly speaking, the hells are powerless over us. If we were actually to see a demon we would be repelled. They are vile, putrid, and threatening. We would never wish to consort with them let alone become one of them. Thus they have no power to entice us. They are the end state of a lifetime of evil-confirming choices. If we were to see them, in the full knowledge that they represented the culmination of our own current evils, we would flee to the Lord immediately. We would quickly seek his mercy and salvation. However, we would do this without resolving our own moral choices, with our own evils intact and un-confronted. Thus, we would not experience the spiritual combats which alone enable us to choose the Lord, in freedom. For this reason, temptations are not put before us at the end of their destructive course, but rather, at the beginning, when they are masked within the comforting surroundings of our world and heart.

In what sense then is it appropriate to talk about the "power of hell"? Hell's power is in the temptation which we feel in the presence of evils which we ourselves love. These loves are in us since birth, they are part of our natural inheritance. They can be excited by the presence of evil spirits and grow in power as we, in our freedom, seek to satisfy and confirm them. The Writings discuss this process of enticement as follows: "it is through the evil one identify-the world of spirits. As a temporary accommodation during this time, the Lord permitted these spirits to dominate the world of spirits because they there maintained external social order; they ruled over cities, conducted church services, preached good works, cared for the young, and maintained civil order. While their motives were primarily hypocritical, they nonetheless provided an orderly context for other spirits who were still in the process of discovering their true loves. We are also told that in this external order the innocence of those in simple good could be preserved and that they could still find comfort there.

This state of the world of spirits during the dying Christian Church could not last forever. Since the existing Church was no longer spiritual, those who entered the world of spirits from it were primarily motivated by the pursuit of honor, reputation, and gain. Because such love of the world is a preliminary manifestation of the love of self, as was discussed previously, such spirits could not transmit the love and light of heaven to those still on earth. In fact, as their love of self became more manifest in them, they often blocked this communication entirely. The Last Judgment on the Christian Church thus became necessary. Swedenborg explains why this came about:

> III. A last judgment exists when a church is at an end, and the end of a church is when there is no faith because there is no charity. There are many reasons why the last judgment exists when the end of the church is. The principal reason is that then the equilibrium between heaven and hell begins to perish, and with the equilibrium man's freedom itself; and when man's freedom perishes, he can no longer be saved, for he cannot then be led to heaven in freedom, but from freedom is borne to hell; for no man can be reformed without freedom, and all man's freedom is from the equilibrium between heaven and hell. (LJ 33)

ing with something in the good. This gives rise to temptations . . . resulting in the struggles that enable good people to be freed from their evils" (DP19). Of course, the tragic possibility also exists that we will embrace these evils, defend and enact them, thus freely choosing the life of hell. We are therefore led to the rather sobering conclusion that the principle source of active evil in the natural world is in the human will. And further, that the power of evil spirits is directly dependent on their access to the proprium of living men.

A human being's spiritual destination is directly affected by the quality of the church dominant on earth during his life. While that church remains fully committed to charity and faith, the number of people entering the spiritual world with love to the neighbor would at least equal the number of spirits entering it whose dominant loves were for self and the world. However, if the church, in this case the Christian church, abandons its spiritual principles and becomes merely another worldly institution, then its ability to lead individuals to a heavenly life is seriously compromised. This inability has profound implications for mankind's freedom and salvation. As only spirits from the world of spirits may approach men in the natural world, they thus bear the essential burden of mediating both good and evil on the earth. They do this as individual spirits with individual men, as was described earlier, and they also do this collectively through auras which they project from themselves into the world. A church necessarily reaches its end when the spirits from it, upon entering the spiritual world, confirm themselves in evil loves and therefore cannot maintain the equilibrium essential to the freedom of those still on earth. As individuals these spirits counsel evil and in concert they emanate auras which appear as dark, noxious clouds and actively block heavenly auras from reaching the natural world. This process, if left unaltered, would totally prevent the light of heaven from reaching the earth, and no one could be saved since all would follow their natural inclinations to hell.

As was mentioned earlier, the Lord permitted the disorderly state of the world of spirits to exist during the Christian Church because it served His Divine end of providing the necessary spiritual equilibrium for salvation. However, when the state of the world of spirits actually interfered with the balance and tended to lead people to hell, the Lord brought an end to it and to the corrupt church which was supplying it. This is what is meant by the Last Judgment of the Christian Church. It occurred in the year 1757. A further explanation of this process is given in the following passage:

IV. Moreover every church in the beginning is spiritual, for it begins from charity; but in the course of time it turns aside from charity to faith, and then from being an internal church it becomes an external one, and when it becomes external its end is, since it then places everything in knowledge, and little or nothing in life. Thus also as far as man from being internal becomes external, spiritual light is darkened within him, until he no longer sees Divine truth from truth itself, that is from the light of heaven, for Divine truth is the light of heaven, but only from natural light. (LJ 38)

This passage makes clear that as it neared its end, the Christian church passed from an internal to an external state. It passed from a life based on charity to a faith based on knowledge. This transition was profoundly tragic. As the church and its leadership turned away from the Divine truth, "spiritual light" was darkened for them and they turned to knowledge derived from "natural light" for confirmation of their authority. It is not precisely clear when this transition occurred in the Christian Church. Perhaps it was the rediscovery of classical Greek philosophy during the Middle Ages. This philosophy provided "rational" grounds for faith but eventually gave the impression that if those grounds could not be maintained the church would be "disproved." Thus began a long and corrosive period of "disputation" which weakened the authority of the church. Perhaps it was brought about by the religious wars of the sixteenth and seventeenth centuries, which forced the church to rely more and more on the power of secular, political forces for its survival. In return, that church would provide its moral influence to support the power of the state. This was a truly perverse bargain, which virtually put an end to the church's independent mission of salvation. The vast devastation and human suffering caused by these wars profoundly undermined the moral claims of the Christian Church. It may also be argued that the critical attitude of the Enlightenment in the early eighteenth century played a crucial role in weakening it. The answer is complex and worthy of intense analysis by New Church scholars. For the present, however, let us focus on the spiritual dimension of the problem.

As the church moved its focus from the internal to the external, it attempted to justify its power and influence in natural ways. In fact, it began to see its power and influence as good in themselves and sought to defend its prerogatives as absolutely necessary for the good of society. The church no longer thought of its wealth for the purposes of charity or its power as a means to facilitate justice. On the contrary, by the early eighteenth century the Christian Church had become a firmly established force, along with the intelligentsia and the state, in virtually every European country. It had become a fully integrated secular institution. As Swedenborg writes, "When it [natural light] is alone and not illuminated by spiritual light, it sees Divine truth as it were in night, and recognizes it as truth for no other reason than that it is called so by the leader, and is received as such by the common assembly" (CLJ 38). Social defining of truth by a leader and the common assembly was a far cry from the original mission of the church. Its spiritual mission was virtually at an end, and it had simply stopped being a real church. Human freedom and salvation were in jeopardy.

At this point the Lord intervened to reopen the living communication between heaven and the human race. He had no alternative: the Christian Church had become Babylon.

> V. *What is meant by Babylon, and what its quality is.* By Babylon are meant all who wish to have dominion by religion. To have dominion by religion is to have dominion over men's souls, thus over their very spiritual life, and to use the Divine things, which are in their religion, as the means. All those who have dominion for an end, and religion for the means are in general Babylon. They are called Babylon because such dominion began in ancient times. (LJ 54)

As can be seen from the above passage, the sin of Babylon is grievous indeed and amounts to nothing less than profanation. Human history is filled with examples of pagan religious systems being intimately connected to the state. It is often the case that the political systems of ancient societies derived from religious roots. This phenomenon is still discernible in our own time.

The Christian Church, however, was not primarily a cultural phenomenon. It was not merely a set of symbols and assertions about the "holy" which guided rituals and legitimated kings. The Christian Church was a true church which was established on earth as a direct consequence of the Lord Himself becoming flesh and dwelling among us. His act of redemption founded the Christian Church and into this church were implanted the real doctrines of Divine order. This church was entrusted with previously unknown truths about the Lord Himself. In addition, the Lord provided countless examples of charity while on earth. He stressed that for the church to remain spiritual it must begin in charity. Concerns for honors, reputation, and gain should not be the prime motivation for charitable acts lest they cease to be charitable at all. Once charity becomes the means to a secular end it loses its spiritual significance and the internal life of the church begins to die. All that then remain are its external forms, rituals, and privileges.

At the beginning of a church its doctrine comes directly from the Lord. It is new and fresh. It has seen a "revelation." It is not derived from philosophies and ideologies current at the time. Instead, it defines itself against those systems. The Lord would often say to His disciples, "You have heard it said, but I say unto you . . .." The words are hardly those of an incremental traditionalist who seeks accommodations. They are stark statements of fresh, Divine truth. Obviously the Lord and His disciples sought to accommodate His words to individual hearers and reach them where they were in their spiritual lives. But while the style and manner of presentation could be adjusted, the content of the Divine truth remained the same.

This was not the case for the eighteenth century Christianity. Various secular, intellectual, and scientific groups arose which based their approach on purely naturalistic grounds. These groups soon set the terms for intellectual discourse. They did this because they could produce empirical results to an increasing naturalistic and external world. The Christian Church, after an initial period of hostility, reached out to these movements and embraced them as the dominant discourse of that time. The principle caveat for the church was that the Enlightenment (as it was ironically called) would not intellectually challenge the formal doctrinal architecture on which the church's secular power rested. Thus deism, as it was known, became the *de facto* theology of both the intelligentsia and church hierarchy. Deism had little spiritual content, but it did preserve the forms of Christianity, and this was the important thing.

The Enlightenment entered into a similar arrangement with the secular state. Many rulers of the time prided themselves on their "rational" and "enlightened" method of rule. However, many of the great projects of this period, both of church and state, were carried out using the instrumentalities characteristic of the pre-Enlightenment era, i.e., slavery, serfdom, titles of nobility, forced labor, sale of indulgences, conquest, bribery, and murder. As was noted earlier, the net effect of this combination of intellectual, religious, and political power was the creation of an impressive structure of external domination and order. The life of genuine charity, which is associated with an internal spirituality, was clearly not a priority within this system.

By the mid-eighteenth century, the Christian Church had reached its spiritual end. It had become a means for those who sought dominion over others through religion. The state enforced political domination while the Christian Church enforced spiritual domination – proclaiming that salvation itself could not be achieved without it. Thus was created a coherent and self-reinforcing system of control. There appeared to be no way out.

As we now know, the Lord had perceived this situation and knew its spiritual significance for salvation. The Last Judgment was being prepared. Its timing was based on spiritual factors.

VI. *Why they (the Christian Church) were there tolerated, until the day of the last judgment.* The reason was that it is from Divine order that all who can be preserved, shall be preserved, even until they can no longer be among the good. Therefore all those are preserved who can emulate spiritual life in externals, and present it in a moral life, as if it were therein, whatever they may be as to faith and love in internals; so also those are preserved who are in external holiness, though not in internal. (LJ 59)

As the purpose of creation is to form a heaven from the human race, the Lord desires as many people to be saved as possible. He knew that even within the degenerated state of the eighteenth century Christian Church there were many who were instructed by its doctrines and comforted by its ceremonies. These "common people" were in simple good and found inspiration in the ordinary life of the church. These people existed both on earth and in the world of spirits. It was for their salvation that the Lord waited until the existence of the Christian Church threatened to cut off the spiritual communication between heaven and the human race entirely. The Lord's forbearance had a positive impact on the salvation of ordinary Christians; we are told that, "Thus many were led to a life of good, and therefore into the way to heaven; on which account also, many of the religion were saved, although few of the leaders" (CLJ 59).

The Lord's solicitation toward all members of the human race is exemplified by His preparation for the Last Judgment. In preparation the Lord sent messengers into the spiritual world who undertook a "visitation" to both the good spirits and evil ones. The messengers presented a final call for all to embrace the life of true religion, fulfilling the Lord's prophecy: "So shall it be in the consummation of the age; the angels shall go forth, and separate the evil from the midst of the just" (Matt. 13.47–49). Like all other aspects of the Lord's Providence, this "separation" was accomplished through the freedom of the participants. This judgment took place on the grand scale of the spiritual world as a whole. However, the visitation and the preservation of the church until its absolute end provided for the salvation of each spirit individually.

VII. All are preserved from one judgment to another, who live a life similar to a spiritual life in externals, and emulate as it were a pious and holy internal; by whom the simple may receive instruction and guidance; for the simple in faith and heart look no farther than to see what is external, and apparent before the eyes. Hence all such were tolerated from the commencement of the Christian Church until the day of the judgment. (LJ59)

How the Lord accomplished the Last Judgment of the Christian Church in the spiritual world will be briefly described below. A fuller description of these events appears in the volumes, *The Last Judgment and Babylon Destroyed* (published 1758), *Continuation concerning the Last Judgment* (published 1763), and *Apocalypse Revealed* (published 1766). Since the current book is focused primarily on the effects of the Last Judgment in the natural world, this account will be limited to a general summery.

The visitation by angels explored the spiritual and moral quality of the spirits, that the good might be separated from the evil. The good were removed to heaven for further instruction while the evil were left behind. Following this there were great earthquakes by which the evil spirits realized that the Last Judgment was at hand. They panicked and fled in all directions. Some tried to escape while others attempted to hide wherever possible. Each one tried to bring with him the objects which his desires led him to value, but these things for which they had sacrificed the life of heaven were destroyed in the ensuing fires and storms. Eruptions from below soon followed, and a great wind picked the evil spirits into the air and carried them, along with the dust which had been their prized possessions, into the hell best suited to their particular love. It was through this series of cataclysms in the world of spirits that the "Babylon" nation was destroyed. But the large numbers of evil societies entering into hell had to be accommodated in such a manner that the overall spiritual equilibrium of creation could still be maintained. We are told that this process took the entire year of 1757 to complete. At the end of the Last Judgment the world of spirits had been cleared of chaos and the pathways between heaven and mankind were reopened.

With such momentous events taking place in the world of spirits, how was life on earth affected? Were there signs and wonders to announce this fundamental change? Surprisingly, the answer is no; the natural world continued on much as it had before. It was as if everything had happened and nothing had happened. Swedenborg describes this situation in the following passage:

> VIII. The state of the world hereafter will be altogether similar to what it has been heretofore, for the great change which has taken place in the spiritual world, does not induce any change in the natural world *as to external form;* so that after this there will be civil affairs as before, there will be peace, treaties, and wars as before, with all other things which belong to societies in general and in particular. (LJ 73; emphasis added)

The conventional expectation, which was in fact the teaching of the Christian Church, was that such great events would be mirrored in

the natural world. That Church still believes that its end will coincide
with the end of earth itself. But this was not in the Lord's Providence
since the work of salvation was not yet complete. There was one more
church to be founded, which was to be the "crown of all the churches."
To this church would be transmitted a new revelation free from the
interference and hostility of the world of spirits. That the Last Judgment
was not accompanied by miraculous happenings on earth was directly
connected to the nature of this new revelation. Mankind would not
be awestruck into shallow declarations of faith. The Lord designed
His New Church to be where human beings could enter freely into an
understanding of the mysteries of faith. Once the spiritual equilibrium
was restored, human minds were prepared for new revelation; there
would now be no further need for explicitly miraculous events to awe
and to terrify. Swedenborg explains this process:

> IX. This does not signify that such things (earthquakes, eruptions, etc.) will
> exist in the natural world: for the Word in its prophecies does not treat of the
> kingdoms on earth, nor of the nations there, thus neither concerning their
> wars, nor of famines, pestilences, and earthquakes there, but of such things as
> correspond to them in the spiritual world; what these things are, is explained in
> *Arcana Coelestia*. (LJ 73)

The above statements treat of things which bear directly on the
Lord's plan for the salvation of the human race. They also are of
profound significance to the present church and its members. These
statements about the earthly ramifications of the Last Judgment can be
introduced under two headings: the social and the physical.

The first statement maintains that after the Last Judgment "there
will be civil affairs as before." There will be peace and war, treaties
and agreements, competition and cooperation as there had been. Thus,
the structure of the social world will continue to be guided by laws
and processes which stretch far back into the past, and there will be no
sudden and visible transformation of the world of everyday life. As a
result, human freedom will not be confronted with massive changes
in how the world appears to work. We can see that these statements
did indeed play out: the entire hierarchical structure of the eighteenth

century survived intact; contracts and labor relations, which existed prior to the judgment, remained after it; marriages were not dissolved; municipal officials stayed in office; the languages and social forms of the people continued. The importance of this continuity cannot be overstated, for it is one of the two core assumptions on which the future of New Church scholarship will be based.

The second statement maintains that the Last Judgment bore no significance to "famines, pestilences, and earthquakes" in the natural world. Thus the structure of the natural, physical world continued to be determined by the constant operation of physical principles and processes which have been in existence since the creation of the natural world. These processes—the organic and inorganic, physical, chemical, and biological—are unchanged. All of these things remained constant. The "physics" of an era may change, but the reality to which it refers stays the same. This constancy of physical structure is the second core assumption for modern New Church scholarship.

With this being said, the essential problem for New Church intellectuals in our time consists in providing an account (or a set of interrelated accounts) of the vast changes in social structures and scientific accomplishments which have occurred between the mid-eighteenth century and today. The issue is quite straightforward: if the social and physical world remained basically unchanged after the Last Judgment, what could have been the intervening variable which will help us to account for the vast changes which have become visible since that time? Both the starting point for that analysis and the clue to its eventual resolution are given to us in the Writings. The following passage addresses this vital point:

> X. But as for the state of the church, this it is which will be dissimilar hereafter; it will be similar indeed as to the external appearance, but dissimilar as to the internal. As to the external appearance divided churches will exist as heretofore, their doctrines will be taught as heretofore; and the same religions as now exist will exist among the Gentiles. But henceforth the man of the church will be in a more free state of thinking on matters of faith, thus on the spiritual things which relate to heaven, because spiritual freedom has been restored to him. For all things in the heavens and in the hells are now reduced into order, and all thought

concerning Divine things and against the Divine inflows from thence; from the
heavens all thought which is in harmony with Divine things, and from the hells
all which is against Divine things. (CLJ 73).

The great change on earth will be in the internal life of the church.
How will these changes be effected? It will be through the ability of the
people of the church to "be in a more free state of thinking on matters
of faith." Therefore, the extraordinary changes we have witnessed
on earth are derivatively related to the fact that, "Spiritual freedom
has been restored to man; and by it interior Divine truths have been
revealed; for man in his former state would not have understood them,
and he who would have understood them, would have profaned them
. . . man has freedom by means of that equilibrium between heaven and
hell . . . man cannot be reformed except in freedom" (CLJ 73).

How spiritual freedom is inexorably connected to human rationality
must be explained. The Writings describe how the Last Judgment in
the world of spirits began a progression of changes, which restored
spiritual freedom and ultimately the possibility of mankind's salvation,
by utilizing the power within the human faculty of rationality.

> XI. Before the last judgment was effected upon them, much of the communication
> between heaven and the world, thus between the Lord and the church, was
> intercepted. All enlightenment comes to man from the Lord through heaven, and
> it enters by an internal way. So long as there were congregations of such spirits
> between heaven and the world, or between the Lord and the church, man could
> not be enlightened. It was as when a sunbeam is cut off by a black interposing
> cloud, or as when the sun is eclipsed, and its light arrested, by the interjacent
> moon. Wherefore, if anything had been then revealed by the Lord, either it
> would not have been understood, or if received, still it would afterwards have
> been suffocated. Now since all these interposing congregations were dissipated
> by the last judgment, it is plain, that the communication between heaven and the
> world, or between the Lord and the church, has been restored. (LJ 11)

Once the "dark interposing cloud" which had formed between heaven
and the world as a result of the growing externality of the Christian
Church on earth was removed, heaven's light, which is Divine truth
and Divine love, flowed into the human mind and strengthened the

only source of rationality. This light, which contains the energy and warmth essential to all natural life, is especially essential to the life of the human mind as it struggles to achieve its goals in the world. The power of this strengthened rationality increased the energy available to the human mind in both spiritual and natural activities.

The fundamental basis of this discussion rests on the relationship between the spiritual and natural aspects of the human mind. This has been made very clear by the Writings in the following passage:

> XII. Our rational faculty is like a garden or flowerbed, like newly tilled land. Our memory is the soil, information and experiential learning are the seeds, while heaven's light and warmth make them productive. There is no germination without these latter. So there is no germination in us unless heaven's light, which is divine truth, and heaven's warmth, which is divine love, are let in. They are the only source of rationality. Angels are profoundly grieved that scholars for the most part keep attributing everything to nature and therefore close the deeper levels of their minds so that they can see no trace of truth from the light of truth, the light of heaven. (HH 464)

It is worth pointing out that the source of human rationality is also present in the lowest hells since the light of Divine truth and love penetrates even there. This is the only reason why its inhabitants retain the faculties of speech and symbolic thought. Rationality is a definitional property of humanity. The capacity for it can never be removed. It persists to eternity in spite of the perversions it has brought about. Rationality itself, however, cannot guarantee that human freedom will be used for good.

The intimate connection between the mind, properly so called, and the Divine life, is so profound that it could be said that the natural world without mind is a "void." This is true even in the presence of life processes at the non-human level. It is human rationality which functions as the creative energy to transform the matter of nature into new and constantly changing objects. Mind has intentions, both material and moral, and the world is both created and destroyed by them. To provide an illustration of this point let us conduct a thought experiment. Imagine that you are sitting in an ordinary room in someone's home. The objects surrounding you are typical of what you would expect in such a setting. Set yourself the following challenge: how many objects could be identified and discovered in that room? You are not limited to only named objects—be creative. Let your imagination carry you away! The objects could include descriptors as well, e.g. spatial relations, temporal relations, color, texture, use, movement, temperature, and activity. A simple example of the process I have in mind is animation. Endow these objects with speech and action. Anyone familiar with children's cartoons will immediately grasp the possibilities. The number of objects and scenarios is virtually limitless. This is precisely the point. By applying an analytical approach plus human creativity you will produce a large list of varied and ingenious objects. The results would be quite fascinating. Now stop and look at the room. Has it changed? Is anything physically different about it as a result of your exercise? Absolutely not! The room remains as it was. There is an excellent reason for this. Taken by itself, without human presence, the room is dead. It will never change as a result of any forces internal to itself. Only external forces, i.e. gravity, temperature, etc., have an impact on it. But adding the human mind to this mix of objects makes them come "alive"; a virtual infinity of projects and questions present themselves. Someone could spend his entire natural life working on our challenge and die before he had exhausted it. This dynamic, human intentionality involves action against and for objects and other actors, with the potential of a complex and transformative result in which a whole new dimension of reality emerges. Here we have the active sphere of human thought. This is the nature of the human life-world. This is the reality in which our spiritual choices are made and carried out.

It is clear that the Last Judgment intensified the communication between heaven and the human race and that this in turn increased the power of the human mind to understand spiritual things. As a man absorbs spiritual influx and orders his intellectual life to take that influx into account, the capacity of his mind to comprehend even natural things is increased. It is not necessary for every human mind to be so ordered for there to be an increased intellectual energy. The collective impact of this influx on secular matters is mediated through the differing receptivity of various members of a given community. This is an extremely complex process which is effected by the various feedback mechanisms by which new information is stored and made available to others. For example, a society possessing organizations promoting "useful knowledge" would be more likely to benefit from this influx than one which did not. Universities and production associations could also fill this feedback function if they were guided by the principles of knowledge development and practical application. One would be justified in suspecting that the area of world culture which would initially experience this influx would be the world of western Christianity. Only in this area was the Last Judgment focused with such profound intensity in the late seventeenth and eighteenth centuries. While it is well beyond the scope of this introductory essay to document this transformation of natural consciousness during the era of the Last Judgment, it remains a fundamental challenge of New Church scholarship to do so.

A further question now presents itself. If the Christian Church had ended, but the Lord required mediation between Himself and the human race so that freedom could be maintained, what earthly vehicle would be available to contain the Lord's restored communication with the world? Swedenborg addresses this vital question in the following passage:

> XIII. Hence it is, that after the last judgment has been accomplished, and not before, revelations were made for the new church. For since communication has been restored by the last judgment, man can be enlightened and reformed; that is, can understand the Divine truth of the Word, receive it when understood, and retain it when received, for the interposing obstacles are removed. (LJ 12)

In the years just prior to the Last Judgment the Lord was preparing a vessel where His renewed influx could be received, i.e. the *Arcana Coelestia* whose eight volumes were published between 1749 and 1756. Immediately following the publication of the last volume in 1756 the Lord began the series of events which would result in the Last Judgment. After that event the new truths revealed by the Lord could be contained in a new revelation which would facilitate their understanding while reducing the probability of their being profaned. The "more free state of thinking on matters of faith" and the text of the new revelation were thus linked in a dynamic and life-giving way.

There were few who were aware of the *Arcana* when it was published and even fewer who received a new revelation. However, the text existed to provide the ground for the eventual enlightenment and reformation of the human race. Swedenborg would produce additional volumes of the Writings throughout the remainder of his life. All of these would serve the purpose of providing a visible expression of the Second Coming of the Lord. This was the "crown of all the churches" and would serve as the specific location of Divine doctrine in the world. Unless this specific church existed on earth, no human being could be saved.

It is clear that as the history of the New Church unfolds, it will see a time of increased material power and intellectual energy in the human race. This will be a period of tension and conflict. It will also be a time of increasing hope. This is because the light of heaven has strengthened mankind's capacity for understanding the new revelation. "Nunc licet" is the motto of the New Church.

The Writings speak forcefully of this spiritual optimism in the following passage. They also invoke the reality of the Lord's resurrection as a comforting parallel to the current state of the church:

XIV. *The state of the world and of the church before the last judgment was like evening and night, but after it, like morning and* day. When the light of truth does not appear, and truth is not received, there is a state of the church in the world like evening and night; that there was a state before the last judgment, may appear from what is said above; but when the light of truth appears, and the truth is received, there is a state of the church in the world like the morning and day. Hence it is that these two states of the church are called "evening and morning" and "night and day," in the Word. Since such things are meant by "evening and night," therefore the Lord, in order to fulfill the Word, also was buried in the evening and afterward rose again the morning. (LJ 13)

It is of essential importance to remember, however, that the moral choices between good and evil remain as they were. The increased power of the mind permits the doing of good or evil on a truly massive scale. Man's freedom is a constant, his evil loves remain, and his increased capacities are no guarantee that he will choose to do good with them. This is the terrible fate of our times. The recent, tragic history of the twentieth century is a brutal reminder that this struggle is a constant one. It will never disappear. It is our calling to be continually and intentionally engaged in it.

Everything is part of the Lord's Providence. The natural world of struggle and anxiety is not the entire story. There is a brilliant light at the end of this night. In fact, we carry this light within us even as we struggle against evil in this world. The spiritual consolation provided by the resurrection of the Lord and the founding of the New Church provide us with the most profound comfort. The laws of Providence and of the Lord's essential charity have now been articulated to us, and we are encouraged to explore the deeper levels of our minds where the truth of heaven lives. Acknowledgement of this deeper level separates us from both nature and natural man and with this there comes a challenge: we are the heirs of the Last Judgment. We are the beneficiaries of the broad and deep changes that have engulfed humanity since the mid-eighteenth century. We, too, are the inheritors of the increased analytical and moral power of the modern world. But we have a precious gift which separates us from the rest of humanity: we know the origin of our time.

The models available to contemporary intellectuals to explain the emergence of the modern world are all based on natural and material premises. Some look to economics, some to technology, others to politics, sociology, or some other combination of natural explanations. There is some truth in all of these approaches. However, they are not the cause of the changes we experience. Rather, they are its effects. The true cause lies elsewhere: in the mediated impact of the Last Judgment on the mental and moral life of mankind. This event, which ended one church and founded its successor, is the true cause of the transformations we see around us.

To bring this perspective into the consciousness of the modern world is a fundamental vocation for New Church scholars. It is a true "calling" in the religious sense—an act of genuine charity. To do this well implies that the New Church scholar must engage the secular disciplines in a competent and respectful manner. We must be knowledgeable and sophisticated in our approach. The papers included in this volume certainly meet these criteria. They advance the dialogue which must continue and be enlarged. There is so much more to be done.

Africa and the Last Judgment
"The World Transformed"

REV. JEREMY F. SIMONS[1]

"The Last Judgment is nothing else than the end of the Church with one group of people and its beginning with another." (AC 3353)

Jesus said to them, "Have you never read in the Scriptures: 'The stone which the builders rejected has become the chief cornerstone. This was the Lord's doing, and it is marvelous in our eyes'?

Therefore I say to you, the kingdom of God will be taken from you and given to a nation bearing the fruits of it." (Matt. 21.42,43)

---

1. In collaboration with the Rev. Ekow Eshun and Brian Smith

Map of Africa. http://www.mongabay.com.

PREFACE

As a child growing up in Bryn Athyn in the 1950s, I spent hours listening to stories about Africa from my South African grandmother, Agnes Edith Pemberton Gyllenhaal. My grandfather, the Rev. Frederick Gyllenhaal, was a General Church minister who became pastor of the church group in Durban, South Africa in 1913. Soon he was approached by Rev. Samuel Mofokeng, representing a New Church congregation in "Basutoland" (Lesotho), as well as a Zulu minister, Rev. Mcanyana, who sought an association with the General Church. Through that beginning he came into contact with many African congregations to whom he preached from the Heavenly Doctrines, often riding on horseback for weeks through Lesotho's mountains. My grandmother's house was full of mementos from her African youth, and my own childhood was filled with her stories.

In 1974, just before my senior year at the University of Pennsylvania my family went to visit Hyland and Beth Johns at their vacation house in Brigantine, New Jersey. On the way there, we picked up our neighbor and friend, Dr. Sig Synnestvedt, at the Philadelphia airport, and took him with us. He was arriving back from a trip.

After a few days on the beach, Dr. Sig called us together and told us about his trip. He had just returned from Ghana, West Africa. He had been sent there by the Swedenborg Foundation to find out why there was such a high demand in that country for Swedenborg's Heavenly Doctrines. The Foundation had a policy of sending a free book to anyone who wrote requesting one. In the 1960s they began getting more and more requests from this particular country. By the late 1960s they were sending them upwards of 10,000 books per year. In a ten year period they had sent over 100,000 books to Ghana and very few anywhere else. Sig Synnestvedt had gone there to find out what was happening to all of those books. What he discovered was that people were reading them, and that they had an enormous appetite for the kind of information that could be found in the Heavenly Doctrines.

His report stunned me. Even having been raised with stories of Africa, I had never connected with the idea that there was any special

interest in the New Church there. I was unaware of what the Heavenly
Doctrines said about Africa. When I heard Sig Synnestvedt's report
and looked Africa up in *The Swedenborg Concordance*, I was amazed by
the number of passages and what they said. I made up my mind to go
there and see for myself.

In 1976, after graduating with a degree in Economics and attending
one year of theological school, I joined the Peace Corps and spent two
years in Togo, a francophone country bordering Ghana. I lived in a
tiny village in a beautiful mountain rainforest region on the Ghanaian
border. I took every chance I got to travel throughout Ghana and the
rest of Africa. I visited hundreds of readers of the Heavenly Doctrines
and speculated about how the New Church was going to grow in the
country. I became friends especially with Pastor Benjamin Garna, of
Ashaiman, a part of Tema.

On my return and continuation of theological school, I did
everything that I could to promote interest in Ghana. Many people in
Bryn Athyn were interested and helpful. People such as Leon Rhodes,
Rev. David Holm, and Rev. Doug Taylor did everything they could.
Dr. Robert Gladish and the Rev. Bob Jungé did not hesitate to begin
bringing students from Ghana to Bryn Athyn for college and theological
school. Bishop King invited Pastor Garna to attend clergy meetings.
The students who came, William Ankra-Badu, Simpson Darkwa,
Martin Gyamfi, and others, were excellent students. They became
ministers and by 1986 the first was back in Ghana beginning to organize
the General Church there. Many General Church representatives went
to Ghana in those years—Geoffrey Howard, Bishop King, Willard
Heinrichs, Alfred Acton, and others. I returned there over the summers
of 1979, 1980, 1985, and most recently in 1999.

The church in Ghana is now well established, with seven pastors, a
theological school, and two large elementary schools. In addition, the
church has been spreading to the neighboring francophone countries
of Togo, Cote D'Ivoire, Burkina Faso, Cameroun, Congo, and others,
thanks to the travels of the Rev. Alain Nicolier from France, and
new pastors Sylvain Agnes in Cote D'Ivoire and Segno Kodjo Ayi in
Togo.

I am amazed to have seen all this occurring over the past thirty years, beginning from the astounding story that Dr. Synnestvedt told me in 1974. His report transformed my world. I dedicate this paper to his memory.

I also wish to thank the Rev. Ekow Eshun, a newly ordained General Church minister in Ghana, and Brian Smith, attending ANC Theological School, who helped gather research for this paper. Eshun's reflections on many of the teachings about Africa are included with the passages about African spirituality.

This is all part of a much bigger story about the Last Judgment, which is the story of the transformation of the world.

THE LAST JUDGMENT

Introduction

In 1980 *Time* magazine noted:

> Many churches in North America and Western Europe have seen their membership dwindle for years. But throughout the Third World, and particularly in Africa, Christianity is undergoing the largest numerical expansion in church history.[2]

The "largest numerical expansion in church history." Twenty-seven years later this dramatic expansion has not slowed down, and it is changing the face of modern Christianity. It is also changing the General Church of the New Jerusalem, as more than a third of all General Church baptisms since 1987 have been African. There is a similar Christian increase going on in Asia and South America, and perhaps we will soon see the New Church rapidly growing in those places as well.

---

2. "Faith in Africa: A Tale of Joyful Numbers," *Time*, January 21, 1980) www.time.com/time/magazine/article/0,9171,952553,00.html.

Is this an effect of the Last Judgment? Passages from the Heavenly Doctrines seem to indicate that this is exactly what the Last Judgment is about. We read that "The Last Judgment is nothing else than the end of the Church with one group of people and its beginning with another" (AC 3353).

Does the apparent movement of Christianity from North America and Western Europe to Africa, Asia, and South America fit this description? Is the church coming to an end with the peoples of North America and Western Europe and moving to these other parts of the world? The Heavenly Doctrines declare that:

> When a new Church is established by the Lord it is not established among those within the Church but among those outside it, that is, among the gentiles. These are referred to many times in the Word. (AC 4747.2)

Who are the "gentiles"? Where do they live? Many peoples worldwide could be called gentiles—peoples who have not been part of the Christian world. Of these peoples the Heavenly Doctrines pay more attention to Africans than any others. One passage says:

> The angels rejoiced that the coming of the Lord was now at hand, and that the Church, which is now perishing in Europe, should be renewed in Africa. (SE 4777)

Is the church perishing in Europe? Is it being renewed in Africa? Is this an effect of the Last Judgment? The Heavenly Doctrines seem to state that Christianity will come to an end in the West and that the New Church will grow among the gentiles. But what we observe is that Christianity seems to be renewing itself in the gentile world, with the New Church remaining unknown. Is this different than what the Heavenly Doctrines teach, or is this seeming renewal a preparation for the New Church?

These questions are the topic of this paper, which explores what the Heavenly Doctrines teach about the Last Judgment, Africa, and the New Church. As we celebrate the two-hundred-and-fiftieth anniversary of the Last Judgment we will look at how the judgment has changed, and is changing, our world.

The Last Judgment

Swedenborg described the Last Judgment this way:

> I have been allowed to see with my own eyes that the Last Judgment has now taken place. I have seen the wicked cast into the hells, and the good raised to heaven, thus restoring all to order and so re-establishing the spiritual equilibrium between good and evil, or between heaven and hell. I was allowed to see how the Last Judgment took place from beginning to end; and also how Babylon was destroyed, and how those who are meant by the dragon were cast into the abyss; and then again how the new heaven was formed, and the new church meant by the New Jerusalem was set up in the heavens. I was allowed to see all this with my own eyes so that I could bear witness. This Last Judgment started at the beginning of last year, 1757, and was fully completed by the end of the year. (LJ 45)

The Heavenly Doctrines clearly state that the Last Judgment is, or was, a spiritual event; not visible in this world. The Scriptural description of worldwide cataclysms communicates the supreme significance of the Last Judgment, but the basis of its significance is spiritual:

> Those unfamiliar with the spiritual sense of the Word have understood only that on the day of the Last Judgment everything in the world we see around us will be destroyed. . . . They ought now to know that it is not the sky we see with our eyes which is to be destroyed nor is it the earth on which we live, both of which will remain in existence; but the "new heaven and new earth" mean a new church, both in the heavens and upon earth. (LJ 1)

Since this kind of Last Judgment is not obvious to the untrained eye, we are marking the two hundred and fiftieth anniversary of an event that few people on earth would acknowledge has even happened. The world has not detected it, and since the Last Judgment occurred life has continued on as though nothing had changed. As the Heavenly Doctrines state:

> The future state of the world will be exactly the same as it has been up to now; for the mighty change which has taken place in the spiritual world does not cause any change in the external appearance of the natural world. So just as before there will be politics, peace-treaties, alliances and wars, and all the other general and particular features of society. When the Lord said:
> "There will be wars, and then nation will rise up against nation, and kingdom against kingdom; and there will be famines, plagues and earthquakes in various places" (Matt. 24.6), He did not mean such events in the natural world, but corresponding ones in the spiritual world. For the Word in its prophecies is not concerned with kingdoms on earth or the peoples on it, so not with their wars either; nor is it concerned with famine, plague and earthquakes on earth, but with the events in the spiritual world which correspond to them. (LJ 73)

The future would be, to all appearances, the same as the past and present. No one on earth, apart from believers in the Heavenly Doctrines, has suspected that the Last Judgment has already taken place as there have been no obvious signs.

This does not mean, however, that there were no signs at all. This same passage declares that people will have "more freedom in thinking about matters of faith" (LJ 73). The truth will come to people's understanding more easily, and they will be able to accept it more easily because the spiritual forces that interfere with this process have been subdued by the Lord.

Are there detectable signs of this kind of freedom? What signs would there be? The long term effects could be enormous, yet so subtle as to be almost invisible. What are these effects? This paper deals with the teachings about and the evidence for the effects of the Last Judgment on the church in different parts of the world, and specifically on the people of the continent of Africa.

What is Happening on this Earth?

Let us step back from the Last Judgment and ask the question, "What is happening on this earth?" What are the most important things that are going on? We might think about the growth of the earth's population, its ability to feed itself, the state of war and peace, and the state of the environment. We might consider the steady advances in knowledge and technology, the increase of education and literacy, the spread of political and economic systems, and the movements and changes in world religions. We might look at the spread and control of disease, crime, pollution, and poverty.

The Lord's perspective is concerned primarily with humanity's spiritual welfare—its state of faith and charity—and therefore its happiness. His Divine Providence "regards eternal ends, and not temporal ones, except as they accord with eternal ones" (DP 214). The Lord's purpose is to improve humanity's welfare for eternal ends. That is, His purpose in creating and guiding the world is a heaven from the human race (DP 27).

When viewed from the Lord's perspective, as this is explained in the Heavenly Doctrines, all of the trends, movements, advances, and struggles that are going on in the world are important only insofar as they affect or coincide with the Lord's eternal ends. The question is about the ways in which the world is becoming a better place; the extent to which the Lord's will is being done on earth as it is in heaven.

The Word is more Widely Distributed than Any Book ever Written

By far the best-selling book of all time is the Bible, the Old and New Testaments. An estimated six billion copies have been printed. Worldwide it is not only far and away the cumulative leader, it has also been the best-selling book every year since printing was invented[3]—and even before. This year, and every year, more Bibles will be distributed among the world's 6.6 billion people than any book on any best-seller list. According to the Heavenly Doctrines, this is why, in providence, writing was invented:

> The main reason was for the sake of the Word, which was able on our planet to be set down in writing. Then, having been written, it could be disseminated to

---

3. Michelle Vu, "Christian Books Still Dominate All-Time Best-Sellers List," *Christian Post*, July 4, 2007, www.christianpost.com/article/20070704/christian-books-still-dominate-all-time-best-sellers-lists/index.html.

all parts of the planet, and once it had been disseminated it could be preserved for all future generations. (AC 9351)

We are told that the Lord works silently and invisibly to reform the human race (DP 186), but in this respect His means are public and quantifiably successful. The Word is widely, almost universally, available on earth, leaving only the issue of who will accept it and who will not. The Word is being spread, and the Lord is extending the Church throughout the world by means of it.

What is the Last Judgment?

The Last Judgment, fundamentally, is a separation of the good from the evil:

> The Last Judgment is the separation of those who live according to Divine truths, from those who do not live according to them. (AE 875)

> The Last Judgment is treated of when there must be a separation of the good from the evil, and the good are to come into heaven, and the evil into hell. (AE 374.15)

The separation occurs as the Lord comes down, as it is His presence that causes the judgment:

> When a last judgment is impending the Lord approaches with heaven, and out of those who are below in the world of spirits no others are able to endure the Lord's coming but those who are interiorly good, and they are interiorly good who shun evils as sins and look to the Lord. (AR 340)

We are specifically interested in the fact that the Last Judgment causes certain changes to happen in the world; most importantly, it brings about the end of one church and the beginning of a new one. It not only separates the good from the evil, but does so for the purpose of restoring order in the church, by beginning a new church. The point is to change the world for the better. It is about setting people free of the norms and paradigms of the past so that more positive ideas and values can become the norm. The whole purpose of this is to bring people into a happier state.

> "Morning" means the time of the last judgment, when those governed by good are to be saved and those ruled by evil will perish. It consequently means the end of a former Church and the beginning of a new Church, which are meant by a last judgment in the Word. (AC 8211)

> The Last Judgment takes place when a church comes to an end, and this happens when there is no faith because there is no charity. (LJ 33)

Many passages point out that the Last Judgment took place because of the state of the Christian world:

> Such is the state of the church to-day; it has no faith because it has no charity. Where there is no charity, neither is there any spiritual good, for charity is the sole source of that good. I have been told from heaven that some people still have good, but it cannot be called spiritual good, only natural good. (LJ 38)

> For the new church that is called the Christian Church, and that was begun by the Lord when He was in the world, and afterwards propagated, has successively decreased down to this time, which is its last time, in which is the judgment. (AE 369)

The Last Judgment is the End of the Church

The Last Judgment took place because of the spiritual end of the church in the Christian world. This sets the scene for the church to be renewed elsewhere:

> The last phase of the Church among one nation is always the first phase of the Church among another. Because a last phase is in this way continued into a first, the Lord is spoken of several times as the Last and the First. (AC 4901)

This is why the Last Judgment is said to be the end of the church with one people and it's beginning with another:

This end with one and beginning with another occurs when the Lord is not acknowledged any longer, or what amounts to the same, when there is no faith any longer. No acknowledgement or faith exists any longer when there is no charity any longer, for faith is in no way possible except with those in whom charity is present. In those circumstances the Church comes to an end and is transferred to others. (AC 3353)

There are also passages that explain why it is that the newly-established must be transferred to others instead of being renewed with the same people—a pattern that has been since the time of the Most Ancient Church. There have been several "Last Judgments":

For a last judgment befalls every Church when it has been vastated, that is, when no faith exists there any longer. A last judgment on the Most Ancient Church took place when it perished, as it did among its final descendants who lived immediately prior to the Flood. A last judgment on the Jewish Church took place when the Lord came into the world. And a further last judgment will take place when the Lord comes in glory. This does not mean that at that time the earth and the world are going to be destroyed, but that the Church is destroyed and, as always happens, a new Church is raised up by the Lord at that time. At the time of the Flood the Ancient Church was raised up, at the time of the Lord's Coming the primitive Church among gentiles; and the same will happen when the Lord comes in glory. (AC 931)

A like judgment has occurred several times on this planet, the first taking place when the Lord's celestial Church, which was the Most Ancient, perished among those living before the flood through the deluge of evils and falsities meant in the internal sense by the flood.

The second judgment occurred when the spiritual Church, which existed after the Flood and is called the Ancient, and which was spread through much of the Asiatic world, reached a point when it had destroyed itself.

The third occurred when the representative of the Church among the descendants of Jacob was destroyed, a destruction which took place when the ten tribes were carried off into everlasting captivity and were scattered among the gentiles, and finally when Jerusalem was destroyed and the Jews too were dispersed. Because the close of that age was reached after the Lord's Coming, many of the Lord's statements in the Gospels about the close of that age are therefore applicable to that nation also; many at the present day do apply statements to it. But though these can be understood in that way, they refer specifically and primarily to the close of the age which is now imminent; that is to say, they refer to the end of the Christian Church, which is the subject also in John, in the Book of Revelation. This will be the fourth last judgment on this planet. (AC 4333)

After each judgment the church died out with one population and moved to another. The "fourth last judgment" (AC 4333), when "a New Church is raised up by the Lord" (AC 931), will end the Christian Church and a New Church will rise and be based on new revelation:

> As this church has come to its end, by the accomplishment of the last judgment, a new church is now being instituted by the Lord, which is called, in Revelation, the "new Jerusalem," to which the things that are being published by me at the present day will be of service; it is also being instituted elsewhere. (PP 401)

"It is also being instituted elsewhere"? Does this mean that there are other revelations? Or simply that, as with every Last Judgment, a new church will be established with people "elsewhere," that is, outside of the Christian world?

THE FUTURE OF THE NEW CHURCH

The Growth of the New Church

The Heavenly Doctrines clearly state that the New Church will grow primarily among peoples who are outside the Christian world as people in the countries where Christianity has existed are resistant to the doctrines of the New Church and will not accept them. The few that will accept them may be considered to be part of the remnant of the Christian Church, and they will be few until the day comes when the New Church becomes widespread in some part of the world outside Christendom.

The following passages demonstrate how frequently the teaching on the spiritual transference of the church occurs:

> When a new Church is established by the Lord, rarely if ever is this effected with those with whom the old Church has been. Instead it is established among those with whom no Church existed previously, that is, among gentiles. This is what

happened when the Most Ancient Church perished . . . It will be similar with the Church existing at the present called the Christian Church. (AC 2986; also 9256.5)

Rarely if ever does the Church remain with those who have truths among them when they have been vastated; but it is transferred to those who know nothing at all about truths; for these embrace faith much more easily than the former.

When the last time of vastation comes upon those who know and do not desire to know and who see and do not desire to see, then a Church arises anew, not among them, but with those whom they call gentiles. (AC 409-410)

A new Church will be raised up in some part of the world, while the present one continues in existence with its external worship, just as the Jews do in theirs. (AC 1850.4)

Consequently when a new Church is established by the Lord it is not established among those within the Church but among those outside it, that is, among the gentiles. These are referred to many times in the Word. (AC 4747.2)

By the holy Jerusalem (Rev. 21) is meant a New Church among the gentiles, after the present church which is in our European world has been vastated. (AC 9407.7)

From all this also it can be seen why a new church is always set up among the Gentiles who are outside the church, which as before said takes place when the old church has closed heaven against itself. For this reason the church was transferred from the Jewish people to the Gentiles, and the present church is also now being transferred to the Gentiles. That the church is transferred to the Gentiles who acknowledge the Lord, is evident from many passages in the Word. (AC 9256.5)

Wonderful to say, the Gentiles worship the one only God under a human form; and therefore when they hear about the Lord, they receive and acknowledge Him; nor can a new Church be set up with others. That the Church is set up again with such, is further evident from the Lord's words in Matthew:

"Have ye not read in the Scriptures, The stone which the builders rejected, the same is become the head of the corner. Therefore I say unto you, The kingdom of God shall be taken away from you, and shall be given to a nation that doeth the fruits." (Matt. 21.42, 43) (AC 9256.7)[4]

4. See also (AC 2910, 3353, 3812, 3898, 4747); (LJ 74); (NJHD 246); (SS 15.3); (SD 4770); (AE 49, 52, 239, 294, 654).

These passages form a clear and direct principle which has been accepted in the General Church. Who are meant by the "gentiles," however, has been unclear and remained subject to interpretation.

What is a Gentile?
Why Does a New Church Grow Up among Them and Not Others?

A gentile can be described as someone who is not a Christian, or perhaps especially, someone who is not from the Christian world. A gentile may also be someone who is not Jewish or Muslim. Gentiles are described as "a church in which there are no truths because they have not the Word" (AR 546). There is nothing inherently good about being a gentile; it is certainly better to know the truth than to be ignorant of it. But gentiles are also free of the false ideas that block the reception of truth. While gentiles have false ideas, they are not deeply rooted false ideas about Christianity. And according to the Heavenly Doctrines, gentiles tend to be more charitable than Christians.

The following passages explain why it is that the Church is to grow among gentiles:

> Gentiles do not possess any false assumptions that are contrary to the truths of faith, for they have no knowledge of the truths of faith. . . . As gentiles do not have such knowledge, there are no stumbling blocks to hinder them. (AC 2986.3)

> Gentiles have not set themselves firmly against those truths because they have no knowledge of them. For this reason those among them who have led charitable lives with one another accept Divine truths with ease, if not in the world then in the next life. (AC 4747.2)

> There is not so great a cloud in the intellectual part with the gentiles as there generally is with so-called Christians. (AC 1059.2; also 1992.4)

> Wonderful to say, the gentiles worship the one only God under a human form; and therefore when they hear about the Lord, they receive and acknowledge Him; nor can a new Church be set up with others. (AC 9256.7)

> A gentile thinks concerning God from religion in his life more than a Christian. (DP 322.5)

Gentiles live a much more moral life than those within the Church; and they embrace much more easily the doctrine of true faith. (AC 1032.2)

More are saved from the gentiles than from Christians. (AC 1059.2; also 2284.5, 2598.3)

These passages describe a state of receptivity in both the intellect and the will. They are not simply ignorant; they are clear thinking, moral, and charitable.

Gentiles and children share certain qualities that make them receptive.

Charity devoid of faith, like that existing with young children and with gentiles who are upright, is simply the ground in which faith is implanted, if not in this life then in the next life. (AC 2839e)

[Gentiles] have not confirmed themselves against the truths of faith, as have very many Christians; and therefore their internal man is not closed, but, as with little children, is readily opened and receptive of truth. (AC 9256.2)

Children accept religious ideas more easily than adults do for the same reason that gentiles do. They have a simplicity that comes from ignorance, and their young hearts have a kind of innocent love of others and of doing what is right, which is fertile ground for religious ideas. Children also tend to be selfish and mischievous if left to their own devices and so need to be taught to behave.

It is important to recognize that gentiles are not good in themselves— "they are indeed in falsities, but from ignorance" (AC 9256.2). If they were good they would not need the New Church. Their mistaken practices and false ideas manifest themselves in cultural characteristics that can be a hindrance to economic success as well as a handicap to living a good life. Attitudes towards employment, honest business practices, the nature of government, and concepts of marriage interfere with individual happiness as well as hindering the smooth functioning of society. The developing nations have many problems, and the most important of these can be traced back to religion and the culture that springs from religion.

Some have questioned whether peoples that Swedenborg considered to be gentiles still are, since Christianity is now so widespread that there are few places on earth where it is unknown; knowledge of Christianity has become almost universal. Nevertheless, the only culture that has been formed and affected for centuries by Christianity is that of "Christendom." In other places, relatively recently influenced by Christianity, the beliefs of the church have not necessarily had time to fundamentally influence their character and culture to the point that they have lost the qualities characteristic of gentiles. As a culture they still long for the truth and have not found it—and despite this, many individuals within any culture may have found happiness in Christianity or even in the New Church.

A Christian culture that has rejected the teachings of the Word does not easily fit the description of a people longing for the truths of faith; Christians do not become gentiles by rejecting Christianity. There has to be charity and an innocent hunger for truths about the Lord. While there are a huge number of people in the United States who know very little about the Word, it is not because that knowledge is unavailable. Everyone has heard of the Bible, and everyone knows that Christians consider Jesus Christ to be Divine. This is a culture hungering for the truth, but they do not recognize that truth in the Bible. The difference between gentiles and these people is the difference between a gentile church and a *vastated* church, both of which are described in the Word as a "wilderness."

A Vastated Church is Not a Gentile Church

The Heavenly Doctrines state that the Church has become a "wilderness." This is not necessarily the same thing as being in a "gentile" state. The term "wilderness" is used to mean both a Church that is at its end and also a Church that never was, that is, a gentile Church. The internal sense of the story of the woman clothed with the sun in Revelation 12 describes what is meant by the wilderness into which she fled:

> "And the woman fled into the wilderness" . . . By a "wilderness" in the Word is signified, 1) The church devastated, or in which all the truths of the Word are falsified, such as it was among the Jews at the time of the Lord's advent. 2) The

church in which there are no truths because they have not the Word, such as it was among the upright Gentiles in the Lord's time. (AR 546)

The people of a devastated or vastated church are different from gentiles because they, for the most part, are not interested in receiving the truths of a new church. They are highly resistant to them, because the truths of the New Church are very similar to what has been rejected. This is why the New Church is at first only among a few:

"And the woman fled into the wilderness" signifies the church among a few, because with those who are not in good, and consequently not in truths . . . . The New Church . . . can as yet be instituted only with a few, by reason that the former church has become a wilderness. (AE 730a)

The former church is a wilderness, not because truths are unavailable, but because people are not interested in them. Swedenborg demonstrated that few people in Great Britain would be interested in the New Church. He sent out books, knowing that some would receive them. Here are his comments after sending out copies of what is, apparently, *Heaven and Hell*:

All these things have been written out in the Latin language, and they have been sent to all the archbishops and bishops of the kingdom (Great Britain), and to some of the nobility; and still not a word has been heard—a sign that they do not interiorly care for the things of heaven and of the Church, and that it is now the very end of the Church, and indeed that the Church is not; for the Church is where the Lord is worshiped and the Word is read with enlightenment. (Preface to *The Athanasian Creed*)

How different would the response be today if this experiment was repeated? The various New Church organizations continually plan and implement this kind of project to let people know about the New Church. They know, however, that only a very small percentage of people in the United States or other Western countries will respond. The reason for this, according to the passages that we have been quoting, is that the church has become a wilderness. Few will respond, but it is worth the effort that it takes to find those few. Still, we should be aware that in other parts of the world, when the time and conditions are right, it is likely that there will be a vastly greater response.

Why are Former Christians Not the Gentiles among Whom the New Church will Grow?

Knowledge, or the lack of it, is never the main indicator of spiritual progress. The primary quality with gentiles who will make up the New Church in the future is charity. If charity were present in the Christian world, the Christian Church never would have come to an end. Many passages in the Heavenly Doctrines harshly and critically describe the Christian peoples as lacking in charity; consider whether they apply today the way they did in Swedenborg's day.

> There are gentiles who when they lived in the world had known from contact and report that Christians live the worst life, in adulteries, hatred, quarrels, drunkenness, and the like . . . . But they are instructed by the angels that the Christian doctrine and faith itself teaches quite differently, but that Christians live less according to their doctrines than gentiles do. (AC 2597)

> Those who come into the other life from the Christian world are the worst of all, hating the neighbor, hating faith, denying the Lord—for in that life what is in the heart declares itself. . . . They are also worse adulterers than all others. (AC 1886.4 pref.)

> Such are Christians at this day as to the interiors, except a few whom they do not know. (AC 3489.2; also 5006.2, 9409.4; SD 590, 2567, 3934, 4843)

> The world called Christian is almost like the antediluvian one. . . . It is worse in that it regards adulteries as nothing. (SD 3598; also 5832e; AE 1008.2)

> Many of the Gentiles abhor the doctrine of Christians because they see their life. Thus it is evident that nowhere does there exist a more detestable life than in the Christian world. (AC 916.3)

> The Christian doctrine prescribes love and charity more than any other in the whole world, but there are few who live according to it. (AC 2596e)

Notice that the religion itself is praised; the criticism is that many people have not followed it. It should be evident from these passages that the Christians who love the Word and follow its teachings are highly praised. The criticized are the unfaithful people of the Christian world. It is clear from many passages that Christians who truly believe and follow the teachings of the Word are the best people in the world and have their place at the center of heaven (cf. SS 105.3; AC 2590). People of this character are likely to accept the Heavenly Doctrines if they are exposed to them. If good Christians were common, however, there would be no need for the New Church, but the assertion of the Heavenly Doctrines is that they are the minority.

Teachings like this occur so frequently in the Heavenly Doctrines they provoked the following comment from some people associated with the founding of the Academy of the New Church:

> There was nothing which struck us so forcibly as the teachings regarding the state of the Christian world. These explained it seemed to us (Frank Ballou and Walter Childs) exactly why the New Church had not been received and why it would be received by but few in the Christian world.[5]

The General Church has been very aware of these teachings from the beginning. Today, however, many question these assertions, saying that their personal experience does not support what is said. Before relying completely on the way things seem to be, however, note what is said in the following statement:

> To those within the Church it is not apparent that this is the condition of the Church, that is to say, that they treat with contempt and loathe everything to do with goodness and truth, and also show hostility towards those things, especially towards the Lord Himself. They do indeed attend places of worship, listen to sermons with some kind of reverence while they are there, go to the Holy Supper, and sometimes discuss these things with one another in a seemly way. (AC 3489)

---

5. Walter C. Childs, quoted in Richard R. Gladish's *Bishop William Henry Benade* (Bryn Athyn, PA: Academy of the New Church, 1984), 228.

This passage describes at length the nature of the ill feelings which reign in the Christian world, and comments that "such are Christians at this day as to the interiors, except a few whom they do not know."

Christian Gentiles

Some people look for support for the idea that the Christian world is moving into a "gentile" state in passages that refer to "Christian gentiles." The Heavenly Doctrines do refer to Christian gentiles, but do not imply that they are the same gentiles who would eagerly embrace the truth if exposed to it. The term is used to mean that they have strayed so far from true worship as to have become idolaters. The point is similar to the one made above in reference to the Church having become a "wilderness."

> The ardor of domineering and getting gain reigns especially in Christian gentilism, where the idols of canonized men are set up to be adored. (AC 9020e)

> Almost all our churches today are like this [making faith the essential thing], with the exception of that which exists in Christian gentilism where people are allowed to venerate saints and images of them. (AC 3447)

> Jacob would [only] acknowledge the Lord as his God if He conferred benefits on him. It was just the same as with Christian gentilism at the present day. (AC 3667.2)

The gentiles have rejected the true church to the point that they are practically heathens—not in a complimentary sense.

What about the Power of the New Light since the Last Judgment?

The increase of light from the spiritual world since 1757 has undeniably been a positive influence for change in the Christian world. Since the Last Judgment the sun of the spiritual world has shone more brightly than before, and the new heaven has been increasing. How much of an effect has this had on the peoples of the Christian world over the past two hundred years?

> After the Last Judgment there was . . . light in the world of spirits, such as was not
> before. . . . A similar light also then arose with men in the world, from which they
> had new enlightenment. (CLJ 30)

> Henceforth the man of the church will be in a more free state of thinking on matters
> of faith, thus on the spiritual things which relate to heaven, because spiritual
> freedom has been restored to him. (LJ 73)

It should noted that this same thing happened after the first Advent.
The light of the spiritual sun alone, however, was not sufficient to keep
the Christian Church from sliding into darkness. My feeling is that the
large scale effect of this new light shows itself only over long periods of
time:

> The Lord, since His advent into the world, appears as a sun in the angelic heavens,
> in stronger radiance and in greater splendor than before His advent. (DLW 221e)

> The sun of the angelic heaven . . . after the assumption of the Human shone out
> with greater effulgence and splendor than before the assumption. This is what is
> meant by the words of Isaiah: "In that day the light of the moon will be as the light
> of the sun, and the light of the sun shall be seven-fold, as the light of seven days"
> (Isa. 30.26). This is said of the state of heaven and of the church after the Lord's
> coming into the world. (DLW 233; cf. AE 401.10)

There can be no question that these things have had a positive effect
on the world, and will continue to exert an always-strengthening force for
good. In *Last Judgment* 74, however, angels who spoke to Swedenborg
about this new power, and the new freedom resulting from it, did not
have great hope that this force would turn things around in the Christian
world. The angels "have slender hope of the men of the Christian church,
but much of some nation far distant from the Christian world, and
therefore removed from infesters." (LJ 74)

Are these "infesters" still a serious problem in the Christian world?
The new light and freedom have their full power only when the power
of the "infesters" has been exposed and removed, which the Heavenly
Doctrines indicate will happen gradually by means of the Word (BE 96,
102). Apparently, the light alone will not change things quickly.

*How Long will the Christian World
Retain the Character of a Vastated Church?*

What indications do we have about how long it takes for a people to fundamentally change their character? Many passages point out how durable the Israelite culture and character has been. A comparison of Christians and Jews may be a flawed comparison, since the nature of the Church with Christians was always distinctly different than it was with the Church that existed with the Israelites only as a representative church. Nevertheless, this comparison is often made in the Heavenly Doctrines (such as in *Arcana Coelestia* 788.2). If the descendants of Jacob retain such a distinct character and heredity after thousands of years, how can we expect the descendants of Christians to change any more rapidly? The following criticisms are made about the Jewish nation:

> This has been so from their earliest forefathers, namely the sons of Jacob, even to the present day. (AC 3881.10; also 9127.6)

> The Jewish nation has been in such love from the first times . . . . This still remains with that nation. (AC 4750.6)

> [The character of that nation] is quite evident from members of it at the present day. (AC 4847.3)

> That nation was such, and also is such at this day (AC 6963.2)

> That descendants . . . are born into affections, thoughts, speech and lives like those of their parents, is clearly evident from the Jewish nation, in that at this day they are like their fathers in Egypt, in the wilderness, in the Land of Canaan, and in the Lord's time; and in that they are like them not only in their minds, but also in their faces; for who does not know a Jew by his aspect? (CL 202.2; see also AC 7051; AE 119.2)

The Heavenly Doctrines' criticisms about the Israelites echo what the Lord says in the New Testament, however, their teachings are even more critical of Christians. The general theme of these comments is also similar to what the Lord says in the New Testament, namely that this is a people which has the Word and does not live according to it, like those who were invited to the wedding feast and refused to come (Matt. 22). Christians are more criticized than Jews because while their religion clearly more teaches love to the neighbor, many still ignore it.

> I have learnt from much experience, that the worst of all the spirits in the ultimate heaven are those who in the world are called Christians. These, for the most part, have no faith, but they persecute and hate all things that are of the true faith, nor do they suffer themselves to be instructed. . . . After the Christians the worst are the Jews. (SE 480)

The fact that Christians have a long history of vicious persecution of Jews may be evidence of this comparison. Historically Christians have discriminated against many peoples and nationalities that were different from themselves. Further example of this behavior is the Christian world's lack of compassion and care for those who are different—the elderly, those with disabilities, and minority ethnic groups. This unpleasant characteristic may be the root of the need to demand rights for various classes of people and the root of the anger that many women feel over their historic treatment by a male-dominated society. Compassion has had to be institutionalized and legislated because, seemingly, it does not exist naturally in the Christian world.

The Strong Effect of Hereditary Evil

Do these uncompassionate characteristics of the Christian world have anything to do with evil, or with the possibilities for the spread of the New Church? How likely is it that such a harsh culture could change so fundamentally in just a few generations? The effect of hereditary evil on churches in the past is the "principle cause of degeneration" (AC 494). The effect of this evil was so strong with those remaining after the fall of the Most Ancient Church that it was not possible to fully establish the Ancient Church, represented by Noah, with them, but only with others, represented by Noah's sons:

> Noah was not the Ancient Church itself, but was as the parent or seed of that church. . . . Every man of the church called "Noah" was of the posterity of the

Most Ancient Church, and with respect to hereditary evil was therefore in a state nearly like that of the rest of the posterity, which perished; and those who were in such a state could not be regenerated and made spiritual as could those who did not derive such quality by inheritance. (AC 788)

The similarity between the situation of those meant by Noah and people of European ancestry at the present day is hard to escape. They "are nearly like that of the rest of the posterity" (ibid.) and therefore it is difficult for the church to be renewed with them. This passage goes on to state that they "cannot so well be regenerated as can the Gentiles, for they have an inherent opposition to faith, not only from principles imbibed from infancy and afterwards confirmed, but from hereditary disposition also" (ibid.). Passages like this may help to explain why it is such a challenge to pass the vision of the New Church from generation to generation in this culture of Anglo-Europeans.

How Much has Changed in Two-Hundred-and-Fifty Years?

In the passages quoted above certain faults are specifically mentioned about the nature of people in the Christian world: atheism, hostility to faith, hatred, quarrels, violence, adultery, drunkenness. Have things improved in these areas since Swedenborg's time? Consider the type of findings and statistics that are routinely published in daily papers, such as the following:

- "One in four adolescents said they were physically or sexually abused in the past year" according to a study published in *Pediatrics Magazine*, October 1994.[6]
- In a recent survey of 17,592 college students "forty-four percent reported bingeing on alcohol, defined as downing five drinks in a row . . . on at least one occasion in the two weeks before the survey."[7]

---

6. David Finkelhor and Jennifer Dziuba-Leatherman, "Children as Victims of Violence: A National Survey," *Pediatrics* 94, no. 4 (1994): 413-420. (quoted from *Chicago Tribune* October 4, 1994, 6).

7. H. Wechsler, A. Davenport, G.W. Dowdall, B. Moeykens, and S. Castillo, "Health and Behavioral Consequences of Binge Drinking in College," *Journal of the American Medical Association* 272, no. 21 (1994): 1672-1677.

- "The Census Bureau estimates that only 39 percent of children born in 1988 will live with both parents until their eighteenth birthday." [8]
- "Within a decade, more than half of the children will be born into families where there has been no marriage."[9]

These and many similar facts do not point to a culture that has become more spiritual or receptive than the one in which that Swedenborg lived.

Swedenborg lived in a world that was basically comfortable and externally orderly, where he could write and publish his books without serious problem. We also live, for the most part, in a comfortable and orderly world, but it is hard, however, to detect the true nature of the church:

> To those within the Church it is not apparent that this is the condition of the Church, that is to say, that they treat with contempt and loathe everything to do with goodness and truth, and also show hostility towards those things, especially towards the Lord Himself. They do indeed attend places of worship, listen to sermons with some kind of reverence while they are there, go to the Holy Supper, and sometimes discuss these things with one another in a seemly way. (AC 3489)

Statistics make it clear that we face problems in the United States, but for most Americans this is not apparent from personal experience. It is very difficult to divorce ourselves from our accustomed cultural prejudices and gain a true and objective perspective regarding what is happening around us.

There are many positive and hopeful signs of spiritual life in the United States. Slavery has been abolished in much of the world. *Time* magazine reported that 69% of Americans believe in angels (December 27, 1993), and another *Time* issue discussed the growing movement to strengthen marriage and prevent divorce (February 27, 1995). While we could choose to see such signs simply in the light of *Arcana Coelestia* 3489, quoted above, it is undoubtedly true that there are many good,

---

8. Carl Thomas, "The Sixties Are Dead: Long Live the Nineties," *Imprimis* 1995, no. 1 (January 1995): 3.

9. Carl Thomas, "The Sixties Are Dead: Long Live the Nineties," *Imprimis* 1995, no. 1 (January 1995): 5. (quoting President Clinton's 1994 State of the Union Address).

well-intentioned, and intelligent people—there is hope for the future. We need to look at all the signs to gain a balanced perspective.

The New Church is Nevertheless Addressed to the Christian Church

Even though the Heavenly Doctrines are critical of the people of the Christian world, the Church is addressed to them, and they are the first to be invited into the New Jerusalem. They are like those invited to the feasts in Matthew 22 and Luke 14; although many did not accept the invitation, the places were nevertheless filled. And when the twelve apostles were first sent out in Matthew 10, they were first sent not to the gentiles, but to "the lost sheep of the house of Israel."

The New Church is addressed to the Christian Church in the same sense that the Christian Church is addressed to the Jews. The New Testament presupposes a knowledge of the Old Testament; the Heavenly Doctrines presuppose a knowledge of Christianity. Passages such as the following invite those in the Christian world to the New Church:

> By [the seven churches] are described all who are in the Christian world, who have religion, and from whom the New Church, which is the New Jerusalem, can be formed; and it is being formed from those who approach the Lord alone, and at the same time perform repentance from evil works. (AR 69)

Other passages make it clear that good Christians are at the center of heaven:

> The Christians, with whom the Word is read, constitute the breast of [the grand Man of heaven]; for they are in the midst of all. (SS 105.3)

> The situation with Christians and gentiles in the next life is that Christians who have acknowledged the truths of faith and at the same time have led a life of goodness are received ahead of gentiles; but such at the present day are few. Gentiles, however, who have led obedient and charitable lives one with another are received ahead of Christians who have not led so good a life. (AC 2590)

There are many good people in the Christian world, and they will be reached if New Church evangelization efforts are what they should be.

"Few" is a relative term—it could include millions of people. General Church experience so far is that "few" is a much smaller number than that, but the teachings should keep us from being discouraged and give us grounds to hope for more success in the future.

Implications for Evangelization

No one claims that evangelization is easy. To succeed against the powers which have enslaved people's minds it is important to have a clear view of where we are and not be like the Pharisees, who could predict the weather but failed to see the "signs of the times." A world view based in reality will keep us from becoming discouraged because we will know what we are up against. It may also help us to make decisions about the kinds of programs that are most likely to be effective.

Two things are implied by the preceding quotations as being very important: First, fellowship within the church organization and New Church education. It is difficult for people to remain committed to the New Church in the skeptical environment of the Western world. The support of others who hold similar beliefs is vital. Similarly, it is difficult for children to become committed to the New Church unless they are taught about it from an early age and experience fellowship and support from their peers.

My hope is that the General Church will accept the idea that the Last Judgment is about the transfer of the church to new populations rather than following our natural inclination to focus on the peoples where the New Church has had its beginnings. The future growth of the New Church is most likely to happen outside of the Christian world. This may be in the near future or the distant future. If we accept this, we will do what we can, within the limitations of the available resources, to promote it, in addition to evangelizing vigorously in the Christian world.

The truth of these teachings is made increasingly obvious through observation of what is happening to Christianity in this world.

What is Happening to the Christian Church?

The statements in the Heavenly Doctrines about the future of the church seem to parallel observations of about what is happening in global Christianity. Phil Jenkins discusses this in *The New Faces of Christianity*:

> Today, there are about two billion Christians, of whom 530 million live in Europe, 510 million in Latin America, 390 million in Africa, and perhaps 300 million in Asia, but those numbers will change substantially in coming decades. By 2025, Africa and Latin America will vie for the title of the most Christian continent. A map of the "statistical center of gravity of global Christianity" shows that center moving steadily southward, from a point in northern Italy in 1800, to central Spain in 1900, to Morocco by 1970, and to a point near Timbuktu today. And the southward trajectory will continue unchecked through the coming century. [10]

The transfer of Christianity from Europeans to the gentiles is especially obvious in Africa:

> The figures are startling. Between 1900 and 2000, the number of Christians in Africa grew from 10 million to over 360 million, from 10 percent of the population to 46 percent. If that is not, quantitatively, the largest religious change in human history in such a short period, I am at a loss to think of a rival. Today, the most vibrant centers of Christian growth are still in Africa itself, but also around the Pacific Rim, the Christian Arc. Already today, Africans and Asians represent some 30 percent of all Christians, and the proportion will rise steadily. [11]

The growth of Christianity in Africa over the last century has been "quantitatively, the largest religious change in human history in such a short period."[12] Meanwhile, the church among the European peoples is in decline, or has stagnated entirely:

> We can predict that by 2050 there should be around three billion Christians in the world, of whom only around one-fifth or fewer will be non-Hispanic whites.[13]

---

10. Philip Jenkins, *The New Faces of Christianity* (New York: Oxford University Press, Inc., 2005), 9.

11. Ibid.

12. Ibid.

13. Ibid.

Looking at various Christian denominations makes the changes very clear:

> The Roman Catholic Church, the world's largest, was the first to feel the impact. Today, two-thirds of its adherents live in Africa, Asia, and Latin America, and that total does not include people of the global South residing in the North. By 2025, that proportion should rise to 75 percent, a fact that will undoubtedly be reflected in future papal elections.
>
> The Anglican Communion—historically, the "English" church—is becoming ever more African dominated, so that the Nigerian branch will soon be its largest representative.
>
> The Seventh Day Adventist Church also epitomizes these trends. In the 1950s, the church had around a million members, mainly concentrated in the United States. Today, the church claims some fourteen million members, of whom only one million are located in the United States; and among even that American million, a sizable share are of immigrant stock.[14]

Is this same process occurring in the New Church as well?

AFRICAN SPIRITUALITY

Early on in the history of the General Church there was a great deal of interest in the New Church in Africa. Christian missions were well established in many parts of the world during this era, but it was still long before any kind of wholesale movement of the church to those populations. New Church missions were established in the early 1900s in South Africa, and in the 1920s considerable resources were devoted to them. The New Church has had reasonable success in South Africa, including the growth of the largest New Church organization in the world: The New Church of Southern Africa. Founded by the Rev. D. W. Mooki, the church currently has 25,000 members, seventy-five ordained ministers, and some 350 congregations. African congregations of the General Church and the Lord's New Church have also grown over the years at a much more modest rate.

---

14. Ibid.

After initial enthusiasm about establishing congregations in Africa, some wondered at their slow growth. Over the past one hundred years, however, the situation has changed Jenkins writes:

> The figures are startling. Between 1900 and 2000, the number of Christians in Africa grew from 10 million to over 360 million, from 10 percent of the population to 46 percent. If that is not, quantitatively, the largest religious change in human history in such a short period, I am at a loss to think of a rival. [15]

This growth has been aided by the spread of education. Since the independence of most African countries was gained during or after the 1950s, the literacy rate has increased dramatically since 1960, "from 9 percent in 1960 to more than 60 percent forty years later."[16]

Since the Heavenly Doctrines assume a well-educated, biblically informed readership, this education factor is especially significant for the growth of the New Church and is an important consideration affecting the timing of the spread of the New Church.

But do the Heavenly Doctrines indicate where the New Church will be renewed? We find an interesting answer in the last passage of *Last Judgment:*

> I had various talks with angels about the future state of the church. They said that they did not know what would happen, because the Lord alone knows the future. What they did know was that the servitude and captivity, in which people in the church have up to now been held, had been taken away, so that now through the restoration of freedom they could better perceive interior truths, if they wished to do so, and thus, if they wished, become interior people. *But they said that they still had only faint hopes of the people in the Christian church, though much better hopes of a people far removed from the Christian world* and sheltered from its attackers, since it was of a nature able to receive spiritual light and become celestial-spiritual people. *They said that at the present time interior truths are being revealed among that people, and they are being received with spiritual*

---

15. Ibid.

16. Paul Tiyambe Zeleza, *The Inventions of African Identities and Languages: The Discursive and Developmental Implications*: (Pennsylvania State University, 2006), http://www.lingref.com/cpp/acal/36/paper1402.pdf (accessed September 7, 2007).

faith, that is, in the way they live and in their hearts; and they worship the Lord. (LJ 74: emphasis added)

Is this saying that the angels have more hope for the church outside of the Christian world in general? Or are they speaking of a particular part of the world? They say "a people far removed from the Christian world," to whom "at the present time interior truths are being revealed." The angels are thinking of a specific people; many passages make it clear that they are speaking of the people of the continent of Africa.

Teachings in the Heavenly Doctrines about Africans

Africans Receive the Truth more easily than Others

The Heavenly Doctrines speak highly of people in Africa: they are more easily enlightened than any other people, they live according to their laws, and a higher percentage of them enter heaven than any other population.

> *Among the gentiles in the next life Africans are liked very much, for they receive the goods and truths of heaven more easily than any others.* Above all they wish to be called the obedient, but not the faithful. They say that because Christians possess the doctrine of faith, Christians may be called the faithful, but not themselves unless they receive it, or as they say, are able to receive it. (AC 2604, HH 326: emphasis added)

> *The African people are more capable of enlightenment than all other peoples on this earth,* because they are of such a character as to think interiorly and thus to accept truths and acknowledge them. (LJ post 118: emphasis added)

> *The African race is the one in this earth which is able to be in illustration beyond all other races,* because they are such that they think interiorly, and receive truths, and acknowledge that they are truths from that ground, differently from other races, for example, Europeans. . . . The Africans in our globe are the ones who are of the genius in which are the angels in the Celestial Kingdom; Europeans, those who are of the spiritual [genius]—the difference in the nature of which may be seen in the [*Arcana Coelestia*].

In a word, the Africans live according to their religion and its laws, which they love; and, therefore, they are of such a character, namely, interior. They were told that Christians do not thus live according to their religion, but according to the civil laws, and only have the doctrinals of religion in the memory, and rarely think from them on account of life, but only on account of doctrine; for they believe they are saved by the faith of doctrine and not by life, nor do they have doctrinals of life. (SE 5518-5518a: emphasis added)

Moreover, the Africans are more receptive than others in this earth, of the heavenly doctrine—which it was given to know from the spirits who are thence. These willingly receive, from the angels, the doctrine concerning the Lord. They, more than others, have it implanted in themselves that the Lord must appear altogether as a man, and that it can by no means happen otherwise. They are in the capacity of receiving not only the truths of faith, but especially its goods. They are of the celestial genius. (SE 4783: emphasis added)

These and the things previously told to me [lead to the conclusion] that *a greater proportion [of people] from Africa, than from other regions of the earth, are introduced into heaven;* for their conscience in these matters is somewhat in the way of truth. (SE 453: emphasis added)

From a great deal of experience, I have learned that the worst of all spirits in the last Heaven are those who in the world were called Christians. Most of them have no belief, but attack and hold in hatred everything having to do with true religion and, unwilling to be taught, persistently trample them under foot. They are so terribly cunning, and contrive such stratagems in opposition to the Lord, and against faith in Jesus, and against believers, that one cannot be amazed enough. And that [wickedness] stays rooted in their disposition and character, for then they live from their own character, and when abandoned to that, are like furies. Mohammedans are really extremely surprised about this, who themselves are easily taught, and allow themselves to be guided, and easily receive the faith. After Christians come the Jews, as well as those who had worshipped Abraham as God, the latter also being quite deceitful. *The gentlest of all are the Africans.* (SE 480: emphasis added)

They say that they do not love their own race only, but all however many there are in heaven, so that they have an ingrained universal love. (SE 453)

This last point is especially evident to people who visit Africa, although naturally, it varies from country to country; the impression one gets is that everyone who sees you is delighted by your presence.

The Ancient Church spread into Africa

African traditional religions, like the ancient religions in many
parts of the world, have their roots in the Ancient Church. A number of
passages state that the Ancient Church was spread into all the countries
of Africa.

> Moreover, this Noachian, or Ancient Church, was diffused throughout Asia,
> especially into Syria, Mesopotamia, Assyria, Chaldea, the land of Canaan and
> the parts adjacent, Philistia, Egypt, Tyre, Sidon, Nineveh, and *also into Arabia
> and Ethiopia*, and in course of time into Great Tartary, and thence downward as
> far as to the Black Sea, *and thence again into all the countries of Africa*. (Coro 39:
> emphasis added)

> Religion has existed from the most ancient times, and the inhabitants of the
> world everywhere have had a knowledge of God, and some knowledge of a life
> after death. This has not originated from themselves or their own intelligence,
> but from the Ancient Word; and in later times from the Israelitish Word. From
> these two Words the things of religion have spread into the Indies and their
> islands, and *through Egypt and Ethiopia into the kingdoms of Africa*, and from
> the maritime parts of Asia into Greece, and from thence into Italy. (SS 117:
> emphasis added)

> The religious beliefs and practices of many nations were derived and transmitted
> from that Ancient Word. For instance, they were transmitted from the land of
> Canaan and from various places in Asia to Greece, and from Greece to Italy,
> and through Ethiopia and Egypt into *several countries in Africa*. (De Verbo 15:
> emphasis added)

> Religious beliefs based upon these two Words spread to the Indies and the
> adjacent islands, and *by way of Egypt and Ethiopia to the kingdoms of Africa;* and
> from the coasts of Asia to Greece and so to Italy. (TCR 275: emphasis added)

> *The second church, which may be called the Ancient Church, was in Asia and in parts
> of Africa;* this came to an end and perished as the result of idolatrous practices.
> (TCR 760: emphasis added)

The following report from Rev. Ekow Eshun in Ghana describes
a fairly typical example of what may be ancient influences on modern
Africa culture.

Comments from Rev. Ekow Eshun

The African Renaissance Movement, which was started about 30 years ago by formerly Catholic Bishop Okomfo Damuah, aimed at re-vitalizing traditional religion. The Afrikania Mission is an organization that champions the movement. It has branches in Ghana and neighboring states such as Togo. It tends to be a political organization, vehemently opposed to the brainwashing and denigration of the African traditional religions. They find Christian conduct reprehensible.

They use water to drive away evil spirits in their worship rituals. (Water signifies truth.)

I had an opportunity to attend a worship service with members of the African Renaissance Mission. At the entrance to the place of worship was a pot of water. Every member who walks in has to dip a finger in the water and make a circle on the forehead. When I asked for the meaning of this sign, I was told that it identifies them with the spirits in the spiritual world.

Just before worship started, two things were done. First, a libation was poured for the ancestors to invoke them to be present with the worshippers. The second ritual involved sprinkling an herbal preparation on me. According to them, this sprinkling protects each person from the attacks of the evil spirits.

In the African traditional religion, there are several kinds of rituals. There are rituals for the dead and rituals for those who commit serious infractions, such as incest, stealing something that belongs to the gods, adultery, murder, breaking tradition, and taboos, etc.

Africans in the Grand Man

A person or group's location in heaven is described relative to the human form or in terms of proximity to a center. African gentiles are less central than good Christians, but more central than many others.

Christians among whom the Word is read form the breast of that grand person. They are also at the center of all. Around them are Roman Catholics. Around these are Muslims, who acknowledge the Lord as the greatest prophet and as the son of God. After these, then, come Africans. And the outmost periphery is composed of nations and peoples from Asia and the Indies. All those who are in that person also face toward the middle. Moreover, the greatest light, too, is found in the middle, where, as said, are Christians who possess the Word, because the light in heaven is Divine truth emanating from the Lord as its sun. (De Verbo 17)

Christians among whom the Word is read constitute the breast of this Man. They are in the centre of all, and round about them are the Roman Catholics; around these again are the Mohammedans, who acknowledge the Lord to be the supreme Prophet and the Son of God. *After these come the Africans,* while the nations and peoples of Asia and the Indies form the outermost circumference. (SS 105; emphasis added)

The Africans and the gentiles in the spiritual world. The gentiles, who know nothing about the Lord, are to be seen surrounding those who do. Indeed the people who occupy the outermost fringes are those who are utter idolaters and worshipped the sun and the moon. Those, however, who acknowledge one God and are scrupulous in observing the kind of precepts that are in the Ten Commandments, are to be seen in the upper region, and are thus in more direct communication with the Christians in the heartland, for this prevents communication being cut off by the Mohammedans and the Roman Catholics. The gentiles too are grouped according to their characters and their ability to receive light from the Lord through the heavens. Some live further in, some further out; this does not depend on their native country, but on their religion. *The Africans are further in than the rest.* (CLJ 73: emphasis added)

The Africans in the spiritual world; also something about other nations. The other nations who know nothing about the Lord are to be seen in the spiritual world further out than those who do. In fact the people who occupy the outermost fringes are those who were utter idolaters and in the previous world worshipped the sun and moon. Those, however, who acknowledge one God and are scrupulous in observing the kind of precepts that are in the Ten Commandments, and so in living in accordance with them, have closer contact with the Christians in the centre; for by this means contact is not interrupted by the Mohammedans and Roman Catholics. Nations are also kept apart in accordance with their characters and their ability to receive light from the Lord through the heavens. Some of them live further in, some further out; this is due partly to their climate, partly to the stock they belong to, partly to their education and partly to their religion. *The Africans are further in than the rest.* (TCR 835; emphasis added)

Africans Believe in Life after Death

My own experience of Africa is that people there have a strong belief in life after death. Many Africans have told me that it is easy to accept the teachings of the New Church about heaven because they are so similar to their traditional beliefs. Only one passage seems to comment on this.

> Roman Catholics believe that their saints are men in heaven, and that the rest are somewhere else; Mohammedans believe the same of their dead; *Africans especially,* and many other races, have a similar belief. Why then do not the Reformed Christians believe this, when they know it from the Word? (DP 274.8; emphasis added)

The Last Judgment and Africa

The connection between the Last Judgment and the establishment of the New Church in Africa is one that the Heavenly Doctrines explicitly make. Here is one example:

> From these things it was evident, what *that signifies which the Lord said where He speaks of the last judgment—that it is called His Coming,* the consummation of the age, when also the temple should be destroyed (Matt. 24.1–3). The angels said concerning the Coming of the Lord, that, as often as a new Church was to be raised up, the Lord Himself should come, and teach, like as when the Most Ancient and Ancient [Churches were established], . . . especially when the Jewish [Church was established]: the Lord then appeared in a bush to Moses, again on Mount Sinai, and also through the prophets by whom the Word, which is from Himself was given so also, now, with those among whom a new Church is to be raised up, whom the Lord Himself teaches by the angels. *Moreover, the Africans are more receptive than others in this earth, of the heavenly doctrine—which it was given to know from the spirits who are thence. These willingly receive, from the angels, the doctrine concerning the Lord.* They, more than others, have it implanted in themselves that the Lord must appear altogether as a man, and that it can by no means happen otherwise. They are in the capacity of receiving not only the truths of faith, but especially its goods. They are of the celestial genius. (SE 4783; emphasis added)

Africans Believe in One God in Human Form and the Doctrine of the Lord

The above passage states that Africans easily receive the doctrine of the Lord and innately recognize that God is a man; this is central to explaining African interest in the New Church. It is also completely consistent with my own experience of Africa. There are no African atheists. People in Africa are especially distinguished by their enthusiastic adoration of the Lord. It can sometimes appear that Africans traditionally worship idols. But these idols are not seen as gods, only as representatives of the ancestors in heaven, all of whom serve the one God. The following passages describe the importance of the African recognition that God is one and that He is in a human form.

> That the Mohammedans, and certain nations in Asia and Africa, abhor Christianity, because they believe that it worships three Gods, is known. (BE 37)

> The rest of the nations in the world, who are possessed of religion and sound reason, insist that God is one: all the Mohammedans in their empires, *the Africans in many kingdoms of their continent,* and the peoples of Asia in several of theirs, not to mention the present-day Jews. (TCR 9.2; emphasis added)

> *That the inhabitants of this earth from the primeval age had an idea of God-Man, or of the Divine Human,* is evident from their idols, also from the ideas of such Gentiles as had interior thought and perception, *like some of the Africans;* likewise from the inhabitants of almost all the earths (as may be seen in a separate small work). Man has such an idea of the Divine because it flows in from heaven, for in heaven no one can think of God except in the human form. (AE 808.4; emphasis added)

> But the idea of God as Man that flows in from heaven is so perverted with many that either a man of the world or an idol is worshiped in place of God, comparatively as the bright light of the sun is turned into colors not beautiful, and its summer heat into foul stenches, according to the objects upon which they fall. But it is for reasons stated above that *the idea of God becomes an idea of a little cloud,* or of a mist, or of the inmost of nature, *ideas that exist among Christians, but rarely among other nations who enjoy any light of reason, as the Africans and some others.* (AE 1118; emphasis added)

> *The inhabitants of all earths have a perception of God in human form,* so also had the wise men of old, such as Abraham, and at the present day *those of interior wisdom such as the Africans.* It is not so with our wise ones, but only with the simple, with whom the general idea about God that comes from heaven has not

been extinguished by perverted reasonings. (*Athanasian Creed* 154; emphasis added)

There is the idea of the Divine Human concerning God in all the earths in the universe (references); *it also exists with the Gentiles of our earth, as with the Africans;* and this from the influx of heaven. But this idea has been destroyed with Christians, especially the intelligent. (*Athanasian Creed* 189; emphasis added)

[Gentiles, especially Africans] *who acknowledge and worship one God as the creator of the universe, have of God the idea of a person.* They say that no one can have any other idea of God. When they hear that many people entertain an idea of God as a kind of small cloud (at the center of the universe), they ask where those people are, and when they are told that they are found among Christians, they say it is not possible. (DLW 11; emphasis added)

Behind these, more to the north, are the places of instruction of various heathen nations who in the world have lived a good life in conformity with their religion, and have thereby acquired a kind of conscience, and have done what is just and right not so much on account of the laws of their government, as on account of the laws of religion, which they believed ought to be sacredly observed, and in no way violated by their doings. When these have been taught they are all easily led to acknowledge the Lord, because it *is impressed on their hearts that God is not invisible, but is visible under a human form.* These in number exceed all the rest, and *the best of them are from Africa.* (HH 514; emphasis added)

Gentiles who in the world have worshipped God in human form, and lived a charitable life in accordance with their own religious beliefs, are associated with the Christians in heaven, since they excel others in their acknowledgment and adoration of the Lord. *The most intelligent of these are from Africa.* (LJ 51: emphasis added)

I was taken again to Africans by a way leading first to the north and then to the west. I saw there what appeared to be a palace with some people about it, and afterward traveled on beyond, where I stopped; and I heard that a great number of emissaries were being sent from the Christian heaven to the people there, who were Africans, and who in that place were ones who in the world had lived according to their religious faith and acknowledged one God in human form. These Africans were told that a person who lives intent on good in accordance with religion possesses as well an affection for truth, because goodness of life desires nothing more than truth, inasmuch as it desires to know how one is to live well. Persons of that character consequently rejoice on being instructed. Moreover, all such persons receive truths from the Lord, they were told, and are enlightened according to the nature and extent of the goodness of their life. The Africans acknowledged this and were delighted by it.

The African people are more capable of enlightenment than all other peoples on this earth, because they are of such a character as to think interiorly and thus to accept truths and acknowledge them. Others, such as Europeans, think only externally, receiving truths in their memory, but not seeing them interiorly in any light of the understanding—a light which they also do not acknowledge in matters of faith.

I told them that few Christians live in accordance with religion, but in accordance with civil laws, and morally and well for the sake of reputation, honors and opportunities for material gain, and that they rarely think to live in accordance with doctrinal precepts, even believing themselves to be saved by faith in their doctrine, and not by an accompanying life. Consequently they also do not have doctrinal precepts governing life.

The Africans were very astonished at this, not wishing to believe it to be so, believing rather that there is no one who does not live in accordance with his religion, and that if he does not, he must inevitably become stupid and evil, because he then does not receive anything from heaven. (LJ post 118: emphasis added)

Africans, too, differ from each other according to their idea of God. Some of them worship an invisible God and a visible one. Some make of these two separate beings; some make them one and the same. Some have been taught by Christians that God was born a man, and they accept this; but when they hear Christians distinguish the Divine into three persons, they go away, believing nevertheless that even if Christians say three, they must still think one; for they do not comprehend what a Son born from eternity is.

Some of the best among them believe that God is altogether a person. They say that those who believed that God was born a man had once seen a bright star in the sky.

The wiser of them believe that God was born in the world as a man and thus manifested Himself. (LJ post 119: emphasis added)

A certain priest, who had supposed no one to be capable of an idea of the Divine Human, was transported into *societies of Africans, and he found that they had no other idea than that of a Divine Human.* (LJ post 121: emphasis added)

The Lord [as conceived] among the Africans. The Africans with whom there is a revelation, do not know, respecting the Lord, that He was born a man; but they know that God is a man, and say that He Himself created Himself Man. On hearing this, it was granted me to talk with Africans; to whom it was stated, that it is true that Jehovah Himself created Himself Man, because from His own proper Power, He had made His Human Divine. (SE 5919: emphasis added)

Children, the simple-minded, women, in a word all who have not destroyed that idea through the causes mentioned above, have the idea of God as of a Man. (6) The same idea remains with all gentiles, *especially with Africans, who cannot conceive what a God who is not Man.* (SE 6057.5: emphasis added)

The clarity of Africans' thought about God and their strong love for Him promotes their reception of the New Church doctrine of the Lord. They easily grasp the necessity of His birth into the world and the means by which He saved the human race, and they take great delight in this information.

Moreover, the Africans are more receptive than others in this earth, of the heavenly doctrine—which it was given to know from the spirits who are thence. These willingly receive, from the angels, the doctrine concerning the Lord. They, more than others, have it implanted in themselves that the Lord must appear altogether as a man, and that it can by no means happen otherwise. (SE 4783: emphasis added)

There are many communities of heathens, especially Africans, who, on being taught by angels about the Lord, say that it was inevitable that God the Creator of the universe should have appeared in the world, because He created and loves them; and that this appearance to the sight of the eye could only have been in human form. When they are told that He did not appear as angels usually do, but that He was born as a man and was seen as such, they hesitate a little and ask whether he had a human father. On hearing that He was conceived by the God of the universe and born of a virgin, they say that this means He had a Divine essence; and because this is infinite and life itself, He was not a man like other men. Later they are informed by angels that He looked like any other man; but when He was in the world, His Divine essence, which is in itself infinite and life itself, threw off His finite nature and the life He had from His mother and thus made Divine His Human, which was conceived and born in the world. *The Africans, because their inward thinking is more spiritual than that of others, understood this and accepted it.* (CLJ 75: emphasis added)

I have heard it reported that the Church today is being established among many in Africa, that they are currently receiving revelations, and that they are receptive of the doctrine of heaven, especially as regards the Lord. (LJ post 115: emphasis added)

Since the Africans surpass the rest in powers of inward judgment, I was able to engage in conversation with them about matters requiring deeper thought. I have recently talked with them about God, the Lord the Redeemer and the interior and the exterior man. As this discussion delighted them, I shall report some of the matters they perceived by inward sight on those three subjects.

About God they said that He had certainly come down and made Himself visible to human beings, because He is their Creator, Protector and Guide, and the human race is His. They said that He sees, examines and supplies every single thing that is in the heavens or on earth; and He regards what is good for them as if in Himself and Himself as in them. The reason is that He is the sun of the heaven of the angels, and is to be seen as high above the spiritual world as the terrestrial sun is above the natural world; and one who is the sun must see, examine and supply every single thing which is below. Because it is His Divine love which appears as the sun, it follows that He supplies to the greatest as to the least the necessities of life, and to human beings the things that concern love and wisdom. Things to do with love are supplied by means of the sun's heat, those to do with wisdom by means of its light. So if you form for yourself an idea of God as the sun of the universe, you will be sure from that idea to see and acknowledge His omnipresence, omniscience and omnipotence. (TCR 837: emphasis added)

Comments From Rev. Eshun Ekow

This is what I have gleaned from the several interviews I've conducted from people who practice the traditional African faith. Their ideas about God fall into four general categories: What God does, human images about God, the nature of God, and people's relationship with God.

Regarding what God does: God is regarded as the Creator. Therefore, God is called by these names: Moulder, Begetter, Bearer, Maker, Potter, Fashioner, Architect, Carpenter, Originator, Constructor. God is also regarded like a chief or king. God created the world "out of nothing." African Traditional practitioners believe that creation hasn't ceased.

Regarding human images of God: People picture Him with human characteristics. Their relationship with the Creator is comparable to the relationship between parent and child. God is pictured as a having the following qualities: He is good, merciful, holy, all-powerful, everywhere, all-knowing, limitless, self-existent, is the First cause, is a spirit, never changes.

Does Christianity add or detract from African Traditional Religion (ATR)? So far, people who practice ATR have a very good understanding of God.

Fundamentally, their understanding about the oneness of God is very admirable. They cannot conceive of the Creator having any rival. They don't consider even the devil as a rival. However, there is a problem with the idea of God being born human. They find this difficult to grasp. On their part, they don't think that the Lord who came in the world over two thousand years ago was the self-same God. To them God is transcendent and cannot come into this material world.

Communication by the Word in Ethiopia

A number of passages speak about Ethiopia, which is often mentioned in the Old Testament, and where Christianity has existed from its very beginning. According to these passages people there possess a written revelation, which is described both as Psalms of David and as their own unique revelation. Several of the following passages appear to describe the same incident.

> *Another time I had with me African spirits, from Ethiopia.* One day their ears were opened so that they heard people singing one of the Psalms of David in a temple in this world. The spirits were moved with such delight by this that they began to sing along with them. But presently their ears were closed again and they no longer heard anything from there; and then they were affected with a still greater delight, because it was a spiritual delight. And at the same time they were filled with intelligence, because the Psalm in its spiritual meaning had to do with the Lord and redemption by Him. The increase in their delight and joy of heart occurred as a result of their communication with a certain heavenly society from the Christian world, and by that communication they came into a similar state. It was apparent from this that a communication with the whole of heaven takes place by means of the Word. (De Verbo 18: emphasis added)

> The same may also be illustrated by the following experience. *There were with me African spirits from Abyssinia.* On a certain occasion their ears were opened that they might hear singing in a temple in the world from a Psalm of David. They were moved by this with such delight that they joined in the singing. However, soon their ears were closed so that they no longer heard anything from the temple. But they were then moved with a delight still greater because spiritual; and they were at the same time filled with intelligence, because that Psalm treated of the Lord and of redemption. The reason for their increased delight was that communication was given them with that society in heaven which was in conjunction with those who were singing that Psalm in the world. From this experience and many others it was made evident to me that communication with

the whole of heaven is effected through the Word. For this reason, by the Lord's Divine Providence, there is universal intercourse of the kingdoms of Europe, chiefly of those where the Word is read, with nations outside the Church. (SS 108: emphasis added)

In African Ethiopia they have several psalms composed in a style similar to that of our Word, and I was told that they sing them in their temples and that spirits experience a resulting communication. In the spiritual sense they have as their theme the one God, the Redeemer of the human race. [De Verbo 18] (LJ post 122: emphasis added)

I was told that in a certain region of Africa they have handed down from ancient time a book which they hold sacred, written in terms of things that correspond in a similar manner as the Word among us. (LJ post 120: emphasis added)

It was granted me to speak with African spirits about various matters, and they absorbed all the truths of the Church with a clear perception. Moreover, when the Word was presented to them, they understood it in its inner, spiritual meaning, and they gave it to their elders, who *said that they have the Word in their possession*, and that it is most sacred. (LJ post 123: emphasis added)

The wiser of the Gentiles, from those who are in Africa, think becomingly about the Lord's Divine Human, and are wise. *They also possess a Book, which is their Word; but it is not like ours. It is written, in like manner, by correspondences. It was written through illustrated men. These are in Africa.* (SE 5809.7: emphasis added)

These passages speak of there being a "book" in one or more parts of Africa with ancient writing like the Psalms or written using the same kind of ancient symbolism. There are surely books like this in existence in parts of East Africa, and possibly elsewhere as well, which have very old religious traditions.

Africans receive Revelations

Several passages state that the people of Africa receive revelations from angels, who instruct them orally. A few imply, as above, that the revelation is written, but most do not address this. These passages are remarkable for their length and number: it is a point of emphasis, not something that Swedenborg described in passing. It is mentioned throughout the Heavenly Doctrines almost every time the subject of Africa comes up, from *Spiritual Experiences* through the end of *True Christian Religion.*

While these passages seem strange and incredible to most Westerners, to Africans and to anyone who is familiar with Africa, they are completely consistent with normal experience. The concept of revelation is universally accepted in Africa, and many people report meaningful visions and dreams as part of their day-to-day lives. When readers of the Heavenly Doctrines describe how they came to read and recognize these books as divine, the answer will not uncommonly include some kind of revelatory experience. One person dreamed of the books and saw light emanating from them. Another was told in a dream to expect a new revelation from Europe, and quickly recognized a book of the Heavenly Doctrines as the thing that he was expecting.

This may seem surprising since the Heavenly Doctrines strictly warn people against contact with spirits, sorcery, and all forms of paranormal investigation:

> Many people believe that a person can be taught by the Lord by means of spirits speaking with him. Those who believe this, however, do not know that it is attended with danger to their souls. (AE 1182.4; see also HH 249, SE 1622, DP 135)

For some reason this danger appears to be less great with people in Africa. It is true that magic and sorcery exist commonly in Africa, and present serious problems. But African's ease with the concept of revelation seems to lessen the danger. In *True Christian Religion* this facility is attributed to their character:

> Since this is the nature of the Africans, at the present time a revelation is being made to them. (TCR 840)

And so we have the following teachings:

> [Gentiles] are informed by angels that He looked like any other man; but when He was in the world, His Divine essence, which is in itself infinite and life itself,

threw off His finite nature and the life He had from His mother and thus made Divine His Human, which was conceived and born in the world. *The Africans, because their inward thinking is more spiritual than that of others, understood this and accepted it.* (CLJ 75: emphasis added)

Since this is the nature of the African in the world too, at the present time a revelation is being made to them, which beginning at the centre is spreading out from there, but has not reached the seas. I heard of the angels' joy at that revelation, that it was opening up communication for them with the human reason, which previously had been closed by the blindness obscuring matters of faith. I was told from heaven that the inhabitants of that country are having dictated to them by angelic spirits the teachings that have just been published in the *Teaching Of The New Jerusalem About The Lord, The Word* and in The *Teaching About Life For The New Jerusalem.* (CLJ 76)

I have heard it reported that the Church today is being established among many in Africa, that they are currently receiving revelations. (LJ post 115)

I was led through several regions in front of me toward the left. After that I saw a large palace, having a spacious courtyard. Someone spoke with me there, saying that a revelation had been promised and that he was awaiting it. Moreover, a luminous glow appeared then surrounded by darkness, which was a sign that a revelation was now to be made. Then, as I was waiting attentively, I heard that the people were anticipating a revelation concerning the Christ, whom they call the one and only man, in consequence of whom every person is human. And then one of the angels spoke with them and instructed them concerning the Lord, telling them that He is the one and only God. They said that they perceived this, but not as yet that He was born a man; but after having been instructed by angels they understood this, too, saying that it happened for the salvation of the human race. They knew in addition many other things about heaven and hell, things of which Christians are unaware. I was told that they were Africans.

I was subsequently shown in a hazy vision how the doctrine of heaven was spreading in Africa, namely, toward the interior parts even to the center, and then continuing toward those who live on the coasts of the Mediterranean Sea, but not reaching the coast, and then after a time turning around toward Egypt.

Angels rejoiced on that account, seeing that the Lord's advent was now at hand once again, and that a new church was now being established with which they could be affiliated.

That doctrine does not reach all the way to Africans living along the coast, since Christians come there who introduce obstacles to its reception, and who have a human concept of the Lord and not a Divine one.

Africans are more receptive of the doctrine of heaven than others on this earth, because they willingly accept the doctrine concerning the Lord. (LJ post 116-117)

The spirits also said that some of them currently speak with Africans in the world and instruct them orally, that their speech with them descends chiefly into their inner perception, and that they sense the influx, thus receiving the revelation with enlightenment. (LJ post 124)

Concerning the New Church. In a wakeful vision, I was conducted through several regions, forwards, a little towards the left, for quite a remarkable distance, until [I arrived] within the tract where are the spirits from this globe. On the way, I was taken possession of according to the minds and nature of the spirits, and everywhere was almost compelled to reflect upon myself and my merit, and to attribute all things which were done by me to myself. The reason was, because the spirits of those regions through which I was conducted, were of such as, in the world, believed salvation to be merited by their works, and this in the particulars, when they have done well from the precepts of religion. There was a region, where, still more conspicuously and manifestly, they attributed all things to themselves or to merit. This region was nearly at the end of the rest; for all these regions were so arranged, that such a faith should go on increasing. There was also a region where they doubted, on account of so innumerable a crowd in infidelity, whether any salvation can be given, but [supposed], that, on account of the multitude of infidels which prevailed and as it were overflowed, the angelic heaven would perish.

After I passed through these regions, I was conducted to a great palace (in appearance, like the castle at Stockholm), and into a spacious court there, extending from one side to the opposite, which is by the sea; and when, at last, I came towards the sea, certain ones spoke, and *said that a revelation was promised which they have long expected, and that now they can scarcely expect it any longer.* Then appeared a certain luminous appearance, as it were in gloom. Hence they conjectured that the revelation is about to come; and, then I was conducted towards that place, I heard those there say that they expect a revelation concerning Christ, whom they called by the name current amongst them, the Only Man. Then, [one] of the angels from the Lord spoke with them, and instructed them concerning the Lord, saying that there is one God, and He is the Lord, and that it is the Father Himself, the Creator, who, when He appears in human form, was, and is, called the Son of God: hence they might have known that the Son of God was from eternity, and that He was the same with the Father, but in a human form. They said that they understand and perceive this; but, that He was born a man, they do not as yet apprehend: wherefore, they were instructed by the angel how this matter was circumstanced; and they, at length, confessed that they apprehend that also, and that it happened for the sake of the salvation of the human race. The same ones who were there, afterwards related that they have long had revelations from heaven, and that thence was their religion, and that it has been promised them that many things should be revealed to them, and, finally, touching God. They knew many things about heaven and hell which Christians are ignorant of. It was perceived that those in the earth, *with whom there is thence communication and influx, were about the region of Africa*, partly also in Asia, rather near the Indian Sea, but not in the immediate neighborhood of the sea.

I was next led from thence towards the right where I also heard people speaking and expecting revelations. With these, angels spoke, and instructed them concerning the Lord, and that they were about to receive the unblemished doctrine of the Church out of heaven, and also that they would receive a Bible, but a new Bible, from the Lord. I heard them saying that it could never be otherwise than that God, the Creator of the universe, has appeared in the world before men, because He created them and loves them, and because there is a life after death, and He wishes thus to save them to eternity; and that that appearance must have taken place, even to the sight of the eye, in human form. Then the spirits spoke together concerning the fact that those who are in the Christian world, at this day, especially the learned, are of quite another opinion, namely, that, inasmuch as the Lord was born a man, and appeared a man, He cannot be, as to the human, the God of the universe, still less the Creator of all things; and that this is a sign that their nature is perverted; for, in those with whom there is anything uncorrupted in the intellectual part, and still more in the voluntary, it is innate that the God of the universe must needs appear altogether as a man. Hence, the ancients called God, when He appeared in the earth, Jehovah, Creator of the universe—for instance, Abraham and the rest; and, likewise, the Gentiles of that time, who were wise above the rest, in Greece, and afterwards in Italy, made all their gods men, as Saturn, Jupiter, Neptune, Juno, Minerva, and many others; likewise the nations wherever they worship idols; because it is innate in them that they see their god, and thus acknowledge him. This arises from the reason that the Divine Truth proceeding from the Lord; puts on the human form, not only in the universal heaven, but also in every angel there; for Divine Truth is, in its form, a man. Hence the correspondences of all things in the heavens, with man, concerning which see nos. [3624-3649, *Arcana Coelestia*]. They spoke such things to each other; and they marveled that, in the tract where the Church is, few of the learned are willing to acknowledge the Lord as God, merely for the reason that He was a man; and that, what it is to make the human Divine, they do not at all apprehend. But I also heard some saying, that it is from permission that certain ones in the Church worship the saints as gods, to the end that the idea of a visible God may not perish; and that they [thus] retain some notion, from nature, that the Divine is in a human form, that is, that the Divine proceeding from the Lord is human in every form.

The ones with whom took place the conversation concerning doctrine from heaven, and concerning a Bible, were a little to the right of the former, as was said; and it was perceived that they were in the entrance to Africa.

It was next shown, in an obscure vision, in what way *that heavenly doctrine would advance in Africa,* namely, from this place towards the interiors of Africa, but, still, not to the middle of it; and, then, should bend itself to the inhabitants who are in interior Africa, nearer to the Mediterranean Sea, and thus go on for a long distance, but not as far as to the coasts; and, then, after a time, should bend its way back through an interior tract as far as towards Egypt; and, also, should then proceed from there, to some in Asia under the government of the Turks, also in Asia round about. *Hence, the angels rejoiced that the coming of the Lord was now at hand, and that the Church, which is now perishing in Europe, should be renewed in Africa;* and that this is done by the Lord alone, by means of revelations, and not by missionaries from the Christians. The people in those countries were also cautioned not to receive any doctrine from Christian missionaries, but that they should indeed hear them, but not believe them. For which reason also, that heavenly doctrine is not divulged to those who are near the coasts, for Christians come thither and introduce scandals; for these surpass all in believing nothing, and living impiously. (SE 4773-4777: emphasis added)

About the African race. About the new heaven and the new earth. About the Last Judgment. It has been previously related, how, from the middle heaven, where those are who are in truths from the Word—thus, where was the college—many were sent to those of the Catholic communion, who, although in darkness, were still in the affection of truth for the sake of truth, by reason of a life of good.

I was now led down to the Africans, first, by a northerly, after by a westerly way—for they dwell in the west far removed from the midst, towards the northern angle there; and, at first, I came to a certain palace, like one of stone on earth, where some people were; and, after that, farther on where I halted, and heard then a vast number [who had been] sent forth from the midst, or from the college, to the nations which were at a distance; and, communication being granted, it was discovered that those nations were Africans, and that they were there who have lived well according to their religious belief, and acknowledged one God, and Him under the Human form.

I spoke somewhat with them about the Lord. They said that they are looking for information, and that they love to know truths. I told them that those who have acknowledged one God under the Human form, and have lived a life of good, are the ones who are able to be instructed and illustrated, since

these are in the affection of truth; for good of life desires nothing more than it
does truth, for it desires to know how to live well: hence those rejoice when they
are instructed: also, that all such receive truth from the Lord, and are illustrated,
according to the kind and amount of their good of life. They acknowledged this
and rejoiced; and, afterwards, I also heard that a great number of spirits and
angels who are instructed in Divine truths from the heavenly Doctrine, were
sent thither. (SE 5515-5517)

The Africans. I was brought by the Lord, through changes of state which went
on for about half an hour, in a southerly direction, *as far as to the wiser African
sort; and it was granted me to converse with them about various matters; and from my
discourse with them, it was granted me to perceive that they knew the truths of the
Church in themselves.* They ran over the things which I knew, and stated that they
knew all these, and more. I imagined that they were of those who indeed perceive
the truths of the Church when they hear others [utter them], but still do not talk
about them; but it was noticed that these likewise speak of them. I also spoke to
them about the knowledges which are representatives and correspondences. Of
these they knew little; but it was shown them what these contribute to wisdom
and happiness—to wit, when they are conjoined. Various things were pointed
out respecting that matter, which things also delighted them much. I was also
informed where their best ones are, namely, at the side towards the sea,
[occupying] more than half of the region, with almost this form:

[Swedenborg's Map of Africa]   [Map of Africa. http://www.mongabay.com.]

Swedenborg's evidently hastily scribbled map, on the left here, is not especially
clear or helpful. It appears to be almost upside-down, with the Mediterranean
indicated at the bottom left, and the Cape of Good Hope, the southern tip of
Africa, at the right. The point he makes in the following passage seems to be
that the populations most receptive of heavenly light are the ones more towards
the middle and west, not so much those at the extreme north, south or east. This

map may not be about populations in the natural world, but a representation of the arrangement of peoples in the spiritual world.

. . . namely, the best of them are in the whole tract, D E, but the worse are towards the Mediterranean Sea, H, and at the Cape of Good Hope, F; so that the kingdoms of the best are D E; but they who are towards D B, that is, towards Asia, are not wise, and are infested by those who come thence, because they speak things which they do not perceive. It is like this almost to C; and those who are still worse are towards A, where Egypt is. They stated that in that great tract D E they all worship the Lord, and are taught by many who communicate with the angels of heaven; that the communication is not through speech by the angels, but through interior perception; and that these are their instructors, whom they perfectly discriminate from all others. They also stated that those from Europe are not admitted to them; and that if they come thither, and are not willing to be their servants, they are sent away from there, by a road at B, and that they are sold by them, in order that thus they may be safe from infestations. When any of the Papal religion come there, they say that they are saints; but they are immediately examined, and they perceive that they know nothing about truth, still less perceive it; wherefore, they are either not admitted, or are sent towards Asia, like the rest. Next they received the Word and read it; and on reading it they perceived nothing of holiness at first, but afterwards more and more of holiness; and then they gave it to their instructors, who said that they have it but have not disclosed the fact. The instructors stated that they dictated it to the men in Africa with whom they have communication, just as the Lord guides [them]. Hence it is evident that there is now a revelation there. Afterwards, also, the work on Heaven and Hell was given to them, which they likewise accepted and preserved; in like manner, also, the ones on *The Last Judgment* and on *The Earths in the Universe,* and likewise those on *The White Horse,* and, lastly, *The Doctrine of the New Jerusalem,*—in order that they may take thence those things which they consider useful. Tranquility prevailed there because they were in order. Certain ones attended on Christians, with whom is the Word, and observed that they perceive nothing of truth from good; and they were led to certain Englishmen, and perceived that they do not receive it; a few [do so] from a certain intelligence, but scarcely anyone from perception. Furthermore, I was conducted in spirit to others in Africa; and this region is known to Europeans, and in the maps is called Ethiopia, where a noble race dwell in tents. (SE 5946: emphasis added)

Since this is the nature of the Africans, at the present time a revelation is being made to them, which is spreading around its point of origin, but has not reached the seas. They reject with contempt visitors from Europe, who believe that a person is saved by faith alone, and by merely thinking and speaking, and not at the same time willing and doing. They say that no one who observes any worship fails to live in accordance with his religion. Otherwise he must inevitably become stupid and wicked, because he then does not receive anything from heaven. Clever wickedness they actually call stupidity, because there is no life, but only death, in it. (TCR 840: emphasis added)

These passages can be interpreted a number of ways. Even if we understand that this phenomenon is common and accepted in Africa, it is still hard to grasp what these teachings imply. Do they mean that the truth from the Heavenly Doctrines will eventually be universally known in Africa apart from the printed books of the Heavenly Doctrines? Do they mean that we should look for groups of people who have New Church doctrine from their own revelation? Nothing like this has been discovered so far. Still, it is common for people to have these types of somewhat obscure individual revelations.

My understanding of these passages is that the revelations are intended to prepare the way for the New Church. They come about because of the nature of people in Africa and because of the spiritual communication that is inherent in that nature. They are generally held individually, not written down, and not used to teach other people. They are not sought, but are accepted as a matter of course. They are not preserved or perceived as something to found religions around. Not that there are not exceptions to this: many in Africa are "seers" and sorcerers.

My expectation is that these revelations will enable people to recognize the New Church when the time is right. They will facilitate its rapid spread once people are prepared, through education and other means, to receive the Heavenly Doctrines.

People in the Interior of Africa

Many passages talk about "the interior," "the center," and "the coasts" of Africa. What do these repeated references mean?

A revelation is being made to them [Africans], which beginning at the center is spreading out from there, but has not reached the seas. (CLJ 76)

I was subsequently shown in a hazy vision how the doctrine of heaven was spreading in Africa, namely, toward the interior parts even to the center, and then continuing toward those who live on the coasts of the Mediterranean Sea, but not reaching the coast, and then after a time turning around toward Egypt.

That doctrine does not reach all the way to Africans living along the coast. (LJ post 117)

It was perceived that those in the earth, with whom there is thence communication and influx, were about the region of Africa, partly also in Asia, rather near the Indian Sea, but not in the immediate neighborhood of the sea. (SE 4774)

It was next shown, in an obscure vision, in what way that heavenly doctrine would advance in Africa, namely, from this place towards the interiors of Africa, but, still, not to the middle of it; and, then, should bend itself to the inhabitants who are in interior Africa, nearer to the Mediterranean Sea, and thus go on for a long distance, but not as far as to the coasts. (SE 4777)

Since this is the nature of the Africans, at the present time a revelation is being made to them, which is spreading around its point of origin, but has not reached the seas. (TCR 840)

The impression given by these passages is that revelations have taken place and are taking place deep in the interior of Africa, and that they are being communicated throughout the continent from the center outwards. Countries such as Congo, Central African Republic, and Chad come to mind as places that are truly in the center of the continent. My belief is that the "interior" is describing the equatorial region, and that the "coasts" are the far north and south of the continent. This seems consistent with the statement in SE 5946 that "the worse are towards the Mediterranean Sea, H, and at the Cape of Good Hope."

Whatever the case, it does not seem as though there is any evidence of this revelation in any organized religious traditions in Africa.

Conjugial Love among Africans

Monogamy does not have a long tradition in Africa. But several passages specifically praise Africans in relation to marriage:

A rectangular screen had been set up in the palace in front of the doors, and behind it stood foreigners from Africa, who called to the natives of Europe, "Permit one of us to present an opinion, too, regarding the origin of conjugial love and its vigor or potency."

All the tables then signaled with their hands permission for him to do so.

Then one of them entered and stood beside the table on which the miter had been placed. He said:

"You Christians trace the origin of conjugial love from the love itself. We Africans, on the other hand, trace it from the God of heaven and earth.

"Is conjugial love not a chaste, pure and holy love? Are the angels of heaven not in an enjoyment of it? The whole human race, and therefore the entire angelic heaven—are they not the offspring of this love? Could anything so wonderful spring from any other source than God Himself, the Creator and Sustainer of the universe?

"You Christians trace the origin of conjugial vigor or potency from various rational and natural causes. We Africans, however, trace it from a person's state of conjunction with the God of the universe. (We call this state a state of religion, but you call it a state of the church.) We trace it from this origin, for when love comes from this source and is constant and lasting, it cannot help but maintain its vigor, a vigor that is like the love, thus also constant and lasting.

"Truly conjugial love is not known except to the few who are near to God. Neither, therefore, is the potency of this love known to others. Angels in heaven describe the potency accompanying this love as the delight of endless spring."

At the conclusion of these words the people all rose, and suddenly, behind the gold table on which the miter rested, a window materialized that had not been visible before. Through it also came a voice, saying, "*The miter will go to the African.*"

The angel then gave the miter to him, handing it to him rather than placing it on his head. And the African went away home with it.

The inhabitants of the kingdoms of Europe also went out and got into their carriages, in which they returned to their companions. (CL 113-114: emphasis added)

On the subject of marriage they [Africans in the spiritual world] said that although their law allows them to marry more than one wife, they do not take more than one, because true marriage love is indivisible. If it is divided, its essence, which is heavenly, is lost; it becomes external and lewd, quickly fading as their virility declines and turning to loathing when it goes completely. But true marriage love is internal and untouched by lewdness, so it lasts forever, growing equally in strength and delight. (CLJ 77)

There are those who are of the conviction there is nothing more honorable than whoredom and adultery, which conviction they then support by many arguments, so that they consider that, with conviction, as a respectable way of life. Such are siren adulteresses, for when convinced of their respectability and devoutness, they can then almost lead angelic spirits astray, but angels are given to recognize them. I spoke with spirits about them, and it was said that such sirens are from Europe, where Christianity prevails, *seldom from Asiatic, African, or American regions.* (SE 3194: emphasis added)

The inhabitants dwelling below the equator, like the inhabitants of this earth in Africa and in the warm zones, go about naked. . . . In a state of innocence, nakedness is not shameful. The shame of nakedness arises from sin, and in fact, from the wiping out of heavenly love. Then follow loves which cause nakedness to be shameful, for which reason Adam also knew at once that he was naked, and also Eve, and they hid themselves.

So it is with those who live on this planet in the equatorial regions. *Nakedness is no great thing to them, for they desire nothing else than to have children, for the sake of heaven.* (SE 566: emphasis added)

My own experience living in West Africa is consistent especially with CL 113, and SE 3194 and 566; the love of God is very consciously the center of thought for people there, just as the African in the story says, and it is also true that there is not the same interest in "nakedness" that Western culture holds so strongly.

Comments from Rev. Ekow Eshun:

Marriage is considered as being a relationship between a man and a woman. Because it is a relationship between a man and woman, I have yet to meet someone whose sexual orientation is homosexuality.

I have spoken with several elderly people about marriages between the same sex. They find it very difficult to conceive. They say it is unthinkable. They say it is reprehensible. On this subject, I want to confidently say that there is no homosexuality in our traditional African way of life. Polygamy? Yes!

People indulge in polygamy for economic reasons. Back in the olden days, the occupation that most people practiced was farming. Because people practiced subsistence farming, parents or families needed more hands to help them in the farm work.

What is the fate of polygamy now? Polygamy is gradually becoming unpopular even in the villages where polygamy used to be very popular. One reason is that the economic situation is becoming unbearable. The cost of living in the villages has become a disincentive for people to participate in polygamy. Besides, there are many of problems with it.

Someone told me that when a man has more than one wife, it is very difficult for the man to remain truthful to the wives equally. There is constant rivalry between the wives. Each of the wives would like to outdo the other so that the man will spend more time with her.

Another person told me that there is problem when it comes to the relationship between siblings. There is a story where someone told me about a wife playing her children against children of the other rival. Such manipulations bring unnecessary confrontation between the children. In some cases, it can lead to murder between siblings.

Marriage is not believed to continue in the other life. It is assumed that it ends when one of the partners leaves this world. Traditional religion has the same mind set as the old Christian church. According to my research, I have yet to meet someone who has said that marriage continues after death, which is not surprising because the old Christianity has not been able to extricate itself from the literalistic interpretation of the Bible.

Visitors from Europe are not Admitted in some Places

These passages are hard to comprehend. The Africa I am familiar with is famously welcoming to foreigners.

> They said that visitors from Europe are not admitted. When any, especially monks, do manage to get in, the Africans enquire into their knowledge, and when they give some account of their religious beliefs, call them rubbish they cannot bear to hear. So then they banish them to hard labour, so that they may do something useful. If they object to doing this, they sell them into slavery, and their law permits them to beat slaves as much as they wish. If they can still not be forced to do anything useful, they eventually sell them for a pittance to humble people. (CLJ 78, see also SE 6095)

> That there is a region inhabited by good people extending from Ethiopia toward the center, into which foreigners from Europe are not admitted, and if they make their way in and are unwilling to serve, the people sell them to Asians. (LJ post 124)

These passages may relate to areas in East Africa that have a much longer history of contact with Europeans than is true of most of Africa. For example, there have long been claims that the Ark of the Covenant is kept to this day in Ethiopia, but foreigners are not allowed to see it. Africa is a large continent and the people are varied—it would be surprising if there were not these regional differences.

Africa and Magic

As the practice of magic is something that is commonly feared throughout the continent, there is quite a bit of evidence as to the truth of the following passage.

> *Concerning the worst magicians of all, who come from Africa*—the cerebral. There was brought, from a certain hell to behind the back, a certain one who was able with great power to inspire fear and horror in the spirits who came. He was placed at my occiput; and all spirits who came under his gaze were terrified and fell back, as it were, out of horror and terror. But, afterwards, there came a certain woman who had, wrapped in a linen cloth, some of the flesh of a leg, which she called a morsel, and which she gave him to eat. He approached and stretched out [his hand]; and from it he was stupefied, as if deprived of his life, nor was he able any longer to think at all, but stood like a statue. Hence I could infer that such were those who are called by the ancients Cerberi, and who were in the entrance to the lower places. This woman was there also. The place corresponds in position to the occiput.
>
> The same woman then went further below, under that place, and there tarried. Afterwards, she raised herself up and poured out something from a bowl, as it were liquor to drink, saying that she gave drink to those that were beneath—of which also they drank; and then those who were the guards, there, began to be insane.
>
> After this, she wished to enter by magical arts into the hells of the sirens, into which no one is admitted. She wished to take certain ones away from thence; and this she effected through dreadful magical arts—by turning herself into various serpentine forms—and, as it were, penetrated in thither. She thus drew to herself those whom she wished to take away from thence, who were the worst of all; but when she had done that execrable deed, she was cast in with violence, and there she lay.
>
> It was discovered whence such characters were. There were enchantresses at a certain height above, in front, who spoke, and said that the former ones inflicted such things by their means. *The angels said that such exist in Africa, and that they are interiorly religious but exteriorly vicious, and that thence they receive influx from the celestials, and turn it into such magic*—for the things by which they

act are correspondences; so that those arts come from an interior sphere, and were irresistible in a lower sphere. (SE 4946-4949: emphasis added)

Concerning kings and queens who believe themselves to have absolute power, and to have the lives of men at their disposal. A profane characteristic.

*There was a queen—it was said that she was from Africa—*who had absolute power, and who believed that she had power over the lives of men, namely, that it had been lawful for her to kill whomsoever she pleased, whether innocent or guilty. Moreover, from her religious belief she knew that there was a God, and likewise acknowledged Him. She was lascivious in an extreme degree, and admitted lovers, but had afterwards caused them to be slain, lest a report should thence spread to the public, that she was of such a character. She was seen. She was black like the inhabitants of that region, with a handsome face, and, also, beautiful hair. It was granted to speak with her, and to say that absolute authority does not confer such power, but that [her power should operate] against those who act contrary to the laws and justice and equity, not against the innocent. But she supposed that she had [that power], because they bestowed it upon her [at her coronation]. It was granted to say, that she knew there is a deity above her, and it would be contrary to the deity and His laws so to do: but she was not then able to withstand this, and was silent. She was profane, because she acknowledged a deity, and yet lived in such a manner. She suffered most grievous punishments, and it was said that her hell was a most grievous one, of the character which is allotted to the profane. [It was also said] that they [the profaners] at length become like skeletons, scarcely holding together, in which there is so little of life as to be scarcely anything; for the state of a profane person has this property from that holiness which coheres with a profane [act]. They [evils and goods] cannot be separated [with these] as with others, but they are torn asunder and, then, the life which is only in holy things, that is, in goods and truths, perishes, or is changed into most abominable stenches, and accompanied with torture. (SE minor 4740: emphasis added)

Comments from the Rev. Ekow Eshun

I interviewed a man who claimed that magic used to be very common in the country before the advent of television. According to this man, as part of community-organized entertainment magicians were put on the bill.

Recollecting his memories about some of these incidents, he claimed that some magicians show their powers in strange ways. He remembered an instance where a magician called someone from the audience. When this person came on the stage, the magician told him that he was going to kill him and would bring him back to life after three days. Lo and behold! After the third day, this magician brought this person back to life! This sounds funny, but, it did in fact occur.

In front of large crowds in the open, these magicians can conjure items from thin air and give these items to people gratias! Some of the items include fabrics, towels, sandals, soaps, expensive cologne, shoes, eggs, etc. The question is, of course, how do these magicians get these strange powers? In Ghana, it's an open secret that magicians work in concert with dwarfs. Dwarfs are believed to be spiritual beings who serve as messengers for the magicians. Dwarfs can go to people's stores and steal items at anytime.

It is very interesting to learn that the magic "fever" is catching on with the clergy in the country.

An incident recently occurred in the second largest city in the country, Kumasi. I missed the incident narrowly, but it has enormous relevance to my subject. I interviewed someone concerning the incident and he told me that a fetish priest has just surfaced in the city of Kumasi and is doing a lot of wonders. According to this interviewee, the priest was commanding currency notes from the air. Just last week, the government introduced new currency notes in the country. Surprisingly, it was one of these currency notes that the priest was commanding from the air. The incident was shown on the television.

As if this wasn't enough, this fetish priest alleged that over 400 pastors in the country have consulted him for powers so that they can perform wonders on the members of their congregation. Some ministers do perform wonders which are very doubtful; in some instances, they stretch their hands on their congregation and members fall down and fume. In certain instances, members roll on the ground and behave in a weird way, reminiscent of a being processed.

These incidents are happening in some parts of the country. Some churches, particularly the well-established ones, such as the Catholic, Methodist, Presbyterian, Baptist, and Anglican churches are beginning to question the source of these powers.

Just last week, I followed a news item in the newspapers which took me to a suburb of Accra. The news was that someone had killed a certain man and the ghost of the deceased was haunting the perpetrator of the dastardly act. Unable to bear the harassment the ghost was giving to the murderer, the murderer consulted a fetish priest to perform some medicine which would protect him from the ghost which was giving him sleepless nights. Unfortunately, I wasn't able to follow through with the rituals that were scheduled for the deceased for the following day.

Africans have a Celestial Disposition

The Africans in our globe are the ones who are of the genius in which are the angels in the Celestial Kingdom; Europeans, those who are of the spiritual [genius]—the difference in the nature of which may be seen in the [Arcana Coelestia]. (SE 5518)

They [Africans] are in the capacity of receiving not only the truths of faith, but especially its goods. They are of the celestial genius. (SE 4783)

Statements about the celestial or spiritual natures of different peoples can be easily be misunderstood; it is important not to confuse teachings such as these about the sense in which every individual, and every group of people, is either more celestial or more spiritual, with the teachings about the Most Ancient Church, which was the celestial church. The people of the celestial church were profoundly different from people today. We read:

> There are in general two Churches—the celestial and the spiritual. The celestial Church exists with the person in whom the will part of the mind can be regenerated or made the Church, whereas the spiritual Church exists with one in whom, as stated, solely the understanding part can be regenerated. The Most Ancient Church before the Flood was a celestial one because there existed with those who belonged to it some degree of wholeness in the will part, whereas the Ancient Church after the Flood was a spiritual one because among those who belonged to it no degree of wholeness existed in the will part, only in the understanding part. (AC 5113)

This description makes it plain that since most ancient times everyone is born with hereditary evils to the point that no one has "some degree of wholeness in the will part," and therefore the celestial church no longer exists:

> The people after the flood, as also the people of the present day, do not possess celestial but only spiritual seed. (AC 310)

> The Lord did not come into the world to save those who are celestial, but to save those who are spiritual. The Most Ancient Church, which was called Man, was celestial, and if this Church had remained uncorrupted there would have been no need for the Lord to be born a human being. But as soon as it began to decline the Lord foresaw that the celestial Church would cease to exist altogether in the world, and therefore a prophecy was given there and then about the Lord's

Coming into the world (Gen. 3.15). After the era of that Church there was no longer a celestial Church but a spiritual Church. (AC 2661)

Not that people cannot become celestial. Everyone is born natural "yet with the capacity to become either celestial or spiritual" (AC 4592). Still, everyone also has an innate character that is either more celestial or more spiritual, as is said of children in heaven:

> In general young children are in disposition either celestial or spiritual. Those of a celestial disposition are unmistakably different from those of a spiritual disposition. (AC 2301; also HH 339, SE 3544)

Also of men compared to women:

> According to what was established from creation, the masculine sex belongs to the class of spiritual qualities, while the feminine belongs to that of heavenly qualities. (SE 1061)

The same thing is meant by this comparison between Europeans and Africans:

> The Africans in our globe are the ones who are of the genius in which are the angels in the Celestial Kingdom; Europeans, those who are of the spiritual [genius]—the difference in the nature of which may be seen in the [*Arcana Coelestia*]. (SE 5518)

This does not mean that Africans *are* celestial, simply that they have a character more *like* that kingdom, whereas Europeans are more like those of the spiritual kingdom.

Further Comments from Rev. Ekow Eshun about West Africa

> I come now to the topic of why Africans love the laws of their religion. There is a strong indication that Africans love their religion because of fear. There are many stories about people who have violated the laws governing African Traditional Religion and have died because of it. Incidents of deaths are so pervasive that the compiled stories about them would fill volumes. The gods

who are responsible for ensuring that society is always kept in order are very retributive.

I am told there was an instance in which someone committed an offence and the results extended into the entire community. After lots of people died the fetish priest was consulted. He revealed that someone had committed an offence and as a result, the gods were bringing a disaster or plague on the people. The only remedy was for the gods to be pacified. In this particular instance, a human being was needed for pacification. When someone volunteered and the pacification was done, the plague stopped immediately.

I am told that there are similar stories all over the country. It is a very serious thing for anyone to break the rules of the gods for fear that they will be killed by the gods. According to my research, the only motivation for people in Africa keep the laws of their country is fear.

The qualities that distinguish Africans are various. In Africa it is often said, "All human beings are children of God, and no one is a child of the earth." What this means is that there is a spark of God's nature in every human being. While elaborating on what constitutes our humanness, someone told me that as Africans we need to show virtues like compassion, generosity and hospitality, caring, and altruism.

Conclusion

The cataclysmic language associated in Scripture with the Last Judgment is no exaggeration. The teaching of the Heavenly Doctrines that the "future state of the world will be exactly the same as it has been up to now" and that "the mighty change which has taken place in the spiritual world does not cause any change in the external appearance of the natural world" (LJ 73) can be misread. It is not that the Last Judgment does not affect the world, only that the effects are not immediately obvious. The truth is that the Last Judgment is transforming the world completely.

In many ways its effects are so subtle that we require scholarly papers to convince us of their existence. The movement of Christianity from the western hemisphere to the southern hemisphere is so dramatic that it is regularly reported in the news. It can not be ignored. The growth of Christianity in Africa over the last century has been "quantitatively, the largest religious change in human history in such a short period."[17]

But is this growth what the Heavenly Doctrines refer to when they say, "that the Church, which is now perishing in Europe, should be renewed in Africa" (SE 4777)? This is Christianity, not the New Church.

My expectation is that the fantastically wide distribution of the Bible, and the similarly amazing expansion of Christianity, are only parts of the process of the future worldwide growth of the New Church. They are among many factors that are preparing the way, joining the spread of literacy and education, of infrastructure and transportation, and political systems that aid, rather than impede, the freedom of thought and action that religion requires.

When the time is right, then, the Heavenly Doctrines will join the Old and New Testaments as the most widely available and commonly read literature on earth.

Is now the time? In the early 1900s New Churchmen seemingly miscalculated when they devoted significant resources to promote the New Church to African populations that, arguably, were not yet prepared to receive them. A hundred years later the literacy rate on the continent has soared, and yet it is still facing enormous political and economic challenges, many of which would seem to stand in the way of the widespread distribution and ownership of the books of the Heavenly Doctrines, and the formation of churches to guide people.

I think, however, that the spread of Christianity and the rapid increase of membership in the African General Church, are indications that the time may be right. How quickly the expansion we see now will speed up is anyone's guess; it may not be significant for a hundred years or more. But we are told that it is certainly happening:

> A new Church is being established by the Lord in which will be the worship of the Lord alone, as it is in heaven. Thus everything in the Lord's Prayer from beginning to end will be fulfilled. (AR 839)

---

17. Philip Jenkins, *The New Faces of Christianity* (New York: Oxford University Press, Inc., 2005), 9.

> This new Church, truly Christian, will endure to eternity. It is to become the
> crown of the previous Churches, because there will be true faith and true charity.
> In this new Church there will be spiritual peace and internal blessedness of life.
> (Coro lii-liv)

While these passages never say that the New Church will be
the dominant religion in this world, other passages do give this
impression:

> The New Church, which is meant by "the woman," is at first amongst a few,
> that in the meantime provision may be made for it among more; until it grows
> to fullness . . . . The number of these in the spiritual world now increases daily,
> therefore according to their increase does that church that is called the New
> Jerusalem increase on earth. (AE 732)

The implication is that this increase will be numerically significant,
and it is hard not to imagine that the New Church will one day be
the religion of all humanity, bringing peace on earth. The imagery of
the Old and New Testaments consistently predicts a future church that
includes "all people." It is beautiful to see this happening.

> The earth shall be full of the knowledge of the LORD as the waters cover the
> sea. (Isa. 9.11)

> All shall know Me, from the least of them to the greatest of them, says the
> LORD. (Jer. 31.34)

> And I, if I am lifted up from the earth, will draw all peoples to Myself.
> (John 12.32)

How should the General Church respond to this? Should we de-
emphasize evangelization in the Christian world and concentrate on it
in Africa, Asia, and elsewhere? I would say that our awareness of what
is happening should lead us to pay attention and devote what resources
we can to the church all over the world. At the same time, the worldwide spread of the church is a long-term venture. We do not know
how long it will take. We can not neglect the church in the former
Christian world even though it is more challenging to be successful

there. The methods of New Church education, community building, and effective leadership and communication models are expensive and labor intensive, but if used effectively they can help spread the New Church in the "global North" until the time is right for it to take off in the gentile world. The Last Judgment marks the end of the Church with one group of people and its beginning with another. This movement will transform and heal the world. We are all part of it, yet it is accomplished by the Lord alone. ⚒

Islam and the Last Judgment

ERIK E. SANDSTROM

INTRODUCTION

In speaking on Islam, I begin by stressing that more than any other religion Islam has an intensity of affective involvement. Correctness has a high premium, and there is an ecstasy of obedience to the *Qur'an*, which is complete, immutable, and self-sufficient. Both Muslims and converts to Islam from non-Arabic nations learn Arabic just to read the *Qur'an* in the original. They justify hearing the contents in the sheer beauty of the sound, and of the script. While the *Qur'an* supplies Islam with internal differences from all other religions, the *Sunna* provides matching outward distinctions. The *Sunna* is the recollection of the words and practices of Muhammad himself, and when written down is called the *Hadith*. This has a couple of different versions. In addition, there is also *ijtihad*, which is personal interpretation of the law, *jima*, which is the correct consensus of interpretation for the *Umma*, the community of Islam as a whole. *Mufti* are legal counselors who issue *fatwas* on the correctness of the *Sharia*, or law. Muslims feel that ecstasy and few if any Muslims leave Islam. Once a Muslim, always a Muslim.

No non-Muslim can claim the same intensity of insight into Islam, so I speak as a mere "Orientalist," that is, someone not of Islam persuasion talking about their religion. However, the Writings allow us to speak fearlessly about any religion, and they provide an inside point of view by revealing the true spiritual nature of humans and giving us to understand the interior aspects of all religions.

Therefore, in dealing with Islam and the Last Judgment, the first part of this paper is about the Writings and Islam. I will then address what the *Qur'an* itself has to say about "last things" or eschatology, namely, what happens when we die, are resurrected, and judged. The *Qur'an* has *surahs* which are in amazing agreement with the New Church doctrine on the Last Judgment. Muslims more than Christians, but similarly to the New Church, take life after death and individual immortality as factual. Finally, I want to look at Islam at the historical time of the Last Judgment in 1757, 250 years ago, and say a few words about Muslim expectations of their own Messiah, bringing their version of the Last Judgment on the world.

The Writings explain that all people have commandments similar to the Ten Commandments (DP 322) and that all people can be saved who live by such laws. However, when he wrote in the Heavenly Doctrines that Muslims after death enter heaven if they lived by the Ten Commandments, Swedenborg was in fact referring to the five pillars of Islam. These are to Muslims what the Commandments are to Christians. The pillars are not duplications of the commandments. Nevertheless, the *Qur'an* indeed mentions Moses and the Law:

> We wrote for Moses upon the tables the lessons to be drawn from all things and the explanation of all things, then bade Hold it fast, take the better course. (*Surah* vii. 145)

> We verily sent Moses with Our Revelation. (*Surah* xiv. 5)

However, the Ten Commandments are not listed in the *Qur'an*, as they are in both the Old and New Testaments; instead they occur separately from the Sinai event. On murder the *Qur'an* says, "Whoso slays a believer of set purpose, his reward is Hell forever. Allah has prepared for him an awful doom" (*Surah* iv. 93). On adultery "As for your women guilty of lewdness, call to witness four of you against them. Confine them to the houses until death take them, or Allah appoint a way" (*Surah* iv. 15). Further, "Marry not those women whom your fathers married. It was ever lewdness and abomination, and an evil way" (*Surah* iv. 22). On incest, "Forbidden unto you are your mothers, your daughters, your sisters and your father's sisters, your mother's sisters" (*Surah* iv. 23). Fornication falls under *haram*, a punishable act. As for the thief, "Both male and female, cut off their hands. It is the reward of their own deeds, an exemplary punishment from Allah" (*Surah* v. 38).

So we see that not only do Muslims know the Ten Commandments, but even assign paradise and salvation to Jews and to Christians also, who are deemed "religions of the book." For Muhammad, as the Writings agree, took from both Testaments for the *Qur'an*. Muhammad actually recommends Muslims to "observe the Taurat (Torah) and the Injil (Gospel)" (*Surah* 5.6–8). Swedenborg had in his own library Herbert's "Travels": *Some Yeares Travels into Divers Parts of Asia and Afrique*, the French version. It describes in detail the Muslims in Iran in the 1600s. It contains a whole section on Jesus and the Ten Commandments of the Muslims, which turn out to be eight in this text. These commandments actually are the five pillars of Islam: Shahada, Salat, Zakat, Sawm and Hajj (commandments 1 to 5) but the text goes on to address how Muslims honor father and mother, and observe the rule against murder, and the Golden Rule. These are commandments 6, 7, and 8. Probably this was one of Swedenborg's earthly sources for saying that Muslims who had lived by the precepts of the Ten Commandments, i.e. have shunned evils as sins, come into the Muslim heaven (DP 255.5). They have lived sincerely and justly in their own good, for in everything sincere and just there is the Divine proceeding from the Lord. "They can in their manner still live faithfully, and gradually be led on to the Lord" (LJ post 97). A Muslim knows "from the *Qur'an* . . . that the evils forbidden in the Ten Commandments must be shunned, and if he does, he is saved" (AE 1180.2).

What was not known at the time of the Writings' publication was that Muhammad was illiterate, and so although the Writings repeat the assumed fact that he wrote the *Qur'an*, still he "did not write" it. Instead, some fifty or so years after Muhammad's death, his followers collected the sayings, accepting those sayings as authorized by the standard that at least one of the four closest companions to Muhammad remembered the saying. But when the Writings confirm that Muhammad was "raised up in providence" (DP 255), i.e. called on to establish Islam, this doctrine legitimizes the well known Muslim accounts of how Muhammad was converted by the angel Jibril, i.e. Gabriel, of his ride to heaven on a small steed named Burak, and of his eye-witness glimpse into the after-life. We in the New Church therefore accept that these things actually happened. Muhammad was indeed a precursor to Swedenborg, as was John the Apostle when he witnessed the Book of Revelation. All three were eyewitness, having their "eyes opened." Therefore, the *Qur'an* is similar to both the book of Revelation and the Writings, in that angels were involved in their composition or contents. There is much spiritual material in all of them, but plainly spoken doctrines are in the *Qur'an* as in the Writings. There is one portion of the *Qur'an* that the Writings say contains a spiritual sense, but they do not identify which.

THE LAST JUDGMENT ON ISLAM

The Writings refer to Mohammedans, Moslems, and Mohammedanism, terms which we can automatically change to Muslims and Islam as the correct modern terms. They were the third category of people to be judged in 1757. The Last Judgment began in December of 1756 and was almost finished by May of 1757, but ran all the way to January of 1758. The whole of the world of spirits was crammed with "false heavens" and for the Last Judgment they were arranged in concentric circles, with Catholics who were judged first in the next circle out from the center, then around them the Muslims, then in a wider circle the Gentiles. At the center were the Reformed, with each Protestant nation at different points of the compass relative to the east, where the Lord is always seen. The Reformed were judged last, since they were the last to have received the baton of the Word of God in the relay race of world religions. They were the last to have the Word, and to read it openly. The Word had been rescued from its tomb by Luther and the Reformation (Inv 24).[1] Without people in northern

---

1. Luther was abetted and indeed saved from the flames by Gutenberg's printing press, an invention fifty years prior to Luther, which allowed pamphlets to be printed with quotations from Scripture, allowing a reasonable support, with Frederick the Wise providentially nabbing Luther for God's ends.

Europe reading the Bible for themselves, how could the Writings have been given 300 years later?

All nations were judged in 1757 by their spiritual lacks, but in the after-life not upon the earth. The false heavens had accumulated from all religions of the world, since the Lord's first advent, right up to 1757 (AE 397). Since the world of spirits is the channel of influx from the Lord and the heavens, these false heavens had a chokehold on the human race. That is why there was a judgment, and why every judgment happens there. The reasons for the long delay since the first prophecies of this event were, first, that the Lord judges no one. It has to happen on its own, by the guilty bringing it on themselves. Secondly, it was delayed until there were enough good spirits to actually form a new heaven. When these two factors "caught up," the wicked at the center of each false heaven thought they had succeeded in entering heaven. It was at this very point that the Lord approached with the intent of actually raising them and everyone else in the world of spirits, into heaven. The format followed the story of Sodom and Gomorrah: angels infiltrated, they called on everyone to cease their evil, but they could only lead the good away, taking them by the hand. This happens at every Last Judgment, but with thousands of angels infiltrating the false heavens, leading all the "good" out by the hand. All interiorly good, whose ignorance had made them easy prey for the wicked leaders who had abused them by means of holy externals, were led out with a 100% success rate. This first stage is called "visitation" (AC 2317). When stage two is reached and only the wicked are left, then being shorn of their innocent victims, they drop the façade. Still, the Lord's more intense outpouring of love and mercy then strives to lift them also up into heaven. "All are called, few chosen." However, their evil loves, which had abused the truths from revelation, made those truths "too hot to handle" so to speak, and so they flung them away from themselves. Since they got rid of all the handles by which they could be raised, and since the Lord's love is received by truths, without any such truth, their evils caused them to sink into hell like stones settling down to their own specific gravity of evil. That is how the evil condemn themselves.

The Muslims were judged this way too, but based on the genuine truths to be found in the *Qur'an*, and whether they had lived in love towards the neighbor. You cannot claim to love God and hate the neighbor. All who live in charity to the neighbor according to their own religion, the Writings explain, receive instruction after death that the Lord is the only God (AC 4721, 2789). Charity to the neighbor is always the main criterion for salvation.

One other criterion for a Muslim to enter heaven, strange to say, is the belief that Jesus was the *Son of God*. Now this phrase is sheer sacrilege to a Muslim. It is *shirk*[2], adding partners to Allah. The *Qur'an* mocks those who have added *partners* to Allah:

> Lo Allah forgives not that a partner should be ascribed unto Him. He forgives all save that to whom He will [sic]. Whoso ascribes partners to Allah; he has indeed invented a tremendous sin, and has wandered far astray. (*Surah* iv. 48, 116)

> It befits not the majesty of Allah that He should take unto himself a son. Glory be to Him. (*Surah* xix. 35)

So how can Muslims accept Jesus as the Son of God? We have to sort this out. First, the main reason Providence raised Muhammad, and let a "new religion arise adapted to Orientals" we read, was to "root out" all the idolatry since ancient times in the regions of the Middle East (DP 255). This eradication of ancient idolatries was why the Lord raised up Islam to begin with, but it has nothing to do with accepting Jesus as the Son of God.

Second, the Writings say that Muslims on earth cannot accept Jesus Christ as the God of heaven and earth, for the reason that "oriental people acknowledge God as Creator of the universe, and could not comprehend that He came into the world and assumed a Human form" (DP 255.4). The Writings explain their difficulty. Since the title *Son of God* to Muslims means "adding partners to Allah" which is *shirk* (sin of idolatry or associating beings or things with Allah), consequently no one who does this can escape a severe penalty. Even the *satanic*

---

2. http://en.wikipedia.org/wiki/Shirk

verses,[3] to which Muhammad had at first added three goddesses Al-Lat, Al-Uzza, and Manat as helpers to Allah, were later retracted. Those goddesses had been worshipped by the Arabs prior to Islam.

So the Son of God as a Christian adjunct, Muslims can never accept. However, when explained in New Church terms as the embodiment of Jehovah, namely a human form raised to Divine glory or glorified, so that in the Risen Lord is both God the Creator and Lord the Redeemer, in One Person, this visible God *is* approachable by Muslims.

Swedenborg addressed Muslims in the other world on this very subject, and this has become a famous quotation in the New Church: "What with man rots in the grave was with the Lord made Divine" (LJ post 87). These words were first spoken to Muslims!

Muslims were told in the after-life that the Lord "was conceived of Jehovah" who is Allah, or the Father, and thus that the Lord was the Son of God from the Divine in Him. He glorified the whole body, so that "that part of the body rejected by those born of human parents, and which rots away in the grave, was with Him glorified and made Divine from the Divine in Itself, and that He rose again, leaving nothing in the tomb." To this, the Muslims listened attentively, and asked, "Why had they never heard that before?" (LJ post 87).

The reason they had never heard that before is that no Christian ever saw it that way, and so could not say it on earth. No one could. Now, post 1757, the Writings have said it, so of course we all can say it. We wonder whether Muslims today would listen to this view that Jesus is *not* a partner added to Allah, but Allah's very *embodiment*, raised to the same Infinite and Divine level as Allah Himself. This would make Allah visible in human form.

However, being Orientals, no Muslim could believe that God Himself could come on earth. Only after death can those who have lived in charity accept Jesus as the Embodiment of Allah, as a theological construct, but not as a Christian phrase. Perhaps the Hindu concept of Avatar might be a vehicle, and Muslims in India in fact find it easy to

---

3. "Now tell me about Al-Lat, Al-Uzza, and Manat, The third one, another goddess. What! For you the males and for him the females! That indeed is an unfair division."

accept how the high Hindi God, Brahman or Vishnu, could come in the bodily form of an Avatar. Indra was an ancient appearance of Vishnu on earth, Krishna later in history. Could Jesus be accepted as an Avatar of Allah? But unlike Avatars, Christ's body was made completely divine. Nothing was in the tomb. This is missing in Hinduism.

Another issue over which Muslims were judged was how they regarded Muhammad himself. They regard Muhammad so highly that they have "little regard for the Lord" (CL 342). Muslims in fact connect Muhammad so closely to Islam and to their religious practice that it verges on idolatry, the very *shirk* which they abhor. Since religion makes the "inmost" of the human spirit, Muhammad himself is commonly seen by Muslims after death (LJ 69). However, as with other famous people, the demand to meet famous people is so great that impersonators take on that role. Muhammad had several impersonators to greet Muslims in the spiritual world.

Some Muslims even end up worshipping Muhammad as a god in the afterlife (LJ post 78). Muslims who revere Muhammad to the point of worshipping him have the incompatible experience of being chased away by the impersonator of Muhammad. He drives the adoring crowd away telling them to go to the Lord who rules the universe (LJ post 73). Muslims would not do that here, but their interior view of Muhammad was of such a nature that after death it comes into the open.

So in summary, Muslims are accepted into heaven if first, they had lived by the *Qur'an* together with charity to the neighbor and second, they had believed God to be one, and the Lord to be in that unity (AE 1180). That unity of God is called *tawhid*.

While adding partners to Allah is *shirk*, and makes a Muslim see red here on earth, can Muslims accept that Jesus, called *Isa* in the *Qur'an*, was born of the Divine Will of Allah? Such a Divine will of the birth of Isa does in fact have supportive wording in the *Qur'an*. When Miriam is told of the forthcoming birth of Isa, the Messiah, the *Qur'an* stresses the virgin birth possibly more strongly than the Gospels. Here is the whole Annunciation:

Lo, Allah gives you glad tidings from Him whose name is the Messiah, Jesus, son of Mary . . . one of those brought near to Allah. He will speak to mankind in His cradle, in His manhood, and He is of the righteous. (*Surah* 3.45, 46)

Miriam asked, My Lord, how can I have a child when no mortal has touched me? He said, So it will be. Allah creates what He will. If He creates a thing, He says unto it only, Be, and it is. (*Surah* 3.47)

Another *surah* repeats it in different wording:

How can I have a son when no mortal has touched me neither have I been unchaste? Thy Lord said It is easy for Me. And it will be that We may make of him a revelation for mankind and a mercy from Us, and it is a thing ordained. (*Surah* xix. 20, 21)

"Be and it is." A "thing ordained." Does the *Qur'an* here pronounce the Divine birth of Jesus? Does this not raise Jesus, or Isa, the son of Mary, to Divinity? Jesus was "ordained" as a "revelation to mankind." Another *Surah* says of Jesus:

And because of their saying (in boast), "We killed Messiah Jesus, son of Mary, the Messenger of God,"—but they did not kill him and nor did they crucify him, but the resemblance of Jesus was put over another man (and they killed that man), . . . But God raised (Jesus) up (with his body and soul) unto Himself (and he is in the heavens). . . . And there is none of the . . . (Jews and Christians), but must believe in (Jesus) before his death. And on the Day of Resurrection, (Jesus) will be a witness against them. (*Surah* 4.157–159)

Here Jesus is called Messiah, who was raised to Allah Himself, and he will be there in the day of resurrection. Perhaps this was known to Swedenborg, who read the *Qur'an* at least in heaven, if not on earth. The Writings insist Muslims who go to heaven "acknowledge the Lord as the greatest prophet" (CLJ 68, SS 105, AE 1180.2, DP 255). The Writings explain in rational terms of doctrine, that the Lord was like other men except that He was conceived of Jehovah but still was born of a virgin mother, and by "birth derived infirmities from the virgin mother like those of man in general" (AC 1414; cf. AC 8909,

TCR 38). However, that he was "the son of Joseph is an insane notion" (TCR 94).

Do the words of the *Qur'an* quoted just now make Jesus to be divinely sent by Allah to teach the human race? Is this the same as calling Him the "son of God," the greatest prophet, and wisest of all? (CLJ 68, LJ post 98). The *Qur'an* does *not* say Jesus was the son of Joseph, but often "the son of Mary" (*Suras* 2.87, 136, 253; 4.157, et. al.). Accordingly, a Muslim also said as much, namely that Jesus

> was not the Son of Joseph, as they believed in the world, but the Son of God Himself, by which was insinuated the idea of unity of the Lord's person and essence with the father. (CLJ 69)

Once they acknowledge that the Lord is "one with the Father," Muslims have a heaven "full of all felicities," and live from the Lord in a spiritual marriage of good and truth" (LJ post 101). Such felicity matches the "paradise" Muslims believe in.

Indeed, some Muslims were shown "The glory of the Lord upon which they fell down upon their faces" (LJ post 71).

On earth, Christian missionaries had persuaded the Arabs that Jesus was a "partner" to Allah, and thus that God was three persons. On earth, Muslims could neither understand nor accept that "there are three persons, each person God, yet God is one" (CLJ 72). Instead Muslims called Christians "fanatics" who say, "God is one, and mutter three" (TCR 831). They complain that the Christians "from Greece" (i.e. Eastern Orthodox Christians) worship three gods, not one (LJ post 100). Rejecting all this, they conclude that the Lord "cannot but be God, because He was conceived of God Himself as the Father. Thus the Divine itself was in Him from conception, and the Divine is indivisible" (LJ post 95).

After death, Muslims can comprehend this:

> that the Trine is in one person, in the Lord; that His inmost is the Father, the existere is the Son, and the life from Him is the Proceeding Holy spirit. This union was effected by God the Father by His advent into the World. Thus He and the Father are one, the Holy Spirit speaks not from itself but from Him, i.e. Jesus. (LJ post 89)

Muslims who after death idolize Muhammad as a "universal human" and "exemplary model" may have confused Muhammad's own message in the *Qur'an* concerning the Holy Spirit, saying

> I am indeed the Messenger of God to you, confirming the Torah that is before me, and giving good tidings [gospel] of a Messenger who shall come after me, whose name shall be *Ahmad*. (*Surah* 61.6)

"Ahmad" may actually be an elusive reference to the Second Coming. However, Muhammad says of himself

> Muhammad is but a messenger . . . like those who passed away before him. Will it be when . . . he [Muhammad] dies or be slain, you will turn . . . on your heels? He who turns back does no hurt to Allah and Allah will reward the thankful. (*Surah* 3.144)

In other words, Muhammad tells Muslims that they will only harm themselves by turning away from Islam upon Muhammad's own death. This is to *prevent* idolizing him. Allah will reward those who remain Muslims even after Muhammad is gone. No idolatry there.

The impersonators of Muhammad in the afterlife consequently raise the question of whether Muhammad himself was saved or not. The answer is ambiguous, as with Luther, since both events are claimed. He was seen as a bodily spirit saying, "I am your Mohammed" (TCR 830, CLJ 70) but elsewhere, he is said to be among Christians who acknowledge the Lord as the Only God (SD 5243).

Besides the three issues of living by the Ten Commandments, accepting the Lord as the Son of God, and not adoring Muhammad himself, there is one more issue regarding Islam and the Last Judgment, namely polygamy.

Polygamy "exhales uncleanness towards heaven," while monogamy between one husband with one wife, "corresponds to the marriage of the Lord and the church" (CLJ 71). Because Muslims accept polygamy—it is after all *taught* in the *Qur'an*—the consequence, the Writings teach, is that they cannot accept interior truths of religion (ibid.). Only monogamy is capable of accepting the full range of truth from the Word. Furthermore, for that same reason the Muslim heavens are segregated from the rest, they only join the other heavens if they accept monogamy.

That was why Muhammad could not be inspired to reveal *interior* truths of religion, such as are found in the Gospels, even in parabolic form. So although the Writings say he was inspired to recite the *Qur'an*, and Providence raised him (DP 255), this enlightenment did not extend to include deeper truths. Indeed the *Qur'an* reads as a primer of basic doctrines.

All who enter heaven receive instruction in the Doctrine of the Lord, and know that the Trinity is in the Lord. Just as others come to their heavens, so Muslims have three heavens, which are "outside the Christian heavens" (CL 342, TCR 832). In the highest heaven are those who acknowledge the "Lord as one with the Father, thus Himself as the Only God." In the second heaven are those who renounce polygamy, and live with one. In the lowest heaven are those being initiated (DP 255.5). This lowest heaven must be closest to the world of spirits, where all gather at first after death, and where last judgments are always executed.

The reason those who practice polygamy are not condemned to hell is that polygamy is not opposite to heaven, as adultery is. It is thus forgivable, but only for non-Christians. Nuns who lived by the Commandments, but thought they were "virgins married mystically to Christ," also live outside heaven. So Muslims who otherwise are upright, also live outside heaven if they cannot give up polygamy. It is the Lord's concession that eternal life is granted, but not the fullness of heaven. So interestingly, the segregation of Muslims in the other world is because "religion separates them" (LJ 50).

It seems that the distinction from other religions that Muslims themselves insist on holds also in the lower heavens after death. The Lord is order itself, and is the source of all order in heaven and on earth. There can be order but no actual heaven. Such are the Muslim lower heavens.

RESURRECTION, LAST DAY OF JUDGMENT

We come now to the eschatology of the *Qur'an*, the *Surahs* which spell out what to expect. It is quite poetic. "It is not righteousness that ye turn your faces to the East and the West; but righteous is he who believeth in Allah and the Last Day" (*Surah* 2.177).

The Day of the Resurrection is in Arabic *Yawm al-Qīyāmah* (Arabic: يوم القيامة) and this equals the Last Judgment in Islam. Belief in Qiyâmah is part of *Aqidah*, a fundamental tenet in Islam. The trials and tribulations associated with it are detailed in both the *Qur'an* and the *Hadith*. Many scholarly authorities, the most well known of which are al-Ghazali and al-Bukhari, describe them in detail. Every human, Muslim and non-Muslim alike, is held accountable for his or her deeds and is judged by Allah accordingly (*Surah* 74.38). Al-Qiyâmah, the Rising of the Dead, is the title of the 75th *surah* of the *Qur'an*.[4] "Nay I swear by the Day of Resurrection . . . Does man think that We shall not assemble his bones? We are able to restore his very fingers!" It will happen "when sight is confounded, the moon is eclipsed, the sun and moon are united . . . Unto thy Lord is the recourse that day" (*Surah* lxxv.1–12).

This version points to a physical resurrection. However, there are obviously spiritual components of what will happen to a person.

The context is life after death, and the "inter-space" that people enter after death, where they may dwell for 1,000 years before either entering paradise or joining Iblis (the name for the devil) in hell, to drink boiling water for the sins committed here. The *Surahs* on this read exactly as the judgment scene of final awareness; all simulations end.

They have foretastes of what their final state will be. Death is the lesser resurrection, and time spent in the grave is a time of growth, transformation, etc. based on the deeds performed in the world. This means that while the body is in the grave, the soul is in the inter-world.

---

4. http://www.nmhschool.org/tthornton/wahhabi_movement.htm

A person is questioned by angels while in the grave. When the day of resurrection comes, the angel Seraphiel blows a trumpet, and a crier calls from heaven: "My servant has spoken the truth, spread out carpets from paradise for him, clothe him from paradise, open a gate for him into paradise." Joy and fragrance of paradise then comes, the grave is made spacious as far as the eye can see, and someone with a beautiful face, garments, and sweet scent comes and says: "Rejoice in what pleases you, for this is your day which you have been promised." The dead one asks, "Who are you?" The answer: "I am your own good deeds."

During judgment a person's own "book of deeds" will be opened, and he or she will be apprised of every action taken and every word spoken (*Surah* 54.52–53). Actions during childhood are not judged. Even minor and trivial deeds are included in the account. When the hour is at hand, some will deny that the Last Judgment is taking place. They are warned that the judgment precedes the "Day of Pining" (distress) (*Surah* 19.39, 30.55–57). If one denies a deed he or she committed, or refuses to acknowledge it, his or her body parts will testify against them.

Throughout judgment, however, the underlying principle is that of a complete and perfect justice administered by Allah. The accounts of judgment are also replete with the emphasis that Allah is merciful and forgiving, and that mercy and forgiveness will be granted on that day insofar as it is merited.

Here is a medley of sayings, speaking for themselves.

Those judged to hell are servants of Iblis, the *Qur'an*'s term for Satan. His servants are the Jinn, or wicked spirits. Human souls are Jinn, and live after the death of the body:

> The Jinn did We create aforetime of essential fire . . . So the angels fell prostrate [before Adam] . . . save Iblis. He refused to be among the prostrate . . . What ails you that you are not among the prostrate? He said, why should I prostrate myself unto a mortal whom you have created? [Allah] said, Then go forth from hence, you are an outcast. And lo, the curse shall be upon you till the day of judgment. (*Surah* 15.27–44)

What happens to the guilty? They will drink boiling water, and

On that day will be linked together in chains, their raiment of pitch, and the fire covering their faces. Allah repays each soul what it has earned. Lo, Allah is swift at reckoning. This is the clear message for mankind that they may be warned . . . and know . . . that He is only One God, and men of understanding may take heed. (*Surah* 14.49–52)

The signs of judgment are given:

Earthquakes, nursing mothers forgetting the nursling, the pregnant will be delivered, mankind shall be drunken but not drunk. (*Surah* 22.1)

When the sun shall be darkened, when the stars shall be thrown down, and mountains set moving . . . when the scrolls shall be unrolled, the heavens stripped off, hell set blazing, when paradise shall be brought nigh, then shall a soul know what it has produced. (*Surah* 81.1–14)

The sun overthrown, stars fall, hills moved, camels abandon young, beasts herded together, seas rise, souls reunited, the girl-child buried alive is asked "For what sin was she slain?," pages laid open, sky torn away, hell lighted. (*Surah* 81.1)

The heavens split asunder. (*Surah* 84.1)

The Trumpet shall blow. (*Surah* 20.100, 50.20, and 78.17)

Jews and Christians . . . both are readers of the Scripture, Allah will judge between them. (*Surah* 2.113)

Who believes in Allah, Last Day and does right—Yahudis, Sabeans, Nasara. (*Surah* 5.69)

Surely their reward is with their Lord, no fear shall come upon them, neither shall they grieve. (*Surah* 2.62)

Who is in charge?

Allah is Owner of the Day of Judgment. (*Surah* 1.3)

Allah will be the Sovereign on the day when the Trumpet is blown. (*Surah* 6.74)

Warn mankind of the day when the doom will come upon them, and those who did wrong will say: Our Lord! Reprieve us for a little while . . . It will be answered: Did you not swear before, that there would be no end for you? (*Surah* 14.44)

On that day, some faces will be whitened and some blackened: did you disbelieve after your profession of belief? Then taste the punishment for you that disbelieved. Those that are whitened, Lo, in the mercy of Allah they dwell forever. (*Surah* 3.106, 107)

Allah has no *partners* who *can* intercede:

On that day He will call unto them and say: Where are My partners whom you imagined? Cry to your so-called partners of Allah . . . they will give no answer . . . and they will see the Doom. If they had but been guided! Who is a God beside Allah, who could bring you light? (*Surah* 28.62–71)

Other passages deal with Allah knowing everything:

They have plotted their plot, and their plot is with Allah, though their plot were one whereby the mountains should be moved. So think not that Allah will fail to keep His promises to His messengers. Lo, Allah is mighty, able to requite the wrong . . . On that day the earth will be changed, and . . . they will come forth unto Allah, the One, and the Almighty. (*Surah* 14.46–48)

It will long that there might be a mighty space of distance between it and evil. Beware of Allah, He is full of pity for His bondmen. (*Surah* 3.30)

Everyone earns his or her own reward:

Every soul will find itself confronted with all that it has done of good and . . . evil. (*Surah* 3.30)

You will see every nation kneeling down; every nation will be called to its record. This day you are requited for what you did. (*Surah* 45.28)

Everyone's eyes will be opened to see reality:

We have now removed from you your covering, so your sight today is piercing. (*Surah* 50.22)

The earth will be shaken with a final earthquake, and yield up her burdens, she will relate her chronicles. Whoso does good one atom's weight will see it then . . . or ill an atom's weight, will see it then. (*Surah* 99.1–9)

They will read the book of their own soul:

Read your book; your own soul is sufficient as a reckoner against you this day. (*Surah* 17.14)

[All] secrets will be divulged. (*Surah* 86.9)

That which is in the breast will be brought out. (*Surah* 100.10)

On that day you shall be exposed, not one secret of yours is concealed. (*Surah* 69.18)

Mankind will be sorted into three classes (*Surah* 56.7). Whether this refers to the three states in the world of spirits, I leave for others to decide.

There seems to be no time there:

On the day when He gathers, it will appear that they tarried an hour, they will have perished who denied meeting with Allah. (*Surah* 10.45)

On paradise:

Who believe and do good works, male or female, will enter Paradise. (*Surah* 4.124)

The truthful will enjoy Paradise. (*Surah* 5.119)

Those who pay heed to *Qur'an* will enter Paradise. (*Surah* 6.127)

Paradise which they enter under which rivers flow, wherein they have what they will, thus Allah repay those who ward-off evil. (*Surah* 16.31)

The Books will be opened, and all will be lined up:

On the day when we remove the hills . . . We gather them together as to leave not one of them behind. We set before Your Lord in ranks, and the book is placed, and you see the guilty be fearful of that which is in it. They say, What kind of a book is this that leaves not a small thing nor a great thing but has counted it! And they find all that they did confronting them and your Lord wrongs no one. (*Surah* 18.48–50)

We shall bring forth for him on the Day of Resurrection a book which he will find wide open. . . . Read your book. Your soul suffices as reckoner against you this day. (*Surah* 17.13)

Allah sees all; everyone's own deeds bring reward or punishment:

Allah is informed of what you do. (*Surah* 3.185)

Taste your torment which you inflicted. (*Surah* 51.14)

Taste what you have earned. (*Surah* 78.30)

Wrong-doers: Taste what you used to earn . . . The evils they earned will appear unto them, and that whereat they used to scoff will surround them. (*Surah* 39.24, 47–48)

On the Day of Resurrection, every soul will be paid in full what it has earned. They will not be wronged. (*Surah* 3.161)

Whoso does evil or wrongs his own soul, then seeks pardon of Allah, will find Allah forgiving, merciful. Whoso commits sin commits it only against himself. [Those] resolved to mislead you, will mislead only themselves. (*Surah* 4.110–113)

They plotted, so Allah struck at the foundation of their buildings, and the roof fell down on them, doom came on them, whence they knew not. (*Surah* 16.26)

No one can hide:

Nothing of them have been hidden from Allah . . . Each soul is requited that which it has earned. No wrong is done this day. (*Surah* 40.16, 17)

Family ties cannot help a person either:

Your ties of kindred and your children will avail you naught upon the Day of Resurrection. (*Surah* 60.3)

There is a separation:

This is the day of separation, which you used to deny. (*Surah* 37.21)

Idolaters go to hell . . . Those from whom kindness has gone forth . . . will be far removed from thence, and not hear the slightest sound of it. (*Surah* 21.98)

Angels come down, but cannot intercede:

Angels are sent down, in a grand descent. (*Surah* 25.22)

Angels stretch their hands: Deliver up your souls, this day you are awarded doom of degradation for what you spoke concerning Allah other than the truth, and scorned His portents . . . You have left behind all We bestowed on you, behold not with you your intercessors, or whom you claimed they possessed a share in you. (*Surah* 6.94)

On that day no intercession avails . . . Allah knows all that is before them . . . he who has done some good works being a believer, fears not injustice. (*Surah* 20.109–112)

We see from this that the expectation of the book of life being opened, and that we ourselves write our own story, is quite clear. The piercing eye, the woe is me what have I done, the penalty being attached to the evil deed, all are clear doctrines also in the Writings.

WORLD SCENARIO IN 1757

Besides the resurrection and the judgment then facing every Muslim, there was also the expectation of the Messiah, or Mashih, exemplified in the al Madhi expectation. We begin with historical events which were contemporaneous with the Last Judgment, and find Wahhab was active at this very time.

I now turn to the world situation around the time of the Last Judgment. We learn from the Writings that the Holy Land, from the Nile to the Euphrates, or even as far as the Indus, was representative. Spiritual qualities of the church were meant by wars and battles where nations which attacked Israel, meaning the church. The nations that conquered Judah and Israel in the Old Testament depict spiritual conflicts of the church, and Israel's conquest of the invaders meant overcoming those evils (DP 251). This however *ceased* to be the case after the Lord's Advent (AC 1000). Still, the same spiritual qualities of the church present among the Biblical nations, were *transferred* to the "nations of Christendom," (DP 251) that is Europe, where Christianity was "about to come" (AR 34). Angels know this well. In fact, all wars in Europe express the spiritual conditions of the church on earth (DP 251), in which case Islam's role in that history also must have a meaning. For Islam entered the historical scene in Europe and so it featured in the same spiritual map. Although angels know how to interpret this very well, we do not. However, let us engage in some speculation.

The wars of Europe are indications of the spiritual states of the church. European history therefore outlines our spiritual battles and temptations. That would include Islam capturing Iberia and then invading Gaul across the Pyrenees. Did Martel stop them by the hand of Providence? Certainly Charlemagne, Martel's grandson features in this spiritual history, since "the noble kingdom of France" is said to be the internal sense of one verse in the Book of Revelation: namely of the Ten Kings who have not received a kingdom (Rev. 17.12, AR 717). El Cid, therefore, who around the same time as the Battle of Hastings, helped to oust the Saracen Muslims from Spain, must also feature in this spiritual scenario. Later, in 1453, Mohammed II Fathi, from Turkey, conquered Constantinople, thereby toppling the Byzantine Empire which had existed since its division from the Roman Empire beginning in AD 395. Constantinople became the seat of the Greek Orthodox Church, and had acted as a "second Rome." With its fall, the honor of being the Second Rome was transferred to Moscow, which some called the Third Rome. Meanwhile, the Muslims expanded west from Constantinople, and by 1683 they threatened Vienna. This was just before Swedenborg was born. King Sobiesky from Poland relieved the siege of Vienna at the battle of Chocim (1683). Did first France and later Poland stand for states of the Christian Church that defended against the spiritual meaning of Islam? Islam has certainly featured in Europe's spiritual history, and so it featured, as we saw, in the Last Judgment.

So is it surprising that there was a "world war" waged on three continents during the very time of the last Judgment? The *Seven Years War* in Europe was called the *French-Indian War* in America (having started a year earlier), and the same war was also fought in India. All the European nations were pitted against each other. England and Prussia were allied against France, Austria, Russia, Sweden and Spain. Hanover was involved as well. In India the factions are almost beyond count, and we do not have time to sort them out here.

In Europe the main players of the war involved Frederick the Great, Prime Minister Pitt, Czar Peter III of Russia, Czarina Catherine the Great of Russia, and the Queen of Sweden. Famous victories include: General James Wolfe of England taking Quebec (September 1756), and Clive taking Chandenagore (January 1757). Captain Robert Clive, British governor, had allied himself with Hindu leaders in Bengal who were dissatisfied with the Muslim Siraj-ud-Dawlah. He arranged for the defection of Mir Jafar, one of the nawab's generals. Clive thus ended the French-Muslim threat in India.

Muslim influence in India had begun in earnest under the Mughal Empire, which lasted from Babur in 1453 through Shah Jahan who in the 1640s constructed the Taj Mahal, on to Aurangzeb ending in 1707. A most zealous and orthodox Muslim, Aurangzeb built beautiful buildings and took the Mughal Empire to its *zenith*. He was the last of the *great* Mughals. Retracting the liberal policies of his forbears, he returned to stricter Muslim law, forbidding all forms of pleasure, suppressing and executing Hindus. That backfired, and in effect finished the Mughal dynasty and any real Muslim influence. He was defeated by invading Persians in 1739.[5] Although the Muslim Mughal Empire

5. http://en.wikipedia.org/wiki/Mughal_dynasty. During this same era, in

went into decline, still Ahmed Shah Bahadur (1725–1775) began as the
fifteenth Mughal Emperor at the age of twenty-three in 1748, but ruled
unsuccessfully for six years. Badly diseased, he retired in 1754. His eyes
were put out, and in January 1754 he was killed in his sleep at the age of
thirty, by Wazir Ghazi-ud-Din, who was quite a character!

This Wazir was earlier Nawab Mir Ghaziudin Khan Bahadur, the
Wazir of the Mughal Emperor Shah Jahan III. He became Paymaster-
General in 1752 and held various Wazir positions until 1759. His titles
read like Arabian fairy tales—*Amir ul-Umara, Imad ul-Mulk, Ghazi
ud-din Khan Bahadur, and Firuz Jang, Nizam ul-Mulk, Asaf Jah*. Finally
he ended up as *Farzari Khan* on 21 February 1757. He was the one who
blinded and imprisoned Emperor Ahmad Shah Bahadur in 1754, and
then went on to assassinate Emperor Alamgir II in 1759. He is as close an
example as anyone can find of a Muslim *culprit* gadding around in India
at the time that Clive destroyed the French, and thus also any Muslim
influence and power. This extraordinary Wazir Bahadur escaped all
punishment by, conveniently, going on a pilgrimage to Mecca.[6]

While Islam was waning in India, at the very same time it was
waxing in Arabia. The same war was also causing skirmishes there.
This was the time also that Wahhab, the name heard so often in
connection with the September 11, 2001 attacks, rose to power. He was
fighting for his own beliefs in Arabia. I have, however, found no direct
link between the simultaneous fighting in India and in the Arabian
Peninsula, except the British connection. If European war reflects
the spiritual states of the church being punished just prior to the Last
Judgment, then Britain, France and the religion of Islam feature both
in India, and in Arabia, where there was a vehement fundamentalist
Muslim revival.

Muhammad ibn Abd al-Wahhab (c.1703–1791), influenced by
Taimiya (d. 1328), used *ijtihad*, a personal interpretation of the *Sharia*,
to analyze the times, and to bring *Qur'an* and *Hadith*, themselves
perfect and immutable, under the scrutiny of *Sharia*, adapted to a

---

1747 Ahmad Shah Durrani united the Pashtun tribes and created the nation of
Afghanistan.
6. http://en.wikipedia.org/wiki/Ghazi-ud-Din

changeable world. His own *ijtihad* adapted the *Sharia* to the Arabian Peninsula's politics. Wahhab was fanatically opposed to any cult of saints, destroying shrines, and wishing even to raze Muhammad's own shrine to the ground, or demolish the *Kaaba* itself as being *shirk*, i.e. idolatry. By extolling the ecstasy of obedience, and *Tawhid*, the unity of the Divine, they called themselves both *Mujtahid* in their exercise of *ijtihad*, an independent legal counseling in *Sharia;* and *Muwahidun* "those who advocate oneness," i.e. strict *monotheists* based on the Islamic doctrine of *Tawhid*. Al-Wahhab understood this oneness of God as the *exclusiveness* of the One God. There was only one way to see it!

In 1744 Ibn al-Wahhab joined forces with a tribal chief, Muhammad Ibn Saud, starting a militant reform movement in Arabia. Many wars came from the *fatwas* (legal opinions) that he issued. With the help, ironically at this time, of the British and through declaring other tribes *Mushrik* (polytheists), the Saud family from Najd became the undisputed tribe in Arabia. Wahhab's religious mission to wage holy war (jihad) against all other forms of Islam resulted in the conquest of his neighbors by c.1763.

Ibn Abdul Wahhab, as mentioned, issued *fatwas* that branded every Muslim in Arabia who was in dispute with the Ibn Saud family, a *K'fir* (infidel) through their *Bidaa* (innovation). However, by one commentary, Wahhab in his alliance with Saud condoned the biggest *Bidaa* in all Arabia. The declaration of hereditary right of the sons of Saud was itself *Bidaa*, an innovation, since this accepted a political *intermediary* to Allah, which met with his condemnation. Perhaps this hereditary right was ensured through the marriage of one of Wahhab's daughters to the Saud family.[7]

Saudi Arabia is Wahhabi to this day, still threatening to level five mosques built by Muhammad's own daughter and by four of his companions (Mosque of Sayyida Fatima bin Rasulillah, Salman al-Farsi Mosque, Abu Bakr Mosque, Umar ibn al-Khattab Mosque, and Mosque of Ali ibn Abi Talib). These structures are unique cultural assets with incalculable historic value, not to mention religious

---

7. <http://www.al-islam.org/encyclopedia/chapter9/7.html>

symbolism.[8] Wahhabis continue today to oppose Sufis, Shiites, and all others deemed unfaithful to the Wahhabis' austere interpretation of the *Sunna* (custom) of the Prophet Muhammad.[9]

On reflecting on Wahhab, it is interesting that his revival of monotheism or *tawhid* and banning of all saints and external manifestations of Allah, took place at the same time as the Great Awakening in Europe and America. They seem linked by their fervor in purity, and a direct link to God or Allah.

AL-MAHDI

In connection with Islam and the Last Judgment, we will now consider the expectation of the Messiah, or Mashih, or Al-Made. If you saw the old movie decades ago of Gordon in Khartoum, you would have heard about the Mahdi. He is also known as Ahmad:

> I am indeed the Messenger of God to you, confirming the Torah that is before me, and giving good tidings [gospel] of a Messenger who shall come after me, whose name shall be *Ahmad*. (*Surah* 61.6)

The Mahdi, the Divinely guided One, is an expectation of a world leader to unite humankind under the banner of Islam. According to the unanimously accepted saying of the Prophet Muhammad, God will bring about a savior before the end of time to establish the global domination of Islam over all religions. In other words, the savior will

---

8. <http://www.beliefnet.com/story/147/story_14732_1.html>

9. In the massacre of Karabalee 1802, Wahhabi regarded Shiites as idolatrous in their use of an Imam and making pilgrimage to shrines. Wahhabis, being similar to Kharijites, who used violence to enforce the Muslim system, and rejecting rational speculation, then massacred an entire village.

establish the Kingdom of God on this earth. In Islamic traditions, that savior is known by the name of "al-Mahdi."

However, there is hardly anything stated directly on the subject, either in the *Qur'an* or in the *Hadith*. There is a promise of the establishment of God's Kingdom on earth at the hand of the righteous:

> We would like to bestow a favor upon those who have been oppressed in the earth and make them leaders and make them inheritors (of the world). (*Surah* 28.5)

He again says,

> Certainly, We wrote in the Psalms (Zabur) . . . "As for the earth, surely My righteous servants shall inherit it." (*Surah* 21.105)

Therefore, a tradition, or Sunna, has developed in Islamic eschatology, that Judgment day starts thirty years before the end of the earth. The coming of the Mahdi (also *Mehdi* meaning "the divinely guided one") will precede the Second Coming of Isa (Jesus) and it will trigger the redemption of Islam and the defeat of its enemies.

The exact nature of the Mahdi differs between Shiite and Sunni Muslims, but both agree that Isa (Jesus) and the Mahdi will together fight evil in the world, cement justice and will unite the Muslims and true Christians under true Islam and abolish all *Jizya* (taxes or tributes). The Mahdi is expected to come from Mecca but will rule from Damascus, Syria. Isa will defeat *Dajjal* (the false Messiah or antichrist), and then shall live on Earth for many years. According to some traditions, Isa will marry and have a family, and then die.[10]

For the sake of providing a wider range of what the messiah means to Islam, we shall mention that the *Ahmadiyya* movement considers that Mahdi is the incarnation of Jesus and Muhammad and at the same time is one of Vishnu's Avatars. This is a modern movement, and there is an Anti-*Ahmadiyya* movement to oppose it. It is based on the Mahdi being preceded by false Mahdis, called *Dajjaal*. The true messenger

10. http://en.wikipedia.org/wiki/Judgment_Day

of Allah can alone help you detect a *Dajjaal*, and say to him "I bear testimony to the fact that you are the Dajjaal about whom God's Messenger (may peace be upon him) had informed us." If the *Dajjall* would then kill you and bring you back to life, that is proof that he is a *Dajjaal*, especially if he tried to kill you again, but cannot do it.

Mahdi (and each one is of course convinced he is *the*, not simply a, Mahdi) will, according to the Islamic traditions, be directed by Allah to restore the Prophetic caliphate and, as such, is not bound by the letter of the Islamic law. For example, both Ibn Tumart and Muhammad Ahmad declared that they alone were capable of interpreting the *Qur'an*, whereby any previous opinions and commentaries were relegated to irrelevance. And of course the opposition to them by established religious figures—both of these men, like most Mahdists, led revolutions against existing Islamic governments—only served to reinforce their Mahdist claims, since only true Muslims could recognize the Mahdi. Anyone claiming to be the Mahdi, then, is largely unfettered by any norms, Islamic or otherwise. Ibn Tumart and his leadership, for example, killed tens of thousands *of their own followers* whom they deemed lukewarm in their support.[11] And Muhammad Ahmad was the one who had Charles Gordon decapitated and his head displayed after taking Khartoum. He might have proved just as bloodthirsty as Tumart had he not died of malaria some six months later.

---

11. Mahdism is believed by many to be the province only of the *Shi'is*, but many of the most successful Mahdist movements in history have been *Sunni*. The *Shi'is* expect only a blood descendant of Muhammad to be the Imam, while the *Sunni* are more eclectic in who is Imam. Most prominent here would be Ibn Tumart's *al-Muwahhid*s (Almohads) who ruled from Portugal to Tunisia, 1130–1269 CE, and Muhammad Ahmad's Sudanese Mahdists—about whom the movie *Khartoum*, starring Charlton Heston and Sir Laurence Olivier was made—who ruled Sudan from 1885–1898. There was another one in 1979: one Juhayman al-Utaybi declared his brother-in-law Muhammad al-Qahtani to be the Mahdi and led several hundred armed followers to occupy the main mosque in Mecca. They were either killed or captured and then executed. Mahdism ends up being a means of expressing dissatisfaction with extant Islamic governments. http://hnn.us/articles/13146.html

Al Madhi ties in with those who are expecting his arrival. They are the *Ismaelis*, called the Seveners, true successors of Muhammad through the line of Ismail, the elder son Jafar al Sadiq. But the Twelver Shiites are called *Imamis*, because of their esoteric concept in an unbroken chain of imams going back to the year AD 874, when they say the last true Imam left us. The most important cosmic force is the divine Light of guidance, "pre-eternal, and the real instrument of creation," which "Light" passed from one imam to the next. Seven and twelve refer to the different lines of succession. However, the last Imam who is infallible and divinely guided, who will do away with the consensus system of law, is in *ghayba* or "occulation." He is alive somewhere on earth, waiting for the right time to show himself.

CONCLUSION

I would like to finish by reflecting on the whole picture. Islam is the subject, the Last Judgment the context. Islam is a strong presence in our mentality today. It is a self-sufficient religious belief, with its own texts, which are sufficiently linked with the Sacred Scriptures to warrant Islam the status of a spiritual religion, capable of saving its sincere followers. But it also has its extremists, as does Christianity.

If the wars at the time of the Last Judgment stood for spiritual states of the church, we can only outline a possible spiritual map. In the world of spirits, England was at the center in the last judgment performed on the Reformed, which took place last, after that performed on the Catholics, Muslim and Gentiles. The European nations that fought in the war at the very time of the Last Judgment were all the nations ranged around England in the world of spirits. England stands for a greater spiritual light, thus the potential of seeing Divine truth in its own light. Judged, however, England would mean the denial of this quality. Prussia (or Germans) stand for obedience to the Word, but a judgment against Prussia, would mean the denial, or disobedience to the Word. And Sweden, identified with the stubborn insistence on faith alone, yet with a superb ability to see truth itself, would in judgment stand for the misuse of these qualities. France is a noble nation because of its independence from the Papacy, and so stands for perhaps the ability to fight for the truth. In its judgment, France would be truth seen as *owned* by people, or subject to prohibition, as happened during the Enlightenment and the inquisition banning literature even up to 1762. Spain was Catholic, and could stand for ruling over others in the name of Christ, but removing the Word itself from the people. Islam then conquered Spain. Was that because the Word was hidden? Then Islam was defeated by el Cid. Was faith in the Word restored? Islam was defeated by Martel. Again, the Word was involved. Islam was defeated together with the French in India. One wonders. And in America, England and France used gentile Indians, remnants of the Ancient Church against each other. All gentiles were also judged in 1757 in vast numbers.

We can only ponder the meaning of the Last Judgment and its effects displayed in that Seven Year War, 1756 to 1763. The states of the church were coming to an end, and in America one quick outcome, via a subsequent revolution, was the separation of state and church as never before or since, anywhere. Only in America is this separation by law.

And why did Wahhab have his rise at this very time? Why did he insist on his own form of *iconoclasm*, casting down idols? The Holy Land had ceased to be representative—events there were no longer outcomes of spiritual dramas. However, there was warfare there too, in 1757, perhaps a distant pantomime of the spiritual conflict in Europe, as were the conflicts in India and America. Whatever else it was, it was a time of culmination. We may ponder on the effect of the spread of the New Church, sufficiently to inform everyone that the Last Judgment has already occurred, historically, and no "end of the world" will come, and no future Messiah either. Instead, god-fearing leaders can arise from all points of the compass, but whose allegiance will be directly to Truth, thus to a justice which surmounts that of all the kingdoms of the earth. ⚹

NOTES

History of the Middle East Database

1744   In the Arabian Peninsula, an alliance was forged between the Muhammad Ibn Saud and Muhammad Ibn Abd al-Wahhab, the leader of the *Muwahidun* ("those who advocate oneness"), better known in the West as the Wahhabis.

1750   By this time, the Ottomans were forced to accept the fact that most of Iraq was under the control of a dynasty of Georgian Mamluks.

1757   British rule over India began following the defeat of the Nawwab of Bengal at the Battle of Plassey. The British went on to take the French settlement at Chandernagor the same year.

1768–

1774   The Russo-Ottoman war was fought over Black Sea territories. The ensuing Treaty of Kuchuk Kainarji opened the Turkish straits to Russia. The Sultan was forced to renounce suzerainty over the Khan of Crimea and over the Muslim Tatars living along the North shore of the Black Sea. The Ottoman Empire was also forced to accept foreign rights of intervention on behalf of Orthodox Christians residing in the Ottoman Empire, an enormous blow to Ottoman Muslim pride. The defeats marked by the treaties of Karlowitz and Kuchuk Kainarji led the Ottomans into a period of introspection during which they began to ask themselves where they had gone wrong. This led to a period of political and religious centralization, administrative reform, and modernization in an effort to recapture lost ground.

1773   In the wake of weakening Ottoman influence in the Arabian Peninsula, the tribe of Saud captured Riyadh. The Saudis drew their inspiration largely from the puritanical Muslim sect known as the Wahhabis. The Saudi-Wahhabi alliance began to spread a political and religious reform movement throughout the Arabian peninsula.

http://www.nmhschool.org/tthornton/mehistorydatabase/safavid_and_
ottoman_eras.php#saudi_wahhabi_alliance1744

Time Line: Muhammad and Islam

570   Born in Mecca
610   Call in cave, Night Journey
       Meccan *Surahs*
622   Hijra, move to Medina
       Medinan *Surah*s
624   Battle of Badr
625   Wounded at battle of Mount Uhud, Medina, Saudi Arabia
       50 Archers left post
       Mixed results
627   War of the Trench: After Muslims are forced to dig trenches,
       battle becomes stalemated. The attacking force of 9,000 lose
       heart, and then a violent two day storm blows over their tents
       and puts out their fires, so they leave. In the aftermath, the
       Jewish tribe of Banu Qurayza are found to be in league with
       the attackers, and so about 900 of their males were slain, and
       women and children were enslaved for treason.
       Vision: return to Mecca.
       Treaty reached with Mecca: return next year for pilgrimage
629   Muhammad and company make pilgrimage as Muslims, to
       Kaa'ba, in Mecca
       Enter, and worship
630–1 Meccans break truce.
       With 10,000, Muhammad takes Mecca mostly peacefully
       Most convert to Islam
632   Died, Medina
632   Abu Bakr, 1st Caliph
634   Umar, 2nd Caliph Shufa: decide on successor
644   Uthmān, ibn 'Affān, was the third Caliph after Muhammad, and
       ruled from c. 579 to July 17, 656. He was one of the sahaba,
       or companions of Muhammad. An early convert to Islam, he

played a major role in the compilation of the Qur'an. He was assassinated after an armed revolt.

656   Ali, 4th Caliph

657   Muawiya, raised Syrian troops to attack Ali, the fourth Caliph after Muhammad. With veterans from the battle of Badr, Ali routed the Syrians, captured the water-front which formed the prize of victory. In the battle of Siffin later, Ali himself mounted on a piebald horse, and wielding his ponderous and two-edged sword, led the charge. Muawiya's defeat ended the threat.

661   Ali murdered

680   Karbala: Husayn, Muhammad's own son, murdered with company as he rose to claim Shia version of Caliph/Imam title Martyr for Shiites

749   The Abbassids from 'Abbas ibn 'Abd al-Muttalib who was Caliph from the 566-c. 653 CE, reached a high point in the Muslim civilization, and was the most developed part of the Arab world, together with Byzantine, China and India. They took control of the Empire, however omitting a direct descendant of Muhammad. Hussain, the grandson of Muhammad, and followers were slain in the Battle or Massacre of Karbala (680 CE), leading to a separate Shiite sect seeking a rightful heir to the Muslim empire rather than the Sunni succession after Ali. Beginning of Sunni.

The Imperative to Find the Ancient Word in China: A Result of the Last Judgment

CHRISTOPHER D. BOWN

Often I meet New Church people who want to find the Ancient Word. It is as if there is a magical challenge the Lord awakens by these words in *Apocalypse Revealed:*

> Ask about it in China, and perhaps you will find [the Ancient Word] there among the Tartars! (AR 11)

These words open our imaginations to adventure and exploration. They also involve a personal and spiritual challenge—to meet people on the other side of the world—in the most populous and quickly developing country on earth today—to come to know them as friends, and to grow together spiritually with them with mutual responsiveness to the Lord.

Because the Lord so passionately loves us, He is always revealing Himself to us, the human family. He is continually trying to tell us things we need to know. He is continually trying to uplift, inspire, motivate, and teach each one of us through all the years of our life. The principal and profoundly powerful way He does this is through the written Word. The Word is the means by which we are reconnected to heaven and to the Lord; it is how we can reach past what would be otherwise a merely natural and selfish life, and up to the truly human life the Lord intends for us. It is the means by which our heart can be touched by the good things of love and our mind can be enlightened

---

1. Maps and photos used in the Last Judgment conference presentation of this paper can be found online at http://web.me.com/chrisbown/AncientWord/.

by the true things of wisdom. The Word helps us grow in loving one another and in loving the Lord.

For the earliest people who woke up to the reality of the living God, the Word was "written" on their hearts, by an inward way. However, since people freely turned their backs on the Lord and focused their lives on themselves, the Lord provided a written Word, in book form, so that through the miracle of reading and living, we can be reconnected inwardly with the living God, with heaven, and with all things truly spiritual and human.

Today we have a written Word that includes the Old Testament, the New Testament, and the Writings. Yet even before Moses received the first part of the written Word we have today (the Ten Commandments written on tables of stone at Mount Sinai), there was a written Word already in existence. In the Writings this earliest written Word is called "The Ancient Word."

The challenge presented to "ask about" and "perhaps" find the Ancient Word has fascinated people of the New Church ever since *Apocalypse Revealed* was first published in 1766. *Apocalypse Revealed* 11 begins by addressing the spiritual significance of Asia. It then adds a special note which discloses to us not only that there was a written Word in west Asia before the Israelite Word, but also that this earlier Word was still in existence more than 3000 years later on the opposite side of Asia. This written Word was preserved and still being used by peoples who lived in the eastern half of what was then called "Great Tartary"—north of the Great Wall of China (figure 1) and specifically in the area from which the emperor of China at that day came.

The passage ends with the words given above. Are they just a suggestion? Or, given that they are written in the imperative, is there a need for us to act, literally, to "ask in China"? Is the suggestion for readers to respond as individuals, as their interest is awakened or quickened? Or, given that these words are written in the plural, is it really that the people of the coming New Church—for whom the whole book *Apocalypse Revealed* is addressed—are being challenged to act as a group?

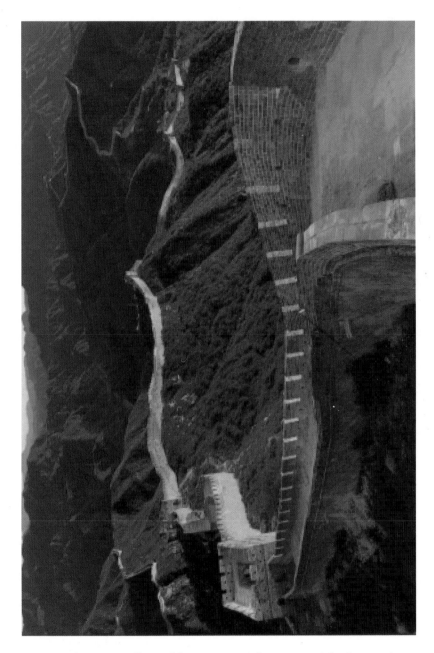

Figure 1. The Great Wall at Badaling. Courtesy of a non-copyrighted postcard.

Figure 2. The Kangxi Emperor, a Manchu who ruled China 1661–1722 and is considered one of China's greatest emperors. This work of art is in the public domain.

The imperative given to us takes on significance in the context of the Last Judgment, which occurred nine years before the publication of *Apocalypse Revealed*. With the Last Judgment of 1757 and the formation of the new heaven in the thirteen years or so that followed, there was a fresh beginning for the whole human family and a reclaiming of the inner stability of heaven itself that will last forever. In view of the presence of heaven and the spiritual world with each of us here on earth, through our unconscious minds the Last Judgment marks a fresh start for those on earth to live what the Lord and heaven stand for.

The events of the Last Judgment and the revelation that followed are the context for the imperative to ask in China for the Ancient Word. In studying this context we can understand the significance of the imperative and we can find the tools for understanding and working with the changes afoot in the Lord's Divine Providence.

THE 1757 LAST JUDGMENT AND ASIA

Often we think of the Last Judgment as involving only the Christian Church. The Christian Church certainly was at its end—the "end of the age" that the Lord many times had predicted would come. The church had ended and was judged in the spiritual world. While this event was invisible to physical eyes, it made a profound impact on the life of the human spirit.

The judgment, along with sorting and ordering the heavens and the hells, involved people from every part of the earth, everyone who had lived from the time the Lord was on earth until 1757. The judgment was not just for Christians; there was a judgment for gentiles as well. Good gentiles were gathered into the new heaven, not incorporated into the early or ancient heavens, where there are people who lived before the Lord's coming on earth two thousand years ago. Rather, the gentiles who lived since then are part of and integral to the New Heaven. The New Heaven is made up of all good people from all churches and religions since the Lord's coming (NJHD 3–4, LJ post—125).

It is important to be alert to this timeline because what Swedenborg learned about the Ancient Word and its being preserved in Great Tartary seems to come from two sources. The first source was people in heaven who lived on earth *before* the Lord was on earth and who then had the Ancient Word. There was a Last Judgment when the Lord was on earth, and He formed "ancient heavens" from all the good people who had lived up to that time. Those specifically who had the written Ancient Word became angels of the heaven of the copper age. The second source was people in heaven who had lived on earth during the time *after* the Lord was on earth up to Swedenborg's day. They were people from Great Tartary, who on earth and in heaven continued to have the written Ancient Word. They, along with hundreds of thousands of other gentiles, were brought up into heaven with the 1757 Last Judgment, and they became part of the new heaven.

Something of the distinct process of the judgment and formation of heaven from the gentiles in 1757 is described in Swedenborg's *Spiritual Experiences,* which he was writing as the Last Judgment was prepared for in late 1756 and as it happened in 1757. The process of the judgment was summarized a year later in the published book *The Last Judgment* (1758), and the outcome of the judgment in the spiritual world was described five years later in *The Continuation concerning the Last Judgment* (1763). Much of the material from this volume was then repeated at the end of *True Christian Religion* (1771) in the supplement about the spiritual world.

The description of the gentiles and their situation in the spiritual world in late 1756, that is, just before the Last Judgment was getting underway, is fascinating.[2] The intriguing part is a story about some gentiles towards the east who were sad because "the Divine does not appear to them," and they said they had been waiting for someone to teach them. An angel replied that they had not seen God because they had not been willing to believe that the living Human God had been born on earth—the most basic of all revelations. Their response was

---

2. It starts with SE 5240 (parts repeated in LJ 48) just after an entry specifying "the last days of the year 1756" and almost 100 passages before one dated January 6, 1757.

that they could conceive of God as being a person, but not as being born a person on earth, because they had no idea of a virgin birth being possible (SE 5244 = LJ post 129).

The concern raised in this story endures today and is a crucial issue for the New Church to face, in both the East and the West. At the Last Judgment the Africans fared better than many others did because they more readily affirmed the Divine Human of the Lord. In the Last Judgment the Lord "sided" with the gentiles, over the Christians, even with their wide range of ideas about God and implications about the Lord (SE 5807–5809—apparently still in 1757).

The events of the Last Judgment itself were concentrated in the early months of 1757, with the ordering of the new heaven as spring arrived in the northern hemisphere, continuing through the year (SE 5762–5763, 5821, 5882). The judgment process was completed within that year. The book *The Last Judgment*, published a year later, states: "This Last Judgment started at the beginning of last year, 1757, and was fully completed by the end of the year" (LJ 45). Likewise "All the predictions in the Book of Revelation are today fulfilled" (LJ 40, 44).

A prediction by the Lord Himself that we often overlook also came true: "Then they shall come from the east and the west, and from the north and the south, and recline in the kingdom of God" (Luke 13.29—cited in LJ 52).

We do not have many details about the 1757 Last Judgment's effects on non-Christians. One chapter in *The Last Judgment* describes the process for everyone (LJ 45–52), with only brief mention of the gentiles beyond Islam (LJ 47, 51). Even then, the account is only basic. It includes all gentiles, with few distinctions given for differing ethnic groups, countries, regions or continents—except Africa. Much of it occurred in only a few days, with huge numbers of people—so many that Swedenborg suggested they could only be counted in groups of 10,000s (LJ 51, echoing SE 5882).

The Last Judgment ends with a chapter entitled "The Future State of the World and the Church" (LJ 73–74). In outward appearance— the physical reality of the world and the common events of human history and life—the world would continue on much the same.

Inwardly, however—in the realm of the human spirit—there would be a profound difference resulting from the 1757 Last Judgment. The people in the church would now have more freedom in thinking about matters of faith, and so about the spiritual matters which have to do with heaven, because of the restoration of spiritual freedom (LJ 73.2; also referred to in TCR 115 as the Lord effecting a "redemption," which is a liberation or setting free of people, Coro 21). At first glance this freedom might seem to apply only to the Christian world, where we might assume "the people in the church" to be. However, the Lord's church is both with Christians and with gentiles (LJ post 125, referring to NJHD 3, 244–246). The earlier draft of this LJ 73 passage states that "In consequence of this, people [i.e. all people] now enjoy freedom of thinking rationally" (SE 5874).

One pervasive and permanent outcome that transforms the whole world we live in is that, "The reception of Divine truth and good . . . [now] is more universal, interior, easy, and distinct" (AE 1217).

When the Last Judgment of 1757 was fully completed all prophecies about that Judgment were accomplished and all things were restored to order and basic stability in the spiritual world—a world not distant on the other side of the universe, but present with each of us today. Furthermore, the freedom of the human spirit was restored to all people on earth, along with a new, easier responsiveness to what is true and good in human life.

THE LAST JUDGMENT OPENED THE WAY
FOR NEW DISCOVERIES AND REVELATIONS

The year 1757 started a transformation—a radical change—of the whole spiritual world. Most simply, "after the Last Judgment the state of the spiritual world has been completely changed" (AE 754.3). That year marked the growth of a new heaven for people from all churches and all religions throughout the earth. With all these good people freely finding their homes and places, and with Swedenborg traveling in spirit to discover what these different peoples were like, there was new and more open communication. This new heaven provided and continues to provide a new underlying order and openness for the whole spiritual world and for everyone on earth. The changes resulting in basic order and deep stability continued for over a dozen years more, right up to the writing of *True Christian Religion* in 1770 (TCR 123.2).

In those years Swedenborg had revealed to him[3] many new things for the New Church. In one sense he learned from spirits and angels, and he participated in making things happen as they did. More deeply he was directed by the Lord and given perceptions of truth through his daily experiences in the spiritual world and his ongoing study of the Word. Included in the discoveries made for the New Church (LJ cont 12, DP 264.4; see also Coro 21) was revelation about the Ancient Word itself, moreover, about the Ancient Word being preserved with the peoples and nations of Great Tartary.

Pre-1757 Perspective on the Ancient Word

Before the 1757 Last Judgment, Swedenborg already knew much about "the Ancient Word," which was affirmed in much of *Arcana Coelestia* (translated today as *Secrets of Heaven*), written and published between the years 1749–1756. Some basic points given there are as follows.

At the beginning of *Arcana*, Swedenborg discussed the earliest people who woke up to the existence of the living God and their humanity from God. They enjoyed making up stories, with elements drawn from nature and their experience, arranged into a narrative or story which conveyed a message about what they were experiencing spiritually. This style was Divinely inspired—it came from the spiritual breath or inspiration of heaven and the Lord—so the made-up stories were part of the Lord's Word for them. At some point Moses came into possession of these stories and included them in the Book of Genesis.

---

3. The "as-of-self" or "apparently independent" reaching up by people to their Creator (DLW 170) but with the Lord really alone teaching (DP 163, TCR 779) suggests that discovery and revelation are two heads of the same coin.

These stories included the creation story, the story of the Garden of Eden, and others (AC 66, 1139).

On the other hand, Swedenborg was aware, as are modern Biblical scholars, that earlier texts and manuscripts which predate the Bible are directly referred to in the Bible we have. For example, Swedenborg knew that the Book of Numbers 21.14–15 refers to the *Book of the Wars of Jehovah* (AC 1664.11; cf. 1659), and that the *Book of Utterances* is mentioned in Numbers 21.27.

Both of these books were written, he declared, in the earliest style, in which people and words were employed to signify (or correspond) to something spiritual, something about the Lord, something more than the actual or literal things given in the text (AC 1756.2). The narratives or stories in that written Ancient Word "were therefore such as came near to a kind of prophetic style, the kind that would allow young children and also simple people to retain things in their memory" (AC 9942.5). It is likely that there was a form of that Word that predated writing, that was collected and handed-down orally, perhaps even dramatically, or by rituals in worship. Eventually the Word was written down and composed into books. Swedenborg recognized that these books of the "Word of the Ancient Church" were of two basic types—narrative (sometimes called "historical") and prophetic—like many of the books of the contemporary Old Testament (AC 2686).

It is important to be aware that there are also other books from that time and those people—called simply "books of the Ancient Church." One example is the Book of Job, which is full of correspondences, but is not the Word because "it has no internal sense in which the one subject is the Lord and His kingdom" (AC 3540.4, 9942.5). In addition there were books written by those not in the church, but also full of correspondences and meaning—such as the ancient Greek myths, or those of the Arabians or Syrians—but again, these are not the Word (AC 4280, 9942.4). While many of those books were known and read by educated Europeans in Swedenborg's day, the Word of the Ancient Church itself, however, was unknown: "In course of time that [written] Word came to be lost" (AC 2897) so that it "is no longer extant" (AC 3432.2, 8273).

Discoveries about the Ancient Word During and After the Last Judgment

As the Last Judgment was occurring, something new came to light which is described in a section of *Spiritual Experiences* about "Books and the Word in the other life, in heaven" (SE 5602). It begins by saying that there are written books in the spiritual world just like on earth, and with similar writings "in Latin, Hebrew and Eastern languages." What Eastern languages? Written in what scripts—Middle Eastern or Asian? The spiritual world has the entire Word that we have, "from beginning to end, so written so that every one can read it" (SE 5603).

Swedenborg also discovered that although it was "lost" and no longer "extant" on earth, the "Word of the Ancient Church" continued to exist in the spiritual world. It included the books mentioned in the Old Testament: the *Wars of Jehovah, Utterances* (or *Enunciations*), and *Propheticals*. Furthermore:

> That Word is so written that they can be instructed in minutest things. It is also inspired: but, inasmuch as it was no longer of service for the people who succeeded them [the ancient Israelites and the Jews], another Word [the Hebrew scriptures] was written. (SE 5605)

Six years later, in 1763, there was a turning point which combined more powerfully than before both the spiritual and historic realities of the Ancient Word. Swedenborg describes this in the section entitled "The Lost Ancient Word":

> Angels of the third heaven have told me that the ancients had a Word among them, written, like our Word . . . but which has since been lost. They also said that this Word is still preserved among them, and is used by the ancients in that heaven, for whom this was the Word when they lived in the world. (De Verbo 15, repeated in SS and TCR; cf. TCR 279)

The Word of the Ancient Church not only *exists* in the spiritual world, it is *kept safe* and *actually used* by the very same people who used it here on earth in ancient times. Later the passage lists the various countries in the ancient Middle East where the people had lived while on earth.

Significantly, two more parts of the Ancient Word are then specified as being part of the Ancient Word: the prophetic *Book of Jasher* and the early made-up stories of Genesis (the first seven chapters, almost word for word). The inclusion of the early chapters in Genesis is again something Swedenborg was told "by angels" (TCR 279.4). This tremendously increases the textual content from the Ancient Word copied and available in the Old Testament.

Swedenborg's next spiritual experience about the Ancient Word is his conversation with Moses: "I asked him about the book *Jasher*. He said that he has seen it; and he told me that Word still exists with the ancients of his day, and is read" (SE 6107, dated late 1764).

The final spiritual experience published several years later in 1768 (in *Married Love* but possibly drafted a year or more earlier in the "lost" work on marriage), involves those ancient peoples and the heaven of the "copper age" where they live:

> There are also sacred halls here, built out of boards of olive wood, and in the middle of them is a sanctuary, containing in an ark the Word given to the inhabitants of Asia before the Word which the Israelites had. . . . The angel then led me to one of the buildings, and looking in, we saw in the middle of it the sanctuary, all bathed in a brilliant white light. And the angel said: "The light comes from that ancient Asiatic Word, for all Divine truth shines with light in heaven." (ML 77)

This heaven, of course, existed during all of Swedenborg's earlier spiritual experiences, but only then, as he hoped to learn about the marriages of earlier peoples, as he journeyed into new spiritual territory, did he come to that heaven and found the Ancient Word central in their lives. All the pre-Advent churches, including the part of the Ancient Church whose people became angels in that copper age heaven, had their Last Judgment when the Lord was in the world. "It came to an end when the Lord came into the world. He then carried out a last judgment on all who had lived from the date on which that church was first set up" (LJ 46). That heaven must have existed for more than 1,700 years.

The people in the heaven of the copper age also know that the Ancient Word existed, on earth, in Great Tartary, with Swedenborg's contemporaries. The angels told him: "in the kingdoms of Asia it has now been lost, and it is preserved only in Great Tartary" (ML 77).

Did Swedenborg already know this? Sometimes it is hard to ascertain exactly when certain spiritual experiences happened, especially narrative accounts in the later books of the Writings. But reading the Writings in the chronological order they were *published* should inform us. *Married Love* was published two years after *Apocalypse Revealed*, in 1768.

Discoveries about the Ancient Word in Great Tartary

Just before the Last Judgment Swedenborg had what might have been his first contact in the spiritual world with people from Great Tartary. The description in *Spiritual Experiences* was not edited and was not repeated in later works:

> I was afterwards brought back, but higher up, where were spirits from the regions of the north part of Asia; and it was perceived that they were of such a disposition, from their life in the world, as to be able to receive the heavenly doctrine of which I have spoken above. (SE 4779)

The "north part of Asia" may refer to Great Tartary. Swedenborg's *Principia Rerum Naturalium* (1734) includes a map of the world in which *Tartaria* (the Latin word we know in English as "Tartary") was highlighted and stretched across north Asia. See figure 3.

Spiritual Experiences 4779 occurs within a series of passages about the beginning of the New Church that occur in *Spiritual Experiences* before the 1757 Last Judgment.[4] This pre-Last Judgment series develops the first extended discussion and the new revelation of the

---

4. It is 440 passages before SE 5239, which mentions the last days of 1756, and also precedes SE 5336, which is dated January 6, 1757.

heavenly doctrine occurring among the Africans.[5] This whole section of *Spiritual Experiences* is seminal in understanding spiritual realities of Africa and Asia then and the hope for New Church growth in those parts of our world today.

The mention of Tartars occurs about six to seven years later, sometime between January 1762 and December 1763 in *Spiritual Experiences* 6077. This passage, modified somewhat, is also used also in *Last Judgment posthumous* (LJ post 132[6]).

It should be noted that often when we do not know much about this world—the numerous and diverse things and people in it, and the history that has taken place—we stumble when we read the Writings, which are nuanced and detailed. Swedenborg's knowledge was more vast than most of ours. In addition, the richness and complexity of life on earth in his day and in the century preceding are reflected repeatedly in what we are told in the Writings.

Such is the case with what is said about Tartars and Great Tartary. Great Tartary was a name used at Swedenborg's day for an enormous stretch of land across much of the Asian continent—an area which contained many distinct peoples and nationalities. Several peoples or nations of Great Tartary lived along and north of the Great Wall of

---

5. SE 4770–4772, 4773–4780 and 4783 are about a new church that would begin once the Last Judgment was effected. SE 4775 is echoed in TCR. The context seems to be revelation of the heavenly doctrine, out of heaven, to spirits from Africa and potentially north Asia—and from there to spirits from other regions of earth and then to spirits of other planets (SE 4780). It is also noteworthy that in the flow of passages, SE 4781f talks about why the Lord was born on this earth, the initial seed for EU 113–117, published several years later, in 1758, the year after the Last Judgment. The seminal points about the Africans are: their easy belief in the Lord being born on earth (SE 4775 and 4783, echoed in TCR 837) and a vision of how the heavenly doctrine would spread in Africa (SE 4777 = LJ post 117 = LJ cont 76 = TCR 840). The series also mentions other parts of Asia: "in Asia, in the vicinity of Africa" (SE 4771), "to some in Asia under the government of the Turks, also in Asia round about" (SE 4777) and "partly also in Asia, rather near the Indian Sea, but not in the immediate neighborhood of the sea" (SE 4774).

6. NBR numbering

China, a system of walls built for over 1,000 years to keep them out of China.

Some have assumed that the first passages to describe Swedenborg's contact with people from Great Tartary in the spiritual world is the same passage about the people with the Ancient Word—only that Swedenborg changed some of the details because he was confused. I suppose this could have happened, but I do not think it was the case.

The report is about "Tartary close to China—Lesser Tartary [or, *Tartaria Minor*]." The people there are described as a peaceful group, not knowing war; very populous; aware of both China and Siberia; friendly with the Chinese (the *Last Judgment* revision adds that they "used to live outside the Great Wall of China"); fearful of the Siberians (the advancing Russians or perhaps other Tungusic people like themselves?); looking for inner qualities and merit in their leaders; and as having an ancient book. The ancient book is the Psalm of David, part of the Hebrew Old Testament that survives in western culture today. They also have the Ten Commandments.

Four hundred years before Swedenborg's time, at the time of Kublai Khan, European Christian missionaries worked with the Mongols (who are one of the peoples or nations of Great Tartary). The missionaries translated the Psalms into Mongolian and taught a choir of boys to sing the Psalms. This passage in *Spiritual Experiences*, then, must be not about the Ancient Word.

Swedenborg's next experience about Tartars, reported in 1766 in *Apocalypse Revealed* is the one that ends with the bold and challenging imperative for all of us.

> Concerning the Ancient Word that used to be in Asia before the Israelitish Word, this new thing deserves to be mentioned: It has till now been preserved among the peoples who dwell in Great Tartary.
>
> I have spoken with spirits and angels who were from there in the spiritual world, and they said that they possess a Word, that they have had it in their possession from ancient times, that they perform their Divine worship in accordance with that Word, and that it consists of nothing but correspondences.
>
> They said that even the Book of *Jasher* that is mentioned in Josh. 10.12, 3, and in 2 Sam. 1.17, 18, is in it; also, that with them are the books, *The Wars of*

Jehovah and the *Prophetical [Enunciations]*, mentioned by Moses (Num. 21.14, 15, and 27–30); and when in their presence I read the words that Moses had quoted therefrom, they searched to see if they appeared there, and found them. From these things it was plain to me that the Ancient Word is still with them.

In the course of the conversation they said that they worship Jehovah, some as an invisible, and some as a visible God.

Afterwards they told me that they do not suffer foreigners to enter among them, except the Chinese, with whom they cultivate peace, because the emperor of China is from there.

Then they also told me that they are so densely populated that they do not believe any region in the entire world is more densely populated; which is indeed credible on account of the wall so many miles long which the Chinese built up a long time ago for their own protection against invasion by them.

Ask about it in China, and perhaps you will find it there among the Tartars! (AR 11)

In addition, in *True Christian Religion* we are told that from having the Ancient Word the peoples in Great Tartary have their Divine worship, right at that day, and also that they draw "precepts for their faith and life" from it (TCR 279.3, 851 Memorable Relations Summary XXXII).

The Ancient Word is the earliest written revelation given to the human family. The discovery that it still exists and is actively used (or was used in Great Tartary in the 1760s), *plus* the imperative for us to go to China and "ask about it" are all the direct outcome of the 1757 Last Judgment and the new revelations made after that.

GREAT TARTARY IN SWEDENBORG'S DAY

Swedenborg knew a great deal about the world we live in. He perhaps knew more than many of us individually today know about our planet, although modern technology and communication make it easier for us.

He knew, for example, about "tigers and lions" in the forests of Tartary (TCR 515). Peter Matthiessen's book about Siberian tigers has a map of the range of tigers throughout Asia which shows the range

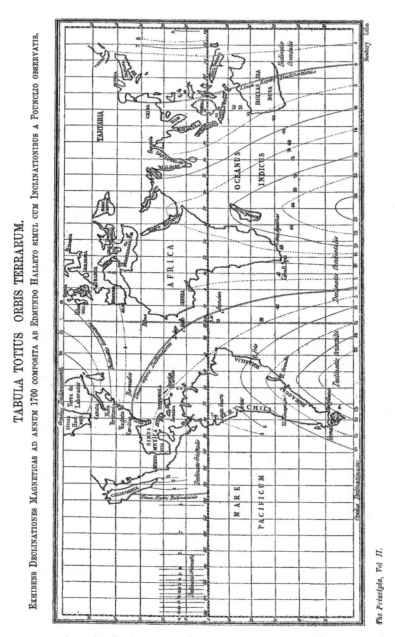

Figure 3. Edmund Halley's 1700 map showing Tartary. Reprinted from Emanuel Swedenborg's *The Principia*. Courtesy of The Swedenborg Society, 1912.

circa 1800 and the range today. It is fascinating that the eighteenth century range includes forests of "Tartary" that cover both the eastern and the western reaches of north China. This confirms Swedenborg's reference to them. In addition, it matches rather well the parts of China that Dr. James Brush and I visited together, during three summers in 1998-2001, searching for the Ancient Word in China.

Apparently there are no lions in Tartary, regardless of all the slightly misshaped stone lions placed outside many restaurants in Beijing and other cities. Swedenborg might be referring to leopards—there are leopards in the forests of Tartary in the east and in the snowy mountains of Tartary in the west.

Swedenborg himself, those he wrote for, and those he corresponded with had some basic shared knowledge about Tartary. His friend Gabriel Beyer knew what he meant when he said that he would prefer to live in Tartary than in Europe if he could not go directly to the Lord there (Letter to Gabriel Beyer, April 12, 1770).

Edmund Halley's map of the world in Swedenborg's *Principia Rerum Naturalium* (1734, showing the variation in magnetic fields on the surface of the earth) contains the basic common knowledge of the early eighteenth century. See figure 3. One of the three volumes of *The Principia* was about copper, which displays Swedenborg's awareness and knowledge about mines in the "Tartary" brought into the expanding Russian empire.

Those who during Swedenborg's day were called "Tartars" are today recognized as part of the Altaic ethno-linguistic group. The Altaic family has three broad groupings: Turkic (in western Asia but extending to Xinjiang in China), Mongol (over large reaches of central or northern Asia), and Tungusic (those in the east, such as the Manchus). Some scholars include the Koreans in the Altaic family.

The idea for this grouping began during the time of Swedenborg's youth, through the questions and research begun by the German philosopher G. W. von Leibniz, who was interested in the underlying unity of the human family. Swedenborg may have learned about this concept through his brother-in-law, Eric Benzelius, an ambitious librarian who communicated with scholars, such as Leibniz, throughout

Europe. It was with Benzelius that Swedenborg lodged when he was a student at Uppsala University between 1703 and 1709.

Following his completion of university, Swedenborg spent five years traveling overseas, in parts of Europe more sophisticated culturally and politically than Sweden and more modern in science and technology. After he returned to Sweden in 1715, Swedenborg actively established himself in the Board of Mines. Part of his initiative was to learn about mining and mines across Europe and abroad.

During the same period, Leibniz' full hypothesis was grounded in comparative linguistic fieldwork by P. J. Strahlenberg. Strahlenberg was a Swede who had been captured by the Russians when the Swedes were defeated at Poltava in 1709. He then traveled extensively in Russia, Siberia and Great Tartary. Strahlenberg's book published in German in 1730, was a best-seller in Stockholm and was translated into many European languages, including English. With the book's popularity and its Swedish authorship, it is difficult to imagine that Swedenborg would not have been aware of it.

Through the seeds sown in the ideas and questions of Leibniz, and the comparative cultural and linguistic work of Strahlenberg, Altaic scholarship developed for over two hundred years. It was pursued mainly by European explorers and travelers until after World War II, when for strategic reasons (the Altaic peoples straddle the border area between China and Russia) it was funded in America, often stimulated by scholars drawn from Europe after the war. That generation of European and American scholars, with their firsthand field experience in "Great Tartary"—Denis Sinor, Walther Heissig, Nicholas Poppe—are now gone.

Altaic scholarship had a strong emphasis on the common religious or spiritual culture shared across the differing ethnic and language groups considered to be part of the Altaic family. Shared religious ideas among the Altaic peoples include ideas of a visible and invisible God (who is heaven), belief in the spiritual world and heaven (called "eternal blue heaven"), belief that one awakens there three days after dying, a strong use of correspondences or symbols, and shamanism.

Shamanism is an archaic form of interaction with the spiritual world that continues in North Asia (our English word "shaman" originates from the Tungusic or Manchu word *saman*) and elsewhere. A shaman has personal access—through rituals, songs, and trance—to the spirit world. The shaman communicates with both the good and the evil spirits there, with the purpose of helping people on earth who otherwise feel helpless and powerless. The shaman, when on the side of what is good, is protected ritually by a bronze mirror (shown to evil spirits); he or she is also protected by trust in the God of heaven, and by the shaman's songs and rituals. In the case of the Manchus, these songs and rituals were written down in books.

This thread of scholarship about the Altaic peoples was a large component of my early contact and research in searching for the Ancient Word in China.

In 1973, having just graduated from university, I spent six weeks traveling through Europe with Charles and Karen Cole. In a bookstore in St. Moritz, high in the mountains of Switzerland, I picked up a small book in German by Walther Heissig with the title: *The Heroes, High Adventures and Outrageous Stories of the Mongols*. The book contained beautiful songs about Gesar Khan, the eternal blue heaven incarnate on earth. In one song he goes forth to slay a fifteen-headed giant king who has invaded his land. In another he comes to find and revive his dead heroes. The songs about Gesar Khan make up the popular and widespread national epic for the Mongols. He is the omnipresent hero, incarnation or son of heaven *(tngri)*, and is thought of as riding a white horse, with the sun as his helmet or having a helmet with the sun and moon on it.

Years later I would read that Heissig had found those two songs in Europe; they were embedded, apparently to be hidden from Buddhist zealots, in a Mongolian wax figure. The figure had made its way to a Catholic monastery in Belgium through priest missionaries who had been sent to eastern Mongolia and the Ordos Desert in the western part of Inner Mongolia (and bordering various ancient sections of the Great Wall). That Heissig found two beautiful new songs of the Gesar epic in Europe is amazing. Just as amazing is the hard work scholars like him have done to locate written texts used right in people's homes and lives. Heissig reports:

> But in those areas in which the Mongols were not affected by Chinese penetration, the Geser [Gesar] Khan cult survived until very recent times. In 1943, when I discovered several volumes of manuscript of Geser Khan songs in the Küriye Banner, a densely settled area in Eastern Mongolia, I asked the owners if I might take the volumes home with me for a few weeks to read through them, compare them with the printed versions in 1716 and photograph them, in case they should contain anything new. After I promised to treat these manuscripts with the utmost respect and never, on my journey, to keep them in an unclean place, I was allowed to take them away.[7]

The story continues that someone soon arrived asking for them back. Their cattle were falling sick at home, and the manuscripts were needed for praying to Gesar Khan for the cattle to recover. Many of the Mongol homesteads in that densely settled area had small chapels to worship Gesar Khan. Heissig returned the volumes and concluded, "I hope the cows in the Küriye banner have been restored to health."

Travelers, missionaries, and scholars have collected or reported songs and stories from Great Tartar for hundreds of years. Perhaps the Ancient Word can be found in a library, museum, monastery, or archives, somewhere in China or even in Europe or America. Perhaps there are books of the Ancient Word in the Old Manchu Archives in the Forbidden City in Beijing, or among the Manchu documents sent to the Vatican by Jesuit priests still in China when Swedenborg was a youth. There may be copies in the basement of the British Museum in London among the manuscripts bought at the beginning of the twentieth century in Dunhuang, at the far western end of the Great Wall, where for centuries they had been stored in a cave. Perhaps part of the Ancient Word is in the collection of Mongolian manuscripts and books at Western Washington University. If one knew what one was searching for and knew the Asian languages necessary, one might even

---

7. Heissig, *Lost Civilization*, 149. See also his *Religions of Mongolia*, 101. His 1716 reference is about the printing of part of the Mongolia Gesar Khan epic in Peking sponsored by the Qing or Manchu emperor then.

find parts of the Ancient Word as books or manuscripts, on a shelf or in a box, by means of a card catalog or index—without going to China.

TODAY'S OPPORTUNITY
IN A WORLD TRANSFORMED

The imperative that ends *Apocalypse Revealed* 11, however, points us in another direction; it points to China and the people who have and use the Ancient Word. The challenge was given over 240 years ago. Some wonder if we might really find it today, given all the transformations that have occurred in China, especially in the last one hundred years. It still may be possible, though, for us to take up the challenge. The specific teachings in the Writings about Divine providence acting in human history are not, as people imagine, about political events per se. They focus mainly on the Word, its revelation, and its progressive preservation, often over many centuries (e.g. AC 9350–9355, SS 13). If the Lord has revealed to the people of the New Church the fact of the Ancient Word being with Tartars in China and He has challenged us to go and ask and find it, then might He not, in His providence, still preserve it, regardless of the vicissitudes of recent history?

Ask about it in China, and perhaps you will find
[the Ancient Word] there among the Tartars! (AR 11)

These words encourage us to search for the Ancient Word in such a way that we will find people who still have it and use it. We will find it among people who are still able to read the books of the Ancient Word; who have their worship of the living God from them (AR 11); who have precepts of life and faith from them (TCR index XXXII). Fundamentally it points to finding people, hopefully even after 240 years, who are still being reconnected to heaven by means of the written Word they have. The people themselves will be a witness to the Ancient Word—and perhaps we are to focus on them, as well as on our finding the Ancient Word.

ASKING IN CHINA TODAY

Asking Requires Good Questions

"Ask about it in China," we are enjoined. So, what do we ask? Here is where we benefit from a clear and flexible understanding of the clues the Lord Himself provides for us. We are flexible and playful in asking questions and exploring with others the religion and holy books that they have or that they know others have.

One set of questions revolves around the titles and texts of the Ancient Word that we have from the Hebrew Scriptures, which are highlighted in the Writings.

To begin with, do we ask people if they have the Ancient Word? The phrase "Ancient Word" is a phrase given in the Writings for the first written revelation here on earth, but the phrase is not the title of a book or set of books. It is not what people in China are likely to call it. It is a description. It is interesting that the Latin word for "ancient" —*vetustum*—does not refer to something old, dusty, and no longer in existence, but to something "earliest and still existing."

Most likely it is not "still existing" as one bound book, like our Bible. It most likely continues, as the various books of the Bible did for most of their history, as separate books and manuscripts. We need to ask questions, therefore, about the books we are told about.

In addition, we should be prepared for various written forms, matching the movement of the Lord in His Divine providence. Writing and printing, for example, were the direct result of the Lord acting in history (AC 9353, EU 115). We might find handwritten manuscripts, or photocopies of them. We should not leave out printed books, whether produced in the eighteenth century, or in the decades since the end of the Cultural Revolution in China. What we are looking for could even be on the internet.

So a better start for our questions is to ask about the books we are told about that make up the Ancient Word. In the Book of Numbers (21.14 and 21.27–30), Moses quotes from books that existed in his day, books called *The Wars of Jehovah* and *Oracles* (or *Utterances* or

Prophetical Enunciations). In Joshua 10.12–13 and 2 Samuel 1.17–18, the *Book of Jasher* is quoted. These three sets of books, along with the made-up stories in the early chapters of Genesis, were part of the written Word that existed before Moses and may still be preserved and used today.

It may be significant that in *Apocalypse Revealed* 11, the *Book of Jasher* is specified as the first part of the Ancient Word. Perhaps we should ask first about that book and the passages that we know from it. However, is it likely that we would find a book in Manchu or Mongol that is called "Jasher"? It is possible, since the Manchu word *doro*— "law"—may come from ancient Hebrew. However, it is more likely that the names were translated, according to root meanings, than that they were transliterated. In this case, the name "Jasher" means "upright" or "just." So would it be more fruitful to ask about a "book of the upright person"?

Likewise, the two available graphic quotations from the *Book of Jasher* might prove to be a more immediately fruitful avenue to ask about than the obscure quotations with difficult place names from the *Book of the Wars of Jehovah* and *Oracles*. One might ask: "Do any of your holy books or stories talk about the sun and the moon standing still?"; "Do they talk about teaching people the bow (and arrow)?"; "Do they have a song called 'the song of the bow'?"

In Numbers 21.14, the *Wars of Jehovah* is mentioned as a single book. In the Writings, though, we are told that the narrative books— that is, several books—were called *Wars of Jehovah* (ML 77, TCR 265). It may be more likely to find the "Wars of Jehovah" as a theme in many books than as the title of one book. If we remember that in the churches before the Lord's life on earth people only knew of the humanity of God by means of the presence of Jehovah in the heavens—that is, by means of the people there responding to the passionate life and love that is Jehovah—perhaps we might ask if there is a theme in their books such as the "wars of heaven."

A second set of questions that we might pursue focuses on details in the Writings about the people who still have and use the Ancient Word. These details are twofold: the details of their religious life taken directly or indirectly from the holy or sacred books they have and the details about the natural or historical circumstances of their lives on earth.

For example: "They worship Jehovah, some as an invisible, and some as a visible God" (AR 11). We might ask therefore, "How do you picture the Life that creates the universe?" Furthermore, since in their heaven "the God of heaven" is mentioned rather than "the Lord" (ML 77), and knowing that heaven itself is an underlying presence in their religions, we could ask, "How do you picture the God of Heaven?" or even "Can heaven be pictured?"

Since the people we hope to find have precepts of life from the Ancient Word, we could ask about specific rules of life; we could ask if they have a teaching about marriage like the one the angels of the copper age have (since those angels are the ones who have the Ancient Word that is still in Great Tartary):

> Children, if you wish to love God and the neighbor, and if you wish to be wise and be happy to eternity, we advise you to live monogamously. If you depart from this precept, all heavenly love will escape you, and with it inward wisdom, and you will become outcasts. (ML 77)

More simply we could ask how important monogamy is for them. Given that the marriages of the good people of the copper age are monogamous (ML 77), the presence of monogamous marriages with the people of "Great Tartary," both today and in the past, could be a strong indicator of continuing spiritual precepts and values from the Ancient Word.

There are many examples of questions about historical circumstances that are mentioned in passages in the Writings or that may not be mentioned and yet are significant for our search. We need to be prepared with much "contextual" knowledge, knowing:

- What Swedenborg and readers of his day (mainly Europeans) may have known about China and Great Tartary
- What was happening in China and Asia at that day

- What has happened in the 240 years since the challenge given in *Apocalypse Revealed* 11
- What is happening in China today

Into the early- and mid-twentieth century, some continued to speak of Tartars and Tartary, referring to peoples and a region in Asia containing the common borders of China and Russia. Peter Fleming wrote about his travels in "High Tartary." Owen Lattimore wrote about the "fish-skin" Tartars. Today, however, we hardly speak at all of Tartars or of Great Tartary.

One aid is the map in the Latin edition of Swedenborg's *Principia* of 1734 (see figure 3). Other contemporary sources offer a more detailed and nuanced sense. One map (see figure 4) shows *Magna Tartaria,* or "Great Tartary," stretching across Asia from the Caspian Sea to Korea, lying between China (and the Great Wall) and the expanding Romanoff empire in Russia and Siberia, with several major Tartar nationalities highlighted in the places where they live (Mosheim, 1741). The famous French *Encyclopedia,* begun at the time of the Writings lists over eighteen different peoples or nations that make up Great Tartary.

One point that opens up definite possibilities for us is the repeated idea that the Ancient Word was still preserved and used, at least in 1766, with several peoples or nations in Great Tartary. We read in *Apocalypse Revealed* 11: "It has till now been preserved among peoples who dwell in Great Tartary." *True Christian Religion* 266 speaks of it surviving among "nations" of Great Tartary—"nations" meaning extended family systems or groups, or using China's modern word, "nationalities." So we should expect the Ancient Word to be a group of books, not one book, and it should be present with more than one people or nationality that lies north of the Great Wall of China, but not necessarily with all peoples or nationalities who live there.

The statement in *Apocalypse Revealed* 11 is that the emperor of China comes from Tartary; it does not necessarily follow then that because the emperor at that day was Manchu, the Ancient Word is only with the Manchus. Rather, we should only expect that the emperor comes from the region (the Latin is simply *inde*—"the emperor of

Figure 4. Map of Great Tartary *(Magna Tartaria)*. Johann Lorenz Mosheim, 1741. *Historia Ecclesiastica Tartarorum*. Gallica Digital Library, 2011. http://gallica. bnf.fr/ark:/12148/bpt6k57547244/f10.image.r=Hugo.langEN.

China is from there") where there are peoples that have the Ancient Word.

In northeast China today there are seven recognized nationalities that would have been considered peoples or nations of Great Tartary in Swedenborg's day. These seven nationalities are called: Manchu, Xibe, Daur, Ewenki, Oroqen, Hezhen, and Mongol. See figures 5–11. Additionally, some of these groups are currently in the far eastern maritime province of Russia, which was part of the Chinese empire in Swedenborg's day, and some of these groups have experienced significant migration to other parts of China. Some have maintained their traditional culture, such as some Mongols in Inner Mongolia and the Xibe people in the far west. The Xibe, originally from what is now Heilongjiang Province not far from Harbin, were ordered to move to the far west of Xinjiang province to protect the border area there. This occurred in the 1760s, just when the information that the Ancient Word was preserved in Great Tartary was being revealed in *Apocalypse Revealed* 11. Their repeated requests to return to the northeast were refused, and they continue in their own autonomous region, with radio and newspapers in their own language—also with several *saman* or shamans not far from what is now the border with Kazakhstan. People from all these minority nationalities are scattered as families and individuals elsewhere in China or even overseas, in the Chinese diaspora around the world.

The reference to "tigers and lions in the forests of Tartary" in TCR 515 may seem whimsical to us. There may be no lions today, (although the reference may be to leopards—Amur leopards in the forests in the eastern reaches of Great Tartary, and snow leopards in the west). But there still are tigers—Manchurian or Amur or Siberian tigers—in some of the mountain forests that serve as a barrier and boundary defining Dongbei, the collective name for China's three northeast provinces.

Figure 5.
To the left, Daur.
Courtesy of non-copy-
righted postcard.

Figure 6.
To the right, Ewenki.
Courtesy of non-copy-
righted postcard.

Figure 7.
Above, Hezhe.
Courtesy of non-copyrighted postcard.

Figure 8.
To the right, Manchu.
Courtesy of
non-copyrighted postcard.

Figure 9.
To the left, Mongol.
Courtesy of non-copy-
righted postcard.

Figure 10.
To the right, Oroqen.
Courtesy of non-
copyrighted postcard.

Figure 11.
To the left, Xibe.
Courtesy of non-copy-
righted postcard.

Benefiting from Current Qing Scholarship

In the past twenty years, a new generation of vigorous scholarship has transformed Qing[8] and Manchu studies. Two of today's leading Qing scholars are Evelyn Rawski at the University of Pittsburgh and Pamela Crossley at Dartmouth University.

Their work supersedes many of the books and articles I had discovered in my own research. During most of the 1970s I regularly searched what was then the largest open-stack library in the world at Princeton University. In the summer of 1976 I had a stack pass that granted access to the closed stacks of the Library of Congress; in off-work hours I searched through dusty shelves in the basements looking for anything that might help regarding the Manchus, Mongols, and Tibetans. Later in 1990 I used the library of the School of Oriental and African Studies in London, England. When in Bryn Athyn, Pa. I used the Academy of the New Church library and its interlibrary loan system.

The recent work of Rawski and Crossley should be the beginning point for the research of new students and scholars seeking the Ancient Word in China.

Some of the books and articles listed in Rawski and Crossley's bibliographies I had looked at earlier. Some of the earlier material has clues that can continue to help us with our research questions (which are not the same as most academic scholars). In addition, the earlier research provides a framework for understanding and appreciating new content and new interpretations.

Their work has given Qing and Manchu studies a fresh and exciting tone. The older generation of Western historians looking at China assumed the Chinese or Han myth that China had a superior, dominant civilization; all other groups encountering it, even those that

---

8. "Qing" is the name chosen by the Manchus for their dynasty which ruled China from 1644 to 1911. During those years the emperor of China himself was not Han but of Manchu stock. Some emperors had mothers or grandmothers who were from other Tartar nationalities from north of the Great Wall. An older rendering of "Qing" is "Ch'ing."

conquered and ruled it, ultimately lost their own identity to it, ending up "Sinified"[9].

While living in Seattle and preparing for my 2001 expedition to China, I began to turn to ideas from the anthropological work done by Steve Harrell at the University of Washington and others, about groups of people creating their own group identities in China.

Until the 1970s it was assumed that to study modern Chinese history one needed only Chinese (Mandarin) language skills—not other Chinese languages or Manchu. Scholars thought that everything important was written in Chinese. This assumption fell away, however, when the new scholars realized that the Manchu emperor and court had carried on extensive and secret communication in Manchu, as the Chinese could not read it.

The recent scholarship not only focuses on the Manchus having their own integrity, it also explores how the Manchu identity was shaped during this period. The Manchus, rather than being Sinified, had kept their own cultural and political identity during the seventeenth and eighteenth centuries.

Perhaps the Manchus were a modern invention during and just before Swedenborg's time. They created a new ethno-linguistic identity in the decades preceding their conquering China. As rulers of China they continued to affirm that "Manchu" identity. By Swedenborg's time the Qing or Manchu emperor was trying to strengthen this identity by sending research expeditions to Changbaai Shan—the Great White Mountain along the border with Korea that the Manchu ruling clan claimed it originated from—to gather the original Manchu shaman songs. Moreover, he promoted the publication of these shaman songs in the 1740s and the 1780s. Handwritten copies are still produced today, often with Chinese characters interlinear, both as a pronunciation guide and as a translation. In the past twenty years or so, many shaman texts have been printed as well in China.

---

9. "Sinified" refers to the assimilation of China's culture into one's own and thereby losing one's own culture in the process. For example, the assimilation of the Chinese identity into non-Han Chinese peoples.

What we know of Manchu *saman jiao*—the Manchu shaman religion—partly reflects developments contemporary to the Writings, where we are told the Ancient Word is still preserved among the Tartars in China. Perhaps the process of preservation is very similar to the idea of progressive preservation of the Old Testament and New Testament texts of the Bible, which began as individual "books" or manuscripts. Our idea of one book, containing all the texts, is the result of a world transformed by the printing press.

Part of the recent scholarship affirms the powerful dynamics present during Qing times, between "Tartar" groups in the regions north of the Great Wall and the Tibetans (who are not Tartars, although the first edition of the *Encyclopedia Britannica* (1768–1771) made that mistake, which has confused New Church members ever since). This is important information for us because we are not interested in the Chinese or Han people but with the Tartars in China, and the Chinese world that included them. The *Apocalypse Revealed* 11 imperative does not lead us, though, to look for the Ancient Word with the Han people or in Tibet.

The new Qing scholarship of Rawski, Crossley, and others opens the door further for New Church explorers and researchers. Additionally there is new freedom to travel widely in China which began in the early 1990s.

Although neither the old nor the new scholarship is looking for anything like the Ancient Word, it provides informed pictures of the context; the relevant details we want still need to be teased out.

Asking implies Learning about Current Scholarship
in China—Scholarship by Modern-day "Tartars"

A critical new dimension of the scholarly work that we need to examine is the work done in China since the end of the Cultural Revolution. Beginning in the 1980s there was an effort to affirm and promote, in a politically non-threatening way, the ethnic identities of various nationalities within China. There are 56 officially recognized nationalities in China, with the Han being the overwhelming group.

There are seven recognized "Tartar" nationalities—that is, ethnic-cultural-linguistic groups with common roots and originating north of the Great Wall in part of what used to be called "Great Tartary."

As this contemporary scholarship is in Chinese it is relatively inaccessible to those of us without knowledge of Chinese. Fortunately during the three summers we traveled together in the last ten years, Dr. James Brush and I gathered significant summaries, through interpreters, from the Chinese scholars we interviewed. Some of them we worked closely with: in one case daily for a week, in another daily for ten days, and in another daily for almost three weeks. The main Chinese scholars that helped us were:

- Dular Chaoke (from Hailar, Inner Mongolia) and Wang Lizhen (from Harbin), a married couple both teaching at the Nationalities University in Beijing. Chaoke also was a member of the People's Congress during the time that we worked with him in the late 1990s. During the 1998 trip Chaoke traveled with us to Shenyang, Dandong on the Yalu River, to Kuandian, a small town in the mountains near North Korea, and to a remote homestead in the mountains where we met Manchu shamans. In 1999 I met up with Lizhen in Harbin.
- Fu Yingren of Ning'an (Heilongjiang Province). Fu Yingren is a former Manchu shaman or *saman*, a retired schoolteacher, and in retirement wrote extensively about Manchu culture and folklore. He helped us in 1998.
- Song Heping, former head of the Chinese Academy of Social Sciences, talked with us over coffee in a modern hotel near her home in Beijing in 1998.
- Zhao Aping of the Manchu Institute in Harbin was helpful in a variety of ways in 1998.
- Fu Yuguang and Wang Honggong of Changchun (Jilin Province). At the end of our 1998 trip we met Fu Yuguang in his home in Changchun (near automobile factory #1). We met there again in 1999, down the Songhua River to a fishing hamlet to meet an old Manchu shaman and his family. That year his associate Wang

Honggong agreed to travel with us for ten days to Xinjiang; first to Ürümqi, then on to meet Xibe shamans in Qapal, an autonomous Xibe district in the Ili Valley bordering the Tian Shan Mountains, with the border of Kazakhstan just miles away. Fu Yuguang himself traveled with us in 2001 for three weeks while we met or learned about the shamans of other "Tartar" nationalities (Mongol, Ewenki, Oroqen, Daur, Hezhe). Together we traveled to Hailar and Inner Mongolia, then to towns in the north of Heilongjiang province, along various stretches of the Heilong Jiang/Amur River bordering Russia.

Some of these scholars had purely an academic or intellectual interest in helping us, but many had personal or family spiritual experiences that made them sympathetic to our search. Some even affirmed the possibility of the existence of the Ancient Word we were asking about and searching for.

It is not insignificant for our quest that four of the seven scholars listed are modern day "Tartars"—three are Manchus, one is Ewenki-Mongol. They also were the ones most personally sympathetic.

All of the scholars gave us copies of their recently published books, in Chinese, about the culture, myths, religion, languages, and history of the minority nationalities we were asking about. In addition, I bought scholarly books, in Chinese, that seemed most significant for our quest and its context.

Asking in China Means Going There and Asking

It has only been twenty years since, for the first time in history, the challenge can be taken up directly in China. The search can be conducted with the ease of modern communications and transportation and with an unheard of level of freedom and access to most ethnic minorities and remote regions of the country. During three summers in the past ten years, Dr. James Brush[10] and I have had the opportunity to

---

10. Dr. Brush is a retired biochemist living in Phoenix, Arizona. Since finding the New Church as a young man he has been interested in the search for the

begin to search together, and he has also traveled extensively in China, Mongolia, and Siberia in the intervening years.[11]

We have traveled to Beijing and met modern "Tartars" who live there. We have journeyed through much of the northeast of China, north of the Great Wall (in what used to be called Manchuria and today is called Dongbei). We traveled out to the far northwest of China, to Xinjiang province and the Tian Shan, the Celestial Mountains. There we entered areas restricted for foreigners and were almost arrested. A couple of years later we traveled into Inner Mongolia. With a Chinese academic host and with appropriate local contacts, we explored the Black Dragon River (the Heilong Jiang or Amur River), a very sensitive border area between China and Russia, and met with other modern "Tartar" ethnic minority groups.

Discoveries Made by Going to China and Asking People

What we discovered in China provides strong echoes of the presence of the Ancient Word with the "Tartar" nationalities, given the clues we have from the Writings. The echoes are numerous, reflecting almost every clue given in the Writings that we could ask about. When taken all together they are simply amazing! They yield avenues for further study with the materials we collected and for further research

---

Ancient Word in China. When his wife passed on, he decided to devote the rest of his life to searching for it in China. He began to learn Chinese. He traveled to China to work on his language skills and to meet modern day "Tartars." For several years he arranged to be a guest research professor at one of the universities in Harbin, so that he could continue the search during his free time. I was encouraged to travel and work with him in China. We travelled over three summers while I taught at Bryn Athyn College and later when I was pastor in Seattle, Washington. He has also traveled to the Russian Far East (due east of China), to Mongolia, and to the regions of Siberia due north of Mongolia.

11. Dr. Brush and I were able to undertake these three summer trips together because of generous research grants from the Carpenter Fund (administered by a committee at the Academy of the New Church in Bryn Athyn, Pennsylvania). Dr. Brush had been funded by the Carpenter Fund previously and has been subsequently. Individually we have also spent personal funds on the project over many years.

in China, and neighboring Mongolia, by those who know well one or more of the several languages required—Chinese, Manchu, Xibe and Mongol.

Echoes that are Basic

(1) As mentioned above, *The Book of Jasher* means "the book of the upright," or the upright person, the upright man.

When asked about the importance of being upright in Manchu culture (not mentioning its connection with one of the books of the Ancient Word we were looking for, but in addition to quoting from an article by Giovanni Stary about Manchu poetry) Fu Yingren, a former Manchu shaman in Ning'an, told us that being an upright man was of vital importance. The book of songs that each Manchu shaman has is the *Book of the Upright Man*. He let us photocopy three of these shaman books. See figure 12 below.

Figure 12. The *Book of the Upright Man* from the Manchu shaman Photo by author with courtesy of Fu Yingren.

Song Heping in Beijing gave us her published book, which contains songs from such Manchu books translated into Chinese.

At the Old Manchu Archives in Beijing, we obtained a copy of a recently published book containing such "songs of God" for the Xibe people. Intriguingly, while in the far west of China, interviewing a Xibe shaman in his home, I noticed that he had a printed book of Xibe shaman songs, which he consulted to verify his chanting. It was a different book than the one we were given at the Old Manchu Archives, but try as I might I could not find this second Xibe shaman song book at any of the bookstores back in Beijing.

(2) In the Hebrew Scriptures there are two specific quotations from *The Book of Jasher*.

In the first quotation from *Jasher* in the Book of Joshua, we find the words, "Sun stand still . . . and moon in the valley of Ajalon" (Josh. 10.12). Fu Yingren said that the Manchu shaman songs spoke of the sun and moon standing still. He showed us his own painting of a red sun in the spirit world, which reflects the Manchu cosmology. In a museum in Hailar in Inner Mongolia, we photographed Mongol shaman clothes with both the red sun and the moon, standing above a valley or field in which deer were grazing. The Hebrew word "Ajalon" seems to mean "deer field." See figure 13.

The second quotation from *Jasher*, David himself quotes: "To teach the sons of Judah the bow" (2 Sam 1.17). This might be reflected today in one of the favorite sports of the Manchus, Xibe, Mongols and other nationalities—archery; even today they are world-class archers. It was intriguing to see a bow and arrow, pointing up into the sky or towards heaven, on top of the Xibe temple for Gesar Khan (Guandi) near Yining in the Ili Valley in Xinjiang.

(3) As mentioned above, *The Book(s) of the Wars of Jehovah* might be found as books of the wars of heaven.

I had found the 1993 English translation of Fu Yuguang's basic essay on the Manchu shaman world view. It highlights that the wars of heaven are a major theme in the Manchu shaman concept of heaven.

Figure 13. Mongol shaman's clothes (in a museum in Hailar, Inner Mongolia) show-ing a red spiritual sun and moon standing still over a valley with a deer in a field. Photo by the author.

On our 1999 visit to him in his home in Changchun, he gave us the 1995 book that he and Wang Honggong had written about the wars of heaven. He also showed us the over 400-year-old manuscript in Manchu that he has about the wars of heaven. See figure 14 below.

Figure 14. Fu Yuguang's over 400-year-old Manchu manuscript about the "wars of heaven." Photo by author.

(4) The largest parts of the Ancient Word text we have are the creation stories and other early made-up stories that are quoted in Genesis 1–7, word for word from the Ancient Word.

In the first verse of Genesis, which is taken from the Ancient Word, we read: "In the beginning, God created the heavens and the earth" (Gen. 1.1). These are the very words that Wang Lizhen recalls her grandmother (a Manchu shaman or *saman* living not far from Harbin) reciting to her when she was a girl. Dr. Brush learned about this from Lizhen before I joined him in China. It helped persuade her to assist in our search.

We have found creation stories, stories of paradise, stories of a flood. In a bookstore in Beijing with extensive holdings for minority nationalities, we bought a book with the creation stories of various nationalities (n.d.) and a book with flood stories (n.d.). Most interesting to find were direct phrases in the Manchu creation story, very similar to what we have in the Book of Genesis: "God created heaven and earth" and words similar to Gen. 1.27, "God created them in His image, male and female." And to my New Church ears, the phrase in the Manchu creation story, "The infinitely powerful God *(abka enduri)* rules both heaven and earth," rings loud and clear.

Suggestive Echoes

The passages from the Writings, especially the story of the heaven of the copper age (ML 77), can produce other questions to ask and more clues.

We found echoes of the *Married Love* 77 story with "Tartars" in China. Given that the story is about an ancient, pre-advent heaven made of up of people with the Ancient Word most likely before it reached Great Tartary, these echoes are more suggestive than directly connected with the Ancient Word in China today. They are more cultural than textual. They suggest links with the Ancient Church times, which provided the world with a basic, simple spirituality. In the copper age story, the people there talk about "the God of heaven." The Manchus also talk about "the God of heaven." The Manchu name for Him is *abka enduri*. Recall the statement from the Manchu creation story, "The infinitely powerful God *(abka enduri)* rules both heaven and earth." Fu Yingren told us that some picture *abka enduri*, while others do not. These points echo also *Apocalypse Revealed* 11 where we read that the Tartars with the Ancient Word "worship Jehovah, some as an invisible, and some as a visible God."

In *Married Love* 77, the people mention that they have from their fathers a "precept of marriage." When that precept was quoted to Fu Yingren and Fu Yuguang, when each was interviewed in his own home, both said that there is a precept similar in the Manchu religion.

Fu Yingren came up blank when asked about an ark or special chest or repository for sacred books (perhaps including old wooden or stone tablets, such as mentioned in *Married Love* 77). Although I do not think he understood what I was asking about.

However, in Beijing, the day before leaving China in 1998, I discovered what I was looking for. At *Tiantan,* the enormous Temple of Heaven complex (see figure 15 below), there were halls at the Imperial Vault of Heaven with shrines displaying sacred tablets with the names of God in Manchu and Chinese painted in gold.

On subsequent trips I noticed shelves high up on the bedroom wall in the homes of shamans (see figure 16 below). The shelves were

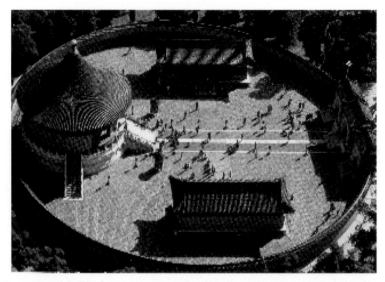

Figure 15. Sidehalls of *Tiantan* or Temple of Heaven in Bejjing, with repositories of tablets with Manchu names of God in gold. Courtesy of non-copyrighted postcard.

Figure 16. A Manchu shaman in a remote fishing hamlet on the Songhua River in Jilin Province retrieves his holy scriptures (and idol) from a special box above the master bed. Photo by author.

for candles and incense, but also held a box containing the shaman's personal copy of holy scriptures. I noticed this in a Manchu shaman's home in a remote fishing hamlet along the Songhua River, several hours northeast of Changchun. That year I saw such a box again in a Xibe shaman's home in the poor Xibe autonomous town Qapal, south of Yining in the Ili Valley, on the opposite side of China.

We also found other, less direct echoes. Fu Yingren told us about the cosmic tree or tree linking heaven and earth, like the tree of life in the garden of Eden (Gen. 2.9). Climbing the tree was often part of the Manchu shaman initiation. In remote areas, he said, they used to carve a tree with a human face, to depict *abka enduri*, the Manchu god of heaven. Taking pen in hand, he drew a picture of it for us.

Fu Yuguang gave us his own book about Manchu shamanism (1998). The picture on the cover is of a tree carved with a human face.

In the book of Xibe shaman songs we got in Beijing, there is a picture of what in the east was the cosmic tree, and now in the west was a ladder of swords. The swords were blunt and covered with yellow paper, we learned in Xinjiang, to make it easier to climb. Giovanni Stary reports that the ladder represents a golden ladder to heaven which played a role in the spiritual initiation of Xibe shamans.

Often I asked people about a photo showing a birch tree carved with a face smiling (in Humphrey and Urgunge's book on shamanism with the Daur Mongols). The face carved in the tree served as a reminder for Daur when they were in the forest about the "mountain god," who they called *bayin achaa* or "rich father," and of his generosity in giving them all the game and other food they found.

Walther Heissig mentions the importance of the "white old man" in the Mongol religion. The "white old man" came to Dular Chaoke several times in dreams, warning him at critical junctures in his life. People also told us that he was part of the initiation dreams of the Manchu and Xibe shamans. His presence is involved in the calling and work of epic singers of many Altaic (Tartar) nationalities. We were told of spiritual contacts who scold and correct the epic singers if they make mistakes in writing, translating, or singing the epics.

It was difficult to find much information in China about the Mongol epic songs and worship of Gesar Khan. As Heissig notes, where the Chinese (Han) penetrated, the Mongol worship of Gesar Khan and the manuscripts of songs about his wars and protection slipped away.

When we asked about it in both northeast China and in Xinjiang in the far west, we got the same answer—the Xibe temple for Gesar Khan, where the bow and arrow on top still point to the sky or heaven, is empty, everything was destroyed in the Cultural Revolution. Unfortunately, we did not make it to the "densely populated" Küriye banner in eastern Mongolia to see what might remain or have been restored. "Densely populated" areas are one of the clues in *Apocalypse Revealed* 11 and might be one of the possible echoes to listen for. Reading Qing period population studies might be a productive approach.

A final suggestive echo might be genealogies and family trees. Remember "the book of the genealogy of Man" (Gen. 5.1) and the long genealogies in early Genesis, taken from the Ancient Word? Each Manchu family and clan has its own set of written "home rules" or rules of life, and a written genealogy. In Fu Yuguang's video about the *saman jiao* (the shaman religion), a genealogy is shown much as a tree—a tree of the clan's life.

GROUPS AND THEIR IDENTITY FORMATION

To "identify" with a group is to feel a kind of oneness with the others in the group. An outside observer may group people based upon his or her own sense of the characteristics that the people seem to share. That may be a valid way to view group identity, but the observer may not recognize the deepest, human group identity or shared oneness.

The Writings address the spiritual world and the place of the gentiles and other groups there. The Last Judgment has taken place and a basic and underlying "order" has been brought into effect in the world of the human spirit.

"Order" for things which are alive and human does not mean that they are static or fixed. Plasticity and transformation are possible. "Order" means that things fit together well, from the inside out, from essential things to superficial things, with the capacity for allowing change to happen. This comes from matching Divine truth—that is, human reality from the Lord.

The simplest picture of group identity appears in the book *The Continuation concerning the Last Judgment* where the "place" of the gentiles in the spiritual world is mentioned:

> The heathen [or gentiles] too are grouped according to their characters and their ability to receive light from the Lord through the heavens. Some live further in, some further out; *this does not depend on their native country, but on their religion.* (CLJ 73; emphasis added)

In the simple picture, religion is the primary determinant for our being part of a given group and part of the whole human family. "Religion" as used in the Writings is more than an organized, historic religion, which is how many people use that word today.

The following are simple descriptions from the Writings about religion:

> What is religion but walking with God? (Coro 40)

> Religion alone makes a person spiritual. (AE 107.3)

> A person can become spiritual, or receive spiritual life, in no other way than by a life according to religion from the Lord. (AE 902.3)

> Religion alone renews and regenerates a person. (TCR 601)

This idea is repeated about seven years later, with significant modification, in *True Christian Religion*:

> Nations [or gentiles] are also kept apart in accordance with their characters and their ability to receive light from the Lord through the heavens. Some of them live further in, some further out; *this is due partly to their climate, partly to the stock they belong to, partly to their education, and partly to their religion.* (TCR 835; emphasis added)

Therefore, common character and identity are defined by holding a *shared*:

- Religion
- Climate
- Family or group biological links
- Education

The Germans in the spiritual world are described (TCR 813), as having a *shared*:

- Leader or king
- Legal system
- Language

Of course the shared characteristics listed here change, in time, for groups, and even for individuals in their own lives. The changes result in the identity or character of a group changing as well—and not primarily from the external factors in and of themselves, but because they lead to and reflect deeper shifts in the human spirit.

At the same time, once a religion has been accepted by a nation or group of people and has been pervasive in its culture, the Lord uses it to lead that group of people: "When once a religion has been established in a nation [ethnic group or family system] the Lord leads that nation according to the precepts and dogmas of its own religion" (DP 254.2).

In addition, religion is known to have an impact on moral decision-making even after commitment to that religion wanes or disappears within a given culture. That is an intriguing hint given repeatedly in Fons Trompenaars' *Riding the Waves of Culture*. While working on a Ph.D. dissertation at the University of Pennsylvania, Trompenaars undertook what at the time was the largest cross-cultural survey of the impact of culture on business, including moral decision-making. He suggests that the religious tradition behind the culture of a country influences how the people there make moral decisions, especially when contrasted with other peoples with different spiritual or religious heritages.

In *True Christian Religion* 816, Swedenborg discusses the people of Hamburg, Germany—a busy commercial shipping city. Perhaps we see ourselves similarly today, in our globally alert and communicative world, as we expand beyond our religious heritage:

> I enquired where the people of Hamburg are to be found in the spiritual world. I was told that they are nowhere to be found gathered into one community, much less into one state, but scattered around and mixed with Germans in various regions. When I asked the reason, I was told it was because their minds are continually looking around and as it were traveling outside their own city, and taking little note of things within it. For the state of a person's mind in the natural world determines its state in the spiritual world. (TCR 816)

In another context, I was reminded of this passage by one of the members of my church in South Africa who was born in Hamburg. A few weeks after that I found Hugo Odhner's insightful observation about it in his discussion of the Last Judgment in his book about *The Spiritual World:*

> Societies in the world of spirits are in constant flux or change, especially after a general judgment such as occurred in 1757. Since that time, the increase in travel and communication has supplied men in the world with a broader outlook, and local loyalties and provincial and national customs are less distinct. Most large modern cities have their cosmopolitan and international colorings, and few have any religious homogeneity. Even in Swedenborg's day, he reports, there was in the world of spirits no city corresponding to Hamburg, because of the cosmopolitan nature of that ancient trading and shipping center. (Odhner 107–108)

Influx from the world of spirits continually affects people on earth, shifting cultural and personal identities, as well as changing group identity and character.

The following is an intriguing passage concerning this topic, from a study about the impact of boarding schools on Mongol youths in Inner Mongolia:

> Since ethnic identity derives from situationally shared elements of a multidimensional habitus, it is possible for an individual to possess several different situationally relevant but nonetheless emotionally authentic identities and to symbolize all of them in terms of shared descent. [12]

Our identities result from shared or common circumstances as well as the deeper unconscious associations with the world of spirits. Additionally, the Writings speak of our associations shifting throughout life's stages, the outcomes of our decisions and the lives we lead, and our individual and group identity.

All this bears on the formation of the Manchus as a distinct people in the seventeenth and eighteenth centuries, on the shifts and transformations for all the "Tartar" nations or Altaic peoples since then, and on the profound changes in consciousness and group identity happening today in China and throughout our global village.

Perhaps the distance that people naturally feel when the deeper current and values of the human spirit are missing or obscure, may be why we are told in one of the final passages about the peoples of Great Tartary having the Ancient Word in the spiritual world: "The reason for this isolation [from Christians at that day] is that the [Tartar angels and spirits in the spiritual world] possess a different Word" (TCR 279.4). Today we have part of the text of that "different" Word. In addition, as we enter into the spirit and life of the Word we have, by way of the heavenly doctrines, we enter into the same spirit and life present within the Ancient Word—in effect, we have the same Word.

The sense of isolation and alienation that is felt, sometimes very personally and tragically, when there are identity shifts in pre-modern or traditional cultures, can be overcome. What can help is a strong sense of our common humanity, a feeling that can be grounded in the living Divine truth pictured in the revelations of the spiritual world after the 1757 Last Judgment—including the revelation about the Ancient Word being preserved and used by the nations or peoples in

---

12. Carter Bentley quoted in Wurlig Borchigud "Modern Mongolian Ethnicity" in Stevan Harrell, *Cultural Encounters on China's Ethnic Frontiers,* 299.

Great Tartary. Those in the New Church have much to share and offer for the "healing of the nations" (Rev. 22.2).

Our ability to answer these questions about shifting identity and its shifting spiritual background may also affect our ability to find and recognize the Ancient Word in China.

It has been suggested that we will not find the Ancient Word with Tartars in China until we identify and engage with the "inner Tartar" in ourselves.[13]

I suggest that if we lived in the eighteenth century and went to Beijing after reading *Apocalypse Revealed* 11, we would find ourselves in a world radically different from our own in America or Europe. It would be difficult to connect to that world, to communicate with empathy and understanding, to recognize and appreciate the Ancient Word, and to participate in finding it. The Lord, however, tells us to find it, and it must be possible, "for with God nothing will be impossible" (Luke 2.37).

Swedenborg's own travels in the spiritual world demonstrate that it is possible and provide an important clue. In heaven, Swedenborg met people from our earth's distant past, although his journey was not always easy or clear. With the help of angel guides sent from the Lord, he got there (consider the stories in *Married Love* 75–77). He was able to travel to distant worlds, beyond our solar system, in the starry heaven, and in some cases it took several days of intense inner spiritual work as preparation (consider the last part of *Earths in the Universe*).

The search for the Ancient Word is more than an adventure of this world, like in an Indiana Jones movie with a series of physical events and a physical treasure to find; the search for the Ancient Word is also a spiritual journey, which the 1757 Last Judgment makes possible, which Swedenborg shows as possible to do, and which in *Apocalypse Revealed* 11 we are challenged to take up.

---

13. Some may suggest from a psychological viewpoint that in searching for the Ancient Word we need to connect with our "inner Tartar." Others suggest it from believing that the Divine truth, as stated in the Writings, is primarily a description of the realities inside each of us, as well as, possibly, reflecting outer objective realities.

In the past ten years we were fortunate to benefit not only from our own personal inner spiritual work, but also from having "angel guides." We worked closely with and traveled to modern-day "Tartars," who were mainly people with simple good will, and who in the possibly abstruse words of Carter Bentley, are likely to have "several different situationally relevant but nonetheless emotionally authentic identities."

- Most of the key scholars in China who were our guides were themselves "Tartars" with dual identities: modern scholars and "inner Tartars." Both identities were at work while they helped us.
- Most of the "Tartar" shamans we met and interviewed were of course in touch with their "inner Tartar," but also had identities, personal or through family members, which bridged to the modern world. This was true in the remote fishing hamlet on the Songhua River, with the family who had a radio and an old beat-up Toyota pickup as its connection to the outside world. China's quest for modernity is present in even in the most remote parts of the country. For example, in Tahe, a remote town at the far northern part of China, only miles from the Russian border, dozens of local teens and young adults spent hours playing online internet games on the banks of new computers filling the internet café.
- The young Korean New Church people, who now often are a part of several worlds may be a help in the search for the Ancient Word in China among "Tartars" there. Some scholars consider Koreans to be part of the Altaic family.
- Young people of the New Church today who are living and working in China are forming bridges to both the Han people and to minority nationalities, setting up in themselves "several different situationally relevant but nonetheless emotionally authentic identities." (Perhaps even just learning another language well enough to communicate and share may help form a new authentic identity that can bridge to others more deeply—consider *True Christian Religion* 813's list.)

The underlying spiritual unity of the human family—the underlying spiritual unity of the Lord's church throughout the world—which now is more clear and possible given the 1757 Last Judgment and the ordering of the spiritual world immediately afterwards, provides an answer. It is easier than some think to be mutually connected as human beings, for since the 1757 Last Judgment "the reception of Divine truth and good"—the elements of the common humanity we all share—"is more universal, interior, easy, and distinct" (AE 1217).

THE IMPERATIVE TO FIND THE ANCIENT WORD
IN CHINA: THE LAST JUDGMENT PERSPECTIVE

The 1757 Last Judgment provides us with a powerfully informed context for viewing the quest for the Ancient Word in China. The imperative to ask about it in China, and perhaps find it with the Tartars, is a direct outcome of the Last Judgment.

The fact that the Ancient Word is still preserved, not only in ancient heavens, but in modern heavens and on earth, and the challenge to find it, are outcomes of an inner stability, oneness, openness, and freedom, made possible by the new communication and revelation of the whole spiritual world after 1757.

The revelation about the Ancient Word in Great Tartary shows the potential the Lord is opening up; it is prophetic of a deeper connectedness of the human family, a unification of His church throughout the world, and the possibility for the life of heaven to become real again on earth. We can live our lives with openness, hope, and trust; we do not have to remain trapped by what is "only natural" or "merely human"—what is parochial and isolated, or indifferent and apathetic, or fearfully focused on a decline and destruction of the world. We can live with a deep inner trust in the goodness of life and in the fact that the living force behind all things and deeply within ourselves is a truly human force of benevolence.

Powerful for us can be a deepened sense not only of Divine providence but also of Divine revelation. The Writings given through

Emanuel Swedenborg are powerful tools for understanding the role the spiritual world plays on the deeper unconscious level present with each of us and with groups of us which form our ethnic and cultural identities, and bridge to peoples of other identities.

These tools can inform our understanding of the process of Manchu identify formation in the seventeenth and eighteenth century. We need to learn about what will restore and renew the use of the religious texts that such ethnic groups already have—texts, which give them precepts for life and faith, and wake them up to heaven. We also need to be aware that these possibilities will vary from group to group.

The strong sense of our common humanity, pictured in the revelations of the spiritual world after the 1757 Last Judgment, provides assurance and comfort for what traditionally was felt as alienation. It provides our hope to join, in time, with all peoples, of all religions, in all lands. The discovery of the Ancient Word will testify to the underlying spiritual or religious unity of the human family on this planet.

There may be also an unspoken hope in the Lord's imperative and challenge for us—the hope that New Church people will become close friends with modern day "Tartars"—people who may be still awake to heaven and what is human in life—people awake in their own way to charity and good works, justice and mercy, love, and tenderness in marriage. Such friendship may be timely and deeply significant. It may help to establish a fruitful field in which the Lord's New Church— even in its broadest, most basic church universal form—may grow and thrive.

It may very well be the peoples of Great Tartary that are being referred to in this pre-1757 passage from *Spiritual Experiences*:

> I was afterwards brought back, but higher up, where were spirits from the regions of the north part of Asia; and it was perceived that they were of such a disposition, from their life in the world, as to be able to receive the heavenly doctrine of which I have spoken above. (SE 4779)

If people of the New Church go to China to meet "Tartars" and become friends with them—mutually responding to the Lord and having their lives changed—then a field for the deeper growth of the

Lord's New Church will be planted with good seed that can grow and bear fruit.

Today, with so many connections to the past already destroyed in the cultural revolution of the 1960s and 70s, and with a headlong rush toward what is modern, what is ancient in China may be but a memory before long. There is hardly anyone who is not participating or at least affected by the rapid and pervasive modernization afoot in China today. Becoming friends with people of the New Church and learning directly from the Lord in His new revelation can profoundly help and support those who have the Ancient Word—or perhaps only remnants or echoes of it—to find ways to participate in and contribute to the spiritual purpose, direction, and values of their own people, to China, and to the whole human family.

The Writings tell us that the gentiles of this day are not very deep; they really are very simple people, spiritually. As ordinary people, even in remote rural areas of China, learn about the world around them through the Internet and other forms of mass communication, and when from simple goodness of religion they affirm the common humanity we share, we should expect doors to open easily and lasting friendships to develop. We have much to offer, and the suggestion— the imperative given in the plural in *Apocalypse Revealed* 11 may point to our responsibility to take initiative. Then the Lord's prediction that came true at the time of the Last Judgment in the spiritual world will also come true here on earth:

> Then they shall come from the east and the west, and from the north and the south, and recline in the kingdom of God (Luke 13.29—cited in *Last Judgment* 52)⁂

BIBLIOGRAPHY

Bown, Christopher. "Expedition to China 1999." Lecture slide show with audio and handout, Bryn Athyn College Swedenborg Library, Bryn Athyn, PA, October 6, 1999. New Church Audio: http://store.newchurch.org.

————. "On the Steppes of Great Tartary. Can We Find the Ancient Word Today?" Lecture transcript. London: Swedenborg Society, April 21,1990.

————. "Searching for the Ancient Word in China." *Academy Journal* (1999): 4–9.

————. "The Tartar Connection, or Searching for the Ancient Word at Swedenborg's Day." Unpublished manuscript.

————. "Where Was Swedenborg's 'Great Tartary'?" *Academy Museum Notes: News from the ANC Museum Association* vol. 1, no. 2. (February 1977): 1–2.

Crossley, Pamela Kyle. *The Manchus*. Cambridge, MA: Blackwell Publishers, 1997.

————. "*Manzhou yuanliu kao* and the Formalization of the Manchu Heritage." *The Journal of Asian Studies* vol. 46, no. 4 (November 1987): 761–790.

————. *A Translucent Mirror. History and Identity in Qing Imperial Ideology*. Berkeley: University of California Press, 1999.

D.J. "Tartares ou Tatars." *Encyclopédie, ou Dictionnaire raisonné des Sciences, des Arts, et des Métiers*. vol. XV. Stuttgart-Bad Cannstalt: Friedrich Frommann Verlag, 1967. [Reprint of 1765 Neuchâtel edition.]

Ekenvall, Asta. *Eric Benzelius d.y. och G. W. von Leibniz*. Linköping, 1953.

Encyclopedia Britannica, Three-volume reprint of the first edition, Edinburgh: 1768–1771.

Fairbank, John K., ed. *The Chinese World Order. Traditional China's Foreign Relations*. Cambridge: Harvard University Press, 1968.

Harrell, Stevan, ed. *Cultural Encounters on China's Ethnic Frontiers*. Seattle: University of Washington Press, 1995.

Heissig, Walther. *Helden-, Höllenfahrts- und Schelmengeschichten der Mongolen*. Zürich: Manesse Verlag, 1962.

————. *A Lost Civilization: The Mongols Rediscovered*. Translated by D. J. S. Thomson. New York: Basic Books, 1966.

————. *The Religions of Mongolia*. Translated by Geoffrey Samuel. Berkeley: University of California Press, 1980.

Hoppal, Mihaly. "Shamanism at the Turn of the Millenium."
http://www.erm.ee/pro/pro8/hoppal.htm
(accessed February 3, 2001).

―――. "Shamanism in a Postmodern Age," *Folklore.*
http://haldjas.folklore.ee/folklore/vol2/hoppal.htm
(accessed January 12, 1999).

Humphrey, Caroline and Urgunge Onon. *Shamans and Elders:
Experience, Knowledge, and Power among the Daur Mongols.*
Oxford: Clarendon Press, 1996.

Larmer, Brook. "Manchurian Mandate." *National Geographic,*
September 2006.

Lee, Robert H. G. *The Manchurian Frontier in Ch'ing History.* Cambridge,
MA: Harvard University Press, 1970.

Matthiessen, Peter. *Tigers in the Snow.* New York: North Point
Press, 2000.

Mosheim, Johan Lorenz. *Historia Tartarorum Ecclesiastica.* Helmstadt
University, 1741.

Odhner, Hugo Lj. *The Spiritual World. Essays on the After-Life and
on the Last Judgment.* Bryn Athyn, Pa.: Academy Publication
Committee, 1968.

Rawski, Evelyn S. *The Last Emperors. A Social History of Qing Imperial
Institutions.* Berkeley: University of California Press, 1998.

―――. "Presidential Address: Reenvisioning the Qing: The
Significance of the Qing Period in Chinese History." *The Journal
of Asian Studies,* vol. 55, no. 4 (November 1996): 829–850.

Smith, Marcia. "Parallel Passages to Emanuel Swedenborg's Spiritual
Diary and three small works on the Last Judgment." Bryn Athyn,
PA: n.d.

Spence, Jonathan. *The Chan's Great Continent. China in Western Minds.*
New York: W.W. Norton and Company, 1998.

―――. *Emperor of China. Self-Portrait of K'ang-hsi.* New York:
Vintage Books, 1975.

―――. *The Search for Modern China.* New York: W.W. Norton and
Company, 1991.

Stary, Giovanni. "A New Subdivision of Manchu Literature: Some Proposals." *Central Asiatic Journal,* vol. 31, no. 3–4 (1987): 287–296.

―――. "The Secret 'Handbook' of a Sibe-Manchu Shaman." *Shamans and Cultures,* ed. Mihaly Hoppal and Keith D. Howard. Los Angeles: International Society for Trans-Oceanic Research, 1993.

Strahlenberg, Philip John. *Russia, Siberia and Great Tartar,* English ed. Germany, 1738. (Originally in German. Library of Congress has reprint of German edition, Stockholm, 1730). Reprint New York: Arno Press, 1970.

Swedenborg, Emanuel. *Principia Rerum Naturalium,* Dresden and Leipzig ed., 1734. Reprint Basel: Swedenborg Institute, 1964.

Swedenborg, Emanuel. The *Principia,* 1734. Reprint London: The Swedenborg Society, 1912.

Trompenaars, Fons and Charles Hampden-Turner. *Riding the Waves of Culture. Understanding Diversity in Global Business,* 2nd ed. New York: McGraw-Hill, 1998.

Winchester, Simon. "Black Dragon River." *National Geographic,* February 2000.

Yuguang, Fu. "The Worldview of the Manchu Shamanism." *Shamans and Cultures,* ed. Mihaly Hoppal and Keith D. Howard. Los Angeles: International Society for Trans-Oceanic Research, 1993.

Possible Consequences of The Last Judgment
On World Religions

ERIC H. CARSWELL

A fundamental definition familiar in meaning to many readers of Swedenborg asserts that all religion has to do with the way a person lives his or her life and the life of religion is to act in ways that are truly good (Life 1). Action or doing is the focus of this definition. The context for any person's decisions about what to do or say is a combination of what that person cares about, the beliefs the person holds, what the person knows and understands, and how that person views the situation immediately in front of him or her. This conference is focused on a constellation of different values, beliefs and ideas that the Lord in His Second Coming has revealed about the Last Judgment that has and continues to influence decisions we make individually and as members of organizations.

How do we look at the world? What is the framework in which we interpret our experience? A person with a strongly prejudiced point of view will be highly unlikely to see a member of a group, nationality, or race towards whom he holds a prejudice in a good light. We know, in fact, that for a person who knows what is true, but has little or no concern for what is truly good and useful, this is a common mental state:

> people with whom faith is separated from charity . . . see nothing else but errors and perversities residing with a person. . . . they see in the neighbor nothing except his evil. Or if they do see anything good they either perceive it as nothing or else place a bad interpretation on it. . . . Especially when they enter the next life, with those who have no charity, a feeling of hatred is manifest in every single thing; they wish to try everyone and indeed to pass judgment on them.

Their one desire is to discover what is evil in them, all the time having it in mind to condemn, punish, and torment. (AC 1079.1–2)

A person like this has a prejudiced outlook on everyone that individual meets. No matter who they are and what they are doing, a person with this kind of faith sees faults and flaws in others. This state of mind is directly contrasted in this description with a very different kind of outlook.

[People] who have faith that inheres in charity are different. They notice the good things, and if they do see evils and falsities they excuse them, and if possible endeavor with that person to correct them . . . those who have charity hardly notice the evil in another person, but instead notice all the goods and truths that are his; and on his evils and falsities they place a good interpretation. Of such a nature are all angels, it being something they have from the Lord, who bends everything evil into good. (AC 1079.1–2)

This second outlook could sound like a Pollyanna view of life—a naive assumption that everything will always work out just fine no matter what. The Lord clearly indicates that there are important qualities in this outlook, which is truly angelic because it reflects the Lord's outlook.

Another passage describes a view on life that we are invited to receive through our reformation and regeneration; this view holds an unflappable peace underlying it in good times and bad.

Peace holds within itself trust in the Lord, the trust that He governs all things and provides all things, and that He leads towards an end that is good. When a person believes these things about Him he is at peace, since he fears nothing and no anxiety about things to come disturbs him. How far a person attains this state depends on how far he attains love to the Lord . . . Peace is at the center of all delight, even within unhappy things for a person governed by good . . . Calmness of mind, contentment, and cheerfulness because things are going right are nothing in comparison [to heavenly peace], for these affect only the outward parts of the mind. But peace affects the inmost parts of all; it affects the primary substances . . . from these it spreads and pours itself out into parts formed from those substances and beginnings of them. It brings a lovely feeling into them; it brings bliss and happiness to the parts where his ideas form, consequently to his ends in life, and so makes his mind into a heaven. (AC 8455)

When we read about the Last Judgment in Swedenborg's theological books, aspects of what is written strongly support the peace and hopefulness described in this last passage. There are other things said, however, that support a far less hopeful outlook. We are taught very clearly that there is evil: evil can exist within us, and evil that exists outside of us results in occurrences which are far distant from the Lord's will. The modern use of the term "apocalyptic," (involving or portending widespread devastation or ultimate doom (*American Heritage Dictionary*), is a reminder of how the book of Revelation describes the destructive nature of evil; an evil that seeks to hide but is seen in all its ugliness and twisted forms of life when the light of heaven shines on it. On the hopeful side, the Last Judgment describes how the Lord can shed light and bring about judgment on even very well disguised evil. On the less hopeful side, the Lord's allowance of this disorder in the church on earth and in the world of spirits for the sake of the preservation of our freedom to choose evil is a sobering reminder of what human beings have done and can do.

We are told of a hierarchy of occurrences that take place under the Lord's universal foresight.

> The Lord however foresees and sees all things and every individual thing; and He provides and arranges the same, though:
>
> 1) Some things arise from His permission
> 2) Some from His concession
> 3) Some from His consent
> 4) Some from His good pleasure, and some from His will. (AC 1755)

Another passage that speaks of these levels of order and permission is:

> All order begins in Jehovah, that is, in the Lord, and it is in accordance with that order that He rules over every single thing. But there is much variation to His rule; that is to say, it may be His Will, or His Good Pleasure, or His Consent, or His Permission from which He rules. Things that have their origin in His will or in His good pleasure are products of laws of order which have regard to what is good, as also do many things that exist by His consent, and even some that do so by His permission. But when a person separates himself from good he subjects

himself to the laws of order which are those of truth separated from good and
which are such as condemn. For all truth condemns a person and casts him down
into hell; but out of good, that is, out of mercy, the Lord rescues him and raises
him up into heaven. From this it is clear that it is a person himself who condemns
himself. (AC 2447.2)

The theological writings of Swedenborg clearly state that hell
exists. Some people repeatedly choose values and ideas that result in
them living to eternity in this unhappy place. Groups of people who
can form the Lord's specific church on earth can also repeatedly reject
the doctrine and life presented in Divine revelation and choose values
and ideas that result in the utter destruction of their ability to serve
as the Lord's specific church. They can also so corrupt that Divine
revelation that it ceases to be a source of spiritual light. When this
happens it is called a "last judgment." One church comes to an end and
another one begins.

The subject of the papers for this topic at the Last Judgment
Conference relates to the question of how the people of that new
church are supposed to view others—both those in the previous church
and those following other religious traditions. The three papers in the
order they were presented are:

1)   Rev. Jeremy F. Simons—African and the Last Judgment
2)   Rev. Dr. Erik E. Sandstrom—Islam and the Last Judgment
3)   Rev. Christopher D. Bown—The Imperative to Find the Ancient
     Word in China: A Result of the Last Judgment
I will discuss them in reverse order of their presentation.

THE IMPERATIVE TO FIND THE ANCIENT WORD
IN CHINA: A RESULT OF THE LAST JUDGMENT

In his paper on the Ancient Word, Rev. Bown addresses the issue
of the world outlook we might draw from our knowledge of the Last
Judgment. Early in his paper he notes "the book *The Last Judgment*

ends with a chapter about "The Future State of the World and the Church" (LJ 73–74)."[1] Summarizing this chapter he asserts:

> In outward appearance—the physical reality of the world and the common events of human history and life, even churches in the Christian world and religions with the Gentiles—the world will continue much the same, we read. Inwardly, however—that is in the realm of the human spirit—there would be a profound difference resulting from the 1757 Last Judgment. The people in the church would henceforth have more freedom in thinking about matters of faith, and so about the spiritual matters which have to do with heaven, because of the restoration of spiritual freedom. (LJ 73.2; also referred to in TCR 115 as the Lord effecting a "redemption," which is a liberation or setting free of people, Coro 21)

This promised freedom of thought is a huge gift. In areas of life in which spiritual darkness inevitably reigned due to the chaos in the world of spirits prior to Last Judgment there is now the possibility of seeing the truth once again. It is impossible to make good decisions when a person is spiritually "in the dark." But who benefits from this new light? Rev. Bown continues:

> At first glance it might seem to apply only to the Christian world, where we might assume "the people in the church" to be. However the Lord's church is both with Christians and Gentiles (LJ post 125, referring to NJHD 3, 244–246). So the apparently earlier draft of this LJ 73 passage has: "In consequence of this, people now enjoy freedom of thinking rationally" (SE 5874)
>
> One pervasive and permanent outcome that transforms the whole world we live in, is, that, "The reception of Divine truth and good . . . is more universal, interior, easy, and distinct." (AE 1217)
>
> The Last Judgment of 1757 is fully completed. All prophecies about that Judgment itself were accomplished. All things were restored to order and basic stability in the spiritual world—a world not distant on the other side of the universe, but present with each of us today. Furthermore, freedom of the human spirit was restored to all people on earth, along with a new, easier responsiveness to what is true and good in human life. That deeper stability and freedom and easier responsiveness to what is human continues for each and all of us today.

---

1. All quotations are drawn from the speaker's paper on the Last Judgment.

These words carry a fundamental optimism about the spiritual light that is possible for all human beings—both those who directly have the doctrinal prose that is the Second Coming of the Lord (TCR 779) and those who do not (SS 104–106).

ISLAM AND THE LAST JUDGMENT

In his paper Rev. Dr. Erik E. Sandstrom observes that:

The Last Judgment began in December of 1756, and was almost finished by May of 1757, but continued to the end of that year, into the beginning days of 1758. During that time, the Catholics were judged first, then the Muslims, then the Gentiles, in ever widening concentric circles around the center. At the center were the Reformed, with each Protestant nation in different points of the compass relative to the east, where the Lord is always seen.

He summarizes how the Last Judgment was brought about and states:

The Muslims were judged this way too, but based on their lives according to the Qur'an, including as with everyone else, their love towards the neighbor. You cannot claim to love God and hate the neighbor. All who live in charity to the neighbor according to their own religions, the Writings explain, receive instruction after death that the Lord is the only God (AC 4721, 2789). Charity to the neighbor is always the main criterion for salvation.

One of the qualities of New Church doctrine that many find appealing is its emphasis that good people from all religions can be instructed in the next life and welcomed into heaven. In many places and among many religions a person who has eyes to see it can recognize the Lord's presence within the charity of people's lives.

Rev. Dr. Sandstrom further notes that there are specific qualities of Islamic doctrine that potentially provide a common basis between a New Church person and a Muslim.

the Qur'an itself has much to say about "last things" or eschatology, namely what happens when we die, are resurrected, and judged. The *Qur'an* has *Surahs* which are in amazing agreement with the New Church doctrine on the Last Judgment. Muslims more than Christians, but the same as the New Church, take life after death and individual immortality as factual.

This common basis is not merely a matter of chance; it reflects part of the Lord's work. It does not, however, make the Qur'an a perfect revelation. He states:

> That was why Muhammad could be inspired to reveal *interior* truths of religion, such as are found in the Gospels, even in parabolic form. So although the Writings say he was inspired to recite the *Qur'an*, and Providence raised him up (DP 255), this enlightenment did not extend to include deeper truths. Indeed the *Qur'an* reads as a primer of basic doctrines.

From his review of Islamic doctrine and life, Rev. Dr. Sandstrom draws both similarities and differences between Islamic doctrine and the New Church, which relate to both Divine guidance and human freedom. They can support an outlook that is ready to see the Lord's role and the hopeful outlook it supports as we look toward religions quite different from the New Church.

AFRICA AND THE LAST JUDGMENT

In his broad and deep study Rev. Simons covers many subjects. He conveys strong optimism for the growth of the New Church among Africans and cites doctrinal passages to support this optimism. For the purpose of this review the concentration will be less on his treatment of African spirituality and its future but instead on the outlook his research and prose indicates in relation to parts of the world historically dominated by Christianity.

He writes about how Christianity has been affected by the Last Judgment:

> A factor that has undeniably been exerting a positive influence for change in the Christian world is the increase of light from the spiritual world in the 250 years since 1757. Since the Last Judgment the sun of the spiritual world has shone more

brightly than before, and the new heaven has been increasing. How much of an effect has this had on the peoples of the Christian world over the past two hundred years? "After the Last Judgment there was . . . light in the world of spirits, such as was not before. . . . A similar light also then arose with men in the world, from which they had new enlightenment." (CLJ 30)

The hopefulness conveyed by this description of a promised new light is similar to that conveyed in Rev. Bown's description of this doctrine. Rev. Simons' prose states that the optimism in this idea is distinctly qualified by other statements in Swedenborg.

There can be no question that these things have had a positive effect on the world, and will continue to exert an always-strengthening force for good. In LJ 74, however, angels who spoke to Swedenborg about this new power, and the new freedom resulting from it, did not have great hope that this force would turn things around in the Christian world:

[The angels] know that the slavery and captivity in which the man of the church was formerly, has been taken away, and now, from restored freedom, he can better perceive interior truths, if he wills to perceive them, and thus be made more internal, if he wills to become so; but that still they have slender hope of the people of the Christian church, but much of some nation far distant from the Christian world, and therefore removed from infesters. (LJ 74)

Are these "*infesters*" still a serious problem in the Christian world? It seems that the new light and freedom really only have their full power when the power of the "*infesters*" has been exposed and removed, which the Writings in other places indicate will happen gradually by means of the Word (BE 96, 102). Apparently the light alone will not change things quickly.

The ideas in *Brief Exposition* 102 referenced in this last paragraph are explained in *Brief Exposition* 103 in which the reader is invited to look at several preceding paragraphs, one of which is *Brief Exposition* 79. This passage describes the "thick darkness" present in the Christian world due to the interior false doctrine related to justification by faith alone. These interiors are somewhat hidden by another quality described in this passage as the exteriors of the thought of people who apparently are traditional Christian preachers:

the exteriors, which do not gain admission, are valuable sayings concerning charity, good works, acts of repentance, and exercises of the law; yet these are accounted by them merely as slaves and drudges, which follow their mistress, faith, without contiguity. But because they know that the laity account these things as equally necessary to salvation with faith, they carefully subjoin them in their sermons and discourses, and pretend to conjoin them with and insert them into justification. This, however, they do merely to tickle the ears of the common people, and to defend their oracles, that they may not appear mere riddles, or like the vain responses of soothsayers. (BE 79e)

This paragraph suggests that the laity it refers to would be shocked if they were told that their church teaches that "charity, good works, acts of repentance, and exercises of the law" were unnecessary for salvation. Who are "the laity" referred to in this passage? Are they the same as "the common people" referred to later? Current experience seems to indicate that some of the laity does adamantly believe in salvation by faith alone. *Brief Exposition* 79 specifically references the predications of the states prior to the Last Judgment and yet it describes laity who would not listen to preachers who spoke only of salvation by faith alone. Should we be surprised to run across such people today, potentially aided in their conviction by the renewed spiritual freedom and light accomplished by the Last Judgment?

Rev. Simons cites a number of discouraging current statistics for the United States related to "atheism, hostility to faith, hatred, quarrels, violence, adultery, drunkenness." He states, "These and many similar facts do not point to a culture that has become more spiritual or receptive than the one that Swedenborg lived in." But he qualifies this by observing:

It is also true that there are many positive and hopeful signs of spiritual life in the United States. . . . While we could choose to see such signs simply in the light of AC 3489, quoted above, it is undoubtedly true that there are many good, well intentioned and intelligent people, and there is hope for the future. We need to look at all the signs to gain a balanced perspective.

What is the appropriate outlook on the Christian world around us and what especially are the implications for evangelization in these ideas? Rev. Simons refers to an outlook that is important.

> No one claims that evangelization is easy. The battle against the powers which have enslaved so many people's minds for so many years is a kind of war. To succeed in it, it seems as though it is important to have a clear view of where we are, and not be like the Pharisees, who could predict the weather but failed to see the "*signs of the times.*" A world view based in reality will keep us from becoming discouraged, because we will know what we are up against. It may also help us to make decisions about the kinds of programs that are most likely to be effective.

What programs are most likely to be effective? What is the reality of what we're up against? The General Church has long had skeptical views of outreach. One strong early statement about it is:

> [The] increase of the New Church, therefore, spiritual and material, will be in the Church itself,—from within outward, not from without inward, from offspring in the Church, and not from proselytism out of the New Church. . . . As in the past, so in the future, there will be a few coming from the Old Church; but that there will be an increase of numbers from that source, is a view that has no basis in revelation or experience; the hope for it is vain, and the work based upon it will be barren of result. (Bishop W.F. Pendleton, Address to the 4th General Assembly, *New Church Life*, 1900, 365)

Rev. Simons also reflects some of the applications or implications of this perspective espoused by Bishop W.F. Pendleton.

> Two implications for me from the teachings quoted above are, first, how important fellowship within the church organization is, and, secondly, how important New Church education is. It is difficult for people to remain committed to the New Church in the skeptical environment of the Western world. The support of others who have similar beliefs is vital. Similarly, it is difficult for children to become committed to the New Church unless they are taught about it from an early age and unless they experience fellowship and support from their peers.

Rev. Simons then states the priorities he draws related to "the slender hope" that the angels have for the people of the Christian Church.

My own hope is that the General Church will accept the idea that the Last Judgment is about the transfer of the church to new populations. We should always be exploring ways to do this, rather than following our natural inclination to focus on the peoples where the New Church has had its beginnings. The future growth of the New Church is most likely to happen outside of the Christian world. This may be in the near future or the distant future. If we accept this, my hope is that we will do what we can, within the limits of the available resources, to promote it.

His prose advocates a policy that would concentrate more energy and resources in supporting the growth of the New Church in developing world countries or at least in countries that have not been traditionally Christian. Based on doctrine about the Africans and their receptivity, Rev. Simons would encourage special focus on that part of the world.

Given the context and strength of this recommendation, it is somewhat surprising that Rev. Simons ends this paragraph with "in addition to evangelizing vigorously in the Christian world." Immediately after this statement, he returns to his fundamental assertion: "The truth of these teachings is made increasingly obvious by observing what is happening to Christianity in this world." Does this translate into an outlook of vigorous effort founded on little hope of positive outcome? It is a rare individual who can believe that effort on an issue is likely futile and continue "vigorous" effort. Given the limits of time and resources that we all face, does not the Lord want us to allocate our effort to the areas of life most likely to bring lasting benefit? The outlook advocated by Rev. Simons is likely to strike some as paradoxical or just confusing. Yet he is confident within its reconciliation in his own mind.

CONCLUSION

How are we to look at the world? What is the framework with which we interpret our experience? The New Church has been given a wealth of ideas and perspective related to the Last Judgment and its implications for our world view. Each of the three papers in this section takes one area of the post-Last Judgment world and reflects on its qualities. In doing so each contributes ideas that can assist others in forming and expanding their own perspectives on this world and the decisions each of us face. ⚔

A New Refrain:
The Child And "Songs Of Innocence"

JANE WILLIAMS-HOGAN[1]

INTRODUCTION

The First Christian Church came to an end in 1757. The details of its demise are described by Emanuel Swedenborg (1688–1772) in his small work *The Last Judgment* (1758). Swedenborg witnessed the tumultuous end of the church as it was taking place in the spiritual world. At the time of its death the Christian Church had become so external that virtually no light from heaven could penetrate the darkness that had descended upon it. The darkness deepened as generation after generation of Christians, both churchmen and laity alike, confined their search for Divine truth to what could be discovered by using the lamp of natural light alone. The more natural light was relied upon, the dimmer Divine truth became, until its light was all but extinguished.

The gathering darkness was spiritual in nature, and black clouds settled over the spiritual world blocking the Lord's communications to his church on earth preventing (genuine) human enlightenment. According to Swedenborg: "All enlightenment comes to man from the Lord through heaven, and enters by an internal way" (CLJ 11, 1763). Conditions in the spiritual world prior to the Last Judgment were so dire that "if anything had been revealed by the Lord, either it would not have been understood, or if received, still it would afterwards have been suffocated" (CLJ 11).

In the eighteenth century, during the final decades of the Christian Church, it is my contention that although the loss of spiritual

---

1. Assisted by Kendra Knight

enlightenment affected every aspect of the Divine with the members of his church, it had its greatest impact on their reception, i.e. rejection, of the most interior quality of heaven—innocence.

Innocence is the essence of love to the Lord, and charity toward the neighbor (SH 5236.2). Innocence has no relationship to self-centeredness and covetousness (HH 277.2). Swedenborg wrote in *Heaven and Hell* that

> Not many people in our world know what innocence is or what its quality is, and people involved in evil do not know at all. It is, of course, visible to our eyes—something about the face and the voice and gestures, especially of infants—but still we do not know what it is, much less that it is where heaven lies concealed within us. (HH 276)

Although Swedenborg stated that the innocence of infants is external and not internal, nonetheless we can learn something about the nature of innocence from it. Infants are not in real innocence because they do not have any internal thought.

> They do not know what good and evil are, or what true and false are, and . . . As a result, they do not have any foresight of their own, no premeditation, and therefore no intent of evil. They have no self-image acquired through love for themselves and the world. They do not claim any credit for anything, but attribute everything they receive to their parents. They are content with the few little things given them as gifts and enjoy them. They are not anxious about food and clothing or about the future. They do not focus on the world and covet much from it. They love their parents, their nurse, and their little friends and play innocently with them. They are willing to be led, they listen, and obey. (HH 277.2)

Swedenborg also discussed innocence in his work *Marriage Love* (1768). In it Swedenborg stated that:

> a sphere of innocence flows into infants, and through them into their parents, and affects them. That [sphere of innocence] also flows into the souls of parents and conjoins itself with the same sphere within infants; and that it is insinuated more especially by touch. (ML 395, 396)

Swedenborg not only stated that innocence is the most interior quality of heaven but he also stated that this is so, because "the Lord is innocence itself" (SH 5608). In an age where people of the church "know practically nothing about heaven and hell or their life after death," (HH 1) even though such knowledge is available in the Word, parents may not sense the innocence in their babe or feel it in their own breast, leading them to act with either indifference or hostility toward their child.

In the waning days of the Christian Church, the influence of the churches on the conduct of their members diminished, leading to an increase in immorality and a corresponding assault on innocence— particularly regarding sexuality, marriage, procreation, and child rearing; and when the churches did hold sway they often reinforced attitudes and actions that stifled a concern for the protection and nurture of innocence.

The Last Judgment occurring in the middle of the eighteenth century swept away the clouds in the spiritual world, and re-opened the communication between heaven and the world, and the Lord and the church. As a result, the light of heaven could again enlighten human minds, and innocence could be recognized, cherished, and protected.

The task of this paper is to explore innocence in relation to the social realities and experiences of infants and children in eighteenth century England before and after the Last Judgment; and then attempt to develop a theoretical explanation of what occurred taking the Last Judgment into account.

SOCIAL ENVIRONMENT 1700–1749

By 1700 in England, the Puritan Revolution had run its course, and the Glorious Revolution of 1688 had created a limited constitutional monarchy that shared power with Parliament and a national Anglican Church subordinate to the Crown. Society remained hierarchical, and was still dominated by a privileged landed aristocracy. However, the grip of the aristocracy on the larger society was weakening, and the emerging commercial, financial, and manufacturing sectors were beginning to challenge the old structure creating new opportunities, openness, and fluidity. The governing partnership was expanding to include the propertied middle class, and the National church was faced with competition from a number of non-conformist Protestant faiths (Bucholz and Key, 2004, 344).

The social structure was divided into the (1) titled aristocracy; (2) the gentry, distinguished into "greater" and "lesser"; (3) the middling sort, made up of merchants, manufacturers, artisans, craftsmen, and professionals; and (4) the ordinary people, comprised of yeomen farmers, husbandmen, laboring people, cottagers, paupers, and vagrants. Less than one percent of the population were titled aristocrats, and ninety percent of the population were ordinary people, leaving the remaining nine percent of the population in the middle with far fewer gentry than artisans and craftsmen. In comparison with other European countries, the English peerage remained far more open to new men than did those on the continent (Bucholz and Key, 350).

Three aspects of British social structure stand out during the eighteenth century: first, that the first sixty years of the century mark the zenith of aristocratic wealth and power made visible by the building or rebuilding of their palaces and castles often set in vast walled parks; second, the increasingly punitive management of the poor by the Parishes of the Church of England, due to a growing fear of the association between poverty and crime; and third, a strengthening of the penal code by Parliament, particularly by increasing the number of capital crimes from fifty (1680) to over two hundred (1820) over the century to deal with the crime and violence "bred" among the lower orders (Bucholz and Key, 350–372).

Another important factor that helped to shape early modern England was the change in agricultural methods, the increase in trade and the growth of national wealth and power. Despite the fact that almost every foreign policy decision from the reign of Elizabeth onward was made to increase and secure British overseas trade, agriculture remained the heart of the British economy through the early modern period. It fed the population, employed at least eighty percent of it, and it enriched England's most powerful members (Bucholz and Key, 346). The proportion of land held by the wealthiest members of society increased, and they began to employ new methods of cultivation that demanded the acquisition of even more land. Improvement in agriculture improved profits. Importing Dutch farming methods, new fodder crops were introduced such as turnips and clover that permitted keeping animals year round. These crops also required different methods of planting and management, necessitating fewer workers and destroying the centuries old small plot system of village agriculture. Two harvests were now possible in a year with these root crops. The use of field flooding and increased applications of fertilizer (manure) resulted in greater yields for wheat, rye, oats, and barley (Bucholz and Key, 346). Surpluses could now be sold on the continent. Not only did aristocrats improve their agricultural yield, but they also took interest in their mineral rights, and became mine and quarry owners. They invested their expanded wealth in their country estates, their London townhouses, finance and trade. Their enrichment came at the expense of small landholders and yeomen, whose debts increased. Frequently they were forced to sell their property to the large landowners, thus becoming either tenants on what was formerly their own land, or moving off the land altogether and into the towns (Bucholz and Key, 346).

Even though trade was not the heart of the English economy, it played an increasing major role in it. According to Bucholz and Key, "overall, British trade expanded in total gross value from £7.9 million in 1663–69 to £14.5 million in 1722–4" (347). In addition, imports surpassed exports. The export of wool was overtaken by the import of sugar from the West Indies. The sugar was then re-exported to Europe, as well as goods brought from Asia. The demand for sugar grew dramatically from £26.2 million in the late 1660s to £92.6 million in the late 1720s (Bucholz and Key, 347). The production of sugar and tobacco in the colonies over time began to rely exclusively on slave labor, which drew the English into trading in slavery.

The development and extension of trade in the early modern period increased the British appetite for the luxury items now available from England's trading partners. England was flooded with "Madeira and port wine from Portugal; figs, raisins, and oranges from Spain; silks and olive oil from Italy; sugar, tobacco, furs, and salt-fish from America; coffee from the Middle East; [as well as cottons, silks, spices, and indigo from India, and tea from China]" (Bucholz and Key, 348). The imports from Asia amounted to thirteen percent of all imports. London managed eighty percent of England's imports and sixty-seven percent of the exports. But the increase of trade also changed the port towns of Bristol, Liverpool, and Glasgow.

The increase in trade, the greater availability of luxury goods, and the building frenzy of the aristocracy all speak to an emphasis on the material world, reinforcing the secularization that was already underway.

THE CHURCH

In the early modern period the Anglican Church was administered by the sons of the aristocracy and the gentry. Their interests did not significantly diverge from their brothers and cousins involved in agriculture, trade, and finance. Religiously, the growth of Deism and atheism (which did exist) was less important as a factor in shaping attitudes than indifference toward the authority of the clergy, the scriptures and moral theology. This indifference was held by the clergy and the laity alike. From Peter Gay's perspective:

> The real source of the trouble, hard to diagnose and almost impossible to eradicate, was a bland piety, a self-satisfied and prosperous reasonableness, the honest conviction that churches must, after all, move with the times. This—the concessions to modernity, to criticism, to science, and philosophy, and good tone—this, was the treason of the clerks. (Gay, 1966, 343)

Deprived of any real power after the Restoration, "even over its own affairs, . . . the church could not avoid becoming involved in politics" (Gay, 343). Parliament wrote all the new cannons, and censured heterodox writings. In addition, the Bishops, as members of the House of Lords, were a constant and reliable source of votes because they had been chosen "to vote right and to talk well" (Gay, 343). Gay reports that in 1733, Walpole was saved by twenty-four Episcopal votes. The device used by the government was called "translation." In this process promising men were selected at first to fill the less desirable bishoprics such as Bristol (£450 per year), if they behaved well, in time they were elevated to a mid-range See, Lincoln, for example for £1000 per year. If he played his cards right eventually he might aspire to one of the more prestigious Bishoprics like Durham at £5000 per annum, or even Canterbury worth £7000 per year, plus additional clerical sinecures as part of the package (Gay, 343). It was a system that worked so well, that in mid-century Horace Walpole (1717–1797) could say:

> There were no religious combustibles in the temper of the times, Popery and Protestantism seemed at a stand. The modes of Christianity were exhausted and could not furnish novelty enough to fix attention. (Johnson, 1976, 345)

With little or no spiritual guidance from the church, the culture gradually became oriented towards the pursuit of pleasure in this world, rather than delaying gratification until the next. Individuals were now free to seek their own pleasure here and now, no longer bound by the strictures of moral theology or tradition. In this atmosphere it is not surprising that individuals developed a callous indifference toward all those unable to take care of themselves, all those in need of protection and support—the weak, the dependent, the immature, and the innocent, including infants and little children.

MORAL CHANGE

The decline of Puritan fervor had an impact on sexual morality and behavior across all the levels of British society. English data from the late Middle Ages through the early Modern period seems to suggest that in the Elizabethan era there was a fairly high degree of indifference toward the sexual mores legislated by the church. According to Stone, the number of prosecutions in the church courts for sexual misconduct was quite high, if the data from Essex County is in anyway representative. In a population of 40,000 people there were 15,000 court cases regarding sexual offences over a forty-five year period from 1558–1603. This is 350 cases per year, involving one percent of the population. Stone reports:

> In an adult life span of 30 years, an Elizabethan inhabitant of Essex, therefore, had more than a one-in-four chance of being accused of fornication, adultery, buggery, incest, bestiality, or bigamy. Even if only half of the charges were well founded, it still suggests a society which was both sexually very lax and also highly inquisitorial, with a great readiness to denounce each other's transgressions. (1979, 324)

However, he also notes that if convicted the penalties were not very severe, with public shaming or public confession being the primary methods of correction. In fact, bigamy, although a church crime, was not a civil crime until 1603.

Other indicators of sexual freedom or license that Stone cites is the astonishment of foreign visitors concerning the common practice of kissing on the lips when greeting one another, and the lewd conversation among the men, after the women retired from the table.

Prior to the early Modern period, sexual conduct was engaged in with two different ends in view, the first was to ensure the procreation of a male heir within the framework of marriage; and the second was extra-marital and focused on love, companionship, and sexual pleasure. In the eighteenth century these two ends began to be fused within the middling level of English society. Religious opposition to extra-marital liaisons declined or the censure of the church was more frequently ignored, while among the gentry and the groups that made up the small middling level increasingly were drawn to the ideal of companionate marriage. The second shift is even more dramatic, and according to Stone:

> [it] was one of the most conspicuous results of the collapse of moral Puritanism as a dominant influence in society after 1660 and of the general secularization of society. This was a release of the libido from the age-old restraints of Christianity, which had been particularly effective in the late sixteenth and early

seventeenth centuries. By the mid-eighteenth century there was emerging a new ideal, which now included sensual pleasure within its scope. (327)

The ideal of sensual pleasure led to an "easy-going" attitude toward promiscuity within aristocratic circles, and, in fact, as it became fashionable, it may have become the norm. Stone cites an anonymous, 1739, author concerning the causes. They were:

> The traditional free and easy ways of the English, corruption by foreign manners, the decay of religion, permissive education with too much stress on "ornament of the body" for girls, marriage for money or sexual passion rather than settled affection and the infidelity of husbands. (330)

This behavior increased the ranks of illegitimate children among the aristocracy. Some of these children were raised by at least one parent, while others were not. It should be noted that at this level of society illegitimacy fell harder on the female sex than on the male, particularly since the only career open to a woman was marriage.

It would appear that either the same degree of laxity toward sexual norms was simultaneously adopted by members of the middling rank, or that they began to ape the lifestyle of the aristocracy, but in any event promiscuity and illegitimacy spread among gentlemen and into the professional classes.

Along with promiscuity came a dramatic increase in venereal disease. James Boswell, Samuel Johnson's biographer, highlights the problem in his lengthy discussions about his own bouts with the disease in his journals and diaries. He had gonorrhea at least seventeen times. Obviously this affliction affected both men and women, and generally it was more a subject of humor than admonishment. When Boswell's father complained about the frequency of his son's infections to a Scotswoman, she merely suggested that the problem was actually quite common (378). The treatment of ingesting mercury was almost as dangerous as the disease itself.

The taken for granted nature of sexual promiscuity and the diseases that followed can be seen in the fact that cures for venereal disease were the most common type of advertisement in the growing eighteenth century newspaper trade, followed by cosmetics (379).

Boswell's journal also throws light on the sexual "under life" of the capital—it suggests that basically all women were prey to the sexual appetites of gentlemen and aristocrats, some willingly and some not! There were actresses, who were willing partners, as well as milliners, shirt and ruffle makers, who might provide services for a monthly fee. In addition, expensive call girls were available and high and low class brothels, some with specialized services, as well as common street prostitutes. Then there were the maids and the serving girls whose virtue was under continual assault in the homes of the well to do, taverns, and eating establishments, if we accept as valid the testimony of the novels and diaries of the period (381). Their vulnerability was enhanced by the fact that underclothing, which possibly could have provided a small degree of protection, was not invented until the nineteenth century.

In his concluding remarks concerning upper class sexual attitude and behavior, Stone suggests that the upper classes set the tone for the rest of society—what they did was the model of how their social inferiors ought to behave and act. He also notes several shifts in sexual values from the late Middle Ages onward. The first phase lasting until about 1600 was one of moderate toleration; this was followed by a phase of repression that coincided with the rise of Puritanism and their acquisition of political power; the waning of their power and the success of The Glorious Revolution ushered in a period of permissiveness and even license that peaked in 1770; at which time he claims that sexual repression slowly gained ground, and in the nineteenth century was reasserted as the norm. He claims that these swings were not just cyclical, but that they were related to changes in religious enthusiasm (339).

The sexual conduct of the lower levels of society did not just imitate the actions of their "betters," but they seem to have been granted greater leeway by the church, in part because the church did not exercise total control with respect to the institution of marriage. Imperfect control led to accommodations to local practices or customs. For example, in the fourteenth century, betrothal followed by intercourse constituted a binding marriage contract; and children born after betrothal but before marriage were considered legitimate; bigamy was condemned in principle but rarely detected or prosecuted. Given the absence of formal marriage registers, prior to 1538 it could be argued that these informal adaptations made some sense. The introduction of church registers for birth, marriages, and death can be viewed as a tightening of control on the part of the clergy, but also may be viewed as a response to effective Protestant criticism of the church. The growth of Protestantism, particularly in its puritanical form, had an impact not only on the formal regulation of marriage, but on attitudes toward sexuality, promoting a "puritanical" approach fully sanctioned by the church (383).

The effect of this attitudinal shift on the poor is unclear, given the fact that one of the obvious characteristics of poverty was overcrowding, a corollary of which would be the complete lack of sexual privacy. Until the Modern period, poor families had at most two rooms into which were crowded not only all the family members, but all the functions of family life from the most intimate to the most public. Sexuality was, therefore, almost never private and was a taken-for-granted part of family life and experience. In such circumstances, it might be difficult to sustain "puritanical" attitudes toward sex (384). In fact, this observation raises the question of the popularity of Puritanism among paupers, because of the absence of the social conditions that could support its adoption.

In order to understand whether or not there were shifts in the moral codes or conduct among the poor in the early modern period, it is useful to explore the relationship between sexuality and marriage prior to and after seventeen hundred. An important question is, how important was it to postpone sexual relations until after the marriage bans were read? If, in practice, it was very important then one would expect that very few children would be born prior to nine months after the wedding ceremony. If it was not very important to wait until after marriage to engage in sexual relations, then the expectation would be that a fairly high percentage of children would be born eight and one half months or less after marriage.

According to Stone:

> It has now been established that the level of recorded pre-nuptial pregnancies in England was low [around twenty percent] in the late sixteenth century and declined lower still in the seventeenth century, certainly well below twenty percent. During the first half of the eighteenth century a startling change took place. The rate of pre-nuptial pregnancies shot up, reaching over forty percent [at mid-century and continuing toward the end of the century]. ... By then pregnancy was proceeding—if not actually causing marriage, not marriage pregnancy. (387–388)

Rates of illegitimacy are much harder to ascertain than pre-nuptial pregnancy, due to various attempts on the part of unmarried women to deal with the situation, including abortion, infanticide, and abandonment; with incidents among married women not included at all. Thus, one can suppose that the rates of illegitimacy are generally underestimated in cultures that value marriage as the legitimate venue of sexual activity, and conversely when marriage is not viewed as the fundamental locus of sexuality, one could imagine both a decrease in the marriage rate and a more accurate measure of illegitimacy.

Stone reports on the changing rates of illegitimacy:

> In the Elizabethan period the rural illegitimacy ratio had been running at the modest level of under four percent. Between 1590 and 1660, however, the recorded ratio fell steadily to the astonishingly low point of one half percent at the height of the period of Puritan control, in the 1650s. It picked up a bit thereafter, but was still under two and a half percent in the 1720s. It then took off rising to four and one half percent in the 1760s and over six percent after 1780 [before it again began to fall]. (389)

The increase in illegitimacy was accompanied by an increase in prostitution. The late eighteenth century social reformer Francis Place (1771–1854) wrote: "chastity and poverty are incompatible" (392). Prostitution in the eighteenth century was fed not only by poverty but also by the growing culture of sexual promiscuity among the very poor. For some prostitution was preferable to working up to sixteen hours a day as a seamstress. It was seen as a means of survival for the growing ranks of un-wed mothers, and it was a "profession" of last resort for mistresses who were caste off by their lovers. Daniel Defoe (1660–1731) wrote in 1725 that: "many more, were members of the huge class of young maidservants in London, who found themselves temporarily our of a job and forced to 'prostitute their bodies or starve.'" He continued: "This is the reason our streets are swarming with strumpets" (392). These girls would go from a good house to a bawdy house, and perhaps back again. Defoe felt that they performed poorly in both situations. However, this belies the fact that there were few employment opportunities available for poor girls with little or no education. They could be seamstresses, Mantua-makers (an intricate dress made of one uncut piece of fabric), house servants, or prostitutes.

Not surprisingly, along with an increase in prostitution was the growth and popularization of pornography. In 1773, the noted social reformer and Judge, Sir John Fielding (1721–1780) decried its indecency and open availability. He wrote: "such obscene books and prints are sufficient to put impudence itself to blush" (394). It was not only sold in respectable bookshops but in all the open book stalls as well.

This review of changes in sexual mores, attitudes, and practices from the late Middle Ages through the early Modern period in England clearly identifies the unique character of the eighteenth century, in which "exceptional freedom was provided for the popular expression of sexuality" (394). When this century is placed in a conventional religious framework, it differs markedly from the Puritan era that preceded it and the Evangelical era that followed. "It was a time when the authorities made very little effort to curb the displays and products that reflected the pagan admiration of virility common to all folk culture" (394). It was not until the end of the eighteenth century that moral reformers began to turn the tide; in part, according to Stone, because of fears brought on by the French Revolution. Nonetheless, by 1800 the public had considerable less toleration for such public displays of immorality, particularly as middle-class morality spread down to the respectable poor through the Sunday Schools (a movement in which the New Church played a considerable role).

The unique and excessively libertine character of eighteenth century England can be explained, in part, by a conventional interpretation of religious, legal, and economic factors.

According to Stone, a change in moral theology regarding attitudes towards the purpose of sex in marriage at the end of the seventeenth century to include comfort and endearment opened the Pandora's box of separating sex and procreation. Once sexual pleasure was recognized as an end in itself, it was not long before it was also pursued outside of marriage. This was obviously not the intent of the theologians, but might be seen as a logical consequence in an increasingly secular age (396).

Stone argues, however, that an even more important factor was the suppression of all the external forms of pleasure associated with "Merry England" by the militant Puritans during the short lived rule of Cromwell. They banned: maypoles, cock fighting, stage plays, horse racing, and bawdy houses. They drastically reduced the number of alehouses, and made adultery punishable by death (396). After the Glorious Revolution of 1688 not only was Parliament made supreme, but the church (neither Puritan nor Catholic, but Anglican) became subservient to the state. In this secular atmosphere, the populace, resentful of the harshness of Puritan rule, readily embraced the public pursuit of pleasure.

Another important factor at the beginning of the Modern era was the separation of sin from law. Civil law began to focus more on violations of property rather than sexual morality. The development of a civil code of conduct focused on the control of violence and public order, leaving matters of sexual morality to the church courts. In a secularizing society, however, these courts became less and less relevant, as fewer cases were referred to them. There is also some evidence, at the local level (Yorkshire), that churchwardens, frightened by reprisals from parishioners, were afraid to bring matters of sexual immorality to the attention of their superiors (398). Since the civil courts left the prosecution of sexual conduct to the church, the ultimate effect was a dramatic decline in any social control of sexual behavior (399).

The concerns of the courts became increasingly economic. While no longer concerned with punishing fornication, the main concern of politicians became which social institution would bear the cost of maintaining the bastards—the parish, the father, or some other social entity. The over-riding concern of every public jurisdiction was to pass on the responsibility of child maintenance elsewhere. This new concern had a negative impact on both the unwed mother and her child. No parish wanted the child to be born within its borders. This attitude at times led to the forcible removal of a woman in labor beyond the boundaries of the parish. That either the mother, the child or both would die in such circumstances was a matter of indifference (401).

Thus, according to Stone:

> The penalties of pregnancy without marriage in the eighteenth century were very heavy for both mother and child. The former was likely to lose her job, might be sent to the House of Correction, and eventually be driven into prostitution. Because of the tremendous incentive to the mother to conceal the birth, the child was likely to be murdered in the first few hours, or abandoned in the street, either to die there or to be dumped in a workhouse, where the prospects of survival were not much better. (401)

Another piece of the economic puzzle is this: why did fathers in much larger numbers no longer chose to marry the mothers of their children or to accept responsibility for their offspring conceived prior to marriage? One explanation is that, in the early Modern period, among the poorer orders propertylessness increased. This would mean that poor men would no longer propose marriage in exchange for exclusive sexual rights to a woman, because he could not guarantee that he could support her and their offspring in the future. Chastity and exclusivity loose currency as bargaining chips, if they are not coupled with the provision of future security. In early Modern England the rise of rural laborers and urban workers without either property or status suggests the growth of a class without a stake in the virginity of its women. Given their lack of a future prudence, planning, and provision become irrelevant. Enclosure and the subsequent growth of towns thus became spurs to impoverishment, prostitution, and bastardry (402).

RISE OF TOWNS

In 1700 the island nation of England was still a predominately rural country, and most of the people lived in hamlets and villages. The dual processes of enclosure and industrialization led to the development of the towns. According to a well known historian of the period, J. H. Plumb, these towns ate up the people—the men, women, and children that were pushed off the land due to changes in agriculture practices, and were then sucked into the towns due to the rise of manufacturing. Conditions in the towns were such that Manchester, Liverpool, Sheffield, Leeds, Birmingham, and Coventry, as well as London, were barely able to maintain their populations, despite constant influx from the countryside (Plumb, 1950, 11).

The towns were ill prepared to receive new inhabitants. There was no sanitation; open cesspools were in the courtyards of the wealthy, while the paupers and working populations used any place of convenience to relieve themselves, and garbage was pitched from windows and doors from homes and from trades and craftsmen, including butchers. The streets were unpaved, narrow, barely six feet wide, and dark, particularly at night without any system of illumination. Torches carried by young "link" boys lit the way. Both the boys and their customers took their lives in their hands on these journeys, for robbery and/or molestation was an ever-present reality. The average houses were hovels crowded together with only one or two rooms, while the houses of the more well-to-do might be deserted, when they moved from town centers seeking healthier surroundings. Towns were "warrens of filth, squalor, and disease" (Plumb, 12). The dwellings and cellars not only housed people but also pigs, chickens, and other livestock. The over-riding reality of the towns was their stench.

The houses were not only crowded together but were themselves crowded. According to Plumb, one room in Manchester often sheltered ten people, frequently with little or no furniture, not even beds. In the winter, the occupants would huddle together for warmth. "Disease was rampant and unchecked: smallpox, typhus, typhoid, and dysentery made death a common place" (Plumb, 12). The poor and destitute were buried by the parishes in uncovered pits in churchyards and other open places. Once dug the "poor's holes," as they were called, were not closed until completely filled with bodies. It is not hard to imagine the effect of the noxious smell that surrounded such holes when it rained or during hot weather on those living near or passing by, as well as the implications of such pits on the health of the community, particularly on the most vulnerable—infants and children.

The population of Britain had increased over the course of the century, from approximately 5.5 to 9.3 million, even though there was an incredible waste of life between 1720 and 1750, both in London and in the mushrooming towns of the North. "In the early part of the century, only about one child in four born in London survived." In the Northern towns the infant mortality was probably higher (Plumb, 13).

At the beginning of the eighteenth century death remained at the center of human experience. Although no age group or class was exempted from its acquaintance, urban poverty assured that the relationship was closer and more intimate; and the infants of the urban poor were unquestionably the group highest at risk due, in part, to culpable neglect. According to Lawrence Stone:

> [Poor] infants in the Early Modern period were exposed by lack of attention by the mother in the first critical weeks; premature weaning; accidental smothering in bed with their parents; the transfer of the infant to the care of a wet-nurse (with the highest probability of death by neglect); abandonment in doorways; or deposit in parish workhouses or foundling hospitals, which were often almost equally lethal if less offensive to the public than the spectacle of dead babies littering the streets. (55)

In the midst of the ever-present specter of death, adults sought palliatives in activities such as gambling, violence, and drink (Plumb, 13). The dependent infants and children of these misguided, self-centered, and addicted adults were the primary victims of these activities. Gambling was a vice indulged in by all the various classes, according to Plumb, "the wealthy favored stocks, cards, and lottery tickets; the poor, crown and anchor, pitch and toss, or bull baiting and cock fighting" (Plumb, 13). While Plumb suggests that violence belonged exclusively to the poor, particularly in the activities of burning, looting, and destruction by urban mobs, and rioting to protest such things as the Gin Act, unemployment, and the building of work houses, unfair wages and other "injustices;" my reading of the record suggests that the treatment of the poor by those in power and authority also constituted a form of "officially" sanctioned violence. "Official" violence took the form of increasing capital offenses that resulted in the hanging of children for petty thievery; transporting them to the colonies against their will, destroying the cottages of the poor, lest they become nests for "beggars brats" and hustling pregnant women out of the parish in order to rid themselves of the cost of maintaining their infants in the future, should they somehow survive.

The third palliative was gin or Lady Geneva as it was called. The toll it took in lives lost was so enormous, particularly from 1720 to 1751, that it would be useful to explore what is known about the "Bills of Mortality" during the century, before returning to a discussion of the rise and fall of Lady Geneva.

THE BILLS OF MORTALITY

According to Dorothy George, the key to understanding the social history of London lies in the change in population—growth or decline, and in the ratio of births and deaths (George, 1965, 21). During the eighteenth century there were differences of opinion on this issue—some thought the population was declining, others saw growth. It was not until the census of 1801 that the matter could be definitively settled. Until that time people relied on the London Bills of Mortality to make their estimates. These Bills originated in the sixteenth century and only contained the list of burials in the various parishes that were contained within the city walls and its "Liberties." They were useful because a rise in burials might give early warning about the plague or other epidemics. Eventually baptisms were included, and after 1629 the cause of death was listed. After 1603 the Bills covered the "out parishes" or suburbs of London, and in 1636 the distant parishes were included—Westminster, Stepney, and South London (George, 21).

For the early modern period the Bills list the births and deaths in the parishes of greater London, but not the areas of London as it expanded to the west, for example Marylebone and St. Pancras. In addition, because it was kept by the Company of Parish Clerks, it did not record the births and deaths of dissenters. The classification of diseases was not very scientific either. However, despite these obvious limitations the Bills give a fairly good picture of the fluctuations in mortality; and despite their inaccuracy, other evidence tends to support the broad picture they painted (George, 22).

By the middle of the eighteenth century they point to one inescapable truth—the deaths in London far exceed the births. As London was the primary destination of an increasingly mobile population, this imbalance was clearly a drain on the whole nation. At the time it was said: "London will not feel any want of recruits till there are no people in the country" (George, 22).

Some used the statistics in the Bills to support the theory that the population of London and of England, as a whole, was declining due the growth of luxury. Samuel Johnson (1709–1784) took offense at this proposition, in a dialog with Oliver Goldsmith (1728–1774) saying, "Sir, consider to how very small a proportion of our people luxury can reach" (George, 23).

The census done in the early nineteenth century demonstrated that both London and England had increased population during the seventeen hundreds. It had grown slowly at first but after mid-century the population increased more rapidly. In order to compare the census data with earlier time periods, population estimates were made for 1700 and 1750. These estimates were made not from the limited data from the Bills, but from parish registers of births. It was assumed that births had the same relationship to the earlier populations as they did to the population in 1801. The figures for London included five parishes that were outside of the Bills (Marylebone, St. Pancras, Paddington, Kensington, and Chelsea). The numbers are: 674,500 in 1700; 676,750 in 1750; and 900,00 in the 1801 census return. If the parishes outside of the Bills are omitted, the slight increase from 1700 to 1750 disappears and, in fact, there is a population decrease of 9000. An examination of the parish-by-parish data shows that some of the newer parishes in the old Bills gained population from 1700 to 1750, but that some of the oldest and most crowded parts of the city had decreased (George, 24). George suggests that if the Bills of Mortality were used the decrease would have even been greater. Both the Bills and the Parish Registers, as well as records of coal consumption, indicate that the population grew until about 1720. After that there appears to be a decline.

Baptisms definitely declined, but it is not clear that this was due to a decline in the population of London. If burials alone are an indication, it shows that the population was increasing, and other evidence, such as maps, shows this as well. Nonetheless, baptisms were decreasing, particularly from 1740 to 1760, while during this period burials increased. George reports that:

> By 1740 it had become evident that burials were increasing and baptisms were deceasing, and many calculations were made of the havoc caused by this waste of life. The figures were indeed alarming. The baptisms increased from the beginning of the century till 1724, when they were 19,370, and then decreased till they reached their lowest point, 13,571 in 1742. They continue at a low level till 1760 and then they began slowly to increase. The burials reached their highest point just when the baptisms were at their lowest, and were 32,169 in 1741. They did not again during the century come within 4000 of this maximum, and after 1760 it was evident that they were decreasing. (George, 24–25)

An examination of the Bills shows that the loss of life was at its worst between 1727 and 1750 (and this was the worst it had been since the days of the plague). In 1728 the Bills began to record the ages of the dead. This information made it clear that mortality was greatest among children. The population of London was sustained only by immigrants who were beyond the very dangerous first years of life. Many old people retired outside of the Bills to die. Nonetheless, in 1750 the percentage of deaths is 1 in 20. It was even higher in 1741 and 1742 (George, 25).

The picture charted by the Bills of Mortality during the eighteenth century is radical. During the first half of the century there were three burials for every two baptisms. During the early years of the 1740s there were two burials for every one baptism. After 1750 the average ratio grew less until finally in 1790 baptisms were greater in number than burials. Using the Bills the numbers were 18,980 baptisms to 18,038 burials (George, 406).

According to George, the principal organizer and man responsible for the census of 1801, John Rickman (1771–1840) calculated the death rates from the parish registers as follows:

In 1700 it was 1 in 25, in 1750 it was 1 in 20; from 1797 to 1801 it was 1 in 35. By 1821 it was 1 in 40 (George, 25).

> The decrease was greatest in the burials of children. For the twenty years from 1730 to 1749 the burials of children under five were, according to the Bills, 74.5% of all children christened. The proportion steadily decreased and from 1790 to 1809 was 41.3%. (George, 26)

Despite the fact that there was general prosperity in England between 1700 and 1757, and London shared in that prosperity until 1720 as seen by the Bills of Mortality, some blight seems to have affected London so dramatically from the 1720s onward that it severely affected the survival rate of children born there for approximately forty years. That blight was gin. Dorothy George writes:

> The only explanation seems to be that usually given by contemporaries—the orgy of spirit-drinking which was at its worst between 1720 and 1751, due to the very cheap and very intoxicating liquors, which were retailed indiscriminately and in the most demoralizing conditions. (George, 27)

THE PALLIATIVE GIN—LADY GENEVA

When James II came to the throne openly as a Catholic in 1685, England was at a crossroad. The English had long thought of themselves as a Protestant nation, despite their disillusionment with Puritanism. The Glorious Revolution of 1688 made it clear that the English would not suffer to have a Catholic on the throne. James II was overthrown and the Protestants, Prince William of Orange and his wife Mary, the eldest daughter of James, were crowned king and queen at the behest of the Parliament. Not long after William III arrived in England, the liquor, gin, became another Dutch import. The name derives from the Dutch word, "jenever" or juniper, one of the distinctive ingredients of the liquor. This soon led gin to acquire the nickname "Lady Geneva."

One of the first acts of William, now King of England, in 1689 was to form a Grand Alliance against the expansionist polices of France. Banning the import of spirits from France was an extension of William's Nine-year War against France. Distilling gin soon became part of William's economic miracle.

Promoting the distilling of corn was vital to the interests of the landed aristocracy. As Daniel Defoe wrote in 1713, before the effects of the policy were visible:

> In times of plenty and a moderate price of corn, the distilling of corn is one of the most essential things to support the landed interest that any branch of trade can help us to, and therefore especially to be preserved and tenderly used. (George, 29)

In fact, beginning during the Nine-years War, everything possible was done to promote the production and consumption of spirits. Charles I (1625–1649) had incorporated the distillers of London in 1638, giving them exclusive rights to the trade. During the Nine-years War, the charter was overridden, and it was no longer obligatory to apprentice in the trade for seven years before opening a distillery. George observes:

Anyone was free to distil on giving notice to the Commissioners of Excise and paying the low excise duty, and anyone was free to retail spirits without the justices' license required for alehouse-keepers. (George, 29)

Clearly, the government gave special privileges to those engaging in the trade. It did not take long for vested interests to emerge in production and retailing gin. The public loved it, because it was cheap and readily available. As distilleries became the retailers of their own product, the line between production and retailing became blurred. Gin may, in fact, have been the very first mass marketed product, as "factory outlet" stores multiplied almost magically in the alleys and lanes in London during the first decades of the eighteenth century.

It was not until 1721 that some of the negative effects of the increased patterns of consumption were noted in the excise returns and in the Bills of Mortality (George, 30). This year also marks the first efforts to curb gin drinking, even though some observers twenty years earlier noted its terrible addicting quality.

By 1721 it was said that: "Nor is there any part of this town wherein the number of alehouses, brandy and geneva shops do not daily increase, though they were so numerous already that in some of the largest parishes every tenth house at least sells one sort or another of those liquors by retail" (George, 31). At this time, drinking spirits, particularly gin, became associated with the increase of poverty, debauchery, and criminality. Concerns about gin and its social effects were brought to the attention of London's local government through the Petty Sessions and Quarter Sessions on an on-going basis.

Government, however, was slow to respond. In 1725 the chair of the court in Middlesex repeated the charges of the social diseases brought about by the consumption of gin, and the response was to make an inquiry into the number of retailers. The next year (1726) the constables reported that there were 6,187 houses and shops that sold spirits in the metropolitan area, not including the City or areas in Surrey (George, 32).

The report stated that in some areas spirits were sold in every tenth house, in some every seventh, and in some every fifth. However, that did not take into account the spirits sold out of wheelbarrows on the streets, or from private houses and rooms. In Holborn, the report stated:

> Geneva is clandestinely brought in among the poor there, and that they will suffer any punishment . . . rather than live without it, though they cannot avoid seeing its fatal effect by the death of those among them who had drunk most freely of it. (George, 33)

This same year the College of Physicians petitioned Parliament to do something about "spurious liquors [that] 'cause weak, feeble and distempered children'" (George, 33). However, it took several more years before any action was taken. In 1729 an Act was passed requiring those involved with compound distillation (gin production) to have an excise license. It had some effect, but it was repealed in 1733 on the complaint of farmers. Not only was it repealed, but the Act stated that it wanted to "encourage making and selling of homemade spirits from the corn of Great Britain" (George, 33).

Another committee was commissioned by the Middlesex Sessions in 1735 to investigate the problem, and it was discovered that the number of retailers had increased to 7,044 (4939 licensed and 2105 unlicensed); however, Sessions thought the numbers were low, because over half of the constables themselves distilled and sold gin (George, 34).

Concerning the impact on women and children, the report said:

> With regard to the female sex, we find the contagion has spread even among them, and that to a degree hardly possible to be conceived. Unhappy mothers habituate themselves to these distilled liquors, whose children are born weak and sickly, and often look shrivel'd and old as though they had numbered many years. Others again daily give it to their children . . . and learn them even before they can go, to taste and approve this certain destroyer. [It continued] Neglected children starved and naked at home . . . either become a burden to their parishes or . . . are forced to beg whilst they are children, and as they grow up learn to pilfer and steal. (George, 34)

At this time, the justices of the Middlesex Sessions petitioned the House of Commons against the excessive use of spirituous liquors.

The petition was successful and the Act carried unanimously. The intention of the Act of 1736 was to stop the retailing of British spirits by requiring a license of £50 per annum and a duty of 20s. a gallon on distilled spirits (George, 34). The fact that the land owning members of Parliament would pass such an Act was stirring testimony to the "evils of gin" (George, 34).

There was opposition to the Bill. It was condemned by some because the suppression of the trade could lead to riots; it was unfair to suppress an activity that had explicitly been encouraged for forty years; it would interfere with the liberties of the people; and it would result in the loss of £70,000 in revenue (George, 35).

In the end, however, the Act could not be enforced. At first consumption was reduced. Nevertheless, it did not take long before there was an increase in the illicit sale of gin, and attempts to report these infractions were dealt with violently by mobs taking matters into their own hands. Informers were intimidated by threats, beatings, and murder. In the course of seven years, only three licenses were issued, and the yearly quantity of spirits sold rose to the incredible amount of 8,000,000 gallons in 1743 (George, 35).

In 1743 the Act of 1736 was repealed, but it was now clear that it would be necessary to suppress gin shops as such. To accomplish this spirit licenses would be given only to those who held alehouse licenses, and the distillers of spirits were forbidden to retail their product. Spirits were to be made respectable and more expensive. This change in strategy had a positive effect and the level of consumption dropped. However, in 1747 the distillers made a plea to Parliament that they be again allowed to retail their product, due to the financial hardships the Act of 1743 imposed. This right was granted provided they took out a license for £5. Immediately the pernicious old patterns emerged. There was a public outcry (George, 36).

In 1751 William Hogarth (1697–1764) printed *Gin Lane*, perhaps his most memorable engraving, and Henry Fielding (1707–1754), Middlesex Justice, published "Reasons for the Late Increase of Robbers" (George, 36). Using the evidence of the Bills of Mortality the House of Commons was bombarded with petitions from every quarter of London: The Corporation of London, the authorities of Westminster, countless parishes, the Bankers' Company, and from the towns of Bristol, Norwich, and Manchester (George, 36). The clear and common message of these petitions was that:

> The use of cheap spirits was destroying the people, shortening their lives, causing irreligion, idleness and disorder, and if not checked would destroy the power and trade of the kingdom. (George, 36)

Parliament passed yet another Act, this time with effect! "The Act of 1751 . . . was a turning point in the social history of London" (George, 36). It is important to mention that this "watershed" is not just a later recognition of historians, but was something observed by those who lived through the change. What made the Act of 1751 stand out was the seriousness of enforcement. An important element in this was Henry Fielding's creation of the Bow Street Runners in 1749. Although initially only a small force of eight men, they were the first professional constables, because they received a salary from the magistrate's court located at No. 4 Bow Street. They did not patrol but were given the responsibility to serve writs and arrest offenders on the authority of the justices. They carried this authority throughout the whole country.

When Henry Fielding retired as the Chief Magistrate in 1754, his half brother John Fielding (1721–1780) succeeded him. John had assisted Henry for four years, and served as a Magistrate for twenty-six years until his death in 1780. During his life, among other contributions to law and order in England, he organized the Bow Street Runners into a more professional police and patrol force. Blinded in a naval accident when he was nineteen, he was known as the "Blind Beak" and it was reported that he knew the voices of over 3,000 criminals.

ASSESSMENT

It is important to mention that the enforcement of this new legislation took place in the face of the vested interests of very wealthy men and in an atmosphere that did not condemn casual drunkenness. The outcry against gin originated among the middle and trading classes, and perhaps can be viewed as the first time that middle-class sensibilities positively affected public policy. Without the enormous pressure from the voices of the reformers, the vested interests of the governing class could easily have been maintained unchecked for an extended period of time. No independent moral voice is heard from the Anglican Church, in fact, nothing is heard from the church at all— only deadly silence in the face of parishes filled with intoxicated souls, enslaved by the poison of distilled spirits rather than freely drinking from the living water of spiritual truth.

As early as 1757 contemporaries were noticing the effect of the Act of 1751. It was observed by George Burrington (1727/8–1784) that, "the lower people of late years have not drank spirituous liquors so freely as they did before the good regulations and qualifications for selling them [were introduced]" (George, 38). By 1760 the consumption of spirits had been reduced to only 2,000,000 of gallons per year, where it remained until 1782 to 1784, when it fell to only 1,000,000 gallon per year. By this time the population had greatly increased, putting the 8,000,000 gallons consumed by a much smaller population in 1743 in stark relief (George, 39). Before turning to examining this and other positive changes that occurred after 1750, it would be useful to examine the effect of the gin craze on the lives of infants and children.

THE IMPACT OF "THE GIN CRAZE"
ON INFANTS AND CHILDREN 1720–1751

Discussions of the evils of the gin trade often begin with showing Hogarth's engraving of *Gin Lane* or with the story of Judith Dufour or both. *Gin Lane's* depiction of a poor babe flying out of her besotted

mother's arms certain to receive severe injuries when she hits the ground
is an image of neglect and moral ruin. The story of Judith Dufour goes
beyond neglect to portray callous wickedness. George quotes from the
Old Bailey Sessions Papers:

> The scene is in St. Giles where in 1750 every fourth house at least was a gin shop.
> Its eighty-two "two-penny houses" were also brothels of the lowest class and
> places for receiving stolen goods. Many of the crimes of the times bear the marks
> of a gin-inflamed insanity. (George, 42)

Here it should be noted that much of the gin that was distilled was
hastily or poorly concocted and was literally poisonous as well as
addictive. The narrative continues:

> There is the case of Judith Dufour who fetched her two-year old child from the
> workhouse where it had just been 'new clothed,' for the afternoon. She strangled
> it and left it in a ditch in Bethnal Green in order to sell its clothes. The money
> (one and fourpence) was spent on gin and was divided with a woman, who (she
> said) instigated the crime. She worked all the following night at a silkthrowster's
> and confessed the deed to a fellow-working woman. "This poor creature was,"
> her mother said, "never in her right mind but always roving." (George, 42)

The fact that London children were dying in large numbers has
already been presented in this paper, and many of them who died
did not have the benefit of being christened or in some cases given
a decent burial. Gin, prostitution, and disease affected the number
of births, as well as the survival of infants born. These factors may
account for the discrepancy in the ratio of burials and baptisms. Thus,
while successful campaigning against gin was one way to reduce the
death rate in London, another was to reduce the mortality rate among
parish children. Sending parish infants and children to workhouses
was begun around 1723 as a movement to improve the lives of children
who were being sent out to wet nurses. Workhouses, however, proved
almost completely fatal to children, and during the gin-craze the
horrors multiplied. The reformer and philanthropist, Jonas Hanway
(1712–1786), described the workhouse women as "indigent, filthy, and
decrepit" (George, 42). If 75% of the children in London died before

they were five, parish children, who were sent to workhouses or nurses, died at an even higher rate—particularly those under twelve months of age, because almost 99% of them died (George, 42, 43).

After working for almost seventeen years to establish an institution to care for the deserted and abandoned children of London, sea captain Thomas Coram (c. 1668–1751) in 1739 was finally able to garner the necessary support. A memorial was prepared for the government that included the following statement:

> No expedient has yet been found out for preventing the murder of poor miserable infants at their birth, or suppressing the inhuman custom of exposing newly born infants to perish in the streets; or the putting out of such unhappy foundlings to wicked and barbarous nurses, who undertake to bring them up for a small and trifling sum of money, do often suffer them to starve for want of due sustenance or care, or if permitted to live either turn them into the streets to beg or steal, or hire them out to loose persons by whom they are trained up in that infamous way of living and sometimes are blinded or maimed and distorted in their limbs in order to move pity or compassion, and thereby become fitter instruments of gain to those vile merciless wretches. (George, 43)

The charter was granted and subscriptions poured in. The first children were received that very year in a temporary dwelling. The permanent building was begun in 1742 and by 1745 one wing of it was in use in Lamb's Conduit Fields in Bloomsbury. William Hogarth was among the first governors, and George Frideric Händel (1685–1759) donated the proceeds of a concert performance of the *Messiah* to the hospital. Until 1756 the number of infants and children admitted was fairly small and the death rate was comparatively low. Until 1756, 1384 children were admitted and of them, only 724 died—a rate of 52%.

The need however, was tremendous, and in 1756 the governors were persuaded to change the policy and to open the doors to anyone bringing children. It was thought that the number of children that would be brought in would be related to the number of children either abandoned or sent to workhouses in local area. However, when the word of open admissions was out, children were left there from all over London and far beyond, from almost any sort of home or situation, and in almost any condition or state of health. Needless to say there were not enough qualified workers to care for them, and their level of health upon admittance was often so poor that many of them died. In fact, some children were left naked, striped of all their clothing. During the period of open admission (three years and 10 months) 14,934 infants and children were brought to the hospital and, of those, only 4,400 survived to be apprenticed or a mere 30% (George, 44,45). While the number is appalling, it was still better than the rate for children sent to parish workhouses or to wet nurses. After 1760 the hospital was gradually reverted to a private charity, and admitted children on a case by case basis. Also after 1760 the death rate was 1 in 4, and as the century progressed it fell to 1 in 6, and after 1800 it was even lower than that (George, 45).

The experience of the foundling hospital taught Jonas Hanway, one of the governors, that such an institution was not the best solution to provide care for neglected and abandoned parish children. An overview of the treatment of such children prior to mid-century will be presented before returning to the solutions of Hanway and others.

PARISH CHILDREN AND POOR APPRENTICES
1700–1760

Parish children were the offspring of London's settled poor. Their parents were entitled to some relief under the poor laws, as one of the categories of defined need was "parents overburdened with children" (George, 215).

It is safe to say that because parishes were required to care for foundlings and illegitimate children should no one else take on the responsibility, they were ambivalent about permitting them in the parish or their survival. Non-resident women were either forcibly removed from the parish or a security deposit was demanded. Parents could also hand over unwanted children for a set fee of perhaps £10. This ensured that no more claims would be made upon them for the care and support of the child. Once the parish was paid, this money was often used for a parish feast, called "saddling the spit." Defoe claimed that parishes often took the money and used it to feast and make merry, assuming that the child might not live more than eight or ten months (George, 216).

The very act of soliciting payment from the father to renounce his claims on his child, as an act of acknowledging responsibility, gave him the possibility of absolving himself from any future responsibility to his own. This was an insidious arrangement, giving the parish the appearance of discouraging men from taking paternity seriously.

Unfortunately, within the framework of this arrangement, the parish officers not only assumed that the child might not live but they conspired (with a "small c") to facilitate such an outcome. A Parliamentary Report of 1716 contains the following observations:

> A great many poor infants and exposed bastard children are inhumanly suffered to die by the barbarity of nurses, who are the sort of people void of commiseration or religion, hir'd by the church wardens to take off a burthen from the parish at the cheapest and easiest rates they can, and these know the manner of doing it effectually. (George, 217)

In fact some nurses or midwives paid security fees to the parish that permitted them to keep or dispose of children as they chose without fear of reprimand or molestation (George, 217). Ideally if these children survived they would then be apprenticed until they were twenty-four years old, if male and, twenty-one or marriage, if female. However, many of them simply became vagrants or beggars.

The defects of this system became more and more obvious, and so in the early 1720s the workhouse movement developed. The aim of the movement was to prevent vagrancy, and the disease and crime that followed. They wanted to give the children a start in life, providing that they did not get a better start than those not being helped. Since work and labor shaped the human condition, children should be trained into it as early as possible. In placing children in workhouses not only would they become accustomed to work, but they would also contribute to their own upkeep though their unpaid or under paid labor (George, 218–220).

It was believed that the workhouses would not only replace the system that was so full of abuses of starvation and misuse, but that it would also make the children better. To quote a 1732 Account of Workhouses:

> and that the children of the poor, instead of being bred up for irreligion and vice to an idle vagabond life, will have the fear of God before their eyes, get habits of virtue, be inured to labour, and thus become useful to their country. (George, 218)

Children, between the ages of six and sixteen, placed in these workhouses began the day at 6:30 with prayers and breakfast, worked from 7:00 AM until 6:00 PM or 7:00 PM with an hour mid-day for dinner and play. Between 7:00 and 9:00 PM in the evening, the children had supper, prayed, and played. They went to bed at 9:00 PM. In the summer they would wake at 5:00 and fit in an extra hour of work. Children who misbehaved were severely disciplined with whippings and confinement. At times, however, the sufficiency of food was some compensation (Pinchbeck and Hewitt, 1969, 164).

Some workhouses, however, were severely overcrowded and the children slept six to eight in one bed and, in one example thirty-nine children slept in three beds. Needless to say, under such conditions, disease was easily spread. While many workhouses advertised some form of rudimentary education, it was often provided by other inmates of the workhouse and was essentially perfunctory (George, 219). In addition there was some effort to teach the elements of Christianity and manners, however, the purpose was mostly to prevent them from appearing like little savages. Children were to stay at the workhouse until they were apprenticed, which usually began before the age of fourteen and lasted until their mid-twenties.

Parish apprenticeships were a form of poor relief, and thus differed legally from ordinary apprenticeships because of the longer term of servitude and the compulsory binding of the overseers. They were universally approved as a means of setting the poor to work, despite the fact that the methods of their masters often left a great deal to be desired. Poor children were generally placed in less skilled and poorly paid trades. In effect poor children were apprenticed in such a way as to relieve the parish of maintenance as quickly as possible (George, 224).

The parish officers, therefore, were not too particular about the qualifications of the master. Parishes and poor parents often paid a £5 fee to the master to take the child. The master would then assume the maintenance costs for the child, in return for his labor over an extended period of time. The attractiveness of the £5 fee often meant that masters would take in children for whom they could not provide (George, 225). In fact, he might take the fee, with the intent of getting rid of the child as soon as possible. To this end he might mistreat the child to such a degree that the apprentice ran away, or the apprentice might be so provoked that his conduct permitted the master to break the agreement without having to return the fee. Or he might not train him in the trade at all, and only keep the child as a household drudge (George, 229). It was also not unusual for a master to hire out his apprentice to someone else, suggesting that the apprentice was, in fact, little more than a slave (George, 233).

In 1738, a report entitled "Enquiry into the Causes of the Increase of the Poor" made the following observations:

> A most unhappy practice prevails in most places, to apprentice poor children, no matter to what master, provided he lives out of the parish, if the child serves the first forty days we are rid of him forever. The master may be a tiger in cruelty, he may beat, abuse, strip naked, starve or do what he will to the poor innocent lad, few people take much notice, and the officers who put him out the least of anybody. For they rest satisfied with the merit of having shifted him off to a neighbouring parish for three or four pounds and the duty they owe to every poor child in the parish is no further laid to heart. The greatest part of those who now take poor apprentices are the most indigent and dishonest, in a word, the very dregs of the poor of England, by whom it is the fate of many poor child, not only to be half starved and sometimes bred up in no trade, but to be forced to thieve and steal for his master, also brought up for the gallows into the bargain. (George, 227)

Not only were apprentices often brought up for the gallows, but they were frequently the victims of murder, manslaughter, and rape. They were sold into press gangs and they were transported overseas against their will. It was not only young boys who were victims but young girls were frequently starved and abused by their mistresses as well. According to Dorothy George, however, prior to mid-century these cases received little public attention and the perpetrators, despite overwhelming evidence against them, were usually acquitted (George, 231).

ASSESSMENT

As this data suggests the only significant change in manner of treatment of poor and illegitimate children by the parishes during the first half of the eighteenth century was the widespread introduction of workhouses for children. It is clear from this data that while there was a desire on the part of some to reform the treatment of poor parish children, the main emphasis of the reforms had more to do with the solvency of the parish, and the appearance of public order than it did with the genuine well-being of the children—they constituted a problem that needed to be addressed and controlled.

While many of the eighteenth century observers and commentators used in this section did in fact see the children as helpless, hapless innocents in need of care and protection, the view they give of English society suggests that their own perspectives were the exception, not the rule. Callousness, indifference, and brutality toward others dominated relationships, particularly toward children. They dominated in large part because the children had neither the self-awareness nor the self-centeredness to demand the loving care and protection their innocence required. Their innocence could go unnoticed by the majority of adults, because the adult's own store of innocence was almost completely compromised by the spiritual tempo of the times. It must be remembered that the children in question were parish children (not borough children), and that the officers in charge of their care and placement were church wardens not government officials. It is interesting to note that the voices of concern over their conditions were all from laymen.

While the self-interested parish church's aim was to rid itself of the children as quickly as possible, it could do so only with countless compromises to decency, justice, and charity, that is, compromises with its professed Christian beliefs. To achieve its goal, the parish appeared willing at every turn to sacrifice the children for the sake of its own economic and material interests. During the first half of the eighteenth century, regarding the treatment of its children, the spiritual voice of the parish is strangely and deathly silent.

MID-CENTURY OBSERVATIONS

At this point, the evils confronting the most vulnerable members of eighteenth century society have been sketched. Much more could be said, but I believe that enough documentation has been provided to understand the enormous scope of the life-threatening and life-challenging problems facing the innocent prior to the Last Judgment. Before turning to examine the social environment of England, particularly London, in the second half of the century, it would be useful to pause and explore observations made about significant changes that occurred in the middle of the century.

M. Dorothy George in her book *London Life in the Eighteenth Century* (1965) provides a carefully researched, richly detailed, and comprehensive picture of eighteenth century urban life in the British capital city. It is an invaluable source and I used it extensively to produce this study. It draws heavily on vital primary data essential to understanding the social environment of London's children. Her work allows the reader to see conditions, events, and important dates through eighteenth century eyes. She makes her own assessment based on the many reports she read, written by eighteenth century Londoners and visitors to the capital. What is her appraisal of changes, and what does she report were the views of those who lived through them?

George makes her assessment clear in the opening paragraph of her book:

The later eighteenth century, according to the more modern school of social historians, is regarded as the beginning of the dark age, in which there was a progressive degradation of the standards of life, under the blight of growing industrialism, while the earlier part of the century is considered a golden age, one of those periods when English working-class prosperity was at its height. The social history of London obstinately and emphatically refuses to adjust itself to this formula. There is a cleavage, certainly, about the middle of the century, but it is improvement, not deterioration, which can be traced about *1750* and becomes marked between *1780* and *1820*. (George, 1)[2]

The improvement which took place however cannot be entirely accounted for by the specific circumstances of London through this undoubtedly had something to do with it. The contrast from the earlier to the later eighteenth century is marked from many directions. The test of the change is in the death-rate, which begins to fall after *1750* and falls more rapidly after *1780*. (George, 3)

The miseries of poor children and parish apprentices began to receive attention about the *middle of the century* and their position was progressively improved. The parish poor no longer begged and starved on minute doles. (George, 3)

George uses the observation of Giuseppe Baretti (1719–1789) an Italian resident in London who "noticed a marked improvement between *1750 and 1760*," to support her discussion of the noticeable change in London life, particularly in areas of health, cleanliness, and the reduction of violence mid-century (George, 3). The observations of the reformer, Francis Place (1771–1854) are marshaled to reinforce the point. He commented that: the transformation of manners in the 1780s, as he remembered it were even then vastly improved since the forties and fifties (George, 4).

Some of these important changes have already been pointed out: the wasting of life was halted in *1750*, legislation against alcoholic spirits became effective in *1751*, there was a marked improvement from that date, and it, in effect, is the date of the turning point of the social history of London. In addition in *1757* the distilling of spirits was banned altogether due in part to a very bad harvest. A total ban was in place until *1760* (Dillion, 2002, 280).

---

2. In this section I have put the dates and references to dates in italics to highlight them.

In addition the first lying-in-hospital for married women dates from *1749*, and three more are built between *1750* and *1757*. The first public book on nursing and mothering, written by Dr. William Cadogan (1711–1797) was published in *1750*. Titled *An Essay on the Nursing and Management of Children* it went through twenty editions in nine years (George, 49).

George's material also notes dates when there was development of, or change in, sentiment. For example, in two places she mentions that the feeling of compassion emerged about *1760*. Compassion toward climbing boys or chimney sweeps, is evident at that time, as well as compassion toward parish children that resulted in legislation. Here it is interesting to note that both "knowledge" and "compassion" increased together. The ameliorative legislation and improved administration is the resulting use.

Also during this mid-century time frame, education was begun to be viewed as a better vehicle than workhouses to improve the lives of parish children and to provide them with the tools to make a usefulness and productive life.

These important and telling observations concerning change emerged in the eighteenth century. However, it is equally important to note observations on the eighteenth century from greater distance. The following views concerning significant dates come from professional historians writing in the twentieth and twenty-first centuries.

The book *The Enlightenment* by Norman Hampson reveals several interesting facts about the eighteenth century. One is that beginning in the seventeenth century and continuing into the next was a widespread sense that the predicted Apocalypse was not far off. Sir Thomas Browne (1605–1682) wrote: "'Tis too late to be ambitious. The great mutations of the world are acted, or time may be too short for our designs" (Hampson, 1968, 21). Hampson also reports that the "scientific and philosophic speculation of the Enlightenment, by the *1760s*, seem to have ended in impasse" (Hampson, 186). To move beyond the impasse he notes a change in attitude that he dates from *1749*. He cites the prize essay of Jean Jacques Rousseau (1712–1778) titled "Whether the restoration of the arts and sciences has contributed to the refinement of morals as the source of this change" (Hampson, 187). However, from the New Church perspective, the publication of the first volume of the *Secrets of Heaven* (*Arcana Coelestia*) is more likely to be the source of the shift.

Another noted British historian of the eighteenth century, J. H. Plumb has made several interesting observations about the middle decades of that century. In an article called "The New World of Children in Eighteenth Century England published in 1976,"[3] he wrote:

> Not only did this new attitude towards children begin to emerge among educationalists in the *middle decades of the eighteenth century*, but we can deduce also from the success of small private academies, for the development of a new kind of children's literature, and from the vastly increased expenditure on the amusements and pleasures of children, that parents, too, were no longer regarding their children as sprigs of old Adam whose wills had to be broken (Plumb, 70; emphasis added).

In this article he also informs us that John Newbery (1713–1767) was a pioneer in the field of books written specifically for the enjoyment of children. His first "Pretty Little Pocket Book" was published in *1744*,[4] and it quickly captured the imagination of the public. His line of children's books was very successful. In *1761* he developed one series of books on science for children written from the perspective of a young boy "Tom Telescope." His most popular book was "Little Goody Two-shoes" published in *1765*. The "Tom Telescope" books went through seven editions, and "Little Goody Two-shoes" went through twenty-nine before the end of the century (Plumb, 219).

No only were books now being written for children but retailing toys for children began during this same time period. Plumb writes:

> in 1730 there were no specialized toyshops of any kind, whereas by *1780* toy shops everywhere abounded, and by 1820 the trade in toys, as in children's literature, had become very large indeed. (Plumb, 87; emphasis added)

In his 1950 book *England in the Eighteenth Century*, Plumb writes:

---

3. Plumb, "The New World of Children in Eighteenth Century England," 64–93.
4. Italicized dates indicate clustering of changes around the 1757 date.

Between *1760 and 1790* it was crystal clear that there were two worlds, the old and the new; the new was the product of technological change and certain of success, certain to bring into being a new and strange Britain. . . . But compared with the centuries which had gone before, the changes in industry, agriculture, and social life of the second half of the eighteenth century were both violent and revolutionary (Plumb, 77; emphasis added).

Ivy Pinchbeck and Margaret Hewitt in their book *Children in English Society*, published in 1969 write:

Yet the *eighteenth century* also saw slowly developing a challenging ideal of philanthropy and humanitarianism which, in relation to children, was devoted to securing them from greed and abuse; to providing institutions for the unwanted child; to training schemes for waifs and delinquents; and to providing some sort of education for the poor child, that at the last, he might not be damned through ignorance of the Christian religion. (Pinchbeck and Hewitt, 311–312; emphasis added)

Lawrence Stone, who wrote *The Family, Sex and Marriage in England 1500–1800* in 1979 focused his commentary on the increasing evidence of rationalism and this-worldly secularization that accompanied the changes in English culture and religion. He writes:

What is significant in religion is not so much the growth of Deism and atheism as the growth of an attitude of indifference towards the authority of the clergy, the scriptures and moral theology. One suggestive piece of evidence of this change is the slump between *1650 and 1740* of the number of editions of the Bible published in England, despite the continued spread of literacy. . . . they [Bibles] had now to compete with novels and with a flood of textbooks on all aspects of nature and the physical world. (Stone, 159–160; emphasis added)

He continues this thought later in his book with the comment:

England in 1650 [at the height of Puritan power] was probably less secular than it ever had been, and in 1780 it was probably more secular than it was ostensibly to be again for over a century. (Stone, 416)

Secularization was also involved in the attitudinal shift over time in which private sin was distinguished from public law (Stone, 399).

Another area of profound change during the eighteenth century was portraiture, particularly portraits of children. Although there were some portraits of poor children painted during this era, the artistic revolution was clearly a development associated with the children of the upper classes. In the book *The New Child: British Art and the Origins of Modern Childhood, 1730–1830* by James Christen Steward written in 1995, he states: "Artistically the British eighteenth century truly begins with the work of William Hogarth around 1730 and continues through the artistic watershed of the *1760s*" (Steward, 17). He continues by saying that "what is 'new' about the 'new child' in Georgian art is his prominence, his centrality, and his emotive quality" (Steward, 17). In the *art of the second half of the century,* Steward notices

> a sudden and unprecedented upsurge of appreciation . . . for works devoted to the subjects of happy family, the education of the child, nursing, the instillation of moral values, and similar themes of childhood. (Steward, 27)

In fact, the portrait could "thus play a central role in developing the newly important attributes of familial love" (Steward, 97).

ASSESSMENT

What these quotations indicate is that profound shifts in almost every sphere of human endeavor occurred in the middle of the eighteenth century, clustering around 1757 but deviating as much as ten to fifteen years on either side. Those living during the era felt that they had witnessed a shift in human consciousness, followed by a shift in social action and behavior. Most modern historians acknowledge that something remarkable occurred in the middle of the eighteenth century and that it had profound effects on mortality rates, law and order, philosophy, social responsibility, human compassion, education, and artistic sensibilities, particularly as they related to ideas concerning the treatment of children. However, it is important to point out that not all historians accept this perspective, including some historians who focus on childhood. Their perspective, what it is based upon, and how it "fits" within the framework of the Last Judgment will be taken up later in this project.

The next section will explore some of the shifts noted above, specifically: reforms and reformers; the involvement of New Church educators in the Infant School Movement in early nineteenth century England; and the "new child" in art.

THE SOCIAL ENVIRONMENT 1750–1800
REFORMS AND REFORMERS

The discussion of the social environment in the first half of the eighteenth century touches on both reforms and reformers, the foundling hospital, the Gin Act of 1751, the organization of "professional constables," to name a few of the reforms; as well as some of the reformers: Coram, the Fielding Brothers, Hanway, and Dr. Cadogan.

The foundling hospital was the inspiration of Thomas Coram, who died in 1751, the same year the Gin Act was passed. After many years of effort, Coram was able to garner support from London's "well-to-do" residents for this private charity. After his death the work was carried on by a Board of Governors, one of whom was Jonas Hanway. Since it would be impossible to document all the reformers and their causes in this project on "Innocence," it would be useful to examine Hanway and his projects to get inside the drive to reform.

Early in his adult life (1743) Hanway became a business partner in a firm that had interests in Russia and other areas in the East. For seven years he traveled for the company and had many adventures traveling to Persia and back to St. Petersburg. Upon his return to England in 1750, he wrote a book describing his travels. After the publication of his travel book in 1753, he focused his interest on philanthropy. He is noted for his involvement with four specific social causes: the Marine Society, the Foundling Hospital, Parish Treatment of its Poor Children, and the Conditions of Climbing boys or Chimney Sweeps.

He founded the Marine Society in 1756, along with Sir John Fielding and several other men (Fowler and Walker) for two purposes: to supply the Navy with men and boys, and to save the boys from a life of vagrancy. The Society very soon began to focus primarily on "friendless boys" and young offenders, sending them off to sea not as convicts but properly equipped for a life at sea. In 1762 six years after the Society was founded, over 5,451 boys had been properly outfitted and sent to sea. They even had a ship school where the boys could be trained. In fact, the school is noted for the introduction of sports for these boys, especially cricket, realizing the social value of recreation (George, 287).

It was Hanway's position at the Foundling Hospital that led to his interest in a broader reform of the treatment of parish children. He was dismayed with the flood of infants and children brought to the Foundling Hospital after open admissions were declared, and the lack of resources available to care for them, and their subsequent high mortality rate. He felt there must be some better way to provide for the parish children. But he believed that first he must document the problem. From 1757 until 1763 he visited every workhouse in London to observe the conditions and to collect statistics. He was interested in the mortality rates. He wrote, "these were so melancholy that they were generally disbelieved" (George, 45). Needless to say, he had a difficult time obtaining accurate statistics because some parish officers did not want to reveal to him that all their children had died (George, 45–46).

In 1762 he was able to have an Act passed that required parishes to keep a register of the infants put into their care. The register was to record their reception, discharge, or death. The registers were to be returned to the Company of Parish Clerks and a yearly abstract was to be created.

He wrote an open letter in various newspapers and magazines in December of 1763 to the vestries and parish officers covered within the Bills of Mortality. The letter shows his level of seriousness and his character.

It is very obvious that this annual register is meant to strike alarm on the breast of those whose humanity and circumspection the lives of these poor babes depends and not simply to inform us that such a number of them died. ... This register is a favorite child of mine, I mean to watch the progress of it, and as far as may be in my power, to do you justice, as well as the poor infants . . . I have already had the pleasure to see the Register productive of great good in some particular parishes. (George, 46)

Hanway's efforts for this cause were indefatigable. His biographer wrote:

Going from one work house to another in the morning, and from one member of parliament to another in the afternoon, for day after day, and year after year, with steady and unwearied patience, enduring every rebuff, answering every objection, and accommodating himself to every humour, for the furtherance of this beneficial design almost without assistance. (George, 46)

Finally in 1766 a parliamentary committee was appointed to investigate the state of "Parish Poor Infants." It examined the registers created since 1762, prepared a report, and incorporated its recommendations into the Act of 1767. Essentially the Act made mandatory the principles developed at the Foundling Hospital and already practiced in some of London's parishes. The recommendations were that:

- All parish children under six be sent out of London to be nursed
- Those under two must be sent five miles from the cities of London and Westminster
- Those under six at least three miles
- Nurses were to be paid at least 2s. 6d. a week
- For children over six at least 2s.
- They were to have a reward of 10s. for rearing children sent to them under nine months (George, 47).

George notes: "the effect of the Act was immediate. [and] it was said that 'that the poor called it the Act for keeping children alive'" (George, 47). In the very first year the reduction of burials in London was 2,100. A parliamentary review of the Act done in 1778 called the

Act very salutary. In addition to reducing the mortality of infants when compared to the earlier figures, the review also noted that more children were reclaimed by their parents. The later figures no doubt directly reflect the real benefit of the Act; they also reflect administrative changes at the local level of the parishes, and also the effect of the Gin Act (George, 47).

The Act of 1767 was very significant, because in it, for the first time, the aim was not on checking extravagancy but "undue parsimony" (George, 47). This not only had a positive effect on its primary goal, the care of infants, but it also had a positive effect on the position of parish apprentices. To cut the mortality rates even farther, improvements were required in medical care and midwifery. In the closing decade of the eighteenth century, important strides were made in these areas as well.

Hanway's last major concern had to do with "one particularly forlorn set of children—the little climbing boys or chimney sweepers" (George, 243). The first notice of their plight was a letter in the *Public Advertiser* in 1760, perhaps written by Hanway. Later in 1767 when he was protesting placing very young children as apprentices, he wrote:

> Among those who have placed out children so young as seven years of age, there are several parishes who apprentice them to chimneysweepers. Chimney sweepers ought to breed their own children to the business, then perhaps they will wash, clothe and feed them. As it is, they do neither, and these poor black urchins have no protectors and are treated worse than a humane person would treat a dog. . . . They often beg in the streets, and seem to be in much more real need than common beggars. (George, 243)

In 1773 the Marine Society investigated the conditions of climbing boys. After they had washed and clothed them, they interviewed nineteen boys. They discovered that the boys were not well supervised or cared for, and thus had a great deal of independence, as well as "much ill treatment" (George, 244). They were often orphans of extremely poor people or illegitimate offspring of the very poor. Their services would be sold for seven years for a mere twenty or thirty shillings. They were sold by the poor who had too many children and not enough food.

Hanway died in 1786 before his campaign on behalf of these boys was successful. The cause, however, was taken up by David Porter, who was himself a chimney sweep and who had worked in conjunction with Hanway on this project. He was finally able to get Parliament to consider an act for the protection of apprentices in 1788. In their testimony before the committee considering the bill, they reported on:

- The excessive number of boys in the trade
- Their low pay of sixpence a day
- Boys who were bound as young as four years old
- Boys who had not been washed for four or five years and some without being washed at all
- Boys who contracted "sooty warts" disease i.e. cancer from not being washed
- Parents selling their children to the highest bidder among the master sweeps because no one else would take them so young (George, 244)

The bill that was finally introduced was a very watered-down version of the bill that had been originally proposed, and did not go far enough to really deal with all the abuses. However, it was better than nothing and at least began to address some of the conditions under which they lived and worked. The matter was again reviewed in 1797 and 1798, and perhaps because public compassion was finally awakened, there were many convictions during Quarter Sessions under the 1788 Act (George, 244–245).

Thus, it is possible to date the emergence of public concern for these children from about 1760—their daily life stood in marked contrast to "golden lads and girls" mentioned in Shakespeare's poem in Cymbeline, even though in the end both groups come to dust (George, 246).[5] Prior

---

5. The lines of Shakespeare's poem read: Fear no more the heat o' the sun, Nor the furious winter's rages; Thou thy worldly task hast done, Home art gone and ta'en thy wages; Golden lads and girls all must, As chimney-sweepers, come to dust. And in Warwickshire, Shakespeare's home region, children call dandelions "chimney sweepers," as their golden head turn grey and can be blown away like dust.

to that time chimney sweeps, link-boys (torch bearers), and Japaners (shoe blacks) had all been regarded as criminals in the making rather than as "innocences" in need of support and compassion.

ASSESSMENT

During the second half of the eighteenth century, a wide range of reform movements were instigated to address the problems of the poor and underprivileged classes and their children living in London. It is interesting to note that the men who became involved in these efforts were cosmopolitan entrepreneurs, writers, and justices. While some had careers in the British Navy, for example Thomas Coram and John Fielding, their socialization took them beyond the typical patterns of the aristocracy and the gentry. They all were all reasonably well educated academically, but it was most likely their practical education that encouraged their reforming spirit. They all appear to have been religious. For example John Fielding had his portrait painted with a book of law, and the Bible resting under one hand, and a document detailing legal reforms written by himself and Henry in the other. Biographies of Henry Fielding identify him as politically liberal in his day and a supporter of the Anglican Church; he may have "earned" his position on the Middlesex bench due to that support coupled with his anti-Jacobean sentiments. Hanway was not only a philanthropist, but wrote many pamphlets and books on religious topics, for example "Essays and Meditations on Life and Practical Religion with a Collection of Proverbs (1762)"; "Moral and Religious Instructions intended for Apprentices, and also for Parish Poor; with Prayers from the Liturgy, and others adapted to private use. To which is added the Right Rev. Dr. Edward Synge's "Knowledge of the Christian Religion" (1767).[6] He also wrote several works encouraging the taking of the Lord's Supper.

---

6. It is interesting to note that this last work has been republished in 2007 and is available on Amazon.com.

One is entitled: "Earnest Advice, particularly to persons who live in an habitual neglect of our Lord's Supper" (1778).

What is clear about these men is that they saw evil and responded to it by taking action to combat it. They were tireless in their efforts, and would not accept defeat. Coram pushed for over seventeen years to establish the foundling hospital; the Fielding brothers changed the legal procedures to ensure enforcement, prosecution, and judicial review; and Hanway labored to scientifically demonstrate the deadly impact of parish administration of the poor laws. He unmasked the church's lack of charity. Because the parishes were unwilling to care for their helpless and innocent charges, Hanway used the authority of the government, first to force them to count their failures and then to require them to financially meet their moral obligations to their own children. It is important to recognize that the state was called upon to be the enforcer, when the church parishes abandoned the clarion call of Christianity "to suffer the little children to come unto me [Christ]" (Mark 10.14). Economic and material considerations had replaced the moral and spiritual life of the church. While a judgment against the church was made in the spiritual world, these reformers also judged the church in the natural world and found it wanting. The reformers benefited from the changing spiritual condition, increased freedom and rationality brought light into the world revealing sins against the innocent.

It would be useful to end this section with a reflection on some changes related to natural health that took place during the eighteenth century. Dr. Thomas Heberden (1754–1843) made the following observations in 1807:

> Anyone who will be at the pains to compare the conditions of London and all the great towns of England during the seventeenth century, with their actual state and note the corresponding changes which have taken place in diseases, can hardly fail to consider cleanliness and ventilation as the principle agents in producing this reform. And to this may be added . . . the increased use of fresh provisions and the introduction of a variety of vegetables among the ranks of our people. The same spirit of improvement which has constructed our sewers and widened our streets and removed the nuisances with which they abounded,

> and dispersed the inhabitants over a wider surface and taught them to love
> airy apartments and frequent changes of linen, has spread itself to the country
> where it has drained marshes, cultivated the wastes, enclosed the commons. . . .
> Few have adverted with the attention it deserves to the prodigious mortality
> occasioned by annual returns of epidemical fevers, of bowel complaints and
> other consequences of poor and sordid living to which we are entire strangers.
> (George, 58)

Clearly problems remained, as we know from reading the novels of
Dickens and others and some of these will be examined in next section
of this paper. Nonetheless, the inescapable fact is that a sufficient
number of changes had occurred during the eighteenth century to
improve the life chances of the poor. The huge increase in population
is an undeniable testament to something wonderful happening—quite
simply more infants surviving!

NEW CHURCH INVOLVEMENT
WITH INFANT SCHOOLS

Charting the spirit of reform in the second half of the eighteenth
century in London has given me a new appreciation of the founding of
the New Church there. The church was founded in 1787; the priesthood
of the church was established in 1788; and the first Conference of the
New Church was held in 1789 in Great East Cheap. Attending the
conference were William Blake, the poet and engraver of *Songs of
Innocence,* and his wife, Catherine. *Songs* was actually published that
same year. To imagine these momentous events for the New Church
taking place at the very time Parliament was considering legislation to
curb the abuse of young chimney sweeps is thrilling. The New Church
could be formed and chimney sweeps could be protected because the
descent of heaven's light and inmost core of innocence illuminated the
need for, and the use of, both actions.

It is not surprising therefore that, in the early days of the New
Church in England, these two uses grew together in the lives of
educators, particularly the educators who were pioneers in the

Infant School Movement. This connection is discussed in a book on educational innovators written in 1967 by W. A. C. Stewart and W. P. McCann. They wrote:

> If the early infant schools can be said to have had any theoretical basis at all, it was Swedenborgianism. It is a remarkable fact that three out of the four pioneers of infant schools—namely Oberlin, Buchanan, and Wilderspin—were members of the New Church or adherents of the Swedenborgian doctrine. (Stewart and McCann, 1967, 245)

In a later book by McCann specifically about Samuel Wilderspin published in 1982, an additional connection is made linking the development of infant schools to concerns about "evils of juvenile delinquency" given the enormous growth of London's population around the turn of the century. Infant schools in England developed during the first quarter of the nineteenth century, and the population grew fifteen percent between 1811 and 1820. Poverty and unemployment rose at the end of the Napoleonic Wars (1815) increasing the number of youths at risk. The 1816 estimate of young thieves in London was two to four thousand, and by 1821, the estimated number rose to between eight and ten thousand (McCann, 37). There was a pressing concern among the governing class to stem the tide and engage in some form of prevention.

The very first infant school was developed by Robert Owen (1771–1858) at the Cotton Mill at New Lanark, Scotland. It was developed to fit Owen's deterministic philosophy, articulated in 1814 in his *New View of Society*. His fundamental belief was "that the character of man is without a single exception, always formed for him." Thus, he stressed the need for and importance of a person's early education. He believed that a child's indelible characteristics were developed in the first year of life, and that his disposition was set before the age of two. He opened an infant school in New Lanark for the women who worked in his mills. He hired James Buchanan (1784–1857), a relatively simple and kind man with a love of infants and the patience to care for them as the instructor. Buchanan was also open to following Owen's philosophy. His views were simple: The children were not to be beaten, they should be spoken to in a soft voice, they should be allowed to play, and should be kind to each other. Owen did not believe in the use of books or toys with the children, ages one to six. He wanted the children to be happy, however, he frequently uses the word "docile" in his writings.

Buchanan worked successfully at New Lanark for two years from 1816 to 1818. Many social reformers became interested in the work at New Lanark and observed the methods being used. Thus, in 1818, Buchanan was invited to London by a group of Whigs and Radicals, to open a school in London. The first infant day school was opened at Westminster, and a second school was open not long after at Brewers Green. Not long after he arrived in London he was attending the New Jerusalem Temple on Waterloo Road. Buchanan was most likely introduced to the Writings by Benjamin Leigh Smith (1783–1860), a Radical MP, whose father was an associate of William Wilberforce (1759–1833). Smith had taught in a New Church Sunday School in his youth. He also employed Buchanan to tutor his eldest child, Barbara. Barbara grew up to found her own very successful but experimental co-educational establishment.

JAMES BUCHANAN

After the school's first year in Westminster, several of the school committee lost interest in the project. Some say it was because of Buchanan's unusual teaching methods. Benjamin L. Smith and Joseph Wilson, a silk merchant with Evangelical leanings, remained interested and Smith had a school constructed on Vincent Square. The school was able to accommodate one hundred children. There were low benches around the walls that held colorful pictures of animals. There were lesson cards with geometrical shapes, and a ball-frame for teaching arithmetic. The pupils were the poor children from the surrounding neighborhood. They were dirty and wild, but Buchanan was able to keep them relatively content and orderly.

Julia Leigh Smith, Benjamin's sister, in a letter to Florence Nightingale recalled his methods:

The first I remember of him is seeing him with a hundred or more little children, for he was very small, and had an infantile expression, one might have called it angelic, when he was leading his troop of little ones marching to the sound of his flute. It was a scene of perpetual bustle, movement and noise, always growing into good humor, and I think a smile was always playing on his features thought it did not look fixed there. He was always alive, not mechanical, and I believe he could have quieted the whole infantry at any moment when he chose with the help of his wife and flute. The poor little things clustering on him like hiving bees, all trying to caress him. (Steward and McCann, 249)

Steward and McCann discuss the effect of Buchanan's religious views on his teaching. They indicate that his Swedenborgianism was so much a part of his life that the doctrines flowed into everything that he did with the children. He taught correspondences, teaching the children, for example that "the circle corresponds with harmony (or truth), and then the angels come and join us" (Steward and McCann, 249). He loved to tell Bible stories and have the children act them out. He was described as innocent, and

he looked upon children as angels and saw evidence of Swedenborg's system of correspondence on country walks. "A straight fir," recalled Barbara Smith Bodichon, "was the subject of a long discourse on a 'righteous man'." (McCann and Young, 1982, 51)

Buchanan also taught his students reading and arithmetic, using words and actions, "but he used no books or slates in his school and all his teaching was done by encouraging the children to sing, recite, and play" (Steward and McCann, 250). Buchanan always took part in these exercises, so much of the learning was through imitation. Julia Smith remembered that this was very effective, because the children became quite good at reading, writing, and counting (Steward and McCann, 250).

It is clear that Buchanan was an effective teacher because he had a true partnership with his wife. She was observed to be "a thrifty, bustling, managing, and shrewd Scotswoman," and "the real bones of the school" (Steward and McCann, 250). In addition, she "was also always patient and good-humoured" even in the face of some of

Buchanan's idiosyncrasies, such as day dreaming or wandering off from time to time. Behavior that was perhaps due to his simple and unaffected nature (McCann and Young, 41).

His school received many important visitors including Queen Victoria, and he was invited to open other schools, one by the Nightingale family in Derbyshire, and one supported by Smith, also in Derbyshire. He also trained several teachers, and remained at the Vincent Square School until 1839. The Vincent Street School was successfully reviewed that year. It remained privately financed and had 170 students, equally divided between boys and girls.

His success, however, did not lead to personal advancement in the field of education. This may have been due to his self-effacing personality, but Steward and McCann suggest that his Swedenborgian beliefs could have contributed to the problem. They suggest that the religious atmosphere in England at the time made it difficult to achieve recognition outside of the prevailing orthodoxies, because regardless of one's actual achievement one's work and activity was suspect. In any case, Buchanan decided to relocate to New Zealand in 1839. Despite all the good that he had done during his twenty-year educational career in London, his method died with his departure because it was so bound up with his personality.

SAMUEL WILDERSPIN

Samuel Wilderspin (1791–1866) was born into a New Church family, and in 1807 began teaching in a New Church Sunday School. He identified this as an important experience in his pedagogical education. During this time he learned how to get and keep the attention of his students. He learned how to adapt to them, to amuse them, and to teach them.

Married to Sarah Anne (1787–1824) in 1811, he worked as a clerk or calenderer until he was asked by a silk merchant in Spitalfields to open an infant school there. He leapt at the opportunity, and moved to Quaker Street in the summer of 1820 with his wife and family.

Spitalfields was one of the poorest districts in London. Wilderspin was initially seen as an outsider, and was pelted with objects and mocked on his way to the school. However, he earnestly wanted to get to know the people he was there to serve, and would walk around the neighborhood disguised in old clothes visiting the place most often frequented by the poor. He observed a lot of crime and delinquency first hand, and became convinced that "most of the crimes committed by infants arise from the neglect of moral cultivation" (Steward and McCann, 256). While initially there was hostility to Wilderspin, his school and his methods in Spitalfields, over time he won the respect of the community. He demanded that the children come to school fed with clean faces, brushed hair, and clean clothes. If they did not come presentable, they would be sent home. This was as revolutionary as were his methods. Gradually the community warmed to Wilderspin, his school, and his methods. When his wife died in October of 1824 after the birth of their son Samuel, the whole community attended the funeral, closing their homes, with the women wearing black ribbons in their bonnets.

When Wilderspin's son Samuel died five months later, his grief was so great that he could not continue at the Quaker street location. In the summer of 1825, he was selected by the recently formed Infant School Society of 1824, to be their agent for the formation of other schools, and master for the projected model school.

Wilderspin was deeply imbued with New Church principles and they animated the tenets of his teaching methods. McCann and Young, in their book on Samuel Wilderspin, were impressed with the extent of the material on infancy in the Heavenly Doctrines. They write:

> One of the most striking aspects of Swedenborg's writings is the amount of attention he devoted to infancy and infants, and the sympathy and benevolence with which he regarded them, a circumstance that might go some way to explain the attraction of infant teaching for members of the New Church. The young child, in Swedenborg's system of correspondence, was the symbol of innocence. A whole chapter of *Conjugial Love* was devoted to the theme "of the Conjunction of *Conjugial Love* with the Love of Infants." The concept of infancy in *Heaven and Hell*, probably Swedenborg's most popular work, foreshadows that found in

the poems of Blake rather than in Protestant treatises (especially the Evangelical variety) of the early nineteenth century. Swedenborg's young children display innocence in their "looks, action and prattle": they possess "no design or reflection," know "neither good nor evil," nor what is true or false, and have no love of self or the world confining their affections to their parents, nurses or little companions. (McCann and Young, 53)

They continue:

this powerful exposition of innocence of childhood acted like a magnet on Swedenborgian teachers, drawing them irresistibly into opposition to the traditional Christian view and positively affecting their treatment of children. (McCann and Young, 54)

I would also add that it was also in opposition to Owen's concept of natural determinism, although both focused on the importance of early education. The New Church practitioners believed in human freedom and Owen did not.

Wilderspin, unlike Buchanan, left a legacy of his educational philosophy in writing. Particularly evocative of his Swedenborgian principles was his *Early Discipline*, published in 1834. He wrote:

Children were active, thinking and feeling beings. The bodily powers of sight, touch and hearing were the instruments of superior faculties which we call the intellectual; mental powers were, however, but agents "acting under the influence of a yet higher impulse, that of the spiritual principle." (McCann and Young, 54)

McCann and Young saw these principles echoing Swedenborg's discussion of human development as a person is lead from natural truths, to intellectual truths, and to celestial truths. For Wilderspin, when an individual acts from Divine light and allows the spiritual principle to guide the lower levels of his life, that person has realized his or her true humanity (McCann and Young, 55).

Wilderspin believed that education should begin with the senses. The duty of the infant school teacher is to provide an atmosphere and a pattern of interaction that encourages the child to examine, compare, and judge at their own level of development. His fundamental principle was "to let the children think for themselves" (Steward and McCann, 257). Wilderspin also believed that education in the past had been focused on using the mind to produce feeling, now he suggested that education should attempt to operate on the mind through the medium of feelings. Using kindness and love would affect both the head and hands.

With his infant schools Wilderspin hoped to create models that would differ from both the dame schools, run by ignorant and old women, and the National and British schools that demanded memorization of facts that were little understood by the students. In contrast to these models Wilderspin suggested large airy classrooms, filled with proper instructional material, staffed by engaged and thinking teachers. In addition, it was essential that a large playground be attached to the school with swings, maypoles, flowers, and trees.

The playground was not just for recreation and play but it also was a venue for moral education. Wilderspin believed that it was on the playground that the lesson of the classroom became apparent or not. Observing the children at play was an important element of their moral education. Play should be freely chosen, because Wilderspin believed that "if they play at what they choose they are free beings, and manifest their character. When they are forced they become slaves, and their faculties are not developed" (Steward and McCann, 259).

With regard to the teacher, character and ability were the essentials. Wilderspin felt he must possess: "patience, gentleness, perseverance, self-possession, energy, knowledge of human nature, and above all, piety" (Steward and McCann, 259) The goals of his educational program were: healthy bodies, active minds, piety, and a caring spirit. Wilderspin's critique of existing schools in England was their inattention to the spirit of morality. He believed that the fundamental principle of the infant schools was *love*. His system of education encouraged students to develop all the simple moral virtues: "unselfishness, love of neighbor, honesty—and the pure and simple morality of the scriptures" (Steward and McCann, 260).

Wilderspin worked tirelessly to establish his system of Infant Schools throughout the nation. His work as a traveling agent lasted for five years, and during that time sixty new schools were established. Many of the people attracted to this new enterprise were Evangelical and this often created tension with Wilderspin's ideals and goals. When the Society folded in 1829, he became a freelance Infant School missionary. He retired to Wakefield in Yorkshire in the mid 1840s. During the last twenty years of his life he attempted to reinvigorate the local Lancasterian school and lectured at the Mechanics' Institute.

ASSESSMENT

Wilderspin's impact on the education of young poor English children is inestimable. By 1835 there were over 2,000 Infant Schools in operation. Nonetheless, he was disappointed because he felt that often the externals of his system were implemented without the corresponding internals. One of the basic problems was in the adequate training of the teachers.

Nonetheless, his accomplishment was enormous. Steward and McCann make the following assessment:

> Whatever the shortcomings of his followers, however, Wilderspin had almost single-handedly created a country-wide system of infant schools and provided a theory and method by which they could be run, and his achievement must be measured against the standards of his time. The institution that Wilderspin's infant schools were designed to replace was the dame-school, and to Wilderspin more than to anyone else do we own the inauguration of professional standards in the education of young children. The key point about Wilderspin is that he started from the very beginning and had to overcome both hostility and indifference. (Steward and McCann, 266–267)

It is important to point out that, despite this, many of his contemporaries recognized Wilderspin's worth and appreciated and utilized his methods. More importantly, one can only imagine the gratitude that his young pupils felt as they were welcomed into a warm, secure and loving environment, and were allowed to play freely in a garden filled with flowers and trees. In this picture, perhaps we see images of heaven, and catch a glimpse of some of Swedenborg's spiritual experiences brought to life. While many of the reforms of the eighteenth century stopped the doing of evil, Buchanan and Wilderspin, utilizing insights from heaven, actually had the opportunity to realize the doing of good. They seized the opportunity not only to protect innocence but also to nourish it.

THE NEW CHILD—ART

In order to explore the shifting perception of innocence in the eighteenth century, this paper has focused almost exclusively on poor, indigent, and illegitimate children and the men of rank and status who recognized their plight and fought to alter the social institutions that governed their survival and wellbeing. At this point, however, it is useful to turn attention to the relationship of elites to their own children, using the paintings they commissioned to capture their images. Let us take a moment and look at these images. Do you see any spiritual qualities or only natural images? Do you see representations of the eternal or merely the timeless? Do you see hope or nostalgia? There are three paintings to consider:

"The Age of Innocence" Sir Joshua Reynolds 1788
"Boy and Rabbit" Sir Henry Raeburn 1786
"The Artist's Daughters Chasing a Butterfly" Thomas Gainsborough 1756

While it is clear that a revolution in this genre occurred around "the artistic watershed of the 1760s," assessing the meaning of this shift is fraught with difficulties. Since the paintings were commissioned and executed by adults, the question arises: what, if anything, do they tell us about the lived experiences of the children depicted? Are we only viewing an adult construction of childhood, even as we think we are seeing the individual child or children? These questions are currently of great importance in the recently developed field of the history of childhood and the social history of children. I will return to these problems when I take up the question of historiography.

Leaving these questions unresolved for the moment, I would like to turn to another question: what value does an examination of these portraits, these family scenes have as we consider the perception of innocence in the eighteenth century? So the first question is, what is innocence? And the second question is, do these pictures reveal it?

Let us return to definitions of innocence presented earlier. A definition of innocence found in *Heaven and Hell* is: lacking

> foresight, premeditation or evil intent; and without a consciousness of self; but possessing contentment, and love for those who care and play with them, and a willingness to be led. (HH 277.2)

Innocence is visible in the face, voice, and gestures, especially of infants (HH 276). Innocence is without guile (HH 278). McCann and Young paraphrase these ideas from the Writings in the following way:

> they possess "no design or reflection," know "neither good nor evil" or what is true and false, and have no love of self or the world, confining their affections to their parents, nurses, or little companions. (McCann and Young, 53)

They write that: "Swedenborg's children display innocence in their looks, action and prattle" (McCann and Young, 53). Innocence as defined by Swedenborg is a spiritual quality—it is, in fact, the inmost of heaven.

So what do we see when we view some of the paintings that make up this genre? Do we see the spiritual qualities of innocence, as defined in the Writings, or do we see "natural" innocence—that is a worldly imitation of it masquerading as spiritual? The importance of making this distinction came to me while reading a discussion of Sir Joshua Reynold's painting *The Age of Innocence* in the book *Pictures of Innocence: The History and Crisis of Ideal Childhood* by Anne Higonnet (1998). The discussion of Reynold's painting sets the stage for Part I of the book called "The Invention of Innocence."

Sir Joshua Reynolds (1723–1792), "Age of Innocence," Ca. 1788, Oil on canvas, 76.5 cm (height) x 63.8 cm (width). Reproduced by permission from Tate Images. Digital image ©2009, Tate Images, London.

Reynolds painted two versions of "Age of Innocence." One version is more accessible at Tate Images, the other version is at the Plymouth City Museum, England. The author, Jane Williams-Hogan, used the Plymouth City version for analysis of the architectural structures in the background. To view the Plymouth City version, go to http://books.google.com, look up the book *Artful Dodgers: Reconceiving the Golden Age of Children's Literature*. The painting is found in that book on page 94, in black and white. (accessed April, 2011)

Sir Henry Raeburn, R.A., "The Boy and the Rabbit"
Ca.1814, Oil on canvas, 103.0 cm (height) x 79.30 cm (width).
Reproduced by permission from The Royal Academy of Arts.
© Royal Academy of Arts, London.

Thomas Gainsborough, (1727–1788),
"The Artist's Daughters Chasing a Butterfly"
Ca. 1756 113.5 cm (height) x 105 cm (width).
Reproduced by permission from The National Gallery.
© 2011 National Gallery, London.

In order to bring the distinction to life, it is necessary for me to quote at length from Higonnet:

> Sir Joshua Reynold's painting *The Age of Innocence* still looks familiar, even though it was painted in the late eighteenth century. True to its title, the image presents an archetype of innocence, one which the late twentieth century continues to cherish. Also true to its title, the painting defines an age—not the child's age, but an age of childhood. *The Age of Innocence* might as well be titled the invention of innocence.
>
> It is a pretty picture. Clever composition allows plants, land, sky and clouds both to show off the child prominently in the foreground and to make her seem reassuringly small. At once aggrandized and miniaturized, the child sits quietly close: face, throat, chubby feet and arms near to us in the picture's space, creamily painted, soft peaches and cream unctuously brushed in round shapes—big eyes, downy cheeks, dimpled hands. We the viewers are being encouraged to take visual delight in this figure, but not in the same way we would enjoy looking at an adult. The parts of the body so prominently displayed are exactly those least closely associated with adult sexuality, a difference reinforced by the child's clothing, which wafts in pure white drifts across what would be adult erogenous zones. The opposite of adult sexuality appears natural. The child belongs so comfortably in nature that she doesn't need shoes, as the picture insists by pointing tiny toes right at us.
>
> Because it looks natural, the image of childhood innocence looks timeless, and because it looks timeless, it looks unchangeable. Yet that image was invented, and not so long ago, by Reynolds, among other British portrait painters. The Age of Innocence began only about two hundred years ago.
>
> The image of the naturally innocent child, which I call the Romantic child, simply did not exist before the modern era. (Higonnet, 1998,15)

First, it is important to point out that Higonnet believes that innocence was invented not discovered or perceived. It is a human social construct, but as she describes it, a construct with little or no substance. It is not "lack of guile," "lack of self-consciousness," "contentment," or "non-worldliness"; rather it is size, color (peaches and cream), clothing, and non-adultness. It is a property associated with continuums not with discrete degrees (or Collingwood's hierarchy of forms). None of the words she associates with innocence are intrinsic to it.

In addition she equates innocence with what is natural, and the natural with what is timeless and unchangeable. It is interesting that she uses the word natural, when what she might be pointing to is "unaffected." There is nothing natural about the painting. As is all art, it is contrived—it is a social construct—both in form and substance. There is nothing natural about a young child in a white dress, sitting in a pose to have her portrait painted. Portrait painting is also a social contrivance, found in some cultures and not others. And, of course, nature is spatial, and is bound by time. Nature is always changing.

However, if the painting were to be described as "unaffected" or "unselfconscious" and "eternal" rather than as natural and unchangeable—one could see spiritual qualities being presented, not invented. The child's closeness to the foreground of the painting, allowing the viewer to almost touch her, may be presenting "The Age of Innocence" as something new, not seen before, so a close-up is necessary, and, in fact, vital. The viewer can't miss it, and must absorb it. The child in the foreground contrasts to the dark background that includes the shapes of castle and spire—state and church. The viewer is called to keep innocence present to himself, in the foreground of his own life, while the institutions of power remain in the shadows.

Higonnet and other authors point to the new and burgeoning field of eighteenth century portraits of children as paintings of loss and nostalgia. She writes:

> The modern child is always a sign of a bygone era, of a past which is necessarily the past of adults, yet, which, being so distinct, so sheltered, so innocent, is also inevitably a lost past. (Higonnet, 27)

The modern eighteenth century era differentiated the child from the adult. This differentiation was marked by special clothing for children, by contrasting the child's body from the adult's body, and by seeing the child as an inhabitant of a distant edenic realm, unconscious of adult desires. She sees the "'Romantic child' as an unconscious child, as one that does not connect with adults, and one that seems unaware of adults" (Higonnet, 28). The children depicted are absorbed in childhood. According to Higonnet, they represent the childhood we cannot reach. Thus, every sweet and sunny image of the "Romantic child" carries within it "a dark side: a threat of loss, of change, and ultimately of death" (Higonnet, 29).

To see the specter of death lurking behind "The Age of Innocence" suggests an unwillingness to read the eighteenth century, particularly the second half of it, on its own terms. The second half of the eighteenth century, even on the natural plane, marked a decline in infant mortality, a rise in population, and a growth of industry, technology, and scientific development. While there were vestiges of fatalism in public discourse about the future, there was also a greater sense of optimism. Human action, human intervention could make a difference. This project has described some of the effects of that spirit that protected and enriched human lives.

The children of the elite were in a position to inherit the earth, but if they were to do so, they needed to be treated differently from adults. Just as the innocent parish children and the chimney sweeps needed to be protected from neglect and indifference in safer and more nourishing environments, so did the children of the elite. While the neglect and indifference of elite children may have been less severe, it nevertheless existed. Social reformers came to the aid of the neglected poor, and created new institutions for their protection. What happened among the upper classes was not social legislation, but a cultural transformation of the institution of the family. The family became more self conscious and more protective of its individual members. The greater natural and spiritual resources of these elite families made it easier for them to nurture the innocent states of their children, and in doing so, the parents were more able to respond to them and express their delight. These paintings capture the awakening of that delight. They express freshness and openness to the guileless nature of children, whose very existence was viewed as a gift.

Thus, in the eighteenth century visual images of the spiritual ideal of innocence were created. It is true, however, that not all of the images painted of children around the time of the Last Judgment focused on the ideal. Some were in fact painted from an adult perspective portraying less than ideal sensual images of children. The painting by Reynold's of *Cupid as Link Boy* (1774) and *Mercury as Cut Purse* (1771) are cases in point.

However, in subsequent generations the spiritual ideal became associated with either over sentimentalized images of children or the repression of children's sensuality. Without a clear concept of the spiritual qualities of innocence, as detailed in the Writings, naturalists have come to question the idea of innocence altogether, and see it merely as a historic invention, not a gift from the Lord.

HISTORIOGRAPHY—HISTORY OF THE CHILD AND CHILDHOOD

There have always been children. Obviously, enough children over the millennia were sufficiently protected and cared for that the human race has persisted on this planet until the present day. And from time to time, memoirs of childhood, observations of children and childhood were published, as well as books of advice for mothers, and novels written from the child's perspective. However, there was scant academic attention paid to the history of children, until 1960, when a French social scientist, by the name of Phillipe Ariès, published *Centuries of Childhood: A Social History of Family Life*. While it was not the first book to tackle the topic of the history of childhood, the pioneering work over time stirred enormous professional response. The eighteenth century historian J. H. Plumb acknowledges the work of Ariès, in his article, "The New World of Children in Eighteenth Century England," but goes on to say: "We have too long neglected some of the most vital fields of human experience, as if unworthy of a professional historian's attention" (Plumb, 1975, 64).

Since the 1970s, childhood and children's lived experiences have been the focus of much study by professional historians, art historians, and sociologists. These works at first drew on and complemented Ariès's work, but later challenged it, and began to ask a different set of questions about children and childhood. Ariès's essential point was that in the pre-modern world it was difficult to distinguish between the behavior of adults and children. As soon as possible in the socializing process, children were dressed like little adults and were encouraged to imitate the actions of adults; who, according to Ariès, behaved more like "children" as we understand that word today, than adults. They were emotional, capricious, and openly libidinal. Although his book is called *Centuries of Childhood*, Ariès documented the emergence of parents as adults who increasingly took responsibility for protecting their offspring from the harsh, sophisticated, and overtly sexual world of adults.

According to Hugh Cunningham in *Children and Childhood in Western Society Since 1500* (1995), Ariès thesis mirrored a 1939 book by Norbert Elias called *The Civilizing Process*. He quotes Elias to underscore the thrust of the much more widely read work by Ariès. "For Elias, 'The civilizing process' involved a control of the instincts, something which was hardly under way in the middle ages when, consequently, 'The distance between adults and children, measured by that of today was slight'" (Cunningham, 1995, 5). "Ariès's work," he writes, "is an extended gloss on Elias's perception" (Cunningham, 5).

Even as Ariès describes the changes he saw in the dress, manners, customs, games, and pastimes from those of medieval society to the eighteenth century, he wrote with a certain sense of nostalgia for what he saw as the communal sociability of the past. Using primarily French sources he comments on the tiresome manners connected to a formal politeness and etiquette that stifled genuine social life. He writes:

> The whole evolution of our contemporary manners is unintelligible if one neglects the astonishing growth of the concept of the family. It is not individualism that has triumphed but the family. But this family has advanced in proportion as sociability has retreated. (Ariès, 1962, 406)

He saw the concept of the family as a manifestation of intolerance toward variety.

Viewing children as naturally innocent was a part of the overall development of the "idea of childhood," articulated by Ariès. This belief in the natural innocence of children, however, he associated with protecting them from anything that might disturb their modesty. From his perspective this led to a kind of moralization that was intolerant and fragmented the undifferentiated sociability of the past.

The initial professional response to Ariès is a trio of books with different agendas: Lloyd de Mause (ed.), *The History of Childhood* (1974); Edward Shorter, *The Making of the Modern Family* (1975), and Lawrence Stone, *The Family, Sex and Marriage in England 1500–1800* (1977). De Mause focuses his analysis on the parent-child relationship. He argues for what he called "the psychogenic" interpretation of history, claiming that it supersedes economics and technology as the fundamental motor force of history. From de Mause's perspective, children can be seen as projections of the unconscious self; thus, they "become" embodiments of one's own "evil" and "fear." This, he suggests is the origin of "original sin." Or the child can be seen as the "parent substitute" in a reversal of roles, in which the child is called upon to nurture a parent who was deprived of love in his or her own childhood. Finally the child may be a subject of empathy. In this relationship the parent sees the child's needs and attempts to satisfy them. De Mause's work has been a part of the contemporary conversation about childhood, but historians have never taken his thesis very seriously. Nonetheless, historians have taken exception to his opening sentence:

> The history of childhood is a nightmare from which we have only recently begun to awaken. The further back in history one goes, the lower the level of child care, and the more likely children are to be killed, abandoned, beaten, terrorized, and sexually abused. (de Mause, 1974, 1)

Shorter focuses on the rise of sentiment as the force creating the modern family. There were changes of sentiment that reordered traditional family priorities in terms of partner selection, mother-infant relations and the nature of the household. Sentiment places personal happiness over economic considerations in mate selection; sentiment places the welfare of the child over the mother's contribution to the economy of the family; and sentiment places family privacy or domesticity over obligations to the broader community

(Shorter, 1775, 17). Shorter sees capitalism breaking up the structure of traditional-agricultural society.

Stone, like Shorter, also argues for the development of sentiment. However, he believed that

> one of the central features of the modern family an 'intensified affective bonding of the nuclear core at the expense of neighbours and kin', was well established in the key middle and upper sectors of English society by the middle of the eighteenth century. But he did not think that this and other features of the modern family spread up to the higher court aristocracy or down to the respectable working class until late in the nineteenth century. (Cunningham, 11)

Stone saw individualism, not capitalism as the motivating source of the change. For Stone, changes in parent-child relations had a more important role to play in the development of the family, than they did for Shorter. However, neither of them put the same emphasis on childhood or children that Ariès did.

Despite differences between de Mause, Shorter, and Stone they all agreed that there were major changes in attitude toward and treatment of, children over time. Their differences had to do with the causes of those changes.

In 1980 Michael Anderson published *Approaches to the History of the Western Family 1500–1914.* He suggested three competing theories of family development: "the sentiments approach," "the demographic approach," and "the household economics approach" (Cunningham, 13). He challenged the "sentiments approach" by suggesting that it made speculation "fact," and they relied too heavily on cultural explanations without paying serious enough attention to economic structures (Cunningham, 13).

In 1982 Linda Pollack attempted a frontal attack on all the existing histories of children and childhood in *Forgotten Children: Parent-child Relation from 1500 to 1900.* She did so in an environment in which central portions of their explanatory frameworks had been called into question by historians. The critiques were totally dismissive of the work that preceded them. The critics labeled them "methodologically unsound, technically incompetent, and in their conclusions wholly mistaken" (Cunningham, 14). Basing her study on actual parent-child relationships as recorded in diaries, Pollack created the new paradigm for the eighties. She concludes that "the evidence does not agree with the arguments of such writers as Ariès, de Mause, or Stone that children were harshly, even cruelly disciplined, but reveals that brutality was the exception rather than the rule" (Pollack, 1982, 199).

Pollack wants to demonstrate the constancy of parental affection toward their children over the centuries. She used sociobiology to make her case that children like primates "require a certain amount of protection, affection and training for normal development," and that parents everywhere try to supply that (Cunningham, 14). Diaries then become her data through which she demonstrates parents supplying the needs for normal development. Her use of diaries as the basis of her revision of the older views can be criticized because her sample is skewed. It reflects only the actions recorded by well educated, literate, economically viable, and religious individuals. It generalizes to the whole society based on the actions of only the upper classes. Despite the fact that she lists the religion of the diary writers in her appendix, she does not seem to take this variable into account in her analysis. Despite her critique of earlier historians, her analysis continues to highlight sentiment as the most important variable in the discussion of the history of children.

Michael Anderson, however, explores the concept of household size. He argues that in the phase of development known as proto-industrialization, the age of marriage fell and the level of fertility within marriage rose. All members of the family had access to employment, including children. In such a society, the family strategy would focus on economics rather than sentiment.

In his *Marriage and Love in England 1300–1840* (1986), Alan Macfarlane's attempts to unite economic concerns with sentiment. He draws on anthropology to understand the difference between societies in which children are viewed as both an economic and emotional benefit, and societies such as England where, since the Middle Ages, they were viewed as a cost to their parents. This led the English to marry late, or not marry, and then spacing the children after marriage.

If households determined whether children entered the labor force or not, when economic conditions improved as they did at some point during Industrial Revolution, they might decide to withdraw the children from the labor force and invest in their children's education. What these historians overlook, according to Cunningham, are philanthropic efforts to rescue children, or laws that changed the conditions under which children could work (Cunningham, 17).

Cunningham reviewed the historiography of the children and childhood in order to put his own approach in context. He suggests that the emphasis on sentiment and household economies places the understanding of the history of children solely with the family, while ignoring the broader political and social structural context in which family life and decisions are made (Cunningham, 17).

Cunningham articulates his position in the following way: first the key changes took place in the eighteenth century.

> Framed by the writings of John Locke at its beginning and of the romantic poets at the end, with the strident figure of Rousseau at centre stage, there seems in the eighteenth century to be a degree of sensitivity to childhood and to children lacking in previous centuries. . . . Children can be classed alongside of slaves and animals as the recipients of the sentimentalism and humanitarianism that characterized the latter part of the eighteenth century. (Cunningham, 61)

He writes:

> The key to these changes is the long-term secularization of attitudes to childhood and children. It was not that people suddenly ceased to be Christian, but that for many their Christianity narrowed in its range, became less all embracing as an explanation for natural phenomena and as a guide to action.
>
> There were numerous and important exceptions to this generalization; Christianity did not give up its claim without a fight, and was on the resurgence in the late eighteenth and early nineteenth centuries. But there was a long term, if interrupted, decline in the belief of original sin, so that by the mid-nineteenth century, it flourished only in the margins of Christianity; and with that decline children were transformed from being corrupt and innately evil to being angels, messengers from God to a tired adult world. They also came to be seen to a greater degree as endowed with a capacity for development and growth whose motor was more nature than God. The art of childrearing became one of

hearkening to nature, giving freer reign to growth, rather than bending twigs to a desired shape. (Cunningham, 62)

Cunningham's review of the historiography of children and childhood and his presentation of his own perspective in which "long-term secularization" plays the key role in creating the conditions for change, provide a necessary and useful platform for the analysis that follows. It provides a necessary platform because this rather lengthy review of the history of children and childhood clearly shows the underlying assumptions, the overall scope, and the limitations of modern historical scholarship of children and childhood. It provides the New Church scholar with a comparative model through which she can assess the contributions that a New Church interpretation makes to the field.

One of first things we learn about reviewing histories of children is that children themselves do not leave many records independent of adults, particularly in the past. In effect they do not write their own history, whether in artifacts, collective actions, or words.[7] Even Pollack, who set about demonstrating continuity of care and concern for children had to rely on parent's comments to gain insight into the every day lives of children. The information available in the diaries was constructed by adults to be consumed or appreciated by adults. One could argue that among other things, that the authors were constructing their views of childhood, as much as they were recording the actual activities of their children.

Thus, it is possible to conclude that children don't make childhood; they participate in childhoods created by adults. They may be interactive participants in that creation, but they do not create either the structure or the rules. Knowing something of the ideals of childhood in any age will, therefore, gives access to the lived experience of children, albeit

---

7. Pollack states that she had access to a few child diaries: one prior to the eighteenth century, written by a Prince Edward Tutor; in the eighteenth century she had access to three British child diaries written by three sisters; and three American child diaries written by three different people. The diaries in question were written by children around the age of eleven. In any case, it is impossible to generalize based on these small numbers.

imperfectly. Suggesting this cuts through the concern of the historians about whether their focus of study is children or childhood; it always is both children and childhood.

Whether sentiment, household economy, politics or social structure is pinpointed as the dominant variable, all the historians in the review take a naturalistic view of historical causes. Religion, if it comes into the discussion at all, is generally viewed in a negative light.

The period of the Enlightenment is preceded by repressive Puritanism and is followed by repressive Evangelicalism. Religion points to non-empirical causes, and is therefore either seen as superstitious or ruled out of bounds. Pollack's list of diaries indicates either the religion of the diarist, if he or she had one (which most did), or says they are "religious" or in few cases the category is left blank. It would be interesting to review her data to see what, if any, role religion played in the lived experiences of the diarists' children. Dedication to a naturalistic perspective often does not permit historians to take even the naturalistic expressions of religion seriously enough to see its effect on both social constructs, such as childhood, and lived lives.

One final point on the review of historiography: except for Cunningham who is in fact interested in the work of philanthropists and law makers on the lives of children, the historians in question did not seem to appreciate the data from the Bills of Mortality except M. Dorothy George, or the efforts of social reformers to better the lives of the parish children and the chimney sweeps. It is hard to envision continuity of care in the face of this type of data. It is also hard to understand their criticism of creating a separate protected world for children.

Now I would like to turn to Cunningham's own perspective and why it creates a platform for a New Church interpretation of the eighteenth century attitude toward "innocence" and the impact of the Last Judgment. Cunningham sees long-term secularization as the key to the changes in the eighteenth century. From the naturalistic perspective he is absolutely right. What else is secularization but the waning of the power of the established churches? What else is secularization but a lessening of the hold of the established churches on the minds of congregants? As Cunningham wrote:

> It was not that people suddenly ceased to be Christian, but that for many their Christianity narrowed in its range, became less all embracing as an explanation for natural phenomena and as a guide to action. (Cunningham, 62)

Secularization is on the natural worldly plane what the prelude to the Last Judgment is on the spiritual plane; or what the consummation of the church is on the spiritual plane. As we have seen, Walpole wrote that "there were no religious combustibles in the temper of the times . . . The modes of Christianity were exhausted and could not furnish novelty enough to fix attention" (Johnson, 345). Written near the date of the Last Judgment, what else is Walpole seeing but the deep impress of secularization in England, despite the institutional trappings of the church? As Walpole is writing about the exhaustion of Christianity, Jonas Hanway is asking the parish officers to account for their treatment of parish children. Both men are dealing with a church dead to the Christian impulse, but Hanway is not deterred. What is the source of his vision—his inspiration? It is surly moral, and possibly spiritual.

THE NEW CHURCH INTERPRETATION— THE IMPACT OF THE LAST JUDGMENT AND SONGS OF INNOCENCE

The New Church historian looks for moral and spiritual causes to explain natural events. Natural empiricists or secular humanists, on the other hand, look for natural causes. They look to explain change thorough sociobiological, demographic, economic, material, technological, scientific, political, and social structural shifts. The New Church historian may look at natural variables but only insofar as they interact with moral and spiritual causes.

Walking through the narrative presented in this project, one walks through the dirty, filthy, crowded streets of London with the stench of sewage and rotting flesh in the air, with no clean water to drink, with bodies of animals, but sometimes human beings, too, old and young, littering the streets. The population of this great city were drinking gin, day after day, by the penny drams; but consuming over the course of the year as much as fifty-six gallons per adult male. Yet the consumption by women and children could not be far behind. This population was not just neglected; they were encouraged by landed vested interests to keep drinking gin, regardless of the consequences to their health and wellbeing, or the wellbeing of their infants and children. One sees *Gin Lane,* by Hogarth and weeps. The scene is not too different from some of Swedenborg's more graphic pictures of hell.

Metaphorically speaking, clearly the light of heaven could not penetrate the smoke generated by fires of the thousands of stills that operated in the city. We know that Swedenborg lived in London in 1749 publishing the first volume of *Secrets of Heaven* (*Arcana Coelestia*)! What did he see, what did he feel?

Two years after the publication of that first volume, the Gin Act of 1751 was passed and real reform began to occur. The Gin Act was moral legislation in the teeth of the vested interests. In 1757, the year of the Last Judgment, Jonas Hanway begins to visit the parishes collecting statistics concerning the children placed in their care. Ten years later a bill was passed concerning the care of parish children, it was moral legislation that overcame indifference. As presented earlier, it was called, by the poor, "the Act for keeping children alive" (George, 47).

Why did Jonas Hanway seize on this cause and other humanitarian ventures, what natural explanations are there, what natural causes? Increased wealth? No. Reputation or honor? Possibly. However, the evidence suggests that his concerns were moral and spiritual, lit by reading the Word and taking the Lord's Supper about which he so often wrote.

He clearly felt the children's innocence, their need for care, their need of protection in the face of much hostility, and took on the responsibility to press the state to legislate, when the church would not act responsibly on its own.

While there are many other points made in this project, this contrast is perhaps the most telling: a resolutely unwilling Anglican Church and a resolute moral champion, Jonas Hanway—a picture of David and Goliath. This stark contrast speaks to the reality of the Last Judgment and its power to bring to earth the light of heaven, which contained within it heaven's inmost—the innocence of the Lord himself. ⚬

BIBLIOGRAPHY

Ariès, Phillipe. *Centuries of Childhood: A Social History of Family Life.* New York: Vintage Books, 1962.

Ariès, Phillipe and Georges Duby, eds. *A History of Private Life. Vol. III, Passions of the Renaissance*, Roger Chartier, ed. Arthur Goldhammer, trans. Cambridge, MA: The Belknap Press, 1989.

Blake, William. *Songs of Innocence and of Experience*. New York: The Orion Press, 1967.

Bucholz, Robert and Newton Key. *Early Modern England 1485–1714: A Narrative History*. Malden, MA: Blackwell Publishing, 2004.

Cunningham, Hugh. *Children and Childhood in Western Society Since 1500*. London: Longman, 1995.

DeMause, Lloyd, ed. *The History of Childhood*. New York: Harper and Row, 1974.

Dillon, Patrick. *Gin The Much Lamented Death of Madam Geneva: The Eighteenth-Century Gin Craze*. Boston: Justin Charles and Company, 2002.

Gay, Peter. *The Enlightenment An Interpretation: The Rise of Modern Paganism*. New York: Norton, 1966.

George, Dorothy. *England in Transition*. Baltimore: Penguin Books, (1921) 1953.

George, M. Dorothy. *London Life in the Eighteenth Century*. New York: Capricorn Books, 1965.

Hampson, Norman. *The Enlightenment: An Evaluation of its Assumptions, Attitudes and Values*. Hammondsworth, Middlesex: Penguin Books, 1968.

Heywood, Collin. *A History of Childhood: Children and Childhood in The West from Medieval to Modern Times*. Cambridge: Polity Press, 2001.

Higonnet, Anne. *Pictures of Innocence: The History and Crisis of the Ideal Childhood*. New York: Thames and Hudson, 1998.

Hogan, Michael with Jane Williams-Hogan. "The Last Judgment and New Church Scholarship: Some Implications for the Future." Unpublished paper, The Cole Foundation, 2005.

Johnson, Paul. *A History of Christianity*. New York: Simon and Schuster, 1976.

Kolata, Gina. "Wet-Nursing Boom in England Explored." *Science*, New Series, vol. 235. Mp/ 4790. (Feb. 13, 1987), 745–747.

McCann, Phillip and Francis A. Young. *Samuel Wilderspin and the Infant School Movement*. London: Croom Helm, 1982.

O'Malley, Andrew. *The Making of the Modern Child: Children's Literature and Childhood in the Late Eighteenth Century*. New York: Routledge, 2003.

Pinchbeck, Ivy and Margaret Hewitt. *Children in English Society*, vol. I and II. London: Routledge and Kegan Paul, 1969–1973.

Plumb, J. H. *England in the Eighteenth Century*. Harmondsworth, Middlesex: Penguin Books, 1950.

Plumb, J. H. "The New World of Children in Eighteenth Century England." *Past and Present*, 67 (1975), 64–93.

Pollock, Linda A. *Forgotten Children: Parent Child Relations from 1500 to 1900*. Cambridge: University of Cambridge Press, 1983.

Shorter, Edward. *The Making of the Modern Family*. New York: Basic Books, Inc., 1977.

Steward, James Christen. *The New Child. British Art and the Origins of Modern Childhood, 1730–1830*. Berkley: University of California Press, 1995.

Stewart, W. A. C. and W. P. McCann. *The Educational Innovators*. London: Macmillan, 1967.

Stone, Lawrence. *The Family, Sex and Marriage in England 1500–1800*. London: Penguin Books, 1979.

Swedenborg, Emanuel. *Arcana Coelestia*. vol. I and vol. VII. West Chester, PA: Swedenborg Foundation, 1997, 1998.

————. *Conjugial Love* (1768) [NCE title: *Marriage Love*]. John Chadwick, translator. London: Swedenborg Society.

————. *Heaven and Hell*. (1758) George Dole, trans. West Chester, Pennsylvania: Swedenborg Foundation.

————. *Conjugial Love*. West Chester, PA:Swedenborg Foundation. 1998.

————. *Heaven and Hell*. West Chester, PA: Swedenborg Foundation. 2001.

————. *The Last Judgment. Miscellaneous Theological Works*. West Chester, PA: Swedenborg Foundation. 1996.

————. *Continuation on the Last Judgment. Miscellaneous Theological Works*. West Chester, PA: Swedenborg Foundation, 1996.

Wrightson, Keith. *English Society 1580–1680*. New Brunswick, NJ: Rutgers University Press, 1982.

Williams-Hogan, Jane. "The New Church in a Disenchanted World: A Study of the Formation and Development of the General Conference of the New Church in Great Britain." Ph.D. Dissertation, University of Pennsylvania, 1985.

The Last Judgment and Women
in the Modern Western World

SONIA SONESON WERNER[1]

INTRODUCTION

Swedenborg claims the Last Judgment happened in the spiritual world in 1757. The Lord ordered the heavens so that people could be enlightened, making it possible for humans on earth to see spiritual truths more directly and more inwardly (TCR 508).

This essay will trace a few of the main events in the past 250 years which appear to have been inspired by new ways of thinking about womens' rights and roles in society. Rather than using a traditional method to analyze the history of women, I will describe and explain human events through the perspective of a developmental psychologist. I believe that it is more thorough to use two theories rather than one to analyze the effects of the Last Judgment on women's roles in the modern western world: a spiritual theory of human development and a feminist theory of development.

Both theories involve descriptions of psychological maturation, which occurs first through complacency, then suffering through struggles, and eventually usefulness to others. Application and synthesis of these two theories help us to more fully appreciate the historical events and to see how major social changes occurred due to the work of key historical figures. Two case studies will be analyzed through these two psychological theories of development.

---

1. With student research assistant Megan Malone.

This essay's focusing point is that analysis of women's history by means of psychological case studies and theories of human development enable the reader to more effectively reflect on her or his own spiritual growth and contributions to humankind. Initially, there will be a brief explanation of the Last Judgment according to New Church doctrines. Descriptions and explanations of the two selected theories of psychological development will follow: the first is a theory of feminist identity development according to Downing (1985), the second is a theory of spiritual development, authored by Moody (1997). These psychological theories were selected for two reasons. Both theories focus on stages of adult development rather than child development. Secondly, the final stages of both theories emphasize usefulness to the neighbor as part of the description of the most fully mature adult. These theories will then be applied to the case studies of two key women who lived following the Last Judgment of 1757: Mary Wollstonecraft and Julia Ward Howe. These women were both directly and indirectly influenced by the Writings of Swedenborg, moreover, both women were deep thinkers whose personal reflections led to public statements that facilitated the women's movement. The essay ends with a comparison and conclusion regarding future research suggestions.

WHAT IS THE LAST JUDGMENT?

According to Swedenborg, his spiritual eyes were opened in the eighteenth century and he was able to witness the reordering of the heavens (TCR 115, 124, 772). Although there were no obvious, natural events happening on earth at that time to mark the occasion, the Lord needed to bring structure to heaven and judgment to people who had abused their power in churches and governments when they had lived on earth (AC 1850).

Smoley, a New Church scholar, states that in the other world a major judgment occurred on the leaders of the Catholic and Protestant churches who had abused their power by distorting truths or promoting faith alone. They had organized the church hierarchy to be intertwined with the European governments, to keep power in the hands of the male clergy. This created an unhealthy dependency and effectively kept laywomen and men like spiritual children unable to fully mature.

The theological Writings of the New Church, penned by Swedenborg, indicate that following this judgment it was possible for people to consider spiritual ideas more deeply, if they chose to do so (TCR 508). As people reflected and thought more for themselves, rather than depending on interpretations from dominating clergy, they eventually began to question the authority of the churches and governments.

The Writings clearly indicate that each person has God-given value. Every single human being is a potential angel and deserves respect, regardless of his or her gender, race, wealth, or social class. The New Church is unique because it describes a "Church Universal" in which anyone who regenerates and searches for God is included, regardless of which church they attend. Another major doctrine revealed in the Writings is the importance of individuals developing their loves, their understanding, and their unique use. Therefore it is essential that people should not think they are saved by faith alone but by the marriage of faith and charity, and that heaven is a society of useful angels serving each other, interdependently (AC 4663).

Downing's Theory of Feminist Identity Development

Prior to the 1970s, there were very few psychologists who payed attention to the unique psychological development of women. Carol Gilligan's (1982) identification of the moral development of girls and women as being different than males led to an entire group of researchers analyzing the similarities and differences between the genders. In 1985, secular psychologists Nancy Downing and Kristin Roush described a new model of feminist identity development:

> It is based on the premise that women who live in contemporary society must first acknowledge, then struggle with, and repeatedly work through their

feelings about the prejudice and discrimination they experience as women in order to achieve authentic and positive feminist identity. (Downing and Roush, 1985, 695)

They identified five stages through which many women progress as they evolve into the adult development of their identity. Later, other psychological researchers studied this theory more thoroughly and came to the conclusion that "the empirical literature is generally supportive of the model's general tenets and is indicative of its promise for application to practice" (Moradi, Subich and Phillips, 2002, 6). In addition, psychologists have developed assessment tools to use when measuring the developmental progress, and to confirm the validity of the theory (Fischer, et al., 2000):

We found good support for the composite instrument's internal consistency, as well as convergent, discriminant, and factorial validity in a sample that included a wide age range and non-student community residents. (Fischer et al., 2000, 15)

In other words, this theory of feminist identity has been described and tested in controlled studies, reported in peer-reviewed psychological journals, and widely applied to a variety of female populations.

Downing and Roush (1985) created a model of feminist identity development which included:

1) *Passive Acceptance* of women's subordinate role
2) *Revelation* or awareness of oppression
3) *Embeddedness* in groups of women, away from men
4) *Synthesis* of new insights and new roles in society
5) *Active Commitment* to social change for other women

"The first stage, Passive Acceptance, is characterized by an acceptance of traditional gender roles, and the belief that men are superior to women" (Fischer, et al., 2000, 15). Women in this stage are often content in their clearly defined roles, especially if there are several benefits to following the norms as defined by the men in their lives. They may also get defensive if people try to nudge them to change.

Male dominated institutions, such as the eighteenth century organized churches, had policies which kept women in certain roles. For example, the clergy burnt women as witches if they discussed spiritual insights.

According to historian Merry Wiesner (1993), both Protestant and Catholic clergy led witch hunts across Europe from the fifteenth through the eighteenth centuries. Weisner estimates that at least 100,000 women were tried and killed for religious, political, sexual, or economic reasons. Women were far more likely than men to be accused of threatening the establishment.

Many national governments had and have laws preventing women from voting or making changes to the way things are. In America, women did not gain the right to vote until 1920. Thus, for the vast majority of voiceless women who seek the approval of society it seems easier to remain passive and accept their lot in life.

According to Downing and Roush (1985) however, some women outgrow this initial stage. Due either to a jolting encounter with a gender-biased policy or sexual harassment of some kind, women may become aware that it will not do to stay passively accepting of things as they are. There is an awareness, or revelation, that women are being oppressed. This stage:

> is preceded by one or several crises that result in a questioning of traditional gender roles, feelings of anger towards men, and dualistic thinking. Women in this stage may also feel guilt over ways that they may have contributed to their own oppression in the past. (Fischer et al., 2000, 16)

It is important to understand the intense feelings and conflicts women experience in this stage. They may be deeply depressed or outwardly very angry at men. It is possible that this will lead to self-hatred or prejudice, or both, against all men. Depending on the extent of the crisis, the feelings may vary. Some women experience abuse or rape and then get blamed for it, while others may be denied promotions at work, because of gender bias. Regardless, the main characteristics of this stage are strong feelings and righteous indignation; there is no turning back to a life of passive acceptance of oppression.

Since women tend to talk to other women when they have concerns (Tannen, 1990), it is no surprise that the next evolution in the feminist identity process is for women to get together. The third stage, titled "Embeddedness" by Downing and Roush (1985), is "marked by feelings of connectedness with other women (and) cautious interaction with men" (Fischer et al., 2000, 16). This is a very common experience and it can be both positive and negative. In some ways women find comfort in realizing that they are not the only victims of abuse, rape, discrimination, harassment or belittlement. They compare notes and start to see patterns beyond their own personal experiences. There may be a tone of hatred of men or at least a sense that women don't need men and can do things on their own. They create an entirely new subculture of women free from male domination. They might need to break social ties to participate in this new social group or operate in secret. Downing and Roush call this stage a time of embeddedness because women fit themselves tightly into this new social group. Many get stuck in this stage for a very long time and are cautious about interacting with men. Sadly, it may take a long time before they trust men again.

Some women do continue to evolve to the next stage, which involves the development of a positive feminist identity. Downing and Roush call this the "Synthesis" stage. "Women in this stage are able to transcend traditional gender roles and evaluate men on an individual basis" (Fischer et al., 2000, 16). These women see that they have options and can make a conscious choice to not revert back to the traditional roles in which men make all their major decisions. These women synthesize all that they have learned from personal experience and what they have observed or learned vicariously from other women. Instead of stereotyping all men as oppressors, they now renegotiate with all the individual men in their lives: father, husband, supervisor, or son. They evaluate the oppressive behaviors, assert themselves calmly, and make their own decisions. Some women sever old ties because renegotiation seems impossible, so divorces from abusive husbands or resignations from oppressive organizations are likely to occur. Women are decisive and confident as they exercise their newly formed positive identities. They feel affirmative about being women and can face the reactions and backlashes which may occur as they change their own behaviors. They are much less fearful and angry than they were in previous stages.

For just a few women it is not enough to change their own personal relationships, they also want to change the opportunities for others as well. Downing and Roush (1985) call this the "Active Commitment" stage. Women who feel called to do so get involved in changing policies and laws which effect entire groups of people. They might write articles for public audiences, make speeches, become lawmakers, or get elected to positions of leadership in order to enact change at an institutional level. This stage is characterized by "a deep commitment to social change and the belief that men are equal to, but not the same as, women" (Fischer et al., 2000, 16). Clearly, a key manifestation of this stage is that these women are willing to speak up and become agents of social change. Mary Wollstonecraft and Julia Ward Howe are examples of such useful contribution and will later be discussed.

Moody's Theory of Spiritual Development

There are several theories of moral and spiritual development defined in the past century by American and European psychologists, theologians and philosophers. In the 1930s, Jean Piaget, the Swiss genetic epistemologist, was one of the first people to describe the early stages of the moral development of children. Following his lead, Lawrence Kohlberg described the six stages of moral development of male adolescents and adults in his landmark study of the 1960s. Kohlberg's student, Carol Gilligan, continued this line of research in her analysis of female moral development in the 1980s. Piaget, Kohlberg and Gilligan all carefully avoided mention of development of faith or spirituality, as it was not considered worth studying by secular psychologists during that era (Santrock, 1991; Gilligan, 1982).

In the 1980s an educator and theologian named James Fowler began outlining stages of faith (1981). This was one of the first non-sectarian descriptions of spiritual growth. He identified six stages which many people experience over the course of their childhood and adulthood, regardless of their particular branch of religion. This work was a major contribution to the study of the psychology of religion. However, the stages are described rather elaborately, making them difficult to remember and apply.

Since then, a philosopher and psychologist who specializes in the aging process, Harry Moody, has created a simpler theory which also includes a description of spiritual growth across the lifespan. It is this more recently defined theory that I will use as a lens for analyzing the effects of the Last Judgment on women. Moody's theory enables us to see the struggle that these women may have experienced during the times that they made a huge difference in the lives of other women.[2]

Moody describes his theory as the *Five Stages of the Soul* (1997):

1) The Call
2) The Search
3) The Struggle
4) The Breakthrough
5) The Return

Moody describes the first stage as the Call, "the first step in the pursuit of spiritual wisdom" (1997, 35). In the modern western world people have religious freedom; they can choose *not* to be religious and/or spiritual at all. For those who choose to focus less on the material world and more on their connection to God, they may sense a calling or an awakening. For some this may happen after a serious disaster or brush with death. For others it might be a quiet wondering about the meaning of life. We only know if a person has entered into this step if she chooses to tell people or write about it in a letter, autobiography or publication. It could remain a very private matter.

In the second stage, the individual will enter into a Search process. She may go to resources to ask spiritual questions and find answers. This might involve an investigation: attending churches, reading doctrinal

---

2. There are fewer published studies of the validity of this theory as compared to the research on the feminist identity theory.

books, studying the biographies of spiritually inspired people, finding tutors, or joining discussion groups.

> On a conscious level, the Search is a quest for a spiritual practice that seems right for us. On a deeper level what we are really looking for is a secret something not easily put into words but that we sense it is out there, somewhere, someplace, waiting for us, calling to us. (1997, 36)

In some church organizations, women are encouraged to pursue these inquiries on their own, but in male dominated organizations women are told to follow the priesthood and not bother with their questions. In fact, the quest may appear as a form of doubt—which seems to be the opposite of faith—and thus may be severely punished.

Those that satisfy their initial appetite about spiritual practices and doctrines may move into the next stage: the Struggle. "Like any seeker on a quest, spiritual heroes and heroines must endure trials, pass tests, and be challenged along the way" (1997, 36). In general, the Struggle stage is full of the difficulties involved in reconciling one's abstract beliefs with the daily tasks of living in this world of time and space. There may be times when life seems to have no meaning or be very disappointing. There may be failures and tremendous discouragement. There is no set length of time that a person will experience the Struggle.

Fortunately, the next stage is quite a contrast to the Struggle. Moody calls this stage the Breakthrough.

> The spiritual forces collecting inside us can no longer be held in check. A sudden surge of energy pushes things to the limit; then follows a burst of vision, and the hidden forces of the world pour into consciousness. Something is changed in us, and we are never the same. (1997, 37)

One gets amazing insights and often feels at one with the universe or part of God's Providence. It all starts to make sense.

According to Moody, some people evolve to a fifth stage called the Return. For those who reach this level of spirituality, they remain involved in everyday life but have a new, deeper level of commitment.

They find ways to serve others in humanitarian projects and social change. They are useful in a state of joyfulness. They may experience the Return by giving back to their families, neighbors, country, culture, or social group. It is not a time of self-service but of giving to others because it is a way to give back to God. Some become courageous mentors to other people who are still in their Struggling stage. In other cases, people in the stage of the Return make persuasive speeches or write compelling works which change the course of human events.

MARY WOLLSTONECRAFT

Mary Wollstonecraft (1759–1797) lived during a turbulent time. Born and raised in England, she was mostly self-educated as there were very few opportunities for females to acquire an education equal to that of men. Through the analysis of historians, she has become most well known for her published work (or essay) entitled *A Vindication of the Rights of Women* (1792). She also wrote *A Vindication of the Rights of Man* (1791), *Maria, or the Wrongs of Woman* (1798), *Original Stories from Real Life* (1788) and the *History and Moral View of the Origins and Progress of the French Revolution* (1793). Many excellent biographies have been written about Wollstonecraft. Several of them have been published in the past thirty years: Gordon (2005), Jacobs (2001), Taylor (1983), Todd (2000), Tomalin (1992), Wardle (1993).

In this essay, I will draw from primary and secondary sources and use Downing and Roush's feminist identity theory and Moody's spiritual development theory to describe and analyze Wollstonecraft's lifework.

Wollstonecraft in the Passive Acceptance Stage

It appears that Wollstonecraft spent very little time in the Passive Acceptance phase in her childhood. Her father was economically unstable, restless, and brutal to the women in his family. As most fathers of the time, he made arrangements for the education of his sons but not his daughters. However, Wollstonecraft observed the neighboring Arden family in which the intellectual father educated both genders of his offspring equally. "Mary yearned for a father like Jane Arden's" (Jacobs, 2001, 21).

She longed to join that family, be treated as worthy of an education, and have opportunities to think for herself. With her strong personality and yearning for fair treatment, Wollstonecraft moved beyond the Passive Acceptance stage as early as nine years old, in 1768.

Wollstonecraft in the Revelation Stage

Although Jane Arden chose to remain a conventionally passive girl, she was intrigued with Wollstonecraft's desire to join in her family's home-schooling projects and receive intellectual stimulation from a more interesting father.

> Jane . . . saved her letters for twenty years. They are unusual letters, a first outlet for Mary Wollstonecraft's frustrations and bold ideas. Awkward at times, always emotional, the letters to Jane are filled with observations that will be refined in her early books. (Jacobs, 2001, 31)

It appears that even before Wollstonecraft was ten years old she noticed that the genders were treated differently; she was not being encouraged by most people to read and to learn. As a daughter from a lower-middle income, English family, she had very few people to talk to who took her seriously. But whenever she could she would obtain books and try to talk to Mr. Arden, local ministers, and older brothers who would not laugh at her curious statements.

She entered the Revelation Stage when she observed her mother's economic dependency on her father. When he could not seem to focus on his vocation and invest in worthwhile endeavors, the entire family suffered—especially when he took out his frustrations by drinking and becoming violent. This outraged Wollstonecraft and she hated seeing her mother and sisters so dependent, when they could have become independent had a proper education or apprenticeship been available to them. The only avenues that seemed open to her were to do domestic service work, become a governess, or serve as a paid companion to wealthy women. Before she was twenty she had tried many of these roles and hated them all. However, whenever she could she taught herself a variety of subjects so that she might become a teacher. When her sister also became a of victim of domestic violence, Wollstonecraft rescued her from a terrible marriage. This added to Wollstonecraft's righteous indignation about the oppression of women. She hated the dependency of uneducated poor women and she had no respect for the wealthy women of leisure who spent their resources on pampering themselves and living the life of the idle rich. Wollstonecraft was angry!

> She was grappling with the great question—Who Am I?—and had an easier time deciding what she was not—not powerful, not free to choose, not loved or happy or valued at her worth. Matters improved somewhat when Mary met her new neighbor. . . . He and his friendly wife invited Mary to come study and live with them. . . . along with another girl he tutored. (Jacobs, 2001, 26)

Clearly, Wollstonecraft was in the Revelation Stage of psychological feminist identity during these adolescent and early adult years. This prepared her for the next stage of her development.

Wollstonecraft in the Embeddedness Stage

After finishing her studies at the Arden household, Wollstonecraft was thrilled to have access to her new neighbor Mr. Clare's library, which was full of philosophy, theology, and Shakespeare. One author who especially intrigued her was Jean Jacques Rousseau. Wollstonecraft had mixed feelings about his ideas of humanity, particularly because of the manner in which he described women. According to Rousseau:

> Woman lives in a more primitive and natural manner than man. She continues to dwell, at least partially, in the premoral state of savages, who could be neither good nor evil because they do not exist as social beings. (Steinbreugge, 1995)

> Women always remain children. They are incapable of seeing beyond the walls of the household . . . . woman's inability to reason like a man reveals itself in a number of ways, among them her inability to understand reasons for religious

belief. That is why every girl must take up her mother's religion and every woman her husband's. (Davis and Farge, 1993, 329)

Wollstonecraft questioned this limited view of women as social and spiritual beings, but her ideas were not yet fully formed. She also read Immanuel Kant, who viewed the genders in the following manner:

> Man must be superior to woman in physical strength and courage and woman must be superior to man in her natural faculty of submitting to man's attachment to her. By contrast, in a state that has not yet reached the level of civilization, superiority resides exclusively with the man. (Davis and Farge, 1993, 333)

While she became deeply embedded in her friendship with Fanny Blood (her fellow tutor student), she cautiously avoided romantic encounters with men. She observed how women interacted with men, but stayed closer to her best girlfriend, and they debated the true nature of women. She was clearly in the stage of Embeddedness; she retreated from suitors and formed her own feminist point of view. Fanny could organize ideas well, which helped Wollstonecraft form her intense, random outbursts of anger about male domination into coherent sentences and paragraphs. There is a marked difference between the style of her writing prior to her studies with Mr. Clare and her style afterwards. She "loved Fanny better than all the world besides" (Jacobs, 2001, 27). Fanny was reflective about what she read but Wollstonecraft was original in her insights and always wanted to assert her will. They enjoyed studying together and expanding their ideas.

Wollstonecraft in the Synthesis Stage

Beginning with her first attempts at writing for a public audience, Wollstonecraft transcended traditional gender roles and formed a positive feminist identity, synthesizing all that she had learned about female roles and reacting against both Rousseau's and Kant's portrayals of women.

During this stage, Wollstonecraft worked and socialized with men in a very productive manner.

For a woman to take up her pen in this way ... was sufficiently unusual to require
a fair degree of hubris on a woman's part; something in which Wollstonecraft
was never deficient. In her case, however, the turn toward professional writing
was also facilitated by a new circle of acquaintances. These were the Rational
Dissenters. (Taylor, 2003, 6)

By 1786, Wollstonecraft met the leader and publisher of this
group, Joseph Johnson, who appreciated talent regardless of gender.
Wollstonecraft appeared to be in the Synthesis Stage as she evaluated
Johnson and negotiated with him for her paid work in his printing
company. For many years to come, Johnson encouraged and challenged
Wollstonecraft to edit, translate, and proofread various articles before
they went to press and also to author her own work. He was a wonderful
mentor who believed in Wollstonecraft's talents.

In addition, a flock of intellectuals welcomed her into their debates
and discussions in London. Over the next three years, Wollstonecraft
interacted regularly with Thomas Paine, William Blake, Richard
Price, Joseph Priestley, Thomas Holcroft, William Godwin and Henry
Fuseli. They seemed to have no gender bias, so she felt valued and
encouraged to try out a role quite different from the ones her female
peers held. These men were involved in challenging the authority of
the churches and governments and they shared what they read and
wrote. They supported each other regardless of the reactions of the
establishments. The American Revolution had already been advanced
by Thomas Paine's pamphlet *Common Sense* (Liell, 2003, 21). A decade
later he was welcomed into this group of Dissenters and Radicals.
Wollstonecraft was inspired by his courage and clarity of his writing.

During this time, another revolution was brewing in France. Paine
and others traveled to France and were highly involved in encouraging
the people of the third estate (lowest socio-economic class) to rebel
against the authorities of the church and government. According to
historian Roger Chartier who seemed unaware of the theological
works of Swedenborg, there was a definite shift in the culture in France
in the 1750s:

After 1750 . . . a critical attitude came into being among a large segment of the population of France. Although not necessarily expressed explicitly in clear thought or organized discourse, this new attitude induced people to abandon their traditional actions, reject inculcated obedience, and perceive sources of power formerly viewed as objects of awe and reverence in a more detached, ironical, or suspicious manner. In this sense, it is legitimate to recognize an erosion of authority in the decades preceding the French Revolution as well . . . That is, it prepared people's minds for the sudden and radical collapse of an order that had already been emptied of its powers of persuasion. (Chartier, 1991, 187)

Wollstonecraft joined in these arguments and felt compelled to write *A Vindication of the Rights of Man* (1790). This was "the first in a general radical onslaught" on defenders of the aristocracy of France (Taylor, 2003, 7).

Her name was bracketed with Tom Paine's; . . . she was commended in France and America, and feted by fellow radicals in England. Conservatives blustered; professional wits sneered . . . it was a marvelous time for a feminist polemicist, and Wollstonecraft reveled in it. (Taylor, 2003, 7)

She had found her voice, her style of writing, her courage, her political framework, and a social group. Initially the people for whom she advocated were the men of the lowest social ranking in France. In 1792, however, she had a stunning awakening: it was time to advocate for her own gender.

Wollstonecraft in the Active Commitment Stage

Even in current times, only a very small percentage of women become actively involved in making changes to social systems. It was even more rare 220 years ago. But Wollstonecraft saw the power of writing and publishing as her medium for change.

Mary Wollstonecraft was the first major feminist, and *A Vindication of the Rights of Women*, written in the western tradition when the issue of the rights of man was bringing revolution to the United States, to France, and threatening to even shake the venerable English Parliament, is the feminist declaration of independence. Wollstonecraft dared to take the liberal doctrine of inalienable human rights, a doctrine which was inflaming patriots on both sides of the Atlantic, and assume these rights for her own sex. . . . She inspired passion, enthusiasm, outrage, admiration, hostility, eulogies and barely printable insults. (Miriam Brody, 2004, ix)

Wollstonecraft was probably the first woman in the modern western world to reach this level of feminist identity development, as described by Downing and Roush. She rejected the philosophers, Kant and Rousseau, for their misogyny. She was disgusted by the frivolous upper class of women she had worked for in England and saddened by the conditions of extremely poor women. She addressed her work to the middle class audience; she assumed that they could read her publications and would benefit from her proposed education reforms. But she genuinely hoped that all women would respond well if they had more legal rights, educational opportunities, and encouragement to be rational human beings. Her great contribution was created at a very young age.

In the next section, Wollstonecraft will be analyzed in terms of her spiritual growth and maturity as demonstrated in her journals and published work.

MOODY'S THEORY OF SPIRITUAL DEVELOPMENT

Moody's *The Five Stages of the Soul* (1997) describes phases that many people in the modern western world appear to experience over the course of a lifetime. The stages are: The Call, The Search, The Struggle, The Breakthrough, and The Return.

Although Wollstonecraft led a relatively short life of only thirty-eight years, it appears that she may have experienced many aspects of this spiritual progression. While most feminist biographers steer away from any mention of theology in Wollstonecraft's emerging point of view, Taylor's (2003) thorough biography of Wollstonecraft concludes that it is essential to include religion. Taylor feels that religion played a central part in Wollstonecraft's life, but that the religious aspect of Wollstonecraft's radicalism is its least explored aspect, yet it is impossible to understand her political hopes, including her hopes for women, outside a theistic framework. (Taylor, 2003, 4)

I have therefore included the theological component in this case study.

Wollstonecraft in the Call Stage

While Wollstonecraft was a young girl she was fascinated with religion, but she quickly became critical of organized religion. It is most likely that during those years of study with Mr. Clare that she learned about many different religions and philosophies and added her own insights about humane ways to treat people of all economic classes and genders, because each human being was a child of God. Wollstonecraft wrote: "For how can woman be virtuous unless freedom strengthen her reason till she comprehend her duty, and see in what manner it is connected with her real good?" (Taylor, 2003, 12) She seemed to experience the Call as a general curiosity and thirst for knowledge, even though she was discouraged by the majority of the people in her life. She started forming the idea that only if women were not dominated by men, could they become spiritually mature adults who answered to God rather than to their husbands, fathers, or priests. She longed for a more direct relationship with God and disliked the thought of being treated like a child for the rest of her life.

Wollstonecraft in the Search Stage

Admirers of Mary Wollstonecraft are often reluctant to see her as a religious thinker . . . . *A Vindication of the Rights of Woman* (1792) is generally located in the tradition of Enlightenment Humanism . . . so it is startling to find that it contains at last fifty religious themes. (Taylor, 2003, 93–94)

If we investigate the inner workings of Wollstonecraft's radicalism we see that she was deeply influenced by the nonconforming British

Protestants (called British Radicals or Dissenters) during the European Enlightenment.

Her Search was activated when she studied the theological books in the library of Mr. Clare and then fueled when she joined debates with the British Dissenters and Radicals as a young adult. One of the key people in this social group who influenced Wollstonecraft was William Blake. He read Swedenborg, joined the first organized New Church in England, debated and argued about Swedenborgian ideas, and created remarkable designs and engravings about the afterlife. Blake knew about Swedenborg's claim that the Last Judgment had occurred. As he wrote in his book *Marriage of Heaven and Hell*: "As a new heaven is begun, and it is not 33 years since its advent" (Blake, 1790, 3). The one common thread among these Radicals in London was that they wanted an end to the abuse of power among the clergy and government leaders. The Last Judgment was primarily about reordering the heavens and judging the clergy who had abused their power while they had been in the world. So we can assume that Blake and other readers felt justified in challenging corrupt authorities. They took ideas such as the one below and felt they could think about faith on their own, without the clergy as interpreters. According to Swedenborg:

> But henceforth the man [or woman] of the church will be in a more free state of thinking on matters of faith, thus on the spiritual things which relate to heaven, because spiritual freedom has been restored to him. For all things in the heavens and in the hells are now reduced into order, and all thought concerning Divine things and against the Divine inflows from thence; from the heavens all thought which is in harmony with Divine things, and from the hells all which is against Divine things. (LJ 73)

This significant change in the way people could think is reflected in the following account from an historian:

> Percolating within the minds of intellectual giants and commonfolk, were the seeds of great political, social, industrial, commercial, scientific, and artistic revolutions of the late 18th century. When these thoughts later became physical realities, such as the American and French Revolutions, they did in fact initiate

a new age of liberty by dramatically changing the institutions of the past . . . in the forms of apocalyptic events. (Bellin, 1988, 101)

As Wollstonecraft shifted her focus from advocating for the rights of the lower class in France to a declaration of the rights of all women, she formulated her theological and political position around a Christian-Platonic ideal. She wanted to see women transcend and transform from degraded objects of male tyranny to self-redeemed females worthy of God's love (Taylor, 2003, 21). She never lost her belief in God even while she challenged the corrupt clergy in both the Catholic and Protestant churches. Like Paine, she believed in God and a hereafter, but wondered about who was running the organized Christian churches on earth. When Wollstonecraft wrote the *Vindication* she called for women to get right with God.

For . . . if they be really capable of acting like rational creatures, let them not be treated like slaves; or like the brutes who are dependent on the reason of man, when they associate with him; but cultivate their minds, give them the salutary curb of principle, and let them attain conscious dignity by feeling themselves only dependent on God. (Taylor, 2003, 94)

In addition to the direct connection to Swedenborg's writings through Blake, Wollstonecraft was also greatly influenced by the theology of Dr. Richard Price and Joseph Priestley. They both interacted at Joseph Johnson's printing house and joined in lively debates on spiritual and political matters. Priestley was a clergyman and chemist who read some of Swedenborg's work and met many devoted followers of Swedenborg. While he admired the followers as good people he still was not convinced that Swedenborg actually talked to spirits (Rose, et al., 2005, 197). Dr. Price served as a minister to this radical group and urged people to reject Calvinism's doctrine of original sin and to think critically about religion (Tomalin, 1992). Future scholars might investigate more deeply the work of Dr. Price to see if he read Swedenborg's theological works, or was just indirectly influenced through Blake and Priestley about the idea of rejecting the corrupt leaders of the churches and seeking direct enlightenment from God.

Wollstonecraft in the Struggle Stage

Due to personal relationships, economic instability, and the political whirlwind of the French Revolution, Wollstonecraft experienced many struggles during the next fifteen years of her life. She had several disappointing relationships and one marriage which ended in her husband abandoning her. She adopted and bore a few children and struggled to find the time and energy to continue her writing. She even faced serious depressive episodes and attempted suicide more than once (Taylor, 2003; Jacobs, 2001).

> To Wollstonecraft, the imagination was a sacred faculty, linking the fantasizing mind to its Maker. Psychic life was the realm not of an isolated 'I' but of a yearning soul reaching towards its God. All Wollstonecraft's struggles for a larger life were framed by this credo, although at times of acute emotional conflict even the divine light occasionally dimmed and she was left floundering in darkness, bewildered and forlorn. (Taylor, 2003, 21)

Wollstonecraft in the Return Stage

Wollstonecraft was surrounded by British Dissenters who constantly debated the value of organized religion. They changed their minds repeatedly, as they read more, reflected intensely, and then sought their own inspirations. This was especially true of Blake (Raine, in Larsen, 1988). "In such an atmosphere Wollstonecraft too gave up church attendance, though she retained a tenuous but stubborn belief in God" (Tomalin, 1992, 103).

In spite of their phases of intense spiritual and political discouragement, Wollstonecraft, along with Blake, Dr. Price, Priestley, and William Godwin kept renewing their hopes for an ideal utopia. They felt their work was part of God's Providence to bring great changes to the world. They loved being part of a divinely led movement which was struggling and constantly moving towards a paradise on earth. In their discussions, speeches, sermons, and writings, they all proclaimed that the Lord was working through their efforts to bring a time of hope and renewal. In Wollstonecraft's book entitled *Mary, a Fiction*, the heroine was eagerly awaiting the great day of judgment when the Lord would reign. Wollstonecraft was optimistic that evil was passing away and a new spirit was coming forth to bring new order to the world. She wanted to see a more perfect form of government which would honor all human rights, and bring a higher state of happiness to all people, including women (Taylor, 2003).

Another piece of evidence that Wollstonecraft was familiar with Swedenborg's work is that in *Vindication of the Rights of Woman* she mentions him in a footnote. She took the position that women have the potential to develop into fully functional separate adults. However, in *Vindication,* she seems to challenge Swedenborg when she writes that leading thinkers of her day described female excellence to include "submissive charms" (Wollstonecraft, 1792, 45). Apparently, she wondered whether Swedenborg's Writings could support a woman in an egalitarian relationship, because she was certain that Rousseau's would not.

Wollstonecraft eventually married William Godwin and they corresponded whenever they were apart. In their letters, which were saved and published posthumously (Wardle, 1966) we can see that Wollstonecraft and William Godwin made every effort to have an egalitarian marriage. Apparently they knew of the ideals of conjugial love and rejected the traditional marriage model involving male domination. They shared idealistic dreams and communicated with love and mutual respect. Their married life was cut short, however when their daughter was born. Wollstonecraft became quite ill and died a few days afterwards. She was not even forty years old.

This modern theory of spiritual development outlined by Moody (1997) provides a unique lens for viewing and appreciating the life of Wollstonecraft. The deepest levels of a person's spirituality can of course never be known, but based on her written documents and letters, we can draw conclusions about the progression through stages that she seemed to experience over the course of thirty-eight years. However, it is a more robust and complete analysis when it is combined with the application of Downing and Roush's Feminist Identity Development Theory (1985). Overall, it appears that Wollstonecraft achieved a highly developed level of both spirituality and feminist identity. The final stages of both of these theories involve useful service to others: Return to God by helping others in humanitarian work (Moody, 1997) and Active Commitment to social change (Downing and Roush, 1985). Wollstonecraft's written contributions were examples of both returning to God and actively promoting social change. Her ideas have continued to enlighten and inspire others for over 210 years and have changed the course of history for women so that there might be true freedom for all. Therefore, I assert that this is one form of evidence of the effects of the Last Judgment on women: the individual efforts of people such as Wollstonecraft.

In the following section another case study will be examined, again using the two developmental theories of feminist identity and spiritual growth.

JULIA WARD HOWE (1819 – 1910)

Ward Howe in the Passive Acceptance Stage

According to Downing and Roush (1985), women who are comfortable with the social system of male leadership in family and legal affairs are still in the Passive Acceptance Stage of Feminist Identity Development. During Julia Ward Howe's childhood and adolescence in America of the early nineteenth century, she was primarily in this Passive Acceptance Stage, as she did not see any other options. Her mother died when she was only five years old so her kind but domineering father was the primary influence in her life. He made almost all the decisions about her daily schedule, her education and her social world. Fortunately, he did encourage her to obtain as much education as possible so her world was broadened through books. Around the time of her coming out into society in her late teens and early twenties, she began flirting with men and attending balls and women's discussion groups. Her father's and brother's passings left a huge hole in her world (Grant, 1994).

Ward Howe in the Revelation Stage

After her father died Ward Howe experienced a period of grief and depression. She had no parents to guide her as she figured out how to become an adult. For the next thirty years, she was in the Revelation Stage of feminist identity development. It was a slow and evolving process. Probably one of the first indications we have of her growing awareness of feminism is that she was fascinated by the Abolitionists who were fighting against slavery. She saw both male and female Quakers voicing their concerns about respect for all human beings. This left a deep impression on her. She saw women making concerted efforts to instigate social change. She often wondered if she could be more active in these great causes. She dreamed of a literary career and tried to write poems and essays on issues of national and theological concern. She longed to be involved and felt confined by the rules that the men in her life had imposed upon her.

She married Samuel Howe (knick-named Chev) whom she had met in the Abolitionist group and who was a director of an agency for the blind. They raised a large family. Over the years, Chev Howe restricted her power to manage her own inheritance or earnings from published works. She also had no choice in where they would live. He often bought and sold houses without her consent. He discouraged her from writing and speaking outside the home, and she wondered if she would ever be able to use her linguistic skills to their fullest extent.

> Chev had internalized the view of womanhood that had emerged in the first few decades of the nineteenth century in New England. He wanted not only a self-denying wife but a creature of domestic perfection who would maintain a serene and happy home far from the perplexing and alienating world of work. Howe, on the other hand, entertained no such notions. She clung to a much broader view of her role. After all, just as this view of women's work was taking hold, she had been growing up without a mother. Howe had no examples for this role. Besides, New York society was not like that of New England . . . as they emulated the ideal of the leisured aristocrat more than that of the domestic matron. . . . These conflicts were like buckets of cold water on Howe's flickering hopes for a happy marriage. (Grant, 1994, 71)

Ward Howe found great respite and relief in reading Swedenborg during these decades of raising the family. She enjoyed her babies, but became overwhelmed with raising so many children without help from her husband or extended family. By midlife, she stopped looking to Chev Howe for emotional support, especially when she learned of his infidelity. This cut deeply into her hopes and she realized she could not depend on him to make her happy. She had to search inward in her theological studies and outward by publishing her writing to feel fulfilled. She still did not have a strong circle of female friends, so she was very lonely.

Ward Howe in the Embeddedness Stage

Ward Howe noticed that throughout her own childhood, and now during her marriage, her family was kept apart from most people so she had rarely experienced the joy of close girlfriends. After the Civil War, her children gradually moved away to start their own lives, and she decided that even if Chev Howe disagreed she wanted to become involved with activities outside the home. She noticed that people who used to be involved in Abolition work were now seeking civil rights for women.

It was a major step in her life to now shift from a private domestic world to a very public life fighting for an international cause. When she was nearly fifty years old, she discovered for the first time the delights of working with groups of other women. Embeddedness was now extremely important to her and no men stood in her way (Grant, 1994). Chev Howe was about eighteen years older than her and so it is not surprising that he passed away around this time, due to illness. Although she missed some aspects of raising a family, she was eager for the chance to redesign her own life. So she committed herself to joining women's groups all over the country.

One of her published poems had previously made her name quite well known, especially when it was set to a familiar tune. Ward Howe wrote the *Battle Hymn of the Republic* (see the next section for an analysis of this poem). When she was invited to come to the front platform at a national meeting for women's suffrage, she was exhilarated. People knew who she was! Based on all her private studies of spirituality, she made speeches that had a philosophy that rang true. Audiences welcomed her inspiring leadership and readily joined the organizations dedicated to women's right to vote and to receive better education. Ward Howe was now embedded in her new close female friendships, no doubt heightened by the fact that she had not had that social connection for her first fifty years of life (Grant, 1994).

Ward Howe in the Synthesis Stage

Ward Howe now felt that she could synthesize her religious philosophy with her longing to help women make political advances. Ward Howe's philosophical studies and writing allowed her to refine her thoughts, to expand her mental vocabulary of images and paradigms, and to fold in the religious feeling that had always been a part of her interior life (Grant, 1994). Because she was so articulate, she gained confidence and this enabled her to interact with powerful men, even if they disagreed with her. She had a very positive feminist identity because she knew that suffrage would not only improve women's daily lives, but also help them develop their full spiritual and moral capacity (Grant, 1994). She was not angry at men for being domineering, so she could stay calm as she voiced her concerns in speeches to legislators. She just simply knew that it was time for a change, because too many women could not fully develop if they were not legally treated like adults.

Ward Howe in the Active Commitment Stage

Ward Howe spent the next thirty-five to forty years actively involved in promoting the women's movement. She was inspired by the concept from Swedenborg that every human being deserves to be free and to feel life as one's own (DP 129). She loved the ideals about the marriage of good and truth, which were reflected in the healthy marriage between a man and a woman. She rejected Calvinist ideas about men acting as the head of the married couple. Also, she loved the Swedenborgian concept of applied religion manifesting as a life of useful service to others (DP 26). Ward Howe felt that:

> Religious ideas showed their true value in their practical applications. Were they useful? Could they advance society along the paths of improvement? The message she had received from Swedenborg she was now ready to proclaim herself. (Grant, 1994, 191)

Now that she had raised her children and her husband was gone, she turned all her attention to influencing lawmakers about women's rights to vote, own property, and be educated. While she set aside her previous materialistic fascination with fancy clothing, she was still welcomed into many of the most fashionable homes. But her role was to urge the women to join clubs and associations that promoted the right to vote. She became the president of the American Woman's Suffrage Association and founded their periodical, the *Woman's Journal*, in 1870. Later she became the president of the New England Women's Club and the Association for the Advancement of Women. In 1893, she became the first president of the Massachusetts Federation of Women's Clubs and then the leader of the General Federation of Women's Clubs.

> Hers was a significant contribution to the rhetoric of that movement. By holding up a vision of women as independent moral agents; she made feminism accessible to middle class women. (Grant, 1994, 192)

Clearly she was a role model for hundreds of other women as she tirelessly worked to change the social and political culture in the United States. Whenever she spoke she made great efforts to inspire people at a moral and spiritual level, and never promoting a specific religion. She always hoped that by liberating women from their confined roles that then they would be able to evolve and fulfill their potential as ethical human beings. "From Swedenborg she had derived the idea of divine inspiration as the source of all moral action" (Grant, 1994, 176). She joined with the other suffrage leaders who cast the vision of women becoming full members of society. Together they wrote:

Declaration of the rights of women: We propose, as the basis of our discussion and subsequent action, the equality of the sexes before God; and the rights of the individual as set forth in the ever-memorable words of the Declaration of Independence: We hold it as self-evident truth also that these principles, applied to women, must produce the best results and that such application is necessary to the normal development of society. (Grant, 1994, 194)

In 1908, only years before she died, Ward Howe was honored by being the very first woman to be elected into the American Academy of Arts and Letters.

Historian, Carol Hymowitz (1978) describes a debate about the effectiveness of the social groups led and organized by Ward Howe and others; the groups were "one of the most important sociological phenomena of the 20th century" (Hymowitz, 1978, 222). Many of the women joined to have social connection, and as their aims were diverse, the goal of suffrage became confused. Hymowitz claims that the "women's clubs did little to advance the cause of women's equality" (1978, 223). Perhaps this explains why it took so many decades to win the right to vote. In recent, western history, women had no experience mobilizing large groups toward a goal: this was their first attempt. Ward Howe was instrumental in reconnecting the various subdivisions of the suffrage movement and helping them become more focused.

Although Ward Howe's theological position has been briefly mentioned in this analysis of her feminist identity, the next section will employ Moody's psychological theory to address her spiritual development.

JULIA WARD HOWE: PSYCHOLOGICAL ANALYSIS IN TERMS OF SPIRITUAL DEVELOPMENT

Ward Howe became active in helping women approximately a century later than Wollstonecraft. However, there are some parallels to draw as we analyze her life through the psychological lens of Moody's theory of spiritual development. As mentioned earlier, the five stages outlined by Moody are: The Call, The Search, The Struggle, The Breakthrough, The Return.

Ward Howe in the Call Stage

Recall that Ward Howe was born in 1819 in New York City to an upper middle class family and that her mother died when she was only five. As an adolescent, Ward Howe was raised by her father, Samuel. He was a protective and worried single parent looking after half a dozen children. We know from Ward Howe's letters and journals that she was an impressionable and sensitive youth. As her father became quite authoritarian and concerned about proper behavior he often restricted her social life. His constant correction of Ward Howe caused her to become intensely worried about conforming to his expectations. However, she felt pulled to the attentions of adoring suitors and longed to be set free from her father's oppressive household.

As a wealthy woman she had much leisure time at home. When she was not permitted to leave the house she devoted her time to her growing interest in theology. Her father approved of this attention to religious studies, although he narrowed his own personal focus to evangelical doctrines. Regarding Ward Howe:

> Religious questions interested her at an early age . . . the difficult ones of her father's orthodoxy, which combined the ideas of conservative Congregationalism with the practices of low-church Episcopalianism. Concern about damnation and salvation sharpened the edges of Howe's sensitivity. Combined with long years of intermediate status, and with her natural emotional intensity, these questions helped precipitate a serious crisis in Howe's life when she was in her early twenties. (Grant, 1994, 30)

Using Moody's theory, we can interpret this as her Call to start a spiritual inquiry. Although Samuel Ward Howe was strict in correcting Ward Howe's social behavior, he was quite liberal in providing a broad education for her. Her formal education ended at age sixteen. When she showed little interest in learning domestic duties proper to a young lady, Ward Howe's father paid for tutors. She studied French, Greek, Latin, Italian, piano, singing and dancing, but learning German opened up a new world of literature and philosophy for her. Ward Howe said: "I derived from the studies a sense of intellectual freedom so new to me that it was half delightful, half alarming" (Grant, 1994, 35). This time period of joyful research with books and tutors helped her establish her lifelong routine of reflecting on spiritual questions and then reading intensely to find answers.

Ward Howe in the Search Stage

According to Moody, an individual will enter into an intense search process during their spiritual development. The person may go to books and resources, ask people spiritual questions, attend churches, read various doctrines, and sort through various theologies and reflect on them. During the 1800s, most females relied on men to address theological issues.

Ward Howe was mostly isolated from other young people and she had the time to pursue intellectual interests if she chose. Fortunately, her family somewhat supported this quest, even if the rest of New York society did not considerate it appropriate.

> Julia determined to begin her studies on her own in good earnest. These studies gave her a way to occupy her time since she was so rarely allowed out of the family circle. They also gave her the opportunity to cultivate her considerable intellectual gifts . . . She buckled down to a daily routine of morning study . . . Since she was by nature unsystematic, and she wished to be efficient and orderly in her studies, Howe asked her sisters to tie her in her chair when she began her daily stint. Only they could unloose her when the hours appointed for study were over. (Grant, 1994, 36)

This humorous picture illustrates the amazing self-discipline Ward Howe imposed upon herself during her adolescence and young adulthood. Her father did not always bother to find out exactly what she was reading, but her siblings thought she was rather peculiar to spend so much time with her books.

> It seemed odd to them that a wealthy young woman would devote so much time to study. Yet Howe's inclination had a certain logic. The study of mathematics,

Latin and philosophy was generally reserved for males. As such, it was a badge of male rationality and intellectual fitness. Furthermore . . . study had been the avenue toward success and public stature. If study had worked for the men in her family, then, Howe hoped, it might serve as the "open sesame" for her. With this training and background, she would be able to not only produce the great work so dear to her heart, but also to have it accepted and recognized by other great minds as an achievement of substantial merit. (Grant, 1994, 37)

Although Ward Howe was not the first woman to piece together her own education, she was certainly rare among the socially elite families in New York City. Eventually she found a network of learners and mentors. They read books and wrote essays. They exchanged their essays, and asked for comments. Although speaking in large public settings was considered a social taboo and was actually illegal for women, there were parlor discussions starting up in Boston, and Ward Howe longed to be part of these groups. "For all these women and for Julia Ward, their education was a triumph over the discriminatory approach to women's education in vogue" (Grant, 1994, 38). Some of the most important influences on Ward Howe's young adult life were the female readers of Swedenborg in the Boston area.

Julia mingled with Boston's literati, including such intellectual women as Elizabeth Palmer Peabody, Fanny Appleton, Margaret Fuller, and Annie Fields. Howe found the literary salons of the Hub a welcome relief from the parlors of New York. She described them as a circle of society composed of warm-hearted, intelligent people, not cold, carping critics, people who are disposed to make the best of you, who have sense enough to perceive your good qualities and charity enough to overlook your faults. . . . Fuller was dedicated to helping women polish their strengths and overcome their limitations by developing their powers of analysis and criticism. All who recalled her remembered the kindness she displayed toward other women on these occasions. (Grant, 1994, 48)

In order to appreciate the importance of Ward Howe's contact with Margaret Fuller, a brief description of her will be included here.

Fuller's approach was instrumental in shaping the lives of several women during the Transcendental period of American culture. Recently, historian Deborah Felder wrote a book about the one hundred most influential women of *all* time (Felder, 2001); Fuller was included in her list. In addition, a biographer, Susan Cheever (2006), recently described Fuller's profound influence on Ward Howe and other women:

> Fuller's work and her life were so affecting because she was dedicated to a revolution on behalf of women in society. Her personal antislavery campaign was supported by her actions and the way she lived her own life, with what was then a shocking degree of independence for a woman. She made her living giving 'conversations' at a time when it was illegal for a woman to do public speaking for pay. . . . She took the kind of jobs that only men had before her. (Cheever, 2006, 55)

Fuller worked along with Ralph Waldo Emerson (a devoted reader of Swedenborg) and Bronson Alcott publishing journals and teaching in progressive schools in order to promote Transcendental ideas. When we analyze the unique concepts that Margaret Fuller expressed during her short life of forty years, we uncover key ideas derived from Swedenborg's works. According to the New Church author, Susan Flagg Poole:

> The nineteenth century women were inspired by Swedenborg's writing because of the value he placed on the qualities of love and understanding in both genders. Traditionally, the idea of woman as a creator of ideas and a problem-solver had not been valued equally to her role as a nurturer. (Poole, 1999, xxi)

Fuller was particularly astute in her description of the effect that Swedenborg's writings had on women in the eighteenth century. "His idea of women is sufficiently large and noble enough to interpose no obstacle to her progress" (Fuller, 1994, 297). In addition, Fuller felt that Swedenborg's works should be praised "for understanding the need for women's fulfillment" (Rendell, 1984, 282).

Fuller was also influenced by the legendary Wollstonecraft and admired her tremendously for her approach to marriage.

> Fuller thought that when equality entered into the partnership [of marriage] then a progressive improvement could be traced, from the practical egalitarian partnership of the good provider and capital housekeeper, to those couples

who in intellectual and religious terms were able to share a common faith and a
common purpose and aspirations towards a true freedom. Mary Wollstonecraft
and William Godwin (and other couples) all presented true examples of an
intellectual partnership. In such partnerships, Fuller does not suggest that the
precise division of labor is of importance. It is the freedom to choose and to
speak that is essential. (Rendell, 1984, 282)

Fuller effectively lived her own religion by treating these aspiring
women in her parlor discussions as full adults with the ability to think
on their own. Elizabeth Palmer Peabody established a "foreign"
bookstore in Boston with a parlor-type room for Fuller to lead these
"conversation" or discussions, for pay. Swedenborgian ideas were
thoroughly discussed, along with other theologies, amongst these
women in this semi-public setting. This was a revolutionary step
in American culture and it had a profound effect on Ward Howe.
Here she could ask her theological questions and be appreciated and
encouraged. She felt no criticism because she was treated as a fully
functioning adult: she could develop her "understanding" side, along
with her "loving" side, and strive to be a complete human being, as
described by Swedenborg.

In Ward Howe's young adulthood, her father and favorite brother
both died. Although this led to serious grief and depression, an outcome
of her recovery from this loss was realization that her strong mental
faculties made her resilient. She was not totally dependent on the men
in her life to develop herself spiritually. She was starting to feel her
own independence.

Although she had a high self-efficacy regarding her intellectual
competency, her knowledge that she lacked skills in the practical
activities of home management distressed her. So, modeling herself
after Margaret Fuller, she boldly started to imagine a career outside
the home setting, which was almost unheard of at the time. She was
not sure her suitors would welcome this notion, so she continued her
private studies and wondered about her future.

One of the advantages of reading primary sources during her
studies was that Ward Howe could sharpen her comprehension and
critical thinking skills outside of the conservative dogma present in

the colleges and churches. Her confidence in her own mental powers was liberating. Now that she was gaining competence in her ability to understand abstract ideas, she longed for a career as a writer in which she could share her thoughts with others. She wanted to be a woman who was understanding, loving *and* useful in the public domain. She saw many difficulties in the world and wanted to make a difference through her written work.

Although Ward Howe had been socially restricted by her father, she did miss him. She recalled that her father consistently communicated a powerful message to Ward Howe and her siblings: he felt people should take responsibility for their own lives and shape their own destiny. Ward Howe observed this behavior in her father, and even after his death, she was strongly influenced by his approach to life. He had also felt that a learned man should take a leadership role in society, and although it was atypical for women to seek leadership roles, Ward Howe spent the next half a century figuring out how to be useful to her generation. It was not a smooth journey.

Ward Howe in the Struggle Stage

Moody describes this third stage of spiritual development as a challenging time. "Like any seeker on a quest, spiritual heroes and heroines must endure trials, pass tests, and be challenged along the way" (Moody, 1997, 36). This is a time of reconciling one's inner yearning for spiritual growth with the daily struggles of life. People in this stage may go through times of doubt and despair, and their faith may be in question. The inner struggle may be the result of a variety of types of difficulties: economic, political, theological, social, medical, or marital. Regardless of the specific details, Moody claims that there is a common psychological theme running through these experiences, when individuals address questions about their relationship with God during the turmoil.

Ward Howe's struggle began with most of the people in her social world telling her that women should not be intellectual or speak in public. On the one hand, "Fuller had even gone so far as to say that

Ward Howe showed a capacity for genius. . . . with genuine inspiration
. . . and urged her to publish her poetry. Here was reassurance indeed"
(Grant, 1994, 50). However, as most of Ward Howe's other friends and
relatives were not so encouraging, she struggled with mixed messages
about how to use her linguistic gifts. With the exception of Margaret
Fuller and other Transcendentalists and Abolitionists, most people told
Ward Howe to be quiet.

Ward Howe held out hope that if she could establish her own
home, she could have a haven in which she could study theology and
discuss important topics with a few sympathetic friends. She opened
herself up to the possibility of getting married in order to make this
dream become a reality. She met a fellow Abolitionist named Samuel
Gridley Howe, knick-named Chev Howe. He seemed so much like her
deceased father: his height, his first name and his confident posture.
She fell in love. Chev Howe was eighteen years older than her and felt
almost like a father figure to her. As they both agreed on the key issues
of ending slavery and employing the disabled, she hoped he would
be like-minded in other liberal areas. But this was not to be the case.
He took a paternal attitude to Ward Howe and called her "the child."
At first, this nickname felt loving and familiar because she missed her
father. But from the time they married in 1843 until he died in 1876, he
undermined every effort she made to speak her mind. He never treated
her like an adult, much less an inspired individual ready to influence
thousands of people. Although Ward Howe had heard from Margaret
Fuller about Wollstonecraft's egalitarian marriage to William Godwin,
this ideal seemed impossible in Ward Howe's marriage.

Ward Howe's particular struggle was on several fronts. She never
developed the usual home-making skills, so she felt incompetent in the
traditional roles of wife and mother. Her husband was domineering
and demanding and he constantly criticized her for this flaw. He did not
encourage her to pursue interests outside the home and did not want
her to have a national reputation as an author or leader.

The Howes loved their six children and raised five to adulthood in
spite of frequent moves, Chev Howe's extra-marital affairs, and their
unstable family economics. Ward Howe yearned for the opportunity to

continue her studies and her writing in the midst of heavy family duties. She was separated most of the time from her network of freethinking friends in Boston, so encouragement was sparse, but she remembered the affirming words of Margaret Fuller. Raising many children made it difficult to find time, but whenever she could she studied and wrote many essays and poems. She was determined to "write some great work or works which myself should leave to the world" (Grant, 1994, 37).

Ward Howe is most well known for authoring the lyrics of the beloved song *The Battle Hymn of the Republic* during the Civil War (Grant, 1994). She wrote the lyrics while she and her family were in Washington DC witnessing the war. Ward Howe was only paid $5.00 for this inspiring work, but upon its publication the song made her instantly famous. The words were set to the well-known tune about the rebel, John Brown, and the ballad was sung repeatedly in churches across the north.

THE BATTLE HYMN OF THE REPUBLIC

Mine eyes have seen the glory of the coming of the Lord
He is trampling through the winepress where the grapes of wrath are stored
He hath loosed the fateful lightnings of his terrible swift sword
His truth is marching on

I have seen him in the watchfires of a hundred circling camps
They have builded him an altar in the evening dews and damps
I can read his righteous sentence by the dim and flaring lamps
His day is marching on

I have read a burning Gospel writ in fiery rows of steel
As ye deal with my contemners, so with you my grace shall deal
Let the hero, born of woman, crush the serpent with his heel
Our God is marching on

He has sounded out the trumpet that shall never call retreat
He has waked the earth's dull bosom with a high ecstatic beat
Oh! Be swift my soul to answer his, be jubilant my feet
Our God is marching on

In the whiteness of the lilies he was born across the sea
With a glory in his bosom that shines out on you and me
As he died to make men holy, let us die to make men free
Our God is marching on

He is coming like the glory of the morning on the wave
He is wisdom to the mighty, he is banner to the brave
So the world shall be his footrest and the soul of his stave
Our God is marching on.

As one commentator has written:

Howe was able to draw on images and ideas about the war that had been circulating through the press but had not yet been fully confronted. New England intellectuals of the period such as Henry James, Sr. [a Swedenborgian] . . . were all sounding similar notes of religion, violence, justice and retribution. They believed that divine energy informed the course of events and transformed ordinary individuals into instruments of God's will. . . . Howe's genius lay not so much in creating the elements of the *Battle Hymn* but in fusing them together.

. . . the poem is a powerful assertion about the war. It demonstrates that Howe had not merely heard all the rhetoric, but had internalized it. . . . Howe was able to make the meaning of the war crystal clear. (Grant, 1994, 137–138)

Fame was a mixed blessing. Ward Howe's name became well known across the country and she was introduced to people in the most prominent social circles when she went to public events. Her husband resented and sabotaged these connections whenever he could.

Ward Howe continued to read Swedenborgian works about eternal marriage and being useful to society, in order to try to find some comfort in her struggle. This led her away from Calvinism and other religious organizations and towards a spiritual way of life that made sense to her.

Howe admitted that she had been bitterly and dreadfully unhappy at times during her marriage and vast and painful longings of [her] soul lay unsatisfied. Nevertheless, she hoped to cultivate a spirit of humility, of gratitude, and the love of uses upon which . . . Swedenborg so insists. By focusing on duty and action, Howe believed she could overcome ill feeling (Grant, 1994, 88–89).

[Swedenborg's] work was increasingly associated with social and religious radicalism. . . . Much of his theory, however, fit into her growing framework of belief. Swedenborg believed in a benign deity, as she did; he saw redemption as a gradual process available to all prospective individuals, as did she. His reformulation of the doctrine of the Fall as an expression of self-love and pride, rather than as total sinfulness, made sense to her. She also appreciated Swedenborg's perceptions of religion as part of one's total life, not merely a set of special obligations practiced at certain times. Like others of her generation, including the senior Henry James, she welcomed the departure from the doctrines of her Calvinist childhood. (Grant, 1994, 117–118)

Ward Howe was very serious about the Old Testament statement that people should listen to the still small voice of God. She quietly paid attention to that voice and she was strengthened from within. As a result, she stayed married to Chev Howe but grew in the confidence that she could study, reflect, think for herself, and receive courage from her direct enlightenment through God's revelations. Her happiness did not completely depend on Chev Howe's opinion of her spiritual quest or her yearning to express herself in poetry and published articles. Ward Howe proclaimed:

> "the inner voice . . . has bidden me to do the greatest thing I could do, to rise to the greatest height I could attain. . . . Thanks to the guidance of Swedenborg" . . . In the early 1850s, Howe had no doubt . . . that the sound was divinely inspired and that she should obey it. (Grant, 1994, 119–121)

During her daily struggles at home, she not only received inspiration from the Old Testament and the theological writings of Swedenborg, but also the New Testament. She viewed Jesus as a courageous and determined being whom she longed to emulate.

> If Howe was going to free herself from Chev's domination and society's expectations, she could only do so by determination—the will to seek the right and to do it. Will was a powerful agent of accomplishment; it meant determination and persistence to Howe. Howe's changed view of the will matched her changed view of Jesus. From Swedenborg, she had derived the idea of divine inspiration as the source of all moral action, and she believed that Jesus's choices in life were the result of God's direction. Now Howe saw the role of the will in Jesus's life, for it had taken a strong will to carry out the divine instructions. Howe saw Jesus as a role model, as the one who chose a difficult path on purpose. . . . By extension, she could regard her own will as a beneficent and not a selfish force. For a daughter of orthodoxy and the wife of a domineering man like Chev, this was an important breakthrough. (Grant, 1994, 176)

Ward Howe in the Breakthrough Stage

Moody states that not every adult experiences a spiritual and psychological breakthrough after a long struggle. Many remain in turmoil and confusion their entire earthly lives. For those that do resolve many of their issues, there is a significant change in the quality of their journey.

> The spiritual forces collecting inside us can no longer be held in check. A sudden surge of energy pushes things to the limit; then follows a burst of vision, and the hidden forces of the world pour into consciousness. Something is changed in us, and we are never the same. (Moody, 1997, 37)

To illustrate how unusual this breakthrough experience is for people, compare Ward Howe's life to that of the twentieth century nun, Mother Teresa. Currently there is a great deal of focus on Mother Teresa, who worked for decades serving the poorest people in India. Apparently, however she privately struggled for over fifty years in a crisis of faith, longing to feel God's love and to see meaning in her life. She wrote about her challenges in journals and letters, which have only recently come to the public's eye through publication. The letters of Mother Teresa give us a glimpse into the psychological and spiritual struggle of this person, one of the most amazing women ever known. As David van Biema wrote of Mother Teresa:

> Everything she's experiencing . . . is what average believers experience in their spiritual lives writ large. . . . scores of people have felt abandoned by God and had doubts about God's existence. . . . Who would have thought that the person who was considered the most faithful woman in the world struggled like that with her faith? (van Biema, 2007, 43)

Using Moody's terminology, we could conclude that Mother Teresa never left the stage of Struggle and experienced the stage of Breakthrough that could bring her peace. On the other hand, there is plenty of evidence to support the view that she did achieve a breakthrough and had progressed to the return stage. Perhaps these stages are not mutually exclusive and people may fluctuate between them.

In Ward Howe's life, some major events happened at both personal and national levels that facilitated her Breakthrough. As she resolved spiritual issues in her own mind she gained the confidence and determination needed to be an inspired leader.

In the decade after the Civil War, many civil rights activists turned their attention from the needs of slaves to the rights of women. Both groups needed courageous leaders to help them change laws, policies, and social customs. Abolitionists such as Sarah and Angelina Grimke became Suffragettes, and Ward Howe joined them in turning the tide. While the Grimke sisters are most noted for being former slaveholders who became Quaker Abolitionists, their major contribution to the women's movement was that they were the first women to effectively speak in public to large American audiences and legislative bodies (Perry, 2001). Their breaking out of that social norm paved the way for Susan B. Anthony, Elizabeth Cady Stanton, Julia Ward Howe, and others who rose up and spoke on behalf of women's political, educational, and economic rights.

In the same decade after the Civil War, Ward Howe's family life changed dramatically. Her children all reached independence and her husband Chev Howe died. She was alone. The demands on her time completely shifted. Although there was a period of grieving for the loss of her roles of wife and mother, Ward Howe readily embraced the chance to be more useful outside the domestic sphere. She wrote in her journal:

> In an unexpected hour a new light came to me, showing me a world of thought and of character quite beyond the limits within which I had hitherto been content to abide. The new domain made clear to me was that of the true womanhood. Melancholy gave way to relief. (Grant, 1994, 198)

> [Others wrote about her saying that] from the moment she came forward in the woman suffrage movement . . . there was a visible change [in Ward Howe]; it gave her a brightness to her face, a new cordiality in her manner, made her calmer, firmer; she found herself among new friends, and could disregard old critics. (Grant, 1994, 198)

Ward Howe diligently helped to organize the first convention of the American Woman Suffrage Association where she was called to the platform, and in reference to her fame as the author of the well-known *Battle Hymn of the Republic*, was introduced as the prophetess of the suffrage movement. Because she longed for all women to become fully moral and spiritual human beings, she was ready to fight for their economic and political rights as a means to that end. In her speech to the convention, she outlined many complaints of women in her generation:

> the partial laws, the unequal judgments, the inferiority of education, the inequality in the distribution of labor, and the greater inequality in the distribution of

wages. We know that one half of the human race has hitherto been negatived by the other half . . . [Suffrage would] at once place woman on the footing of a noble and conceded equality with man. It would open to her at once the avenues of thought and action, of art, of culture, of educational and political efficiency. It would do this in justice to individuals, and to society which they compose . . . suffrage would grant to women the freedom of action and decision that would allow them to be fully moral beings . . . And we, the representatives of women, rise up, and appeal back to the bond of Christian brotherhood, which allows no human being to oppress another. We say, Christian men and women, the present way of the world has been hitherto held to be the right way, but it is the wrong way. In debarring conscience from her final action, you debar her from her final exercise. If I, a woman, may not do what I think most virtuous, useful and honorable, without deference to usage and prescription, neither may I think it. Others must think it for me, and I must be content to adopt their errors for my intuitions, and to take their abuses in place of my uses. (Grant, 1994, 199)

The concepts at the heart of her persuasive speech were that women needed to vote and receive a full education. She knew that more political and economic freedom could lead to more moral and spiritual freedom. Ward Howe knew that if a woman:

could not see the choices then she could not exercise her conscience to the fullest. Unless women could see, face, and grapple with moral choices themselves, they were lesser human beings. Suffrage thereby [becomes] not merely a question of justice or improving woman's daily lot, but of recognizing her full moral capacity. (Grant, 1994, 200)

Ward Howe was not the only reader of Swedenborg who saw the connection between theology and the social changes happening in the modern western world. According to Ralph Waldo Emerson, the doctrines of Swedenborg were one of the two most profound influences in changing the world for women. He gave an important speech about women's suffrage, before the Civil War, in which he predicted that the spread of Swedenborg's new revelation about men and women could have a huge impact.

I think another important step [towards achieving women's rights] was made by the doctrine of Swedenborg, a sublime genius who gave a scientific exposition of the part played by man and woman in the world, and showed the difference of sex to run through nature and through thought. Of all the Christian sects, this is at this moment the most vital. (Agonita, 1977, 215)

Emerson sensed that change was coming but he did not know who would be the instruments of this revolution. Clearly, Julia Ward Howe emerged as one of the public voices for this key religious influence. Her efforts helped to transform the ancient view of woman as an under-developed human or men's property, to the new concept of woman as a fully functioning moral and spiritual adult.

Ward Howe in the Return Stage

Not everyone has the determination to enter into the Return Stage of spiritual development. Moody posits that the people who reach this advanced stage of spiritual growth reach a deeper level of spirituality and return their gifts to humanity by serving in their neighborhood or family. These people tend to be serene as they joyously serve others.

It is probably just a fraction of these spiritually mature people who have the courage to also become major change agents, and attempt to improve the lives of a nation of citizens. Ward Howe was one of these people.

Julia Ward Howe had not always been dedicated to improving the status of women. She began her career at the age of 49, after a sheltered adolescence, and 25 years of domestic life . . . To many, then it seemed peculiar that Howe was selected, in November 1868, as the first President of the newly formed New England Woman Suffrage Association. . . . She brought thousands of women to the cause because she knew how to talk to them out of her—and their—experience. Loneliness, isolation, depression, and a lack of an outlet for talents were frequently women's lot. Howe knew this well, and she devoted the last 40 years of her life to its remedy. . . . If the pursuit of philosophy and religion reinforced the private dimensions of Howe's existence, they also nourished her self-esteem and her ability to think, judge and operate independently. Moreover, the fruit of all this study would become the core of Howe's feminist theory. She came to believe in the primacy of individual conscience, the absolute necessity for free action of individual moral will, and the role of both sexes in advancing human progress. (Grant, 1994, 3)

Ward Howe appears to have evolved through all five of Moody's stages of spiritual development. During her lonely adolescence, she responded to the call by pondering issues. Her curiosity about theological questions led her to serious study to find answers. Through her Search, she discovered the theological writings of Swedenborg. The ideas there opened her eyes to a loving God who valued people of all races and both genders. She learned about the gradual process of regeneration in contrast to the Protestant doctrine of instant salvation. She yearned to develop her own will and understanding and to perform new uses. She was inspired to face her Struggles and serve others. During her Breakthrough, it became absolutely clear that she could directly listen to God's still small voice, without reliance on male clergy or relatives. She experienced the Return by using her skills in writing, leading, and speaking in the woman's suffrage movement. Although she died several years before women gained the right to vote in America, she was a catalyst in the work to gain that right. In the last forty years of her life she served as the organizer and president of countless women's groups and associations. She published hundreds of articles in national periodicals and for four decades annually, formally addressed legislative bodies. She started the international event called Mother's Day for Peace, in order to honor women who cared about peace in the world. Ward Howe helped other women find their strength in groups and coached them to find their own voices so that they could obtain legal and economic rights, as full citizens of their country/ nation.

COMPARISON OF MARY WOLLSTONECRAFT AND JULIA WARD HOWE

Wollstonecraft and Ward Howe were both major contributors to the advancement of women in the modern western world. There were some similarities and differences in their lives that are worth noting. Some similarities:

Both were deprived of the formal education provided to their brothers, but arranged their own home studies in spite of the social norms restricting the education of women. Both mastered several languages and deeply studied philosophy, politics, and theology.

Both had literary careers which they combined with family responsibilities, including raising children.

Both retained a strong belief in God, yet distanced themselves from organized religions because of the male clergy's domineering attitudes and limited social activism. Neither were active members of Swedenborgian societies.

Both learned of Swedenborgian ideas from liberal minded peers.

Both faced disapproving backlash when they were outspoken, but were not deterred from their missions.

Both based their feminist declaration of political and educational rights on theological ideals, derived from Swedenborgian doctrines.

Both worked for decades to inspire others towards social change, and publicly challenged governments that oppressed women.

Both lived during a major war that had a huge impact on their lives. Wollstonecraft lived during the French Revolution and witnessed it firsthand in the streets of Paris, writing about the enormous social changes in the *History and Moral View of the Origins and Progress of the French Revolution* (1793). Ward Howe lived during the American Civil War, and was directly exposed to the atrocities of war near Washington DC. As a result she wrote the *Battle Hymn of the Republic* and started the first International Mother's Day for Peace event.

Some differences:

Wollstonecraft's most significant contribution to the women's movement was done in a solitary manner through her *Vindication of the Rights of Woman*. Ward Howe's greatest achievement was her inspiring leadership of groups of women.

Wollstonecraft's feminist identity development progressed more quickly than that of Ward Howe. As a result Wollstonecraft's stages of Embeddedness and Synthesis occurred during her adolescence and young adulthood. In contrast, Ward Howe's stages of Embeddedness and Synthesis did not happen until she was nearly fifty years old. It is possible that Wollstonecraft's feminism started earlier as it was triggered by the brutality of her male relatives. Ward Howe's father was strict but not abusive.

Regarding their spiritual maturity, Wollstonecraft's Struggle stage appears to have occurred after she wrote the *Vindication,* and lasted less than a decade. Ward Howe's Struggle stage lasted for nearly thirty years and occurred before her work as a leader of women's organizations.

Wollstonecraft never quoted Swedenborg's Writings directly. Ward Howe did repeatedly.

Wollstonecraft pushed for equality in her personal relationships with men and established it among British Radicals such as William Blake and more particularly in her marriage with William Godwin. Ward Howe learned of Wollstonecraft's intellectual and spiritual relationship through Margaret Fuller. Unfortunately, Ward Howe never experienced equality in her own relationships with her brothers, father or husband. Wollstonecraft's Synthesis stage could therefore have been more satisfactory on a personal level than Ward Howe's. Perhaps they both understood the dream of conjugial love.

CONCLUSION

This essay has offered the perspective of a developmental psychologist in analyzing the effects of the Last Judgment. This study has focused on the social changes of women's rights in the past 250 years, by focusing in on the case studies for two key women. Their personal and professional biographies have been described and explained by means of two developmental theories: feminist identity and spiritual growth. Each theory includes five stages that may occur over the course of a lifespan. Based on biographies, letters and published documents, I have concluded that to all appearances both Wollstonecraft and Ward Howe progressed through all five stages of feminist identity and all five stages of spiritual growth (with the understanding, of course, that an external evaluation of another's psychological or spiritual state can never be considered certain).

Both women were determined to share their theological and political reflections on the status of women and to fight for social change. Both searched for truth, developed their gifts, and did good works that eventually helped millions of women achieve their potential.

In the future, other scholars of the direct or indirect effects of the Last Judgment might pursue the following topics about the social and psychological changes for women created by this event:

- Educational reforms
- Employment opportunities
- Ordination
- Literary achievements
- Mental health
- Communication patterns in marriage
- Parenting styles
- Roles of women in established Swedenborgian organizations

In addition, the following case studies would be worth analyzing in terms of the direct or indirect influence of the Last Judgment and the doctrines of the New Church (many of these women fought for women's rights and/or the abolition of slavery):

- Lydia Maria Child
- Angelina and Sarah Grimke
- Harriot Hunt
- Anna Cora Ogden Mowatt
- Sarah Orne Jewett
- Jessie Willcox Smith
- Lydia Fuller Dickenson
- Ednah Silver
- Mary Lathbury
- Ellen Spencer Mussey

Besides utilizing developmental psychology, future scholars could also employ theories and tools from other branches of psychology. For example, the recent surge of research about physiological psychology informs us about the way people learn, reflect and make important decisions. This might be a fruitful endeavor to investigate how the brain works when people are "entering intellectually into the mysteries of faith" which is now possible since the Last Judgment and the reordering of the heavens (TCR 508).

Another valuable direction for future researchers is a comparison of the Swedenborgian doctrine of repentance and Moody's theory of the *Stages of the Soul*. Swedenborg writes (TCR 567) of several stages of repentance which seem to more thoroughly explain the Struggle Stage identified by Moody. The five stages described in the Writings of Swedenborg can be summarized in this manner:

1) Self-examination
2) Acknowledgement of one's mistakes and owning the guilt
3) Confessing to the Lord and praying for His help
4) Stopping the bad behavior
5) Resisting the temptation the next time

Moody's Struggle Stage description might be too vague and individuals might benefit more from Swedenborg's detailed outline of repentence. I suggest that future scholars investigate how to synthesize Moody's theory with the Swedenborgian doctrine of repentance. This work could be quite helpful for case studies as well as for use in therapy.

Further efforts to combine these two theories will provide a richer understanding of the significant difference in human lives that has occurred since the Lord led the Last Judgment in 1757. I leave it to the reader to apply these two specific theories from developmental psychology to current situations. Self-awareness about one's own development can lead to a deeper search for spiritual inspiration, resulting in new active commitments. This could lead to new improvements in the conditions for all women across the globe. 🔚

BIBLIOGRAPHY

Agonito, R. ed. (1977). *History of ideas on woman*. New York: Perigee.

Anderson, B. S. and Zinsser, J. P. (1988). *A history of their own: Women in Europe from prehistory to the present*. New York: Harper.

Bellin, H. F. and Ruhl, D. eds. (1985). *Blake and Swedenborg: Opposition is true friendship*. West Chester, PA: Swedenborg Foundation.

Benz, E. (2002). *Emanuel Swedenborg: Visionary savant in the Age of Reason*. West Chester, PA: Swedenborg Foundation.

Beswick, S. (1870). *The Swedenborg rite and the great Masonic leaders of the 18th Century*. Montana: Kessinger.

Blake, W. (1790). *The Marriage of Heaven and Hell*. London: William Blake.

Block, M. (1984). *The New Church in the new world*. New York: Swedenborg Publishing Association.

Brock, E. J., Glenn, E. B., Odhner, C. C., Odhner, J. D., Walker, C. H., and Williams-Hogan, J. K. eds. (1988). *Swedenborg and his influence*. Bryn Athyn, PA: The Academy of the New Church.

Brody, M. (2004). *Mary Wollstonecraft: Mother of Women's Rights*. New York: Oxford University Press.

Chartier, R. (1991). *The cultural origins of the French Revolution*. Durham, NC: Duke University Press.

Cheever, S. (2006). *American Bloomsbury*. New York: Simon and Schuster.

Davis, N. Z. and Farge, A. eds. (1993). *A history of women in the west: Renaissance and Enlightenment paradoxes*. Cambridge, MA: Harvard University Press.

Downing, N. E. and Roush, K. L. (1985). From passive acceptance to active commitment. *The Counseling Psychologist*. vol. 13, 4, 695–709.

Emanuel Swedenborg: Herald of a new era. (1989). Sydney, AUS: The Swedenborg Lending Library and Enquiry Centre.

Emerson, R. W. (1977). Woman's suffrage. In. R. Agonito ed., *History of ideas on woman* (209–224). New York: Perigee.

Emerson, R. W. (2003). *Emerson on Swedenborg: Introducing the mystic.* London: Swedenborg Society.

Fay, E. A. (1998). *A feminist introduction to romanticism.* Malden, MA: Blackwell.

Felder, D.G. (2001). *The 100 most influential women of all time.* New York: Citadel Press.

Fischer, A. R., Tokar, D. M., Mergl, M. M., Good, G. E., Hill, M. H., and Blum, S. A. (2000). Assessing women's feminist identity development: Studies of convergent, discriminant and structural validity. *Psychology of Women Quarterly,* 24, 15–29.

Fowler, J. W. (1981). *The stages of faith.* New York: Harper Collins.

Gabay, A. (2006). The Reverend Jacob Duche and the advent of the New Church in England. *The New Philosophy, CIX,* 381–394.

Gilligan, C. (1982; 1993). *In a different voice.* Cambridge, MA: Harvard University Press.

Gordon, L. (2005). *Vindication: A life of Mary Wollstonecraft.* New York: Harper Collins.

Grant, M. H. (1994). *Private woman, public person: An account of the life of Julia Ward Howe from 1819 to 1868.* New York: Carlson.

Hallengren, A. (1998). *Gallery of mirrors: Reflections of Swedenborgian thought.* West Chester, PA: Swedenborg Foundation.

Hoover, K., Marcia, J., and Parris, K. (1997). *The power of identity: Politics in a new key.* Catham, NJ: Catham.

Hymowitz, C., and Weissman, M. (1978). *A history of women in America.* New York: Bantam.

Jacobs, D. (2001). *Her own woman: The life of Mary Wollstonecraft.* New York: Kensington Press.

Josselson, R. (1983). *Finding herself: Pathways to identity development in women.* San Francisco, CA: Jossey-Bass.

Larsen, R. ed. (1988). *Emanuel Swedenborg: A continuing vision.* New York: Swedenborg Foundation.

Lawrence, J. F. ed. (1995). *Testimony to the invisible: Essays on Swedenborg.* West Chester, PA: Swedenborg Foundation.

Liell, S. (2003). *46 Pages: Thomas Paine, Common Sense, and the Turning Point to Independence.* Philadelphia: Runing Press Book Publishers.

Marshall, M. (2005). *The Peabody sisters: Three women who ignited American Romanticism.* Boston: Houghton Mifflin.

Mill, J. S. (1997). *The subjection of women.* Mineola, NY: Dover.

Moody, H. R. (1997). *The five stages of the soul.* New York: Anchor Books.

Moradi, B., Sublich, L. M. and Phillips, J.C. (2002). Revisiting feminist identity development: Theory, research and practice. *The Counseling Psychologist,* 30, 1, 6–43.

Opdycke, S. (2000). *The Routledge historical atlas of women in America.* New York: Routlege.

Perry, M. (2003). *Lift up thy voice: The Grimke family journey from slaveholders to civil rights leaders.* New York: Penguin Books.

Poole, S.F. (1999). *Lost legacy: Inspiring women of 19th century America.* West Chester, PA: Swedenborg Foundation.

Rendell, J. (1984). *The origins of modern feminism: Women in Britain, France and the United States.* New York: Schoken Books.

Rose, J. S., Shotwell, S., and Bertucci, M. L. eds. (2005). *Scribe of heaven.* West Chester, PA: Swedenborg Foundation.

Rousseau, J. J. (1968). *The social contract.* London: Penguin.

Santrock, J. W. (1997). *Life-span development.* Dubuque, IA: Brown and Benchmark.

Saxton, M. (1995). *Louisa May Alcott: A modern biography.* New York: Noonday Press.

Sigstedt, C. O. (1981). *The Swedenborg Epic.* London: The Swedenborg Society.

Smoley, R. (2005). The inner journey of Emanuel Swedenborg. In J. S. Rose, S. Shotwell, and M. L. Bertucci eds., *Scribe of Heaven* (3–52). West Chester, PA: Swedenborg Foundation.

Steinbrugge, L. (1995). *The moral sex: Women's nature in the French enlightenment.* New York: Oxford University Press.

Strachey, R. (1928). *The cause: A short history of the women's movement in Great Britain.* London: G. Bells and Sons.

Swedenborg, E. (1961). *Last Judgment and Babylon destroyed*. London: Swedenborg Society.

———. (1970). *Apocalypse Revealed*. London: Swedenborg Society.

———. (1972). *True Christian Religion*. New York: Swedenborg Foundation.

———. (1978). *Arcana Coelestia*. New York: Swedenborg Foundation.

———. (1979). *Heaven and Hell*. New York: Swedenborg Foundation.

———. (2003). *Divine love and wisdom; Divine providence*. West Chester, PA: Swedenborg Foundation.

Tannen, D. (1990). *You just don't understand*. New York: Ballantine Books.

Taylor, B. (1983). *Eve and the new Jerusalem: Socialism and feminism in the 19th century*. New York: Pantheon.

———. (2003). *Mary Wollstonecraft and the feminist imagination*. New York: Cambridge University Press.

Todd, J. (2000). *Mary Wollstonecraft: A revolutionary life*. New York: Columbia University Press.

Todd, J. ed. (2003). *Mary Wollstonecraft: The collected letters*. New York: Penguin.

Toksvig, S. (1948). *Emanuel Swedenborg: Scientist and mystic*. New York: Swedenborg Foundation.

Tomalin, C. (1992). *The life and death of Mary Wollstonecraft*. London: Penguin.

van Biema, D. (2007, August 23). Mother Teresa's Crisis of Faith. *TIME*.

Wardle, R. M. ed. (1966). *Godwin and Mary: Letters of William Godwin and Mary Wollstonecraft*. Lincoln, KS: University of Kansas.

Weatherford, D. (1994). *American women's history*. New York: Prentice Hall.

Weisner, M. E. (1993). *Women and gender in early modern Europe*. New York: Cambridge University Press.

Wollstonecraft, M. (1992). *A vindication of the rights of woman*. New York: Knopf. (Original published 1790, London: Joseph Johnson).

————. (2001). *Original stories for real life: 1791*. Washington DC: Woodstock. (Original published 1788, London: Joseph Johnson).

————. (2005). *Maria or the wrongs of woman*. United States: Echo Library. (Original published unfinished posthumously (1798), London: Joseph Johnson).

TIME LINE: MARY WOLLSTONECRAFT

Dates	Age	Events	Feminist Identity	Spiritual Stages
1759	0	birth	—	—
1767	8	childhood	Passive Acceptance	—
1768	9	abused	Revelation	—
1770s	teen	tutored and left home	Embeddedness	Call
1779	20	met Blake and heard of Swedenborg and employed as an editor	Synthesis	Search
1792	33	published *Vindication*	Active Commitment	Search
1790s	30s	travel and start family French Revolution	Active Commitment	Struggle and Breakthrough and Return
1794	35	second marriage: William Godwin		
1797	38	death		

TIME LINE: JULIA WARD HOWE

Dates	Age	Events	Feminist Identity	Spiritual Stages
1819	0	birth	—	—
1824	5	mother dies	—	—
1820s	child	home schooled	Passive Acceptance	—
1830s	teen	tutored, met Margaret Fuller (read Swedenborg)	Revelation	Call and Search
1841	22	father dies	Revelation	Search
1843	24	married to Chev: Samuel Howe	Revelation	Struggle
1840–1860s	20–40	raised children	Revelation	Struggle
1860s	40s	Civil War and *Battle Hymn*	Revelation	Struggle
1870	50	joined suffrage movement	Embeddedness	Breakthrough
1870s		leader in groups	Synthesis	Return
1876	57	husband dies	Active Commitment	Return
1870s–1910	50–90	national leader and speaker and published author	Active Commitment	Return

From Thought to Action:
the Last Judgment, Swedenborg
and the Antislavery Movement

BRIAN D. HENDERSON

INTRODUCTION

In the American South, slavery was euphemistically referred to as the "peculiar institution" during the nineteenth century. During the eighteenth century, however, "freedom, not slavery," wrote Seymour Drescher, "was the peculiar institution" (Drescher 1986, x). Virtually every state in Europe practiced some form of enslavement, either at home or in some part of its territory. Britain and France had built their colonies on slave labor. Most of Russia, Prussia, and Austria lived under the yoke of serfdom. According to one estimate, close to three quarters of the world's population was in bondage of one type or another during this century (Hochschild 2005, 2).

The eighteenth century man or woman, looking back across the expanse of history, would have seen the consistent presence of slavery as an accepted part of human history, which stretched back virtually unbroken from ancient times. For more than four thousand years—from Ancient Egypt, Babylon, and Assyria to classical Greece and Rome, to medieval Europe, in India, China, and the Muslim world—the legal condition of the slave had remained virtually unchanged. The human slave was legal property to be bought and sold, required to work for the benefit of his master. So prevalent had the practice of slavery been throughout human history, many scholars consider those societies that did *not* practice slavery to be anomalies.

It is not surprising then that historian Adam Hochschild claims:

> If . . . [in 1787] you stood on a London street corner and insisted that slavery
> was morally wrong and should be stopped, nine out of ten listeners would
> have laughed you off as a crackpot. The tenth might have agreed with you in
> principle, but assured you that ending slavery was wildly impractical: the British
> Empire's economy would collapse. (Hochschild 2005, 7)

Perhaps what *is* surprising is how quickly slavery as a legal institution was brought to an end; by the end of the nineteenth century slavery had been legally abolished virtually everywhere in the western world. In slightly more than one generation, the antislavery movement which had begun in late eighteenth century England had accomplished its goal: the legal abolition of slavery in Europe, its possessions, and its former colonies.

In England this abolition movement represented a group of people who fought for close to fifty years for other people's rights—a feat all the more amazing when one considers that close to ninety-five percent of Englishmen and no Englishwomen possessed the right to vote (Hochschild 2005, 96). "Without this most basic of rights themselves," asks Adam Hochschild, "how could they be roused to care about the rights of other people, of a different skin color, an ocean away" (Hochschild 2005, 97)? Likewise, David Brion Davis asks:

> Why was it that at a certain moment of history a small number of men not only
> saw the full horror of a social evil to which mankind had been blind for centuries,
> but felt impelled to attack it through personal testimony and cooperative action?
> (Davis 1966, vii)

As we recognize not only the 200th anniversary of British Parliament's ending of the British slave trade, but the 250th anniversary of the Last Judgment, it is important to reflect on possible answers to these questions. It is universally recognized that antislavery movements arose almost simultaneously in Britain, France, and North America in the second half of the eighteenth century. What is less clear is *why* it was that these movements sprang to life precisely when they did. Why didn't they appear in the sixteenth or seventeenth centuries? What was it about the second half of the eighteenth century that caused these movements to suddenly spring to life? While historians continue to struggle to formulate and agree on an answer to these questions, we can look to the nature of the Last Judgment and its effects on the natural world for answers. We can also look to see how the Lord's revelation through the Writings of Emanuel Swedenborg inspired individuals to take up the cause and play a vital role in the fight against slavery and the slave trade.

Before that is undertaken, however, it is useful to understand how firmly rooted slavery was in western culture at the end of the eighteenth century and how widely accepted the arguments used in its defense were, as well as to see when and how criticisms against slavery turned into antislavery action. Only then can it be seen how the spiritual effects of the Last Judgment affected the chain of events in the natural world. A case study will also be made of how one individual, inspired by Swedenborg, played a critical role in the fight to abolish the British slave trade.

THE HERITAGE OF EUROPEAN SLAVERY

The first textual evidence of slaves dates from the civilization of Sumer in 1200 BC (the Ur-Nammu tablet), and there is general agreement that slavery appeared independently in Europe, Asia, and Africa as early as 1000 BC. In classical Greece, Athens possessed roughly an equal number of free male citizens and slaves. One estimate places the proportion of slaves in fourth century Athens as high as that of the American South in 1860, with a higher percentage of Greeks owning slaves than nineteenth century southerners (Davis 1966, 35). While most Greek slaves were non-Greeks purchased from traders, the vast majority of slaves in the Roman Empire were enslaved captives, brought back to Rome by their conquering legions. With an estimated two to three million slaves in Italy alone (Hochschild 2005, 2), Rome foreshadowed the American Deep South with its slave markets, where slaves were examined and forced to display their agility (Davis 1966, 36).

With the dawning of the medieval period and the feudal system, slavery disappeared in the interior of Europe. But even as serfdom replaced slavery, the continuing heritage of Roman law, particularly its definition of slaves as personal property subject to the will of their master, blurred the line between slave and serf. In France, for example, serfs were limited to virtually the same legal rights as Roman slaves (Davis 1966, 37, 46). David Brian Davis argues that by the end of the medieval period, when the labor shortages and rising wages resulting from the Black Death and Hundred Years' War "threatened to undermine the entire manorial system in the late fourteenth century . . . the ancient principles of servitude justified severe laws to keep workers on the land." Davis claims

> the legal principle of slavery survived as a weapon of social control. In 1547, for example, it was possible to enact a temporary law stating that vagabonds who attempted to escape from enforced service were to be branded on the forehead with the letter "S," which signified that they would be "slaves" for the rest of their lives. (Davis 1966, 40)

Throughout the Middle Ages slavery continued on the periphery of Europe, particularly in areas that maintained military or commercial contact with the Byzantine Empire and the Islamic world. By the late Middle Ages slave societies existed along virtually all of the main trade routes from Russia and Egypt to Venice and the south of France. In Spain, Christians and Muslims enslaved one another as they waged religious war for more than six hundred years. In the Mediterranean the slave trade flourished from the thirteenth to the fifteenth century. Venetian merchants sold slaves from the Dalmatian coast to the Muslim world, creating a trade that was, according to Henri Pirenne, "as vital to Venetian prosperity as was the later Atlantic slave trade to the economies of Britain and France" (Davis 1966, 42). According to Davis, during these centuries the Venetians and Genoese established a slave trade system in the Black Sea and the Mediterranean that would serve as a model for the Atlantic African slave trade:

Arriving on the coasts of the Black Sea in the thirteenth century, they ultimately established bases or factories which became thriving markets for the purchase of slaves. Like the Portuguese who built forts in West Africa, the Italians were not required to seize slaves on their own. . . . The Italians not only created stock companies, commercial bases or *fondachi*, and a highly organized slave trade, but in the colony of Cyprus they established plantations where imported bondsmen were employed in the cultivation of sugar cane. By 1300 there were Black slaves on Cyprus, which had become virtually a prototype for the West Indian colonies. (Davis 1966, 42)

By the end of the fifteenth century the fall of Constantinople to the Turks had closed off the slave markets of the Black Sea, gradually extinguishing the trade of the Genoese and Venetian merchants and ultimately ending commercial slave trade in the Mediterranean (Davis 1966, 44). The chain of slavery would continue, however, as the Portuguese made contact with Africa, breaking the monopoly of Arab traders and importing the first African slaves. As early as mid-sixteenth century, Portuguese merchants were shipping black Africans to Castile. By the end of the century, the slave trade shifted from the Black Sea and the Mediterranean to Africa and the coast of Portugal. The discovery of the New World and the establishment of sugar plantations in the West Indies brought an insatiable demand for African slaves.

While estimates vary, most place the number of slaves imported into the New World from the fifteenth to early nineteenth century somewhere between ten and fifteen million, or three to four times the number of white immigrants who made the voyage across the Atlantic (Pieterse 1992, 52). By the late eighteenth century nearly eighty thousand Africans experienced the Middle Passage each year (Hochschild 2005, 2). For three and a half centuries European nations competed with one another in the lucrative slave trade. While slavery had continued virtually uninterrupted from the Ancient World to the settlement of the New World, what had changed by the sixteenth century was the addition of skin color to the institution.

Prior to the eighteenth century, there was little need for Europeans to establish an elaborate defense of slavery. The justifications for slavery that did exist were largely philosophical in nature, relying on a combination of classical tradition, medieval theological dualism, biblical authority, and an emerging view of the inferiority of those who were black.

The classical defense of the slavery, particularly of foreign "barbarians," was that slaves were part of a fixed natural social order. According to Aristotle, "Humanity is divided into two: the master and the slave" (Hochschild 2005, 3). The masters possessed reason while the slaves, lacking reason, were inferior by nature and needed to be guided by their masters. Slavery, Aristotle argued, provided the only way for the enslaved to fulfill his or her function in life. In short, for some men, "slavery was natural to their being" (Outram 2005, 60). While skin color was not necessarily a determining factor in Greek and Roman slavery, both turned relatively quickly to enslaving foreigners, and evidence exists that both saw blackness as different and inferior.

The theological notion of dualism, developed during the Middle Ages, emphasized the distinction between the physical body and the spiritual mind. This separation led to the argument that it did not matter whether the physical body was enslaved as long as the spiritual mind was free. As long as slaves were Christianized their spiritual minds would be free, thereby minimizing the impact or significance of the enslavement of their physical bodies.

The Bible had proven to be a long-lasting source for the defense of slavery. Not only was slavery present in the stories of the Old Testament, but the curse of Ham had become widely accepted by the seventeenth century as not only an explanation for black skin color, but a justification for the enslavement of black Africans (Pieterse 1992, 44). In Genesis 9.18–29 Noah curses Ham's offspring for his sinful failure to cover his father's nakedness. By his words, "Cursed be Canaan a servant of servants shall he be unto his brethren," Noah was seen to curse the sons of Ham to eternal obedience and slavery. While the Bible nowhere mentions that Ham's offspring were black, a connection between Ham and blackness developed during the Middle Ages and became a powerful argument for the enslavement of black Africans and other people who they considered to be "less than white."

It was commonly held, therefore, that slavery was sanctioned by God and that black Africans could be made slaves because of their inherent inferiority. Deirdre Coleman states:

> European perceptions of the inferiority of Africans were so ingrained in this period that some went so far as to argue that Africans were "doomed by the almighty to the sufferings they underwent, and the [Europeans] were merely the instruments of the divine vengeance." (Coleman 2005, 97)

SLAVERY AND THE "SCIENCE OF RACE" IN THE ENLIGHTENMENT

Dorinda Outram argues that by the eighteenth century "assertions that black Africans formed a 'race' whose characteristics uniquely fitted them for slavery and justified its imposition as 'natural', had become common" (Outram 2005, 67). One explanation for this tendency to "link slavery and race" is the fact that from the second half of the seventeenth century, as white indentured servitude declined and was all but eliminated in the British colonies, virtually all of the slaves being shipped to Europe's possessions in the New World were black Africans. But another factor must be given at least as much consideration—the growing interest during the Enlightenment in scientifically classifying all things in the natural world, including mankind (Outram 2005, 67). Over the course of the two previous centuries, European exploration had resulted in an outpouring of accounts of new lands, plants, animals, and human beings. These discoveries required some "logical framework" if man were, as Winthrop Jordan argues, "to continue to make sense of the world" (Jordan 1974, 99).

The desire to systematize and categorize the discoveries of new plants and animals, and ultimately to scientifically study the place of mankind in nature and the physical differences between the races, was indicative of the shift that took place during the eighteenth century away from religion and the issue of salvation toward scientific discovery. "Viewed in the broadest terms," Winthrop Jordan argues, "this growing interest in the physical distinctions among human beings was one aspect of the secularization of the west" (Jordan 1974, 99).

In Greek antiquity, geographic differences had divided humans into those who were "cultured" and those who were "barbarians." These distinctions continued into the Enlightenment. As Emmanuel Eze notes:

> Aristotle, for example, defined the human being as a rational animal, and supposed that the cultured people (such as the male, aristocratic Greeks) were capable of living in a reasonable way and organized their society accordingly (democratically), while the "barbarians," the non-Greeks, incapable of culture and lacking the superior rational capacity for the Athenian-style democratic social organization, lived brutishly and under despotism. European Enlightenment thinkers retained the Greek ideal of reason, as well as this reason's categorical function of discriminating between the cultured (now called "civilized") and the "barbarian" (the "savage" or the "primitive"). (Eze 1997, 4)

The accounts from the so-called "New World" described people with "strange" habits, reinforcing the European view of themselves as "civilized" and those outside Europe as "primitive." The question of the differences between races, however, became increasingly important because in the eighteenth century people still saw nature in terms of a great hierarchy, or "Great Chain of Being," in which everything had a "naturally assigned position and status" (Eze 1997, 5)—from inanimate objects, to the lowest forms of life, to animals, to mankind, up through heaven, culminating in God.

As early as the late seventeenth century Sir William Petty (1623–1687) distinguished between the races on the basis of physical distinctions:

> I say that the Europeans do not only differ from the . . . Africans in Collour, which is as much as white differs from black, but also in their Haire . . . [and] in the shape of their Noses, Lipps, and cheek bones, as also in the very outline of their faces and the Mould of their skulls. They differ also in their Naturall Manners, and in the internall Qualities of their Minds. (Jordan 1974, 102)

By the early eighteenth century Carl Linnaeus (1707–1778) and Comte de Buffon (1707–1788) began to classify everything in nature—plants, animals, and humans according to the "naturally" ordered hierarchy of the Great Chain of Being. Buffon believed that all of mankind had originally been white and that darker skin color was the result of climate, thereby implying that racial characteristics were not fixed by God in their creation, but could be altered through a change of environment (Outram 2005, 68).

By the second half of the eighteenth century anatomists such as Peter Camper (1722–1789) and Johann Friedrich Blumenbach (1752–1840) began to focus not only on skin color, but on the skeletal structures of various races, thereby providing scientific "evidence" to the "notion of a natural hierarchy of the races on the strength of natural form, cranial angles and skin pigmentation" (Outram 2005, 69). In other words, the differences between the races could not be changed simply by altering the environment; the differences were distinct and unchangeable.

In 1781 Blumenbach distinguished five races of mankind: Caucasian, Mongolian, Ethiopian, American, and Malay. Of the Ethiopian race he wrote:

> Color black, hair black and curly, head narrow, compressed at the sides; forehead knotty, uneven, molar bones protruding outwards; eyes very prominent; nose thick, mixed up as it were with the wide jaws; alveolar edge narrow, elongated in front; upper primaries obliquely prominent; lips puffy; chin retreating. Many are bandy-legged. To this variety belong all Africans, except those of the north. (Pieterse 1992, 46)

While he argued that the five races were merely variations of the same species, he placed these "variations" within the "naturally" ordered hierarchy by "allott[ing] the first place to the Caucasian [whose] stock displays . . . the most beautiful race of men" (Eze 1997, 79).

Camper perhaps best illustrates the desire of eighteenth century intellectuals to use science to categorize the races within the hierarchy of nature. By measuring the profile of the human head, Camper was one of the first to use scientific instruments to "measure" racial differences.

The so-called "Camper facial angle" measurement determined that there was a spectrum from apes to black Africans to Europeans, with Africans placed lowest among humans because they possessed the smallest "facial angle" (Pierterse 1992, 46). While categorizations such as Camper's clearly acknowledged that black Africans were human beings and not "beasts," the belief that they were on the boundary between animals and humans became widespread.

In essence these anatomists created theories explaining the difference between the races that defenders of slavery could use to argue that science supported, and even strengthened, the old Aristotelian argument that "barbarians" were "natural slaves" who when enslaved were living according to their own true nature. In short, they used these "scientific" theories to argue that slavery could "be seen as maintaining the order of nature" (Outram 2005, 69).

The defenders of slavery also used the writings on race by such philosophers as David Hume (1711–1776) and Immanuel Kant (1724–1804) to strengthen their position. Eze argues that in these writings,

> "Reason" and "civilization" became almost synonymous with "white" people and northern Europe, while unreason and savagery were conveniently located among the non-whites, the "black," the "red," the "yellow," outside Europe. (Eze 1997, 5)

David Hume (1711–1776) not only professed that blacks were inferior to whites, but argued that the African people demonstrated limited intelligence and ingenuity.

> I am apt to suspect the negroes and in general all the other species of men (for there are four or five different kinds) to be naturally inferior to the whites. There never was a civilized nation of any other complexion than white, nor even any individual eminent either in action or speculation. No ingenious manufactures amongst them, no arts, no sciences . . . there are NEGRO slaves dispersed all over EUROPE, of which none ever discovered any symptoms of ingenuity . . . In JAMAICA indeed they talk of one negro as a man of parts and learning; but 'tis likely he is admired for very slender accomplishments like a parrot, who speaks a few words plainly. (Kramnick 1995, 629)

Immanuel Kant (1724–1804) argued in *Observations on the Feeling of the Beautiful and Sublime* (1764) that different races or nations have "different aesthetic and moral sensibilities" (Eze 1997, 49), with Germans at the top and Africans at the bottom. In this essay Kant writes:

> The Negroes of Africa have by nature no feeling that rises above the trifling.... So fundamental is the difference between these two races of man, and it appears to be as great in regard to mental capacities as in color. The religion of fetishes so widespread among them is perhaps a sort of idolatry that sinks as deeply into the trifling as appears to be possible to human nature. A bird feather, a cow's horn, a conch shell, or any common object, as soon as it becomes consecrated by a few words, is an object of veneration and of invocation in swearing oaths. The blacks are very vain but in the Negro's way, and so talkative that they must be driven apart from each other with thrashings. (Kant 1764, 638)

When speaking of a Negro who offered an opinion on how whites treated their wives wrote

> And it might be that there were something in this which perhaps deserved to be considered; but in short, this fellow was quite black from head to foot, a clear proof that what he said was stupid. (Kant 1764, 639) (Kramnick 1995, 637–639)

Edward Long (1734–1813), a British colonial administrator and planter in Jamaica, offers a description of African slaves in his book *History of Jamaica* (1774) which echoes the views of Hume and Kant:

> We find them marked with the same bestial manners, stupidity, and vices, which debase their brethren on the continent, who seem to be distinguished from the rest of mankind, not in person only, but in possessing, in abstract, every species of inherent turpitude, that is to be found dispersed at large among the rest of the human creation, with scarce a single virtue to extenuate this shade of character, differing in this particular from all other men; for, in other countries, the most abandoned villain we ever heard of has rarely, if ever, been known unportioned with some good quality at least in his composition. It is astonishing, that although they have been acquainted with Europeans, and their manufactures, for so many hundred years, they have, in all this series of time, manifested so little taste for arts, or a genius either inventive or imitative. Among so great a number of provinces on this extensive continent, and among so many millions

of people, we have heard but of one or two significant tribes, who comprehend
any thing of mechanic arts or manufacture; and even these, for the most part,
are said to perform their work in a very bungling and slovenly manner, perhaps
not better than an *orangutan* might, with little pains, be brought to. (Kramnick
1995, 644–645)

It was through writings such as these, Eze argues, that these
philosophers, "played a strong role in articulating Europe's sense not
only of its cultural but also *racial* superiority" (Eze 1997, 5).

THE EMERGING DEBATE OVER SLAVERY
IN THE EIGHTEENTH CENTURY

By the eighteenth century, as the authority of religion was eclipsed
by that of science, these emerging scientific and environmental
arguments began to replace the theological and biblical defenses of
slavery. The "science of race" was not the only defense of slavery,
however, as slavery forces drew on concepts of natural rights as well
as legal, economic, and even humanitarian arguments to support their
cause.

The fact that slavery continued to exist largely unchallenged by
any organized force during the first half of the eighteenth century
when so many intellectuals were concerned with the issues of equality,
freedom, and controls on arbitrary power seems a paradox. In fact,
some of the leading figures of the period, while opposed to slavery
in theory, stopped short of advocating for its elimination or acting to
bring about its end. While many believed that slavery would not exist
in an ideal world, they accepted it as the "reality" given its importance
to national economies and the material greed and lust for power that
existed in the world. The *Philosophical Dictionary* (1764), included
the following: "The human race constituted as it is, cannot subsist
unless there be an infinite number of useful individuals possessed of no
property at all." Likewise, Adam Smith wrote, "[It] has been universal
in the beginning of society, and the love of dominion and authority
over others will probably make it perpetual" (Hochschild 2005, 87).

John Locke (1632–1704) wrote

> Slavery is so vile and miserable an estate of man and so directly opposite to the generous temper and courage of our nation that it is hardly to be conceived that an "Englishman" much less a "Gentleman" should plead for it. (Greenidge 1958, 127–128)

Yet, Hochschild points out, he invested £600 in the Royal African Company. Voltaire (1694–1778), who criticized slaveholders in *Candide*, "accepted with pleasure," writes Hochschild, "when a leading French slave ship owner offered to name a vessel after him" (Hochschild 2005, 87).

The defenders of slavery even made use of the words of Montesquieu (1689–1755), the first of the philosophers to offer a harsh criticism of the institution of slavery, to support their position. Montesquieu argued that slavery was an extension of despotism and that it was "against natural law, by which all men are born free and independent" (Merriman 1996, 405). However, he also wrote that slavery was more acceptable in despotic societies where everyone was already subject to tyranny, since one would lose little by willingly choosing enslavement in the face of despotism. Proslavery propagandists twisted Montesquieu's words to support their cause, arguing that since most African tribes were despotic, the slaves in European colonies were, in effect, better off. Addressing how defenders of slavery used the principles of the Enlightenment to defend slavery, Davis states:

> A belief in progress and natural rights might lead, of course, to antislavery convictions; but if history seemed to be on the side of liberty, slavery had attained a certain prescriptive sanction as a nearly universal expression of human nature. Men who had acquired an increasing respect for property and for the intricate workings of natural and social laws could not view as an unmitigated evil an institution that had developed through the centuries. (Davis 1962, 214)

As the eighteenth century progressed, supporters of slavery began to develop more elaborate defenses of the institution based on legal, economic, and even humanitarian arguments. In England, defenders argued that slaves had been legally purchased under British law and were therefore the rightful property of their owners. Not only were slaves legal property sanctioned by British law, they argued, but the entire slave system benefited the national economy. England could not remain competitive with Spain and France if they freed their slaves. Without slavery, planters would not be able to provide England with its vital raw materials. More dangerous still, if the entire colonial economy could collapse, the welfare of the nation itself would be endangered. They even argued that the slaves themselves would suffer from a collapse of the colonial economy.

Responding to growing humanitarian calls for more humane treatment of slaves, defenders of slavery argued that many enslaved Africans had in fact been saved from certain death in Africa and that by being brought to the Americas they were taught European "civilized values" such as hard work. Some even went so far as to compare the conditions of slaves to those of English servants and workers, asking their opponents why their humanitarian principles appeared not to extend to their own countrymen.

Many of these arguments were direct responses to the growing criticism of slavery which, began to emerge from both sides of the Atlantic during the eighteenth century. By the second half of the century, intellectuals such as Jean-Jacques Rousseau (1712–1778), who argued that no man should "submit to a human master but rather to the common good" (Ackerman 2005, 5), began to condemn slavery as a violation of the natural rights of man. As Wayne Ackerman argues, "along with new ideas about the worth of the individual and the rights of humanity came questions about the morality of slavery as an institution" (Ackerman 2005, 5).

At its foundation most of the emerging criticism focused on the inhumane treatment of slaves and therefore the slave trade, rather than on slavery itself. If the slave trade could be ended, they reasoned, the supply of new slaves would be greatly reduced, thereby encouraging slave owners to treat their slaves more humanely.

This spirit of humanitarianism, which ultimately led to the emergence of antislavery activity, was born out of religion. Religious revival had begun in the previous century as religious thinkers began to search for the true purpose of God's creation and the proper role and place of mankind. An important result of this religious revival was the development of "new ideas about sin, salvation, God himself, and, later, slavery" (Ackerman 2005, 6). These ideas included the belief that God's Providence controlled the moral order and could "punish those that did not live according to God's standards" (Ackerman 2005, 6). Specifically, English evangelicals' belief that Providence would punish Britain as a nation if it did not begin to address some of its moral issues lead to an array of social reform efforts, including opposition to the slave trade. Evangelicals began to view slavery as "detrimental to humanity" and "incompatible with their religion." At the root of this emerging religious opposition to slavery was the changing idea of sin.

In 1737, the Quaker Benjamin Lay called slavery a "Hellish practice," a "filthy sin," the "Capital Sin," "the greatest Sin in the World, of the very nature of Hell itself, and is the Belly of Hell" (Davis 1966, 291). Previous religious belief held that all men were condemned by original sin—that slavery was part of the punishment for Adam's sin and that by nature some men were required to work harder in their enslavement than others. It was the bondage to sin that mattered, not physical slavery. As Davis writes:

> men could not fully perceive the moral contradictions of slavery until a major religious transformation had changed their ideas about sin and spiritual freedom. (Davis 1966, 292)

Quakers and others began to emphasize the notion that man was created with free will, that is, with the ability to choose between good and evil. Mankind, they argued, could only achieve moral perfectibility through free choice, which was destroyed by slavery. All men were not enslaved as a consequence of original sin, and therefore slavery was not part of the natural order. Rather, it was "contrary to nature as well as to Scripture" (Davis 1966, 316). It was inconceivable to them that a good, loving God had condemned mankind, and especially one particular race, to perpetual slavery.

Despite this emerging religious belief that slavery was a sin and the resulting humanitarian criticism of the treatment of slaves as morally wrong, most of the attacks against slavery remained individual calls for reform. It was not until the second half of the eighteenth century, particularly after 1770, that organized efforts to end the slave trade began to appear.

Trying to capture the state of the slavery debate during this period, Hochschild writes:

> No major thinker defended slavery, but few spent real effort attacking it. . . . A latent feeling was in the air, but an intellectual undercurrent disapproving of slavery was something very different from the belief that anything could be done about it. (Hochschild 2005, 85)

While it should be noted that antislavery legislation was to appear in the young United States during the 1780s, as Pennsylvania, Rhode Island, Connecticut, and others began gradual emancipation, these efforts were limited to individual states that possessed very few slaves. Hochschild offers an interesting analogy between the issue of antislavery in England in the mid-eighteenth century and that of environmental awareness today:

> An analogy today might be how some people think about automobiles. For reasons of global warming, air quality, traffic, noise, and dependence on oil, one can argue, the world might be better off without cars . . . Even if you depend on driving to work, it's possible to agree there's a problem. A handful of dedicated environmentalists try to practice what they preach, and travel only by train, bus, bicycle, or foot. Yet does anyone advocate a movement to ban automobiles from the face of the earth? Similarly, despite the uneasiness some people in late-eighteenth century England had about slavery, to actually abandon it seemed a laughable dream. (Hochschild 2005, 85–86)

And yet organized antislavery movements appeared simultaneously in the United States, France, and England in the last quarter of the eighteenth century and in less than one generation legislation was passed outlawing the slave trade in each of these nations.

THE EIGHTEENTH CENTURY
ANTISLAVERY MOVEMENT IN ENGLAND

To understand the monumental shift that occurred in the movement against slavery during the last quarter of the eighteenth century, it is important to pinpoint the moment of transition from individuals questioning the morality of slavery and even condemning the existence of the institution, to organized groups working to abolish first the slave trade and then the institution itself.

Virtually all historians point to the events in England in the 1780s and to the organized movement begun in the previous decade by the Quakers as the critical turning point. The Quakers in particular are given credit for serving as the vital link between the period of antislavery thought and antislavery action because of their ability to build a far-reaching organizational structure that could not only build broad-based popular support for legislative change but also provide the funding necessary to support such an effort. Prior to 1770, however, the Quakers faced the same contradiction as many of the other critics of slavery in the first half of the eighteenth century.

Some Quakers may have begun to see slavery as a sin but many, especially those in the southern colonies of British North America, continued to own slaves. Even George Fox, who condemned the notion of slavery and urged masters to treat their slaves with love, felt "compelled to accept slavery as part of the natural order" (Ackerman 2005, 7). William Penn owned African slaves, Pennsylvania law included strict slave codes, Quaker merchants continued to import African slaves as late as 1730, and such notable Quakers as David and Alexander Barclay were members of the Royal African Company (Davis 1966, 304–305).

It was not until the middle of the eighteenth century that the Quakers, led by such men as John Woolman (1720–1775) and Anthony Benezet (1723–1784), began to take action first against the slave trade and then against slavery itself. Historians argue that this transition to action was surprisingly sudden. Interestingly, this shift seems to have taken place at the London Yearly Meeting of 1757, when the

Meeting ruled that "all members who bought or sold Negroes were
to be excluded from business meetings or from making financial
contributions to the Society" (Davis 1966, 330). In 1761 the London
Yearly Meeting "announced that slave dealers merited disownment"
(Davis 1966, 330).

By the 1770s English Quakers had begun to express their opposition
to slavery beyond the Society of Friends, printing and distributing
their first antislavery pamphlets (Ackerman 2005, 9). In 1783 the
Quakers established the structure necessary to carry out the protracted
fight against slavery when a six-person committee was formed for the
purpose of "agitat[ing] against slavery and the slave trade" (Hochschild
2005, 78). This committee submitted articles to newspapers, distributed
pamphlets throughout the country, and sent a fifteen-page pamphlet to
the king (Hochschild 2005, 78). In the same year they presented the
first of what was to become many petitions to the House of Commons
calling for an end to the slave trade. For antislavery supporters, this
was an important first step. A society established for the purpose of
attacking slavery had sent a petition to Parliament calling for an end to
the slave trade. Politically the petition had minimal impact. Not only
did Lord North fail to support the petition, believing "it would not
suit economic interest to push for a cessation of the trade" (Ackerman
2005, 9), but not a single Member of Parliament was "persuaded to
take up the cause," with many discounting the effort out of hand since
it came from the Quakers, whom they saw as "powerless oddballs" and
"conspicuously different" (Hochschild 2005, 78).

Four years later, in 1787, the Quaker antislavery organization
broadened its membership, welcoming non-Quakers for the first
time, including abolitionists Thomas Clarkson and Granville Sharp.
This new group, which was to become the core of the Society for
the Abolition of Slavery, formed the first national, nonsectarian
antislavery organization. With Clarkson and Sharp as its leaders, the
Society brought together Quakers, evangelicals, members of literary
and philosophical societies, academics, and other intellectuals to fight
against slavery; it could no longer be dismissed as being "controlled by
a fringe sect" (Hochschild 2005, 95).

While the Quaker organization provided much of the initial force, the establishment of the Society for the Abolition of Slavery, whose declared purpose was to "procure and publish such information as may tend to the abolition of slavery" (Greenidge 1958, 132), is universally seen as the true beginning of the organized antislavery movement. As Hochschild writes,

> If we were to fix one point when the crusade began, it would be the late afternoon of May 22, 1787, when twelve determined men sat down in the printing shop a 2 George Yard, amid flatbed presses, wooden trays of type, and large sheets of freshly printed book pages, to begin one of the most ambitious and brilliantly organized citizens' movements of all time. (Hochschild 2005, 3)

The members of the Society ultimately sought the abolition of slavery, however they decided to "proceed with caution" and first target the slave trade. Their goal was to spearhead a popular movement that would ultimately pressure Parliament into passing legislation banning the slave trade. This was not an easy task given the general acceptance of slavery and its perceived importance to the national economy. Perhaps more importantly, they faced the reality that a significant number of the Members of Parliament were financially tied to the African slave trade.

To achieve their goal of antislavery legislation the Society needed support within Parliament, which they soon received in William Wilberforce, Charles Fox, and William Pitt. Historians credit Clarkson's determined collection of evidence of the brutal realities of the slave trade, Wilberforce's relentless efforts to keep the issue alive in Parliament, and the Society's ability to build popular support against the slave trade for the ultimate success of antislavery legislation.

In 1788 the Abolition Society organized its first nationwide petition campaign, resulting in the presentation of over one hundred petitions attacking the slave trade to Parliament. Parliament refused to take specific legal action, as most members continued to fear the impact that ending the slave trade would have on the British economy, but on February 11, at the request of William Pitt, Parliament appointed a Trade Committee of the Privy Council to consider the state of trade with Africa with particular attention to the slave trade. In preparation for the council's hearings the Abolition Society, with Clarkson at the fore, sought out witnesses who could present hard evidence of the horrors of slavery. The testimony of these witnesses was effective. When the Privy Council's Report was published in April 1789, "its effect was damning" (Greenidge 1958, 135). In March the House of Commons had resolved itself into a committee of the whole to inquire into the slave trade and on May 12, 1789 the inquiry commenced with Wilberforce standing before the House of Commons and, for the first of what would become many times, calling for a resolution to end the slave trade.

Unsuccessful, he pushed for the appointment of a select committee of the House of Commons to hear further evidence against the slave trade in January 1790. After testimony and evidence was presented, Wilberforce proposed a bill to end the slave trade from the English world on April 18, 1791. All the while the Abolition Society continued to build popular support, resulting in a campaign that sent 519 petitions, representing every English county, to Parliament. While Parliament voted the bill down 163 to 88, the antislavery forces appeared to have won a significant victory when a clear majority of the House of Commons resolved that the slave trade ought to be gradually abolished. Members of Parliament, however grew increasingly nervous about the potential radicalism of the growing popular movement against slavery, particularly given the violent turn of the French Revolution. As a result, when Parliament reconvened the following year they declined to renew discussions on a gradual end to the slave trade.

In France a group of liberals, including the Marquis de Lafayette (1757–1834), had been corresponding with the English Society for the Abolition of Slavery and had established a similar society: *Les Amis des Noirs* (Society of the Friends of the Negro) in 1789. While Wilberforce had hoped to visit Paris to support the new society, it was determined that Clarkson should go instead since it may not have been prudent for a member of the British government to travel to France given the growing unrest of the French Revolution (Greenidge 1958, 135).

Meanwhile, Wilberforce continued his efforts in Parliament, but it would take another six years for a notable victory—the passage of a bill in 1799 limiting the number of slaves per ton permissible on British slave ships (Ackerman 2005, 12). It would be another five years before Wilberforce made significant progress toward a legislative ban of the slave trade itself. The Abolition Society, dormant since 1795 largely as the result of Clarkson's ill health, was revived with the infusion of new members in 1804. With the support of the rejuvenated Society, Wilberforce introduced a new bill, which this time passed the House of Commons only to lose by seven votes in the House of Lords (Greenidge 1958, 137). Wilberforce gained another victory when both houses of Parliament passed a bill on June 24, 1806 that abolished slave trade to territories taken by the British during the Napoleonic Wars and prohibited British slave ships from taking slaves to foreign colonies (Ackerman 2005, 13).

The final step toward the complete abolition of the slave trade took place the following year. On January 2, 1807, Lord Granville introduced a bill stating:

> from and after January 1, 1808, all manner of "dealing and trading in slaves" in Africa, or their transport from Africa to any other place, should be prohibited and unlawful. (Greenidge 1958, 138)

On March 16 Members of Parliament rose and cheered Wilberforce, and by March 25, 1807, the English slave trade had been officially ended. Twenty years after its establishment, the Society for the Abolition of Slavery had achieved its first goal and by 1833 it achieved its second— the abolition of slavery in all English possessions.

Over the course of the nineteenth century the institution of slavery, which had gone virtually unchallenged before 1757, was officially abolished throughout the western world. In France colonial slavery was temporarily outlawed in 1794, although Napoleon's repeal of the law in 1802 caused slavery not to be permanently abolished in France and her territories until 1848. In the United States the slave trade was ended in 1808 and slavery was abolished with the passage

of the thirteenth amendment in 1865. Spain outlawed slavery in all
of her territories by 1820 and the emerging independent republics of
Latin America followed suit—Chile (1823), Mexico (1829), Bolivia
(1831), Uruguay (1842), Equador (1851), Argentina (1853), Venezuela
(1854), and Peru (1854). In 1861 Tsar Alexander II abolished serfdom
in Russia. By 1888, when Brazil officially abolished slavery, the efforts
begun by twelve men gathered in a London print shop a hundred years
earlier were at last completed.

THE CAUSES
OF THE BRITISH ANTISLAVERY MOVEMENT
AND THE LAST JUDGMENT

Historians continue to seek an answer as to why an organized
antislavery movement suddenly emerged in the second half of the
eighteenth century. As Howard Temperley asks,

> The problem is easily stated: What was it, in the late eighteenth and early
> nineteenth centuries, that made men turn against an institution which, in one
> form or another, had existed since time immemorial? Why was slavery attacked
> *then?* Why not in the seventeenth century, or the sixteenth? Why, indeed, was it
> attacked at all? (Temperley 1981, 21)

The traditional answer has been that the eighteenth century
antislavery movement was the culmination of a long line of intellectual
inquiry. That is, antislavery ideas, originally expressed in relative
isolation by individuals beginning in the sixteenth century, finally
coalesced and were channeled into a popular movement in the late
eighteenth century. In *History of Abolition* (1808), Thomas Clarkson
attempted to describe this progression of ideas, showing how the "tiny
springs and rivulets" of individuals in the sixteenth and seventeenth
centuries "converge[d] to become rivers, eventually swelling the torrent
which swept away the slave trade" (Temperley 1981, 21). Ultimately
this approach argues that individuals acted against slavery, whether
for religious or humanitarian reasons, because it was the morally right

thing to do. In recent decades, however, historians have begun to question this approach. They argue that this view fails to meaningfully connect the progression and development of ideas to the realities and events of the period—it fails to explain what in paticular about the late eighteenth century made men adopt antislavery views and act upon them (Temperley 1981, 23).

The competing explanation is that the antislavery movement resulted from specific economic forces at work in the late eighteenth century. While these historians do not totally discount the role of morality, they argue that slavery was abolished when it was no longer profitable. Eric Williams, for example, argues that it was not benevolence but greed and self-interest that brought an end to slavery. By the late eighteenth century, he argues, slavery was not only "becoming less important to the British economy . . . that it was inefficient and unprofitable" (Engerman 1981, 6). Critics of this view argue that slavery was not failing but expanding and increasing in importance to the British economy in the late eighteenth century. In fact the number of slaves imported into the Caribbean, Brazil, and the British colonies reached its height during the middle of the eighteenth century. Outram argues that slavery and the slave trade in particular were: "essential to the increasingly integrated world economy of the Enlightenment," and that the abolition of the slave trade meant "the dismantling of a profitable, successful, and globally organized economic structure." (Outram 2005, 63–65)

A third approach, put forth by Howard Temperley, tries to reconcile these two contradictory explanations (Temperley 1981, 22). Temperley's answer is that in the late eighteenth century people began to believe for the first time that it was *possible* to eliminate slavery. Until this time, as we have seen, slavery was almost universally seen as a part of the natural order. "Before slavery could become a political issue—or even in the proper sense, a moral issue, what needed to be shown was that the world could get along without it" (Temperley 1981, 29). Temperley argues that this evidence presented itself in the rapid growth of the free-labor economies of England and New England.

In short, people began to see that material prosperity and individual freedom did not have to be mutually exclusive. Slavery was already increasingly being seen as inhumane and morally unacceptable and could now been seen as "removable" and ultimately as an impediment to human progress.

Historians continue to search for a clear and meaningful answer to why an antislavery movement seemed to suddenly appear in the late eighteenth century, New Church historians can offer critical insight into why this may have been the case. In particular, an understanding of the Last Judgment can shed light on why people came to not only see slavery as a sin, but be able, as Temperley argues, to see slavery as "removable." It is significant that historians identify the second half of the eighteenth century as the critical turning point in the transition from antislavery thought to antislavery action. It is intriguing that some point to the London Quaker Yearly Meeting of 1757 specifically as the beginning of this shift.

The Writings of Emanuel Swedenborg tell us that the Last Judgment took place in the spiritual world in 1757. Prior to the Last Judgment "much of the communication between heaven and the world . . . was intercepted" (CLJ 8) which resulted in people losing the ability to both recognize and distinguish between truth and falsity and freely choose between good and evil. By means of the Last Judgment, the equilibrium between heaven and hell was restored, clearing the air, as it were, for the Lord's influx to again flow freely into the world and restore man's freedom. The result was that people could again be enlightened to see the truth around them, to recognize the false ideas that were in their midst, and to freely choose between them. As Swedenborg writes

> For since communication has been restored by the Last Judgment, man can be enlightened and reformed; that is, can understand the Divine truth of the Word, receive it when understood, and retain it when received, for the interposing obstacles are removed. (CLJ 12)

Swedenborg also states, however, that the Last Judgment took place in the spiritual world and that:

> The future state of the world will be exactly the same as it has been up to now; for the mighty change which has taken place in the spiritual world does not cause any change in the external appearance of the natural world. (LJ 73)

The changes that took place in the natural world were internal and as such do not necessarily appear so obvious or immediate. One of the important effects of the Last Judgment, however, was that evils present in the world, such as slavery, could be more easily recognized and that people could freely chose what was true and good. Swedenborg tells us that the Last Judgment brought one era to an end and allowed a new era to begin. It was precisely at the end of the eighteenth century that humans began to identify slavery as a sin and recognize that it could and should be removed. Within one century a new era *was* born—an era founded not on slavery but on free labor. Prior to the middle of the eighteenth century slavery had gone virtually unchallenged. Even when individuals began to oppose slavery, most still accepted that it was an unchangeable part of the natural order. As historian J.M. Roberts writes:

> In the middle of the eighteenth century most people . . . could still believe that the world would go on much as it seemed always to have done. The weight of the past was everywhere enormous and often it was immovable. (Johnson 2007, 8)

Yet, by 1787 only thirty years after the Last Judgment took place in the spiritual world, a society was organized in England for the express purpose of eliminating slavery. Within a century slavery had been legally abolished throughout the western world.

THE SWEDENBORGIAN INFLUENCE
ON THE BRITISH ANTISLAVERY MOVEMENT

While the nature of the Last Judgment and its effects can provide insight into the question of why the antislavery movement began when it did, it is also important to recognize that the truths revealed in the Writings of Emanuel Swedenborg (1688–1772) inspired individuals to play an active role in the fight against slavery. Marguerite Block notes that even though Swedenborg does not specifically address the institution of slavery, a significant number of his early followers found in his Writings the "inspiration for their attack upon it" (Block 1984, 55). One such individual was Carl Wadström (1746–1799), who came to play an important role in the English antislavery story.

Born in Stockholm on April 19, 1746, Wadström began his career working in Sweden's Government Surveying Office in 1766 before he was appointed to the College of Mines three years later, where, like Swedenborg, he eventually served on the Board of Mines. An interesting chapter in Wadström's early career involved a covert mission to Prussia, where he was sent by King Gustav III (who was contemplating hostilities with Russia) to discover the secret of their sword making. Caught and imprisoned, Wadström managed to escape and return to Sweden with twenty-seven sword makers, which earned him honors from the king (Acton 1943, 2–3). Two years later, Wadström traveled through Germany, France, Holland, and England as the tutor to Adolf Ulrik Grill, whose father Klas Grill had business connections to Swedenborg. During this trip Wadström took careful notes on the mines, factories, machinery, and farming in these nations (Acton 1943, 4). As a friend noted after his death in 1799:

> As a scientist, Wadström had genius and deep insight, especially in mineralogy, mechanics, natural history, and political economy. He sketched with unusual ease and correctness, and was thoroughly familiar with English and French. (Acton 1943, 5)

His insight in these areas, and particularly his talents for sketching, came to play an important part in the antislavery drama.

Like Swedenborg, Wadström left his scientific pursuits and his career in the College of Mines to dedicate the rest of his life to a different path. Wadström created a colony in Africa and put an end to the slave trade.

While it is not clear when Wadström was introduced to Swedenborg's Writings, Acton speculates that it was most likely late in 1778 or early in 1779 (Acton 1943, 5). It is clear from a letter sent by Augustus Nordenskjöld to his brother on March 30, 1781 that Wadström had at that point deeply committed to Swedenborg's Writings. Nordenskjöld writes in his letter:

> Director Wadström is one of the most solid receivers of whom I know, and engages in much activity and conversation in all companies, wherever he can bring up the subject. He also gives his testimony modestly and frankly. (Acton 1943, 6)

One such "activity" was the establishment of a group of men who shared his interest in Swedenborg's Writings. In a detailed account of the meeting of this group in the *New Jerusalem Magazine* (1790), Wadström clearly states that these men came together as a direct result of Swedenborg's teachings regarding the African people. He writes:

> In the year 1779, a society of affectionate admirers of the Writings of that extraordinary man Emanuel Swedenborg assembled at Norrköping in Sweden, in consequence of reflecting on the favorable account this eminent author gives, both in his printed works and in his manuscripts, of the African nation. (*New Jerusalem Magazine* 1790, 70)

While we do not know which passages in particular drew the interest of these men, we do know that with regard to the nature of the Africans, Swedenborg differed markedly from the many philosophers of the century who emphasized the racial superiority of the European and likened the African to beasts. As we have seen, Hume (1711–1776) not only believed "the negroes . . . to be naturally inferior to the whites," but wrote of one Black African in Jamaica: "'tis likely he is admired for very slender accomplishments like a parrot, who speaks few words plainly" (Kramnick 1995, 629). Kant (1724–1804) suggested that the religion of Africans was a type of idolatry and used color as proof of their lack of intelligence: "this fellow was quite black from head to foot, a clear proof that what he said was stupid" (Kramnick 1995, 639). Likewise Long (1734–1813) wrote that Africans "are said to perform their work in a very bungling and slovenly manner, perhaps not better than an *orangutan* might, with little pains, be brought to" (Kramnick 1995, 645).

In stark contrast to these depictions, Swedenborg writes that the spirits he visited with in the spiritual world who had lived in Africa were more capable of enlightenment than were Europeans because of their ability to think interiorly.

> The African people are more capable of enlightenment than all other peoples on this earth, because they are of such character as to think interiorly and thus to accept truths and acknowledge them. Others, such as the Europeans, think only externally, receiving truths in their memory, but not seeing them interiorly in any light of the understanding—a light which they also do not acknowledge in matters of faith. (LJ 118)

Swedenborg also calls the Africans "the most beloved" of the heathens in heaven because of their ability to "receive the goods and truths of heaven more readily than others" (HH 326), noting specifically that "when the Word was presented to them, they understood it as to the internal spiritual sense" (LJ 123). He noted not only the Africans' willingness to receive the Word and their ability to see God as a Man, but their celestial nature:

> Moreover, the Africans are more receptive than others in this earth, of the heavenly doctrine . . . . These willingly receive, from the angels, the doctrine concerning the Lord. They, more than any others, have it implanted in themselves that the Lord must appear altogether as a man, and that it can by no other means happen otherwise. They are in the capacity of receiving not only the truths of faith, but especially its goods. They are of the celestial genius. (SE 4783)

Addressing the state of the church and Africa, Swedenborg writes:

> Hence the angels rejoiced that the coming of the Lord was now at hand, and that the Church, which is now perishing in Europe, should be renewed in Africa. (SE 4777)

Inspired by Swedenborg's Writings, Wadström and the Norrköping society determined to eliminate the African slave trade and establish a new society on the west coast of Africa which was founded on "true Christian principles." Wadström wrote of their intentions:

> I esteemed it as one of the happy events of my life, the being present on this remarkable occasion . . . . Before this memorable meeting was dissolved, every one present expressed his warmest and most cordial assurance, to labor, each in his particular station, unceasingly to exert his utmost abilities in concerting and carrying into execution a plan, not only for the abolition of that execrable trade, but for the general civilization, founded on true Christian principles, of those uncultivated and hitherto abused nations. (*New Jerusalem Magazine* 1790, 70)

These followers of Swedenborg, whose primary objectives included the abolition of the slave trade, predated the Quaker antislavery society in England by four years and Clarkson's Society for the Abolition of Slavery by eight years.

With regard to establishing a colony on the coast of Africa, the Norrköping group sought to create a society founded on the principles of Swedenborg's Writings. Based on agricultural trade and free of slavery, this society would eliminate the "Lust of Dominion" and "Lust of Possession" which the group believed had corrupted Europe (Coleman 2005, 68) and of which Swedenborg wrote, "Dominion from evil and falsity consists in desiring to make all slaves . . . . [and] destroying all. From which it is evident that dominion from evil and falsity is of the devil" (AC 1749[3]). These goals were later formalized by Augustus Nordenskjöld and published in *A Plan for a Free Community upon the coast of Africa under the protection of Great Britain; but Entirely Independent of All European Laws and Governments* (1789), which Wadström signed along with two others.

Getting to the coast of Africa, however, proved an arduous task for Wadström and his friends. Their first attempt was late in 1779, when they presented a petition to King Gustav III seeking support in establishing "a commercial and farming colony" (Acton 1943, 10). While this effort failed due to the tensions surrounding the American Revolution, the king gave his consent on September 27, 1781, granting a charter by which "they were empowered to organize their own government, to enact their own laws, and to establish a society in all respects independent o[f] Europe" (Wadström 1794, 185). But this effort again failed when they could not attract enough colonists, despite Augustus Nordenskjöld's trips to England and France to recruit volunteers.

With plans for colonization stalled, Wadström and Nordenskjöld decided to make an exploratory voyage to Africa. Again their initial efforts did not come to fruition, this time of their own choosing. In May 1784 they had received an offer from French merchant Jacques Chauvel who proposed sailing to the Senegal River where they could transfer to a smaller ship and sail to Gallam, 700 miles up the river. Wadström and Nordenskjöld refused the offer when it became clear that Chauvel planned to transport slaves on the voyage (Acton 1943, 12–14).

Wadström finally achieved success in 1787 when he received a subsidy from King Gustav III to travel to Africa, with instructions to investigate an appropriate site for a future colony with the hopes of establishing gold mines and developing trade with the Africans. King Gustav required that Wadström be accompanied by Professor Anders Sparrman (1748–1820), a natural scientist, and Lt. Carl Axel Arrhenius, Sweden's most distinguished Swedish chemist and mineralogist (Acton 1943, 20). Wadström said of the expedition, "the king loved gold, my worthy companions loved natural history, and I loved colonization" (Wadström 1794, 187).

They eventually secured passage on a French ship owned by the slave-trading Senegal Company (Acton 1943, 25). Having landed on the French Island of Gorée, near Dakar, Wadström and his companions made several trips to the mainland coast. It was there that Wadström witnessed the horrors of the African slave trade firsthand. One of the scenes Wadström describes in his work *Observations on the Slave Trade* (1789) was the brutal condition of slaves he saw being unloaded from a sloop that had brought them from Sallum to Gorée.

> The greater part of them were women and children. Notwithstanding this, they had been thrown into the sloop as if they had been articles of lumber, and devoid of feeling. Obliged, moreover, from too close a stowage, to lie on the inequalities and protuberances of the bare planks, without being able to change their position they had in the course of only eight days ... been very materially

hurt; for when I saw them brought out of the sloop, they had several contusions on various parts of their bodies, and in others their flesh was severely cut. A poor child in particular, about two years old, had a very deep wound in his side, made in the manner above stated. He lay afterwards, upon being landed, with the wound contiguous to the ground, so that the sand getting into it, put him to exquisite pain. I mention this instance, only to give an idea of what are thought to be rooms of accommodation for slaves, and of that inhumanity, which naturally springs out of the prosecution of this trade. (Wadström 1789, 14–15)

Wadström describes another occasion on which a number of slaves were brought by French soldiers to the coast.

These consisted of men, women, and children . . . . The women . . . vented their sorrow in shrieks and lamentations. The children, in a state of palpitation, clung to their mother's breasts. Their little eyes were so swelled with crying, that they could cry no more. During all this time, the captors, to shew their joy on the occasion, and to drown the cries of their unfortunate fellow-subjects, were beating large drums. To this was added, all the noise that could be collected from the blowing of horns, and the human voice. Taking in the shrieks and the agony of the one, and the shouts and joy of the other, with the concomitant instruments of noise, I was never before witness to such an infernal scene. (Wadström 1789, 11–12)

Finally, he describes the horrific conditions in the slave prisons.

They were confined in prisons or dungeons resembling dens, where they lie naked on the sand, crowded together and loaded with irons. In consequence of this cruel mode of confinement, they are frequently covered with cutaneous eruptions. Ten or twelve of them feed together out of a trough, precisely like so many hogs. (Wadström 1789, 29)

The hostility of the Senegal Company, which prevented them from gaining access to the interior, and the outbreak of hostilities between England and France, caused Wadström and his companions to leave Africa after only three months. Whether it was because of the antislavery developments beginning to take place there or word that followers of Swedenborg were taking steps to establish their own church, Wadström decided to return home to Sweden by way of England (Johnson 2007, 2). Wadström arrived in London in March 1788 and on Christmas day he was baptized in the first New Church place of worship, a rented chapel in Great East Cheap (Acton 1943, 33).

He would soon meet the leaders of the English antislavery movement—Thomas Clarkson, Granville Sharp, and William Wilberforce—bringing him center stage in the Abolitionist Society's efforts to end the slave trade. In 1789 Wadström published his now famous engraving of the slave ship *Brooks* along with a description of the inhumane seizure of African slaves.

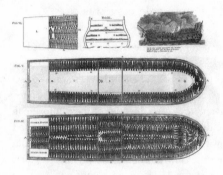

Of the engraving of the slave ship, Wadström wrote:

The plan and sections annexed exhibit a slave ship with the slaves stowed. In order to give a representation of the trade against which no complaint or exaggeration could be brought by those concerned in it, the *Brooks* is here described, a ship well known in the trade, and the first mentioned in the report delivered to the House of Commons by Captain Parrey, who was sent to Liverpool by Government to take the dimensions of the ship employed in the African slave-trade from that port. (Wadström, *Description of a Slave Ship*)

Later that year he also published *Observations on the Slave Trade and A Description of Some Parts of the Coast of Guinea* (1789), the purpose of which he wrote in the preface, was to expose "to the world the atrocious acts committed in that part of the globe to which I have been eye-witness."

He received his first chance to expose the horrors of slavery in 1788 when he and Dr. Anders Sparrman were as eyewitnesses asked by

Clarkson and Wilberforce to testify before the Trade Commission of the Privy Council. Clarkson wrote of Wadström and Sparrman:

> It so happened that by means of George Harrison, I fell in unexpectedly with these gentlemen [professor Sparrman and Wadström]. I had not long been with them before I perceived the great treasures I had found . . . They showed me their journals . . . (in which were) a number of circumstances minuted down, all relating to the slave trade. I obtained a more accurate . . . knowledge of the manners and customs of the Africans from them than from all the persons put together whom I had yet seen. (Acton 1943, 28)

Wadström was called on again to testify in 1789, this time before the committee of the whole of the House of Commons in 1789, where he presented twenty-seven pages of testimony, which included not only a description of the methods used by the Senegal Company for procuring slaves but the charge that the slave trade caused the natives to go to war with one another in order to sell slaves to the Europeans for goods. He described the Africans as:

> quiet, inoffensive people, happy in themselves, and in one another, enjoying the comforts of life, without the intervention of toil and trouble. (Wadström 1789, 6)

He went on to testify that:

> They had a great inclination for trade and industry, and, without doubt, would farm their land well, if only the slaves dealers did not occupy all their thoughts. (Acton 1943, 34–35)

He was called yet again to give testimony a third time in 1790, when Wilberforce had succeeded in calling for a select committee of the House of Commons to hear further evidence. The following year Wilberforce and Fox drew on Wadström's evidence in their critical speeches before the House of Commons on April 18, 1791. These speeches introduced the bill to abolish slavery from the British world, which, while officially voted down, helped convince the House of Commons, at least temporarily, that the slave trade ought to be gradually abolished (Acton 1943, 45).

Three times between 1789 and 1791 Wadström had been asked by Clarkson and Wilberforce to provide critical testimony before the Privy Council and the House of Commons. In addition, his engravings were displayed in the Parliament buildings, where they helped to build awareness and sympathy for antislavery among Members of Parliament (Acton 1943, 40). Clarkson had also taken 500 copies of one of Wadström's engravings with him when he traveled to Paris to support the newly formed Society of the Friends of the Negro in 1789. The eyewitness accounts of the inhumane brutality of the slave trade and the visual images of the horrors of the slave ships helped sway a critical portion of Parliament to the antislavery cause. Wadström's reputation also began to spread among the antislavery forces in France.

In 1793 Wadström wrote his famous two-part *An Essay on Colonization, particularly applied to the Western Coast of Africa, with some Free Thoughts on Cultivation and Commerce* (1794), which made him one of the most recognizable antislavery figures in England and throughout Europe. His *Essay*, for which he had two hundred and eighty-five advance subscribers (Acton 1943, 50), included his first-hand descriptions of the cruelties of slavery; several engraved plates, including a reprint of his famous cross-section of a slave ship; a description of the possibilities for colonization on the coast of Africa; and an argument that the Africans were more economically valuable to Europeans as trading partners and free laborers than as slaves.

Unfortunately the cost of printing far exceeded estimates, and Wadström was forced to turn over all proceeds to the printer. This combined with the heavy financial loss he suffered from a cotton mill he had established left him disillusioned and in financial difficulty (Acton 1943, 52). Refusing to abandon his original goal of establishing a colony in Africa (first established as part of the Norköpping group in 1787), he moved to Paris in 1795, where he saw in the French Revolution the possibilities of a new freedom, and of a national spirit which would eagerly sympathize with his dreams of a colony where a truly free government would be established. (Acton 1943, 54)

Upon his arrival in Paris he addressed the French Directory, calling upon them to join with England in abolishing all slavery (Acton 1943, 55). Two years later he played an active role in reviving the Society of Friends of the Negro, which had been established in 1789, and to which Clarkson had brought copies of his engravings. Sadly, Wadström would not live to see the fruits of his labor. He died in 1799, eight years before Wilberforce's victory in British Parliament brought an end to the English slave trade.

Having been made an honorary citizen, Wadström was given a French state funeral with ceremonial honors. In 1861 the Royal Academy of Sciences struck a medal in his honor. On the reverse side of the medal was the image of an African sitting under a palm tree reading with his cast-off chains at his feet, with the inscription: "Libertas meritas est mihi facta tuis [Liberty had become mine, by thy services]" (Acton 1943, 64).

CONCLUSION

As we recognize the 250th anniversary of the Last Judgment in the spiritual world, it is important to inquire and reflect on the many changes that have occurred, and do occur, as the result of the Lord's influx being able to flow uninhibited into the natural world, restoring our free ability to distinguish and choose between good and evil. Almost immediately following the Last Judgment, dedicated individuals suddenly began to recognize that the evil of slavery, an evil which had remained virtually unchallenged most of its history, was not immovable. And so they worked tirelessly to bring it to an end. The second half of the eighteenth century marked a critical shift from individual antislavery *thought* to organized group antislavery *action*, and ultimately to the legal abolition of slavery. While New Church men and women cannot claim to have started the antislavery movement, there were individuals, such as Carl Wadström, who were inspired by the Writings of Swedenborg and played a critical role in the early antislavery movement. Wadström's testimony and graphic illustrations of the cruelties and horrors of slavery provided leaders such as Clarkson and Wilberforce the evidence they desperately needed to turn the hearts, and legislative authority, of British Parliament.

There is important research to be done by New Church scholars to continue to discover the vital role that the Writings played in inspiring men and women to take up the fight against slavery in England, in the United States, and elsewhere in the world. We need to continue to build on the foundations laid by previous scholars in their work on such individuals as Augustus Nordenskjöld, who worked closely with Wadström; Thomas Goyder, the New Church minister in England who called on his parishioners to sign a petition in 1833 demanding an immediate end to slavery in the British Empire; Robert Carter, who freed his four-hundred and fifty-five slaves, more than any other American; Rev. John Hargrove, who in addition to preaching before members of Congress twice, delivered an antislavery poem to an abolitionist society; Lydia Maria Child, whose *An Appeal in Favor of the Class of Americans Called Africans* (1823) thrust her and the Swedenborgian argument against slavery into the antislavery debate in the United States; Alexander Muravyov, who helped to orchestrate the emancipation of the Russian serfs; and many others.

It would be useful to consult what the Writings have to say about the English people when considering the vital role the fight to abolish the English slave trade played in creating the impetus for broader antislavery movements. Is it significant that the Writings speak of England's freedom of speech, freedom of press, and freedom of thought (TCR 807, LJ 40)? Could this be why the antislavery movement found much of its origins in England?

We must also remember that the effects of the Last Judgment continue to be played out, even now, in the natural world. While slavery was legally abolished virtually everywhere in the western world within slightly more than a hundred years of the Last Judgment, it continues to haunt us today. iAbolish, an American antislavery organization, placed a recent estimate that there are twenty-seven million slaves worldwide in countries on six continents, including as many as 17,000 being trafficked into the United States each year.[1] As we celebrate not only the 250th anniversary of the Last Judgment, but the 200th anniversary of the end of the British slave trade, we should all be cognizant of the many around the world who are still not free and ask ourselves what can and should be done to ensure that slavery does not become, once again, a morally wrong, yet "immovable" reality. ⚮

BIBLIOGRAPHY

Ackerson, Wayne. *The African Institution (1807–1827) and the Antislavery Movement in Great Britain.* Lewiston, New York: The Edwin Mellon Press, 2005.

Acton, Alfred. "Carl Bernard Wadström." Bryn Athyn, PA: The Swedenborg Library, 1943.

Block, Marguerite. *The New Church in the New World.* New York, NY: Swedenborg Publishing Company, 1984.

Brown, Christopher Leslie. *Moral Capital: Foundations of British Abolitionism.* Chapel Hill, NC: The University of North Carolina Press, 2006.

Coleman, Dierdre. *Romantic Colonization and British Anti-Slavery.* New York: Cambridge University Press, 2005.

Davis, David Brion. "The Emergence of Immediatism in British and American Antislavery Thought," *The Mississippi Historical Review* 49, no. 2 (September, 1962): 209–230.

Davis, David Brion. *The Problem of Slavery in Western Culture.* New York: Oxford University Press, 1966.

Dole, George F., David B. Eller, Olle Hjern, Robert Kirven, Jean-François Mayer, Frank S. Rose, Jonathan S. Rose, Alice B. Skinner, Richard Smoley, and Jane Williams-Hogan. *Emanuel Swedenborg: Essays for the New Century Edition on His Life, Work, and Impact.*

1.http://www.iabolish.org/slavery_today/primer/index.html.

Edited by Jonathan S. Rose, Stuart Shotwell, and Mary Lou Bertucci. West Chester, PA: Swedenborg Foundation, 2005.

Drescher, Seymour. *Capitalism and Antislavery: British Mobilization in Comparative Perspective.* New York: Oxford University Press, 1987.

Engerman, Stanley. "Some Implications of the Abolition of the Slave Trade." In *The Abolition of the Atlantic Slave Trade: Origins and Effects in Europe, Africa, and the Americas,* edited by Davis Eltis and James Walvin, 3–17. Madison, WI: The University of Wisconsin Press, 1981.

Eze, Emmanuel Chukwudi, ed. *Race and the Enlightenment.* Cambridge, MA: Blackwell Publishers, 1997.

Greenidge, C.W.W. *Slavery.* London: George Allen and Unwin Ltd., 1958.

Hochschild, Adam. *Bury the Chains: Prophets and Rebels in the Fight to Free an Empire's Slaves.* New York: Houghton Mifflin Company, 2005.

iAbolish: The American Anti-Slavery Group. *Modern-Day Slavery Fact Sheet.* (accessed July 7, 2007). http://www.iabolish.org/slavery_today/primer/index.html.

Jennings, Judith. *The Business of Abolishing the British Slave Trade 1783-1807.* Portland, OR: Frank Cass and Co., 1997.

Johnson, Patrick L. "Slavery, Its Abolition and Carl Bernard Wadström." *Things Heard and Seen: Newsletter of the Swedenborg Society* (July, 2007): 1-3.

Johnson, Patrick L. "What Happened after 1757?" *Things Heard and Seen: Newsletter of the Swedenborg Society* (July, 2007): 8-12.

Jordan, Winthrop. *The White Man's Burden: Historical Origins of Racism in the United States.* New York, NY: Oxford University Press, 1974.

Kant, Immanuel. *Observations on the Feeling of the Beautiful and Sublime.* 1764. Trans. John T. Goldthwait. Berkeley:University of California Press, 1961, 2003.

Kellow, Margaret M. R. "Swedenborg's Influence on Antebellum Reform: The Case of Lydia Maria Child" (Paper, annual meeting of the American Academy of Religion, Kansas City, MO, November 23, 1991).

Kramnick, Isaac, ed. *The Portable Enlightenment Reader.* New York, NY: Penguin Books, 1995.

Merriman, John. *A History of Modern Europe: From the Renaissance to the Present.* New York: W. W. Norton and Company, 1996.

Northrup, David, ed. *The Atlantic Slave Trade.* Lexington, KY: D.C. Heath and Company, 1994.

Outram, Dorinda. *The Enlightenment.* 2nd ed. New York, NY: Cambridge University Press, 2005.

Pieterse, Jan Nederveen. *White on Black: Images of Africa and Blacks in Western Popular Culture.* New Haven, CT: Yale University Press, 1992.

Rotberg, Robert I. "The Swedenborgian Search for African Purity." Review of *Romantic Colonization and British Anti-Slavery,* by Deidre Coleman. *Journal of Interdisciplinary History* (Autumn, 2005).

Swedenborg, Emanuel. *Arcana Coelestia.* vol. I and vol. VII. West Chester, PA: Swedenborg Foundation, 1997, 1998.

Temperley, Howard. "The Ideology of Antislavery." In *The Abolition of the Atlantic Slave Trade: Origins and Effects in Europe, Africa, and the Americas,* edited by Davis Eltis and James Walvin, 21-35. Madison, WI: The University of Wisconsin Press, 1981.

Wadström, Carl B. *An Essay on Colonization: Particularly Applied to the Western Coast of Africa with Some Free Thoughts on Cultivation and Commerce.* 1794. Reprint, New York: Augustus M. Kelley Publishers, 1968.

————. "Letter I," *New Jerusalem Magazine or a Treasury of the Celestial, Spiritual, and Natural Knowledge* (February 1, 1790): 70-73.

————. *Observations on the Slave Trade and a Description of some Part of the Coast of Guinea During a Voyage Made in 1787, and 1888, in Company with Doctor A. Sparrman and Captain Arrhenenius.* London: James Philips, 1789.

Williams-Hogan, Jane K. "Swedenborg in Russia: West Meets East." (unpublished manuscript).

Possible Consequences of the Last Judgment
on Society

Rev. Göran Appelgren

Discussant of the following three papers:

A New Refrain: The Child and 'Songs of Innocence,' Jane Williams-Hogan, Ph.D.

The Last Judgment and Women in the Modern Western World, Sonia Soneson Werner, Ph.D.

From Thought to Action: The Last Judgment, Swedenborg and the Antislavery Movement, Brian D. Henderson

INTRODUCTORY THOUGHTS

Knowledge about a certain thing is impossible without observation. What color are your eyes? There is no possible way to make the observation necessary to give you that knowledge, because you need your eyes to observe color. You can't hear or smell the color of your eyes. You must provide different means to make the observation possible. You can ask someone else, or you can look into a still water surface, and beyond primitive times you can use a mirror, a camera and so on. But left to yourself alone with no tools you cannot make the observation necessary. Dr. Williams-Hogan has a similar thought: "Children don't make childhood, they participate in childhoods created by adults."

Another example: If you were to be asked what the most critical question of our time is, you would not be able to give the correct answer. Because you stand in the middle of it, you cannot observe it. We are blind to major changes that are still in their seedbeds. We can at best guess but not even that would come close to the correct answer. If you say the most critical issue today is global warming, you are only repeating already existing knowledge. If you say disintegration of family values, you are again simply repeating existing knowledge. If you say the carbon atom will soon mutate in such a way that it will not any more be able to be the carrier of organic life, then you maybe have found the right answer, but no one will believe you, because there are no observations to support your conclusion. There are always changes under way that we cannot be aware of. No one in this world could see the Last Judgment coming. Still, it happened and changes resulting from it are taking place today. Only gradually do we become aware of major changes—by observation and in a kind of hindsight, and there we can be slow or quick to respond. The quicker we are, the better will the knowledge be, and our readiness to meet the challenges that come from the changes. From observation follows knowledge, from knowledge awareness, and from awareness action. Some of the people described in the three papers were quick to respond, to gain knowledge and to act.

Examples to illustrate this: effects of diseases have been observed, knowledge gained and action been taken. Environmental threats against biological systems have been observed, knowledge gained and action been taken. Take any example you want. But at one point people were totally blind to the coming changes.

From the Word we have another example. It is from chapter eleven in Revelation. The "beast" thought it had all power. It could kill the "two witnesses." A big change was under way. The beast, because it was the beast, had no chance of seeing the change coming. The prophecy of the two witnesses made no impression on the beast. The beast was taken by surprise. Looking into the future it saw nothing. When—after three and a half days—looking back it saw defeat because something unawares had taken place—a Last Judgment on false ideas about the Lord and His commandments.

If we now turn these ideas around in a time line, we will see that existing normal applications, say immunization or emission controls, are taken more or less for granted. They are part of our daily life. But before they were integrated and taken as a given they emerged from somewhere. The cell phone did not just appear from one day to the next. There was a time before the cell phone, then something happened, and after that we live with the cell phone as an integral part of our daily life.

To summarize this, if we look into the future it is hazy, uncertain and impossible to guess what is going to happen. And if we look to the present, we take things for granted, things that slowly grew out of what at first were uncertain observations, maybe bold and crazy reflections on scattered observations of seemingly unimportant data. Looking into the future, and looking back from the present, we must draw the conclusion that in things that have developed to something that is part of people's lives, there must have been a *Before*, an *After* and something *In-between* that we can call the turning point.

One of the beauties of historical studies is that we get to see the elements that contributed to a certain event. There is a cause and effect relationship that we find fascinating. We get excited about details and can think "What if this hadn't happened?"; "What if the coup against Hitler had run its course to the full?"; and so on.

A challenge in historical studies is that we know how it ended. Imagine trying to write a history book about the nineteenth century and mentally excluding everything you knew about the twentieth century and its two world wars, or writing the history of the World War I and brain-washing yourself to the extent you have no recollection of the Second World War. It is impossible, and yet, that is how it should be done, if you really want to describe what was "in the air" at the time before the big event or change took place—writing history as if you did not know what was going to happen next.

An interesting illustration of this thought can be found in a book written in 1883. The author, Rev. Bayley, looks back on the first hundred years of the organized New Church. It is hard to find a quote from the book that exactly captures the tone. Because the tone of voice is of someone, who expects nothing but progress after the Last Judgment. If he had been told that there would two terrible world wars, genocides on a massive scale and more, he would have said: It is impossible (cf. Bayley, 71, 127, 149).

The Last Judgment conference dealt with the effects of the judgment. Has there ever in historical studies been a more clear case of a *Before* and an *After* and something *In-between*! And have there ever been more arcane circumstances to which to direct the inquisitive eye!

These are my comments to the charge for this conference which says: "The assessment of the Last Judgment's natural effects presents New Church scholars with an exciting array of research challenges. These challenges are enhanced by the fact that the effects of the Judgment were not readily observable at that time."

If we look at the three papers we can use these reflections to think about the treatment of children. Walk into that time and think of them as almost not human. After all, most of them died within weeks or months in the middle of the 1700s in London. Mankind lived in disorder. They were not able to see with the eyes we see. It is all too easy to judge the past from values of today. Go back, be like them. Give dispassionate descriptions of ordinary life. The Germans during the holocaust would write an orderly report full of facts just like a salesman on his return to the office would write a report on all the new customers he had lined up with the company. Only afterwards can we, who are more enlightened and do not share the ideology of Nazi Germany, be upset about the facts of life at that time.

To get a grasp of the tremendous social changes that have taken place after the Last Judgment we should seek to find a way to find facts and describe the world at the time in as dispassionate way as possible. Such dispassionate descriptions will—because of their dispassion— create a strong emotional reaction in the reader, because the reader cannot but look at the facts from a post-Last Judgment position.

The point I am trying to make is that we will better see the impact of the Last Judgment if we can see the *"Before"* as if we did not know the *"After"* and even less the acting agent *"In-between."* "How could they?" should be the appropriate reaction when reading about the

"*Before.*" And when reading about the "*After*" the reaction should be "Thank you, good Lord, for intervening."

Such was the theme of the conference and it might work well in the future as a model for study of other areas of life where we look for a specific "*Before*" that we can compare with a pretty obvious post-Last Judgment "*After.*"

All three papers had this outlook. The three authors have chosen different ways to lead the reader to see the upsetting circumstances before the Last Judgment in order to compare with the situation after. But before we comment on these different ways of relating past to present we will give a summary of the papers, where the main theme, the research, the method and the authors' conclusions will be highlighted.

SOME THEORETICAL CONCEPTS IN GENERAL

In order to draw conclusions of effects of the Last Judgment on the state of the world after 1757, we need values or specific ideas as an a priori statement in our discussion, e.g.:

- ideals of conjugial love
- the concept of innocence and it's importance as a preparation for a decent life and even more for the necessary process of regeneration
- human freedom as a starting point for the development of the gifts each individual has from God
- moral revival as based on the Ten Commandments and rejecting faith alone
- a pronounced love of the neighbor seen in active and unselfish duty to the benefit of others
- visions of a new world order

At the core of this conference was the question of a "*Before*" and an "*After.*" See the illustration below. If we take the papers in order it would have to do with the way children were treated *Before* and *After* (rectangle), the way women were treated *Before* and *After* (triangle), and finally how slaves were treated *Before* and *After* (ellipse). Before the Last Judgment there were black clouds of falsities intercepting the light from the Lord. Spirits in the world of spirits were confused, and that affected people on earth. After the judgment the light could reach both spirits and people on earth.

The following chart describes the model:

	Before		After
Light and heat from the Lord	⇓ ⇓ ⇓		↓ ↓ ↓
World of spirits	☹☹☹☹☹☹	Last Judgment	☺☺☺☺☺☺
Uses, occupations on earth	▮ ▲ ⬤		▯ △ ⬭

The Last Judgment was indeed a big shift. A new era was made possible. All three presenters have touched on this. In the Writings it is expressed in several places, e.g.: "The reason why this doctrine [of the Lord] was not, is, because if it had been, it would not have been received; *for the Last Judgment was not yet accomplished*, and prior to the Last Judgment the power of hell prevailed over the power of heaven; wherefore, if the doctrine had been given before from the mouth of the Lord, it would not have remained with man" (Lord 65, emphasis added).

Another mental view to help understand the discussion in the papers is the triad of end, cause and effect.

The end is the Lord's love for mankind, the cause what He did to change the conditions for His Love to reach mankind and that is the

Last Judgment process. Finally the effect is neighborly love reaching mankind. We see that as improvements in the lives of people on earth, of which we have three good examples in the papers.

INTRODUCTORY REMARKS TO ALL THREE PAPERS

The general thesis is that there is an added element, the *In-between*, the Last Judgment that would change the life of children, women and slaves.

In the three papers we see generally two different methods. Dr. Williams-Hogan and Prof. Henderson use statistical and demographic data to describe the before and the *After*. Dr. Werner uses biographical data and two psychological models.

Dr. Williams-Hogan and Prof. Henderson try to find a measurable unit like the "treatment of children or slaves." Then they make observations roughly at the situation around the year 1700, 1750 and 1800. No such measurable unit is used in Dr. Werner's paper. Therefore, if the reader is aware of the two styles used it may make the reading easier.

If we go to the list of a priori statements of values as above, we can see that the subject of Dr. Williams-Hogan includes values such as innocence, freedom, moral revival and unselfish duty. The subjects chosen by Dr. Werner includes freedom, morality and indirectly ideals of conjugial love. Finally, the subjects in Prof. Henderson's paper are values like freedom, morality and visions of a new world order.

In what follows, there is a summary for each paper, an analysis together with suggestions for further study, and a conclusion.

SUMMARY OF DR. WILLIAMS-HOGAN'S PAPER

The author of the first of the three papers was Dr. Jane Williams-Hogan. Her subject was:

A New Refrain: The Child and "Songs of Innocence"

Dr. Williams-Hogan opens her paper with a black and white picture of the church, being a dead church, before the year of the Last Judgment, 1757. "At the time of its death the Christian Church had become so external that virtually no light from heaven could penetrate the darkness that had descended upon it" (p. 189). She then adds that they only had recourse to natural light, not spiritual light to find answers to theological questions. And more precisely she connects this state with the rejection of the key concept of her paper—innocence. "It is my contention that . . . [the Last Judgment] had its greatest impact on their . . . rejection, of the most interior quality of heaven—innocence" (p. 189). After a description of the qualities of innocence Dr. Williams-Hogan says the Last Judgment "re-opened the communication between heaven and the world, and . . . innocence could be recognized, cherished, and protected" (p. 191).

Then the author explains her study in this way: "The task of this paper is to explore innocence in relation to the social realities and experiences of infants and children in eighteenth century England before and after the Last Judgment; and then attempt to develop a theoretical explanation of what occurred taking the Last Judgment into account" (p. 191).

The time periods analyzed are roughly 1700–1750, the mid 1700s, and 1750–1800. The *first period* was marked by the changes of the social structure after the Glorious Revolution in 1688. The influence from the Puritans had gone away. The aristocracy gradually had to give up some of their control of society to the propertied middle class. Poverty was widespread and had increased, seeing the rise in crime punitive measures. There was a death penalty for 200 crimes. New agricultural methods and land reforms led to the unemployment of many people in the countryside. The Church of England had lost power and all new cannons were written by the Parliament. The bishops were weak and the majority of the priesthood came from the privileged classes and paid little attention to their parishioners. Therefore, "with little or no spiritual guidance from the church, the culture gradually became oriented towards the pursuit of pleasure in this world, rather than delaying gratification until the next" (p. 195).

A moral change was under way. "The decline of Puritan fervor had an impact on sexual morality . . . across all the levels of British society" (p. 195). Court cases show that many people were charged regarding sexual offenses, but still the consequences were mild. The gradual secularization of society led to "a release of the libido from the age-old restraints of Christianity" (p. 196). Promiscuity spread and the number of illegitimate children among the aristocracy was on the rise. One author that is quoted claims that the "period of permissiveness . . . peaked in 1770; at which time . . . sexual repression slowly gained ground" (p. 198). The Puritan spirit had been lost and the poor people followed the example of the aristocracy. Illegitimacy rose dramatically as did prostitution. "Chastity and poverty are incompatible" (p. 200).

Moral theology had gradually changed. The purpose of sex in marriage came to include endearment and comfort. In those secular times this unfortunately led to a misuse of the idea of pleasure, something not intended by the theologians. "Once sexual pleasure was recognized as an end in itself, it was not long before it was also pursued outside of marriage" (p. 202).

The number of children born without a stable family environment grew dramatically. This led to enormous challenges for the parishes, which were expected to care for all these infants and children. "No parish wanted the child to be born within its borders" (p. 203).

The growing poverty and total lack of property also changed the way men and women thought about married life. "Poor men would no longer propose marriage . . . because he could not guarantee that he could support her" (p. 203) .

With the rise of towns, other dreadful problems came about. Rural England quickly changed. Big numbers of unemployed people came from villages into towns. The conditions were unbelievable. Sanitation was unheard of and crime was rampant. This made life in a town a challenge, which showed up in statistics of the number of dead. "Death remained at the center of human experience" (p. 205). Infant mortality was fearfully high, one in four or even more.

From the Bills of Mortality one can find proof of this situation. These Bills were first started in the sixteenth century and contained a list of burials. Later on baptisms were added too. A horrendous truth can be discovered from these Bills: "By the middle of the eighteenth century . . . the deaths in London far exceed the births. . . . This imbalance was clearly a drain on the whole nation" (p. 207). From 1700 to 1750 the total population decreased by 90,000 people. "The loss of life was at its worst between 1727 and 1750" (p. 208). Dr. Williams-Hogan points out that "mortality was greatest among children. The population of London was sustained only by immigrants" (p. 208). And "1730 to 1749 the burials of children under five were . . . 74.5% of all children christened" (p. 209).

Dr. Williams-Hogan then describes in detail the *laws surrounding the production of spirits, especially gin,* in England. It is a sad story of how money takes command over morality. Vested interests made sure Parliament would not pass laws that would stop them from making money on distilling and selling gin. One problem was that the producer also was allowed to distribute their products. This led to an increase in the number of places where you could buy gin to very high figures. "The public loved it, because it was cheap and readily available" (p. 211).

Eventually reports on the situation were collected. For instance "the College of Physicians petitioned Parliament to do something about spurious liquors [that] 'cause weak, feeble and distempered children'" (p. 212).

A committee reported in 1735 as follows: "Unhappy mothers habituate themselves to these distilled liquors, whose children are born weak and sickly, and often look shrivel'd and old as though they had numbered many years. Others again daily give it to their children . . . and learn them even before they can go, to taste and approve this certain destroyer" (p. 212).

Acts were passed and repealed in Parliament, but the Act of 1751 had an effect. Another improvement was the creation of a more modern police force. Something had happened: "The outcry against gin originated among the middle and trading classes, and perhaps can be viewed as the first time that middle-class sensibilities positively affected public policy" (p. 215).

Of course the *"The Gin Craʒe" had an impact on children* born in this period. They not only died en masse, they were also treated in the most inhumane ways. A memorial to the government speaks about "murder of poor miserable infants at their birth . . . [or] exposing newly born infants to perish in the streets" (p. 217). Something had to be done. In 1739 Thomas Coram was granted a charter to start his own set of homes for abandoned children, the Foundling Hospitals.

The background for such an initiative is that "parishes were required to care for foundlings and illegitimate children should no one else take on the responsibility" (p. 218). This, however, did not work very well. The care provided was next to nil, and a lot of abuse was reported. The chances to survive were not high. Something had to be done and the answer was workhouses. The children could stay till the age of 24 and during that time they would learn a trade and they could work for the workshop. Again there were reports of abuse and misbehavior. "The apprentice was little more than a slave" (p. 221).

The church had failed completely: "The parish appeared willing . . . to sacrifice the children for the sake of its own economic and material interests. During the first half of the eighteenth century, regarding the treatment of its children, the spiritual voice of the parish, of the church, is strangely and deathly silent" (p. 223).

Following on from this Dr. Williams-Hogan has collected a number of mid-century observations from different authors.

There is evidence of a cleavage about the middle of the century showing improvement, which can be traced to about 1750 with a peak between 1780 and 1820. The death rate begins to fall after 1750 and more rapidly after 1780. The miserable situation for poor children received attention about the middle of the century. The waste of life was halted in 1750, legislation against spirits became effective in 1751, there was a marked improvement from that date, and this is the date of the turning point of the social history of London. A total ban on distilling spirits was in place in 1760. The first public book on nursing and mothering was published in 1750. Education was begun to be viewed as a better vehicle than workhouses to improve the lives of parish children. A new kind of children's literature developed. There were books written specifically for the enjoyment of children. Retailing toys for children began.

One author says that "between 1760 and 1790 it was crystal clear that there were two worlds, the old and the new" (p. 227). Dr. Williams-Hogan draws our attention to the fact that the first volume of *Arcana Cœlestia* was published in 1749 and that this may be the reason for the change. She concludes this part of the paper by saying:

> What these quotes indicate is that profound shifts in almost every sphere of human endeavor occurred in the middle of the eighteenth century clustering around 1757 but deviating as much as ten to fifteen years on either side... Most modern historians acknowledge that something remarkable occurred in the middle of the eighteenth century, and that it had profound effects... particularly as they related to ideas concerning and treatment of children. However, it is important to point out that not all historians accept this perspective. (p. 228)

Next Dr. Williams-Hogan describes the social environment 1750–1800 and some of the reforms and reformers. Jonas Hanway was involved in several projects. He visited all the workhouses in London and managed to have an Act passed in 1762 that "required parishes to keep a register of the infants put into their care" (p. 230). And in 1766 Parliament investigated the state of Parish Poor Infants. The result was recommendations that improved the condition for such children. The effect was immediate and major. "The poor called it 'the Act for keeping children alive'" (p. 231). Hanway was also involved in providing improvements for "climbing boys or chimney sweeps" that worked for the parishes under harsh conditions.

Dr. Williams-Hogan sums up by saying that "it is possible to date the emergence of public concern for these children from about 1760" (p. 233).

In the following analysis Dr. Williams-Hogan underlines that these people saw a need and they responded, whereas the church did nothing, and "the inescapable fact is that a sufficient number of changes had occurred during the eighteenth century to improve the life chances of the poor" (p. 236).

The next section of the paper deals with infant schools, something the New Church was involved in from the beginning. A historian says, "If the early infant schools can be said to have had any theoretical basis at all, it was Swedenborgianism. It is a remarkable fact that three out of the four pioneers of infant schools—namely Oberlin, Buchanan, and Wilderspin—were members of the New Church or adherents of the Swedenborgian doctrine" (p. 237).

The time frame is a bit later here. The infant schools developed in the beginning of the 1800s. The first school began in Scotland. James Buchanan was hired as a teacher. When he moved to London in 1818 he was introduced to the New Church. In his Westminster school he had 100 children. "Swedenborgianism was so much a part of his life that the doctrines flowed into everything that he did with the children" (p. 239). In 1839 he moved to New Zealand.

Another pioneer was Samuel Wilderspin who came from a New Church family. In 1807, aged sixteen, he began teaching in a New Church Sunday school. In 1820 he moved to a poor area in London to work in an infant school just started up. Later on he said in writing that "children were active, thinking and feeling beings" (p. 242). In his method he "suggested large airy classrooms, proper instructional material, engaged and thinking teachers . . . a large playground . . . with swings, maypoles, flowers, and trees" (p. 243). The playground was also for the moral education. He traveled the country and established sixty new schools. "His impact on the education of young poor English children is inestimable. By 1835 there were over 2,000 Infant Schools in operation" (p. 244).

Dr. Williams-Hogan points out that people who have studied Wilderspin's schools and methods are struck by how much Swedenborg speaks about innocence. They say that "this powerful exposition of innocence of childhood acted like a magnet on Swedenborgian teachers, drawing them irresistibly into opposition to the traditional Christian view" (p. 242).

In the next section Dr. Williams-Hogan discusses the way children are depicted in paintings in the middle of the 1700s. Most of the paper has dealt with poor children and the changing conditions for them leading up to a protection of childhood and the quality of innocence. Now the focus is turned to the rich people who could afford to have a painting made of their children.

Dr. Williams-Hogan discusses whether the painting *The Age of Innocence* by Sir Joshua Reynolds shows a natural image or spiritual qualities, and if the painter and people of the time could see a new spiritual quality. It seems clear, she says, that there was a big change in this kind of painting with 1760 as a watershed. One author says that what came to be called the Romantic child "simply did not exist before the modern era" (p. 251). One theme in the discussion is non-adultness. The proportions, the colors differ from paintings of adults. Another aspect was the growing sense of family being a much stronger unit than before. "The family became more self-conscious and more protective of its individual members" (p. 253). Dr. Williams-Hogan ends this section by saying: "Without a clear concept of the spiritual qualities of innocence, as detailed in the Writings, naturalists have come to question the idea of innocence altogether, and see it merely as a historic invention, not a gift from the Lord" (p. 254).

We now turn to a chapter on historiography, the history of childhood. Until the 1960s there was not much academic work done on trying to understand the concept of childhood. Dr. Williams-Hogan goes through some of the literature in order to find models that can work for New Church scholars in this field. It is only in the modern world that a clear distinction between childhood and adulthood can be described. The idea of family in a modern sense is connected with this. Hugh Cunningham is the author Dr. Williams-Hogan mentions as most promising for providing a "platform for a New Church interpretation of the eighteenth century attitude toward "innocence" and the impact of the Last Judgment" (p. 261). He writes: "The whole evolution of our contemporary manners is unintelligible if one neglects the astonishing growth of the concept of the family. It is not individualism that has triumphed but the family" (p. 255).

He and the other authors all agree "there were major changes in attitude toward and treatment of children over time" (p. 257). Dr. Williams-Hogan talks about different ways to assess what actually went on in children's lives, since all records come from adults. She says that "children don't make childhood, they participate in childhoods created by adults" (p. 260).

Her final point in this section is that secularization meant that the Church at the time got less and less relevant and that other models of explaining life appeared. So what was the inspiration for those courageous men who stood up for the betterment of childhood—moral or also spiritual?

In the conclusion there is a New Church interpretation of the impact of the Last Judgment on the concept of innocence. Explanations of natural empiricists look elsewhere than a New Church historian who has to look at moral and spiritual causes along with natural ones. We get a quick walk through this study with the filthy streets of London with its poor children, a time when the first volume of the *Arcana Cœlestia* was published. The Gin Act was passed and a courageous individual, Jonas Hanway, promoted new ways to care for the children. "It was moral legislation that overcame indifference" (p. 263). The church had failed. But with the light from the Lord shining again into people's minds progress could be made. "This contrast is perhaps the most telling, a resolutely unwilling Anglican Church and a resolute moral champion, Jonas Hanway . . . the Last Judgment and its power to bring to earth the light of heaven, which contained within it heaven's inmost—the innocence of the Lord himself " (p. 264).

ANALYSIS OF DR. WILLIAMS-HOGAN'S PAPER

In the call for papers we could read in the introduction: "The assessment of the Last Judgment's natural effects presents New Church scholars with an exciting array of research challenges. These challenges are enhanced by the fact that the effects of the Judgment were not readily observable at that time."

This paper has taken on that challenge and met the goals of this conference very well. As is, or will be, obvious in my comments to the three papers the question of a *Before* and an *After* is crucial to the question of cause and effect. In this paper we have a clear division of the material used. Evidence of the situation in England in the first half of the eighteenth century is presented in much detail and of a varied kind. Dr. Williams-Hogan then uses an interesting method to describe in a condensed form the turning point, the middle of the century, which is to quote several writers who have covered that part of history. It gives compelling proof of a change in society in many ways at that specific point in time. The third part, the *After*, is then dealt with in such a way that the applications described fit well into the material presented in the first two parts.

We can never know, but it is the assumption and the reason for doing New Church research of this kind that there was a new force acting into mankind from 1757. Within that assumption we would expect to see changes in the area we study. One problem though is that we are locked into a set time frame. To put it in simple terms— before 1757 everything was bad and afterwards it got better. That is the pattern we use in order to "prove" that the Last Judgment had an effect on the subject matter in the research. Dr Williams-Hogan's facts unfortunately predate 1757 in many cases. That is maybe why she uses 1749 and the publication of the first volume of the *Arcana Cœlestia* to push back the set time frame by eight years. She does not discuss this problem and maybe that is more for someone else like a discussant to do rather than the presenter of the paper. Let me quickly say that I don't think this is a big problem in the study. This comment has more to do with making us alert to the danger of trying to fit the data to the expected outcome. I think the solution to the problem lies on a higher, more arcane level.

We know that there are precursors to almost everything new that appears. Leonardo da Vinci and Swedenborg constructed airplanes long before there was synthetic energy, which is needed for flying an airplane. Michael Servetus described the Trinity in correct terms long before the Last Judgment and the Second coming of the Lord. I don't know, but maybe we can think of a *precursing* force in connection with the Last Judgment. After all the case was not that all people on earth were all evil up to 1757, and after they were all good. There is room for latitude, and let that be my thought that eases out the problem of the data being a bit too early in this study.

The amount of detail that is presented is praiseworthy. It gives the reader a very good sense of daily life in the streets of London and the miserable life of infants and children, and in fact of mothers and fathers as well. How dreadful to imagine being one of those parents!

We learn of the economic changes that make people pour into the towns, about the deplorable regulations around distilling and distribution, about the moral morass due to indifference from the clergy and the Church, and the confusion in which the new middle class was left. The curious fact that the death penalty was used so broadly could reflect both a sense of having lost control of the rapid changes in society and of the failure of the Church to teach the Ten Commandments. For example there was a death penalty for robbing the mail, killing a sheep or destroying trees for profit (Bayley, 61).

Poverty, drinking and loose morals created a mass of people that were poor, starving and dying. That is the background for the analysis of the God-given quality of innocence that was either not acknowledged at all or was trampled under foot. In my introductory remarks I discussed to what extent we could know about feelings of people in other times. In this case, can we know whether the parents felt guilt and suffered morally when they saw their children starve and die? Maybe the change that is so clearly described in this paper is not only a change seen with our own eyes. We can see how dreadful it was before and how much better it became. But maybe it was also a major shift in people's perception of what a decent and fulfilling life would be. Yes, I think this has been said in the paper but the thought is worth highlighting.

An interesting point that is made is the deadness of the Old Church. By Church I understand Dr. Williams-Hogan to mean the theology as such and its most prominent representatives and to some extent its servants all over the country but not necessarily all of its members. It is bad enough as is described. The callous way in which the Church "cared" for the children in their custody seems to be echoed in these words from Ezekiel: "For after they had slain their children for their idols, on the same day they came into My sanctuary to profane it; and indeed thus they have done in the midst of My house" (23.39). But we should still be a bit careful in painting in black and white. Jonas Hanway is an example of a good member of the dead Church. However, Dr. Williams-Hogan's approach does make us think more astutely about the fact that many ordinary people who were not part of the ecclesiastical monolithic Church started the improvements after the Last Judgment.

That leads me on to talk about two aspects or two kinds of evidence of the Last Judgment, one being influx into all people willing to react, and the other being people who are directly inspired by the Writings. We will see this discussion repeated in the analysis of the other papers as well. Hanway and others knew nothing of the Writings and still they reacted and acted. The light shining anew was for all people to receive. "The light of the sun will be sevenfold, as the light of seven days, in the day that the LORD binds up the bruise of His people and heals the stroke of their wound" (Isa. 30.26). Wilderspin on the other hand is someone who was inspired directly by the Writings as far as we can tell. He was a young man when he first started teaching in a New Church Sunday school. There may therefore be an element of influx also for him, if we assume that he had not studied the Writings as to its particulars about innocence and then made the connection with raising and educating children in order to protect their innocence. At any rate the paper shows clearly the two ways the Last Judgment can affect people.

In the part of the paper where Dr. Williams-Hogan talks about what people did to improve the condition for children she takes us into three different areas. Hanway improved the conditions in the orphanages, "the Act for keeping children alive." Buchanan, Wilderspin and others started infant schools that spread massively over the country. And the third application is art. It is maybe not as critical as the others but it is a good application of the idea of a spiritual change that carries results that are new to the world. She discusses to what extent spiritual qualities can be seen in art work, and if we can assume that the artist intended to express something otherworldly. Later in the nineteenth century the artist Howard Pyle (1853–1911) most definitely "associated light with truth" (Brock, 445).

In the section on historiography Dr. Williams-Hogan tries to set a reliable theoretical platform for further study. The concept of secularization is used as well as the development of the idea of what a family is. The secularization of society is in this study and this time frame is seen more or less as a result of the fall of the Old Church. "The modes of Christianity were exhausted and could not furnish novelty enough to fix attention" (p. 195). Fascinating aspects appear out of those thoughts. The New Church, the fifth and final of the Churches will not be a monolithic, authoritarian Church but it will be a Church that people have within them. Out of the secularization we must hope that a true internal Church develops. This part of the paper is a bit loosely attached but I think it is important. The thrust of the paper is to show how closed the door was to a true Christianity and how the hells had blocked access to the most dear element of a true faith, innocence. True innocence is only possible if each individual discovers the Lord and follows His commandments. That will be the deepest real effect of the Last Judgment.

In these last comments lie also the seeds of further study:

- liberation of the human mind such that it, in full freedom, can follow the Lord;
- studies of developmental stages of the child and how innocence can be furthered;
- addiction and the problems it creates and how we can deal with that in a New Church perspective, taking into account that the twelve step program is spreading around the world as a beacon against all kinds of evils destroying people's lives;
- as suggested by Dr. Williams-Hogan a completely new way to describe and analyze childhood with an understanding of

innocence, family and conjugial love as potential qualities to be made real in society;

• study of paintings and sculptures to see if spiritual qualities can be read into them, and see how this changes over time.

CONCLUSION FROM DR. WILLIAMS-HOGAN'S PAPER

Dr. Williams-Hogan's paper describes a *Before* and an *After* with the mystical *In-between* we call the Last Judgment as the pivotal point. Her evidence gives us sufficient support for the hypothesis that the Last Judgment is the cause of the effect, namely the big changes in social life in England, particularly the treatment of infants and children. The paper also displays the two sides of the effects of the Last Judgment, people responding to a general influx and others from direct inspiration from the Writings.

SUMMARY OF DR. WERNER'S PAPER

The author of the second paper was Dr. Soni SonesonWerner. Her subject was:

The Last Judgment and Women in the Modern Western World

Dr. Werner's perspective is women and the changes made possible due to the Last Judgment. She focuses on two women, one in England and one in America. By looking at the lives of the two women she draws conclusions about the general change in attitude towards women, their growing independence and ability to shape their own destinies, free from the domination of the men surrounding them, foremost fathers and husbands.

Dr. Werner also expresses a wish that the female reader of the paper will reflect on her own spiritual growth and her contributions to womankind: "enable the reader to more effectively reflect on her or his own spiritual growth and contributions to humankind" (p. 268).

She also describes the content of the paper in a few words: "This essay will trace a few of the main events in the past 250 years which appear to have been inspired by new ways of thinking about womens' rights and roles in society" (p. 267).

The paper begins by setting out the thesis which reads: "This essay's focusing point is that analysis of women's history by means of psychological case studies and theories of human development enable the reader to more effectively reflect on her or his own spiritual growth and contributions to humankind" (p. 268).

After that we get a quite brief introduction to the concept of the Last Judgment, with which the reader of these proceedings should be familiar by now. True to her thesis Dr. Werner says that "in the other world a major judgment occurred on the leaders of the Catholic and Protestant churches who had abused their power by distorting truths or promoting faith alone. They had organized the church hierarchy to be intertwined with the European governments, to keep power in the hands of the male clergy. This created an unhealthy dependency and effectively kept laywomen and men like spiritual children unable to fully mature" (p. 269).

She then goes on to explain her method. She uses the biographies of two women, Mary Wollstonecraft and Julia Ward Howe and runs them through two developmental theories. The reason for this method is explained in this way: "I believe that it is more thorough to use two theories rather than one to analyze the effects of the Last Judgment on women's roles in the modern western world: a spiritual theory of human development and a feminist theory of development. Both theories involve descriptions of psychological maturation" (p. 267).

She presents the two theories, actually the second one on feminist development first. In 1985 Nancy Downing and Kristin Roush "described a new model for feminist identity development" (p. 269). The focus is on the development of a pronounced feminist identity. The theory describes five stages through which women progress to reach a full feminine identity. The theory presupposes that this will be a lifetime development. It can start early or later. Each step can be quick or be extended over several years.

The five stages are as follows:

1) Passive Acceptance of women's subordinate role
2) Revelation, or awareness of oppression
3) Embeddedness in groups of women, away from men
4) Synthesis of new insights and new roles in society
5) Active Commitment to social change for other women

In the first stage women are satisfied with the roles they find themselves in, partly because they can see benefits from staying in that position. A drastic example of seeing the benefit is the following: "For example, the clergy burnt women as witches if they discussed spiritual insights" (p. 271).

The second stage describes a growing awareness of the oppression. The women do not want to stay passively accepting of the circumstances. This is the stage called Revelation. Tensions will occur, since they see two sides of reality. "Regardless, the main characteristic of this stage are strong feelings and righteous indignation; there is no turning back to a life of passive acceptance of oppression" (p. 271).

In the third stage, Embeddedness, women seek other women and share their experience for the first time. It is a kind of subculture of women (p. 272). Some women do not get further but some do. They go to the next stage, Synthesis, which means they "are able to transcend traditional gender roles and evaluate men on an individual basis" (p. 272). They look upon themselves more affirmatively and they "renegotiate with all the individual men in their lives: father, husband, supervisor, or son" (p. 272).

They have freed themselves from the former oppression, and that has given them a feminine identity, but in this theory there is still another step, Active Commitment, which means they also go out to do things for other women. Both women in Dr. Werner's study come to this stage.

Harry Moody formulated the second theory used in the paper in 1997. His theory is called *Five Stages of the Soul*. It tries to describe the spiritual development of a person. The five stages are these:

1) The Call
2) The Search
3) The Struggle
4) The Breakthrough
5) The Return

The call is the first step when a person accepts that there is a spiritual or moral dimension to life. This leads to the second step, the Search, which is to go and look for answers to spiritual questions. In the context of the thesis of this paper Dr. Werner says that "in male dominated organizations women are told to follow the priesthood and not bother with these questions. In fact, the quest may appear as a form of doubt—which seems to be the opposite of faith—and thus may be severely punished" (p. 275).

When a person has found good answers the third stage begins, the Struggle. This stage "is full of difficulties involved in reconciling one's abstract beliefs with the daily tasks of living in this world of time and space. There may be times when life seems to have no meaning or be very disappointing" (p. 275).

Many people may recognize these steps, where the fourth stage, the Breakthrough, is when the beliefs that have been built up for a while take hold of the person and where there is no way back to the old ways of thinking and living. This is a satisfactory stage but there is one more, the Return, the fifth and last.

In the Return stage the person wants to give back to those people he or she is connected to or to the whole of society. Also in this case the two women discussed in the paper reach this final stage.

The paper then goes on to analyze the lives of two women according to those two theories, first the feminist identity theory, and then the spiritual development one. We get a matrix of four blocks: Mary Wollstonecraft analyzed by the two theories, and Julia Ward

Howe analyzed the same way. Since biographical data are the basis for the analysis according to the two theories, the data are sometimes repeated in the two blocks for each of the two women. Here we will, however, for briefness give a short description of the life of each one prior to presenting the findings from the two theories.

Mary Wollstonecraft lived in England 1759–97. Her father was "economically unstable, restless, and brutal to the women in his family" (p. 276). She got no education through him. However, their neighbors, the Ardens, had a different lifestyle, and Wollstonecraft was invited to take part in the education that was going on there. After the Ardens she found another neighbor and could use the library to study philosophy and theology. In her social life she got acquainted with members of Rational Dissenters and Radicals, some of which were active in the French Revolution, as well as those instigating the New Church, William Blake among others. She wrote a poem that became famous, *A Vindication of the Rights of Women*, and a book called *Mary, a Fiction*.

As to family life she "had several disappointing relationships and one marriage, which ended in her husband abandoning her. She adopted and bore a few children" (p. 286).

Dr. Werner first goes through the feminist theory and its five stages. She points out that he Passive Acceptance stage was short due to her brutal father. The Revelation phase was from about age 9–16 and had to do with the Arden family. Her mother's sad life certainly played a part. "She hated the dependency of uneducated poor women" (p. 278).

In her Embeddedness stage she found a close friend, Fanny Blood, and also "cautiously avoided romantic encounters with men" (p. 279). This stage lasted the rest of her teens.

In her Synthesis stage she was lucky to find men who had other ideas, the Radicals and Dissenters, among which were also New Churchmen. How much Wollstonecraft read Swedenborg is not known.

Wollstonecraft died young, at the age of 38, but still got to the final stage, Active Commitment. Only very few women had the chance at the end of the eighteenth century to contribute to changing the fabric of society. With the poem *A Vindication of the Rights of Women* she can be seen as the first major feminist. She addressed the middle class women, since "She was disgusted by the frivolous upper class of women she had worked for in England and saddened by the conditions of the extremely poor women" (p. 282).

Next step in the paper is to analyze Wollstonecraft according to the spiritual development theory.

For Wollstonecraft religion was important from an early age. The first stage, the Call, was there from the beginning.

The Search stage started when she met the Dissenters and the Radicals and lasted for more then ten years. Ideas of freedom were at the center. Dr. Werner says: "The one common thread among these Radicals in London was that they wanted an end to the abuse of power among the clergy and the government leaders. The Last Judgment was primarily about reordering the heavens and judging the clergy who had abused their power while they had been in the world. So we can assume that Blake and other readers felt justified in challenging any corrupt authorities" (p. 284).

Her Struggle stage, the third, lasted for about 15 years. "Due to personal relationships, economic instability and the political whirlwind of the French Revolution, Wollstonecraft experienced many struggles during the next fifteen years of her life" (p. 286).

In the final stage, the Return, we find Wollstonecraft more at peace with herself. She married William Godwin, one of the people she had known for a long time among the people who sought new ways of thinking about how a good society should be organized. They seem to have "made every effort to have an egalitarian marriage" (p. 287).

Dr. Werner concludes the analysis of Wollstonecraft by saying that "Overall, it appears that Wollstonecraft achieved a highly developed level of both spirituality and feminist identity" (p. 287). She also draws a far-reaching conclusion going back to the thesis of the paper and the theme of this conference:

"Wollstonecraft's written contributions were examples of both returning to God and actively promoting social change. Her ideas have continued to enlighten and inspire others for over 210 years and have changed the course of history for women so that there might be true freedom for all. Therefore, I assert that this is one form of evidence of the effects of the Last Judgment on women: the individual efforts of people such as Wollstonecraft" (p. 288).

The second woman, Julia Ward Howe, lived in the next century, 1819–1910. She lived in New York and Boston, and the Civil War happened during her lifetime. When she was five, her mother died. Her father was kind, gave her a good education in a home schooling setting including several languages, literature and philosophy. He died when she was 22. She lived under good circumstances. After the death of her father she met with Quakers and Abolitionists, later also Emerson. That is where she met her future husband, Samuel Howe. She gave him many children, but he "wanted not only a self-denying wife but a creature of domestic perfection who would maintain a serene and happy home far from the perplexing and alienating world of work" (p. 289). After many years of looking after her family she had many more years to devote to active work outside of the home all geared towards furthering the rights of women. She was a public figure and wrote a famous poem, *Battle Hymn of the Republic*, many articles and held many, many speeches. She met women who belonged to a Swedenborg reading group, among them Margaret Fuller.

Again, for Howe, Dr. Werner first goes through the feminist theory and its five stages. The first stage, Passive Acceptance, was a relatively normal life with home schooling and social life as expected. She spent a long time, 30 years, in the Revelation phase, beginning with the death of her father. The people she met allowed her to see new ways to think about society, but her marriage stopped her from moving too fast. We know that she "found great respite and relief in reading Swedenborg during these decades of raising the family" (p. 290).

Her Embeddedness stage started when her children began to move out. She began to work with groups of other women interested in the civil rights of women. It also helped that her 18 years older husband died.

The Synthesis stage meant that she could interact with powerful men without being denied her independence or being looked down on.

"She was not angry at men for being domineering, so she could stay calm as she voiced her concerns in speeches to legislators" (p. 291) .

In the last stage, Active Commitment, she "turned all her attention to influencing lawmakers about women's rights to vote, own property and be educated" (p. 292). She became the president of the American Woman's Suffrage Association. Later she took on other similar key roles.

Following the structure of the four blocks the next step in the paper is to analyze Howe according to the spiritual development theory.

Authoritarian upbringing, restrictions in her social life and conformity in thinking seems to have been the background for her Call, the first stage. Because she had a strong interest in philosophy and theology, she entered into an intense Search, the next stage. Fairly isolated from people her age she had a lot of time to follow her intellectual appetites. She had an amazing self-discipline in her studies. "Julia mingled with Boston's literati" (p. 296). Margaret Fuller had a strong influence on her. Howe began to see the possibility of doing something important outside of the home.

Next stage, the Struggle, lasted for a couple of decades. Her husband called her "a child" and others denied her ambition to develop her intellectual side. The song she wrote became very famous, but she was still neglected by her husband for her wits.

Next step, the Breakthrough, came after the end of the Civil War. Many turned their attention to other issues like women's rights. When her husband died she was free to follow her star. During this time she confessed she was thankful to "the guidance of Swedenborg" (p. 304).

The final stage is the Return. Howe was one of the people who had "the courage to also become a major change agent and attempt to improve the lives of a nation of citizens" (p. 308). For 40 years she served in important positions as a leader for countless women's groups.

Dr. Werner then shows us a comparison of the two women, listing similarities and differences. Then we have the conclusion. Dr. Werner points out that both women went through all stages in both theories, and they were both "determined to share their theological and political

388 REV. GÖRAN APPELGREN

reflections on the status of women and to fight for social change" (p. 312).

Finally Dr. Werner has a list of topics for future study and ends by saying: "Self-awareness about one's own development can lead to a deeper search for spiritual inspiration, resulting in new active commitments. This could lead to new improvements in the conditions for all women across the globe" (p. 313).

ANALYSIS OF DR. WERNER'S PAPER

One question in assessing the paper is to ask is whether the two theories were handled with care and followed the intent of the creators of the theories. My answer to that is that they definitely were. The five stages in both theories were traced in both biographies with a good search for relevant details. It is tempting to look for the results you want to find and neglect information that speaks against the intended result. I do not see any such tendencies. Both women came to the final stages both of feminist identity and spiritual development. Although the life span of Mary Wollstonecraft was much, much shorter than that of Julia Ward Howe, we can see that the theories apply in a reasonable way to both of them.

Another question is whether these two cases were good cases to use. Could there be other women whose lives could have given a result that could have supported the thesis in a stronger way. The answer is probably that we cannot know for sure. First of all, as Dr. Werner, points out, there are not that many more or less complete biographies to choose from. Secondly, we would have to make a full study, just like the one at hand, to find out, which leads me to the next question.

A study broader than two biographies would have given a more reliable result. Ideally you would have liked to have twenty, fifty, or a hundred cases. That would have been very difficult both because of lack of data and of the enormous amount of work to compile all the data in a way that you can compare. But theoretically it would be possible.

Connected with this question is whether the material used is too diverse to be used to draw conclusions. Wollstonecraft was in the Embeddedness stage (feminist identity theory) for roughly five years whereas Howe was there for almost thirty years. With more cases we would come up with a consistent pattern.

Something that would be impossible, however, would be to this: Imagine one and the same life that was lived twice, the first time, say, 1700–1770 and the second time 1760–1830. Suppose you could come up with a woman's life that would be something like being married to a lieutenant in the army, having five children, having a good fortune invested in a big estate or a town house, where there would be six servants. Then you would make a comparison of the two lives, one before and the other after the Last Judgment.

No, it is impossible, but my example is meant to point to the difficulty of drawing conclusions from the study of biographies, when you discuss and compare conditions in two different periods of time.

The theories used by Dr. Werner are meant to describe and analyze a person's life from a focal point like feminine identity—for women—or spiritual development—for both male and female. Those theories are not meant to provide support for conclusions about the change of conditions under which those two kinds of development took place.

What we see in Dr. Werner's paper is a presumption of the Last Judgment having had an effect on how well women could make their voices heard in society. There is nothing wrong in the ambition to "prove" that such is the case. The problem though is—as I have discussed in more general terms in the beginning—that the facts used in the study do not enable us to make a comparison. That is why I used the absurd example of two lives being lived twice to illustrate what it would be like to find results from time period one and two and then to compare them.

There could also be other ways to find out about women's freedom in society before and after the Last Judgment. One method would be to look at hard facts.

To the extent that there would be records we could for instance compare events in the year 1700 and 1800, for example:

- how many witches were burnt at the stake
- how many women were killed by their husbands in their homes, or
- what was the punishment for that crime
- how many marriages were arranged
- how many girls or young women attended higher education

You can make a long list. Based on those facts we could draw conclusions that might indicate that a change in attitudes had taken place. With the a priori knowledge we have from Swedenborg we could then from deduction draw the conclusion that the Last Judgment caused that change in attitude.

I think it is fair to say that Dr. Williams-Hogan and Prof. Henderson do just that. They focus on and use the concept of a "*Before*" and an "*After*." If we apply this to the paper at hand we could make statements like these: In the "*Before*" period of time an independent woman was considered to be a witch and was burned at the stake. In the "*After*" period of time an independent woman the same kind of woman would be considered to be just normal and therefore have her right to shape her own destiny.

Dr. Werner comes close to saying just that: "the clergy burnt women as witches if they discussed spiritual insights" (p. 271). That is the "*Before*" state. Obviously in the paper we have proof that that was not the case after 1757. I dwell on this because it is crucial for studying the effects of the Last Judgment. It is tempting, as I said; to draw conclusions that are as it were already in the cards.

But let us see what we can do although we do not have this *Before* and *After* as a ruler. Dr. Werner draws the conclusion that "Wollstonecraft's written contributions were examples of both returning to God and actively promoting social change. Her ideas have continued to enlighten and inspire others for over 210 years, and changed the course of history for women so that there might be true freedom for all. Therefore, I assert that this is one form of evidence of the effects of the Last Judgment on women: the individual efforts of people such as Wollstonecraft" (p. 288).

Can we really be sure about that? The effect of the Last Judgment makes people like Wollstonecraft go out and do active work to change the world for women. That is the assumption, but have we seen proof of it in the paper? Could this not have happened before 1757 must be the question as long as we do not have a study of the *"Before"* state. After all there are women who have not been burnt at the stake and who have inspired women to change their lives. Saint Birgitta in Sweden (1303–73) is one example. Another is Julian of Norwich in England (1342–1416). She redefined the concept of motherhood with spiritual connotations and had differing views on theological tenets. The Church did not persecute her. Some have called her a precursor to Luther and the Reformation. On the other hand you could also argue that there were men like Jan Hus (1372–1415), Michael Servetus (1511–53) or Galileo Galilee (1564–1642) who held theological or scientific views that were not accepted by the hierarchy of the Church. The male dominated clergy did not only hit against women.

The stress on a "male priesthood" rather than priesthood or corrupted priesthood is in my view therefore a simplification. Everybody was confused, laity and priesthood. As an effect of the Last Judgment men changed too, especially within the laity, but within the priesthood as well. The Methodist pastor James Hindmarsh should be a good example. Of those who strived to change the situation of the slaves the majority were men. And in her paper Dr. Werner also states that Howe's father both provided well for her studies and accepted that she had other ambitions than the more traditional ones: "He was quite liberal in providing a broad education for her. . . . When she showed little interest in learning domestic duties of a proper to a young lady, Howe's father paid for tutors. She studied French, Greek, Latin, Italian, piano, singing and dancing" (p. 294).

And we in the New Church would not hesitate to see the founders of the New Church body as enlightened people with a new way of thinking, a thinking that most likely would also include a more modern view on women. "Wollstonecraft pushed for equality in her personal relationships with men and established it among the British Radicals such as William Blake" (p. 311). Had they not been different from pre-

Last Judgment men, her push would have been rejected. Theoretically that idea can undermine conclusions that heavily stress the importance of the deeds of a few individual women. "I assert that this is one form of evidence of the effects of the Last Judgment on women: the individual efforts of people such as Wollstonecraft" (p. 288). Let us imagine that after the Last Judgment men changed to such an extent that they would never think of stopping a woman from speaking publicly in favor of women's rights to vote, own property and be educated. I am not saying that such was the case, but in building a theory and looking for evidence we might just not leave that question out.

This takes me to another question, which has to do with the New Church concept of influx, dealt with in the introduction.

When she says that Howe went out to influence lawmakers, she means influencing men. Without the effects of the Last Judgment in general, through a spiritual influx into all people on earth, including the male lawmakers, nothing of the changes she envisioned would have come about. This is the main thesis of the paper, and it illustrates that both specific inspiration and general influx went hand in hand.

Finally a major theme in the Doctrines revealed in the Lord's Second coming is conjugial love. Ideas in that doctrine that have a bearing on the question of the liberation of women are the new concept of equality between the sexes. The concept is new compared with the ideas of the time, ideas that had their origin in early Christian theology of which most was based on Paul's epistles. Woman was considered to be inferior to man, and man was to be the head of the family. In the Writings this idea is rejected. Both husband and wife are equal and the Lord is the head of them both. In this paper we do not see a lot of this Doctrine being explored. We hear that Wollstonecraft and her husband "made every effort to have an egalitarian marriage" (p. 287), but otherwise this important aspect of the freedom of women is not dealt with.

For further study I can suggest the following:

- A challenge in the kind of theme Dr. Werner has chosen is the question of being able to compare the *Before* with the *After*. Research can be done both on finding methods that would help such a study, and also on finding the hard data to support the evidence of a *Before* and an *After*.
- Family life and love between married partners are definitely areas worth research in the spirit of this paper, since the emancipation of women in the end is not a goal in itself separate from married life but a step on the way to the ideals of conjugial love as set out in the Writings.
- The Swedish nineteenth century writer C. J. L. Almqvist who was a Swedenborgian, wrote a book called *Det går an (It Is Acceptable)* that deals with the previous item—a new way of looking at marriage.
- There are other women, e.g. the writer Ednah Silver (1838–1928), the physician Harriot Hunt (1805–75), the actress Anna Mowatt (1819–70) mentioned in the book *Lost Legacy* (Poole) and others, who could be included in a further study to solidify the tenants in this paper. Silver used a phrase that somehow embraces both female independence and the ideal of conjugial love: "The heart may be larger than the home" (Poole, *Lost Legacy,* 73). Others are of course Florence Nightingale (1820–1910) or Clara Barton (1821–1912) who started the American Red Cross.

CONCLUSION FROM DR. WERNER'S PAPER

Dr. Werner's paper gives us interesting biographies of two women in two countries in different centuries after the Last Judgment and with different family and educational situations. Through two models we get to see how they developed as to their feminine identity and their spiritual progress. This is helpful in understanding the times and the situation for women and it sheds light on how the Last Judgment created a considerable change in the conditions shaping a woman's life in the eighteenth and nineteenth centuries. Some further study illuminating the *Before* state would give more weight to the conclusions drawn about an opening for the emancipation of women.

The paper also displays the two sides of the effects of the Judgment, Wollstonecraft who primarily responded to a general influx and Howe who quite clearly was inspired directly from the Writings.

SUMMARY OF PROF. HENDERSON'S PAPER

The author of the third and last paper was Prof. Brian Henderson. His subject was:

From Thought to Action: The Last Judgment, Swedenborg
and the Antislavery Movement

Prof. Henderson introduces the subject by quoting a phrase from Seymour Dresher: "Freedom, not slavery was the peculiar institution" (p. 321) during the eighteenth century in Europe. That is the background for the antislavery movement in Europe. The norm was to have slaves, not the opposite. And this was the case not only in the eighteenth century: "Many scholars consider those societies that did *not* practice slavery to be the anomaly" (p. 321).

Having said that Prof. Henderson states that it "*is* surprising how quickly slavery as a legal institution was brought to an end" (p. 322). He then makes the point that the legal abolition of both slave trade and slavery was accomplished. The point is worth noticing. He reminds us that slavery is still rampant in our day but under different forms.

The sudden appearance of the movement and the thorough result is surprising, he says. Historians have pointed out the perplexing fact that so many people rose to the occasion and cared for other people they did not know, of a different skin color and oceans away. And it happened at the same time in England, France and North America.

The year 2007 is both the 200th anniversary of British Parliament ending the British slave trade and the 250th anniversary of the Last Judgment, and therefore "it is important for us to reflect on possible answers to these questions" (p. 322).

Prof. Henderson gives us the background for the institution of slavery by looking back into history. The earliest evidence recorded is from 1200 B.C. As early as 1000 B.C. slavery existed in Europe, Asia and Africa. Surprising facts are given about slavery in the sophisticated state of Athens. "the proportion of slaves in fourth century Athens was as high as that of the American South in 1860, with a higher percentage of Greeks owning slaves than nineteenth century southerners" (p. 323). In Athens they bought slaves, whereas in the Roman Empire the slaves were enslaved captives.

In medieval Europe the feudal system replaced the ordinary form of slavery, serfdom being the institution to follow. Slavery was practiced in the more remote areas of Europe though and in neighboring territories, the Byzantine and Islamic areas for instance. The Venetians traded slaves in the Black Sea area. "By 1300 there were Black slaves on Cyprus, which had become virtually a prototype for the West Indian colonies" (p. 325).

With the fall of Constantinople in 1453 the Turks cut off the trade routes and put a stop to the trade, but slavery continued with the Portuguese who made contact with Africa. Black Africans were shipped to Castile. And finally "the discovery of the New World and the establishment of sugar plantations in the West Indies brought an insatiable demand for African slaves" (p. 325).

Prof. Henderson then goes on to discuss to what extent the slave traders and owners had to defend what they did. The answer is basically No. There were several ways of explaining why slavery was not seen as a problem. From Aristotle and others there was the notion of a fixed natural social order with masters and slaves. Notice that skin color is not in issue here, although most slaves were foreigners. The theological arguments built on a dualistic idea. Body and soul were separate. Even if the body was ill treated the soul could remain in a state of freedom. And the Bible was used as well with stories from the Old Testament, especially the story about Noah cursing the sons of Ham. The conclusion is that "it was commonly held that slavery was sanctioned by God and that black Africans could be made slaves because of their inherent inferiority" (p. 327).

Further on in the paper Prof. Henderson draws our attention to the growing connection of slavery and race. "Virtually all of the slaves being shipped to Europe's possessions in the New World were black Africans" (p. 327). In antique times the dividing line went between the cultured ones and the barbarians. Now, in the eighteenth century, there was a growing interest in scientific research and a tendency to systemize and categorize. From new plants and animals the step was not long to human bodies. They "distinguished between the races on the basis of physical distinctions" (p. 328). The Africans were judged as inferior in all respects. Only one scholar stood up against the mainstream opinions when he said the color could have something to do with the climate.

The commonly held view was, again, that there is a naturally ordered hierarchy, and the European, white race takes the first place. Blumenbach named it "Caucasian" in 1781 along with four other inferior races.

But also philosophers chimed in with philosophical or pragmatic arguments. David Hume, Immanuel Kant and Edward Long are said to have used expressions like "naturally inferior" (p. 330), "the difference . . . appears to be as great in regard to mental capacities as in color" and "bestial manners, stupidity, and vices" (p. 331).

This is the background for an emerging debate about slavery in eighteenth century. So far there hadn't been a need to defend slavery as an integral part of society. In the first half of the eighteenth century, however, there was a growing interest in ideas about freedom, equality and participation in the governing of a country. Therefore, at first the debate about slavery was kept on an intellectual plane. Many were those who advocated the abolition of slaves, but at the same time they acted contrary to their beliefs in the real world. Diderot in France argued that slaves had the right to be free but he said at the same time that the slaves were too important to the well being of the French nation.

Locke, who had changed his opinions, sent the same double message. And so did Voltaire.

The one who seems to have kept a straight line was Montesquieu. But others to support the system misused his arguments against slavery.

But the tide was swaying. "Along with new ideas about the worth of the individual and the rights of humanity came questions about the morality of slavery as an institution" (p. 334).

Here we can also see how the question begins to be split in two. One is slavery itself, the other is the slave trade. Some people could see that the slave trade led to an inhumane treatment of people but did not attack the system of slavery. "If the slave trade could be ended, they reasoned, the supply of new slaves would be greatly reduced, thereby encouraging slave owners to treat their slaves more humanely" (p. 334).

During this time arguments based on religion were used more and more. They began to talk about slavery as a sin and that Divine providence would punish those who practiced it. Ideas of free will and free choice were also used. Slavery kept a person from following God's plan for every individual.

Up to now the criticism increased but there was not yet a movement. The wind had turned though. No one any longer defended the system, but as yet only a few attacked it. That was about to change.

The critical point is when it goes from antislavery thought to antislavery action. This happened in the 1770s and 1780s. It was relatively speaking not a slow change but a monumental one. Historians are united in this observation. "Historians argue that this transition to action was surprisingly sudden. Interestingly, this shift seems to have taken place at the [Quakers'] London Yearly Meeting of 1757" (p. 337). The turning point is strongly associated with the Quakers who are given credit for paving the way for this strong and forceful movement. They had a big organization that could provide the structure for popular support and they could come up with the funding for it.

They printed antislavery pamphlets and in 1783 they set up a committee with the sole purpose of agitating against slavery. As a first important step they sent a petition to the House of Commons. In 1787 they welcomed non-Quakers as members. Among them were the key players-to-be Thomas Clarkson and Granville Sharp. They formed the first national, nonsectarian antislavery organization, the Society for the Abolition of Slavery.

They began by attacking the slave trade, although they were set on fighting slavery itself as well. In Parliament they received support from William Wilberforce, Charles Fox, and William Pitt. In 1788 they had their first national campaign. Wilberforce forced the Parliament to form a committee to hear evidence against the slave trade. In 1799 they won their first victory with "the passage of a bill in 1799 limiting the number of slaves per ton permissible on British slave ships" (p. 341).

There is no turning back, and Prof. Henderson describes how one law after the other was passed till finally on January 2, 1807 "Lord Granville [Sharp] introduced a bill stating that, 'from and after January 1, 1808, all manner of 'dealing and trading in slaves' in Africa, or their transport from Africa to any other place, should be prohibited and unlawful'" (p. 341). In 1833 also the institution of slavery saw an end.

We then get a summary of events in other countries where slavery was also forbidden.

Prof. Henderson then looks at factors involved in this movement that can be traced back to effects of the Last Judgment. He first lists theories of why this happened during such a short period of time. Of course people who have no inkling of what is said in the Writings cannot come up with other than philosophical and economic reasons for the change. But as "Historians continue to search for a clear and meaningful answer to why an antislavery movement seemed to suddenly appear in the late eighteenth century, New Church historians can offer critical insight into why this may have been the case" (p. 344). Prof. Henderson suggests that the clearing of the air in the world of spirits made it possible to receive the influx from the Lord and to see the truths around them. This change in the spiritual world would also mean "evils present in the world, such as slavery, could be more easily recognized" (p. 345). And he continues: "Humans began to identify slavery as a sin and recognize that it could and should be removed. Within one century a new era *was* born—an era founded on free labor and not on slavery" (p. 345).

The British members of the Society for the Abolition of Slavery were not Swedenborgians but may have been influenced by the effects of the Last Judgment. There was, however, a figure that most definitely was a member of the New Church. Prof. Henderson presents to the reader the life and deeds of Carl Wadström (1746–1799). He came to play a most important role in what transpired in the English antislavery movement.

He was born in Stockholm and just like Swedenborg worked on the Board of Mines. He was a skilled engineer but had other talents that would serve him well, like speaking English and French and being good at sketching. He found the Writings in 1778 and soon formed a reading group in Norrköping. This group "came together as a direct result of Swedenborg's teachings regarding the African people" (p. 347). Unlike Hume, Kant and Long, Swedenborg had a very different view on Africans.

The resolve of the reading group was "determined to eliminate the African slave trade and to establish a new society on the west coast of Africa that was founded on 'true Christian principles'" (p. 348). From 1779 and on they sought the support of the king of Sweden to go to Africa to establish a colony of free Africans. In 1778 they finally sailed to an island outside Senegal from where they made several trips to the mainland.

This was the first time Wadström got to see for himself what he had only heard about before. Later he was to describe this in his *Observations on the Slave Trade*. Prof. Henderson writes: "One of the scenes Wadström describes . . . was the brutal conditions of slaves he saw being unloaded from a sloop" (p. 350).

He could stay for only three months, and when he returned to Sweden he went through London. Here he got to meet the leaders of the antislavery movement, Clarkson, Sharp and Wilberforce.

Clarkson later wrote about the eyewitnesses he met: "They showed me their journals . . . (in which were) a number of circumstances

minuted down, all relating to the slave trade. I obtained a more accurate
... knowledge of the manners and customs of the Africans from them
than from all the persons put together whom I had yet seen" (p. 353).

Wadström got to testify before the House of Commons three
times 1789–91, something that had a definite effect on the law making
in Parliament. "The eyewitness accounts of the inhumane brutality
of the slave trade and the visual images of horrors of the slave ships
helped sway a critical portion of Parliament to the antislavery cause"
(p. 354).

During the last years of his life Wadström spent time in France.
He hoped France and the French Revolution would be the springboard
for renewed efforts to establish a colony in Africa. As he had done in
England he addressed the Parliament and he "played an active role in
reviving the Society of Friends of the Negro" (p. 355). Unfortunately
he died eight years before the British Parliament passed the law to
abolish the slave trade. As an honorary citizen of France he got a state
funeral.

Prof. Henderson in his conclusion points to the idea of influx being
reinforced after the Last Judgment to inspire people to take action
against injustices as well as to individual people like Wadström who
were directly inspired by the Writings of Emanuel Swedenborg. He
emphasizes the critical shift from antislavery thought to action and also
the sudden awareness of the backsides of an institution that had existed
for thousands of years.

Finally he outlines possible subjects for further study. We know
of New Church people who did take action against slavery but we can
learn more about them. Names mentioned are:

Augustus Nordenskjöld, Thomas Goyder, Robert Carter,
Rev. John Hargrove, Lydia Maria Child and Alexander Muravyov.

Another interesting aspect is what the Writings say about the
spiritual state of the English people at the time of the Last Judgment and
the question of how that made England be the center of the antislavery
movement.

He also points out that slavery still exists and that we should not
just look at these things as passed historical facts but as something that

always has to be monitored and not let it once more become something "immovable." He refers to an organization existing today in America that works for the abolition of slavery in a new disguise within today's very different world.

ANALYSIS OF PROF. HENDERSON'S PAPER

In this paper we get a very clear structure of the situation *Before* and *After*. "Historians argue that this transition to action was surprisingly sudden." There was a long, long tradition of both slavery and slave trade. It was part of the social fabric. Why would it suddenly change? Prof. Henderson gives good evidence of what the situation was before 1757, and of the growing awareness of and action against slavery. The result is compelling. We can almost see it written on the wall: The Last Judgment did this.

However, we must be careful in with such conclusions, and I think Prof. Henderson is. We are dealing with a delicate hypothesis—that the Last Judgment is the reason for all these changes. No matter how compelling the result is we must not make it too easy for ourselves. Prof. Henderson has done very well in fulfilling the purpose of this conference. We have been looking for evidence that can support the hypothesis that a change in the spiritual world has made mankind think and act in ways that promote freedom, both collectively and individually. There is a *Before* and an *After* in this study and we, who believe the Writings tell us the truth, can well believe that the cause of the effect is the Last Judgment. Still we need to leave the door half open. Prof. Henderson asks: "What was it about the second half of the eighteenth century that caused these movements to suddenly spring to life?" And he gives us evidence that point to the thesis of this conference. He has used the evidence but not overused them. This inspires to further study.

The paper is interesting in that it points to the two sides of what we understand the Last Judgment to be, both a general influx from the Lord into all people who are prepared to receive it, and a particular inspiration from the Writings of Emanuel Swedenborg. The men in England acted from influx and Wadström and his friends in Sweden acted from being directly inspired by the Writings. It is moving to think about the fact that Wadström left his employment in order to follow the call he got from reading the Writings. Striking is also the description of how the first hand evidence of Wadström and Sparrman swayed the opinion of Clarkson. The person acting from direct inspiration from the Writings went the furthest to explore the circumstances and could then give a more substantial support to those who acted from general influx.

I think it is very important to keep both of these effects of the Last Judgment in mind. See what I say further on this matter in my concluding remarks.

An interesting aspect of the phenomenon we call influx is the fact that movements against slavery appeared simultaneously in several parts of the world. "It is universally recognized that antislavery movements arose almost simultaneously in Britain, France, and North America in the second half of the eighteenth century."

The paper shows the complexity of the issue. The reasons behind the defense of slavery changed over time. Actually they went back and forth. There were philosophical and theological reasons as well as other more pragmatic ones or economic and scientific. By the time we see the change the theological arguments had come back into the discussion.

What we could have heard more about in the paper is a discussion about the distinction between slavery as such and the slave trade. I found myself not thinking about this distinction to start off with. You may notice that the antislavery movement in the beginning was an anti-slave trade movement, and that the legislation in England first attacked the slave trade and after that slavery itself.

Another interesting question has to with the Quakers. "Virtually all historians point to the events in England in the 1780s, and to the organized movement begun in the previous decade by the Quakers as the critical turning point." It is interesting because of the records we have about the Quakers in the Writings, where the Quaker faith is debased (cf. LJC 83–85, 88; TCR 378.2). And still they have contributed to many good things in this world including the abolition of the slave trade.

Not that much has been said about Divine providence in this section of the conference, but I think in Wadström we have a very good case. He found the Writings and was particularly inspired by them in terms of the fate of the Africans. The king—acting out of selfish motives, namely gold—decided to finance Wadström's trip to Africa. There he got first hand information, and by chance (!) he decided to go via London on his way back to Sweden. Wadström's contact with the English abolitionists most definitely swayed the opinion. It might have happened without Wadström, but it would probably have taken even longer. Bergquist says in his biography on Swedenborg: "His battle is regarded as having contributed to the British decision in 1807 to put an end to slavery in the British Empire" (Bergquist, 430).

For further study I can suggest just what I said in the last paragraph:

- We have been given a very good description of Wadström's background and his direct inspiration from the Writings. But what about the key players in England, Thomas Clarkson, Granville Sharp, William Wilberforce, Charles Fox and William Pitt? They must have been touched by the general influx, but are there other interesting factors that made them take a stand against the slave trade and slavery?

- Another interesting area to explore is the situation in France and especially the Society of Friends of the Negro. Since Wadström played a key role also in France this makes it the more interesting.

- A third area to study could be the concepts of serf and slave and the system in Europe. Russia in the 1800s did not have slaves, only serfs and they were relatively well treated, of which there is plenty of evidence. In Sweden there was a system of strong dependence of a certain kind of farmers that could almost be called serfdom. It was abolished as late as in 1945. (!)

CONCLUSION FROM PROF. HENDERSON'S PAPER

Prof. Henderson's paper is as I can see it the clearest example of describing a *Before* and an *After*, thereby seeing cause and effect in a clear light. He has got clear evidence to support his thesis, and we get to see both influx and direct inspiration from the Writings presented to view.

THE DISCUSSANT'S ADDRESS TO THE CONFERENCE

The Last Judgment—a Mighty Reaction Against Faith Alone

THE TWO GREAT COMMANDMENTS
AND THEIR DESTRUCTION

In my address to this conference I will use the two great commandments as my theme, and we begin by hearing a conversation between the Lord and a scribe:

> Then one of the scribes . . . asked Him, "Which is the first commandment of all?" Jesus answered him, "The first of all the commandments is: 'Hear, O Israel, the Lord our God, the Lord is one. . . . And the second, like it, is this: 'You shall love your neighbor as yourself.' There is no other commandment greater than these." So the scribe said to Him, "Well said, Teacher. You have spoken the truth, for there is one God, . . . and to love Him . . . and to love one's neighbor as oneself, is more than all the whole burnt offerings and sacrifices." So when Jesus saw that he answered wisely, He said to him, "You are not far from the kingdom of God." (Mark 12.28–31)

In this conversation Jesus and the scribe agree on the two basic principles of religion, loving the Lord and loving the neighbor. At the end we also see a promise for the man who talked to the Lord: "You are not far from the kingdom of God" (Mark 12.31).

The conclusion is that a person enters the kingdom of God by loving the Lord and the neighbor. Now, that sounds pretty self-evident, but there are two things needed for this to happen. One is to understand who God is and to understand whom the neighbor is. The other is to let these two loves take precedence over other possible objects for a person's love.

Let's start with the second point, the object of one's love. Observing our daily life we can see that we turn our attention and energy to things of this world to a large extent. Often we prefer to nurture our own needs rather than the needs of others. Sometimes we are downright selfish, and it is all about ourselves. We call these two kinds of love: love of the world and love of self. These two stand in opposition to the love of the Lord and the love of the neighbor.

The right order is for the loves that are self-centered to be subordinated to the two higher kinds. But the question is to what extent a human being is able to make that happen. We go back to the first point—the two good loves.

Suppose a person has a very vague or strange idea of who God is. It is not easy to tune into loving that God. Imagine that you begin to describe this God in such terms that you simply don't know Whom to turn to. Imagine that some people begin to think of God as more than One—in complete opposition to what Jesus and the scribe talked about. Imagine they say there was a greater God in heaven who also had a Son, and one day that greater God would get so upset about the evil state of mankind that He would have to send His Son to be ill-treated and finally slaughtered by people on earth and then be taken up to heaven again. It is easy to see that it would be hard to love a God Whose image has been distorted in such an ugly way.

It is the same thing with the love of your neighbor. In every religion there is a set of rules, much like the Ten Commandments, to tell people how to live good lives. Imagine that some people came up with the idea that loving your fellow human beings is not important, and that the person you look to for spiritual guidance tells you your soul will be safe to all eternity, if you just repeat a memorized dogmatic statement: Jesus died for our sins. If you then go and cheat on your wife or husband or steal from your neighbor, you can rest assured this wouldn't do you any harm. Imagine such a situation, and you can see it would be difficult to understand how to love your neighbor.

The awful truth is that this happened. The Christian Church managed to destroy the fundamentals of a true faith, the one Jesus talked to the scribe about. This is the poison of the *dragon* of the Book of Revelation.

That poison is to make people believe that you only have to believe in "the blood of Jesus" to be saved. Thereby the two essentials of the church are destroyed. The two essentials or the *two witnesses* in chapter 11 of Revelation, the two olive trees and the two lamp stands, signify living according to the Ten Commandments and believing in the One only God Jesus Christ (AR 490). The dragonists made the Ten Commandments of no value, and the unity of God was destroyed. The Church on earth was destroyed from within, and love of the neighbor was given a lesser and lesser chance to inspire people in their daily lives (AR 500).

That in itself is sad and disturbing, but what is worse is that the effects of this lingered for centuries. Had the people who were responsible for this been taken away soon after they left life on earth and thereby not being able any more to affect others in the world of spirits, it would have been better. But this could not happen. This is the explanation in the work *The Last Judgment:*

> There were many reasons why such . . . were tolerated; the principal reason was, that . . . by external sincerity and justice, they were conjoined with the simple good, who were either in the lowest heaven, or were still in the world of spirits and not yet introduced into heaven. For in the spiritual world, there is a communication, and thence a conjunction, of all with their like. The simple good, in the lowest heaven, and in the world of spirits, look principally to externals, but are not interiorly evil. If these spirits therefore had been forcibly removed before the appointed time, heaven would have suffered in its ultimates; and yet it is the ultimate, upon which the superior heaven subsists, as upon its own basis. This was the reason they were tolerated until the last time. (LJ 70)

Therefore these spirits were allowed to influence good spirits and good people on earth like this for centuries, up to just about 250 years ago. They set up for themselves *imaginary heavens* that became more and more false. The two good loves were contaminated with the two evil loves, and the confusion got worse and worse. Man-made rules replaced Divine precepts. The Lord points to this in Mark:

> Well did Isaiah prophesy of you hypocrites, as it is written: "This people honors Me with their lips, but their heart is far from Me. And in vain they worship Me, teaching as doctrines the commandments of men." (Mark 7.6–8)

TWO COMMANDMENTS—TWO KINDS OF DEVIATION

The two great commandments had been destroyed. They are the two witnesses in Revelation. In chapter 11 we can read about how they were attacked, and lay dead "in the street of the great city which spiritually is called Sodom and Egypt, where also our Lord was crucified" (Rev. 11.8).

The opposite of these two witnesses are two deviations of the two great commandments. The love of the Lord turned into its opposite which is the love of self. The love of the neighbor had its opposite in the love of the world. There were two kinds of evil active in the Christian Church, each having to do with one of these two principles. The Catholic form of religion represents the love of self and is depicted by the great whore of Babylon and has an urge to control other people's minds. The Protestant or Reformed Church stands for the love of the world, in particular for the evil of pride of self-intelligence. The *dragon* represents this Church.

The two great commandments would never again have been practiced by people on this earth if those two forces were not to lose their influence. The Last Judgment is all about that. The Book of Revelation addresses all of Christianity at the time of the Last Judgment, and the charge is to repent and receive new life from the Lord (Ps. 87). Throughout the Book of Revelation, in the literal sense but certainly in the explanation of the spiritual sense in the Heavenly Doctrine, we meet a complete—a complete!—resistance on the part of those who are totally engrained in these two kinds of evils (Rev. 16). In Dr. Williams-Hogan's paper we heard this phrase: "A resolutely unwilling Anglican Church." But in the judgment process the Lord approaches them step by step and tells them the truth about who they are. In Revelation the turning point is chapter 11, where the two witnesses were killed. But as with the Lord Himself, the Divine could not be killed. The last verse in that chapter reads: "Then the temple of God was opened in heaven, and the ark of His covenant was seen in His temple" (Rev. 11.19). The hells were defeated. Divine truth was now in a position to dispel falsities and let the light of truth shine again.

In the next chapter we get the powerful imagery of the two signs, the woman clothed with the sun and moon and stars, and the great dragon. The restoration of the two great commandments has begun. Chapter 12 points to chapter 21 where the holy city New Jerusalem descends. A new light and a new understanding of the Word of God is born in the Church, and once the judgment process had come to an end, that light would descend on earth and bring a new revelation to the world, the Writings for the New Church, and new light to those people in all religions who seek guidance from the Divine (Isa. 30.26; AR 53.2).

The end in view in all this was to take away the power from the evil spirits who had stopped good spirits in the world of spirits, and people on this earth, from understanding clearly what love of the Lord and of the neighbor truly is.

The Last Judgment restored the ability to honor both of the two great commandments.

WHAT HAPPENED DURING THE LAST JUDGMENT

What happened during the Last Judgment has been said and will be repeated during these two days, but let me just include this quote from the Apocalypse Revealed which in a few words sums up the process of the Last Judgment in the spiritual world:

(20.11) Something must be premised concerning the universal judgment here treated of. From the time when the Lord was in the world . . . it was permitted that they who were in civil and moral good, although in no spiritual good, whence in externals they appeared like Christians, but in internals were devils, should continue longer than the rest in the world of spirits . . . and at length they were allowed to make there for themselves fixed habitations, and also by the abuse of correspondences, and by phantasies, to form to themselves as it were heavens, which also they did form in great abundance. But when these were multiplied to such a degree as to intercept the spiritual light and spiritual heat in their descent from the higher heavens to men on earth, then the Lord executed the Last Judgment, and dissipated those imaginary heavens; which was effected in such a manner, that the externals, by which they simulated Christians, were taken away, and the internals, in which they were devils, were opened; and then they were seen such as they were in themselves, and they who were seen to be devils, were cast into hell, everyone according to the evils of his life; this was done in the year 1757. (AR 865, cf. AR 330, 886.1)

After that the way was opened for people on earth to respond to the influx of Divine light and heat through the heavens and the world of spirits. People could once again take a position in favor of righteousness and truth and keep that position without being violated or spiritually destroyed by the dragon or by Babylon, the two kinds of evil that destroyed the two great commandments. Spiritual freedom was restored. The concept of freedom permeates all three papers. Dr. Williams-Hogan says: "The reformers benefited from . . . increased freedom, and rationality brought light into the world revealing sins against the innocent" (see chart in this paper: p. 366). And Dr. Werner quotes the two women she has studied: "If they [women] be really capable of acting like rational creatures, let them not be treated like slaves." And from Prof. Henderson's paper: "Following the Last Judgment, dedicated individuals suddenly began to recognize that the evil of slavery . . . was not immovable."

AFTER THE LAST JUDGMENT—
POSSIBLE TO FIND LIGHT GUIDING THE WILL

After the Last Judgment it was therefore possible to find spiritual heat and light to guide the will and the understanding. This is expressed in the prophecy in Isaiah with these words:

> The light of the sun will be sevenfold, as the light of seven days, in the day that the LORD binds up the bruise of His people and heals the stroke of their wound. (Isa. 30.26)

It is a shift from almost complete darkness to a situation where the light of truth is available in abundance. This has had a tremendous effect on what has taken place in the world after 1757. The examples we have heard of in the three papers presented testify to this. But let us continue to explore this in terms of the two great commandments.

THE YOKE IS BROKEN,
BREAKING FORTH IN GOOD ACTIONS

We can understand that from now on it would be easier to get a true picture of who God is. But more important is that it is now possible for people on earth to truly love the neighbor. We know that the Writings teach that a new Church starts from good.

> The church which begins from faith has nothing to direct it but the understanding, and the understanding nothing but what is hereditary in man, that is to say, the love of self and of the world. . . . It is otherwise with the church which begins from charity: good is its director, and in good the Lord . . . and faith is from (the Lord) through good. (AC 4672)

What this is saying is that faith develops from wanting to do good. I think this is a key point in understanding the effects of the Last Judgment in the world of today. Many, many people want to do good.

When they do, they will start searching and in time find their faith. First good deeds and then a living faith.

It is not only good that is the beginning of a new Church but also the source or inspiration of seeking good, namely innocence: "The faith of the church in its rising is in the good of innocence like an infant" (AC 10087.3). It is particularly interesting that one of the papers points to this aspect of the Last Judgment. Dr. Williams-Hogan writes: "They seized the opportunity not only to protect innocence but also to nourish it."

There is always the temptation to pay more attention to ideas and thoughts more than affection, innocence and good will. We will explore that aspect a bit more now.

AFFECTION, PERCEPTION, THOUGHT

In my reading of the Writings I have many times come across three concepts being tied together. They are "Affection, Perception and Thought." It may be a useful tool in trying to understand the changes that have been taking place in the world after 1757.

We just said that a living faith or a New Church starts from wanting to do good. Expressed in a different way we can say it starts with an affection for doing good. About Hanway we hear that he "was dismayed with . . . the lack of resources available to care for the infants, and their subsequent high mortality rate" (Williams-Hogan). And Wollstonecraft said "she hated the dependency of uneducated poor" (Werner). Wadström's detailed reports and "the visual images of horrors of the slave ships helped sway a critical portion of Parliament to the antislavery cause" (Henderson).

Such affections are kindled by God, or by an influx from Him that is not intercepted in the world of spirits. The next step is that the affection leads to a perception of the circumstances around the object of the affection. Perception is an awareness or an insight beyond words and even beyond thoughts. It is all happening in the will part of the mind. Next step is when this mental or spiritual activity passes into the understanding. A thought is there produced and the previous two steps, affection and perception, become visible in the mind. The person begins to think, and from thinking the person can begin to act. But it all started with love and a strong wish to see good be done.

The following quote from *Arcana Cœlestia* can be used to illustrate this starting point:

> The affections of truth and good well forth as from their fountains, from charity toward the neighbor, and from love to the Lord. (AC 4018.3)

And here is an example:

Affection	Perception	Thought
Wanting to see goodness in people's lives	"Something is wrong" "There must be a better way"	"I will do something about it" "I must find some people who can do something"

What the three papers have shown is people who have had a longing for healing, peace and harmony in the world, because they were affected by goodness—I dare to say from the Lord. Therefore they perceived what good could be done and what needed to be done. From having responded to an urge from within to seek goodness, they began to find the right understanding to deal with the different issues. From this followed action (ISB 1.3).

The plan for action, the thoughts that lead the action become powerful, effective when they begin in the right place, in the heart:

"Truth receives its essence from good, and consequently its life, from good" (AC 4301.1). And I may add—from the Lord. We may think that it all starts with the truth side, but it does not: "Without affection (or without the delight which is of love) nothing can enter into man" (AC 4205.2, about Jacob and Laban). A good thought cannot enter if there isn't at first a good affection. Affection, perception, thought. This is how it is said in *Arcana Cœlestia*:

The thought of angels who are with man . . . flows in . . . only with those who are in the good of love . . . for it flows in through good. With these this perception produces thoughts." (AC 5228, cf. 4977, 4967, 5478, 5497; AR 914.1)

TWO INNER SENSES IN THE WORD

Let me just add a thought that I think is also vital in the context. In the New Church we tend to talk about the inner or spiritual sense of the Word, and we tend to see that as something intellectual. It is something we can understand. It is about thought and not so much about affections. But the full truth is that there are two inner senses, the spiritual and also the celestial. The point is that one is for the intellect and the other for the will. Light from the Lord comes with heat. When we read the Word He touches us with light in our understanding, and with heat in our will.

From the Lord proceed two things: Divine love, and Divine wisdom . . . and in its essence the Word is both of these; . . . the man who reads (the Word) from the Lord . . . is filled by it with the good of love and the truths of wisdom; his will with the good of love, and his understanding with the truths of wisdom. (SS 3)

The truths . . . are in the spiritual sense of the Word, and goods . . . in its celestial sense. (SS 40.1,2; WH 10; TCR 191)

Another way to put this is to say that there is both light and heat in the bosom of the Word, and the soul is affected by both.

The light gives life to the understanding, and the warmth gives energy and power to the will. The person who reads the Word "is in light according to his affection for truth, and in heat according to his affection for good" (BE 92, AE 1088).

This is summarized in these words of the Lord: "I am the Bread of Life; he who comes to Me shall never hunger, and he who believes in Me shall never thirst" (John 6.35). And "My words are spirit and they are life" (John 6.63).

As I indicated before about affection, perception and thought, the will side is in fact more important than the understanding side, at least if the latter is not kindled to go into action. Listen to this:

"The Word is the doctrine of good, because it is the doctrine of love to the Lord and of love toward the neighbor." (AC 9780.2) In short, the Word points towards action, good deeds, loving the neighbor. Through the Word the Lord inspires a willing heart to act.

GOOD CHRISTIANS AND GENTILES

The three papers have shown examples of people who have taken action, many of them clearly inspired by the Revelation in the Lord's Second Coming like Wilderspin (Williams-Hogan), Howe (Werner) and Wadström (Henderson), but many others without knowing anything about them, Hanway (Williams-Hogan), Wollstonecraft (Werner) and Clarkson (Henderson).

We have seen that there has been a shift in attitudes, values and ways of affecting how the world develops after the Last Judgment. If we think in black and white and say everything was bad before 1757, and all of a sudden it got much better, we must think that there must have been a lot of people to make that happen, a lot of people. We must then also think that it did not happen because there were a few, very few indeed, who belonged to the organized New Church. No, people outside of the organized New Church did most of the good works that were done.

It is a challenging idea to think about the speed at which the world changed for the better and the fact that the New Church grows slowly (TCR 784). The conclusion must be that the change in the spiritual world in 1757 affected lots of people on this earth. The sun shone sevenfold. The Divine light and heat shone into their hearts and minds. And they reacted. Prof. Henderson says: "The abolitionists fought for someone else's rights." Those people were kindled from within. Affection, perception, thought. And they reacted from a willingness to do good. Dr. Williams-Hogan has these words: "These men saw evil and responded to it by taking action to combat it."

We can all learn from this, and I am so grateful to this conference for putting light on that. The world is changing as a result of the Last Judgment in 1757. It is changing because of what the Lord did. And it is changing because people on this earth react, many people, masses of people. This is an application of the reasoning in the beginning of end, cause and effect—Divine Love, Last Judgment and good deeds. Those masses of people, all the way throughout these 250 years, have reacted to the new, stronger influx. Their good deeds, the cause, go back to the Lord's love for mankind, the end, and to the fact that He changed everything around, the cause. Those people used their common sense, and finally they had *not* confirmed themselves in the abominable doctrine where God is divided in three and the Lord in two (AR 563), i.e. they had not maliciously destroyed the image of God, and therefore they are open to the influx, and if not in this world they will gladly receive the truth about the One only God in the other life.

And secondly they did follow the second of the two great commandments and did good works. The courageous people we have heard about in the three papers are therefore examples of those who are called "the earth that opened its mouth and swallowed up the flood which the dragon had spewed out of his mouth" (Rev. 12.16). They are the good people who remain among *the dragonists* without being led astray any more. This is how it is explained in the Writings:

> The church that is called the New Jerusalem is to tarry among those who are in the doctrine of faith separate while it grows to fullness, until provision is made for it among many. . . . [Those] who live the life of faith, which is charity, are not dragons, although they are among them, for they do not know otherwise than that it is according to doctrine that faith produces fruits, which are good works . . . The church consisting of those who are not dragons is meant by the "earth" that "helped the woman and swallowed up the river that the dragon cast out of his mouth" . . . It is by [them] that the New Church which is called the Holy Jerusalem, is helped and also grows. (AE 764.2)

My point is this. Good Christians, or Gentiles if you wish, are touched by the heat and light in the Word, or the Bible as they would call it. Their affections are kindled and they perceive and they act. Affection, perception, thought. They have been moved into action by an inner dictate from the Lord. "The harvest truly is plentiful, but the laborers are few. Therefore pray the Lord of the harvest to send out laborers into His harvest" (Matt. 9.37). In Dr. Williams-Hogan's paper we heard this sentence: "What is clear about these men is that they saw evil and responded to it by taking action to combat it."

CONCLUSION

In conclusion let me say that as a result of the Last Judgment the two great commandments are being restored to their original purpose, because the dragon and Babylon have been defeated and cast out, and because "the earth opened its mouth and swallowed up the flood which the dragon had spewed out of his mouth" (Rev. 12.16). That "earth" represents lots of people around the world who respond to the new influx made possible through the Last Judgment in 1757. They do that by seeking what is good for their neighbor. All three papers have demonstrated this.

If you think about it, the world is a wonderful place. It works fantastically. Yes, there are imperfections here and there. There is war going on continually somewhere around the world, but think about the millions, billions of small good deeds that are done every day, yes, every hour, every minute, deeds that keep the world going. Next time you go shopping food or go on a trip, think about how many people actually serve you. Count them! Count how many good deeds are done to you just going shopping food for the week. You'll be amazed. It is a miracle that you can buy goods from far away by sending them information about your credit card. There is so much trust and good will around the world. The vendor does get his money and the customer does get his goods. And add to this the endless number of people working unselfishly in charity organizations; all the people who bend over to promote good education, to give young people a sense of usefulness in their lives; and people in all kinds of movements that look towards establishing freedom, independence, decency and human values around the world. Yes, there is fraud and theft, but it is so little in comparison with the overwhelming amount of good deeds. On the massive scale there is so much trust, so much good will. The world would simply not function if the majority of people were selfish and evil. The world is a wonderful place, and it is the Lord's doing through the Last Judgment and through many, many people who have responded and keep responding to His call for unselfish service to the neighbor. All those people are co-workers with us in establishing the kingdom of God. Prof. Henderson ended by saying: "We should ask ourselves what can and should be done to ensure that slavery does not become, once again, a morally wrong, yet 'immovable' reality." The Lord looks for action, laborers of the harvest. Make sure we follow His call!

APPRECIATION

Finally I want to say a warm thank you to Drs. Williams-Hogan and Werner and Prof. Henderson for all the good work they have put into researching, composing and presenting their papers. They have made the Last Judgment come alive as something that is part of our lives and our world from 1757 up till today. Thank you very much!

Celebrating the 250th anniversary of the Last Judgment is probably the most arcane thing I have taken part in but also the most inspiring. Therefore I want to thank Mr. Michael H. Hogan warmly for taking the initiative to this exciting and uplifting conference. ⚡

BIBLIOGRAPHY

Bailey, Jonathan, *Swedenborg Verified by the Progress of One Hundred Years*. London: James Spears, 1883.

Bergquist, Lars, *Swedenborg's Secret*. London: Swedenborg Society, 2005

The Bible, New King James version.

Brock, E. J., ed., *Swedenborg and His Influence*. Bryn Athyn, PA: The Academy of the New Church, 1988.

Poole, Susan Flagg, *Lost Legacy*. West Chester, PA: Swedenborg Foundation, 2007.

Swedenborg, E., *Arcana Cœlestia*

————., *The Last Judgment*

————., *The White Horse*

————., *New Jerusalem and Its Heavenly Doctrine Concerning the Lord*

————., *New Jerusalem and Its Heavenly Doctrine Concerning the Sacred Scripture*

————., *Continuation of the Last Judgment*

————., *Apocalypse Explained*

————., *Apocalypse Revealed*

————., *Intercourse of the Soul and the Body*

————., *Brief Exposition*

————., *True Christian Religion*

The New Jerusalem Come Down to Earth

REUBEN P. BELL

ABSTRACT

This paper sets out to establish the context of the Last Judgment—not just what it was, but why it was, why it occurred when it did, and what it was supposed to accomplish. These are essential to our understanding of the subtle nature of its manifestation in the natural world. Rising and falling spiritual fortunes are a cyclical reality of the human experience, and the Last Judgment of 1757 was a predictable event in an undulating chain of spiritual readjustments since the fall of the Most Ancient Church. Keys to understanding the natural expression of the spiritual Last Judgment are the incremental increases in human freedom and the evolution of human consciousness in conjunction with these changes. This new consciousness is contagious, and is slowly spreading still, manifesting itself in many of the radical developments of the modern era. Developments in modern history, politics, literature, the arts, religion, philosophy, education, and most particularly the natural sciences, can all be interpreted as either an extension of, or a reaction to, the continuing descent of the New Jerusalem into human minds. The restoration of spirituality to science is the ultimate expression of this New Jerusalem come down to earth.

> The Tree of Knowledge leading to the tree of life. Science is the key to natural things whereby heavenly things are opened up. (Swedenborg 1745, *The Messiah About to Come*, chap. X)

PROLOGUE

The search for signs of the New Jerusalem in the natural world following the Last Judgment of 1757[1] cannot begin with that event. We must start with a prologue to establish the natural world context into which this event descended. Without this perspective the Last Judgment makes no historical sense, and might appear to have no logical cause.

We start not with the Last Judgment of 1757, and not with the Lord's first advent into the world either, but at the beginning of the human narrative, with the first "last judgment," which was the fall of the human race into the knowledge of good and evil.

> Now the serpent was more cunning than any beast of the field which the Lord God had made. And he said to the woman, "Has God indeed said, 'You shall not eat of every tree of the garden?'" And the woman said to the serpent, "We may eat the fruit of the trees of the garden; but of the fruit of the tree which is in the midst of the garden, God has said, 'You shall not eat it, nor shall you touch it, lest you die.'" Then the serpent said to the woman, "You will not surely die. For God knows that in the day you eat of it your eyes will be opened, and you will be like God, knowing good and evil." So when the woman saw that the tree was good for food, that it was pleasant to the eyes, and a tree desirable to make one wise, she took of its fruit and ate. She also gave to her husband with her, and he ate. Then the eyes of both of them were opened, and they knew that they were naked; and they sewed fig leaves together and made themselves coverings. And they heard the sound of the Lord God walking in the garden in the cool of the day, and Adam and his wife hid themselves from the presence of the Lord God among the trees of the garden. Then the Lord God called to Adam and said to him, "Where are you?" So he said, "I heard Your voice in the garden, and I was afraid because I was naked; and I hid myself." And He said, "Who told you that you were naked? Have you eaten from the tree of which I commanded you that you should not eat?" Then the man said, "The woman whom You gave to be with me, she gave me of the tree, and I ate." And the Lord God said to the woman, "What is this you have done?" The woman said, "The serpent deceived me, and I ate." So the Lord God said to the serpent: "Because you have done

---

1. This refers to the Swedenborgian doctrine of a spiritual Last Judgment, foretold in *The Revelation* of the New Testament, as an accomplished event which occurred in the spiritual world in 1757 as reported by Emanuel Swedenborg in his theological works.

this, You are cursed more than all cattle, and more than every beast of the field; on your belly you shall go, and you shall eat dust all the days of your life. And I will put enmity between you and the woman, and between your seed and her seed; He shall bruise your head, and you shall bruise His heel." (Gen. 3.1–15)

The internal sense identifies the last verse of this passage as the earliest prophecy of a Redeemer[2] who would come into the world, in answer to the devolution, over time, from the "knowledge of good and evil" to immersion into evil itself.[3] What happens here will eventually require the first advent of the Lord. We find that something like this will happen again at the end of the Christian Church, necessitating yet another coming of the Lord into the world. These first two events are described in *Arcana Coelestia* 2034:

> After everything celestial with man perished, that is, all love to God, so that as a result the will for what is good existed no longer, the human race was separated from the Divine. For nothing other than love effects conjunction, and when love has been reduced to nothing, disjunction has taken place. And when the latter has taken place destruction and annihilation follow. At that point therefore a promise was given concerning the Lord's Coming into the world, who was to unite the Human to the Divine, and by means of this union was to join [to the Divine] the human race that was abiding in Himself through faith grounded in love and charity. From the time of that first promise given in Genesis 3.15, this kind of faith in the Lord who was to come was conjunctive.
>
> But once faith springing from love did not remain any more in the world the Lord came and united the Human Essence to the Divine Essence so that these were completely one, as He Himself states explicitly. At the same time He taught the way of truth to the effect that everyone who believed in Him, that is, who loved Him and what was His, and who abided in His love, which is a love directed towards the entire human race and so towards the neighbor, would be conjoined and thus saved.

---

2. See AC 250–260 for Swedenborg's exegesis of Genesis 3.15, with a detailed exposition of the spiritual sense, by means of the correspondences embedded in the verse.

3. For an explanation of this descent into evil along a "slippery slope" from doubt to denial to defiance of what is good and true, see Swedenborg's CL 444.

With the addition of the Last Judgment of 1757 to these two other spiritual branch points, the idea of Redemption emerges not as a single historical event, but as a cyclical phenomenon over time, with smaller cycles within the larger ones, of falling away and Covenant renewal. In order to square with human experience, our spiritual history needs to be understood in this evolutionary way. The Last Judgment of 1757 was not an isolated event, but was the culmination of a chain of identifiable spiritual and natural events from the earliest days of human history.

THE EFFECTS OF THE FIRST ADVENT

The most fundamental outcome of the first advent was the glorification of the Lord's Human.[4] Returning to *Arcana Coelestia* 2034, we learn the significance of this event.

> Once the Human had been made Divine, and the Divine made Human in the Lord, an influx of the Infinite, or the Supreme Divine, took place with man which could not possibly have manifested itself in any other way. Also by means of that influx the dreadful false persuasions and the dreadful desires for evil were dispersed with which the world of spirits had been filled and was constantly being filled by souls streaming into it from the world; and those who were actuated by such persuasions and evil desires were cast into hell and so separated. Unless this had been done the human race would have perished, for it is by means of spirits that the Lord rules the human race. They could not have been dispersed in any other way because there was no activity of the Divine by way of man's rational concepts into his inner sensory awareness, for these are far below the Supreme Divine when not so united.

This last judgment brought about a housecleaning in the spiritual world—the world of spirits was cleared of its overflowing stock of

---

4. The enormity of this fact of glorification startled Anglican minister John Clowes (1743–1831) into an almost Pauline conversion to the New Church. A spiritual epiphany on the significance of *Divinum Humanum* led him to become a patriarch of the early New Church in England. This story was related in an address by the Rev. Samuel Noble in 1831 and preserved in Tafel, R. L., *Documents Concerning the Life and Character of Emanuel Swedenborg*, vol. II, part II (London: Swedenborg Society, 1877), 1166–1168.

evil souls, and a separation between heaven and hell ushered in a new spiritual order. This produced a beneficial effect on the natural world as well, as peoples' minds were no longer subject to the involuntary influence of evil spirits. Of equal importance was a development that is often overlooked: a higher degree of freedom was a part of this new order, an emergent human trait that would play an essential role in a spiritual judgment yet to come.

The Glorification served as a major preparatory step for this judgment to come, particularly in the arts and the natural sciences. "Heaven and earth" were now truly conjoined, the "earth" no longer a degree of reality in potential, but brought fully into the contiguum of creation. The mechanism of this conjunction was the induction of spiritual influx, with natural afflux in reciprocation. Now there was a fully functional middle place for the human being to stand, with the spiritual mind and natural body united in unanimous action. Even this far ahead, the Glorification set the stage for the arts and sciences of the New Christian Era.

What changed? All the earth, and the human mind along with it, as a result of the change in natural matter itself. A new degree of intellectual influx could now descend fully into it, to bring a new level of understanding, both spiritual and natural. The New Testament was a new kind of revelation for this new era, accommodated to this new kind of mind. This brought about a new level of freedom—"if you continue in My Word, then you are My disciples indeed, and you shall know the truth, and the truth shall make you free" (John 8.32)— and the stage was set for a new Christian era to begin. But because of the very nature of freedom itself, what brings great human potential, can also bring great calamity. The Writings for the New Church plainly state that "the origin of evil is in the abuse of the faculties proper to man, called freedom and rationality" (DP 15). This radical change at the first advent was also the cause of the "destruction and annihilation" described in *Arcana Coelestia* 2034 above, leading up to the second advent. Freedom is a volatile element; it makes trouble wherever it goes. As we shall see, it is freedom that becomes the driver of the Lord's second advent, and the essence of the New Jerusalem itself.

Now the stage is set—with freedom comes a burst of human spiritual development and the rise of naturalism to counter it. At work here is the perennial tension between good descending into the world and evil rising up to meet it.[5] Swedenborg made dire predictions about naturalism, the intellectual offspring of the Age of Reason, that promised even then to be the corrosive force it has become.[6] The great good of the New Jerusalem descends into the midst of an impressive alliance of opposing forces, and the intellectual, political, and religious landscape of our world is transformed by the apocalyptic struggle that has finally come.

After the first advent and a good three hundred year start came the slow, steady decline of the first Christian Church. In place at its vastation in 1757 was the new era of freedom foretold in John's *Revelation*, finally come to pass with the descent of the New Jerusalem. But it was not readily visible to the natural eye. The "kingdom of heaven" had come, but it did not meet the expectations of the Christian world. This "kingdom" was the Lord's church on earth, and nothing more, and the churches had not ostensibly changed at all. Science had made marvelous progress, but was losing its moorings to spirit. In constructing a method for getting at natural truth by combining inductive reasoning with empirical investigation, Francis Bacon's *Novum Organum* (1620) removed Aristotle's *final cause*[7] from his new, "scientific" chain of cause and effect alone, and naturalism was

5. See the Writings for the New Church on the concept of spiritual equilibrium. The mechanism involves evil at work in the world, but in the Lord's divine providence this evil is put to use as one of two equalizing forces allowing a person complete freedom to move towards good or evil. Central teachings include AC 1857, 3628; HH 292, 293, 541, 593, 594; LJ 33, 34; TCR 475–78.

6. See AC 3024.4, 3108; AE 575; CL 415; TCR 13.4, 75.7, 339, 771, and ISB 2 for core teachings on the threat of naturalism and its potential for harm to the culture.

7. Of Aristotle's four causes (material, formal, efficient, and final), it was the final cause that involved the thing's purpose, or reason for being. As this involved speculation, Bacon abandoned it in favor of only those attributes than could be confirmed by objective observation. See Aristotle, *Physics* bk. II, chap. 3 and *Metaphysics* bk. A, chap. 3 for his complete treatment of these philosophical concepts. Jonathan Barnes ed., *The Complete Works of Aristotle*, Bollingen series

strengthened by this new authority. *Creatio ex nihilo* became the axiom of the day, and all things of nature were now from nature alone. His own religious beliefs notwithstanding, René Descartes' *radical skepticism* helped fuel this secular departure, and the stage was set for the Enlightenment to finally do away with the need for spiritual connection altogether. It was precisely here that Swedenborg saw and reported the dawn of another era, which could finally apply a rational spiritual/natural model to the sublime natural philosophy of the day. There was a growing need to restore the dissolution of science and religion, and the New Jerusalem he proclaimed was coming down to do just that.

EFFECTS OF THE SECOND ADVENT

The Last Judgment of 1757 appeared right on schedule, and just as Swedenborg observed, all those apocalyptic images of John's *Revelation* came to pass. But how were these events in the *spiritual* world manifested in the *natural* world of human experience? Almost not at all. The descent of the New Jerusalem into this world is gradual, cumulative, and spiritual, and not natural at all. But translated into human terms, *spiritual* becomes *mental*, as the highest degree of the human mind is spiritual in structure and in function. This fact will eventually emerge as the solution to the problem. The New Jerusalem steps down from heaven, through the successive degrees of the human mind, to find expression in the natural world of experience.[8] Swedenborg explained this "trickle-down" process in terms of the evolution of the New

---

71.2, 2 vols., (Princeton, NJ: Princeton University Press, 1984), 332–334 (*Physics*), 1555–1557 (*Metaphysics*).

8. The human mind exists as a series of degrees or levels, from the sensual to the celestial, across which spiritual substance is able to interact in an orderly manner with the natural matter of the brain. The crucial mechanism is the operation, by spiritual/natural correspondence, between these two levels. See AC 1999.3; ISB 8.4; DP 220.3; TCR 8; HH 39; LJ 25; SE 5548; WE 919. The best summary of this multi-level structure of the human mind is found in Hugo Lj. Odhner's *The Human Mind* (Bryn Athyn, PA: Swedenborg Scientific Association, 1969).

Church on earth as a function of the gradual replacement of the first Christian church by the descending New Jerusalem.

> It is in accordance with Divine order that a new heaven should be formed before a new church is established on earth, for the church is both internal and external, and the internal church makes one with the church in heaven, thus with heaven itself; and what is internal must be formed before its external, what is external being formed afterwards by means of its internal . . . Just so far as this new heaven, which constitutes the internal of the church with man, increases, does the New Jerusalem, that is, the New Church, descend from it; consequently this cannot take place in a moment, but it takes place to the extent that the falsities of the former church are set aside. (TCR 784)

In terms of everyday experience, the world went right on with its vastated business, while the Last Judgment silently came and went. But just as in the first advent, things changed, and the world would never be the same. What was now descending into the highest degree of every human mind would gradually find expression in a rapid succession of radical ideas that would change the world forever.

What changed? In the "judgment" of the Lord's first advent it was the nature of matter itself, which effected a change in the substance of the brain as physical platform for the mind.[9] This judgment of the first advent set the stage for the last. The key to understanding the Last Judgment of 1757 is to see it as a mutation, not of matter (as in the first), but of human consciousness a discrete degree above matter. Human consciousness mutated into a contagious agent of spiritual change. Contagion progresses slowly at first, in a linear way, but will increase geometrically if the environment can support it. According to the model for bacterial and viral growth, there is first a long lag phase with a gently upward-sloping curve. But with sufficient nourishment, and if other necessary environmental conditions are met, proliferation enters an exponential phase, with an almost vertical slope of astonishingly rapid

---

9. This is not the first time we have seen a change in the substance of the human brain: AC 4326.3 explains that after the fall into evil, the Lord effected a change in the human brain that brought about a reversal of the communicative pathways between cerebellum (the seat of the will) and cerebrum (the understanding). This represents a major developmental event in human spiritual evolution.

reproduction. But despite the impressive outcome, the start is always very slow. And unlike the fate of natural organisms, the exponential phase need never end if the supply of nourishment is spiritual and thus infinite in supply.

SIGNS

What concrete historical events can be traced directly from causes put in motion by the Last Judgment two hundred fifty years ago? What has really changed from 1757 to today? It is much easier to see the things that have not changed.

- Naturalism marches on, and it is developing a disturbingly militant edge. The world religions are no longer just the preoccupation of harmless, soft-headed delusion. Now they stand accused of being hazardous to the health of the human race, and are identified as the cause, not the cure, of human suffering. An impressive collection of atheist polemics has entered the marketplace of ideas, and religious writers have been put on notice that their irrational spiritual rambling will no longer be tolerated by the "Brights" among us.[10]
- The Christian world view is ostensibly still in place; the church you drive by today will likely not be a Church of the New Jerusalem. Things still look the same. But this world view has eroded, leaving an ambiguous, uncertain sense of where things are going, and little sense of purpose beyond the emotional, the political, and the politically correct. There is a great divide between the blind certitude of biblical literalism on one side, and the myopic solipsism of religion as consecrated social work on the other. The Christian

---

10. Following the lead of philosophers J. L. Mackie and Daniel Dennett, mathematician Francis Crick and others, scientist-turned-polemicist Richard Dawkins has recently called for an end to all religions for the good of humanity. He calls himself and like-minded atheists "Brights," (enlightened ones), and in his *God Delusion* (New York: Houghton Mifflin, 2006) we find not just overweening hubris, but the Orwellian rhetoric of an ideologue as well. This is new, and it heralds an unsettling change for future science-religion "dialogue."

compass is broken, and as this becomes increasingly apparent in the culture around us, the Brights are increasingly emboldened. In their defense, they are hearing no credible answers to their reasoned challenges to Christian faith.

• Science continues to defend its rejection of Aristotle's *final cause* for natural things. Despite the significant epistemological challenges of causation being raised by emerging discoveries in quantum physics, the question of purpose for a natural thing remains a *non-sequitur* for a Dennett or a Dawkins. As these questions of the new science continue to accumulate, resistance to them becomes less reasoned and more emotional, less measured and more heated, less polite and more threatening. The temperature is rising in the rhetoric of science as it considers the increasingly tenuous nature of its old, comfortable, and neatly-limited Newtonian universe. Naturalism has traded detached condescension for a kind of reactive militancy—a dangerous development for the new millennium. And yet, despite his distinction as ostensible spokesman for the cause, Dawkins' arguments against spiritual causes for natural things are specious and worn.

• The dissolution of traditional institutions—academic, religious, governmental, and cultural—continues apace. Is this just destructive entropy at work in the world of the human experience, or might this chaos represent something providential, and more optimistic, quietly at work? Concerning the descent of the New Jerusalem, the Lord clearly predicted, "Behold I make all things new" (Rev. 21.5). What would things look like if "all things" were being "made new"? Tranquil or chaotic? The Maggid of Mezerich[11] made this observation about the mystical transformation of becoming new:

> Before an egg can grow into a chicken, it must first totally cease to be an egg. Each thing must lose its original identity before it can be something else.

---

11. Dov Baer (1710–1772), the Maggid of Mezerich, was chief disciple and public voice for Baal Shem Tov, the founder of Hassidic Jewish mysticism.

Therefore, before a thing is transformed into something else, it must first come to the level of No-*thing*ness.[12]

For one brief moment, the thing that is to become new is neither one—lost in time—perhaps not really there at all. And to the casual observer, that no-*thing* state might look more like chaos than becoming new.

• Spiritual malaise is all around us. From the impotence of leaders in every sector of our lives to the doctrinal drifting of our churches, from the absence of moral outrage to the nihilistic darkness of the media that create our culture, there is pathology that unravels the fabric of society. And paradoxically, spiritual malaise increases in the face of prosperity and security, the two most obvious characteristics of American life.

These are the things that have not seemed to change since the Last Judgment of 1757. And yet, through the lens of the New Revelation, all of these can be held up as evidence for the New Jerusalem, slowly trickling into human consciousness.

Looking back 250 years from the perspective of a New Church paradigm, we can see the New Jerusalem at work in a changing world. The signs are there if we wish to see them.

• The Romantic movement in the arts: Born on the cusp of the Last Judgment, this late eighteenth century intellectual movement provided early evidence that something mental and spiritual was afoot in the world. It was a radical departure from the artistic rigidity of the past, and the Romantic Movement may well represent, in retrospect, the slow lag phase of the consciousness of spiritual-natural correspondence, just beginning to spread throughout the intellectual world.

• The freedom movements: From the American and French Revolutions to those that continue to the present, the notion of

12. Perle Epstein, *Kabbalah: the Way of the Jewish Mystic,* (Boston: Shambala Publishing, Inc., 1978), 118.

individual freedom as an "unalienable right," with which we are
"endowed by [our] Creator" is a very new idea indeed. In the six
thousand years of human social development leading up to the
cultural forms of this day, the radical notion of individual freedom
is only a few seconds old. Yet it is embraced as an age-old tenet
wherever it falls to earth. It is a spiritual principle, and its source is
in the New Jerusalem.

• The autonomy of women: Women were *property* 250 years ago.
Their autonomy speaks for itself as an event of the Last Judgment
of 1757. The subjugation of women in the West has simply fallen
apart from exposure to the rational ordering of the New Jerusalem
coming into the world.

• The death of slavery: Slavery is an institution that went from
"curious" to untenable and has identifiable roots in the early
work of the Church of the New Jerusalem. Block and Hallengren[13]
identify the earliest anti-slavery movements in Europe and the
West Indies as that of the Exegetic-Philanthropic Society, an
organization led by philanthropist-activist Charles Wadström,
and founded on the principles of the New Jerusalem. Only in the
most savage corners of the globe does slavery still exist, and soon
it will fall victim everywhere to the inexorable contagion of human
freedom.

• There is no more clearly visible manifestation of the New Jerusalem
than the Internet, the astonishing development of which denotes its
correspondence to something very powerful in the spiritual world.
The Internet, an ethereal and almost spiritual thing, is the essence
of freedom in organic form. Leaderless, multi-nodal, and driven by
individuals in unanimous action, this form is the next phase of the
New Church coming into the world. It is modeled on the spiritual
principles of freedom and variety that make heaven a paradise;

---

13. Marguerite Block, *The New Church in the New World* (New York Octagon
Books, 1968), 54; Hallengren, Anders, *Gallery of Mirrors: Reflections of Swedenborgian Thought*, (West Chester, PA: Swedenborg Foundation Publishers,
1998), 51.

and yet, true to form, it permits evil to express itself as well.[14] The responsibility to use this powerful instrument wisely falls on individuals, not the government or the church, as an exercise in our regeneration. As the printing press was the instrument that brought the New Church into being, so will the Internet propel the New Jerusalem into all the world.

- Even the decline of New Church denominations in the world— in numbers, in influence, and in doctrinal integrity—is evidence that the Last Judgment is finally breaking through the Old Church forms that their well-meaning but short-sighted founders imposed on such a universalizing force as the New Jerusalem. This dissolution—so worrisome to New Church men and women around the world—will be a blessing to the New Church in the world to come, no longer burdened by buildings to maintain, catechisms to defend, and endowments to protect. The New Church will thrive as it was intended to do, as the contagion of love and wisdom at work spreads into the world, and people learn to apply these locally, in their own ways, in all things of life.

- Science, despite the reactive opposition of its orthodoxy, and despite the "science wars" that capture our attention, is converging towards the "omega point" of a new spiritual-natural axiom, with the final cause of creation restored. New discoveries require deeper explanations than naturalism can supply, and the shift to this new axiom will finally happen from necessity, not compulsion. Deep science will finally meet the deep theology of the New Jerusalem, and the true purpose of the Last Judgment of 1757 will be revealed. Once separated from its spiritual roots, once stripped of final cause, science will finally embrace the rationality of the New Philosophy and build a powerful new paradigm to accommodate both sensory experience and spiritual truth. The restoration of the left and right

---

14. HH 56 states that the perfection of heaven is from the variety of the worship there, and it is the freedom of association that determines its social structure.

brains of human intellectual activity—the *tikkun*[15] of the ages—is
the coming of the New Jerusalem.

The signs are there to see. The pulse of human culture quickened in
1757, and the notion of human freedom, once radical, is commonplace
today, in all its permutations. All things are becoming new—cultural
forms and content, immediate communication, access to information,
and a personal spiritual inclination of the human mind. But the science
demands a deeper look.

Once separated from its spiritual roots and determined to maintain
this separation, scientific discoveries themselves are causing scientists
to rethink the separation. Causality is no longer a linear proposition
in a quantum universe with uncertain boundaries, and the simple state
of being is not simple any more. Science, calm and confident on its
surface, is unsettled at its philosophical base; change (and the fear that
comes with change) is in the air.

The separation of spirit from nature was the greatest calamity
of human intellectual development, a product of the Enlightenment,
curiously the period of our greatest intellectual advancement. It has
given us a post modern world view of a purposeless, mechanistic
universe, where humanity plays no major role. Observing the fallout
from this calamity, Einstein remarked that "Science without religion is

---

15. Restoration is a major theme of the Jewish mystics, from Zoharic to Lurianic
Kabbalah, but it is an ancient concept, and common to all religions. From a starting point of unity, there is a separation from the Divine (*Shevirat ha-Kelim*, or
the breaking of the vessels, in Kabbalistic lore). The central theme of spiritual
transformation then becomes *tikkun*, the restoration of the pathways to the Divine. In Buddhism this is the delay in final liberation until all souls are free. In
Christianity it is the coming of the Messiah. To the Gnostics it was the liberation
of the Divine Spark, trapped in earthly bodies. In the New Jerusalem, an era of
a rational spirituality, it becomes the restoration of the two receptacles of truth
and good in the collective human mind, as science and spirituality are reunited
in the New Philosophy. Gershom Scholem, *Major Trends in Jewish Mysticism*
(New York: Schocken Books, 1974); *Tikkun Olam: the Spiritual Purpose of Life*,
at www.innerfrontier.com.

lame; religion without science is blind," but he offered no solution.[16] Others have sensed the anxiety that separation brings, but their solutions tend to be sectarian and dichotomous; winners win and losers lose, and there is no *tikkun*. The key is restoring Aristotle's final cause with freedom built right in—spiritual truths accommodated to each person's place and state. This the New Jerusalem can do, when its universalizing principles of spiritual-natural correspondence are fully understood.

THE SCIENCE WARS:
A MESSAGE FROM THE FRONT

I work in a typical university, with typical university faculty, who are typically immersed in liberal political ideology and scientific materialism. Today's *scientific materialism* is the direct descendant of *naturalism,* which Swedenborg predicted would get a lot worse over time. He was correct in his prediction. By either name it is a way of life in the intellectual circles of academic life, and it is gaining momentum, not just as an attitude, but as a movement. Religion is withering before it, and there is blood in the water of the science wars.

Emanuel Swedenborg was born on January 29, 1688. Despite this considerable historical distance, by looking at Swedenborg the man and his scientific works before his theological Writings, we find a powerful antidote to this naturalism that still drives the learned world today. Naturalism is the belief that nature is from Nature, and that science is the key to understanding all. I work in a place where this philosophy is the order of the day, and in this environment, in self-defense, I have developed a method for talking to my fellow professors about how the world works and how it is that from a scientist I could become a theologian. The "method" was there all along; it has been in plain sight for 250 years. But because of the unassuming nature of Swedenborg's

---

16. Albert Einstein, 1941, *Science, Philosophy, and Religion, A Symposium,* in *The Oxford Dictionary of Quotations,* Fourth ed. (Oxford, UK: Oxford University Press, 1992), 268.

quaint eighteenth century science, it took me a while to see the forest for the trees.

A RATIONALE

First some boiler-plate New Church doctrine: We are told in John's *Revelation*, Chapter 21 that there are twelve gates into the New Jerusalem. The number twelve in the internal sense signifies "all things of faith" (AC 2089), faith signifies the implantation of truth (AE 813), and this, we are told, is the beginning of the work of God (Ibid. 226).

New Church people have always taken "the twelve gates" to mean that there is a gate to suit the particular needs of every person who is seeking spiritual truth, each gate serving as some unique manifestation of "all the knowledges of truth and good" (AR 916). Since "twelve" signifies all things of faith we can assume that the number of gates equals not a literal twelve, but the number of people needing to get in. That's an infinite number in spiritual terms, and that is no doubt a good thing.

One of these gates—the one we are looking at here—is the natural truths of science. Swedenborg used that gate. From a grounding in natural philosophy, Emanuel Swedenborg was drawn through that gate into the deeper truths of the spiritual causes of natural things. He explained this process to German theosophist Friedrich Oetinger, who was fascinated with Swedenborg's philosophy of heaven and earth. In the last passage of *Soul-Body Interaction* (1769) Swedenborg explains

> how I, a philosopher, became a theologian. . . . this happened in the same way that fishermen were made disciples and apostles by the Lord . . . that I too was a spiritual fisherman from my youth. When my companion heard this, he asked what a spiritual fisherman was. I answered that in the Word, a fisherman in the spiritual meaning indicated a person who hunts out and teaches natural truths.
>
> Afterward, I showed him the source of this meaning of fishermen from *The Apocalypse Revealed*—that is because "water" means things that are true on the natural level (AR 50, 932), so also does a river (AR 409, 932), "fish" means people who are involved in things that are true on the natural level (AR 405), and therefore "fishermen" means people who hunt out and teach truths.

On hearing these statements, my questioner said quite loudly, "Now I understand why the Lord chose fishermen to be His disciples! So it does not surprise me that he has chosen you as well, since as you have said, you have been a fisherman in a spiritual sense from your early youth, that is, a hunter of natural truths. Your present occupation of pursuing spiritual truths is because these latter are based on the former."

"Besides," he continued, "what Christian theologian is there who has not studied philosophy in his school days? Where else could he gain intelligence?" (ISB 20)

There is a lesson in this beyond the obvious. Science today is confirmed by the limiting world view of naturalism, which cannot explain the purpose of existence. This has caused a crisis of identity and meaning for the people of the earth. There is chaos at hand, and I suggest that scientific materialism is largely to blame. Naturalism leads to what the Writings for the New Church call "the negative principle," that it eventually denies all things, submits to no authority, and ends up as a kind of insanity.[17] From this come two great challenges: (1) The "traditional" Western religions—Christianity (from fundamentalist to liberal) and Judaism in its visible forms—do not have the theology to answer and support the recent surge of interest in spirituality by some scientists. They are asking penetrating questions that the "religious establishment" cannot answer. (2) Scientists think and ask questions in the language of science, and sublime, high-end New Church theology cannot answer them in kind. This is something that New Church people fail to understand. Our theology sounds fine as long as we are preaching to the choir, but a specialized language of religion is not the language of science. These are problems of our time, but they are not really new at all. Swedenborg responded to this same dilemma in his time by presenting a *scientific* system in which spirit is prime mover. Nature is not from nature but from spiritual substance (thus having a purpose beyond itself), but the objectivity and language of science are inherent in it. He showed the scientists of his day a rational approach to the question of spiritual causes for natural things. I suggest that this same rationale is effective for the scientists and philosophers of this

---

17. AE 575, TCR 13.4, AC 2588.2.

day as well—more effective, perhaps, because the science of the new millennium has finally pushed itself to limits that only purpose can explain.

Naturalism cannot explain the purpose of existence. It is not allowed to even raise the question. Worse still, traditional Judeo-Christian theology cannot explain it either. And although the Writings for the New Church address this question in an intellectually defensible way, they explain it in a language apart from the language of science.

A SPIRITUAL MODEL OF ACCOMMODATION

In Exodus and *The Acts of the Apostles* we find a spiritual model to help us understand this predicament. It is all about language, perception, and accommodation. In Exodus Chapter 4, we find Moses doing a very un-Mosaic thing. He is trying to get out of his assignment, from Jehovah Himself, to go back to Egypt and help the children of Israel out of their misery. And he uses some pretty lame excuses! Exodus 4.10–16:

10   Moses said to the Lord, "O Lord, I have never been eloquent, neither in the past nor since you have spoken to your servant. I am slow of speech and tongue."
11   The Lord said to him, "Who gave man his mouth? Who makes him deaf or mute? Who gives him sight or makes him blind? Is it not I, the Lord?
12   Now go; I will help you speak and will teach you what to say."
13   But Moses said, "O Lord, please send someone else to do it."
14   Then the Lord's anger burned against Moses and he said, "What about your brother, Aaron the Levite? I know he can speak well. He is already on his way to meet you, and his heart will be glad when he sees you.
15   You shall speak to him and put words in his mouth; I will help both of you speak and will teach you what to do.
16   He will speak to the people for you, and it will be as if he were your mouth and as if you were God to him.

Next, we find Paul, that other Apostle, spreading the Good News in Athens, the intellectual capital of the ancient world—a Harvard,

Oxford, or UCLA Berkeley of the ancient world. He entered the Areopagus there, and challenged the smartest Epicurean and Stoic philosophers of the place: "All the Athenians and the foreigners," it says "who lived there [and] spent their time doing nothing but talking about and listening to the latest ideas." Just like your typical university. How did Paul do in that arena?

22   Paul then stood up in the meeting of the Areopagus and said: "Men of Athens! I see that in every way you are very religious.

23   For as I walked around and looked carefully at your objects of worship, I even found an altar with this inscription: TO AN UNKNOWN GOD. Now what you worship as something unknown I am going to proclaim to you."

24   The God who made the world and everything in it is the Lord of heaven and earth and does not live in temples built by hands."

25   And he is not served by human hands, as if he needed anything, because he himself gives all men life and breath and everything else."

26   From one man he made every nation of men, that they should inhabit the whole earth; and he determined the times set for them and the exact places where they should live."

27   God did this so that men would seek him and perhaps reach out for him and find him, though he is not far from each one of us."

28   For in him we live and move and have our being. As some of your own poets have said, 'We are his offspring.'"

29   Therefore since we are God's offspring, we should not think that the divine being is like gold or silver or stone—an image made by man's design and skill."

30   In the past God overlooked such ignorance, but now he commands all people everywhere to repent."

31   For he has set a day when he will judge the world with justice by the man he has appointed. He has given proof of this to all men by raising him from the dead."

32   When they heard about the resurrection of the dead, some of them sneered, but others said, "We want to hear you again on this subject."

33   At that, Paul left the Council.

34   A few men became followers of Paul and believed. Among them was Dionysius, a member of the Areopagus, also a woman named Damaris, and a number of others.

Paul didn't set the place on fire, but neither did he fail. He had the courage to engage his intellectual opponents that day. They were the best; and he held his own against them. How? He got them to listen because he talked to these philosophers in their own language. And he got a few to see the light. How many? "Dionysius, Damaris, and a number of others." We will return to these stories.

THERE ARE TWO FOUNDATIONS OF TRUTH.
WHY NOT USE THEM BOTH?

How can science be a gate into the New Jerusalem? Swedenborg himself had learned the hard way that you cannot climb *up* the ladder of being from the natural world to the world of spiritual causes; it has to be scaled downward, from the top. But as he told Professor Oetinger, concerning science and religion, the one state precedes the other. Swedenborg the scientist did not fail in some way, only to be rescued by the Lord for some higher purpose. His call to be a revelator came as he found himself at the top of his game, with no place to go from there. It was his science that took him to that jumping-off-place. So jump he did, leaving his science books behind. I suggest that he didn't do all that work for nothing, and after studying his science books, I am convinced that he left them for us in this time, for tools to end the science wars. Note well that the word here is *tools*, not weapons. It is time to get to work; we have had enough of war. Why do I believe this to be the case? Swedenborg tells us that there are "two foundations of truth,"

> one from the Word, the other from nature or from the truths of nature. The foundation from the Word is for the universal heaven, thus for those who are in the light of heaven; but the foundation from nature, is for those who are natural and in natural light. . . . But, still, [these two foundations of truth] agree the one with the other. Since the sciences have shut up the understanding, therefore, the sciences may also open it; and it is opened so far as people are in good. . . . all things of heaven constantly have their foundation in the laws of the order of nature, in the world and in man, so that the foundation remains permanently fixed. (SE 5709)

The Writings for the New Church remind us of the causal relationship of spirit to nature, and of nature's purpose as anchor for the spiritual world in ultimates. What better way to bring natural people—scientists included—into the New Jerusalem than by the gate of their own natural philosophy?

Swedenborg's scientific corpus has been largely disregarded by the learned world over the past 250 years. But in providence, it lies ready to use on a new crop of skeptical scientists who would believe in spiritual reality, if they were only shown a rational and plausible way to go about it. Swedenborg's science is a marvelous gate into the New Jerusalem, neglected over time, but ready now to manifest its purpose.

A VERY MODERN PROBLEM

In order to address the problem of modern science and religious faith, let's first provide a description of science as it exists at this moment in history. After three centuries of "progress," science has fallen victim to its own limitations. Science, like so many other institutions in these early days of the New Jerusalem, is in a state of radical change, with no clear sense of where it is headed. Here is how things stand: Naturalism, described by Swedenborg in the eighteenth century, is still going strong. But because of its built-in denial of purpose for the things of nature (Aristotle's *final cause*) science cannot pursue the epistemological and teleological questions raised by certain scientific disciplines themselves. Problems of knowing and being, of complexity and design and diversity, are beginning to plague the disciplines of quantum physics and cosmology, evolution, and molecular biology in the twenty-first Century. There are questions emerging that demand attention to the metaphysical considerations of "why" as well as "what." The leading edge of science begs for explanations that the rules of science do not allow.

Science, which must be objective above all things, is dealing with some unsettling phenomena. The Heisenberg Uncertainty Principle and Bell's Theorem of "spooky-action-at-a-distance," challenge the received notion of objectivity. Force carriers come and go, in and out of "reality," as matter at its lowest (or is that highest?) level redefines objectivity. And Richard Dawkins' red face notwithstanding, certain levels of complexity in biological forms strain the limits of the Neo-Darwinian Synthesis to explain. Worse yet, science—honest, hard-working science—is under fire as never before by Christian fundamentalists, whose battle plan is to take no prisoners. The "Science Wars" are going strong, and scientists who only a few years ago might have been neutral on issues of spirituality are now understandably reactive to anything that sounds religious in tone. Once burned is twice shy. Who could blame them for their reactivity?

Yet, despite the reactive environment that prevails, there is new and genuine interest in the interface of spirituality and science. Inspired in part by the John Templeton Foundation in recent years, the inclusion of spiritual possibilities alongside physical laws is a new but no longer startling development in our culture. "Science and religion" is no longer an oxymoron, and finding the two together in conversation has become an ordinary thing. But the boundaries between this new culture and the vicious, anti-intellectual agenda of the "religious right" are lost on scientists who see only danger when religion enters. Reactivity becomes backlash, and a new spirit of active atheism is on the rise, animated by the energies of anger and indignation. The Science Wars are heating up. The "dialogue" is in danger of collapse.

A new intelligentsia is arising, calling for the end of religion as a menace to the human race, and an impediment to human understanding. Theirs is an impressive voice. A list of major players includes J. L. Mackie (*The Miracle of Theism*, 1981), Francis Crick (*The Astonishing Hypothesis*, 1994), Daniel Dennett (*Breaking the Spell*, 2005), and Richard Dawkins (*The God Delusion*, 2006). These books increase in vitriol over time. Reasoned scientific and philosophical arguments are giving way to emotional outbursts by scholars who have been ravaged by Christianity's militant fringe, and who now are looking for revenge. They are organizing on a university campus near you. There are websites and foundations springing up to encourage people to throw off the ancient yoke of religion and join the "Brights" as they smugly call themselves, in the building of a new and harmonious (but one-dimensional) world.[18]

Why this surge of anti-religious energy from scientists and philosophers? First, we really do have our evangelical friends to thank for poking that snake of science; it is hard to see Christian charity at work in the tactics they employ. But that is not really it at all. It is the New Jerusalem, coming down out of heaven, from God, one mind at a time, that has got the scientific world in such a state. Since 1757, that is a lot of minds. And it is the vastation of the Christian Church, finally unraveling after 250 years. The old stuff just isn't working any more. Fear of loss manifests itself as anger, not fear, and anger shuts off the higher levels of the mind.

One thing more. There is just no plausible religion in the mainstream for scientists or philosophers to consider, were they so inclined. The religion they see at work in the world is a straw man, easily demolished with well-aimed questions—questions that traditional Judeo-Christian theologians cannot answer.

The last part of Chapter 4, "Why there almost certainly is no God," in Richard Dawkins' *God Delusion*, is a perfect example of the trouble in which we find ourselves. [19] We find a big problem here, as Dawkins describes his experience at a Templeton Foundation conference at Cambridge on science and religion, a gathering at which he says he was the "token atheist amongst the eighteen invited speakers." There he challenged the participants to respond to his point that "a God capable of designing a universe, or anything else, would have to be complex and statistically improbable."[20] Describing the response, he says,

---

18. See the Appendix, 375–379, to Richard Dawkins' *God Delusion* entitled "A partial list of friendly addresses, for individuals needing support in escaping from religion." Dawkins has moved from polemicist to evangelist here, with this impressive listing of anti-religion organizations. Dawkins, Richard, *The God Delusion* (Boston: Houghton Mifflin Company, 2006).

19. Ibid.

20. This argument against the existence of God, showcased in *The God Delusion*, is his best shot, which turns out to be little more than the tired old "infinite regress" argument dressed in an Armani suit.

> The theologians were *defining* themselves into an epistemological Safe Zone where rational argument could not reach them because they had *declared by fiat* that it could not. There are other ways of knowing besides the scientific, and one of these must be deployed to know God. The most important of these turned out to be the personal, subjective experience of God.

It is easy to feel his annoyance at the exclusivity of the ground rules and it is easy to identify with his frustration at this obvious manipulation of the process.

Dawkins says that he was eventually attacked by name-calling ("nineteenth century"), which he assumed was in retaliation for his asking, "Do you believe in miracles?" "Do you believe Jesus was born of a virgin?" and "Do you believe in the resurrection?" But the questions he asked were perfectly fair game. He broke through the customary barrier of politeness and asked Christian theologians if they believed the core doctrines of their own religion. According to Dawkins, "it embarrassed them because their rational minds knew it was absurd, so they would rather not be asked."

Dawkins says he left the conference "stimulated and invigorated," but from a close reading of this narrative, I believe that he left with his feelings hurt. His hatred of all things religious was not diminished by the experience.

Did you find the problem here? Despite his editorializing, Dawkins is right on all counts. Traditional theology (which is all that these traditional theologians had at their disposal) could not respond *in kind* to his perfectly rational challenge (infinite regress), and these traditional theologians could not answer his direct challenges to the tenets of their faith. They stone-walled him; they retreated into the rarified air of "subjective experience." In doing so, they made him the winner of the encounter. But they lost his respect.

So what is the answer to this predicament, with the theologians circling their wagons, and Dawkins and Co. on top, with confidence in their own human ingenuity growing by the day? Good religion, right? The obvious answer is deep, wide, New Church theology to provide these people with a rational basis for spiritual belief. But as counter-intuitive as it may seem, that would be wrong. Scientists will not (many, such as Dawkins apparently cannot) engage in high-end theology, so they do it poorly when they try. Why? Because they are scientists, not theologians. They lack the vocabulary, the training, the experience, and the specialized vocabulary for doing deep theology. Scientists are no more conversant with these specialized things than theologians with genetics, or molecular biology. So why expect them to be?

The disconnection comes at the level of expectations—ours and theirs. They ask scientific questions. They expect scientific answers. This is to say they are looking for answers in their own language, because that is what they expect and understand. What is wrong with that? Dawkins likes to taunt his religious enemies by saying (incorrectly for that matter) that the existence of God is a *scientific* question. If someone—anyone!—were to answer him in his own terms, I predict that he would at least stand and listen. It is time that someone did.

AN AGE-OF-REASON SOLUTION
FOR A VERY MODERN PROBLEM

Swedenborg confronted this challenge from the beginning of his career, so he set out to give scientists and philosophers scientific and philosophical answers to their rational challenges to faith. He did this very well in the scientific works that he wrote before his call. They are rich with meticulous description and reasoned speculation. They are rigorous in method and the terminology is precise. They are everything that scientific works should be, and more. Here we find good science applied from the axiom that the human body is a dynamic spiritual-natural unit, animated by a soul, and created for a purpose. But there is no magic in these works, only rational arguments from experience. They model an effective method that we can learn to use.

Contrary to the conventional wisdom of a hundred years of New Church culture, Swedenborg did not "abandon science" at his call. He had not "failed" at anything, although he still had lots of work to do. He had accomplished his major goal, which was to lay out an intellectually defensible model for spiritual-natural interaction in the human body, in the language of science, to leave behind for generations to come. Then the Lord moved him to a different place, where he could continue to work out the same great problems, but from the top down, and this time in the language of spirit.

When Israel was a child, I loved him. And out of Egypt I have called my son (Hosea 11.1). In the Word, Egypt signifies natural truths. At some point a person is able to move up from his or her foundation of natural truths into the universalizing knowledge of spiritual reality. But most of us start out in Egypt. Isn't Egypt the right place for natural people to begin?

Scientists and philosophers want science and philosophy that makes sense, and Swedenborg's scientific and philosophical works are just what they will understand. In those "scientific works" lie the core theological doctrines of the New Jerusalem: influx, degrees and series, forms, and correspondence. Here is *formative substance,* flowing in from the spiritual world bringing human form to matter; and here is the soul's descent into the body, bringing life to even the smallest parts. Here is a spiritual-natural paradigm—not in the arcane language of New Church theology, but in the everyday language that scientists will recognize and understand. It's all there, in scientific terms, to fit their states, and to meet their expectations. It is a wide and visible door into the New Jerusalem.

Not everyone will want to jump through that door. But some will, and all will see how it is possible to enter with the understanding into the mysteries of faith. That is worth a lot. Is this work easy? No. Sometimes we will be apprehensive that we won't know the right things to say, or that people will reject our ideas. But then we remember those stories about Moses and that other apostle, Paul.

TIKKUN

The Lord told Moses not to worry about what to tell the people of Egypt. He said, "I will help you speak and will teach you what to say." But for whatever reason in the literal sense, the Lord saw that

His truth would require a "stepping down," *through* Moses, *to* Aaron, who could accommodate it to the perceptive requirements of those people at that time—the same message, but on a different level, and in the language of its receivers.

This is a powerful spiritual model for the healing of the Science Wars of our day. Scientists speak their own language and see things according to their own cognitive structures. The language of theology is foreign to them, and kindles resentment in some; many scientists have experienced only irrational religious systems, and are not receptive to ideas couched in religious terms at all. But if divine truth were to come to them in the language of science and philosophy, and if it were able to bring rational answers to their penetrating questions, then Aaron will have spoken from the inspiration of Moses, whose wisdom was from the Lord Himself. This is the New Jerusalem stepping down to earth.

Won't people reject religion out of hand? Some surely will; that is what freedom is all about. But look what happened to Paul in Athens. "A few men became followers of Paul and believed," it says, "among them Dionysius, a member of the Areopagus, also a woman named Damaris, and a number of others." That is a start, and it beats the dismal showing of traditional theology against the heated rhetoric of scientific materialism. If nothing else, it could bring a new level of civility to the conflict.

Look at what happened to Swedenborg himself, who never set out to be revelator or a theologian, but who chose to devote his time and energy to natural philosophy. Natural truths eventually became his doorway—his personal gate—into the next level: from philosopher to theologian, from scientist to spiritual fisherman.

Swedenborg's science—his natural philosophy—has been neglected long enough. It is effective in addressing the questions that scientists are asking, and in answering their demands that any claims to spiritual causes for natural things be made in the language of logic and experience. I suggest that we, the keepers of this flame, teach it for what it is, and prepare our New Church scientists to use it for the tool it is, that they can take to any university or areopagus of the modern world. That may have been the idea all along, as Swedenborg watched his scientific works receding in the rear-view mirror, on his way to meet the New Jerusalem.[21] ⚔

BIBLIOGRAPHY

Bacon, Francis. *Novum Organum*. 1620. Peter Urbach trans. John Gibson ed. Chicago: Open Court Publishing, 2000.

Barnes, Jonathan ed. *The Complete Works of Aristotle*. Bollingen series 71.2, 2 vols. Princeton, NJ: Princeton University Press, 1984.

Block, Marguerite. *The New Church in the New World*. New York: Octagon Books, 1968.

Dawkins, Richard. *The God Delusion*. Boston: Houghton Mifflin Company, 2006.

Epstein, Perle. *Kabbalah: the Way of the Jewish Mystic*. Boston: Shambala Publishing, 1978.

Hallengren, Anders. *Gallery of Mirrors: Reflections of Swedenborgian Thought*. West Chester, PA: Swedenborg Foundation Publishers, 1998.

Holy Bible. New Kings James Version. Nashville: Thomas Nelson Publishers, 1982.

Odhner, Hugo Lj. *The Human Mind*. Bryn Athyn, PA: Swedenborg Scientific Association, 1969.

The Oxford Dictionary of Quotations fourth ed. Oxford, UK: Oxford University Press (1992): 268.

Scholem, Gershom. *Major Trends in Jewish Mysticism*. New York: Schocken Books, 1974.

---

21. That this was the actual case is suggested by the inscription chosen by Swedenborg for his *Dynamics of the Soul's Domain* (1740), a quotation from Seneca's Epistles, lxxix: *That man is born merely for a few, who thinks only of the people of his own generation. Many thousands of years and many thousands of peoples will come after you; it is to these that you should have regard. Malice may have imposed silence upon the mouths of all who were alive in your day; but there will come men who will judge you without prejudice and without favor.* In his own day the silence had begun, and Swedenborg apparently knew full well that he was writing to the scientists of the future.

Tafel, R. L. *Documents Concerning the Life and Character of Emanuel Swedenborg* vol. II, part II. London: Swedenborg Society 1877.
Tikkun Olam: the Spiritual Purpose of Life www.innerfrontier.com.

The Liberation of Mathematics
and the Last Judgment

FORREST DRISTY

In the year 1758 a series of five rather esoteric books were published in London. They dealt with topics such as heaven and hell, spirits from other planets, and an internal meaning in certain books of the Bible. All were in Latin, the international language of scholarship throughout Europe, and the anonymous author was clearly a person of extraordinary learning. They all made copious references to the massive eight volume work called *Arcana Coelestia* which had appeared in bookstores, volume after volume, during the previous decade. These books of profound Biblical exegesis were also published anonymously, and obviously the more recent five were by the same exceptional author. People who knew of these books and who were also acquainted with Emanuel Swedenborg, the prominent Swedish scientist and philosopher, had little difficulty in coming to the correct conclusion that he was the unknown author.

In this paper I will be concerned primarily with one of the 1758 books: the one whose title, translated into English, is *The Last Judgment and Babylon Destroyed*. (I will refer to this book as LJ.) In this small volume Swedenborg made the amazing claim that the event all Christians had been awaiting for centuries, the cataclysmic, world-ending last judgment, had been entirely misunderstood. Throughout all of his theological works he had consistently stressed the fact, which for him was repeatedly verified by his own (spiritual) senses, that the spiritual realm is real and substantial. The natural world, by comparison, is *less* real than the spiritual world, and the deeper meaning conveyed in sacred scripture pertains to that more real realm of spirit. Thus the Biblical prophecies of a last judgment, in order to be correctly understood, must be understood in a spiritual sense rather than a literal natural sense. So now, in his book about the last judgment, Swedenborg explained that this prophesied event referred to a complete reorganization of the spiritual world which had already been accomplished by the Lord during the previous year, 1757.

A few years later, in 1763, Swedenborg published another small, twenty-eight page booklet called *Continuation concerning the Last Judgment* (CLJ). This booklet was published in Amsterdam, still anonymous. In the New Century Edition being produced by the Swedenborg Foundation, it is called *Supplements*.

It is not my purpose to produce analysis of Swedenborg's description of the last judgment or to review the contents of his remarkable reports of this event. I do wish to consider briefly a few of his comments about the worldly effects of this major spiritual event. The primary goal of this paper is to indicate how these effects may well have included a major change in the nature of mathematics—a change that can be viewed as a liberation. Some of Swedenborg's remarks can be paraphrased as follows:

- The duration of the last judgment, or at least of his observation of it, coincided closely with the calendar year 1757. (LJ 45)
- The last judgment did not occur in the natural world but only in the spiritual world. (LJ 29)
- There will be no immediate change in worldly conditions or even in the external condition of the church. But the internal nature of the church will be changed dramatically to give people greater freedom in thinking about spiritual matters. (LJ 73)
- Before the last judgment people on earth could not be enlightened because of disorders in the spiritual realm which blocked the influx of truth in a way similar to the blocking of sunlight by dense clouds. After the last judgment communication between heaven and earth was restored. (CLJ 11, 13)

The eighteenth and nineteenth centuries were filled with political and social changes that have extended human spiritual, intellectual, and personal freedom in such profound ways that it is not difficult to attribute them to the effects stemming from the great spiritual event of 1757. We need not dwell on obvious examples such as the movement begun in 1776 toward the founding of a democratic nation and the process of abolishing slavery. My purpose here is to show that even in the discipline of mathematics, abstract and theoretical as it may be, there were occurring at the same time developments that can also be viewed as liberating. They too can be included in the category of events resulting from the last judgment. In support of this view, I will look at the state of mathematics in the middle of the eighteenth century and trace the development of certain ideas that led to the gradual liberation of mathematics.

MATHEMATICS IN 1757

Even before the year of the last judgment, the eighteenth century proved to be a period of great mathematical progress. Mathematicians were making unprecedented progress in their application of the methods of calculus, which had been developed by Newton and Leibniz several decades previously, to all manner of physical problems. The applications ranged from basic engineering to astronomy. This kind of mathematics, exploiting the brilliant techniques of the relatively new calculus, was known as analysis; it was by far the most active and notable aspect of the mathematics of that day. It was characterized by its close connection to the physical world and its rather deplorable (by today's standards) lack of rigor. The rigor was at last developed in the post-judgment decades, which was also when the bonds that had tied mathematics to the physical world were finally severed.

The preeminent mathematician in 1757, and for many years before and after, was Leonhard Euler (1707–1783). Euler was a native of Switzerland who spent nearly all of his adult professional life at the scientific academies in two foreign cities: St. Petersburg and Berlin.

FORREST DRISTY

In 1757 he was fifty years old and at the peak of his power. In the current year of 2007, as Swedenborgians are commemorating the 250th anniversary of the last judgment, mathematicians all over the world are celebrating the 300th anniversary of Euler's birth. This year the Mathematical Association of America, for example, is publishing not one but *five* books about Euler and his mathematical contributions. He is known as the most prolific of mathematicians; his mathematical writings were so widespread and so voluminous that the task of collecting, editing, and publishing them is still going on today, some 224 years after his death. The number of volumes of his collected works is currently seventy-seven and is still growing.

Euler does not, however, play a major role in the account I will give here of what I have called the liberation of mathematics; I have mentioned him primarily to show that in 1757 mathematics was a burgeoning enterprise and to point out the interesting coincidence that this foremost mathematician had his fiftieth birthday in the year of the last judgment.

The story that I intend to tell involves the efforts of several other mathematicians who were men of great genius even though their reputations did not match that of Euler. Their efforts were made not in the ascendant realm of analysis but rather in the relatively quiet areas of geometry and algebra. In 1757 each of these two branches of mathematics were struggling with its own long-standing problem which seemed to defy solution. In each case the following years would bring the unexpected result that the problem was in fact insoluble, thus bringing to a close an era in each subject's history. And in each case the negative result, while disappointing at the time, led to the opening of a new era of far greater opportunity and potential for advancement than could have been dreamed of previously. In this way both geometry and algebra were liberated from previous narrow restrictions. In due course the liberation was extended to all of mathematics. The fact that the origins of this liberation occurred in the late eighteenth century suggests that it was a result of the increasing intellectual freedom stemming from the great spiritual reorganization of 1757.

GEOMETRY

First I will consider the case of geometry. During the eighteenth century, geometry was nearly synonymous with the work of Euclid, whose famous book *Elements* (written around 300 BC) had been the definitive text on the subject for millennia. Euclid's work had been lost to European culture for the centuries during the dark ages but had been rediscovered and restored to its preeminent position during the Renaissance. In *Elements*, geometry was presented as a unified body of knowledge derived, by strict logical reasoning, from a set of supposedly self-evident postulates. It was without doubt a masterpiece of human thought, and it was avidly studied not only by mathematicians but by all scholars who wished to become proficient at careful reasoning. We who live today in an era of constant change can hardly imagine the long-term status Euclid enjoyed. Even in the English-speaking world his presentation of geometry remained standard through the end of the nineteenth century, some 2,300 years after it was first composed.

The problem in geometry mentioned earlier concerned the postulates that Euclid had chosen as the basis for his derivation of geometrical knowledge. There were five of them:

1) A straight line may be drawn connecting any two given points.
2) A straight line may be extended continuously in a straight line in either direction.
3) A circle may be drawn with any given point as center and passing through any given second point.
4) All right angles are equal to one another.
5) If a straight line falling on two straight lines makes the interior angles on the same side together less than two right angles, the two straight lines, if extended indefinitely, meet on that side on which the angles are together less than two right angles.

Looking at these postulates, one notices immediately that the fifth one is of a decidedly different character than the other four. It is longer, more complicated, and lacks the self-evidence the others hold. Why did Euclid choose it? Would it not be more appropriate to have this kind of statement appear as a derived theorem rather than a postulate? As a theorem, it was excellent, as a postulate it was ugly. Aesthetics is an important consideration in mathematics.

So despite the great respect, even reverence, geometers held for Euclid, the fifth postulate was regarded as a scandalous defect in an otherwise nearly perfect work. This feeling was not a new one. Even in ancient times geometers were dissatisfied with the fifth postulate, and it is likely that Euclid himself was not entirely happy with it. He avoided using it in the proofs of his first twenty-eight theorems, but sheer necessity finally compelled its use in order to derive the full content of geometry as he wanted it. Through the centuries numerous attempts were made by various mathematicians to perfect Euclid's noble work by showing that the fifth postulate could in fact be proven from the other four, or failing that, it could be derived from the other four together with another simple and self-evident postulate. By the early eighteenth century interest in such attempts were running high. We will look at one of the most notable attempts.

Girolamo Saccheri (1667–1733) was a Jesuit professor of theology, philosophy, and logic. In his book, *Logica Demonstrativa*, he wrote about the method of logic known as *reductio ad absurdum*, a method related to proof by contradiction in mathematics. Saccheri became fascinated with Euclid's work and studied it thoroughly. He was well versed in the attempts of others to remove the "blemish" from *Elements*, and he had found the errors that defeated some of them. Thinking that he could succeed where others had failed, he published a book in 1733 in which he applied *reductio ad absurdum* to the long-standing problem of the fifth postulate. The title of his book translates from Latin into English as *Euclid Freed of Every Flaw*.

Saccheri's goal was to show that the fifth postulate was a theorem that could be proved from the other four postulates. His strategy in using *reductio ad absurdum* was to make the assumption that the fifth postulate was *false*. If he could show, using the other postulates, that this assumption led to a contradiction or "absurdity," it would then follow that the *assumption* was false and that the postulate must therefore be true. The way he chose to execute this strategy was by means of a rectangular figure as shown below, a figure known in his honor as a Saccheri quadrilateral. It will be referred to as an SQ in what follows. This geometrical construction consists of a base line AB on which two perpendicular segments of equal length AC and BD have been constructed. Using the first four postulates Saccheri could show that the angles at C and D were equal to each other and so there were three possible cases:

Case 1) The angles C and D are both right angles.
Case 2) They are both obtuse, that is greater than right angles.
Case 3) They are both acute, that is less than right angles.

He could also prove that whichever of these cases held for *one* SQ would hold for *all* SQs and that Case 1 was logically equivalent to the fifth postulate—the statement that he hoped to prove by his method of contradiction.

His strategy of denying the fifth postulate amounted to the assumption that either Case 2 or Case 3 is always valid. He then needed only to show that each of these cases led logically to a contradiction. With Case 2 he was indeed led to a contradiction, but only because he used the tacit assumption, not strictly justified by the first four postulates, that straight lines are infinite in length. He does not deserve much criticism for this infraction because many other mathematicians, including Euclid himself, made the same mistake.

In dealing with Case 3, Saccheri was faced with a more formidable task. He filled many pages with careful reasoning establishing strange proposition after strange proposition, apparently confident that he was closing in on an actual contradiction. He never did come to an actual contradiction, but he finally brought his labors (and his book) to an end by making a feeble and unjustified claim that his final propositions involving hazy notions about infinity contradicted the nature of lines. Thus ended the book in which he claimed to have proved, by *reduction ad absurdum*, that the fifth postulate is a consequence of the other four and could be properly placed among the theorems where it belonged.

As noted before, Saccheri was just one of a great many mathematicians who attempted to prove the fifth postulate. An indication of how widespread this effort was is provided by the fact that in 1763 a German graduate student by the name of G. S. Kluegel wrote a dissertation in which he carefully examined thirty such claimed proofs only to conclude that each and every one was defective.

Saccheri's work appears to have failed to convince the mathematicians of his day, for it was soon forgotten. It was not until more than a century and half later, long after it had been rendered obsolete by the work of others, that it was rediscovered and again brought to the attention of the mathematical community. By this time it had long been shown that the fifth postulate is in fact *independent* of the other four: neither it nor its negation contradict those first four postulates. Moreover, by this time a whole new field of non-Euclidean geometry had been developed using, in place of the fifth postulate, its negation. The great irony in this story is that the strange propositions that Saccheri had proved in his 1733 book were valid theorems in the new kind of geometry. If he had proclaimed them as such, instead of claiming that some of them contradicted the nature of lines, he would today be regarded as the first non-Euclidean geometer. He had been doing non-Euclidean geometry, but because of some mental block that he shared with all mathematicians of his day, he was unable to realize what it was that he had done. Could his lack of recognition of the nature of his own work have been caused by obstructions in the spiritual realm, obstructions that were soon to be removed in the coming reorganization of 1757? Discoveries made in the next several decades suggest that this could well be the case.

In 1829 there appeared a paper that is today regarded as the first publication in the field of non-Euclidean geometry. It was written by Nicolai Lobachevsky, a professor at the remote University of Kazan in Russia. Because it was written in Russian and published in a very obscure journal it attracted almost no attention among mathematicians or anyone else. But Lobachevsky was not the only person thinking along non-Euclidean lines. As often seems to be the case, when the world is ready for an idea it tends to appear in the minds of more than one individual. In this case, one of the other individuals was János Bolyai, a Hungarian army officer and a mathematician. His thoughts pertaining to the possibility of a real, authentic non-Euclidean geometry began as early as 1823, but it was not until 1829 (the year of Lobachevsky's publication) that he got his results ready to be considered for publication. He submitted the manuscript to his own father, Farkas Bolyai, who was also a mathematician. As Farkas was in the process of preparing a book of his own for publication, János Bolyai's work on non-Euclidean geometry appeared in 1832 as a twenty-six page appendix to his father's book on another subject. It was not a publication destined to attract immediate attention, but from these humble beginnings in the obscure publications of Bolyai and Lobachevsky the subject of non-Euclidean geometry finally saw the light of day. At the time it caused no stir. The authors were not well known, and the subject seemed too fantastic to be of real interest to serious mathematicians. But in the decades to come this new kind of geometry grew into a major intellectual revolution contributing to what I have called the liberation of mathematics. The consequences of this revolution, which are far too numerous to discuss in this paper, are being increasingly felt as we proceed into the twenty-first century. A single example of these consequences is Einstein's theories of special and general relativity, which depend for their expression on mathematics resulting from non-Euclidean concepts.

It may seem that the sixty-six years from the Last Judgment in 1757 until 1823, when Bolyai is first known to have been thinking in a non-Euclidean way, is an unduly long time for these liberating ideas to have been delayed. In fact, this delay was actually shorter, as it is known that non-Euclidean ideas were actively engaged in the mind of Carl Friedrich Gauss as early as 1792, reducing the time interval to just thirty-five years. Gauss (1777–1855) was for most of his life a professor at the University of Goettingen in Germany. He was a rare example of a child prodigy who not only retained his mental ability but extended it throughout a relatively long life. His mathematical achievements were such as to make him a towering giant in the whole history of world mathematics. He surpassed even Euler in this regard. Even while still a teenager, Gauss is known to have been thinking along the lines of creating a geometry in which the fifth postulate would not be true.

But as Gauss hated criticism and controversy, he was hesitant to publish anything that could result in either. In his day the opinions of philosophers were extremely important in the universities of Europe; the influential philosophers considered it definite that Euclidean geometry was an innate part of the human mind. It was preposterous for anyone, even a respected mathematician, to suggest that there could be a valid geometry in which the long-established theorems of Euclid failed to be true. So Gauss, not wanting to be subject to scathing criticism or involved in bitter and prolonged controversy, declined to publish anything about his revolutionary thoughts on geometry. His aversion to those ordeals resulted in an unfortunate delay in the birth of non-Euclidean geometry. Not only would his publication initiating the new geometry have been decades earlier than those of Lobachevsky and Bolyai, but it would almost certainly have been better organized and it definitely would have caught the attention and respect of a far wider circle of mathematicians. But, as we have seen, non-Euclidean geometry was nevertheless finally launched and changed the history of mathematics, science, and the world.

ALGEBRA

In the field of algebra in the eighteenth century there also existed a very difficult problem that had stubbornly resisted all attempts to solve it. This problem pertained to finding the solutions of polynomial equations, that is, equations of the form:

$$Ax^4 + Bx^3 + Cx^2 + Dx + E = 0$$

The *degree* of a polynomial is the highest exponent appearing (in this case 4). Therefore this polynomial equation is said to be of fourth degree or a *quartic* equation. The simplest case is that of a first degree, or *linear*, equation: Ax + B = 0. Its solution is easily seen to be x = -B/A. Even second-degree, or *quadratic*, equations, which look like

$$Ax^2 + Bx + C = 0$$

are relatively easy to solve, and beginning algebra students learn that the two solutions (the number of solutions being equal to the degree of the equation) are given by

$$x = \frac{-B + \sqrt{B^2 - 4AC}}{2A} \quad \text{and} \quad x = \frac{-B - \sqrt{B^2 - 4AC}}{2A}$$

Even in ancient times quadratic equations could be solved, but as the convenient algebraic notation that we take for granted today was not available then, solving a quadratic in those days would not have been a task for a beginning math student.

When we come to the consideration of third degree, or *cubic* equations, the subject becomes decidedly more challenging. Note that in any polynomial equation you can always make the leading coefficient (that is, the coefficient of the highest power of x) equal to 1. If it is not already 1 to start with, you can merely divide both sides of the equation by whatever it happens to be, and the result will be an equivalent equation whose leading coefficient *is* 1. Thus you can think of the general cubic equation as being of the form

$$x^3 + Px^2 + Qx + R = 0$$

It was a major struggle for the mathematicians of the Renaissance to come up with an algebraic formula, something like the two expressions above for the case of quadratics, that would provide the solutions for the cubic equation. Part of the difficulty was due to the appearance of supposedly non-real entities such as square roots of negative numbers. It was discovered, however, that the equation could always be modified by means of a simple substitution to obtain an equivalent equation in which there was no second degree term. Attempts to find the solutions could then be concentrated on the so-called "depressed cubic equation" of the form

$$x^3 + px + q = 0$$

The competition among sixteenth-century mathematicians to find an algebraic expression for the solutions of this simple-looking equation is a fascinating episode in the history of mathematics, however, the details of this story will be omitted here because they are not relevant to this paper. I will be content to report that such an expression was finally found. There are of course three solutions since this is a third degree equation. Here is the simplest example of what this long-sought answer looks like:

$$x = \sqrt[3]{\frac{-q + \sqrt{q^2 + (4p^3/27)}}{2}} + \sqrt[3]{\frac{-q - \sqrt{q^2 + (4p^3/27)}}{2}}$$

Considering the great difficulties that were encountered in finding the algebraic solutions of the general cubic equation, we might expect that the general quartic equation, the one shown at the beginning of this section, would involve even more strenuous and prolonged efforts to solve. Surprisingly, this is not the case. As quartic equations can be reduced to cubic ones, the results already obtained for the latter could be applied to the former. Nevertheless, the final expressions for the four solutions of the general fourth degree equations are considerably longer and more complicated to write than the ones for the third degree case.

In 1545, solutions for both cubic and quartic equations were published in a book called *Ars Magna* by a colorful Italian mathematician named Girolamo Cardano (1501–1576).

Thus, by the middle of the sixteenth century, with the general cubic and quartic equations satisfactorily disposed of, mathematicians could turn their attention to the next equation: the general equation of fifth degree, also known as the quintic equation.

$$Ax^5 + Bx^4 + Cx^3 + Dx^2 + Ex + F = 0$$

This equation does not appear to be more difficult than the quartic. Surely in a few years, perhaps a decade, algebraic expressions for its solutions could be found. (By *algebraic* in this context we mean expressions involving only the four arithmetic operations of addition, subtraction, multiplication, and division as well as the extraction of roots of all orders.) Mathematicians made an enthusiastic assault on the problem. In fact, they made many such assaults using every kind of algebraic ingenuity they could imagine. Over two centuries later, however, right up to 1757 and beyond, their heroic efforts had gotten them nowhere near the desired goal. Even the exalted Euler himself made more than one serious attempt at solving the frustrating problem, but his efforts were unsuccessful. As late as 1762 he published a paper "On the Solution of Equations of Arbitrary Degree," in which he suggested a kind of canonical form that all solutions of such equations might fit. Although he did not determine any actual solutions, the fact that his canonical form was clearly an algebraic expression makes it obvious that he was of the opinion that general polynomial equations of every degree have solutions of the kind that mathematicians had been seeking for over 215 years. As it eventually turned out, he was wrong in that opinion.

It was almost the end of the eighteenth century, some four decades after the year of the Last Judgment, that a light began to dawn in the minds of a few mathematicians, who were finally beginning to suspect that the big problem posed by the general quintic equation did not have a solution. In other words, that there was no algebraic expression which provided solutions for that equation. Among these few was a little-known Italian algebraist by the name of Paolo Ruffini (1765–1822) and a soon-to-be renowned mathematician named Carl Friedrich Gauss. While Gauss was doing his graduate studies in the year 1799, he expressed in his dissertation the negative opinion that turned out to be correct. He offered nothing, however, by way of proof.

Ruffini apparently had arrived at that opinion earlier then Gauss. He not only expressed the opinion, he claimed to have a proof of it, which he published in 1799, the same year in which Gauss gave the opinion with no supporting evidence. Of course, Gauss was not one to give "supporting evidence." He was not likely to publish any evidence short of a watertight proof. Unfortunately for Ruffini, his proof was not convincing to his fellow mathematicians, and was not taken seriously. In later years he published revised and presumably strengthened versions of his proof, but they met the same fate as his first.

It was not until 1826 that the problem of the quintic equation was finally settled once and for all when a young Norwegian mathematician by the name of Niels Henrik Abel (1802–1829) published a complete and convincing proof that there exists no algebraic expression for the solution of the general quintic equation. It was published in the first issue of a new mathematical periodical called the *Journal of Pure and Applied Mathematics*, which is still being published today, over 180 years later. Abel's proof was an excellent example of the method of *reductio ad absurdum* that Saccheri had applied in geometry nearly a century earlier. An interesting sidelight is the tragedy that accompanied Abel's life, the extreme poverty and hardship that he endured while pursuing his mathematical studies (which extended far beyond polynomial equations), and his death from tuberculosis before reaching his twenty-seventh birthday.

Nearly seventy years had passed since the year of the Last Judgment, 1757. Is it reasonable to think that it would have taken that much time for spiritual enlightenment filter down to the understanding of such a natural-world subject as polynomial equations? I think the answer to this question is affirmative when we consider the slow but necessary advances that were occurring along the way. Even before

Ruffini's work in 1799 there were ideas whose appearance contributed to the final result, although their authors were unaware of the negative conclusion they were leading to. As early as 1771 Joseph-Louis Lagrange (1736–1813) published a paper "Reflections on the Algebraic Solution of Equations" in which he applied the concept of permutations of all the solutions of an equation—a key concept in Abel's proof. Ruffini's work, which had been done at least a quarter century before Abel's, came over time to be regarded as considerably more valid and worthy of recognition than had previously been the case. In recent years some historians of mathematics, in a belated attempt to accord Ruffini some well-deserved credit, are referring to Abel's result as the Abel-Ruffini Theorem.

As we can see now, the negative result for the problem of the quintic equation was the end of an era in the history of mathematics— but it did not cause much excitement. Recall that the same was true regarding the negative outcome pertaining to the fifth postulate. Part of the reason for this was that at the time the active and exciting part of mathematics, where new advances were being made with increasing rapidity, was analysis, where the amazingly fruitful concepts of calculus were still being exploited for comparatively easy results. For most mathematicians there was no need to struggle with centuries-old abstract problems which carried no likelihood of practical application. But algebra was about to undergo a metamorphosis that would greatly expand its significance in the world of mathematics.

In order to comprehend the manner in which algebra was destined to change its role, we must proceed a little further into the nineteenth century. Although Abel's paper (and perhaps even Ruffini's earlier ones) took care of the *general* quintic equation by showing that it had no algebraic solution, there were still *specific* quintic equations (as well as specific equations of even higher degree) that did have algebraic solutions. So there was still a challenging problem facing algebraists: how can you distinguish those polynomial equations that do have algebraic solutions from the ones that do not? Finding the answer to this question led to the discovery (or invention, depending on your philosophical attitude) of those algebraic structures that are today called permutation groups. This discovery was made by a most unusual and colorful young mathematician, Evariste Galois.

Galois was born in 1811 and was killed in a duel with pistols before reaching his twenty-first birthday in 1832. Although we are interested primarily in his contribution to mathematics, his life was so extraordinary in its brevity and tragic ending that time and space must be taken for a brief biographical comment. This unusual young French genius lived during tumultuous times in the political history of his country. His strongly held and loudly proclaimed republican views kept him in a constant state of stress and included periods of incarceration. Moreover, he was also continually frustrated because his amazing mathematical talent, which in hindsight is quite apparent, was not often recognized during his lifetime. This may have been due in part to his uncompromising and somewhat belligerent personality, which was unrestrained by polite tactfulness. The precise circumstances leading to the duel are not known, but a common account has it that his offence occurred at a boisterous public political gathering. It is said that he proposed a toast interpreted by some as a threat on the life of the sitting monarch. He was consequently challenged to the duel by a monarchist. In keeping with nineteenth century standards of honor he could not decline and so he accepted the challenge, quite certain that he would not survive. It is not known who his opponent was.

To turn to Galois' mathematics, recall that the Abel-Ruffini result left many loose ends. Although it established the fact that the *general* quintic equation had no algebraic solution, it did not address the conditions under which certain *specific* equations of degree five and higher *would* have such solutions. This is where Galois's work enters; his results make it possible to determine whether or not an algebraic solution exists for any polynomical equation. But this outcome is not what makes his contribution important in the history of mathematics. The importance lies in the algebraic superstructure which he built in order to obtain the result. Taking the idea of permuting the set of all solutions, which had been used by Ruffini, Lagrange, Abel, and others, and regarding the collection of all possible permutations of solutions as a set whose elements could be combined (something like numbers can be multiplied together), he pushed these concepts to a new level and established the rudiments of what is today known as group theory. Galois showed that any specific polynomial equation, of whatever degree, would determine its own permutation group (as it is called today) whose properties would depend on the coefficients in the polynomial. These properties would also answer the question of whether or not the equation had an algebraic solution.

Galois' work was destined to change the nature of mathematics, but this was not apparent to the mathematicians of 1832. This work remained unknown to all but a handful of people for many years after his death. It was a decade before another Frenchman, and mathematician of some reputation, Joseph Liouville (1809–1882), finally recognized the importance of what Galois had done and announced his result to the French Academy in 1843. In 1846 Liouville published all of Galois' work in a new journal he had started himself. From this point on, with ever increasing rapidity, algebra became a whole new game: it became an enterprise in which new abstract structures could be invented as needed—or desired.

As an indication of what is meant by an abstract structure, we will consider the concept of a group as it is regarded today. A group G is a collection of "elements" which can be "combined" with each other in some way. We will use a, b, c, etc. to denote the elements and + to denote the action of combining. These four axioms are required to be satisfied:

- Closure. The result of combining two elements in the collection is always another element of the collection. That is, a+b is always in G.
- Associativity. For all elements a, b, c: a+(b+c) = (a+b)+c.
- There is an identity element i such that i+a = a for all a.
- Every element has an inverse. For each a there is some b such that a+b = i.

From these remarkably simple axioms springs the branch of modern mathematics known as group theory. In this way an algebraic structure has properties that are determined by a set of axioms in a manner that reminds us of the geometry done by Euclid in ancient times.

The group concept was just the first of many algebraic structures which were to be devised during the nineteenth and, even more so, twentieth centuries. Algebra became a field for the invention of new entities, just as geometry, after the first sight of its non-Euclidean version, became a field in which all manner of new and exotic geometries could flourish. The major new algebraic structures that came into being in the nineteenth century include fields, rings and vector spaces, and many others.

GEOMETRY AND ALGEBRA TOGETHER

A review of the similarities that existed in the development of geometry and algebra in the decades following 1757 is as follows:

- In each case there had been a long-standing problem that seemed frustratingly difficult. For geometry the problem was proving the fifth postulate, which was complicated and lacking in self-evidence, from the other four, which had the simplicity and obvious validity expected of postulates. For algebra it was the problem of finding an algebraic solution for the general quintic equation, a seemingly reasonable next step following the solution of the general cubic and quartic equations some two hundred years before.
- There was a very gradual dawning, *after* 1757, that these problems might be impossible to solve. In the case of geometry, the earliest known inkling of this impossibility occurred to teenage Gauss during the 1790s. In the case of algebra, the first inkling must also have occurred in the 1790s, but in this case to two people: Ruffini, who actually published in 1799 what he thought was a proof of the non-existence of the quintic solution, and Gauss (again) who in his dissertation of the same year expressed his opinion that there was no solution while offering no proof.

- General acceptance among mathematicians that these two famous problems had no solutions came about very slowly. For geometry it was not until the end of the 1830s that the non-Euclidean work of Lobachevsky and Bolyai gained credence, and even then there was no appreciation of the momentous consequences their ideas would have. For algebra it was Abel's 1826 paper that finally convinced most mathematicians that the search for the solution to the quintic was futile (However, for another decade papers were still being presented claiming to have found the long-sought solution. See Derbyshire, 130).

- For both geometry and algebra it was obvious that an era had ended. There was no need to persist in the attempt to do the impossible. But for each a new and far more glorious era was beginning, arising in both cases with the help of ideas that had been developed in the assault on those impossible problems. In one case this meant the creation of new geometries in which the valid theorems were the same as the seemingly preposterous conclusions which the former geometers such as Saccheri had deduced in their attempts at *reductio ad absurdum*. In the other case it meant using the concept of permutations of the solutions of a polynomial to create a new algebraic structure, later called a group, the first of many to come.

The new era that began for geometry and algebra during the early decades of the nineteenth century can be regarded as a liberation for these subjects; they were no longer bound to the physical world and to the so-called real numbers that had been used to quantify it. Henceforth mathematics would be open to all manner of newly devised structures that could be studied for their innate beauty as well as for their ability to model physical reality. This freedom brought with it a stronger commitment to logical rigor in the proof of accepted theorems. Mathematical proofs could no longer make use of subtle tacit assumptions derived from the senses like the older proofs (including Euclid's) did.

MATHEMATICS IN THE NEW ERA

In both cases, the revolutionary nature of the transformations which had occurred in geometry and algebra was not immediately recognized. It was not until 1846 that Galois's achievement was given due respect by mainstream mathematicians, and even then its recognition was due primarily to the efforts of one man: Liouville. In the case of geometry, it was Bernhard Riemann (1826–66) who first saw clearly the amazing possibilities implicit in geometry freed from its Euclidean mold. By applying the methods of calculus to the study of geometry itself, he extended the work of Gauss in the field of differential geometry, making possible all sorts of new geometries with any number of dimensions and with curvature that could vary with location. His famous lecture, given at Goettingen, Germany, in 1854, "On the Hypotheses Which Lie at the Foundations of Geometry," set the stage for the theory of relativity and the field of modern cosmology.

It would be fair to say that by the year of this lecture, 1854, the liberation of geometry and algebra had spread throughout mathematics as a whole. Yes, nearly a century had passed since 1757, but Swedenborg *had* foretold that the effects of the last judgment would appear in the natural world slowly. From this time forward mathematics gathered increasing momentum.

The English mathematician Arthur Cayley (1821–95) took up the study of abstract groups, creating a well-organized framework for explaining and extending Galois's brilliant insights. The resulting field of group theory is still growing in content and application. The so-called imaginary numbers (square roots of negative numbers), which had been lurking around the fringes of algebra for many decades and were regarded with deep suspicion by respectable mathematicians, were finally welcomed into mainstream mathematics and even accorded a position of honor.

Sir William Rowan Hamilton (1805–1865) was so impressed with the two-dimensional complex number system (formed from real and imaginary numbers together) that he struggled mightily to construct a three-dimensional number system. When that goal proved to be impossible, he founded instead a four-dimensional system of "numbers" that he called quaternions. These entities, strange as they were, never endured the ostracism that was suffered in earlier times by their comparatively ordinary cousins, the imaginary numbers.

Late in the eighteenth century the study of analysis situs, the ultimate level of abstraction in deaing with the concept of space, came into being. It is now called topology. The eminent French mathematician Henri Poincare (1854–1912) applied algebraic structures to the study of topological spaces, and created algebraic topology. Geometry and algebra became more and more freely combined, a process that continued throughout the twentieth century to the benefit of all mathematics. Such subjects as algebraic geometry, algebraic number theory, topological groups, combinatorial geometry, and many others developed into important parts of the mathematical enterprise.

Sir Michael Atiyah, a notable contemporary English mathematician, remarks in his 2001 survey of twentieth century mathematics on the ancient mathematical dichotomy between geometry and algebra. He calls them "the two formal pillars of mathematics" (Atiyah, 657). Their primary importance in the structure of mathematics is more clearly evident today than it was in the middle of the eighteenth century. In hindsight it all seems quite natural that their hard-won emancipation from the tight bonds of tradition should in due course lead to the liberation currently enjoyed by all mathematics. The timing of those first halting steps toward freedom, coming as they did in the final decades of the eighteenth century, suggests that they were consequences of the spiritual reorganization that Swedenborg identifies with the Last Judgment. ✻

BIBLIOGRAPHY

Atiyah, Michael. "Mathematics in the 20th Century," *American Mathematical Monthly* 108 (2001): 654–666.

Derbyshire, John. *Unknown Quantity: A Real and Imaginary History of Algebra.* Washington: Joseph Henry Press, 2006.

Eves, Howard. *Great Moments in Mathematics (After 1650)*. Washington: The Mathematical Association of America, 1981.

Livio, Mario. *The Equation that Couldn't Be Solved*. New York: Simon and Schuster, 2005.

O'Shea, Donal. *The Poincare Conjecture: In Search of the Shape of the Universe*. New York: Walter and Company, 2007.

Stillwell, John. *Mathematics and Its History*, 2nd ed. New York: Springer-Verlag, 2002.

Stillwell, John. *Yearning for the Impossible: The Surprising Truths of Mathematics*. Wellesley: A. K. Peters, Ltd, 2006.

Swedenborg, Emanuel. *The Last Judgment and Babylon Destroyed*. 1758. London: The Swedenborg Society, 1951.

Ideas for
Swedenborgian Mathematical Illustrations

NEIL SIMONETTI[1]

ABSTRACT

Emanuel Swedenborg was an eighteenth century scientist and philosopher before he was called to his use as a theological revelator. His background in science allowed him to draw on this knowledge to illustrate divine truths. Swedenborg states in [11] that "the Divine is everywhere," so this author investigates what analogies Swedenborg may have used if he had a stronger background in mathematics.

ASYMPTOTES AND PARABOLAS

As one of the advanced scientists in his day, Swedenborg uses images from science throughout his theological works to illustrate divine truths. He compares the growth of trees and plants to human prolification [20], he uses the heat and light from our sun to illustrate the nature of Divine Love and Divine Wisdom [12], and he draws on his knowledge of the human form frequently to describe the interconnectedness of heavenly systems [16] often referred to as the *Grand Man* [9].

But what if Swedenborg had been a stronger mathematician than a scientist? What kinds of images might he have used to explain divine concepts?

---

1. Assisted by Robert Cooper.

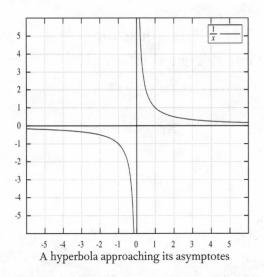

A hyperbola approaching its asymptotes

Swedenborg does use concepts in mathematics to illustrate the perfection of angels, but I get the impression that he was not very comfortable with these concepts. In [18], he states:

I said to the spirits around me that no one, save the Lord alone, is perfect. The angels are not perfect, for heaven is not holy before the Lord [Job 15.15]; nevertheless, the angels can become better and better even to eternity, but they can never become holy in themselves or as to their proprium. Because this seemed strange to the spirits when represented in a spiritual manner, it was therefore elucidated by like things in nature, namely, that there are approximations to infinity, as they are called, which nevertheless do not reach infinity, as for example, between the *asymptotes of the parabola*. But these things must be passed over because they are not understood by many. . . . (emphasis added)

Is it possible that the mathematical concepts were "passed over" because he didn't have a strong mathematical background himself? Perhaps Swedenborg thought his audience would be more familiar with less abstract analogies in science, so he may have intentionally avoided using abstract mathematical analogies. Swedenborg did make a mathematical error here: parabolas do not have asymptotes, but their close relatives, hyperbolas, do. Unlike this example from his diary, Swedenborg was very careful not to make such a mistake in a published work, as seen in [15], where he correctly attributes the asymptotic property to the hyperbola when illustrating the continual perfection of angels:

> Although the wisdom of a wise man in heaven increases to eternity, yet there is no such approximation of angelic wisdom to the Divine Wisdom that it can reach it. It may be illustrated by what is said of a *straight line drawn about a hyperbola*, continually approaching but never touching it and by what is said about squaring the circle. (emphasis added)

Swedenborg used parts of his *Spiritual Diary* as a rough draft for works intended for publication many times [7], so errors like attributing asymptotes to parabolas left in the *Spiritual Diary* should not alarm Swedenborgian scholars. Swedenborg had summarized the basic mathematical knowledge of his day in his notebook [17], so I can imagine Swedenborg consulting his notebook or one of his mathematician friends before sending his work on Divine Providence to the publisher.

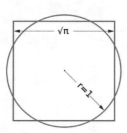

Squaring the Circle

The reader may have also noticed his reference to *squaring the circle*, a classical geometrical problem of using a straight edge and compass to produce a square with the same area as a given circle. In Swedenborg's time, there were algorithms that could get close, arbitrarily close with enough effort, but no exact solution was known. It was proven to be impossible in 1882 when Carl Louis Ferdinand von Lindemann discovered that π was not an algebraic number. [5]

CONTINUOUS AND DISCRETE

So what opportunities could Swedenborg have taken to bring in mathematical analogies? One opportunity that stands out is his discourse on continuous and discrete degrees, found in [14]:

> Continuous degrees are defined as lessenings or decreasings from grosser to finer, or from denser to rarer; or rather as growths and increasings from finer to grosser, or from rarer to denser, exactly like gradations of light to shade, or of heat to cold. Discrete degrees, however, are quite different. They are like things prior, posterior and final, and like end, cause and effect. These degrees are called discrete, because the prior is by itself, the posterior by itself and the final by itself, but yet taken together they make one. The atmospheres from highest to lowest, or from the sun to the earth and which are called ethers and airs, are separated into such degrees. They are like simple things, collections of those, and again collections of these which taken together are called a composite. These degrees are discrete because they exist distinctly and these are understood as degrees of height, whereas the former degrees are continuous because they increase continuously, and these are understood as degrees of breadth.

While using gradations of light to shade to illustrate continuous degrees and levels of the atmosphere to illustrate discrete degrees is effective, the number line gives a natural analogy as well. The field of integers, commonly called *whole numbers*, are discrete entities, while the field of real numbers, which includes fractions and decimal numbers, are continuous entities.

Both systems of numbers are well-ordered, meaning that given any two different numbers, one is "higher" or "larger" than the other. This comparative operator is transitive, meaning that if a is larger than b, and if b is larger than c, then a must be larger than c.

But the two number systems have one key difference which distinguishes the discrete nature of the integers from the continuous nature of the reals. Given an integer, such as 37, you can easily distinguish the next higher integer, 38, just as when you select an atmosphere, such as the stratosphere, there is the next higher atmosphere, the mesosphere. But if you are given a real number, such as 23.7, there is no "next" higher real number. Whatever larger number you choose, such as 23.7000001, there will always be

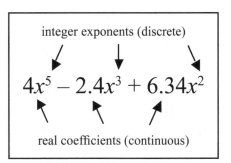

An example of a polynomial

a real number between the two, much like it appears that there can always be a shade of light between two different degrees of brightness.[2]

To see these concepts working together to make a whole, consider the family of polynomial functions. Each term of a polynomial is discrete, as it can be labeled by its integer exponent, yet each term has a continuous variety by having any real number serve as the coefficient. Both the discrete element and the continuous element are needed to define the family of all polynomials. Furthermore, if you expand the family of polynomials to include infinitely many terms (but still

---

2. It has been noted [2] that while Swedenborg outlined his theological revelations, his knowledge of sciences was not more advanced than the other scholars of his day. The field of physics has changed quite a bit since Swedenborg's time, and the discovery of photons, a discrete particle responsible for electromagnetic radiation including visible light, would allow us to categorize different shades of light and darkness as discrete degrees, not continuous degrees, even though the "distance" between these degrees is smaller than the human eye can distinguish.

$$e^x = 1 + x + \frac{x^2}{2!} + \frac{x^3}{3!} + \frac{x^4}{4!} + \cdots$$

$$\sin x = x - \frac{x^3}{3!} + \frac{x^5}{5!} - \frac{x^7}{7!} + \cdots$$

Two functions written as
infinite polynomials

a countable infinity, since the terms are discrete), then Taylor's Theorem shows that every smooth (infinitely differentiable) function, such as the sine and exponential functions, can be defined as a polynomial, with its continuous and discrete portions.[3] [4]

THE GREATEST AND LEAST

Another concept with an accessible mathematical analogy is found in [13]:

> That the Divine is the same in things greatest and least, may be shown by means of heaven and by means of an angel there. The Divine in the whole heaven and the Divine in an angel is the same; therefore even the whole heaven may appear as one angel. So is it with the church, and with a man of the church. The greatest form receptive of the Divine is the whole heaven together with the whole church; the least is an angel of heaven and a man of the church. Sometimes an entire society of heaven has appeared to me as one angel.

The whole of heaven can be seen in the human form. A single society can be seen in the human form. A single person can be seen in the human form. All greatest and least things can also be seen as such.

Even the functions of a single cell can be organized by systems found in the human body: Lysosomes carry out digestion; the mitochondria act as the muscular system; the cytoskeleton forms the cell's skeletal system and acts as a circulatory system; and centrioles carry out the cell's reproductive activities. [1]

Mathematical objects known as fractals, named for their fractional dimensions, can display this concept extremely well, since

---

3. In some cases, the intervals on which these infinite polynomials converge to the function may be finite. As an extreme case, it is possible to construct functions where this interval of convergence is a single point.

the components of a fractal are built by
copying the larger structure. No matter
how far you "zoom in" on a portion of
the fractal, the same patterns continue to
emerge.

Consider the "Minkowski Sausage,"
named by Mandelbrot to honor this
Russian-born mathematician [6], constructed by replacing a single line segment
with eight segments each one quarter of
the original's length as shown here. To
calculate the dimension of this fractal,
determine the ratio of the number of
segments changing at each step (one
segment is replaced by eight), and the
ratio of the size of the segments changing
at each step (the old segments are four
times as long as the new segments), then
divide the logs of these ratios: $\log(8)/\log(4)$
= 1.5. Therefore the dimension of the
Minkowski sausage is 1.5.

To illustrate the idea that "the Divine
is the same in things greatest and least,"
one can see that looking at any part of this
fractal is identical to looking at the entire fractal. There is no loss of
detail as we zoom in or out.

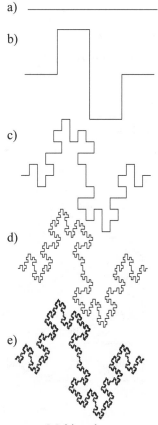

Making the
"Minkowski Sausage"

DIVINE INFINITY

Most people consider infinity to be a quantity without limit. The
quantity of positive integers is one example. If you started counting
today (1, 2, 3, . . .) and had an eternity of time to spend, there is no
number you would not eventually reach, but you would never be able
to count them all. Still, because there is no number that is out of reach,

this infinity is called a *countable* infinity by those who study set theory. A *countably infinite set* is a set that can be lined up, one-to-one, with the positive integers. [4]

Examples of countably infinite sets are shown in the following chart. The pattern shows how they may be lined up with the positive integers. Since all of these sets can line up, one-to-one, with each other, mathematicians consider all these sets to be the same size. You might find it odd that that selecting only the odd integers gives a set the same size as all the integers, when common sense would tell you the set should only be half as big. But what would half of infinity look like if it were different from infinity?

Set	Example
Positive Integers	1 2 3 4 5 6 7 8 9 10 . . .
Odd Positive Integers	1 3 5 7 9 11 13 15 17 19 . . .
All Integers	0 1 –1 2 –2 3 –3 4 –4 5 . . .
Prime Numbers	2 3 5 7 11 13 17 19 23 27 . . .
Rational Numbers in (0,1)	$\frac{1}{2}\,\frac{1}{3}\,\frac{2}{3}\,\frac{1}{4}\,\frac{3}{4}\,\frac{1}{5}\,\frac{2}{5}\,\frac{3}{5}\,\frac{4}{5}\,\frac{1}{6}$ . . .
Pairs of Positive Integers	(1,1) (1,2) (2,1) (1,3) (2,2) (3,1) (1,4) (2,3) (3,2) (4,1) . . .

Similarly, it is not intuitive that the rational numbers between zero and one would be a countably infinite set, since, unlike the integers, these numbers make up a continuous spectrum. Like the fractals, their pattern is indistinguishable as we "zoom in." Still, by ordering these numbers from smaller to larger denominators, they may be lined up with the set of positive integers.

Swedenborg talks of a *Divine Infinity* as something beyond this notion of infinity in [10]:

> People inevitably confuse Divine Infinity with infinity of space. And because they do not conceive of infinity of space as anything other than nothingness, as indeed it is, neither do they believe in Divine Infinity. The same applies to Eternity. They cannot conceive of it except as an eternity of time, but it is manifested continually by means of time to those who dwell within [space and] time.

Is there really an infinity larger than this? That is, is there an infinite set so large that if you attempt to line up the elements of the set, one-to-one, with the positive integers, you are guaranteed to fail, and something will be missed? Swedenborg tries to illustrate this notion in [19]:

> [The Word's] contents are countless, so that not even the angels can exhaust them. Anything found there can be compared to a seed, which planted in the ground can grow into a great tree, and produce an abundance of seeds; these again produce similar trees to form a garden, and their seeds in turn form other gardens, and so on to infinity. The Word of the Lord is like this in its details, and such above all are the Ten Commandments.

This outlines a geometric progression, where if each tree produces, say, ten seeds, each generation would have ten times the seeds as the previous generation. If you number every seed from each tree with a digit from zero to nine, then a seed's genealogy could be represented as a finite decimal number between zero and one. For example, ".142857" would represent one of the sixth generation seeds. These finite strings of digits can also be proven to be countable, since they form a subset of all rational numbers, which can be linked to a subset of all pairs of integers. But the Divine Truth in the Word has infinite depth, so the set of Divine Truths could be compared to decimal numbers which may be infinite in length, such as ".33333333..." or ".14159265...." These can be linked, one-to-one, with the set of real numbers between zero and one.

Is the set of real numbers really bigger than the set of rational numbers, which are countable? There are examples of real numbers that are not rational, like π and $\sqrt{2}$. But like comparing odd integers to integers, this does not make the set bigger.

In 1891, Georg Cantor published his diagonalization argument, an elegant proof that shows that the infinity of all real numbers between zero and one is bigger than the infinity of the positive integers. [3] The idea presented is rather simple.

Suppose that there existed a complete list of real numbers that could be matched, one-to-one with the positive integers. Form a number by taking the digit one higher than the first digit of the first number, then the digit one higher than the second digit of the second number, then the digit one higher than the third digit of the third number, and continue in like fashion. The result is a number between zero and one, call it n. In the example shown, we selected 6, one more than 5, then 8, one more than 7, then 1, and so on. If n were on the list, say in the 724th position, then n's 724th digit would not

$$
\begin{aligned}
&1 - .\underline{5}849204783\ldots \\
&2 - .4\underline{7}59938705\ldots \\
&3 - .50\underline{0}0000000\ldots \\
&4 - .141\underline{5}926535\ldots \\
&5 - .4142\underline{1}35623\ldots \\
&6 - .71828\underline{1}8284\ldots \\
&7 - .618033\underline{9}887\ldots \\
&\vdots
\end{aligned}
$$

$$n = .6816220\ldots$$

Cantor's Diagonalization

adhere to the rule for constructing n, requiring that n's 724th digit be the digit one higher than the 724th number's 724th digit. This problem would arise no matter where you attempt to find the number n on our complete list, and so n cannot be in this list, meaning the list is actually not complete. Since we are able to create this n given any attempt at making a complete list, there cannot be a complete list, and therefore the infinity of real numbers from zero to one is bigger than the infinity of positive integers.

OMNIPRESENCE

Related to our infinite friends, the concept of omnipresence can be a little hard to grasp. In [8], Swedenborg gives a quick definition: "Omnipresence is infinite circumspection and infinite presence." So how can something be everywhere without constantly getting in the way?

Mathematics has a notion of a *dense set:* Given a numeric interval J, a subset of this interval S is called *dense* if every subinterval of the original interval J contains at least one element from the set S. If we choose our interval J to be the set of real numbers from zero to one, one might think that the only dense sets possible would have to be the same size. A smaller set, it would seem, could not have the coverage to be "omnipresent," or dense, within the original interval *J*.

As mentioned earlier, the size of *J*, the set of real numbers from 0 to 1, is infinitely larger than the countably infinite set of integers, or the countably infinite set of rational numbers. Yet, the rational numbers are dense within *J*. To prove this, I must show that if I am given an arbitrary interval inside *J*, no matter how small, there must be a rational number contained within this arbitrary interval.

Proposition: The set of rational numbers in the interval from 0 to 1 is dense within the set of real numbers in the interval from 0 to 1.

Proof: Let *K* be an arbitrary interval within the set of real numbers from 0 to 1, and let k_1 and k_2 be the left and right endpoints of the interval *K*, respectively. This

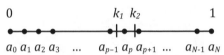

One element from the sequence, a_p, must be inside the interval.

makes k_2 bigger than k_1. Let *x* be the difference, $k_2 - k_1$, of the endpoint values. Think of *x* as the *width* of the interval *K*. *x* cannot be zero, otherwise *K* would not be an interval, it would just be a point, so we can assume that $x > 0$. This allows us to choose *N* to be the next integer larger than $1/x$. Since $N > 1/x$, we also know that $x > 1/N$, so $1/N$ is a quantity smaller than the width of *K*.

Now define a sequence of numbers a_i by defining $a_i = i/N$ for each integer *i* from 0 up to *N*. The numbers in this sequence form a set of equally spaced numbers, $1/N$ apart, that span the interval from 0 to 1. The first number a_0 is equal to zero, so it is either in the interval *K* (when $k_1 = 0$) or it is left of the interval *K* (when $k_1 > 0$). Similarly the last number a_N is equal to one, so it is either in *K* (when $k_2 = 1$) or it is right of the interval *K* (when $k_2 < 1$). If none of these points, a_i, were in the interval *K*, then, since the first one is left of the interval and the last one is right of the interval, the sequence would have to "jump over" the interval *K*. But since the points in the sequence are spaced more narrowly than the width of the interval *K*, this is impossible. So the first point of the sequence to pass k_1, call it a_p, must be in the interval K. Since $a_p = P/N$, a_p is a rational number in the interval K.

This proof can be found in most introductory analysis textbooks, like [4], but more importantly, it shows that the concept of "omnipresence" is not something that Swedenborg made up to describe something that would otherwise be indescribable. ✳

NOTES

[1] Campbell, N., J. Reece, L. Mitchell, M. Taylor. *Biology: Concepts and Connections*, 4th edition. (San Francisco: Benjamin Cummings, 2003).

[2] Coke, S. "More Canons of Interpretation." *Studia Swedenborgiana* 12 (2001): 2. 12.2.

[3] Dauben, J. *Georg Cantor: His Mathematics and Philosophy of the Infinite.* (Princeton: Princeton University Press, 1979).

[4] Gaughan, E. *Introduction to Analysis,* 4th edition. (Pacific Grove, CA: Brooks/Cole Publishing Company, 1993).

[5] James, G. *Mathematics Dictionary,* 4th edition. (New York: Van Nostrand Reinhold Co, 1976).

[6] Lauwerier, H. (trans. S. Gill-Hoffstadt). *Fractals.* (Princeton: Princeton University Press, 1991).

[7] Odhner, G. "The Crossed-Out Passages in the Spiritual Diary," *New Church Life* 97 (1977): 612–614.

[8] Swedenborg, E. (trans. Whitehead) *Apocalypse Explained,* 282.

[9] Swedenborg, E. (trans. Elliott) *Arcana Coelestia,* 550.

[10] Swedenborg, E. (trans. Elliott) *Arcana Coelestia,* 1382.

[11] Swedenborg, E. (trans. J. Ager) *Divine Love and Wisdom,* 8.

[12] Swedenborg, E. (trans. J. Ager) *Divine Love and Wisdom,* 12.

[13] Swedenborg, E. (trans. J. Ager) *Divine Love and Wisdom,* 79.

[14] Swedenborg, E. (trans. J. Ager) *Divine Love and Wisdom,* 184.

[15] Swedenborg, E. (trans. Dick and Pulsford) *Divine Providence,* 335.3.

[16] Swedenborg, E. (trans. Harley) *Heaven and Hell,* 59.

[17]Swedenborg, E., *A Philosopher's Notebook*, trans. Alfred Acton, (Philadelphia, PA: Swedenborg Scientific Association, 1931).

[18] Swedenborg, E. (trans. Buss) *Spiritual Diary*, 883.

[19] Swedenborg, E. (trans. Chadwick) *True Christian Religion*, 290.

[20] Swedenborg, E. (trans. Chadwick) *True Christian Religion*, 585.

All pictures can be found on Wikimedia Commons:
http://commons.wikimedia.org

Possible Mathematical and Scientific Consequences
of the Last Judgment

GREGORY L. BAKER

INTRODUCTION

The premise of the 2007 conference on the Last Judgment was that:

> The end of the Christian church and the second coming of the Lord in the spiritual world in 1757 profoundly changed the reality of the spiritual state of mankind . . . it was . . . profoundly important for all human life. Doctrinally we would expect an event of such vast spiritual magnitude to "break into" human history here in the natural world on a number of dimensions.

And therefore "presenters were asked to focus on the probable natural consequences of this spiritual event."[1]

Rather than immediately embarking upon a discussion of the papers in the session, it seems important to make some general comments on this premise as stated. Understanding the scope and validity of this premise will allow us to assess, with some precision, the degree to which the speakers can realistically meet the objective of delineating "natural consequences of this spiritual event." Do the boundaries of the original premise limit what can reasonably be expected of speakers in their attempts to meet the stated goal?

---

1. The quotations are taken from a memo to discussants by Michael Hogan, the conference organizer.

THE BOUNDARIES OF THE PREMISE
OF THE CONFERENCE

While the Last Judgment was an event of crucial importance to the spiritual welfare of humanity, it was an event that occurred in the spiritual world. The exposure of legions of hypocritical souls to the Divine judgment and their subsequent consignment to Hell, together with the consequent freeing of generations of good spirits from spiritual tyranny, was indeed an act of cosmic spiritual proportions. Yet perhaps the effect of the Last Judgment in this world is more nuanced than what is suggested by the stated premise of the conference. Did this spiritual event actually "break into" human history in the natural world? In the work *Last Judgment*, Swedenborg writes:

> The state of the world hereafter will be quite similar to what it was before, for the great change which has taken place in the spiritual world does not induce any change in the natural world as to external form; so that after this there will be as before civil affairs, peace makings, treaties, and wars as before. (LJ 73)

Could one then argue that improvement in the human condition after 1757 was the result of a general progressive evolution rather than due to a distinct bifurcating event in human history? For example, the first limitation of royal power was famously marked with the signing of the Magna Carta in AD 1215, and subsequent events over the next few centuries slowly increased the amount of freedom in England; a freedom that Swedenborg himself used in order to publish his non-conventional theological works. Was the growth of freedom in Europe a many centuries-long process or did freedom take a quantum leap forward after 1757? Another example, with a shorter temporal pedigree, is the growth of physical and mathematical science from the sixteenth century. In fact the seventeenth century is often called the "golden age" of classical physics. Newton's great discoveries of the classical laws of dynamics and optics, together with his and Leibnitz's discovery of the calculus all occurred prior to the Last Judgment in the eighteenth century. Were these examples indicative of a steady progression in the human condition or, alternatively, were they necessary precursors to a significant shift in that progression? In the latter case, for example, one could argue (but not prove) that the post Last Judgment mathematics of Pierre Simon de Laplace (1749–1827) was significantly more sophisticated in concept and technique than earlier work exemplified by Newton's 1687 *Principia*.

New Church theologians, as noteworthy as Hugo Lj. Odhner, have given voice to the notion that the Last Judgment precipitated *indirect* effects in the natural world.

> Yet the crisis in the spiritual world has obviously had many indirect results in the natural realm, and the aftermath of judgment may be seen in every field of human life.[2]

Odhner contends, for example, that technological advances in all areas have improved communication significantly and thereby have lead to the creation of a human community not completely unlike that found in the after-life. Thus, we humans can talk to each other easily, travel to see each other easily, and perhaps even resolve differences more easily, because of significant scientific and technological advances whose roots may be attributable to the Last Judgment. Such easy communication, Odhner says, mimics, albeit imperfectly, the sort of communication found in a heavenly spiritual community. By inference, he connects this progress to the Last Judgment.

In passing, we also need to recognize that as New Church people, we naturally seek validation of our faith in life and in the events of history. The reality of the Last Judgment is foundational to our faith and therefore we expect and look for tangible manifestations of it. The above quote from *Last Judgment* not withstanding, our human need to support our belief forces us to seek evidence for the spiritual reality described in revelation. Nevertheless, awareness of such need should not inhibit our enquiry into how human history does support this spiritual event. The foundations of our faith will only be made stronger through critical examination. But in this process there needs

---

2. Hugo Lj. Odhner, *New Church Life* (Bryn Athyn, PA: The General Church of the New Jerusalem, August 1957), 370.

to be an awareness of the psychological pressure on our collective New Church psyche.

The question is, should we expect to find evidence, direct or otherwise, for the Last Judgment, in human affairs? It seems to me that the answer is heavily conditioned by the absolute need to preserve human freedom in spiritual matters. One strong message to the New Church is that people can only be truly religious in a state of freedom. Commitment to a life of service to God and to the neighbor is only real if that commitment is freely and rationally given. No external or internal pressure, no miracles, no foreknowledge; nothing must interfere with human freedom to accept or reject the reality of the Lord's creation and His guidance in human affairs. This condition then suggests that by definition the speakers at the conference will be unsuccessful in unambiguously demonstrating natural consequences of the Last Judgment. On the other hand, it is quite possible for a speaker to give *plausible* arguments for a certain advance being at least partly conditioned by the reality of the Last Judgment. It therefore seems appropriate to look for some *reasonable* connection between the events or developments described by the speaker and the spirit of the Last Judgment. It may then be in the context of plausibility that we can fairly examine the degree to which speakers succeed.

We necessarily must enquire as to what the generally expected natural outcomes of the Last Judgment might be—outcomes in human affairs and development. We know that the Last Judgment led to a restoration of freedom in the spiritual world and to the furtherance of the salvation of already good spirits. Therefore one expects from the restoration of spiritual freedom a resulting general enhancement of freedom. "henceforth the man of the church will be in a freer state of thinking on matters of faith" (LJ 73). As a corollary, this freedom of thought should extend to all areas of human endeavor, including scientific and mathematical thought. We can consider this issue in the context of our three papers. The other aspect of the Last Judgment, the restoration of continuing spiritual progress to good spirits, suggests that in human affairs we might see improvements in peoples' natural and spiritual condition. We might expect that science would increasingly work for the betterment of the economic and material welfare of all peoples. We might expect that the criterion of "use," so prominent in the Writings, would become a strong benchmark in assessing human activity. These two possibilities greater freedom of thought and greater useful material prosperity could be plausible, positive, and indirect manifestations of the Last Judgment.

There may also be negative manifestations. Greater freedom can also bring greater license for the machinations of those with evil intent. As well as expanding material prosperity, advances in technology and science bring the potential for deadly consequences. Humanity now has the capability, quickly through nuclear weapons, or more slowly through destruction of the environment, to destroy itself. The world wars and the increasing pollution of the recent and current century are vivid examples. On another level, increased material prosperity can be a distraction from essential attention to spiritual matters. Worse, material prosperity can lead to an intellectual arrogance that makes human achievement supreme and deletes God as irrelevant to reality.

In one sense, it may seem that there is not much that we cannot attribute to the Last Judgment. But on the other hand, it seems not only extravagant but not intellectually productive to attribute all good and bad outcomes of the past two hundred and fifty years to the Last Judgment.

Where does that leave us in regard to the assessment of each of the pieces given for this conference? My own criterion for whether a speaker has met the connective burden is, in the end, rather subjective. If a speaker has made a plausibility argument that his or her particular example has some relevance to the Last Judgment, and if that argument resonates with me then, for me, that speaker has met the aim of the conference. In this way each member of the audience and each reader of this volume is free to form his or her own conclusion. Given that the Last Judgment enhanced freedom, perhaps this subjective approach is fitting, as well as being both necessary and sufficient.

The general topic of the papers in the following session was possible connections with or consequences of the Last Judgment as evidenced in mathematics and science.

IDEAS FOR SWEDENBORGIAN
MATHEMATICAL ILLUSTRATIONS

Simonetti's paper begins with an interesting question raised in the following context. Swedenborg used a great many scientific examples, especially biological examples, to explain and illustrate spiritual ideas. The question is, "why did Swedenborg not use more ideas from mathematics to illustrate spiritual ideas?" Simonetti posits two possible answers to this question. His first is the suggestion that Swedenborg was not a strong mathematician. His second is that Swedenborg thought his audience would be less comfortable with abstract analogies from mathematics as compared to the more concrete images of biology.

In support of the notion that Swedenborg was not a strong mathematician, Simonetti points to *Spiritual Diary* 883 where Swedenborg erroneously refers to a parabola as having asymptotes. In regard to the second suggestion, that readers were less familiar with mathematics than with concrete images from biology, we need only point to the fact that even our contemporary universal public system of education has not led to universal mathematical literacy. How much more prevalent would mathematical illiteracy have been in Swedenborg's day! The question of Swedenborg's mathematical competence is perhaps less easily answered. The scientific biographer of Swedenborg, David Duner, suggested in a communication to this writer that Swedenborg did know the calculus, surely a contemporary mark of mathematical competence. And according to an 1858 article in the *National Review* on Swedenborg, he was offered a professorship in mathematics at the University of Uppsala. On the other hand, in an address to the Swedenborg Scientific Association, May 14, 2005, Duner suggests that Swedenborg's *Geometry and Algebra*, published in 1718 was actually written in 1713–14 and was based on a text by the French mathematician, Charles Reyneau (1656–1728), and that Swedenborg might also have had supervisory help from another French mathematician Pierre Varignon (1654–1722). Duner bases his conclusion on the fact that Swedenborg owned a copy of Reyneau's work and that *Geometry and Algebra* was written at a much higher level than Swedenborg's other writings on mathematics.

Nevertheless, while Swedenborg seems to have been a competent mid-level mathematician for his day, his focus did not reflect that of a frontline mathematician. For one thing he did not spend significant time on mathematics. In his pre-theological works Swedenborg had shown himself to be much more interested in biology and especially the anatomy of the human body (see, for example, *The Brain* and *The Economy of the Animal Kingdom*). Aside from Swedenborg's own direction of scientific study, there is the question of the relative bulk of existing mathematics and existing biology during his era. Mathematics of the early eighteenth century was not as rich a subject as was contemporary knowledge of human anatomy and physiology. Mathematics therefore provided less of a concrete basis for the sort of correspondences that Swedenborg would need in his exposition of the Heavenly Doctrines. Furthermore, many of the illustrations and correspondences would seem to lend themselves to biology rather than mathematics. For example, it is difficult to imagine how Swedenborg might have explained the grand man concept without using the science of the human body.

However, as Simonetti demonstrates, there are concepts that are well suited to mathematical illustration or analogy. His examples are: discrete and continuous degrees, self-similarity of fractals or "greatest and least," infinity, and omnipresence. But observe this fact: with the possible exception of the illustration of both continuous and discrete quantities in the structure of a polynomial, all these mathematical illustrations would not have been available to Swedenborg when he introduced the corresponding theological concept. Ideas about fractals or infinite sets, countable or otherwise, are less than a century and a half old.

Simonetti addressed questions that were somewhat outside the scope of the conference, making no direct attempt to suggest that his mathematical examples were in some sort of cause and effect relationship to the Last Judgment, because a few of them actually pre-dated the Last Judgment. Thus Simonetti avoided the burden of the conference, neither supporting nor countering its premise. However, one must admire the effort to look at an alternative approach, a mathematical approach, to the illustration of theological or philosophic concepts found in the Writings. Simonetti's efforts also support the notion that theology can be illustrated in many ways and by the many intellectual disciplines which reflect human discovery of the created world. Furthermore, this approach also suggests the various ways that each reader of the Heavenly Doctrines can gain insight. A mathematician sees illustration of the Heavenly Doctrines in mathematics. Others will see different illustration.

Questions for further study do arise from this paper. For example, let us suppose Swedenborg had penned the Writings in the twenty-first century. What other scientific examples might he have used to enhance his explanations of spiritual phenomena? Would Swedenborg have relied as heavily on anatomy and physiology in a twenty-first century version? Would mathematics, for example, have played a stronger illustrative role?

These and other questions remind us of the importance of considerations such as those found in Simonetti's enjoyable and thought-provoking paper.

THE LAST JUDGMENT
AND THE LIBERATION OF MATHEMATICS

We now turn to the paper by Dr. Forrest Dristy, *The Last Judgment and the Liberation of Mathematics*. We might summarize the paper as follows. The period leading up to the Last Judgment was a prolific one for mathematics and included the discovery of the calculus. The period after the Last Judgment was even more fruitful for the opening up of traditional branches of mathematics, including algebra and geometry. The questioning of Euclid's fifth postulate in regard to parallel lines leads to a completely new and incredibly rich area of non-Euclidean geometry. Similarly, in algebra, the discussion of the existence of solutions to fifth degree polynomial equations was a turning point and new approach. This discussion set the stage for work that began in the early nineteenth century, which tremendously expanded the scope of algebra to include set theory, group theory, logic, and other fields. Furthermore, mathematical proof, which had been heavily tied to physical intuition prior to 1750, eventually freed itself from the constriction of the physical world and gradually became more rigorous and perhaps more abstract after the Last Judgment. While perhaps not *directly* attributable to the Last Judgment, it seems remarkable that these traditional mathematical disciplines of algebra and geometry should markedly expand in both scope and intellectual depth fairly soon after 1757. That such a discrete change in mathematics should happen during the era of spiritual transition seems more than just coincidental.

Dristy's paper is tightly reasoned and leaves little room for challenge. His discussion of the relevant developments in mathematics is accessible and sufficiently complete for his purposes. He also clearly lays the groundwork for his argument by quoting from the Writings those portions that delineate the Last Judgment as being a spiritual event whose effects restored communication between heaven and earth.

Dristy emphasizes the gradual nature of the changes in mathematics after the Last Judgment but argues that the basic liberating notions were "in the air" within only a few decades of 1757.

It would be interesting to have a more detailed description of the development of rigorous proof after the Last Judgment as compared to the use of intuition and physical reality that buttressed proofs in earlier mathematics. This is a possible area for future study as it might provide insights into progress made by the mind during this transitional era.

The Writings particularly emphasize the concept of *use*. One wonders if this new emphasis on use is reflected by any sort of transition in the history of mathematics. In an essay entitled "The influence of the Five Churches on the History of Mathematics,"[3] Nina Kline, supporting the notion that pure mathematics considerably expanded in scope and concept, since the time of the Writings, also points to the tremendous

---

3. Gregory L. Baker, ed. *New Reflections from Academia* (Bryn Athyn, PA: Academy of the New Church, 2002), 140–147.

use of mathematics in the natural sciences and computer science as evidence for the importance of "use" for modern mathematics.

Finally, we ask if Dristy's paper met the burden of the conference purpose. Did this paper demonstrate a plausible connection between the revealed effects of the Last Judgment and the history of mathematics? For this writer the answer is a strong positive one. The fact that it is mathematics for which this connection is especially apparent is appropriate because, in its purest form, mathematics is an activity of the mind, the mind is the seat of human spiritual activity, and it is this spiritual activity which was opened by upheaval of the Last Judgment.

Let us close this section on the two mathematical papers with the following statement by Herbert Turnbull (as quoted in Kline's piece).

> There is a largeness about mathematics that transcends race and time: mathematics may humbly help in the market place, but it also reaches to the stars. To one, mathematics is a game (but what a game!) and to another it is the handmaiden of theology. The greatest mathematics has the simplicity and inevitability of supreme poetry and music, standing on the borderland of all that is wonderful in science, and all that is beautiful in art. Mathematics transfigures the fortuitous concourse of atoms into the tracery of the finger of God.[4]

THE NEW JERUSALEM COME DOWN TO EARTH

We come to the final piece in the section, "The New Jerusalem Come Down to Earth" by the Rev. Dr. Reuben P. Bell.

Unlike the previous two papers, Bell's paper cuts a very wide swath through the history of human events and spirituality. He begins with the first prophecy of the Lord's first advent, made necessary by the fall of man as represented by the eating of the forbidden fruit. He goes on to discuss the effect of the Lord's glorification as a cleansing of the world of spirits from evil spirits and a separation of heaven and hell. This first "last judgment" significantly increased spiritual freedom in

---

4. Herbert W. Turnbull, "The Great Mathematicians," in James R. Newman, *The World of Mathematics* (New York: Simon and Schuster, 1956), 8.

both the natural and spiritual worlds. Bell continues by noting that this new freedom brought with it the seeds of the second "last judgment," the latter being necessitated by the abuse of freedom in the rise of naturalism and the decline of spiritual life in the Christian Church. In the meantime, the gradual rise of science provided the beginnings of a new age of freedom which would be ripe for a new rational revelation. Then in a change of emphasis Bell lists what he sees as phenomena that have not changed since 1757. These include continuing naturalism, continuing activity of conventional Christianity, rejection of a final cause by science, the gradual dissolution of traditional institutions, and spiritual malaise. Bell lists events and changes (signs) that suggest positive effects of the Last Judgment: the Romantic movement in the arts, significant increases in human freedom, autonomy of women, the death of slavery, the growth of global communication through the Internet, the decline in current New Church growth (an idea we will discuss more fully), and Bell's own feeling that science must move toward incorporation of final causes.

At this point, Bell provides a description of some of his personal interactions with other scientists, holding forth at some length on the evils of scientific materialism as the successor to naturalism, and hints at the inability of current New Church theology to meet this challenge. He suggests that some of the important concepts in modern science—including the uncertainty principle in quantum physics, complexity, and related issues—are signs of problems in science rather than, as most scientists would conclude, opportunities for new knowledge. Bell speaks of the "heating up" of science wars which pits atheism versus fundamentalism, and that the answer to the questions of the atheistic scientist is to provide a religion or a religious philosophy that can deal with the currently unanswerable questions of science. Finally, he sees Swedenborg's scientific writings, as opposed to the theological writings, as a philosophy of science that some present-day scientists will understand and respond to positively.

The tone of Bell's paper is decidedly that of an advocate for change. My sense is that he sees much that is wrong with the entire human condition and believes that current efforts to remedy that condition are ineffectual at best. His paper ranges broadly over a great many topics and is therefore difficult to analyze in detail here. However, a few comments can be made.

We first ask if this paper meets the burden of the conference purpose. Did the paper provide an acceptable argument showing that some area of human endeavor or development could have plausibly resulted from the Last Judgment? The section on "Signs" of the Last Judgment did state a variety of areas, "if we wish to see them . . . in which the New Jerusalem (is) at work." As noted above, the list begins with the Romantic Movement in art and includes the Internet. Although the arguments for each element of the list are not particularly exhaustive, the fact that several members of the list would seem to be self-evidently connected in a plausible fashion to the Last Judgment, means that the paper has met this burden.

One area of interest to members of the various organizations of the New Church and alluded to above, is something Bell suggests as a positive outcome: the decline in "numbers, in influence, and in doctrinal integrity" of New Church denominations in the world. His claim is that so-called Old Church forms were initially imposed on the organized New Churches and therefore the present organizations will and should wither. He suggests that the New Church (unorganized) will thrive as "the contagion of love and wisdom . . . as people learn to apply these locally, in their own ways, in all things of life." Earlier in the paper Bell suggests that the Internet models the form that the next stage of the New Church will take "leaderless, multinodal, and driven by individuals in unanimous action." Those who pour their efforts and treasure into growing the current organizations will undoubtedly disagree. My purpose here is not to debate his statement (although I think it is vulnerable on several counts). Rather, I simply point to the fact that Bell has made this controversial statement and suggest that readers may wish to further ponder this issue. Bell claims that one hundred years of "New Church culture" held the view that when Swedenborg answered the Divine call, he not only "abandoned science," but that he indeed had failed at science. It would have been helpful to see this opinion documented, because this writer does not have that same impression. While I am not exactly sure what is meant by "New Church culture," but my impression is that most thoughtful New Church people think that Swedenborg simply answered a higher calling. Whether he had successfully created an "intellectually defensible model for spiritual-natural interaction" is perhaps another question. Again, most thoughtful New Church people would feel that true success only came later with the help of Divine revelation.

This leads to my last, somewhat more involved, comment on the substance of the paper. I infer that Bell is proposing a stronger role for Swedenborg's philosophic/scientific works in the New Church scientists' dialogue with present day intellectuals and scientists. He believes that the "meticulous description and reasoned speculation" will appeal more than the "arcane language of New Church theology." He further suggests that New Church scientists "use it for the tool it is, that they can take to any university or areopagus of the modern world." This is a controversial issue in the New Church. As a medical scientist, Bell is undoubtedly very impressed with Swedenborg's insights about the brain and other human biological systems. And certainly that particular contribution has been duly acknowledged in modern times. On the other hand, Swedenborg's speculations about the system of elementary physical particles as described in the *Principia* and elsewhere do not have the same standing with modern physicists.

Even granting that Swedenborg's scientific works contain a significant number of insightful speculations, as time goes on. They will be regarded more as some part of the history of science rather than as works that will advance modern science. This development is simply a result of the need to maintain human freedom in regard to anything related to the revelation given by the second coming. There cannot be anything that hints at forcing religious belief as I argued in the earlier section of this paper entitled "boundaries on the premise of this conference." There cannot be anything in the scientific works that suggests special foreknowledge (such as whether string theory is valid) on the part of the eventual author of the Heavenly Doctrines. Foreknowledge, either in the Writings or the scientific works, would impact human freedom to believe or not believe. One way to look at this question is to momentarily interchange Swedenborg with Newton. We know that Newton's scientific publications, especially his 1687 *Principia*, are held in high regard. Yet no scientist today would consider using Newton's *Principia* as an aid to research in elementary particle physics or nanophysics, or any other modern field. Although the issue may not be as clear with Swedenborg's scientific work, the same principal applies. His scientific works are principally of historical interest rather than guides to productive modern science. This does not mean that the scientific works are not worthy of study and preservation especially, as Bell notes, for their elucidation of the concepts of degrees, correspondence, forms, and so forth. It simply means that they have limited utility as an introduction of New Church thought to the contemporary scientific community.

A further thought using Newton as the frame of reference: although not a well-publicized fact, it is true that Newton actually wrote more words about religion than he did about science. His exegesis of Daniel and Revelation gives a detailed explanation of those books based upon his somewhat biased reading of the history of the Christian Church. Yet the tone of those works is polemical and does not convey a spirit brimming with Christian love. As a structured, comprehensive, and compelling theology, Newton's religious works hardly do the job. No reputable theologian or philosopher takes those works seriously as theology per se. It therefore seems clear that there is a significant disconnect between the respect accorded Newton's scientific publications and that given to his religious publications. The reputation of his scientific work does not rest on the reputation of his religious works. Similarly, I would argue that the validity of the Heavenly Doctrines rests only marginally on Swedenborg's scientific works. Our only concern would be that the writer of the Heavenly Doctrines shows, in his earlier works, a rational approach, and a consistency with the knowledge of his day. Furthermore, we are gratified to see that earlier ideas are not generally reversed or nullified by concepts found in the Writings. In other words, the pre-theological works demonstrate that the revelator is, at the least, a developing person of knowledge, perception, and brilliance.

New Church persons hope that the highest respect is be accorded Swedenborg's religious writings. But it seems almost delusional to expect that those who accord scholarly respect to his scientific works will *necessarily* accept the validity of the Writings. Acceptance of the reality of world described in the Heavenly Doctrines requires both emotional and intellectual acceptance. Furthermore, full acceptance requires life affecting and life changing behavior which goes well beyond the sort of intellectual respect that one might accord to the pre-theological works. Thus while agreeing with Bell that the preservation and study of the scientific works is important, I disagree with the notion that they represent a generally viable route to the mind of the modern scientist.

One cannot leave this discussion without at least touching on possible connections of science and religion. Again, I raise this particular issue in the context of religious freedom and categorically state that the Writings are not going to help us do specific research in modern physics. But a realistic spiritual understanding of the overall picture of creation is important. Thus, a grasp of and belief in the sort of reality described in *Divine Love and Wisdom* must be helpful, at least as an over-arching intellectual background for the working scientist. One place where science and religion do *specifically* meet is in the realm of correspondence, and these correspondences are many and various and, I believe, often highly individualistic. They are not provable, but like the plausibility criterion suggested earlier, they are extremely valuable to the individuals who see them. There are correspondences between natural and spiritual structures. There are correspondences between natural and spiritual processes. In this latter case, I note that correspondences between occurrences in the history of science and the spiritual development of a person are plausible and have been discussed elsewhere.[5] One of my special interests is in correspondences between natural and spiritual *limitations*. These include limitations in

---

5. Forrest Dristy, "The Two-fold Nature of Mathematics," *New Philosophy*, vol. 80 (Bryn Athyn, PA: Swedenborg Scientific Association, 1979), 63–69. See also Gregory L. Baker, *Religion and Science: From Swedenborg to Chaotic Dynamics* (New York: Solomon Press, 1992), 153–157.

mathematics, quantum physics, and relativity theory that, respectively, can be seen to correspond to various limitations in spiritual knowledge.[6] Certainly one can affirm that there are indeed two complementary foundations of truth, as described in *Spiritual Experiences* 5609, and quoted in Bell's paper.

What of future study? Because of the broad scope of Bell's paper, there are many avenues to explore. We mention only a few possibilities. It would be interesting to discuss further the question raised about the future "form" that the New Church might take, bearing in mind that the Writings have specific things to say about the role of a priesthood and distinction between ecclesiastical and civil uses. Another area that could give rise to further insight would be to ask, as we did with Simonetti's paper, about the types of illustrations that might occur in a twenty-first century version of the Heavenly Doctrines. For example, if Einstein had been the revelator, would the illustrations have been from relativity theory and the almost unified field theory? Or further on Einstein, would he like Newton have been sufficiently famous that human spiritual freedom would have been abridged if he were to have been the revelator?

Bell writes with passion, providing the reader with challenges and even provocation. Certainly this paper is never dull, and I have enjoyed thinking about the many areas upon which he touches. This paper goes well beyond the agenda of the conference and points to priorities that are important to him as a New Church theologian and scientist. It is evident that I do not always agree with Bell in substance or even tone, but we may be grateful to him for challenging us to consider the many important issues that he addresses.

With these remarks I conclude my commentary on the work of the speakers. In this final sentence, let me express my gratitude to all three speakers in this session for the effort and creativity they have brought to the conference and for their important contribution to the success of these proceedings. ⚶

---

6. Ibid., chap. 9.

Preparation for the Last Judgment:
John Locke and Emanuel Swedenborg

ANDREW DIBB

The Most Ancient Church occasioned the Lord's first advent. The first prophecy, given in Genesis 3.16, promised that the Lord would take on a human form and thereby save humanity. However, He could not come immediately—the Most Ancient and the Ancient Churches had to run their courses before the world was ready for the first advent. The Old Testament was a prophecy of the Lord's coming and His states of life in this world, which were fulfilled in the process of glorification and redemption.

In addition to the Scriptural preparations, other things also had to develop to make the first advent possible: spiritual and moral decline took place within an environment of increasing technological advancement, particularly in the Roman world. Although the Roman conquest of her empire was brutal, it brought benefits for the infant Christian Church. The Roman Empire provided the external environment into which the Lord was born. This profoundly affected the course of the Lord's life itself, and also shaped the course of the Church, leading to its decline and judgment in 1757. It does not take much argument to point out that the Christian Church would have developed very differently in another environment. It can also be argued, however, that since the majority of that Church existed within the Roman influenced world, that the foundations of that society were as carefully directed to the advent and growth of the Christian Church and the writing of the New Testament as the foundations of ancient middle eastern societies were directed to the writing of the Old Testament. It is possible to consider the Word as the seed of redemption, and the Roman Empire as the receptive ground in which that seed grew.

For New Church people, the question obviously arises whether similar preparation took place with regard to the New Church. A similar argument can be used to show that certain developments had to take place or it would have been impossible either to conceive of or to disseminate the Heavenly Doctrine. It is the assumption of this essay that such groundwork indeed had to be laid. Under these circumstances, it would follow that developments were carefully provided according to Divine Providence.

Since the study of Christian history is vast, this study will be restricted to preparations for the Last Judgment in England. There are reasons for this:

First, many of the developments crucial for the Last Judgment to occur were pioneered in England. This is particularly true in the political, scientific and philosophical arenas. England differed substantially in many regards from the rest of Europe during the seventeenth and eighteen centuries. This is particularly true in freedom of religion, which was prized to such an extent that it led to the development of personal freedoms of worship and speech that were not duplicated in most European countries until the nineteenth century.

Next, Swedenborg visited and had a high regard for the English, their political and religious freedoms, and especially their freedom to think according to their consciences. This freedom did not come easily, and was only achieved during Swedenborg's own lifetime. It allowed him to publish many books of the Heavenly Doctrine there, only interrupting this during the 1760s when Sweden was at war with England. He also had books translated into English and disseminated at his own expense.

Third, New Church organizations also at first grew in England, and as in the case of the Christian Church taking root in and reflecting her Roman roots, the New Church today still shows her British origins in many aspects. For example, there is English influence in the liturgy of the various church organizations.

Perhaps the greatest contributions to the environment of the New Church arising in England can be reduced to four: the translation of the Bible, the discovery of the circulation of the blood along with other scientific discoveries, religious freedom, and the development of religious and philosophic thought at the end of the seventeenth century. Although countless other details could be considered as part of the overall preparation, these four are mile markers along the path to the Second Advent. This paper will treat the first two propositions briefly, and then concentrate more fully on the philosophic, religious and political thought of the late seventeenth century when the final preparations were made, many of them in Swedenborg's own lifetime.

TRANSLATION OF THE BIBLE

While the Old Testament served as a foundation for the first advent, so the whole Word provided the base for the Second Advent. However, the Roman Catholic Church had systematically removed access to the Word from the people, partly by insisting that it only be available in Latin, and partly by reserving to itself the right to read and interpret it. Unless this changed, the Lord could not come again, for at the second coming He did not come in person, but by means of the internal sense of the Word (TCR 776, 779). In order for this to happen, the Word had to be restored to people in languages they could read and understand.

The Word had been translated into vernacular languages during parts of the early Middle Ages, but the Roman Catholic Church had greatly strengthened her grip on the Vulgate in the thirteenth and fourteenth centuries, becoming increasingly intolerant of dissent. By suppressing access to the Word, they ensured their own religious and political supremacy. As the Last Judgment loomed in the future it became increasingly necessary for the Word to be returned to the people. In England this need was initially filled by John Wycliffe (1324–1384), a professor at Oxford.

Wycliffe challenged the Roman Catholic Church on many fronts. His stance on the Word led him to begin translating it into English. He believed that the Word was intended for everyone:

> The New Testament is full authority, and open to the understanding of simple men, as to the points that are most needful to salvation . . . He that keepeth meekness and charity hath the true understanding and perfection of all Holy Writ, [for] Christ did not write His laws on tables, or on skins of animals, but in the hearts of men . . . The Holy Ghost teaches us the meaning of Scripture as Christ opened its sense to His Apostles.[1]

His plea for people to read the Word in their own language was nothing short of a revolution against the existing Roman Catholic system.

Wycliffe's work raises the question of why the Reformation did not begin at that point. The answers point to the gradual preparation for the Second Advent: the world was not yet ready. Powerful natural forces kept the impact of Wycliffe's work to a minimum. First, he had no way of duplicating the English translation. The Catholic Church could employ countless monks in monastery scriptoria to copy books by hand, but there were few outside the Church to do that work. Without a means of duplication, the Word could not be disseminated. Wycliffe's translation did not spark the Reformation because the technological equipment necessary had not yet been invented.

A second reason was simply because people were not ready for it. In spite of ecclesiastical abuses, there is little evidence that people wanted change. During the fourteenth and fifteen centuries there was a surge in piety and devotion, demonstrated by the increase in religious practice, building and art. People were simply not interested in religious change. The world had to go through a period of spiritual disillusionment before it would be ready for a change.

However, Wycliffe's work sparked a small grassroots religious revival, which although persecuted, played an important role in the English Reformation in the sixteenth century, which in turn provided

---

1. Wycliffe in Estep, *Renaissance and Reformation*, 65.

much of the impetus for the movement towards freedom of worship in the seventeenth. While the English were more tolerant than most other European countries, there was still nothing approaching the religious freedom that would allow Swedenborg to fulfill his role as revelator and publisher of the Heavenly Doctrine. Nor were scientific and natural ideas sufficiently developed to contain and express the new teachings.

INCREASE IN SCIENTIFIC KNOWLEDGE

A primary difference between the sixteenth and seventeenth century lay in the exploration of science and the development of philosophic thought. In spite of its many advances, the sixteenth century was essentially medieval in its outlook. People attributed the vast array of unexplainable natural phenomena to direct divine influence. Ancient Galenic texts and astrological divination controlled the medical world, and the simplest scientific facts, those taught in elementary schools today, were unknown. It would have been impossible for the Heavenly Doctrine to have been given at that time—the vocabulary of ideas simply did not exist. However, as the seventeenth century progressed, scientific discoveries changed the way people thought. Thus both the discoveries themselves *and* the changes in outlook were an important part of the preparation for the Last Judgment.

Early in the seventeenth century, men like Francis Bacon established an important principle: truth can be known by observation. Gradually ancient theories devoid of any real evidence were challenged and began to fall away. By mid-century Ptolemy's ideas were dead; Copernicus, Galileo and Tycho Brahe had disposed of them. In England, Oxford University led the way in scientific study.[2] The natural world provided a cause and effect relationship linking things that had previously been considered isolated.[3] Without these scientific discoveries and the resultant change in thinking, it would have been impossible for

2. Hill, *The Century of Revolution 1603-1714*, 180.
3. Ibid., 182.

Swedenborg to have described the end/cause/effect relationship of discrete degrees. Nor could he have had the natural model from which he could understand the spiritual sun. If key ideas like this were abstracted from the Heavenly Doctrine, the teachings may have focused on regeneration, but they could not have explained the structure of the spiritual world.

A fundamental shift in understanding came in 1632 when William Harvey demonstrated the circulation of the blood and broke the medieval reliance on ancient masters, especially Galen. It would require centuries for these discoveries to take full effect, but he opened enough of a crack in the door so that some of the light of natural truth could shine in. This example shows the careful work of Divine Providence. Without Harvey's discovery it would have been impossible to use the analogy of the heart and the lungs to describe the relationship between good and truth, which would have deprived the doctrine of the powerful scientific support it gets in these matters. Harvey's discovery led to a far truer understanding of the human body, which by the end of the Christian era in 1757 was growing increasingly accurate. Considering the detailed references to anatomy in the doctrine, especially regarding the Grand Man, and it becomes apparent that the Last Judgment could not have taken place without them.

The Lord carefully laid the foundations for the Last Judgment. It would have been impossible for Swedenborg to reveal the internal sense of the Word had it still been blocked by the Catholic Church. Similarly, he could not have understood the relationship of love and wisdom, or of the Grand Man, and so of the "geography" of heaven had it not been for the medical advances begun in the seventeenth century. The mere fact that Swedenborg from youth onwards familiarized himself with the most current thought available, and used that knowledge as a foundation from which he could express the truths of the Heavenly Doctrine, indicates that these developments were carefully provided for under the auspices of Divine Providence.

JOHN LOCKE

A study of Messianic prophecy shows progressive clarity developing as the time of the advent drew closer. The obscure prophecy given to Adam and Eve in Eden eventually becomes clarified in the prophecies that the Lord would be born of a virgin in Bethlehem, that He would be crucified and rise again as the Savior. It is indicative of the state of the church that the closer it comes to its consummation, the more clearly truths need to be expressed, partly to keep hope alive for the simple good, and partly to provide the final materials necessary for the infant church to grow.[4]

There were no prophecies at the end of the Christian Church comparable to those at the end of the Jewish Church. The Old and New Testaments were to be laid bare, not added to. The Sense of the Letter was complete in them; there was no need of further revelation by means of correspondences. The restoration of the Word, in the vernacular, made Biblical studies more popular than was possible before. At the same time scientific knowledge developed during this "run-up" prelude to the Last Judgment, so there also had to be a concomitant change in the outlook of people. The centuries-old view of the human being that had characterized medieval Christianity had to change into what is essentially the modern mindset. This meant relinquishing certain concepts of God, of people, and of the relationship between them.

In England, John Locke's philosophy and religious writing introduced or championed ideas that were an important part of this process. They seem to foreshadow the Writings in a way similar to the clear prophecies of the late Old Testament era. Many of Locke's ideas were not original to him, but his work reintroduced them to the

---

4. Bishop N.D. Pendleton expressed this concept in an article in *New Church Life:* "A study of the several historical prophecies concerning the advent of the Lord, from the book of Genesis to that of Daniel, reveals the very interesting fact that there is an apparent progression of development of the Messianic idea—that from a first obscure beginning the idea grows and expands until a picture of the Messiah is presented of marvelous beauty and grandeur." Bishop N.D. Pendleton, "The Messianic Prophecies," *New Church Life*, October, 1904.

thinking public with remarkable effect. Even Swedenborg read Locke, and it is within the argument of this paper that Locke contributed to Swedenborg's, as well as the readers' of the Writings, ability to receive the Heaven Doctrine. Swedenborg uses many of Locke's concepts, albeit in different ways, to express the truths of the Heavenly Doctrine.

John Locke's life is a fascinating study in itself. Educated at Oxford, immersed in Aristotelian philosophy and imbued with the scientific orientation of his age, he was also involved in the politics of his time—which necessitated his flight from England to the Netherlands just before the revolution of 1688. His political, philosophical and religious thought illustrate how concepts preparatory to the Last Judgment entered public thought, and how without those ideas neither Swedenborg nor the reading public could have received the Heavenly Doctrine.

Although he is regarded a major philosopher, Locke only published his work towards the end of his life. There is a definite sequence of thought in his work. In the wake of the "Glorious Revolution" of 1688, when King James II was ousted for his Roman Catholicism, Locke published *A Letter concerning Toleration* in 1689. This was followed in 1690 by a flurry of works, *A Second Letter concerning Toleration* and *Two Treatises of Government* in 1690. During that same year he shifted his focus from politics to epistemology and published his seminal book, *An Essay Concerning Human Understanding*, begun in 1671. In 1693 he published *The Reasonableness of Christianity*. His other religious works were only published posthumously: *A Paraphrase and Notes on the Epistles of St. Paul* (1705) and *A Discourse on Miracles* (1706). Interspersed among these were many other works, but these are sufficient for the sake of this article.

Broadly speaking, Locke's published writings that are particularly important for the preparation of the Last Judgment fall into three categories: political, epistemological and religious. Interestingly, they follow this sequence, almost as if Locke was building up to the important religious ideas that set him apart from the mainstream of the Church of England in his day. His work affects the three major areas of the Heavenly Doctrine, the civil, moral and spiritual. Locke's political works on freedom and government affected the environment in which the Doctrines were presented, and spoke directly to some of the most basic issues of civil life. He outlined principles of freedom of worship, of speech and of tolerance that appear to be confirmed in the pages of the Doctrine. The epistemological work redraws concepts of the human mind, which supports the concepts of freedom of choice and the development of rational thought. Again, the processes Locke describes presage the teachings of the Heavenly Doctrine, and since we know that Swedenborg read this work, it may be entirely possible that he did so under Divine guidance, in order to break free from the Cartesian assumptions that formed so much a part of his education. This epistemological part, in describing the formation of the mind, addresses many issues connected with the moral level of the mind. Finally, Locke turned his thoughts to religion, which formed a capital on the pillar and base of his epistemology and political beliefs. His religion, simple, forthright and to the point, seeks to scrap the encrustations of seventeen hundred years of Christian theology. He endeavored to read the New Testament simply, in the terms in which it was written. As such he closed the circle opened by Wycliffe three hundred years before, when he began to translate the Word precisely so that people would read and be instructed by it without the interference of the Church.

POLITICAL THOUGHT

The Letters of Toleration

The Last Judgment could not have taken place in 1657 for the simple fact that there was no religious freedom at that time. In most of Europe the religious wars were barely over, the issues "solved" by the agreement that rulers determined the religion of their country. England was still governed by the puritanical Oliver Cromwell. Anglicanism was suppressed in favor of a more Calvinistic Protestantism, the Quakers persecuted, and Catholicism prohibited. In Europe, the French enjoyed a modicum of freedom under the *Edict of Nantes,* and the Netherlands some greater freedoms.

The tentacles of state religion extended into every detail of people's lives. Not only was the church a major landowner and influence in government, but also it controlled vital areas of daily life. The church issued licenses that today are governed by the state: the right to practice as teachers, midwives, and surgeons was granted by the church. Marriage, separation and divorce, likewise were administered by the church. On another level, the church controlled much of the government's propaganda through their pulpits.[5] They also controlled censorship, effectively curtailing any published material considered subversive to religion or morals. The lines of distinction between where the government ended and where the church began were very blurred. Anyone who dissented from the church was excluded from public life, from universities and certain occupations. The situation was to worsen before it could get better. In 1685 Louis XIV revoked religious freedom, plunging France into religious turmoil as thousands of Huguenots (Protestants) had to flee to other Protestant countries. In England King James II was on a collision course with Parliament and the people over his Catholicism. His insistence in placing Catholics in high and sensitive places led directly to the "Glorious Revolution" of 1688—the year of Swedenborg's birth.

The situation was quite different at the time of the Last Judgment, at least as far as England was concerned. Anglicans worshipped side by side with Quakers, Methodists, Moravians, Lutherans and Jews. Aside from lingering bans on Catholics, more for political than theological reasons, there was an acceptance of diverse religions on a scale unequaled anywhere else in Europe, including Sweden. In Divine Providence, a country had been prepared in which freedom of worship prevailed and where the Writings could be both written and disseminated.

How could changes made in a single century upset hundreds of years of precedent? John Locke was a key influence in the movement

---

5. Waller 2000, 286.

that turned England around on the subject of freedom. His *First Letter on Toleration* outlined his philosophy on the separation of church and state. In this work he lays down not only the role of civil and ecclesiastical order, but outlines an approach to religion that is a major departure from the form which had not only brought bloodshed and war, but was damaging to the development of the human soul.

Interestingly, Locke begins by defining the church, not the state. While he does not say this outright, his inference is that the Church of England had overstepped the mark by taking on a governmental role. Toleration could only come when the church resumed its true use as a promoter of spirituality. He described several characteristics of what he believed should constitute a true church.

The first characteristic for a true church is "toleration."[6] Toleration is the willingness to let people chose in freedom what they want to believe and how they wish to practice that belief. He contends that while the goal of all true religion is to lead people to heaven there may be differences in how people interpret and practice the Word to achieve this. In the final analysis, because the goal is the same, churches will have more in common than people generally believe.

For Locke this tolerance was not merely a matter of political peace, it was a function of religion itself. Tolerance was the mark of true charity, and therefore a mark of true Christianity: if anyone

> be destitute of charity, meekness, and goodwill in general towards all mankind, even to those who are not Christians, he is certainly yet short of being a true Christian himself.[7]

In terms very familiar to New Church people, he points out that

> true religion . . . is not instituted in order to the erecting of external pomp, nor to the obtaining of ecclesiastical dominion, nor to the exercising of compulsive force, but to the regulating of men's lives according to the rules of virtue and piety.[8]

---

6. Locke, *A Letter Concerning Toleration*, 13.

7. Ibid.

8. Ibid.

True Christianity is an internal thing, a state of faith and charity, of believing and doing.[9] A Christian does not begin practicing Christianity by attending church, nor even by the doctrine of the church, but rather by an a conscious decision to actually use the teachings given by the Lord: "Whosoever will list himself under the banner of Christ, must, in the first place, and above all things, make war on his own lusts and vices."[10]

Locke was not trying to eradicate church organizations. Christians who are moved by the teachings of the Lord will band together for common worship and support. External churches are a very necessary part of human life. But rather than the formalized state church with its powers of enforcement over people's lives, he wrote,

> A church then I take to be a voluntary society of men, joining themselves together of their own accord, in order to the public worshipping of God, in such a manner as they judge acceptable to him, and effectual to the salvation of their souls. . . . No man by nature is bound unto any particular church or sect, but every one joins himself voluntarily to that society in which he believes he has found that profession and worship which is truly acceptable to God.[11]

Because church organizations are voluntary societies, the people who join them accept the terms and conditions of the society. Every society has the freedom to admit or expel people who do not conform to their belief or behavior. But that freedom belongs to the individual church, not to the state, nor to a state church. The freedom to comment does not extend beyond anyone who has not voluntarily joined the church.

This means that church organizations need to view each other with charity and toleration, just as the individuals within the church need to do. Every church believes itself to be in possession of the truth, and wishes to be allowed to practice that truth. If one organization does not extend that permission to other churches around them, then they cannot expect it to be extended to themselves. The result is the

9. Ibid., 14.
10. Ibid., 13.
11. Ibid., 22.

destructive intolerance that shook Europe for the first part of the seventeenth century. Locke's solution was to recognize that while one believed one's own church to be true, it is charitable to grant that other churches have the same opinion of themselves:

> For every church is orthodox to itself, to others, erroneous and heretical . . . .
> So that controversy between these churches about the truth of their doctrines,
> and the purity of their worship, is on both sides equal; nor is there any judge,
> either at Constantinople, or elsewhere on earth, by whose sentence it can be
> determined.[12]

By the time the Doctrines were revealed, these principle divisions were widely accepted by the British government and people, which made possible the publishing and dissemination of the Heavenly Doctrine.

If the movement toward freedom of religion had indeed been inspired for the sake of the Last Judgment and the subsequent initiation of the New Church, then it should come as no surprise to find these same concepts enshrined in the Heavenly Doctrine as an ideal for all religions. The separation of church and state enshrined in the United States law is a direct descendant of Locke's philosophy, which in turn has allowed the New Church to flourish here for over two hundred years. This religious freedom can only be maintained if there is a complete separation of church and state into distinctly different areas of responsibility. Locke wrote

> I esteem it above all things necessary to distinguish exactly the business of civil
> government from that of religion, and to settle the just bounds that lie between
> one and the other. If this is not done, there can be no end put to the controversies
> that will always arising (sic) between those that have, or at least pretend to have,
> on the one side, a concernment for the interest of men's souls, and, on the other
> side, a care for the commonwealth.[13]

---

12. Ibid. 29.
13. Ibid., 18.

If the work of the church is the salvation of the human soul, the work of the "magistrate"—Locke's term for political authority—

> is by the impartial execution of equal laws, to secure unto all people in general, and to every one of his subjects in particular, the just possession of these things belonging to life.[14]

The magistrates cannot legislate for the human soul, although they can admonish and exhort, but not compel people in spiritual matters.[15] He points out that if magistrates could pass laws regulating spiritual life, then, since spiritual life is from God, all the laws would be the same. Yet they obviously are different in different countries, indicating that magistrates legislate material and worldly things, and not spiritual. This does not mean that the state abdicates all responsibility on the civil level. Magistrates have the power to admonish and exhort people in moral issues, but they cannot compel people to believe, to worship or to love their neighbor. However, they can pass legislation for the good of society, and that legislation is as binding on the church as it is on an individual. Thus the laws against murder, for example, enacted on the civil plane would equally prevent human sacrifice by the church. The church is both honor and duty bound to obey the laws of the country.

The distinction between church and state allows freedom of worship and conscience. It imposes order and allows each to act as partner with the other. As in any dance, each partner serves the other to make a whole. So while Locke says that it is necessary to distinguish between religion and government, he also says

> A good life, in which consists not the least part of religion and true piety, concerns also the civil government: and in it lies the safety both of men's souls and of the commonwealth. Moral actions belong therefore to the jurisdiction both of the outward and inward court . . . I mean, both of the magistrate and conscience.[16]

---

14. Ibid.
15. Ibid., 20.
16. Ibid., 56.

Locke published his *First Letter on Toleration* in 1689, the year in which the British Government passed the *Act of Toleration*. In this remarkable law nearly all religions (except the Roman Catholic) were given freedom of worship. There were still restrictions on the sects, but a new level of freedom was laid down. By today's standards it was not perfect religious freedom, but it was a stronger beginning than had been made in any other country.

The impact of these ideas on the Last Judgment was enormous. Swedenborg, growing up in Lutheran Sweden, could not have been exposed to the ideas and religious practices of the people he describes in the Heavenly Doctrine if they had not been free to practice their faiths without fear of the law. People only reveal their true quality when they are unafraid of the consequences of them, and the principle holds true for churches. Each variant sect of Christianity needed to be free to run its course, partly so that it could be confronted with truth during the last judgment and respond according to its nature, not by any imposed restraint.

It is indicative of the importance of the ideas Locke summarizes in his *Letter Concerning Toleration* that the concepts he outlined are enshrined in the Heavenly Doctrine and echo in the teachings on the relationship of the state and the individual freedom of human conscience to follow its own faith.

Consider the passage in *New Jerusalem and Its Heavenly Doctrine,* where it is said that

> There are in human beings two sets of things which need to be well ordered: those of heaven and those of the world. Those of heaven are called church affairs, those of the world affairs of state. (NJHD 311)

Priests administer the affairs of heaven, magistrates those of the state. In the Doctrines these are quite distinct from each other:

> Priests ought to teach the people, and to lead them by truths to the good of life, but still they ought to compel no one,[17] since no one can be compelled to believe

---

17. Priestly compulsion is interpreted as the ability of priests to persuade, make

contrary to what he thinks from his heart to be true. He who believes otherwise than the priest, and makes no disturbance, ought to be left in peace; but he who makes disturbance, ought to be separated; for this also is of order, for the sake of which the priesthood is established.[18]

The civil state, likewise, has no right to compel people in religious matters, although it can exhort morality and punish breaches of the law. The work *Divine Providence* spends several passages explaining the doctrine of compulsion, which simply summarized, is that no one can compel another in spiritual things. Compulsion from external sources merely serves to bring the external into a state of compliance, without benefiting the spirit at all (DP 136). When compulsion is extended to religious observance (as it was in the seventeenth century when people were fined for missing church on a Sunday), *Divine Providence* points out that

> Worship that is forced is corporeal, lifeless, vague and gloomy: corporeal because it is of the body and not of the mind, lifeless because there is no life in it, vague because there is no understanding in it, and gloomy because there is no heavenly delight in it. (DP 137)

THE HUMAN BEING

Turning his focus from freedom on a macro-level to the nature of the mind, in 1690 Locke published a book he had been working on

---

rules and enforce them. In the current milieu this is only possible within church organizations. However, when seen from a seventeenth century point of view, it may well imply external compulsion: literal loss of honor, reputation, gain and even life. At that time the church had legal rights of compulsion. It is very different today.

18. NJHD 318. My italics. Note the similarity of this passage with Locke's statement that, "And first, I hold, that no church is bound by the duty of toleration to retain any such person in her bosom, as after admonition continues obstinately to offend against the laws of society. For these being the condition of communion, and the bond of society, if the breach of them were permitted without any animadversion, the society would immediately be thereby dissolved" (*A Letter Concerning Toleration*, 26).

sporadically for many years. His *Essay on the Human Understanding* built
on the philosophical ideas of Aristotle, Hobbes, Descartes and other
philosophers into which he introduced new ideas on the development
and function of the mind.[19] Locke's primary philosophic foundation was
Aristotle, whose teachings permeated Oxford University at that time.
He was particularly attracted to Aristotle's concept that every person
is born with a blank mind, which is molded by the experiences of life
into an individual, conscious, rational mind.[20] He was also influenced
by Hobbes, who held that nature, the source of human experience, was
corrupt, and needed to be eradicated. Locke rejected this concept and
saw nature as the hand of God by which He wrote onto the developing
consciousness.

Perhaps the greatest influence, however, was René Descartes; the
French philosopher who stimulated Locke to rebel against the received
ideas of the day and to consider the implications in people's lives. The
result marked him as an independent thinker.[21] In spite of Descartes'
influence, Locke did not agree with his reductive philosophy, which
held, in part, that people were born with innate ideas, which expressed
themselves as a person grew up.[22] Innate ideas are universal to all people
until they are affected by circumstances. Also, Descartes held that innate
ideas enabled people to understand things they had not experienced—
the idea born with the individual allowed a pre-knowledge that was not
dependent on experience. A primary example of an innate idea was the
belief in God.[23] Little children, who had no experience of God, believed

---

19. Hill, *The Century of Revolution*, 295.
20. Sahakian, *History and Systems of Psychology*, 51.
21. Ibid.
22. http://www.creatorix.com.au/philosophy/t03/g033.html Will Durant
dismisses this saying, "Apparently the stimulus to the Essay was the contention
of the Cambridge Platonists . . . that we derive our ideas of God and morality not from experience but from introspection, and that these ideas are innate
with us, part of our mental equipment, however unconscious, at our birth. This
view, rather than Descartes' incidental statements on 'innate ideas' led Locke to
consider whether there were any ideas . . . not the result of impressions from the
external world" (*The Age of Louis XIV*, 583).
23. Sahakian, *History and Systems of Psychology*, 51.

in Him in all simplicity. Wickedness and evil later in life turned people
to denial, but the denial was acquired through outside sources, not the
original idea of God. Another example of a Cartesian innate idea is
his famous dictum "cogito, ergo sum," I think, therefore I am. People
need no facts to prove their existence, in fact the exercise of disproving
one's existence proves it, for it needs thought to disprove existence and
the mere fact that one is thinking proves that one exists.[24]

Locke rejected this Cartesian idea. He agreed with Aristotle that
the mind at birth was a completely blank slate, a *tabula rasa*, upon
which life experience wrote the raw material of human thought. He
rejected the idea of innate knowledge on several grounds, beginning
with the concept that innate thoughts account for the commonality of
belief among people:

> This argument, drawn from *universal consent,* has this misfortune in it, that if
> it were true in matter of fact that there were certain truths wherein all mankind
> agreed, it would not prove them innate, if there can be any other way shown
> how men may come to that universal agreement, in the things they do consent
> in, which I presume may be done.[25]

For Locke, the hole in Descartes' argument was that of course
not all people believed the same thing, which is obvious. Further, if
ideas were innate, then children and "idiots" would agree to them, for
they would be natural to the human mind. He asked that if ideas are
naturally known, then why are some people ignorant until they are
taught (1.2.21). If knowledge were innate people would know things
without being taught.[26] Locke argued persuasively against innate ideas,
examining and rejecting the arguments in favor of them one by one,
until he came to his final, clearly stated position:

---

24. Ibid., 52.
25. Locke, *An Essay Concerning Human Understanding* 1.2.3. All future references to this essay will be parenthetical containing book, chapter and section.
26. An example would be a person from a remote island who has no concept of
God. If the idea of God was innate, this should not happen.

the truth is, ideas and notions are no more born with us than arts and sciences, though some of them indeed offer themselves to our faculties more readily than others and therefore are more generally received, though that too be according as the organs of our bodies and powers of our minds happen to be employed: *God having fitted men with faculties and means to discover, receive, and retain truths, accordingly as they are employed.* (1.4.23; italics Locke's)

The final point in this quotation is of utmost importance. If people were born with innate ideas, they would be pre-programmed by God. The concept has enormous ramifications on freedom of choice, for what choice is there except to reject God, and failing that, one accepts God by default. This only allows for the negative side of freedom, which essentially is no freedom at all. In rejecting the concept of innate thoughts, Locke focuses on a vitally important aspect of the human being: people are created in the image and likeness of God, and in that they are "fitted with faculties and means to discover, receive, and retain truths." The human being is no mere passive agent in the relationship with God and other people, but an active participant who is fully responsible for his or her own discovery, reception and retention of truth. Locke's statement places the responsibility for spiritual life and its natural expression squarely on the shoulders of the individual.

A great deal of the *Essay on Human Understanding* is dedicated to the process by which people come to exercise their God-given faculties. He began by inviting us to "suppose the mind to be, as we say, white paper void of all characters, without any ideas" (2.1.2). Such is the mind at birth. Rather wryly he wrote

He that attentively considers the state of a child, at his first coming into the world, will have little reason to think him stored with plenty of ideas that are to be the matter of his future knowledge. It is by degrees he comes to be furnished with them. (2.1.6)

It does not take long for ideas to develop as the child grows. Locke's complete rejection of Cartesian innate ideas required him to state an alternative: "two are the fountains of knowledge, from whence all the *ideas* we have, or can naturally have, do spring" (2.1.2). These sources are experience and reflection.

Sensations begin to mark the "white paper" immediately after birth, even before the infant is consciously aware of them (2.1.6). Colors, flavors, words, and so on flow into the opening senses of the newly born, accelerating as the child matures and is exposed to more and more sensations. People have no control over this influx, they cannot stop seeing, hearing, feeling, smelling, making their minds a passive receptacle of sensual influx, all of it is stored in the memory (2.1.6). As these sensations multiply, people begin to learn to tell the difference between them, some are pleasurable, some not. Gradually patterns of groupings of sensations begin to form in the mind; the "white paper" is becoming covered with the script of life. However, sensation is merely the first step in the process of developing the mind. Locke continues:

> The senses at first let in particular ideas and furnish the yet empty cabinet; and the mind by degrees growing familiar with some of them, they are lodged in the memory, and names got to them. Afterwards, the mind, proceeding further, abstracts them, and by degrees learns the use of general names. In this manner the mind comes to be furnished with ideas and language, the materials about which to exercise its discursive faculty. And the use of reason becomes daily more visible, as these materials that give it employment increase. (1.2.15)

Sensation or experience only provides the foundation from which ideas develop. Ideas develop when "the understanding turns inwards upon itself, *reflects* on its own *operations*, and makes them the object of its own contemplation" (2.1.8). Experience is like any raw data, it has to be organized and ordered to be useful. This is the second function of the mind, which Locke calls "reflection." He defines it

> to mean that notice which the mind takes of its own operations and the manner of them, by reason whereof there come to be ideas of these operations in the understanding. (2.1.4)

Reflection sets the data in order, linking experience, grouping subjects, generalizing, abstracting and forming connections between sensations flowing in.

Reflection on sensation and on the contents of the memory is really what allows ideas as we might understand them to develop. Reflection furnishes a new selection of things drawn from, much higher than sensations,

> such are *perception, thinking, doubting, believing, reasoning, knowing, willing* and all the different actings of our own minds: which we, being conscious of and observing in ourselves, do from these receive into our understanding as distinct ideas as we do from bodies affecting our senses. (2.1.4)

The ideas that come from reflection are intrinsically people's own, for while people are passive in regard to what assails their senses, they have complete freedom to develop the ideas of reflection.

Summed up, then, Locke's point is that not only are there no innate ideas, but people cannot even begin to think until their minds have been furnished with the data stored in the memory, for until then the mind has no vocabulary with which to formulate thought (2.1.20). As people learn and mature more, their minds progressively develop higher and more complex thoughts, but all of them can be traced back to sense data reflected on and reorganized as a conscious thought process. Simple ideas are formed from reflection on sensual information, complex ideas arise when the mind exerts its power over simple ideas, which it can do in three ways:

1) Combining several simple ideas into one compound one
2) Bringing two ideas together and not combining them
3) Separating them from other ideas accompanying them in their real existence (2.12.1)

Complex ideas, such as "beauty, gratitude, a man, an army, the universe" are made up of single ideas, and yet when they are combined they take on a single name, and the individual thinks of this grouping of simple ideas as a single whole, which essentially becomes a new simple idea. In this way thought opens up to new ranges of ideas that would be impossible without the foundation of the senses. These complex ideas may at times seem innate to people, especially when the subject is agreed on, for example, when people agree that sunsets are beautiful, they do not reflect that the ability to appreciate the sunset comes from repeated sense data, not only of seeing sunsets, but of having been told that they are beautiful, and perhaps comparing them unconsciously with things they do not consider beautiful. Agreement on things often seems as if the agreed on subject is common property to all people, and since people think similarly on the subject, the knowledge is therefore innate. Locke disagreed. Without experience and reflection, people could not grasp the beauty of a sunset. His point is simply that even though the mind can think in a complex manner, it cannot think apart from the original sense experience. People cannot think about something they know nothing about.

Locke introduced another concept into this mix. People are passive when it comes to the impact of sensation on their senses, for example, one cannot chose to see green as red. Green is green. To some degree, people are also passive in the formation of the ideas generated from experience. But the mind is not totally passive in this area, and becomes less and less so as the mind mounts to higher and more complex thoughts. What determines the development of ideas from experience and reflection is a second faculty he calls "volition or willing" (2.6.2).

Locke was determined that people understand the concept of "faculty" properly. The "faculty of willing" is the ability to will. It does not mean that a person wills or does not will, but simply that a person is able to chose thoughts that appeal. Thus the faculty of will allows people a freedom to choose. Locke insisted that there is a difference between a faculty for will and that the will is free. It is false to assert that the will is free, for the will is merely an ability to chose. Freedom is the exercise of that will (2.21.1ff). He also stressed the difference between freedom and liberty: freedom is the power to exercise the choices presented by the will, liberty is the ability of carrying those choices into action. Common experience shows that people are always in freedom to will whatever they please, but they do not always have the liberty to express it in action.[27]

---

27. (2.25.25) For example, people are free to choose a course of action but limitations of the law, of personal ability, or circumstance, may prevent them from doing so. A man is free to jump from a building in an attempt to fly, but is limited by his physiology and by gravity, and therefore while he has the freedom of

The faculty of the will provides more than freedom: it is the home of human emotions, which are the proximate cause of choices people make. The emotions resident in the will: desire, uneasiness, and so on, form a personal backdrop against which to measure experience and gives people a personal yardstick of measurement. People do things they deem pleasurable and avoid those that are painful. According to Locke, uneasiness is perhaps the greatest incentive to acting in freedom. When people feel uneasy as they reflect on experience, they seek to alleviate their unease by searching for further experience. Further reflection connects experience into more complex ideas. Thus uneasiness leads to growth. Growth slows when a person grows easy about experience. People seldom question things they like and are comfortable with, although they look for ways to enhance or replicate the pleasurable experience. Again, they connect new experiences, enriched by reflection, with other reflections to form complex ideas. Reflection leads the mind back in a circle, however, so that experiences with uneasiness leads to misery, while experiences that satisfy lead to happiness.

There is, then a complete connection between the experience of the senses, the reflection and reduction to abstraction in the understanding, and the involvement of the emotions of the will. In Locke's system the mind works as an integral unit, each part identifiable and definable, but completely dependent on each other part in order to function in the formation of ideas.

The *Essay* contains far more material than can comfortably be contained in this paper. However, it is sufficient at this point to merely point out the brief outline of his argument.

---

choice, he doesn't have the liberty to fly. There is an interesting correlation here to the teaching in Divine Providence 81, which says that people who believe things allowable, do them internally even if they do not do them externally. Thus people have the freedom to choose the things they would do, even though they may not have the liberty of doing them. In the final analysis, the choice, not the action, determines the affection, indicating that lack of liberty limits but does not remove free will.

The *Essay* was both refuted and acclaimed in Locke's own lifetime. There were those who believed him to be toying with atheism by stressing that experience, not God, is the source of thought. This assertion was not strictly true, for, aside from being a practicing Christian, Locke wrote that while experience gives rise to thought, God attaches delight to peoples' ideas (2.7.3). Delight plays a primary role in how people order their thoughts.

In spite of detractors, many others defended Lock's teachings. The *Essay* went through four editions in fourteen years. It was translated into French in 1700 and played a seminal part in the enlightenment of the eighteenth century. This enthusiastic reception should be considered as one of the final states of preparation for the Last Judgment, giving as it did an entirely new view of the way the human being functions. It is difficult to imagine how the truths of the Heavenly Doctrine could have been revealed if people still thought that their belief in God and their moral life were innately present in them from birth. What happens under those circumstances to freedom of choice? How does one reconcile the differences between people and nations, their views of God and practice of morality, except to label anything contrary to Western Christianity as the product of evil and sin—as indeed was the attitude of the Christian Church when, in the post Last Judgment Era, she began her proselytizing of Africa, Asia and the Americas.

Acting like a philosophic prophecy, Locke's epistemology finds powerful expression in Swedenborg's philosophic thought and later in the Heavenly Doctrine. The close similarity between Locke's thought and the development of Swedenborg's concepts of the mind supports the thesis of this essay that there had to be a development of ideas before the Last Judgment could take place, so that the truths which precipitated the Judgment could be both expressed in revelation and received. Locke's epistemology is an important part of this process, partly because of the change in the way people thought of human beings, and partly because it opened doors to further thought and research, much of which was done by Swedenborg himself during his own preparation for the work of revelator.

As in the case of Locke's writings, Swedenborg's epistemology is too vast for the scope of this essay. He initially developed a system to explain how people acquire ideas and develop thought during his pre-enlightenment stage. The roots of his inquiry lay in Descartes' question of how the mind and body, comprised of two distinct substances, could work together since they are utterly and completely different, one spiritual, the other material.[28] Locke's solution provided some starting points for the discussion, but it needed further development. Swedenborg provided physiological material about the brain that was unknown to Locke, and refined the process of how the senses acquire information and translate them into ideas. However, he was unwilling to totally abandon the notion of higher realms of the mind which influence the way people learn from their senses. After his spiritual eyes were opened, he saw the structure of the mind, adding hidden spiritual components that Locke could not have known about before they were revealed. Inge Jonsson described Swedenborg as trying to bridge the divide "between the rationalistic belief in innate ideas in man and the empirical belief that our consciousness is entirely formed by sensory experiences."[29]

Swedenborg was a product of his own time and training. Locke was considered to be one of the first empiricists, that is, he based his understanding of things on observation and the evidence of his senses. His argument, therefore, begins with the senses and works upward into the higher functions of the mind. Swedenborg was also an empiricist in both his pre-theological and enlightened state. Much of his argument on the development of ideas stems from his biological research in the brain itself. Being equipped with far more efficient scientific instruments and a fund of previous researches, Swedenborg was able to examine the human body and draw conclusions about the function of the mind that were closed to Locke. During his spiritual experiences he was able to examine first hand the workings of the higher degrees of the mind in the light of the next world. His empiricism therefore crossed the line from the natural to the spiritual world.

---

28. Odhner, *The Human Mind*, 6.
29. Jonsson, *Emanuel Swedenborg*, 78.

Swedenborg explored the relationship between these two aspects of the mind in his 1741 work *Economia Regni Animalis,* translated as *The Economy of the Animal Kingdom*. In this work he is indebted to Locke and refers to him in glowing terms as "the illustrious Locke, in his golden *Essay concerning the Human Understanding*" (EAK II 212). At this point, Swedenborg pays tribute to Locke's "profound investigation of the powers of the mind" (EAK II 212), but his real interest is Locke's conclusions at the end of the *Essay* that he "discovers at last, as if by divination, that there is yet another and profounder science" (EAK II 212). He quotes Locke's idea that it should be possible for people to discover the "connection and agreement" of the essences of ethics, and from that come to "certain, real, and general truths" (4.12.8). The idea inspired Swedenborg as a challenge to find a unifying and overarching system to explain the old dilemma of the interaction of mind and body. Reflecting on Locke's comments he wrote:

> That to such a science, seen so obscurely, yet so desirable, any other way can lead than the doctrine of order, or of the series and degrees, existing in the world and nature, I cannot be induced to believe. (EAK II 212)

Locke, in his analysis of the acquisition of knowledge, provided a springboard for Swedenborg to develop in the pre-theological works the beginnings of a system of degrees which was essential for his reception of the Heavenly Doctrine, and therefore essential for the Last Judgment to take place. He saw the solution to the problem of the relation of mind and body as *the Doctrine of Series and Degrees,* which describes "the distinction and relation between things superior and inferior, or prior and posterior." The spiritual substances of the mind are superior and prior; those of the body are inferior and posterior. The concept of degrees makes communication possible between them.

Thus Swedenborg sought to bridge the gap between those who, like Descartes posited the idea of connate ideas, and those like Locke who insisted that all ideas originate in the senses. He agreed with Locke that all ideas begin in the senses, but this does not negate higher, internal states of mind, which affect the conscious external. To defend the influence of higher thought, he quotes Locke directly:

> His words deserve to be quoted, and are as follow: "The other fountain, from which experience furnisheth the understanding with ideas, is the perception of the operations of our own minds within us, as it is employed about the ideas it has got; which operations, when the soul comes to reflect on, and consider, do furnish the mind with another set of ideas, which could not be had from things without." (EAK 294)

Swedenborg's interpretation of this passage is that "the soul is a faculty distinct from the mind, and is born into such perfection as to be the order, truth, science, and art of its kingdom" (EAK 294). This higher soul-life, or intelligence, is present at birth, and is the human quality itself. In order to descend into the conscious mind, this intelligence needs to be furnished with the requisite knowledge drawn from the senses, in the manner described by Locke. Thus the soul "knows" all things,

> but not so the mind, which before it can be illuminated by the light of the soul, must be imbued with principles *a posteriori*, or through the organs of the external senses. (EAK 296)

Could it have been possible for Swedenborg to have articulated this early statement of series and degrees, and so provided a working model for the Heaven Doctrine if he had not read "the illustrious Locke"? If these ideas had to exist in order for the Last Judgment to take place, then they would have found their way into the study of epistemology in one way or another. In providence, however, the ideas were set out by John Locke, an early empiricist, in a way that appealed to and challenged the equally empiricist mind of Swedenborg. Perhaps the fact that Locke was an Englishman, whose ideas on this subject permeated English thought, was also in Divine Providence, for they provided a philosophic environment into which the Heavenly Doctrine could be born.

Like the wise men from the east who saw and followed the star to Bethlehem, Swedenborg saw the possibilities in Locke's *Essay* and used it as a springboard into the theologically central teaching of degrees. As his mind was opened during the exercise, so Swedenborg was able to both understand and convey the final spiritual truths about the make-up of the mind.

What he was to discover in the next world, was that the mind was not very different from how he had pictured it on its natural level and in relation to the senses and brain. Seen in the light of heaven, he discovered that the mind was in fact arranged into three degrees, each higher degree communicating with the one "below" it by correspondence. These higher degrees are in their order, and so, in a sense "know" all things relating to love and wisdom. In spite of this, these higher degrees of the mind are closed and unconscious with people during their lives in this world.

Consciousness only exists in the natural mind, which functions very much in the way Locke described, but with one major difference. In the Heavenly Doctrine, the natural mind built on the senses and experiences of the world exists to serve a higher purpose: the inflowing of love and wisdom from the higher two degrees of the mind. Each detail of information acquired through the senses operates as a receptor of higher things. Every detail of the memory communicates in this way with either heaven or hell, with the result that the human being stands as a foundation for the whole spiritual world. The fact that people are unconscious of this connection keeps them in freedom to chose to reflect on, and to act on thoughts and feelings. Although, as Locke said, they may not have the liberty to carry these out.

Like Locke, Swedenborg rejected the idea of any innate thoughts, a point he asserts many times in the Heavenly Doctrine. People at birth are lower than animals, for animals have inborn instincts to direct their lives.

> It is only man who at birth has no such knowledge, having *no innate* knowledge at all. He has only the ability and inclination to receive matters relating to knowledge and love. If he does not get these from other people, he remains lower than an animal. (CL 350)

While Locke ascribed the enjoyment of the senses to God's presence in people's lives, the Writings point out that it may come from other sources.

If people do not have innate thoughts, they still have innate inclinations towards certain things. These inclinations are the hereditary inclinations towards evil passed on from generation to generation which predispose people to regard, avoid and be interested or uninterested in any particular thing. At first glance it might seem as if these inclinations are little more than connate ideas, but in reality they are merely predispositions which cannot come into being without having a mental "vessel" prepared by means of sense experience. One can reflect on the fact that even these hereditary inclinations themselves are founded on sense experience, for as hereditary evils are passed on from generation to generation, they are strengthened or weakened by the conscious activity of people in this world. Even people's hidden motivators are based on sense experience, acquired in much the way Locke described.

To sum up, then, Locke laid the groundwork for much of Swedenborg's pre-theological epistemological thought. Without this foundation, Swedenborg would either have had to create the same system himself, or rely on someone else to have thought it up in the interim. The pre-theological systems described in the *Economy of the Animal Kingdom* and *Rational Psychology* find a fuller expression in the Heavenly Doctrine. While it can be argued that there is a progression of ideas from Locke to the pre-theological thought, for it is all based on empirical evidence, there is no progression from either of these to revelation. The Heavenly Doctrine is able to describe functions of the mind that could never be found by observation. Yet, when these are considered closely, one finds that they rely on the natural, observed functions of the mind and brain. One cannot exist without the other, as long as people live in this world. It is possible, then to conclude that knowledge of these things must have existed in order for the Last Judgment to take place.

LOCKE'S THEOLOGICAL THOUGHT

The sequence in Locke's progression goes from freedom from religious restriction and state imposed choices to the freedom of the mind from determinative innate ideas. The overall movement is towards human responsibility. Under his system it is the individual, not the state, who determines morality and spirituality. On another level, while people cannot control the experiential impact on their lives, they can control the direction their reflections take them as they resolve sense experience into rational thought. There is no place for the control of innate ideas in his system. When one considers the emphasis on individual freedom in the Heavenly Doctrine, this progression becomes extremely important. The Heavenly Doctrine defines freedom in several ways: civil, rational or moral and spiritual (DP 73). The rules of appropriation of good and evil declare that only things chosen in complete freedom remain with an individual and determine his or her place in the next world. The Last Judgment is eminently about freedom as the shackles of Christian thought are broken.

It follows as in a logical sequence that having dealt with the development of the human mind, including how people come to have higher, abstract ideas, morals and values, that Locke turned his mind to religion. Locke was a devout and practicing Christian, but his views were hardly orthodox, so much so, that he is often described as the father of deism.[30] While the *Essay* places its focus on reason developed through experience, Locke does not disregard God's activity in human life. For example, he states that the delight people feel in their experiences comes from God (2.7.3); his was not the naturalistic deism of the eighteenth century.

Deism is often seen as negative, as a rejection of God and the beginnings of naturalism. However, as a thought process it was vitally important: it provided a set of principles within which the Heavenly Doctrine could be written and flourish. Briefly put, deism is the concept that the universe was made by God in a precise and orderly

---

30. Sahakian, *History and Systems of Psychology*, 54.

manner that can be discovered through empirical observation. Once He had created the universe, God ceased to remain involved in the world—He left things to run their course according to His laws, which could be discovered by reason.[31] The flaw in deism lies in its strength, for if God does not interfere in His order, conceptually He became increasingly separated from the ordered, created world. He created, set the world into motion and absented Himself. However, in spite of these shortcomings, deism allowed people to look at God in a different way from the arbitrariness of the medieval concept. Deism made it possible for Swedenborg to describe divine and spiritual realities in orderly terms. God is order itself. He never breaks that order. The works on *Divine Love and Wisdom* and *Divine Providence* are essentially deist in nature because they show us the orderly creation and government of the world, although, as in Locke's system, God remains intimately involved in the progress of things without disturbing His underlying order.

The development of deism was profoundly important for the Last Judgment. First, it broke the medieval concept of an arbitrary God. Before deism took hold of western thought, God was considered to have the power to act in miraculous ways, suspending the laws of nature at will. A great deal of worship was aimed at convincing Him to suspend the natural consequences of things, to miraculously heal, deliver, cause or prevent drought, famine, plague and so on. People believed that anything that happened to them was either punishment or reward doled out by God. Deism swept this away.

As the seventeenth century progressed and both science and philosophy explored natural causes that were once held to be mysterious and miraculous, so it became increasingly necessary to reassess concepts of God. Locke rested his arguments on the evidence of empirical reasoning. The universe works because it is a system of regulated parts. The system does not break down, and nothing can change the inevitable trajectory of its course. From this perspective it would seem that God was absent from creation, like the clock-maker

---

31. Sahakian, *History and Systems of Psychology*, 34.

who wound the clock and left it to run its course. But this is not the sum total of Locke's philosophy. Deism did not destroy or remove his faith in God; it simply refocused it from a belief in miraculous intervention to a reasoned and justifiable recognition of God's role in the universe and people's ability to discover it.

While Locke is credited with founding deism, it can legitimately be asked if he was actually one or not. His attempts to explain Christianity are less about the immanence of God in creation, and more about the kind of life people need to lead in order to have a happier one in the next world. In keeping with his teaching in the *Essay,* Locke believed that God "has put within the reach of [people's] discovery, the comfortable provision for this life and the way that leads to a better" (1.1.5). Some of this knowledge can be received by reasoned thought, but some of it is outside human experience, and so needs to be revealed in order to become known. In the *Essay* Locke draws an important distinction between reason and faith.

> *Reason* therefore here, as contradistinguished to faith, I take to be the discovery of the certainty or probability of such propositions or truths, which the mind arrives at by deductions made from such ideas which it has got by the use of its natural faculties, viz. by sensation or reflection.
>
> *Faith,* on the other side, is the assent to any proposition, not thus made out by the deductions of reason, but upon the credit of the proposer, as coming from God in some extraordinary way of communication. This way of discovering truths to men we call *revelation.* (4.18.2)

The fact that he embraced reason did not destroy his need for faith. On the contrary, it seems to have bolstered it, for as he grew older, Locke became increasingly religious.

When Locke examined the religions of his day, he found it impossible to accept the doctrinal developments that colored the understanding of the Word. The Christian Church had developed doctrinal statements and positions which not only dictated how one could read the Word, but they actually obscured the true meaning itself. Then, drawing on the power of the state to support them, the Church compelled people to conform their beliefs to the officially recognized teachings. Locke teachings. Locke rejected this powerfully. In the Preface to his 1695 work, *The Reasonableness of Christianity*, he undertook to set aside any preconceived notions about the Gospels and simply read them in their own light:

> But I cannot allow to them, or to any man, an authority to make a religion for me, or to alter that which God hath revealed.[32]

He began by considering the reason for the Gospel, the notion that since Adam sinned, and since all human beings were therefore condemned because of it, Christ had to enter the world to remove sin and so redeem the human race. Locke summarily dismisses this encrustation of the Gospel as

> derogatory to the honor and attributes of that infinite being; and so [makes] Jesus Christ nothing but the restorer and preacher of pure natural religion; whereby doing violence to the whole tenor of the New Testament.[33]

He further points out that if the fall of Adam was the reason for the advent, then it is strange that Jesus Himself never mentioned it, since it was so momentous a reason.[34]

At this point Locke resumes his overall theme of human freedom. People are responsible for their own sins; they cannot blame Adam, the state, or innate ideas. Responsibility is a key concept in Locke's "theology." He does not reject the fallen state, and is willing to accept that Adam's initial sin introduced it, but he cannot accept that people are responsible or condemned for sins of which they are innocent. People can only be condemned for their own sins.

For Locke the only way to take responsibility for one's spiritual life is to embrace faith in Jesus Christ. Faith bridges the gap between the failure to conform to God's laws and ultimate redemption.[35] "By the law of faith, faith is allowed to supply the defect for full obedience;

---

32. Locke, *The Reasonableness of Christianity*, 165.
33. Ibid., 1.
34. Ibid., 4.
35. Ibid., 15.

and so the believers are admitted to life and immortality, as if they were righteous."[36]

However, one is left wondering where this faith originates. Ideas and thought come from experience, but experience can only show people the things of this world. Higher things, the purpose of life, the relationship with God, salvation itself, are things revealed by God.[37] Believing them is the essence of faith.

> The law of faith, then, in short, is for every one to believe what God requires him to believe, as a condition of the covenant he makes with him; and not to doubt of the performance of His promises.[38]

Since faith needs object, Locke turns to Jesus as the giver of the Gospel. Setting aside the Christian doctrines, especially the Nicene Trinity, he embraces Jesus as the Messiah, the miracles establish His Messiahship, His teaching and preaching confirm it. This was the Apostle's central message when they went out to preach. For various reasons, mostly to prevent an early death, which would shorten His message, the Lord concealed the fact that He was the Messiah.[39] Yet He did not conceal it entirely, and it was widely recognized.

Acknowledging Jesus as Messiah meant recognizing His kingship, which, in light of the clear teachings of the Gospel cannot simply be a matter of faith, but needed also to be one of life. He saw the Gospels as teaching two things: faith and repentance, which "are the indispensable conditions of the new covenant, to be performed by all those who would obtain eternal life."[40] At this point Locke returns to the subject of Adam, for if Adam introduced death into the world, Jesus bestows eternal life, reversing Adam's sin. It is interesting to note that in this reversal, Locke never explicitly mentions the idea of atonement: people

---

36. Ibid., 22.
37. Ibid., 26.
38. Ibid., 25.
39. Ibid., 62.
40. Ibid., 72.

are not saved by atonement, but by their own repentance and the works they do.[41]

In essence Locke's theology is very simple. He develops no systematic structure, nor does he tackle the major Christian themes. All these are encrustations on the Gospel that he simply ignores, as they are not directly taught in the Gospels. In their stead he considers how humans can be reconciled to the Messiah. His approach is practical rather than theological, and while he rejected orthodox teaching, he embraced the central tenets of the New Testament. Locke's study of the Gospels was no mere philosophical exercise; he incorporated his beliefs into his own life, becoming increasingly religious as he aged.

There is no evidence that Swedenborg read *The Reasonableness of Christianity*. However, as in the case of the *First Letter of Toleration* and the *Essay*, there are some remarkable similarities. The dis-encrustation of the Gospels is a first step, as is the rejection of the idea of corporate original sin. In the Heavenly Doctrine, faith must always be carried into action and life, beginning with repentance and ending with the good of life as one applies the tenets of the Word. Even a cursory reading of *The Reasonableness of Christianity* will resound with familiar concepts to the New Church reader.

CONCLUSION

The Lord always works in a progression. Human conception, gestation, birth, growth and death follow each other in a regular sequence. So do repentance, reformation and regeneration. In every progression, the earlier stages lay down the foundation for those which follow. The case is no different with the history of the Christian Church. It was foreseen from its very inception that the Christian Church would decline and fall, not necessarily because of the evil of human hearts, although that certainly flourished in the process, but because the only revelation the Lord could give at the time of His advent could

---

41. Ibid., 180ff.

not explicitly reveal the inner secrets of heaven. The simplicity of the Gospel story contained within it the seeds of the demise of the Christian Church. Thus the Last Judgment was prophesied in fullness within a few decades of the Lord's resurrection. No one was condemned as a result of the state of the Church, but there were those who used it to their own ends, to manipulate the doctrine for wealth or power. They may well have done exactly the same thing had they known the truth. On the other hand, there were those in simple good who, in spite of the state of the Church, continued to believe in the Lord and endeavored to live what they thought was the life He taught. The book of Revelation describes great multitudes of Christians caught up into heaven.

Yet historically the Christian Church could not stand. The New Church had to be born, its truths revealed to an increasingly sophisticated audience. The thesis of this paper is that those truths could not have been revealed, either to Swedenborg or to the people of this world unless suitable groundwork prepared the way. It required a complete shift in human thought processes to break the hold of medieval superstition and allow for a more rational, almost mechanistic expression of the Divine workings to be revealed.

Revelation could not have happened without the Word translated into the vernacular and freely available in at least some parts of Europe. The translations themselves would have been very restricted if Gutenberg had not invented the printing press. Thousands of people died in this endeavor. But the process was necessary for the sake of the judgment to come.

By the time the seventeenth century dawned, the Christian Church was well on the road to judgment, but in many ways medieval thought still held sway. Science had to show something of the logic of creation, philosophy had to open the doors of exploration into the nature of things, most particularly of the human mind. Finally, God had to be shown as a God of law and order, who imposed order on all things.

The groundwork was laid step by step, with the philosophy of John Locke being one of the most important steps. This essay only outlines the basic principles of his thought, and yet these are the obvious steps needed to finally break with the past and begin the embrace of the future. Each step is echoed in the Heavenly Doctrine, from the relation of church and state, to the development of the mind, to the religion of belief and obedience. Each is a key building block within the Heavenly Doctrine itself.

There are other more subliminal teachings there as well, for example, the whole concept of human responsibility in all things, the idea that people need to act in freedom, that no one can dictate morality or spirituality for others, for only things chosen in freedom can rightly be called one's own.

As the Last Judgment approached more rapidly in the decades following Locke's death, so philosophy and science raced further ahead than anyone could have imagined. The human body was studied with finer instruments and in more detail than ever before, and Swedenborg enthusiastically participated in the process. Sometimes he did his own dissections, sometimes he worked from descriptions of other men's work, but slowly, step-by-step the natural world was shown, empirically, to be a world of order. God was closer to the deist model than orthodox Christian belief. There were no miracles, only the workings of a finely created, perfectly balanced, divinely maintained machine.

The Last Judgment could take place within this environment. The carefully crafted works of the Heavenly Doctrine could peal away layer upon layer of Christian thought and theology, showing the falsity, the *unreasonableness* of each layer. As the truth was gradually exposed, so a picture emerged, in which Jesus Christ is the Messiah, the one sent by God to redeem the world. He did so, not by any vicarious atonement, but by showing people the *reasonable* path of repentance, reformation and finally regeneration. Along every step of the way, people could understand the rationale of their Messiah, of how He created in orderly ways, of how He manages creation by the immutable Laws of Providence that even He never breaks.

The primary difference between eighteen-century deism and New Church doctrine rests in the presence and activity of the Lord. His commitment to human freedom is so great that He keeps His presence hidden, which allows for naturalism. In reality He is present and active in each and every detail of all creation, constantly making sure that the structures and balances are right, that people are free to respond to Him.

The Last Judgment could have taken place in no other environment. It could not return to the direct command of the ancient Jews, nor to the mystery of Christianity. For religion to truly progress and serve the states of the human mind, it had to embrace reason on both a spiritual and natural plane.

John Locke, like a philosophical prophet, moved thought substantially in that direction. Swedenborg acknowledged his indebtedness to him, at least in the *Essay*. We see many elements of his teachings confirmed in the Heavenly Doctrine. It is no great leap of faith to maintain that he was called to play a part in preparing for the Last Judgment. ⚹

BIBLIOGRAPHY

Durant, Will and Ariel. *The Story of Civilization VIII. The Age of Louis XIV.* New York: Simon and Shuster, 1963.

Estep, William R. *Renaissance and Reformation.* Grand Rapids: William B. Eerdmans Publishing Company, 1986.

Hill, Christopher. *The Century of Revolution 1603-1714.* New York: W.W. Norton and Company Inc., 1961.

Jonsson, Inge. *Emanuel Swedenborg.* Trs. Catherine Djurklou. New York: Twane, 1971.

Locke, John. *An Essay Concerning Human Understanding.* John W. Yolton ed. London: Dent, 1961.

———. *A Letter Concerning Toleration.* Amherst, NY: Prometheus Books, 1990.

———. *The Reasonableness of Christianity, with A Discourse of Miracles and part of A Third Letter concerning Toleration.* I.T. Ramsey ed. Stanford: Stanford University Press, 1958.

Odhner, Hugo Lj. *The Human Mind, its faculties and degrees. A study of Swedenborg's Psychology.* Bryn Athyn: Swedenborg Scientific Association, 1969.

Pendleton, N.D. 1904. *The Messianic Prophecies. New Church Life,* October 1904.

Sahakian, William S. *History and Systems of Psychology.* New York: Wiley, 1975.

Swedenborg, Emanuel. *True Christian Religion.* Trans. Wm. C. Dick. London: The Swedenborg Society, 1950.

————. *Angelic Wisdom Concerning the Divine Providence.* Trans. Wm. C. Dick and E.J. Pulsford. London: The Swedenborg Society, 1949.

————. *New Jerusalem and It Heavenly Doctrine.* New York: The Swedenborg Foundation.

————. *Conjugial Love.* Trans. Chadwick. London: The Swedenborg Society.

————. *The Economy of the Animal Kingdom, considered anatomically, physically and philosophically.* Trs. Augustus Clissold. New York: the New Church Press, 1955.

Waller, Maureen. *1700. Scenes from London Life.* New York: Four Wall Eight Windows, 2000.

Yolton, John W. *Locke, an Introduction.* Oxford: Basil Blackwell Inc., 1985.

Removing Obstacles:
Why Swedenborgian Theology
Recasts Christian Concepts of the Last Judgment
and the Singularity of the Earth[1]

ALLEN J. BEDFORD

I. INTRODUCTION

The material examined in this study is the intersection of New Church teachings on the plurality of worlds and on the Last Judgment, teachings that are in opposition to beliefs held by many Christian churches. New Church doctrine holds that human life exists on planets other than planet earth, and that the Last Judgment foretold by Jesus in the Gospels was an event that took place in the spiritual rather than the natural world. These two teachings, while not connected in obvious ways, result from central New Church beliefs—that the purpose of the natural world is to populate the spiritual world (SH 6697, OP 4),[2,3] and, so that this purpose could

1. This study was supported by the Academy of the New Church research committee and was based in part on earlier work funded by the E. Bruce Glenn research fund.
2. The title *Other Planets* (OP) is different from the title given this work in other English translations. The work has been translated into English with two different titles: *Earths in the Universe* and *Worlds in Space.*
3. Citations of Swedenborg's theological works (referred to collectively as the "Writings") in this paper are given by parenthetical reference to work title followed by section (rather than page) number. The work titles used are those given the books by the Swedenborg Foundation's *New Century Edition* (NCE) project. In some cases these titles refer to works that are not yet published by the NCE effort and whose title is different from title given to the work in pub-

continue, the Lord's second coming established a new church on earth (TC 772–773).[4]

This study traces two intersection points of the Last Judgment and plurality-of-worlds teachings within the New Church canon— the theological writings of Emanuel Swedenborg (1688–1772). At the first, Swedenborg used the concept of the plurality of worlds to develop a new perspective on the Last Judgment. At the second, the Swedenborgian perspective of the Last Judgment raises questions about Swedenborgian information about life on other worlds. At both of these intersections, the only material we have to work with is what Swedenborg left us.

According to Swedenborgian theology, the Last Judgment took place in the spiritual world in 1757 (LJ 45),[5] dramatically affecting that realm while producing no obvious result in this one. If it were not for Swedenborg's accounts of the event, it is unlikely that anyone dwelling on the earth since 1757 would imagine that Jesus' predicted Last Judgment had occurred in that year.

And, although the possibility of life elsewhere in the universe has captured human imagination since the time of the Copernican revolution, if it were not for Swedenborg's narratives of his encounters with beings said to be from other planets of this solar system, it is extremely unlikely that anyone today on the earth would imagine those planets to be peopled as Swedenborg describes.

Those who accept either or both of these beliefs do so not on the basis of any physical evidence,[6] but on a trust in the veracity of

lications that are currently available. In those cases the difference is noted at the first citation. *Secrets of Heaven* (SH). Consult the "works cited" section for bibliographic information.

4. The first volume of *True Christianity* (TC) has been published in the NCE. The second volume is to be available in 2011. The title given this work in other English translations is *True Christian Religion*.

5. Swedenborg recorded that the Judgment started in the last days of 1756 (SE 5336).

6. However, there is supportive evidence through the lack of negation. There is no physical reason that human life *cannot* exist elsewhere in the universe, and the earth has not witnessed the Judgment as predicted in the Gospel accounts—the

Swedenborg's theological writings. That trust is strengthened by the reasonableness of Swedenborg's theology, especially when viewed in contrast with eighteenth-century Christian doctrines.

At the time when Swedenborg penned his theological writings (1748–1772), the Christian churches, both Catholic and Reformed, believed, as they still do today, that the Last Judgment had not yet occurred, and that it would be unmistakable when it did. Catholic and Reformed theology of that time, and mostly today also, had no provision for allowing human life elsewhere in the universe, since they saw all humans as descended from Adam and Eve, made guilty by the Fall, and redeemed by Christ's sacrifice. The presence of people on other planets would raise difficult questions about the extraterrestrials' relationship to Adam, and to Christ.

From the sixteenth through the eighteenth centuries, the earth-bound nature of Christian theology became more and more at odds with advances in human understanding of the natural world. In a Copernican universe, widely accepted in the eighteenth century, how could life be confined to the earth alone if the cosmos contained countless numbers of earth-like planets? And in the Day of Judgment, how could that entire universe, stars and peopled planets, fall to the earth? The churches reacted to these persuasive questions with a stubborn refusal to rethink their doctrine. Faith, in short, was dying.

Into this context Swedenborg introduced a new form of Christian theology, a theology that differentiated natural and spiritual substance. In this new theology the spiritual heavens are distinct from the natural universe; the spiritual and natural worlds exist at different levels of creation—the one cannot be seen from the other, and therefore the visible stars of the natural universe do not make up heaven. Unlike the purely natural substance of the physical world, God created human beings to exist in both the natural and spiritual levels, though people are mostly unaware of this while they live in the natural world. At the death of the natural body, people awaken with their spiritual bodies into the spiritual world. Those who in their natural lifetime chose in

---

sun has not darkened, nor the stars fallen, nor have people seen the Son of Man "coming on the clouds of heaven" (Matt. 24.29–30).

freedom to accept and return God's love come to live in the spiritual heavens, but *all* after death live in the spiritual world. The natural world, therefore, is not all there is to God's creation, but serves as a nursery for peopling the spiritual world.

This new theological view of the universe in many ways agreed well with the prevailing, natural view. Swedenborg's theology allowed the physical universe to be enormously large, filled with stars and planets, all obeying the laws of physics, chemistry, and biology, including those laws that allow life to exist on the earth—and therefore on other planets also. Furthermore, in this theology, in which the natural and spiritual worlds coexist, there is no need for God to end the natural world in order to create heaven. A physical end-time would be counterproductive. The expected Day of Judgment would be an event in the spiritual, rather than the natural, world, and would be required whenever good and evil became so mixed in the spiritual world that they could no longer be differentiated. This confusion of good and evil in the spiritual world could result from the church's corruption in the natural world, and, in eighteenth-century Europe, many believed that the Christian churches were corrupt.

In addition to introducing a theology that allowed human life to exist on other planets and did not require a physical end-time on earth, Swedenborg took the next step in both of these subjects. He reported that he encountered spirits from other planets while he was conscious in the spiritual world, and, even more profound for the Christian world, he reported that he witnessed the Last Judgment as it took place in the spiritual world.

The purpose of this paper is: to explore why it is important in New Church revelation to address Christian expectations about the Last Judgment and the possibility of life elsewhere in the physical universe; to reflect on why Christian expectations arose in these two areas that had, over time, proved less and less tenable; to consider the possibility of mistaken expectations among those who accept Swedenborg's works as divinely inspired; and to reflect on how a community develops trust in the New Church Word.

II. SWEDENBORG'S REVELATION
AND THE NEW CHRISTIAN AGE

Over a period of more than twenty-five years, Emanuel Swedenborg claimed to have special access to the spiritual world, seeing the heavens and the hells and talking with spirits and angels. Even more remarkable, he states that this access allowed him to serve as the means by which the Lord fulfilled his promised second coming (TC 779), and that the Lord's second coming is not in person but in a new revelation of the Word (TC 776). The new revelation is an unveiling of the Word's spiritual sense, and this unveiling brings the Lord's presence (TC 780). Swedenborg stated that he could serve this call because he was able to "receive the doctrines of this Church with his understanding, . . . [and could] publish them by the press" (TC 799). To establish the validity of that doctrine, that it was from God and not from himself, Swedenborg wrote

> I . . . testify that from the first day of my call, I have not received anything pertaining to the doctrines of that Church from any angel, but from the Lord alone while reading the Word. (TC 779)

And in his theological works, Swedenborg validates the revelation by careful citation of the Old and New Testaments and by explanation of the spiritual sense, which he shows runs continuously throughout those texts.

The point of view of this study is one of accepting Swedenborg's claim, cited above, that he was able to be present, consciously, in the spiritual world and communicate with angels and spirits, and that this spiritual consciousness was granted him by the Lord, the Creator of the universe, for the purpose of bringing about the Lord's second coming.

Those who accept Swedenborg's claims see themselves as living in a new age, or perhaps the dawning of a new age. The consummation of the Christian Church in the spiritual world has afforded the minds of human beings on earth greater freedom and the potential for enlightenment than had been possible since early in Christian history (LJ 73.2). In this post-Apocalypse world, our challenge is not to prepare ourselves for an earth-bound judgment but to search diligently for the Lord's new presence with us. We are to cooperate with him as he changes our lives and establishes, through people living the two Great Commandments, the just and peaceful society predicted by the biblical prophets. The promise of the New Church is that the Lord can be present with us in rational thought (TC 508)—that one does not have to stop thinking to remain faithful. What makes this promise possible is the clearing away of false ideas about God and religion that had accumulated since the founding of the Christian Church, and even before.

According to Swedenborgian theology, human minds exist at least partly in the spiritual world (LJ 9.1), and our minds are therefore sensitive to favorable and unfavorable conditions there. Much of the thrust of Swedenborg's theological works is to challenge Christian theology, both Catholic and Reformed, and to replace that theology with one based on the Lord's revelation given in the spiritual sense of the Word—the Old and New Testaments. Because of the way in which they clear away false ideas, both in the natural and spiritual worlds, Swedenborg's theological writings are an important agent of the Lord's second coming.

III. RESHAPING CHRISTIAN EXPECTATIONS

In the theological works *Other Planets* and *Last Judgment,* Swedenborg addressed Christian expectations concerning the singularity of the earth as the only "world" and the Last Judgment as taking place on that world. These works were published in London in 1758, a time and place where Christian expectations were facing ever increasing challenge during the Enlightenment. Christ, as Savior of the world, became a strained concept with the acceptance of the Copernican cosmos—a cosmos occupied by countless worlds. And Christ's expected second coming on this now un-singular world, raising the dead to physical life and establishing heaven on earth, became likewise subject to doubt.

By redefining what the Lord accomplished while living as a man on the earth, and by introducing the concept of degrees, levels, or planes of existence, Swedenborgian theology offered a view of Christ's first and second comings consonant with the possibility of human life on other planets and with the stability of natural law on this planet and throughout the universe. Rather than destroy faith, improvements in human understanding of the natural world and application of reason, in its best sense, can, in this new theology, inspire greater understanding of and reverence for God, so long as believers avoid the pitfalls that undermined traditional Christian theology.

Swedenborg's treatment of the Last Judgment and the plurality of worlds supporting human life in the universe are examples of how it is possible to take into account rational conclusions based on physical observations while maintaining faith in what the Lord tells us in the Word.[7] More important and remarkable, the theology of the New Church presented by Swedenborg in the Writings *requires* that the Last Judgment *not* be an event taking place in the physical world that raises the dead to a blessed existence on the earth. Instead, New Church theology *requires* that human life *not* be restricted to planet earth alone.

New Church theology establishes these requirements while holding firm to the same sacred texts that had been the basis of forming the opposite conclusions in the Jewish and Christian churches. The difference in outcome results from a difference in approach to those texts. Core to New Church theology is the belief that the Bible is written in correspondences, that its stories are woven with threads of spiritual meaning. The redemptive truth of the text is not necessarily

7. The biblical story of Abram pitching his tent between Bethel and Ai can be seen as a metaphor of our mental landscape, a place between the natural and spiritual worlds and properly under the influence of each. See "Chemical Education between Bethel and Ai" (Bedford 2004) for an analysis and application of this metaphor.

the physical events narrated but in the things to which the narration corresponds or calls to mind.

A. The Last Judgment and the Spiritual Sense of the Word

In the opening passage of the work on the Last Judgment, Swedenborg related the danger of interpreting the Bible with an eye set only upon the most obvious, physical meaning—that this causes many heresies. He stated also that these heresies can be forgiven because "no one . . . has known that in . . . each part of the Word there is a spiritual sense, or indeed, what a spiritual sense is" (LJ 1). Swedenborg then very briefly reinterpreted passages from Isaiah and Revelation that say that heaven and earth will perish and a new heaven and earth will be formed. According to Swedenborg, the passages are not referring to the visible heaven and earth; they will remain. Instead, the passages are referring to a new church that will be formed both in the spiritual heavens and on earth.

Swedenborg derived this new interpretation using the spiritual sense that had been revealed to him and that he had spent years expounding in the writing of his monumental, multi-volume work *Secrets of Heaven*,[8] an interpretation of the books of Genesis and Exodus. *Secrets of Heaven* serves in some ways as a primer to the spiritual sense of the Word. In this spiritual sense, "earth" in the Word refers to the church.

The heaven referred to in the *natural* sense of the cited biblical passages is not heaven, the spiritual realm of angels, but the starry sky above the earth. In the natural sense, the passage predicts the end of the visible cosmos without any reference at all to a realm beyond what our senses detect. In the natural sense the imagery is based upon an archaic understanding of that cosmos, a cosmos in which the stars are small enough to fall onto the earth.

In the spiritual sense, the heaven referred to in the passage *is* the spiritual realm of angels or spirits. But if this is the case, why would it pass away? Would not the realm of the blessed be permanent?

---

8. This work is not yet available in the *NCE*. The title given the English translation referred to here is *Arcana Cælestia*.

Swedenborg explained that this first heaven consisted not of angels but of spirits "from a varying religion" (LJ 2). This first heaven is not a true heaven, but a place that, like the earth, consisted of a mixture of people who had good and evil intentions, the "sheep and goats." The Last Judgment predicted by the Word, therefore, is a spiritual event that clears away this first heaven and establishes a new and pure one. The remainder of the work *Last Judgment* deals with the nature of that Judgment in the spiritual world, why it was needed, why it was delayed, how it happened, and the new state of the world and the church as a result of it. An outline of the Swedenborgian description of the Last Judgment appears in the section *Swedenborgian View of the Last Judgment* below (p. 556).

B. The Plurality of Worlds

Before publishing his work on the Last Judgment, Swedenborg wrote about his visits with people in the spiritual world who had lived on other planets. Swedenborg sought out this contact because of his own curiosity at a compelling and new question of his day: are there people on the other planets of this solar system, and if there are, whom do they worship?

The question of life on other planets—pluralism—could not be raised until people saw the planets, the "wandering" stars, as terrestrial bodies like the earth, and that was not possible until people accepted the Copernican view of the cosmos, first described in 1543.[9] Galileo's publications in 1610 and 1632 eventually led many in the seventeenth century to adopt Copernicanism. Popularization of pluralism by authors such as Fontenelle (1657–1757) in 1686 and Huygens (1629–1695) in 1698—both works going through several editions and translations through the first half of the eighteenth century—spread this intriguing idea throughout Europe and America. Christian churches of the day could not accept the idea of extraterrestrial human life because of the

---

9. For a review of the other worlds question see my "Planets and Perspectives: New Church Theology and the Plurality of Worlds Debate," and works cited therein (Bedford 2006).

complications such a reality would have for the doctrine of original sin and Christ's atonement for that sin. By the 1750s, contradictions between Christian theology and the Copernican cosmos raised significant challenges to Christian belief and led many toward deism (Crowe 1986, 37, 164).

At the time of the Lord's revelation to Swedenborg, the incompatibility between traditional Christian theology and ideas about the natural world including Copernicanism and pluralism had brought about a crisis of faith. A new revelation at that time would have to deal with these questions, and Swedenborg rose to that challenge early in his career as revelator.

Swedenborg first published his experiences with spirits from other worlds in 1753, in the sixth Latin volume of *Secrets of Heaven*, the first volume dealing with the book of Exodus. He continued publishing information about other worlds through the end of *Secrets of Heaven*, the final volume published in 1756. He then extracted the material from *Secrets of Heaven* and published it separately in 1758 as *Other Planets*. Five years before first publishing information about extraterrestrials, in an entry in his diary of spiritual experiences dated January 11, 1748, we find Swedenborg's first record of encountering information in the spiritual world about extraterrestrial life (SE 460). Within two weeks of that first encounter, Swedenborg recorded conversations with spirits from Jupiter (SE 519-518[10]).

In *Secrets of Heaven*, Swedenborg provided several reasons for his pursuing and publishing this extraordinary information. He wrote that he had a "desire to know about the inhabitants of other planets" and that the things he learned "deserve to be recorded" (SH 6695). Citing the purpose of creation—populating heaven—Swedenborg argued that people should believe that there is human life elsewhere in the universe (SH 6697) and even claimed that "Where a terrestrial body exists, so does the human being" (SH 9237). Further, Swedenborg argued that reasonable people who possess faith will conclude that the universe must have life all through it (SH 6698, 9237, 9441). These arguments

---

10. The section numbering in this part of the diary is scrambled. The sequence is 519, 520, 521, 517, 517 ½ , 518, 522.

are echoed in *Heaven and Hell*, published in 1757, in a section on the infinity of the heavens (HH 415–420).

If from this logic people conclude that there must be inhabitants on other worlds, then they must also wonder about the relationship these inhabitants have with God. The central theme of the material Swedenborg published about life on other planets deals with that subject (SH 6700, 7477, 8543, 8547, 8949, 9694). In particular, Swedenborg's conversations and experience with spirits from other worlds establish for him that the Lord Jesus Christ is the God of the entire universe and that he is seen throughout the universe in human form (SH 7173, 7252, 8541, 8949, 9359, 9694, 9971, 10159, 10377, 10737). Looking back at what he published in *Secrets of Heaven* and *Other Planets,* Swedenborg wrote that the information about other worlds was revealed to show that the Lord is recognized everywhere as the God of heaven (HH 417).

C. The Written Word on Earth

But if the Lord is the God of the entire universe, why would he be born into this particular world? Swedenborg provides a surprising answer. The Lord was born on this planet because this planet alone has writing, and therefore this planet alone has the written Word. The Word in written form can be preserved and passed down to all future generations, spread over the entire globe, and even carried into the spiritual world and to all those from the entire universe who are there (SH 9350–9356). The importance of the Word is that it "constitutes a union of heaven and the world" (SH 9357) because it

> teaches people about the existence of God, of heaven and of hell, and of life after death, and above all teaches them how they must live and believe in order to enter heaven and so be happy for evermore. (SH 9352)

The Word has an essential function because it is the means by which humans can come to know why they exist and what their Creator asks of and does for them. The "first and most essential truth for the sake of which the Word exists" is to teach that God is in human form and even was born in that form on the earth (SH 9355).

In addition to the earth's having a special role in all the universe in that it has writing and therefore the written Word, people on and from the earth are also the outermost part of the "Grand Man," the form in which the Lord sees all people in the entire creation (SH 9360). By being born on the earth and uniting his human nature with his Divine nature, the Lord joined the innermost with the outermost form of creation and therefore encompassed all of it, and "became the Redeemer forever" (TC 127).

According to Swedenborgian theology, the Lord's birth on earth does not need to be repeated elsewhere. In this view, the earth holds a unique role not as the geographical center of the entire universe but because it is home to those who developed writing and who focus on the external aspect of creation. Because of these traits, the Lord's advent on earth bridged the entire gap from the Lord himself to the most distant or external part of his creation, and, because the world on which he was born could record that event, the news of it spread to all lands and even to the spiritual world.

Swedenborgian embrace of the plurality-of-worlds idea is deep and complex, resulting in and from many key theological ideas such as:

1) The Lord Jesus Christ is the universal Supreme Being (OP 65)
2) The purpose of creation is a heaven from the human race (DP 27)
3) We are not condemned by Adam's sin, but by our own choices (DP 83)
4) The Lord's mission on earth was not to serve as a sacrifice to appease the Father's anger (TC 114)
5) The laws of salvation are the same throughout the universe (DP 325)
6) The physical and spiritual worlds are discrete degrees apart (DLW 184). The physical heavens, the stars and planets, are not the same as the spiritual heavens.

7) The Word has an internal sense (SH 1–5). The first chapters
of Genesis are not to be taken as a literal history of the world's
creation, nor do they describe the physical nature of the cosmos.

This last point, that the Word has an internal sense, is the
fundamental, constructive element of New Church theology. By
turning to the spiritual and internal sense of the Word, Swedenborg
was able to address misshapen Christian and Jewish expectations,
stripping away interpretations that return us to our self-centered
nature, and establishing a new set of beliefs and expectations that
return us to God.

D. The Internal Sense of the Word

The opening sentence of *Secrets of Heaven,* the first published book
of New Church revelation, reads: "The Word of the Old Testament
contains heavenly secrets, with every single detail focusing on the
Lord" (1). The conclusion of the second paragraph of that work
provides a criterion that defines the true Word: "Any expression in the
Word that fails to embody [the Lord] within itself, or does not in its
own way go back to Him, is not Divine" (2). And the third paragraph
connects the status of the Word with the status of human beings:

> Without such life [from the Lord] the Word as regards the letter is dead, for
> it is the same with the Word as it is with man, who . . . is internal as well as
> external. The external man if parted from the internal man is just a body and
> therefore dead. It is the internal man which lives and imparts life to the external.
> The internal man is the soul of the external man. The same applies to the Word
> which as to the letter alone is like the body without a soul. (3)

Swedenborg's theology is built, piece by piece, by linking the
internal spirit of the Word to its external letter. This reconnection *is*
the revelation for the New Church. In the concluding paragraph of his
introduction to the entire theology, Swedenborg wrote that no one can
possibly know about the internal sense of the Word unless it is revealed
by the Lord. Swedenborg then stated that by the Lord's Divine mercy

he had been able to "share the experiences of spirits and angels" and, the reader can infer, through this experience saw the Word as the angels saw it (SH 5).

As stated in the previous section, the essential function of the Word is to reveal to humans why they exist and what their Creator asks of and does for them. One can see an example of this in the opening story of Genesis. In the literal sense the story describes the formation of the heavens and the earth with its living forms. It is a compelling piece of Hebrew metaphor, of God hovering and speaking creation into existence. The physical imagery, if taken literally, describes a cosmos quite different from our contemporary concept. The physical nature of the creation outlined in this story does nothing to show readers what they are to do with their existence. But the internal sense of this story, familiar within the New Church, is about our regeneration—how we can respond to the Lord positively and allow ourselves to be reformed. The internal sense points directly to our Creator and our relationship with him.

Going to the text to find out how the world was formed misses the point. Why would the Word tell us about the mechanics of earthly construction? But if we go to the story looking for what it tells us about ourselves, we are likely to find something useful. In addition to the grand sweep of the internal meaning of the story—regeneration and reformation—we can see the narrative as an allegory about our own physical and mental development. For example, the advent of light into what was just emptiness could refer to the spark of life coming into natural material. The vault separating the waters above from the waters below can be the space made for us in the waters of our mother's womb. The dry land appearing could be the formation and birth of our body. The stars, sun, and moon can be driving loves and distant ideas that motivate and guide us. The fish and birds could be developing thoughts borrowed from others that swim around and fly over us. The emergence of animals on the land could be loves and ideas that we make our own, that rest on us. And the creation of humans could be us at an age and development in which we are in possession of ourselves. Seeing the story as an allegory about our physical and mental development, and in correspondence with what the Lord is calling us to do, seems much more applicable and convincing than seeing the story as a description of the earth's creation.

Who is the Lord, and what does the Lord want from me? Those are the kinds of questions that we should bring to the Word. In the treatment of the plurality of worlds, Swedenborg shows us that we on earth are one among many worlds that participate in God's purpose for creation. Swedenborg also shows how it is possible that the Lord, the God of the entire universe, could choose to come in person on this earth. The main reason given—that it was for the sake of the Word— is in line with the very center of New Church theology.

And we may wonder if it is true that our world is really the only one in the entire universe that has writing, or is focused especially on what is external. At present, I find it enough to conclude that humans on earth fit that description, but that the earth may in fact be one among several planets that do. Does it matter in the way that I respond to God whether or not planet earth really is unique in those characteristics? In the work *Last Judgment* there is an implication that the earth may indeed not be unique. Swedenborg wrote that should the human race on the earth die out entirely the human race in the natural world will continue elsewhere, "for there are some hundreds of thousands of earths in the universe" (LJ 10). If the earth is unique in having writing, and if writing serves an important, divine purpose, then that function and quality would have to be present or transferred elsewhere if human life on earth should come to an end. This leaves open the possibility that we on earth share with other planets the role of being creation's outward covering.

But what is most important about what is said about why the Lord came on earth is not whether or not the earth is unique. What is most important is what that explanation says about the Lord's and our nature, and how the Lord's presence is connected to the Word.

E. The Last Judgment and the Plurality of Worlds

In at least two important ways, Swedenborg's view of the plurality of worlds informs his view of the Last Judgment. The first relates to accepting Copernicanism and pluralism. In a Copernican universe the stars and planets cannot fall to the earth. And further, if there are people on other planets, why should a judgment of our earth require the destruction of theirs? The second is more subtle. Because there are people on other planets, the Lord's purpose in creation is not ended by the failure of a particular earth. In fact, it is against the Divine plan to destroy the natural world. Human life on earth may end, but human life in the universe will go on.

IV. SWEDENBORGIAN VIEW OF THE LAST JUDGMENT

What was the Last Judgment? Why was it spiritual and not natural? Who was judged? Why did it occur in 1757, and why did the Christian Church not notice it? What are the results of the Last Judgment, and why was the event revealed to Swedenborg? In his works *Last Judgment* and *Continuation Concerning the Last Judgment*,[11] Swedenborg addressed these questions. Because it is the primary material of this study, it is important to outline what Swedenborg presented to his readers about the Last Judgment. I do so here with minimal commentary and with a focus on those parts that are relevant to this study. Others have provided comprehensive study of the topic.[12]

---

11. The short title for the work *Continuation concerning the Last Judgment* used in the NCE is *Supplements* (SPL)

12. See for example Michael Hogan's "The Last Judgment and New Church Scholarship: Some Implications for the Future" (2005), and Hugo Lj. Odhner's *The Spiritual World* (1968).

A. The Last Judgment was a Limited, Spiritual Event

Swedenborg opened his book on the Last Judgment with this heading: "The Day of the Last Judgment does not mean the Destruction of the World" (LJ 1). Referring the reader to the spiritual sense of the Word, he raised our minds to consider the spiritual rather than the natural world. In the subsection above: *The Last Judgment and the Spiritual Sense of the Word* (p. 548), we noted that Swedenborg showed that the destruction of the heaven and the earth mentioned in the Bible referred to false heavens in the spiritual world and to the church, both on earth and in the spiritual world. The new heaven and earth mentioned in the Word referred to the establishment of a new church on earth and in heaven.

The Last Judgment was a judgment on the false heavens in the spiritual world that had formed since the beginning of the Christian Church, and contained spirits of a mixture of states and motives, some heavenly and some hellish (LJ 2). False heavens were gatherings of spirits who were outwardly in order but inwardly in disorder. They built for themselves places that seemed like heaven, and these places were often on mountains (SPL 9, 20, LJ 69). The Last Judgment destroyed these false heavens. For example, Swedenborg reported seeing their mountains overturned and cast into the sea (LJ 61).

Destruction of the natural world would have limited the Lord's purpose in creation, and in that limitation the "infinite would perish" (LJ 13). The natural world serves as a foundation for heaven, and so destruction of the natural world would destroy heaven also (LJ 2). No angels or devils were created in heaven or hell but came to those places after living as people on earth (LJ 14). Therefore, the only way to build the heavens is through continuing human reproduction in the physical world. Furthermore, birth in the physical world is necessary because in order to be human we must have both a natural body and a spiritual mind—we are connected to both the natural and the spiritual worlds (LJ 9.1). Since the spiritual and natural worlds cannot exist apart from each other it is against reason that the natural world should be destroyed (SPL 9.3).

Because the Last Judgment is a judgment of spiritual character, it cannot take place until the spiritual character is unveiled, which happens when people enter the spiritual world. The natural part of us "is not guilty of any blame or accusation because it does not live from itself, being only the agent . . . through which the spiritual man acts" (LJ 30). The proper time and place for the judgment, therefore, is in the spiritual world where people from many ages are together and their interior natures expressed (LJ 28, SPL 5).

The Last Judgment was limited in several ways. It was a spiritual rather than a natural event; it affected only those who were confused about good and evil rather than already committed to one or the other (LJ 49, 59); and it applied only to those from this planet and whose lives on this earth were in the Christian era (LJ 46, 67). Two previous "last judgments" had occurred on spirits from this planet, one on the ancients represented by the flood, and one at the Lord's advent (LJ 46).[13]

In addition to these communal "last judgments," we each face a "last judgment" after we enter the spiritual world.

Given the limitations of the Last Judgment that occurred in 1757, we should be cautious with our terminology. When we speak of "the Last Judgment" our words imply a singular event, but, according to Swedenborg, the judgment of 1757 was one of several and may not be the last. Judgments made upon spirits from other planets also occur (SH 10810).

B. Conditions Requiring a Judgment

Judgments occur when disorder in the spiritual world extends to such an extent that communication between heaven and the earth is lost (SPL 8). This happens when evil and falsity in the false heavens cloud thought in the spiritual world, which then clouds thought on earth also

---

13. In the first Latin volume of *Secrets of Heaven*, published nine years before *Last Judgment*, Swedenborg provided a list of four rather than two "last judgments" (1850.2–3). The two additional judgments were between the flood and the Lord's advent.

(SPL 11). The disorder results from a loss of charity in a church, and the loss of charity removes faith also. A church comes to its end when it no longer has any faith and charity (LJ 33).

When a church ends there must be a judgment, because human freedom on earth depends on an equilibrium in the spiritual world between heaven and hell. The church serves to counter the forces of hell, and so when the church is no longer there, equilibrium and freedom are lost (LJ 33). A judgment clears the way for a new church to be established that will restore spiritual equilibrium and open communication again between heaven and earth.

Although the Last Judgment did not occur until 1757, the Christian churches had been, according to Swedenborg, in decline for a long time before that. What delayed the Judgment was the semblance of order among church leaders, and through that order the Christian churches were able to lead many people to heaven. So long as outward behavior remained orderly, corruption within could be tolerated (LJ 59). The Lord could preserve false heavens so long as people in those false heavens preserved at least outward order (LJ 59).

Another reason for delaying the Last Judgment was that the false heavens were connected with the lowest parts of the true heavens because they were outwardly similar. If the false heavens were carried away before the outward similarities were broken, the lowest heaven "would have suffered" (LJ 70).

C. How was the Judgment Accomplished?

The key to bringing about a judgment is to make spirits' interior motivations visible. This took place in steps that involved bringing the higher heavens closer to the lower and false ones, and in visitations by angels in which, like the biblical prophets, they warned of the coming destruction. As heaven drew closer, the interior nature of the spirits became more obvious and infighting began. Many then rejected "the Lord, the Word, faith, and the Church" and they began acting from their interior motivations. When this happened, their palaces and other splendors were destroyed (SPL 23–26).

D. What are the Results of the Last Judgment?

In the spiritual world the Last Judgment cleared away the darkness that had been intensifying there, and this new light in the spiritual world also brought new enlightenment to people on earth (SPL 30). But Swedenborg predicted that the Last Judgment would bring about no obvious, outward changes in the world (LJ 73). The church on earth, however, would change. It would remain similar in outward appearance but its inner nature would be new (LJ 73).

Because spiritual freedom would be restored on earth, there would be greater freedom of thought in spiritual matters. However, Swedenborg lamented, people on earth would not notice this change since they do not "reflect upon it at all nor . . . know anything about spiritual freedom, nor about influx" (LJ 73.2).

One result of the Last Judgment was that it enabled formation of a new church on earth through unveiling the spiritual sense of the Word. Revelation of this before the Last Judgment would have failed to bring people into order because "in his former state, man would not have understood these truths, and if he had understood, he would have profaned them" (LJ 73.2). The situation changed after the Last Judgment:

> After communication has been restored by a last judgment, man can be enlightened and reformed, that is, he can understand the Divine truth of the Word; understanding it, he can receive it, and receiving it, he can retain it, *for intervening obstacles have been removed*. (SPL 12; emphasis added.)

Heaven and the Church depend on three essentials: the Lord's divinity, the Word, and charity (SPL 88). The Last Judgment restored enlightenment in the spiritual world and on earth, and this made possible a commitment in both places to these three essentials.

E. Why Was the Last Judgment Revealed on Earth?

False ideas about the Last Judgment damage faith and cause some to reject the Word (LJ 15). Even among the faithful, the inability to understand some part of the Word may lead to its rejection, and since the Apocalypse deals with the Last Judgment, that book in particular could be lost if not properly understood (LJ 42, 60).

Because the Last Judgment was a spiritual event, people on earth would have no way of knowing about it if it were not revealed. In this state of ignorance, people on earth would be waiting perpetually for something to happen on earth that had already happened in the spiritual world (LJ 45).

F. Why does the Christian Church Expect an Earth-Bound Last Judgment?

Because the Church was unaware of the levels or degrees of creation, people did not realize that eternal, spiritual life takes place out of sight of the natural world (DLW 173–174, 188). They also did not realize that the spiritual and natural worlds depend on each other and that therefore the natural world and human reproduction must continue (LJ 6).

The Church also held false beliefs about the soul, thinking of it as a puff of wind rather than a spiritual body. Puffs of wind cannot be judged, and so people thought that the soul would have to return the body for judgment to happen (SPL 3). With a proper understanding of the soul as spiritual body, with all the senses and abilities of a natural body, people can conclude that the Last Judgment would be a spiritual event where all are gathered together and where people's spiritual nature is apparent (SPL 3, LJ 28, 30).

The reason why people held false ideas about the soul and the Last Judgment was that their thought was too much confined to the natural world (LJ 15.5). Educated thinkers saw humans as nothing more than speaking animals (SPL 33), and the church understood the Word in its literal sense and did so without illustrating or explaining the sense of the letter by using "genuine doctrine derived from the Word" (LJ 14). What was lacking was a belief in life after death.

Swedenborg wrote that people could have found evidence for life after death in the Bible. He noted that Bible stories depict people seeing angels and even the Lord after his resurrection. The angels and the Lord were not puffs of wind but were in human form and could speak and even eat with them (SPL 34). Because of misunderstanding some passages in the Word, the church thought of angels and devils as being created from eternity in heaven or hell rather than having once lived as people on earth (LJ 14).

In summary, it is not surprising that the Christian Church did not recognize the Last Judgment. The church's lack of information about the Lord's purpose in creation, the necessity of having spiritual and natural worlds, the fact that these worlds must be separated by level of creation and be invisible to each other, and that the soul is a spiritual body rather than a disembodied puff of air, made it impossible to think of the Last Judgment as a spiritual event that could take place without involving any physical change on the earth.

As Swedenborg pointed out, information was available in the Word that could have indicated that their thinking about the nature of spiritual life was out of order. Information about the natural world also provided evidence that their picture of reality was askew. But, apparently, the thinking in the church had become so solidified that only a judgment and revelation could free it (LJ 40, 56, 60). What brought the church to this dark state?

For most in the Christian Church, the mistaken expectations they held about the Last Judgment resulted from what they were taught, and what they were taught was at least partially useful. The expectation of an earth-bound judgment prompted people to be mindful of their behavior, knowing that they would eventually be judged by their Creator. Since they could not picture judgment in the spiritual world, picturing it on earth was a workable substitute.

For Christian Church leadership, this situation may have been different. Their vision of what the Last Judgment would be like was one that increased their power. As information about the natural world accumulated that was opposed to the Church's world view, the Church leadership responded by resisting that new information rather than by using it to question their own assumptions. One motivation for maintaining the status quo was that it served them. Another is the higher motive of holding to faith in spite of intellectual confusion. Swedenborg's witness of the spiritual world indicates that craving for power had much to do with the falsity that clouded the Christian Church and blinded it from seeing the Lord's purpose and presence.

V. EXPECTATIONS FOR THE NEW CHRISTIAN WORD

Jewish and Christian church history suggests that it is possible for an established church to miss entirely the Lord's presence. Unless Swedenborgians attend to the lessons of that history, we are likely to repeat it. What expectations about their revelation did the previous two churches hold that prevented them from seeing the Lord in the Advent or in the Parousia? What expectations about the revelation through Swedenborg might lead to similar blindness? What sort of relationship with sacred text should we nurture?

A. Empowerment of Local Expectations

Many Jews could not accept Jesus or the Christian revelation because they were expecting a Messiah devoted to their wellbeing above all others. Jewish leaders rejected Jesus on the grounds that he came from Galilee, that he did not obey all of their laws of purity or Sabbath observance, and that he ministered to gentiles. The people rejected him because he took no steps to overthrow the Roman occupation and establish a new and all-powerful Jewish state. Both the leaders and the people could justify their rejection based on sacred text.

For similar reasons, many Christians were unable to perceive the Lord's second coming and the Last Judgment. Like the Jews before them, Christians thought that the Lord put them in a special position that would give them power over all the world. At the Last Judgment Christ would wipe out all those who did not accept Christian doctrine and authority. The possibility of world domination is tempting, tempting enough to blind many eyes to other ways of interpreting the Lord's purpose and presence. And as the Jewish Church before them,

Christians could point to their sacred texts to reject any notion that the judgment could be a spiritual rather than a natural event.

Given how self-focus has shaped expectations of many in the Judeo-Christian culture, it is possible that Swedenborgians might develop expectations of the New Christian Word that lead implicitly to empowerment of their clan rather than openness towards much wider possibilities. A belief that this new Word carries no appearances of truth but is actually true in every respect, with no need of interpretation, may be an example of this tendency. If the Swedenborgian Church did possess such a flawless revelation, then its congregations would command insurmountable power over all other people because they would possess the unambiguous Truth while all others would have something less than that. As God did not give that sort of power to the Jewish or Christian Churches, it is likely that God has not vested it in the New Church either, and so we are probably mistaken if we seek to gain that sort of power from the Word.

We might ask ourselves what are we looking for when we open our sacred texts? What power do we give the text?

B. Authority of Sacred Texts

Sacred texts must have authority to be effective. It is necessary that readers be willing to change in response to the text rather than change the text in response to self. When we accept a text as having Divine authorship, and therefore Divine authority, we treat that text carefully and are slow to question its meaning. This is a respectful and commendable position, but this approach taken too far can also stagnate thought, leaving us unchanged by our encounters with the text because we are not grappling with it. Indeed, learning to question the text appropriately, to enter into dialogue, can enhance the text's authority because in that dynamic, engaging relationship we open ourselves to the life that the Writings tell us lies within the text (SH 3). Rather than any logical proofs or arguments urging that the Writings are the Word, it is this tug, the spark of life transferred when we are open, which brings us that assurance.

A challenge for Swedenborgians today is to chart a relationship with the New Church Word. This is a task of tremendous proportion. On the other hand, it is as easy as reading with a humble spirit. Many New Church scholars have worked to describe the new Word.

One very recent contribution is Bishop Alfred Acton's study on New Church paradigms (2007), in which he offers a set of assumptions about the nature of the Writings and then discusses several consequences of those assumptions. Acton's description highlights issues regarding the authority of the Writings.

Acton's assumptions about the nature of revelation and the Writings are:

1) "The Writings are the Word of God and have Divine authorship" (172)
2) The Writings have a literal sense
3) The Writings reveal the internal sense of the Bible and add new doctrine
4) The Old Testament, New Testament, and the Writings all have a spiritual sense—the sense the angels see
5) Written revelation is finite and therefore limited (Acton, 2007, 172–176)

Acton also describes six categories of finite limits to revelation:

1) The mechanics of writing—what is necessary to record and copy revelation (268)
2) Language[14] (271)
3) The revelator's mind (275)
4) The culture and context of the time when the revelation was given (306)
5) "The limits of angel's knowledge" (312)
6) The nature of the way Lord appears in the Word (313)

---

14. For an analysis of this topic see Kristin King's insightful "The Power and Limitations of Language in Swedenborg, Shakespeare, and Frost" (1999).

Acton concludes that because of the necessary limitations imposed on revelation, the Writings contain fallacies (176). That the Writings contain fallacies is a problem only if we "confuse a fallacy with a spiritual reality" for when we do that "we turn the fallacy into falsity" (177). Acton's assumptions, categories of limitations, and his conclusion all strike me as a reasonable and helpful way to consider what the Writings are and are not.

1. Fallacy and Genuine Truth in the Writings. The General Church[15] has had a tendency to deny that the Writings are fallible because the church sees the Writings as a rational, rather than an allegorical or symbolic, revelation. And, because the revelation took place relatively recently and because Swedenborg possessed extraordinary knowledge of the natural world, difficulties resulting from the limitations of Swedenborg's mind, time, and background are remarkably few, and represent a vast improvement over the contradictions between biblical descriptions of physical reality, and contemporary, scientific descriptions of reality. To a large extent, the Writings appear flawless. However, there are glaring exceptions. Perhaps the most dramatic are Swedenborg's predictions about life on other planets in this solar system, but if one searches for them one can find at least trivial problems throughout.

The way to avoid turning a fallacy into a falsity, Acton argues, is to "make a right comparison of passages to unfold the doctrine of genuine truth" (315), and another New Church scholar, the Reverend Grant Odhner, recently published a study on that subject.

In his "Responding to the Lord's Word," Odhner builds a compelling and beautiful case for seeing the Writings as the Word, which, like the Old and New Testaments, have both veiled and unveiled truths. The function of the Writings, he shows, is to reveal genuine truth (2007, 130). Genuine truths are teachings that are vital for salvation: the essentials of faith, such as the Two Great Commandments (SH 2225). In a collection of passages (e.g. SH 2225, 3440, 9034.2, 10400.3–40)

---

15. The General Church of the New Jerusalem is one of a handful of church organizations worldwide that accepts Swedenborg's theological works as Divinely inspired.

Odhner shows that genuine truths are what the internal and spiritual senses teach, and are apparent in the literal sense (226–228). Readers of the Writings, he concludes, must search out these plain truths in the Writings in the same way that we are taught in the Writings to look for them in the Word (229, 232).

Acton's and Odhner's analyses are invitations to explore and build our own relationship with the Writings, a relationship that is sensitive to the topography, the landscape, of the Writings. In becoming sensitive to that landscape, we are giving the text the authority and power to shape our minds, and, applied to our lives, our hearts also.

2. Sacred Text and its Community. Phyllis Bird, professor of Old Testament Interpretation at Garrett-Evangelical Theological Seminary, has written a powerful analysis of biblical authority for the *New Interpreter's Bible*. In it she argues that the authority of the Bible is not something established by fiat, but develops over time and "involves an element of trust and trustworthiness" in relationship with a community (1994, 36). Theological debate and diversity are natural and necessary expressions of a community engaging with its sacred texts and indicate that the community holds the text in authority (43, 63).

Interestingly, Bird sees community dialog as essential to developing and responding to biblical authority. She writes that "the church is obligated by the form of its Scriptures to listen for the voice of God in the dialog of a community," both the community in the text and the community of readers (63). For her, the community who generated and received the Scriptures is integral to the meaning of those Scriptures.

3. The Writings and their Community. The development of the Old and New Testament Scriptures was very different from the development of the Writings. The Scriptures won their status over time as they addressed a community's spiritual needs. The text itself was shaped and reshaped by community, changing, albeit carefully, in response to changes in the community's circumstances. The books of the Bible we have today result from the work of many human minds working through more than a thousand years, and writing for communities in various circumstances. After original authorship, these texts went through untold layers of manipulation, recombination, redaction, and addition. The Writings do not share that history. They result from the work of one man writing almost entirely in isolation and over a period of about twenty five years. And in the intervening years between their authorship and today, the community has accepted almost none of the manipulations that trimmed and sequenced the Scriptures. The Writings offer a very large set of, as it were, primary data that unravel the internal sense of the Scriptures and, as Acton and Odhner show, bring forth new doctrine.

If Bird's analysis is correct, the Writings gain authority in our lives as we engage with them as Odhner and Acton ask us to do: by setting "particular ideas in a larger framework" (Odhner 2007, 233); by making "a right comparison of passages to unfold the doctrine of genuine truth" (Acton 2007, 315); and by the resulting community dialog.

Because of the way in which the Writings came to us, there is no mechanism for the sort of manipulation that shaped the Scriptures. However, there is room for sorting the books and manuscripts into categories, for example by publication status, intended audience, subject matter, and developmental context. The Reverends Jonathan Rose, George Dole, and Frank Rose each contributed essays along these lines in the Swedenborg Foundation's *New Century Edition* essay volume on Swedenborg (2005). In our studies of Swedenborg's writings it is important not to lump all the works into one bin because when we do that we are ignoring basic contextual information such as noting that some were written before and some after the Last Judgment, that some were carried to publication and some abandoned, that some were written for theologians and others for philosophers. Awareness of context and audience is necessary also for us to hear the way the Writings engage readers. As Bird argues, we are to "listen for the voice of God in the dialog of the community." Each work of the Writings has an immediate community it is addressing. We need to know that community and its concerns to better hear what the Lord is saying because part of what the Word is, is God's response to a community's questions and concerns.

When we read *Other Planets* and *Last Judgment,* we should know that Swedenborg wrote these works for a community that did not know about spiritual and natural levels of creation, that expected a judgment on earth and therefore could not understand how there could be life on other planets, and that was wrestling with the new ideas that there could be life on other planets. It was a community struggling with the tug of naturalism and deism and the Enlightenment's critique of Christianity. The works were written for readers living in an age whose scientific reasoning had turned the cosmos inside out. In large part, both *Other Planets* and *Last Judgment* address and correct Christian expectations. If it were not for a community having those expectations, the works would not have been written.

Since the community of readers within the church today does not hold those same expectations or experience, there is a level of disconnect between the text and its community that we should ponder. The texts were relevant at the time they were written, and are relevant to Swedenborgians today. But what makes them relevant in those two eras is different.

A validation of the text's authority would be to show how over time the text addresses communities' concerns. In order for the text to be relevant in evolving community contexts, what the community gets from the text must be capable of evolving also. Do the Writings have an inherent flexibility or were the doctrines fixed as soon as they left Swedenborg's pen?

C. Topical Development in the Writings

We can consider evolutionary capacity in the Writings in two ways. One would be to examine how the Writings address concerns of various communities separated by time or culture. Another would be to look within the Writings themselves to see if doctrines and other information there develop over time. This analysis is possible because Swedenborg wrote his theological works over an extended period and often treated the same topic in various books. Here, we consider developments in Swedenborg's treatment of the plurality of worlds and the Last Judgment.

1. *Developments in Describing and Addressing the Last Judgment.* Swedenborg's two main publications on the Last Judgment were *Last Judgment,* published in 1758, and *Continuation concerning the Last Judgment* (called *Supplements* by the NCE), published in 1763. Both works open with an explanation of why people expect a judgment that will destroy the earth. The explanation given in the first work centers on people's lack of knowledge about the spiritual sense of the Word (LJ 1). The subsequent work repeats this central reason and expands upon it, emphasizing that people have a mistaken view of the soul, thinking it just a puff of air (SPL 3). Since people cannot imagine how a judgment can take place on a puff of air, they conclude that the soul must reenter the body in order to be judged. Swedenborg's argument develops from being impersonal—spiritual judgment must take place in the spiritual world—to addressing the reader very directly—you will rise in the spiritual world with a spiritual body, more real and solid than your natural body, and you will be judged.

Swedenborg also wrote about the state of the world and the church before and after the Last Judgment. The 1758 work predicts that people's thinking will be freer as a result of the judgment "because spiritual freedom has been restored" (LJ 73). The 1763 work goes further, saying that before the Last Judgment communication between heaven and hell was nearly entirely cut off, and that afterwards communication was restored (SPL 8). "This is why," Swedenborg reports, "after the last judgment, and not before, revelations for the New Church have been made" (SPL 12). In the 1758 publication Swedenborg did not write anything about *communication* between heaven and the earth,[16]

---

16. Though the 1758 work does not describe any communication between the spiritual and natural worlds, it does describe connections between the two, stating that people in the natural world cannot exist apart from angels in the spiritual world, and that angels cannot exist apart from people in the natural world (LJ 9).

although the last paragraph of that work relates from angels' testimony "that interior Divine truths are at this day being revealed" among a "nation set asunder from the Christian world" (LJ 74). Both works predict that thought, particularly in spiritual matters, will be liberated by the Last Judgment, but the later work again takes a more personal tone than the former work, the 1763 publication inviting the reader to open him or herself to communication, in some sense, with heaven.

In *True Christianity*, his last major theological publication, Swedenborg relied on the descriptions he provided in *Last Judgment* to make a point about why the Lord had to be born into the natural world in order to save us. In making this point, which has to do with reordering the heavens and hells, he wrote that he could not describe this before "because the restructuring of the heavens and the hells has been going on since the day of the Last Judgment until the present time and is still going on" (TC 123). The "present time" was 1771, fourteen years after the Last Judgment. More than a decade after the Last Judgment the structure of the spiritual world was still fluid. We should bear this in mind when we read Swedenborg's descriptions of places he visited in the spiritual world, both before and after the Last Judgment.

In this passage from *True Christianity* Swedenborg directs the reader to his 1758 work on the Judgment to get an idea of what a judgment does in the spiritual world. The passage is noteworthy for several reasons. It is an example of how Swedenborg restricted himself to describing only those things for which he had evidence, and, what is unusual, the tone of the passage carries some of Swedenborg's frustration at people's lack of awareness:

> No one knows the situation [of how hell was attacking the world of spirits] at the time of the *First* Coming, because it has not been revealed in the literal sense of the Word. I have been allowed to see with my own eyes the situation at the time of the Lord's *Second* Coming. One can draw conclusions about the earlier situation from that. I described this situation in the little work *Last Judgment*, published in London in 1758. . . . My eyewitness accounts appear in that little work, but copying them here would be a pointless exercise because it is in print and there are still many copies available at the printer's in London. (123)

In addition to acknowledging Swedenborg's situation as a witness to an event of immeasurable importance that no one else seemed to notice, the passage also shows that Swedenborg was satisfied with the details of the judgment given in the 1758 book, even though the reordering of the spiritual world was still going on.

The examples given above of augmenting his 1758 arguments in 1763 to include a more personal dimension for his readers, considering the nature of the soul and the possibility of communication between heaven and hell, suggest that Swedenborg's understanding of the Last Judgment and its consequences grew as he witnessed its effects over several years. But in 1771 he also referred to specific information published more than a decade earlier and so must have been satisfied with those details even after the benefit of developments in the spiritual world and in his understanding.

That the Last Judgment remained an important topic after 1758 is clear because references to it occur throughout the published theological works. Five works contain at least 20 numbered paragraphs on the topic: *Secrets of Heaven* (1749–1756), *Last Judgment* (1758), *Continuation Concerning the Last Judgment* (1763), *Apocalypse Revealed* (1766), and *True Christianity* (1771).

2. *Developments in Describing and Addressing Pluralism.* The development of the topic of extraterrestrial life in the published works is remarkably different from the continuing attention that the topic of the Last Judgment receives. Pluralism enjoys much attention early in these works, appearing in at least 350 paragraphs of *Secrets of Heaven* and of course in the entire work *Other Planets*, for a total of at least 528 numbered paragraphs. But the topic hardly appears at all in other works published in 1758 or later, and none of the references to this topic in later books provide any information about where the spirits are from or how they live. See Table 1 for details.

Table 1. Occurrence of Pluralism in the Published Writings

Book	Publication Year(s)	Number of Paragraphs	Treatment
Secrets of Heaven	1749-1753	313	Detailed accounts of extraterrestrial life
Other Planets	1758	178	Repeat of material in *Secrets of Heaven*
Heaven and Hell	1758	6	415–420: Immensity of the heavens
Last Judgment	1758	5	10, 13, 26, 46, 67: General information that there is life elsewhere
The Lord	1763	1	Preface lists *Other Planets* as among books published
Marriage Love	1768	1	532: Pluralism listed as a revelation for the New Church
True Christianity	1771	4	32: Refers to *Other Planets* 64: Illusion of time and space illustrated 769: Some think that after death they go to another planet 846: Parallel to *Marriage Love* 532

3. *Source Material for* OTHER PLANETS *and* LAST JUDGMENT. Swedenborg
kept a private diary of his experiences in the Spiritual World, published
posthumously as *Spiritual Experiences*. Swedenborg made entries in
this diary (actually a collection of diaries) from 1745 to 1765, with most
of the material written from 1747 to 1749, and relatively few entries
after 1758. Enough dates occur in the text to place experiences in time.

Many of the experiences described in the published works appear
first in the diary. Because of this, Swedenborg's diary allows us to
trace many of his reports in published works back to the time he had

that experience. We can see also how much time he spent dealing with a particular subject. Using this process to examine Swedenborg's witness of the plurality of worlds and of the Last Judgment reveals a substantially different time frame for these two topics, even though the two published works on these topics appeared in the same year.

As noted in the subsection: *The Plurality of Worlds* (p. 556), Swedenborg's first mention of spirits from other planets is in an entry dated January 11, 1748, and is under the heading, "About the adroitness of spirits in making up things that appear to be true" (SE 460):

> From one experience today, I was able to realize how spirits can counterfeit the truth, and thus play with human minds. The case in point was their depiction of the inhabitants of Saturn, whom they claim to be little people, for the most part small in stature but still good in character. They say they meditate more than they speak, that they live in a cold climate, that they cast out from their midst those who are evil . . . that they worship God the Creator of the universe, and similar concoctions having the appearance of truth.
>
> However, I was able to deduce from these things that the inhabitants of that planet, though they did not know Christ Jesus, must nevertheless have been taught by some Divine Word, so as to have a knowledge of Him. (SE 460)

When Swedenborg wrote this he had not yet had the experiences with the spirits from Jupiter that demonstrated to him that the Lord Jesus Christ is the God of all creation, a realization that caused Swedenborg to adopt the name "the Lord" for God.[17]

When Swedenborg published information about the spirits and inhabitants of Saturn in *Secrets of Heaven* some six years later, he reported that they are small in stature and are upright (SE 8948), that they worship the Lord (SE 8949), and that they separate out those who "refer to the light at night . . . as the Lord" (SE 8951). The information is not identical to what Swedenborg recorded for himself in 1748, but it is close. Clearly, Swedenborg was feeling his way through his spiritual experiences and was not always sure how to understand them.

---

17. I described this transition recently (Bedford 2006), based on the Reverend Dan Goodenough's analysis, which he presented in a paper to the General Church Council of the Clergy in 1989.

What he took as misinformation earlier he accepted later as worthy of publication.

Reports of encounters with spirits from other worlds take up at least 189 numbered paragraphs written in 1748. After 1748, just four more paragraphs in *Spiritual Experiences* deal with pluralism: paragraph 4431 on Mercury and memory; paragraph 4673 on "universe dwellers"; paragraph 4742 which mentions communication with spirits from Jupiter; and paragraph 6057 which refers to *Other Planets*. The topic of pluralism is nearly dropped from the diary after 1748, and after 1752 we find no information about extraterrestrials—only a reference to the work published in 1758.

The inverse is the case in diary paragraphs referring to the Last Judgment. From 1747 to 1756, 22 paragraphs refer to it, and 48 from 1756–1757. Not surprisingly, diary entries about the Last Judgment increase as the Last Judgment takes place.

The contrast between the way the topics of the Last Judgment and the plurality of worlds develop in the Writings is remarkable. Pluralism, a topic that took up a large amount of attention in 1748 and was published alongside all the chapters in *Secrets of Heaven* on Exodus and was extracted and published again in *Other Planets,* is not developed at all after 1752,[18] while treatment of the Last Judgment continues to the end of the last published work.

4. *The Disappearing Solar System.* The most controversial part of Swedenborg's reported contact with spirits from other planets is that he identifies groups of them as being from planets in this solar system. One might wonder how he could make this assignment. How could he know what planet a spirit is from? The way he does this is that he actually sees in the other world a replica of our local solar system, and he is able to travel to the planets he wishes to visit. One of the remarkable things about this spiritual solar system is that it is earth

---

18. *Other Planets* was published in 1758, but all of the information presented there about life on other worlds was extracted without addition from *Secrets of Heaven.*

bound—the point of view is from the earth. Why should a heavenly view of the solar system be from the earth's point of view?

Swedenborg described this spiritual solar system as "the way planets are aligned in spirits' and angels' ideas about them" (SH 7171). He also referred to it as the "mental picture that spirits have [of the solar system]" and explained that the:

> expression "mental picture that spirits have" is used because neither the sun in this world nor any planet there is visible to any spirit. Spirits have only a mental picture of them; they see them as they exist within that mental picture. (SH 7247)

The repetitious last sentence results probably from the tremendous difficulty Swedenborg faced in describing this mental image. But difficult as it is for Swedenborg to describe and us to understand what this image is, Swedenborg's assignment of spirits to various planets depends entirely on this "mental picture" of the solar system, and all references to this "mental picture" occur prior to the Last Judgment.

Swedenborg reported that the spiritual world contained many appearances of things before the Last Judgment: fantasy cities with engineering marvels, artificial light, and "devices set before the eyes of those standing at a distance, which do not actually exist among those who are in those devices" (LJ 58). Swedenborg also described these illusions as "splendors" displayed by "arts unknown in the world" (SPL 18). All of these illusions were constructed by spirits' imagination, and all were destroyed by the Last Judgment. It is speculative but plausible that one of these constructions was the "mental picture" that angels and spirits have of the solar system.

Why would spirits construct an imaginary solar system? In the years after the Copernican revolution when people realized for the first time that the planets were earth-like rather than star-like, they also began to wonder if there was life on the planets. This idea is compelling and took possession of the imagination. Upon finding themselves in the next life and wondering about the solar system, it is conceivable that these spirits found a way to see what they believed was there, just as other spirits built for themselves high places and palaces with their imagination.[19]

We may wonder if there was sufficient time for enough spirits to accumulate in the spiritual world from the time of Copernicus and Galileo to 1748 to make such an elaborate construction, but the evidence Swedenborg reported suggests that there was. Consider that the Reformed Church had its start in 1517 and grew to compete with the Catholic Church in the sixteenth century. This gave at most 240 years between the start of that Church and the Last Judgment, and yet Swedenborg reported that the Reformed actually held the central positions in the false heavens. There had been enough time for them to construct cites and elaborate "splendors" in the other world (SPL 18).

If the solar system that Swedenborg reported seeing was actually an artificial construct of spirits' imagination, then Swedenborg's means of assigning home planets for the extraterrestrial spirits he visited would be unreliable. Perhaps the information Swedenborg gave about specific planets (Jupiter, Saturn, and so on) really is not about those specific planets but about unknown planets. This speculation does not necessarily call into question whether or not Swedenborg met spirits in the other world who came from other planets; it merely questions the assignment of spirits to specific planets in this solar system. While Swedenborg dropped planet-specific information from the Writings, the idea of pluralism remains all the way to the end of *True Christianity*, and, as discussed earlier, pluralism is necessary in a Swedenborgian view of the cosmos.

Why might Swedenborg report information that was unreliable? It is possible that Swedenborg was unaware of the full import or context of what he saw. But after the Last Judgment if the spiritual

---

19. Perhaps one motivation spirits had for producing an image of the solar system was to lead people away from Christianity. Swedenborg used the mental image to lead people back. He did this by showing that it is the Lord Jesus Christ who is worshipped on all those planets. If the spirits' mental image of the solar system had been set up to oppose Christian teaching, then Swedenborg's use of the image could be similar to the way Jesus used traps set against him to entrap instead those who set them (e.g. Matt. 15.1–12; Matt. 21.23–27).

solar system disappeared, we might expect Swedenborg to note that. There are several possible reasons why he might not, the most obvious being that he was not concerned about it. Even if he lost the image of the solar system, Swedenborg may have concluded that the planetary assignments he had made were still correct. In Swedenborg's lifetime there was little if any conflict between scientific ideas and the idea of life on the other planets of this solar system. Unless Swedenborg had been presented with evidence to the contrary, there would be no reason for him to question what he had concluded earlier, even if he could no longer see the spirits' picture of the solar system.

Another possibility is that Swedenborg may have thought the planetary assignments questionable but unimportant in what was essential to the message about life elsewhere. He is almost dismissive of the particular information about life on other planets even as he publishes it. In the closing pages of the seventh Latin volume of *Secrets of Heaven*, Swedenborg wrote a prelude to information he would publish in the next volume on life beyond this solar system, both enticing the reader to the next volume and, at the same time, almost scolding readers for being enticed by such things:

> The majority in the Church at the present day have no real belief regarding the life after death, and scarcely any regarding heaven or regarding the Lord . . . . For this reason . . . [I have been able to] be present . . . with angels in heaven, and . . . to see the astonishing things there, and to describe them. This has happened to prevent people from saying from now on, Has anyone come to us from heaven and told us of its existence . . . ? But I realize that those who . . . have already refused to believe [in these things] . . . will also be wholly unreceptive . . . . For it is easier to make a raven white than it is to cause people to believe something once they have at heart banished belief. But let those things which have been shown up to now regarding heaven and hell, and regarding life after death, be for the few in whom belief is present. As for everyone else however, in order that they may be led to some recognition of those things, I have been given consent to mention the kinds of details that gratify and attract the curious. Those that are about to be stated concern the planets in the universe. (SH 9439)

Swedenborg made a similar statement in *Continuation concerning the Last Judgment* as he introduced information about the spiritual nature of nations:

> Because it has been granted me to be in that [spiritual] light, and . . . to see the internal quality of men from one kingdom and another . . . it behooves me, *because it is of interest*, to make it known. (SPL 39, emphasis added)

Swedenborg wanted to help people find the Lord in the Word. He realized that one way to do that was to appeal to people's natural curiosity, and so he provided information to satisfy that curiosity and gave cues, here and there, not to take that information too seriously.

Watching and guiding this process, our Creator must have future readers in mind also. As the current community of readers struggles with a text that in some ways is in conflict with current information about the solar system, we might reflect on how that conflict is useful in terms of bringing people closer to the Lord.

D. Humility and Flexibility in our Approach to Sacred Texts

At the time and place of their writing, *Other Planets* and *Last Judgment* dealt immediately with a powerful reason people were using to abandon Christian faith. People came to see the cosmos itself as an indictment against what the Christian churches taught.

One of Swedenborg's tasks was to save faith in the Age of Enlightenment. To do that he would have to publish a faith that was not at variance with the cosmos. New Church theology accomplishes that and more. Not only are populated planets and the lack of an earth-bound Last Judgment allowed in this new theology, they are requirements of it. Suddenly, instead of opposing Christian theology, the cosmos "declares the glory of God" (Ps. 19.1). This accomplishment, the alignment of faith and reason in the eighteenth century, is revolutionary.

Astounding as this accomplishment is, if the new theology cannot transcend the limitations of time then it cannot establish a long-standing church. Now, some 250 years after the consummation of the Christian age, we are beginning to see whether or not it can.

The New Church teaching regarding the Last Judgment, or better put, the teaching on the nature of communal judgments—that they are spiritual events occurring when a church on a planet comes to an end because it no longer behaves in accord with the two Great Commandments—is timeless and strikes many people when they hear it as reasonable and attractive, and more plausible than the old Christian belief in the destruction of the world.

The New Church teaching that human life exists in many places throughout the universe also is timeless, and many people who hear it find this idea also sensible and attractive.

However, Swedenborg's reports that there are people on Mercury, Venus, the Moon, Mars, Jupiter, and Saturn, and also on the satellites of those planets, is space and time specific and strikes many people as unreasonable and even repellent. Remembering that Swedenborg included this sort of information to entice the curious, it would be ironic if it resulted today in pushing people away. The presence in the Writings of specific information about the plurality of worlds is an opportunity for reexamining our relationship with the New Christian Word.

1. *Protection.* A fundamental flaw of human nature is arrogance—thinking of oneself as being more special and deserving than anyone else. Many of us want to think of ourselves as especially chosen by God, and in the extreme we want to be god. Without the Lord's presence with us in revelation we would have no chance to overcome the powerful currents of our own selfishness. However, the "possession" of a revelation from God can feed our arrogance since we may feel that the revelation gives us special status. If God, the knower of the human heart, is the source of sacred texts, then it is reasonable to conclude that the texts would contain guards against fueling our arrogance and would lead us instead into humility.

One of the characteristics of sacred texts is that in many cases the most immediate and obvious interpretation of what the text means is fallacious. The perplexity this causes among a text's community of readers can encourage a sense of humility about how well the community understands its revelation, and it can entice the community to look beyond the surface for deeper meaning.[20]

To make this point clear, imagine that science confirmed what Swedenborg wrote about the planets of this solar system—that Mercury, Venus, Mars, and the Moon have human life on them, and that Saturn and Jupiter are solid bodies and also have human life. Imagine the euphoric feeling of self-righteousness Swedenborgians would feel as we trumpet our proven-correct revelation. That situation would probably be damaging to the Lord's plan for creation. Not only would it induce tremendous arrogance within our community, but it would also invalidate all those channels the Lord uses to connect with cultures all over the world.

To see how invalidation of revelation might feel, imagine that science demonstrated the factual nature of the creation story, or Noah's flood, or worse yet, imagine that the second coming actually happened as expected by the Christian fundamentalists. If we were not destroyed by the event, we would probably abandon what we have been calling the New Church to join the "real" New Jerusalem.

2. *Reinterpreting the Old and New Testaments.* If planet-specific information in the Writings functions to place a check on our arrogance and prevent invalidation of revelation to other communities, it is just one more example of many in the Word that function similarly.

God, in the Old Testament, made a promise to Abraham and then repeated it again and again to Abraham's descendants: God would give them the land of Canaan and this land would overflow with food and drink, and would be peaceful. Instead of realizing this promise Abraham's descendants never possess the whole land, and the

---

20. In her analysis of biblical authority, Phyllis Bird points out that the early Christian theologian Origen of Alexandria (c. 185–254) realized that the Bible's purpose is in saving us rather than satisfying our curiosity about the world (49). For Origen, the difficulties in the literal sense were signs that we should search for the Bible's higher purpose and meaning.

land was repeatedly under the threat of "sword, famine, and plague" (e.g. Jer. 21.9). Foreign nations took the descendants away into captivity. In this crisis they turned to their prophets and sacred texts, which gave them hope of a coming Messiah who would restore their lands and that they, in Zion, would lead all the people of the world. In the eyes of many Jews today, neither of these promises have been fulfilled.

Rather than living in bitterness at God's "failed" promises, many Jews have found it more fruitful to interpret these promises in less obvious ways. The last 3,000 years of history demonstrate that God's revelation in the Old Testament is not true in the most obvious, literal sense. That same history also demonstrates that, in spite of the contradiction between expectations and reality, a people of faith can preserve and revere documents they receive as sacred, and that these documents affect their listeners powerfully. The Jewish texts have a timeless power that exceeds expectations. Would this have been true if Zion was as God said it would be?

And it can be argued that the Lord's promise to Abraham has been fulfilled. The Lord told Abraham:

> Leave your country, your people, and your father's household and go to the land I will show you.
> I will make you into a great nation and I will bless you;
> I will make your name great, and you will be a blessing. (Gen. 12.1–2)

Prior to Abram's call the world was polytheistic. Through Abraham, not just Canaan but very nearly the entire world has become monotheistic. "Hear, O Israel, the Lord your God is One!" (Deut. 6.4).

In the New Testament the Lord made promises to the Christian Church that in a literal sense also have not been realized. Jesus told his disciples that their generation would not pass before he would come again to judge the world (Matt. 24.34, Mark 13.30, Luke 21.32). This expectation was so strong in the early Christian communities that no effort to record the Gospels took place until that generation had nearly entirely passed away. The final chapter of John contains a reinterpretation of Jesus' words that had given an expectation that John would see him come again. This reinterpretation was necessary because John had died (21.23). It is amazing to think that people who believed that they had actually shared meals with the Lord of creation would not immediately seek to record all they could about what Jesus did and what he was like. Why did they not do this? It was because they felt that the end of the world was near. There would be no need to preserve this information for future generations because there would be no future generations. But as the generation that walked with Christ died off, the early church faced its first major disappointment: the judgment they were seeking was not happening.

This disappointment resulted in important progress for that church. The Gospels were written and the followers of Christ realized that the task of establishing a church, rather than simply spreading the good news, rested on their shoulders. With the Gospels came organized bodies to decide on a canon. The phenomenal growth of the Christian Church and its success in shaping much of world history over the next 2,000 years resulted from the realization that the early expectations were incorrect and too limiting.

In each of these cases, communities of faith had at first accepted God's words in an immediate sense that turned out to be unreliable. In the case of the Jewish and Christian churches, these challenges resulted in reshaping and empowering the impact their revelations had on their lives.

Today, Swedenborgians are reexamining their sacred texts as changing conditions make wider the differences between expectations of the faith, and reasoned conclusions based on evidence. In no area are these differences more obvious than in dealing with extraterrestrial life.

3. *Reinterpreting the Writings.* Reinterpretation of the Old and New Testaments is the foundation of New Church doctrine. As stated in subsection *The Internal Sense of the Word* (p. 553), New Church theology is built up through linking the internal spirit of the Word, the internal sense, to its external letter. By turning his readers' minds

to the internal sense, Swedenborg removed obstacles to faith that had developed through overly-literal and self-referential interpretation of biblical text.

The Reverend Grant Odhner in his "Responding to the Lord's Word" invites New Church readers to apply to the Writings what Swedenborg teaches about acquiring a doctrine of genuine truth from the letter of the Word (2007, 232). Not all of the information presented in the Writings is of the same importance. Just as with the Bible, there are primary truths that illuminate all the rest. The two Great Commandments are an example. The Word connects us with the Lord, and the Lord gave these Commandments. Whatever we take from the Word must be considered alongside these Commandments. Passages that speak harshly of a group of people need to be seen in the light of the commandment to love the neighbor. And information that has little or nothing to do with primary teachings, information such as the name of the planet that spirits come from, should, correspondingly, carry less weight.

Readers should be on guard especially for interpretations that empower self or one's group over others. The mistaken expectations in the Jewish and Christian churches regarding the way the Savior would return were shaped, consciously or not, by self-importance. Expectations in the New Church about possessing special information about the natural world can be linked to a desire for self-importance and could also be linked to a desire to benefit the neighbor.

Increasing our contextual awareness of the Writings, setting "ideas in a larger framework and alongside each other" (Odhner 2007, 233), and building slowly a doctrine of genuine truth from the Writings, gives the community opportunities to develop its relationship with the text and become more supple in response to the text's authority and call.

In *Continuation concerning the Last Judgment*, Swedenborg gave an example of what happens when people do not have a supple response to their doctrine:

> The Dutch cling more closely than others to the principles of their religion . . . .
> If they are convinced that this or that is not in accord, still they do not say so, but
> turn their backs and remain unmoved. In this way, they remove themselves from
> an interior intuition of what is true, for they *imprison* their rational or spiritual
> things under obedience. (SPL 49; emphasis added)

Similarly, Swedenborg reported that certain Jews in the other world
"are unwilling to know that, in the Word, by "the land of Canaan"
is meant the Church, by "Jerusalem" the Church as to doctrine, and
hence by "Jews" *all* those who will be of the Lord's Church" (SPL 82,
emphasis added). These Jews were so locked in their thinking that they
did not realize that they were in the other world and they were still
expecting the Messiah to "march at their head, glittering with diadems,
and lead them into the land of Canaan," with Christians begging them
to be admitted (SPL 82).

And some Catholic spirits, Swedenborg wrote, "strenuously
insisted" on the idea that Peter was given "the Lord's power over
heaven and hell." They could not accept any other meaning to that text
because the teaching is a "fundamental of their religion." They told
Swedenborg that "there was not any doubt about it since it is clearly
stated" (LJ 57).

Inflexible, spiritless text interpretation causes problems. And on
the other extreme, developing doctrine apart from the foundation of
the text also leads to difficulties. At the end of *Continuation concerning
the Last Judgment,* Swedenborg wrote about Quakers in the spiritual
world whose

> religiosity gained such complete possession of them that they believed themselves
> to be enlightened and sanctified beyond all others. Wherefore, indeed, they
> could not be withheld from their religiosity. (SPL 83)

And some Moravians in the spiritual world had "an interior confirmation
of their dogmas" (SPL 90), but that confirmation came from

> visionary spirits who confirm in man all the things of his religiosity, and . . .
> [these spirits] enter more closely with those who . . . love their own religiosity
> and think much about it. (SPL 90)

Responding too much to interior perception without engaging with the Word is an invitation for being overwhelmed by one's own unenlightened "religiosity."

The approach Swedenborg models for us is careful attention to the text along with open-mindedness to the internal sense of that text. Now that the Last Judgment has taken place, communication between heaven and the earth has been restored and so people "can be enlightened and reformed . . . [and] can understand the Divine truth of the Word . . . [because] intervening obstacles have been removed" (SPL 12).

4. *Developing Trust.* As readers of Swedenborg, we need to remain sensitive to several lines of evidence. The Old and New Testaments and the Writings bring us evidence of who the Lord is and what the Lord wants from and for us. Our own immediate experience is also evidence of what works and does not work in bringing happiness to us and to those around us.

Swedenborg assures us that the doctrine of the New Church that he is revealing is not from any angel but from the Lord alone and that the doctrine came to him while reading the Word (TC 779). We can trust Swedenborg in this statement but we should also ponder it. What are the doctrines to which he is referring? What do we do with all those statements Swedenborg reports from "angels' lips" (e.g. LJ 14)? We cannot trust the text simply because we are told to. We must find ways to connect the text to our experience and concerns, and learn to trust it as we discover how it helps us move toward the Lord.

We must refrain from asking ourselves or anyone else to believe things for which they or we have no evidence. Dismissing evidence or ignoring its power places obstacles along the path toward true faith, obstructing people's ability to develop real trust. Instead, we should nurture a spirit of openness and engagement in our community, being patient with one another as we use all the tools the Creator has given us and struggle to find our way back to God.

E. Questions for Further Study

Organizers of the Last Judgment Conference asked presenters to develop a list of questions that invite further study. This study engages a question that can be approached from many angles. Here, it is approached in terms of faith and reason. This question is, What obstacles block people from living in faith, and can those obstacles be removed? The questions listed below deal with that central issue.

1) What is a New Church community? How does that community develop a trusting relationship with the New Church Word?

2) How can we present the faith of the New Church with minimal obstacles to belief? How can we present "genuine doctrine" to people who have not accepted Swedenborg?

3) How do the Writings address mistaken expectations in the Jewish and Christian Churches?

4) Are there mistaken expectations among New Church communities? If so, why do they arise and how can they be corrected?

5) How do genuine truths help us avoid turning "fallacies" into "falsities"? How do we find genuine truth in the Writings?

6) What is enlightenment in the New Christian age? How can people experience the reality of the Lord's presence in their lives?

7) What does Swedenborg's statement, "I have not received anything pertaining to the doctrines . . . from any angel, but from the Lord alone while reading the Word" (TC 779), mean?

8) How did Swedenborg acquire information for the revelation?

9) What were the criteria Swedenborg used to decide whether or not to publish information?

10) In what ways are the concerns and expectations of Swedenborgian readers the same and different in the eighteenth and twenty-first centuries? How do we read the text today to address our concerns and questions?

11) Do the Writings have inherent flexibility or were the doctrines fixed when they left Swedenborg's pen? If there is flexibility, how do doctrines in the Writings evolve from book to book and over time?

12) How is the conflict between the text and the current view of the solar system useful in terms of bringing people closer to the Lord?

VI. CONCLUSION

In this study we have considered the relationship between two doctrinal topics. The two topics are the nature of the Last Judgment, and the idea that the universe supports human life on many planets. The questions addressed by this study were: why does New Church revelation address Christian expectations about the Last Judgment and the possibility of life elsewhere in the physical universe; why did mistaken expectations arise in these two areas; are there mistaken expectations among those who accept Swedenborg's works as divinely inspired; and how can a community develop trust in the New Church Word?

The issue central to the entire paper is the way that faith can be, ironically, weakened by a need many people feel to strengthen their faith by insistence that natural reality comply with their particular and inflexible understanding of spiritual reality. This need has led to the development of and insistence upon several false ideas. One example is the idea that the Lord will come onto the earth and judge it, destroying it in its present form and establishing in its place heaven-on-earth. Another example is the idea that the entire universe is centered on the earth, the only terrestrial region of the universe, and that all human beings in the universe are descended from Adam.

The churches' insistence on these two ideas, the Last Judgment and the singularity of the earth, in eighteenth-century Europe led many to question or abandon faith. Swedenborg addressed these two points in his theological works, replacing these church teachings with a new vision of why the Lord created the universe and how the Lord saves us. The Writings address pluralism and the Last Judgment in order to restore faith in the Lord and the Word.

The revelation of the Word's internal sense is the fundamental, constructive element of New Church theology. Applied to the Last Judgment, the internal sense of the Word showed that the Last Judgment was not the cosmological event that the churches were expecting. The Last Judgment would not destroy any part of the natural world.

In addition to using the internal sense of the Word, Swedenborg relied also on the eighteenth century view of the cosmos, complete with peopled planets, to argue the impossibility of a judgment actually on the earth. Incorporation of the plurality-of-worlds idea was useful in terms of helping people understand the Last Judgment.

However, along with his writing that human life exists on other planets, Swedenborg named planets of this solar system that are peopled, and even described the nature of life on those planets. These descriptions are wholly unsupported by contemporary, scientific evidence. This inconsistency between information present in revelation and information available through scientific investigation has recreated the conflict between faith and reason concerning the nature of the solar system. This conflict, if engaged inappropriately, can once again erect obstacles between people and faith.

The method Swedenborg used to assign spirits to particular planets depended entirely on a "mental picture" he saw in the spiritual world. There are no reports of that mental image appearing after 1757, and so it is possible that the image was one of many illusions that existed in the spiritual world prior to the Last Judgment.

When we understand the presence of the pluralism topic in the Writings as a means to defeating a false and obstructive idea in the eighteenth century Christian church, we should be on guard not to use that information to create another false and obstructive idea in a twenty-first-century, new Christian church. Swedenborg liberated people's thinking from the confines of the natural world by revealing the internal sense of scripture. It is this lifting up from literal interpretation that is needed now.

We make a mistake when we go to the Word for information about the natural world. Using the Word to understand natural rather than spiritual reality is what led many in the Jewish Church to see their occupation and control of a particular geographical landscape as a Divine right. It also caused them to expect a Messiah who would help them capture and control that land, giving them a special Divinely-sanctioned place at the center of all the people of the earth. Similarly, many Christians have interpreted the Word in natural terms, expecting natural events in the world to occur as described in that book. Expecting sacred text to be reliable in the natural sense is not itself a mistake, but often the expectation goes beyond innocent trust in the Word. Often the expectations take enormous proportions that, in the end, serve both to confirm the believers' sense of self-importance and deny the validity of any other group's connection to their Creator. Too often, natural interpretation of sacred text evolves to justify and strengthen love of self and of the world. In addition to damaging the spiritual lives of those who take their beliefs to these natural extremes, the focus on natural interpretation of revelation while simultaneously ignoring physical evidence creates obstacles to faith.

A temptation we all face is the lust for power, and there is nothing more powerful than having special access to God. Intentionally or not, churches have used their scriptures to validate their own power over others. The revelation for the New Church could be manipulated similarly. If the information about specific planets in this solar system turned out to be true in a literal sense, then this would invalidate all those other channels the Lord uses to connect with cultures all over the world. It is a blessing that the physical reality of this solar system is substantially different from what Swedenborg described.

The Word in all its forms and senses is central to fulfilling the Lord's purpose in creation—filling the heavens. New Church writers have begun the task of exploring the landscape within the Writings. Not everything said in the Writings is of equal importance in fulfilling the Lord's purpose. By seeking and applying the doctrine of genuine truth, we can begin to understand the terrain and map those landmarks that help us find our way. Without attending to those landmarks we could repeat the mistakes of the past by seeking natural confirmation of our faith, unwittingly expecting our sacred texts to elevate ourselves above all others in creation.

At one level the promises in the Old and New Testaments that the descendents of Abraham would occupy the land of Canaan, and that the Lord would return before that generation died were not true. But in another way, those promises were fulfilled. Throughout the world, monotheism has replaced polytheism. And the resurrection the Lord promised is better than expected—it happens immediately after death and places us in a world of greater possibilities than this one. In both cases, what the Lord promised is much fuller and more generous than people at first realized. The same can be true with promises given for the New Church. ⚡

BIBLIOGRAPHY

Acton, Alfred, II. "Paradigms Revisited" *New Church Life* 127 (2007): 168–179; 268–279; 306–319.

Bedford, Allen J. 2006. "Planets and Perspectives: New Church Theology and the Plurality of Worlds Debate." *The New Philosophy*

———. 2004. "Chemical Education in a New Church College." Dan A. Synnestvedt, ed. *Faith and Learning at Bryn Athyn College of the New Church*. Bryn Athyn, PA: ANC Press.

Bird, Phyllis A. 1994. "The Authority of the Bible." *The New Interpreter's Bible*. Nashville: Abingdon Press vol. 1, 33–64.

Crowe, Michael J. 1986. *The Extraterrestrial Life Debate 1750–1900: The idea of a plurality of worlds from Kant to Lowell*. Cambridge: Cambridge University Press.

Dole, George. 2005. "Swedenborg's Modes of Presentation, 1745–1771." *Emanuel Swedenborg: Essays for the New Century Edition on His Life, Work, and Impact*. West Chester, PA: Swedenborg Foundation 99–115.

Galileo Galilei. 1610. *Sidereus Nuncius, or the Sidereal Messenger.* Reprinted. Albert van Helden, trans. Chicago: The University of Chicago Press, 1989.

Goodenough, Daniel. 1989. "From 'God Messiah' to 'Lord.'" Unpublished paper to the General Church Council of the Clergy. Bryn Athyn, PA.

Hogan, Michael H. and Jane Williams-Hogan. 2005. "The Last Judgment and New Church Scholarship: Some Implications for the Future." Bryn Athyn, PA: The Cole Foundation.

King, Kristin. 1999. "The Power and Limitations of Language in Swedenborg, Shakespeare, and Frost." *Studia Swedenborgiana* 11: 1–63.

Odhner, Grant H. 2007. "Responding to the Lord's Word" *New Church Life* 127 (2007): 130–140; 183–193; 226–238.

Odhner, Hugo Lj. 1968. *The Spiritual World.* Bryn Athyn, PA: Academy of the New Church.

Rose, Frank S. 2005. "Swedenborg's Manuscripts." *Emanuel Swedenborg: Essays for the New Century Edition on His Life, Work, and Impact.* West Chester, PA: Swedenborg Foundation, 117–148.

Rose, Jonathan S. 2005. "Swedenborg's Garden of Theology: An Introduction to Swedenborg's Published Theological Works." *Emanuel Swedenborg: Essays for the New Century Edition on His Life, Work, and Impact.* West Chester, PA: Swedenborg Foundation, 53–98.

Swedenborg, Emanuel. 1749. *Arcana Cælestia* [NCE title: *Secrets of Heaven*]. vol. 1. Reprinted. John Elliott, trans. London: The Swedenborg Society 1983.

———. 1749. *Arcana Cælestia* [NCE title: *Secrets of Heaven*]. vol. 2. Reprinted. John Elliott, trans. London: The Swedenborg Society 1984.

———. 1753 *Arcana Cælestia* [NCE title: *Secrets of Heaven*]. vol. 9. Reprinted. John Elliott, translator. London: The Swedenborg Society 1993.

————. 1754. *Arcana Cælestia* [NCE title: *Secrets of Heaven*]. vol. 10. Reprinted. John Elliott, trans. London: The Swedenborg Society 1995.

————. 1756. *Arcana Cælestia* [NCE title: *Secrets of Heaven*]. vol. 11. Reprinted. John Elliott, trans. London: The Swedenborg Society 1997.

————. 1756. *Arcana Cælestia* [NCE title: *Secrets of Heaven*]. vol. 12. Reprinted. John Elliott, trans. London: The Swedenborg Society 1999.

————. 1768. *Conjugial Love* [NCE title: *Marriage Love*]. Reprinted. John Chadwick, trans. London: Swedenborg Society 1996.

————. 1763 *Divine Love and Wisdom*. Reprinted. George Dole, trans. West Chester, PA: Swedenborg Foundation 2003.

————. 1764 *Divine Providence*. Reprinted. George Dole, trans. West Chester, PA: Swedenborg Foundation 2003.

————. 1843 (posthumously). *Emanuel Swedenborg's Diary, recounting Spiritual Experiences during the years 1745 to 1765*. vol. 1. Reprinted. J. Durban Odhner, trans. Bryn Athyn, PA: General Church of the New Jerusalem 1998.

————. 1758. *Heaven and Hell*. Reprinted. George Dole, trans. West Chester, PA: Swedenborg Foundation 2000.

————. 1758. *Last Judgment*. Reprinted. Doris Harley, trans. London: Swedenborg Society 1961.

————. 1771. *True Christianity*. vol. 1. Reprinted. Jonathan Rose, trans. West Chester, PA: Swedenborg Foundation 2006.

————. 1771. *True Christian Religion* [NCE title: *True Christianity*]. vol. 2. Reprinted. John Chadwick, trans. London: Swedenborg Society 1988.

————. 1758. *The Worlds in Space* [NCE title: *Other Planets*]. Reprinted. John Chadwick, trans. London: Swedenborg Society 1997.

Naturalism and the Last Judgment

DAN A. SYNNESTVEDT*

"It must be thought that either God or nature governs all things"[1]

INTRODUCTION

Frederick the Great became king of Prussia, just across the Baltic sea from Sweden, in 1743. Frederick liked to call himself "the *philosophe* of Sans Souci" (his palace at Potsdam). The king "rejected and disliked Christianity and all revealed religion, predicting that Christianity would not last more than another two hundred years."[2] Little did he know that, at least spiritually speaking, the first Christian church would not last another twenty.

After putting aside his career as a scientist and philosopher and following his call to be a revelator, Emanuel Swedenborg, a contemporary of Frederick the Great, wrote *The Last Judgment* and *Continuation concerning The Last Judgment.*[3] In these books he records the things he heard and saw in the spiritual world and asserts that "all the predictions in the Apocalypse are at this day fulfilled," including the end of the first Christian church. Both books sound hopeful notes regarding the future of the human race on this planet in the universe. Order has been restored to the spiritual world. Spiritual captivity and slavery have been removed. Spiritual freedom has been reinstated so that people can "better perceive interior truths" and thus "be made

* The author would like to thank Skye Kerr for her editorial assistance as well as the Academy Research Committee for funding and comments on a draft of this paper.

more internal" (LJ 74). There is now a joy in heaven and also "light in the world of spirits, such as was not before" (CLJ 30). "A similar light also . . . arose with men [people] in the world, from which they had new enlightenment." (Ibid.) "The state of the world and of the church before the Last Judgment was like evening and night, but after it, like morning and day" (CLJ 13). To those familiar with the eighteenth century, this sounds simply like more liberty-loving Enlightenment optimism and luminescent metaphor.

The nineteenth and twentieth centuries saw the growth, spread, and domination of the worldview known as naturalism. Naturalists hold that nothing spiritual or supernatural exists: there is only nature and natural ways of knowing it. If, as a result of the Last Judgment and Second Coming of the Lord, there is new light in the world constituting a bright fresh mental morning, then why has naturalism been the dominant worldview for Western intellectuals? One would think that with the enlightenment available to the human race, we would see the growth of spiritualism, not naturalism.[4] This is puzzling. True, Swedenborg also wrote that "the state of the world hereafter will be altogether similar to what it has been heretofore" (LJ 73). Concerning the civil aspect of life, there will continue to be politics, peace, and war. As for ecclesiastical matters, the "divided churches will exist" as before, teaching their doctrines, and the "same religions as now will exist among the Gentiles" (LJ 73). These predictions have certainly come to pass. But given the growth of naturalism and the momentous events reported by Swedenborg, it can seem as though the previous two centuries constitute a rather gray dawn in this world.

Out of the variety of worldviews that existed in the eighteenth century, naturalism is the one that is specifically cited in the Heavenly Doctrines. Passages containing concepts related to a number of worldviews can be found in the Doctrines, and Deism (the idea of a Grand Mechanic who wound up the clockwork universe) is particularly relevant since it was a very popular worldview among some intellectuals during Swedenborg's lifetime. Despite its existence in public writing since at least 1682, the term for Deism is, surprisingly, not used in the Heavenly Doctrines.[5] So the explicit use of the terms for naturalism in both narrative and expository passages in the Heavenly Doctrines is significant.

This leads to several important questions which this essay will answer: does "naturalism" in the Heavenly Doctrines refer to the same thing that philosophers today call "naturalism"? Is it the same thing as "materialism"? Are there any significant differences between naturalism and atheism? Some Christians are today aware of naturalism and claim that it is a "secular faith." Do philosophical naturalists agree? Do the Heavenly Doctrines agree with this?

Naturalism existed prior to the Last Judgment and it has not only continued to exist after it, but has grown. Why? Is there one cause of naturalism, or are there multiple causes? As we will see, the Heavenly Doctrines point to not just one cause, but many. Interestingly, one cause would strike any professional philosopher, at first glance, as non-theological, non-intellectual, and far-fetched: adultery.[6] This raises a new set of questions. Is there a link between the history of marriage, or sexual relations in general, and the rise of naturalism? One contemporary Christian theologian has argued that such a link exists.[7] Can a New Church thinker concur? It is at this point, when naturalism affects how we think of ourselves, how we treat one another, our views on love, family, and society that it ceases to be merely a matter of intellectual curiosity and becomes a vital concern for every human being.

We will begin to answer these questions by first considering the status of naturalism among today's philosophers. After defining naturalism in relation to materialism and positivism, we will briefly examine what Swedenborg the philosopher and some of his contemporaries had to say about the topic in part two. In the third section of the essay we explore what Swedenborg the theologian reveals concerning naturalism, both its causes and its effects. This is followed by a section in which we strive to understand the reasons for the growth of naturalism after the Last Judgment. Arguments both for and against naturalism are considered in section five. Section six includes a brief consideration of the future prospects of both naturalism and its opposing worldview, spiritualism.

DEFINING NATURALISM

That naturalism is the reigning worldview among Western philosophers there can be no doubt:

> [S]cientific naturalism is the current orthodoxy, at least within Anglo-American philosophy. . . . Naturalism has become a slogan in the name of which the vast majority of work in analytic philosophy is pursued, and its pre-eminent status can perhaps be appreciated in how little energy is spent in explicitly defining or explaining what is meant by scientific naturalism, or in defending it against possible objections.[8]

Barry Stroud, past president of the Pacific Division of the American Philosophical Association, states that "what is usually at issue is not whether to be a naturalist or not, but rather what is and what is not to be included in one's conception of 'nature.'"[9] The same thing is asserted by a leading naturalist, David Papineau. Naturalism "is widely viewed as a positive term in philosophical circles—few active philosophers nowadays are happy to announce themselves as 'non-naturalists.'"[10] Christian philosopher Charles Taliaferro states that today "the goal is either to accommodate consciousness, minds, value et al, as denizens of a physical world or to eliminate them. Either way materialism [a form of naturalism] is the order of the day." Quoting William Lycan, he continues: "Few theorists question the eventual truth of materialism."[11]

THE GENERAL CONCEPT

"Naturalism" is a word that is used broadly in the sciences, arts, and humanities. The term can refer to someone who studies nature, especially by direct observation. A botanist or zoologist is sometimes labeled a "naturalist." The famous ornithologists, John James Audubon and William MacGillivray are called "naturalists." In literature and art the term means a faithful adherence to nature, a realistic portrayal of something. For example, in the nineteenth century there was a group of writers, including Emile Zola and Gustave Flaubert, that adhered to principles of naturalism, meaning that a writer should apply objectivity and precision in his or her observation and description of life, without idealizing or imposing value judgments. One might say that this was an attempt to import some of the techniques of modern science into literature.

Naturalism in philosophy has some of the same connotations as "naturalism" and "naturalist" in other contexts, especially the scientific study of nature, but it is more all-encompassing. As philosopher Michael Rea states, the question, What is philosophical naturalism? is difficult to answer. It is "vexed by the fact that the house of naturalism is a house divided. There is little agreement about what naturalism is, or about what sort of ontology it requires."[12] Indeed, a number of terms—scientism, materialism, physicalism, reductionism, positivism—related to naturalism have been coined and these require some sifting as well. There are several forms of, or themes within, naturalism too: ontological, methodological, epistemological, and semantic. Like the terms "theism" or "Christian" we will find that the meaning of "naturalism" is complex.

We will begin with "perhaps the most familiar definition" of naturalism, namely, "the rejection of supernatural entities such as gods, demons, souls, and ghosts."[13] Most commonly, naturalism is defined as anti-supernaturalism.[14] This is consistent with an older definition, which is labeled the "negative" definition of naturalism. John Herman Randall, Jr. states that naturalism can be defined negatively as "the refusal to take 'nature' or 'the natural' as a term of distinction."[15] It is:

> opposed to all dualisms between Nature and another realm of being—to the Greek opposition between Nature and Art, to the medieval contrast of the Natural and the Supernatural, to the empiricist antithesis of nature and Experience, to the idealist distinction between Natural and Transcendental, to the fundamental dualism pervading modern thought between Nature and Man.[16]

In other words, naturalism has no room in it for any *other* kind of entity, substance, cause, force or process besides nature. It is a form of monism, the position that reality is one, or is composed of one kind of thing (substance, force, etc.); this one thing is natural or Nature. So if one has some notion of what supernaturalism is, and theism, deism, spiritualism, and forms of transcendentalism are all kinds of supernaturalism, then one can understand naturalism by thinking of it as the *opposite* of supernaturalism, spiritualism, theism and forms of transcendentalism. This "negative" definition of naturalism arose first because forms of spiritualism constitute humanity's ancient worldview.

In contrast to the negative definition of naturalism, there is what is often called the "positive" definition and it is more complex. "Positively," Randall explains, "naturalism can be defined as the continuity of analysis—as the application of . . . 'scientific methods' to the critical interpretation and analysis of every field." "There is no 'realm' to which the methods for dealing with Nature cannot be extended."[17]

Here is a very brief definition of naturalism of the positive sort. Naturalism is

> In general the view that everything is natural, i.e. that everything there is belongs to the world of nature, and so can be studied by the methods appropriate for the studying of that world, and the apparent exceptions can be somehow explained away.[18]

Two themes in this definition, and in naturalist writings in general, can be discerned. One is ontological (concerning the being of nature): "a commitment to an exclusively scientific conception of nature," and the other is methodological and epistemological (concerning authentic knowledge): "a reconception of the traditional relation between philosophy and science according to which [the method of] philosophical inquiry is conceived as continuous with science."[19] The methodological commitment of naturalists is reflected in Roy Bhaskar's definition of naturalism, which is that

> there is (or can be) an essential unity of method between the natural and the social sciences. It must be immediately distinguished from two species of it: *reductionism*, which asserts that there is an actual identity of subject-matter as

well; and *scientism*, which denies that there are any significant differences in the methods appropriate to studying social and natural objects.[20]

In other words, the naturalist holds that society and individual human beings, or anything else one cares to name, can be, and moreover *ought* to be, studied in the same way as the rest of nature. If something is not studied according to scientific methodology, then it ought not to receive our epistemic assent (it is not "real" knowledge).

These two elements of naturalism also appear in the summary of it given by Wagner and Warner. Importantly, they link them to one of the aspects of naturalism that most appeals to the modern mind: objectivity.

> Contemporary naturalists may take either an epistemological or an ontological starting point. Basic to the epistemological approach are the epistemic merits of science . . . . Underlying the ontological approach is the idea that reality is physical reality. The thrust of naturalism on this view, is that we should believe only in physical things. Although many philosophers combine these ideas (indeed, an entailment seems to run at least from epistemological to ontological naturalism), they represent somewhat distinct fundamental intuitions. A likely source for this bifurcation is the possibility of emphasizing either of two elements in the conception of objectivity . . . . A focus on the idea of an objective world may lead to an ontological formulation of naturalism. Focusing on the process of scientific inquiry would tend to yield an epistemological version.[21]

This definition is helpful because it is given in sympathetic language, one that emphasizes that naturalism is rooted in human beings, their intuitions, and their decisions regarding what it is most important when formulating a position. While there is significant philosophical debate and confusion surrounding the term "objectivity," Wagner and Warner are correct in associating this concept with naturalism.[22] Naturalists tend to think of themselves as being objective, while regarding spiritualists or theists as having fallen victim to subjectivity, or wish-fulfillment, and many people in Western culture think approvingly of natural science as the home of objectivity.

The definitions we have explored thus far have contained a methodological, or epistemic, commitment and an ontological commitment. However, according to Christian philosophers William Lane Craig and J.P. Moreland, naturalism usually contains not just two, but three commitments:

> (1) different aspects of a naturalist epistemic attitude (for example, a rejection of so-called "first philosophy" along with an acceptance of either weak or strong scientism); (2) a Grand Story which amounts to an etiological account of how all entities whatsoever have come to be told in terms of an event causal story described in natural scientific terms with a central role given to the atomic theory of matter and evolutionary biology; and (3) a general ontology in which the only entities allowed are those that bear a relevant similarity to those thought to characterize a completed form of physics.[23]

This definition includes both the methodological (in 1) and the ontological aspects (in 3) of naturalism. Craig and Moreland adding the narrative aspect indicates that naturalism is not merely an academic position, but a worldview. As a worldview it contains implications for ethics, politics, our understanding of human beings and the meaning of life. The narrative aspect of naturalism appeals to the imaginative and affective aspects of people, something that makes it more than just "dry" metaphysics or methodology.

Craig and Moreland mention "scientism" in their definition and this, too, is an important term. Science plays a dominant role in all things naturalist, especially the positive and methodological definitions. "Most naturalists would affirm Wilfrid Sellars's slogan that 'science is the measure of all things: of what is that it is and of what is not that it is not.'"[24] This statement, which is based on an ancient Sophistical saying of Protagoras, captures "the heart and soul" of naturalism.[25] According to Mario de Caro and David Macarthur,

> Perhaps the most common reason cited in favor of this view [naturalism] is some version of what might be called the "Great Success of Modern Science Argument." It argues from the great successes of the modern natural sciences in predicting, controlling, and explaining natural phenomena . . . to the claim that the conception of nature [given by] the natural sciences is very likely to be true and, moreover, that this is our *only* bona fide or unproblematic conception of nature. It is the latter claim that earns scientific naturalism the label of "scientism."[26]

De Caro and Macarthur are not alone in making this assertion. Linda Wiener and Ramsey Eric Ramsey state that they join with other authors in defining scientism as the view "that science is the proper and exclusive foundation for thinking about and answering every question" which becomes "a worldview characterized by its authoritarian attitudes, its totalizing drive to encompass every question, and its disregard and disdain for alternative views."[27] This is similar to the position held by the British philosopher Tom Sorell. He defines scientism as

> the belief that science, especially natural science, is much the most valuable part of human learning—much the most valuable part because it is much the most authoritative, or serious, or beneficial. Other beliefs related to this one may also be regarded as scientistic, e.g. the belief that science is the only valuable part of human learning, or the view that it is always good for subjects that do not belong to science to be placed on a scientific footing.[28]

To illustrate the way that scientism and naturalism are intertwined, the last notion in Sorell's definition is often referred to as "naturalizing" something. For example, epistemology, the study of knowledge and belief, is one of several fields within philosophy. Following Kornblith, one can say that the question, How ought we to arrive at our beliefs?, is, on the traditional view, best left to philosophers.[29] The non-normative question, How do we arrive at our beliefs?, is assigned to psychologists. The question, Are the processes by which we do arrive at our beliefs the ones by which we ought to arrive at our beliefs?, is supposed to be answered by comparing the answers to the first two questions. Kornblith takes "the naturalistic approach to epistemology to consist in this: question 1 cannot be answered independently of question 2."[30] So naturalism can mean greater inter-disciplinary cooperation and, for philosophers, a systematic attempt to pay attention to and use empirical research that relates to one's area of specialty. However, he observes that the most radical kind of naturalized epistemology was promoted by the famous Harvard professor W.V.O. Quine, who held that epistemology "simply falls into place as a chapter of psychology, and hence of natural science."[31] Epistemology is replaced by a rigorously scientific psychology, one modeled on physics and chemistry.

Naturalism sounds like a very modern worldview, and, to the extent that it is exclusively tied to modern science, it is. However, naturalism in both its negative and positive meanings is at least as old as the Roman philosopher Lucretius (99–55 BC) who in his poem *De Rerum Natura*, set out to persuasively transmit the teachings of two Greek philosophers: the hedonist Epicurus (341–271 BC) and the atomist Democritus (born c.460 BC). Lucretius rejected a supernatural existence of the gods, the soul, and a life after death. Moreover he attempted to provide natural, or "scientific" (in the ancient sense) explanations for a variety of phenomena. The influence of this ancient naturalism has been ably traced by George D. Hadzsits (in 1935) and more recently by Benjamin Wiker (in 2002).[32]

The goal of converting parts of philosophy into natural science continued into the 1990s, yet not everyone held to scientism. At *Reasons to Believe: An Interdisciplinary Conference on Naturalistic and Non-naturalistic Perspectives* at Elizabethtown College in 1997, Owen Flanagan, an academic who specializes in the philosophy of mind, gave several meanings of the word "naturalism," ranging from the least controversial to the most controversial. His description includes both positive, negative, and scientistic elements. Naturalism can mean that

- Philosophers should respect and accept the claims of scientists
- When philosophical claims and scientific claims conflict, the scientific claims should be accepted
- Philosophical questions do not differ from scientific questions except in their level of generality
- Only science and a science-oriented philosophy can explain reality
- There is no room or need for immaterial forces, events, objects, or beings
- Ethics can be done without theological or other transcendental (e.g. Platonic) foundations
- The only viable view of reality is materialism or physicalism

Flanagan categorized himself as a naturalist in the sense that he holds to a non-reductive form of materialism when it comes to explaining the human mind (a reductive form is physicalism, i.e., everything is a form of physics and can be explained by physics).[33] The editors of *Naturalism in Question* draw the same distinction between naturalism and physicalism:

> Although every physicalist . . . is committed to scientific naturalism, not every scientific naturalist is a physicalist. On a pluralist conception of science, a scientific naturalist might think there are entities such as acids or predators or phonemes that chemistry or biology or experimental psychology commits him to that are not (reducible to) physical entities, and that, consequently, the explanations of say, biology are not reducible, even in principle, to the explanations of physics.[34]

However, Wagner and Warner observe that "since self-described physicalists also endorse chemistry, ecology, neuroanatomy, and the like, the line between the two classifications [physicalism and naturalism] blurs."[35] Notice that Flanagan must specify that he holds a materialist form of naturalism. This is because "it is no good simply to identify the supernatural with the immaterial, since there are many immaterial things that we are perfectly happy to countenance: for example, concepts and numbers."[36] Ever since Plato launched his theory of the Forms, the ontological status of concepts, numbers, and geometric entities has been in continuous dispute.

A very comprehensive definition of naturalism was published in 1967 by Arthur Danto. It includes the elements of other definitions we have reviewed and amplifies them. He specifies fourteen tenets of this worldview.

1) "The entire knowable universe is composed of natural objects" which exist within the spatiotemporal and natural causal orders.
2) "we need never go outside the system of natural objects for explanations of what takes place within it. Reference to non-natural objects is never explanatory."

3) "A natural process is any change in a natural object or system which is due to . . . natural causes. There are no non-natural processes."

4) "Nature is in principle intelligible in all its parts, but it cannot be explained as a whole. For this would presumable require reference to a natural cause, and outside nature . . . there are no natural causes to be found."

5) Natural method is "(a) explaining natural processes through identification of the causes responsible for them and (b) testing any given explanation with regard to consequences that must hold if it is true." "The natural method is the way in which one set of natural objects—men—operate upon the rest of nature."

6) "natural processes are *regular*. The natural method seeks, accordingly, to establish natural laws."

7) "all philosophers must function in the natural order as other humans do and, in order to do this successfully, must spontaneously apply the natural method." People from various walks of life seek natural explanations.

8) "Reason is the consistent application of natural method, and natural science is the purest exemplar of reason."

9) "Knowledge of the world at a given time is what science tells us at the time about the world." But since this may be revised or rejected in the light of further applications of the natural method, "there is nothing ultimate or eternal about knowledge."

10) "If the formal sciences [e.g. math, logic] are about anything, it will at least not be a realm of timeless numerical essences, and at any rate logic and math are appreciated in terms not of subject matter but of function, as instruments for coping with this world rather than as descriptions of another one."

11) "To say that outside science there is no knowledge to be had is not to say that it is only through science that people should relate to nature, for there are many ways of experiencing the world. Nevertheless, the only mode of experience which is *cognitive* is scientific."

12) It is not "the aim of naturalism to insist that all natural objects are really reducible to one favored *sort* of natural object or that only

the objects or the descriptions of objects recognized by the natural sciences are *real*. All natural objects are equally real."

13) "The universe at large has no moral character save to the extent that it contains human beings among its objects and thus contains entities that have and pursue values." "The natural method alone, not some special moral intuition, provides the key to dissolving moral disputes, and moral theories may be treated no differently from scientific theories with respect to determination of their strength through testable consequences. Naturalism, although otherwise morally neutral, *is* committed to institutions that permit the operation of natural method in moral and political decision."

14) "Naturalistic philosophy, unlike other philosophies, claims no special subject matter and uses no special tools. Its method is the natural method."[37]

How much of this definition could a New Church person agree with? Not much. Later on we will see the extent to which Swedenborg knew about and rejected naturalism, but let us make a preliminary accounting of the matter using Danto's fourteen points. A Swedenborgian could agree with some points in 1, 5, 6, (that the space-time universe is knowable by natural methods which lead to natural laws) and the last part of 9 (scientific knowledge can be revised) quite readily. All other tenets are incompatible with the New Church worldview. As for point 12, that all natural objects are equally real, I think that since the New Church metaphysic includes discrete degrees as well as continuous degrees in the natural world, this must be rejected.[38] Certainly ordinary English usage rejects this metaphysical egalitarianism; a piece of plastic fruit is less real than one that was just picked from a tree. I suppose a naturalist would assert that this merely shows that ordinary language is stuck in its anthropocentric pre-scientific past and should be reformed. Point number 8, that science is the purest exemplar of reason, is highly contentious just from a philosophical standpoint alone. Why shouldn't logic or mathematics be granted this honorific title? Probably because it might lead to a kind of transcendental Platonism, which Danto rules out in point 10. But is it the case that this value judgment concerning science as the best exemplar of reason can be established by the natural method? Even if one could do so, the process seems circular. Insofar as Danto's, or any other naturalist's, message is "Pay attention to science and make use of its findings," a Swedenborgian can agree. To this extent, Swedenborg himself was a naturalist!

Danto's tenets of naturalism were written forty years ago and the definition of naturalism has not significantly changed since then. The most current description of naturalism is written for the online *Stanford Encyclopedia of Philosophy* by the naturalistic philosopher David Papineau who states that naturalism can be separated into an ontological and a methodological component.

> The ontological component is concerned with the contents of reality, asserting that reality has no place for "supernatural" or other "spooky" kinds. By contrast, the methodological component is concerned with the ways of investigating reality, and claims some kind of general authority for scientific method.[39]

Papineau's definition is consistent with Danto's and, as we have seen, with other's definitions. His "methodological naturalism" is consistent with what other philosophers have called epistemic naturalism, which is the view that science and philosophy have the same aims and methods. These are "to establish synthetic knowledge about the natural world ... and to achieve this by comparing synthetic theories with empirical data."[40] By "science" Papineau means "natural science." He notes that the term "methodological naturalism" has been used in other ways, namely that "natural science itself requires no specific attitude to religion, and can be practiced just as well by adherents of religious faiths as by atheists or agnostics." This, it seems to me, is a statement of historical fact.

Naturalism, however, is not merely a set of methodological tenets or dull guidelines without consequences. In fact it is so much more, and this is important to bear in mind. According to John Herman Randall naturalism is an attitude and temper. . . . It undertakes to bring scientific analysis and criticism to bear on all the human enterprises and values so zealously maintained by the traditional supernaturalists and by the more sophisticated idealists.[41]

Naturalism has personal and cultural dimensions. Randall says that naturalists have their opponents: naturalism should "marshal its resources" for its tasks and clear the "obstacles which anti-naturalism would set in its way."[42] Naturalism is an action plan with an agenda. Naturalists want to surpass supernaturalists at explaining life, guiding behavior, educating young minds, and influencing public institutions and debate. This is reflected in Danto's tenet number 13 above. Religious people, at least the supernatural ones, are benighted opponents. They can be overcome by arguing against their claims for a transcendental God and personal survival after death, by conquering territory previously held by "spirit," by naturalizing religion itself, and by naturalists being friendly, helpful, artistic, and promising that naturalism will be as fulfilling for human beings as supernaturalism or as idealism ever was. Once supernatural religion is defeated, it will be replaced by what amounts to the "religion" of naturalism and the "church" of science. Note well Randall's use of religious language:

Men must have a *faith* in the ultimate principles of scientific verification." "What Church, or what Party, can proclaim a Truth or Good which measured by its power—and it is the politics of power we are discussing, the power to bring knowledge and wisdom and to render men steadfast in their *devotion*—can compare with the principles of scientific verification . . . ?"

Assuredly, the anti-naturalists are right: our world is perishing for want of *faith*. The faith we need, the faith that alone promises *salvation*, is the faith in intelligence.[43]

Not everyone writes as fervently about the aspirations of naturalists and the promise of naturalism as John Herman Randall, (in fact contemporary naturalists and secular humanists would be embarrassed by this use of religious language) but Randall's language echoes that of the first major American naturalist.

John Dewey (1859–1952), the leading American pragmatist philosopher of the early to mid-twentieth century, proposed that society disconnect the religious values with which he agreed from supernatural religion, and instead make a scientific understanding of humanity and democracy our new religion. Dewey urged people to make this new faith "militant."[44] This is the beginning of what has become known as "secular humanism" in the U.S.[45] And the effort to promote naturalism in all aspects, especially as a cultural force, continues today. This is clear from the activities of Prof. Paul Kurtz and those associated with the Council for Secular Humanism. This group, which is dedicated to ushering in a completely secular society, publishes two magazines, many books, including ones for children, secular humanist manifestos and declarations, holds regular conferences, lectures, meetings, and summer camps for families, and has established "Centers for Inquiry" in New York, Indiana, Michigan, and Canada. Commenting on the last federal elections, Kurtz writes that

> [a]lthough the Religious Right lost the battle, I reiterate that it is surely not the end of the Culture War. . . . We need to be prepared for the continuing Culture War that seeks to overturn the Enlightenment and all that it represents in our democracy.[46]

NATURALISM, MATERIALISM AND POSITIVISM

As we have already seen, there are different kinds of naturalists: some are physicalists, others are materialists (and there are different kinds of materialists).[47] Just as "naturalist" can refer to positions outside of philosophy, so can the term "materialist." In common parlance a "materialist" is someone who holds that comfort and wealth are the highest values in life, and so has a tendency or commitment to be more concerned with attaining natural, as opposed to spiritual, goals and values. The bumper sticker on the back of a luxury sport utility vehicle, "The one with the most toys wins," sums up this kind of materialism nicely. Most philosophical materialists want to dissociate themselves from the air of greediness that permeates the term "materialist" and instead emphasize their assertion that everything that exists is made of matter and can be explained only in terms of matter (broadly construed). They would not deny that they reject spiritual values and goals, or that they endorse the material nature of ethics, politics, aesthetics and other realms of value, but they would deny that such rejection leads to greediness.

The ancient Greek materialist view, atomism, has been overturned by the findings of modern science, especially Einstein's physics. So today's materialists, when asked what matter is, simply defer to today's physicists for the answer to that question. Today's materialism is not simplistic; it can be as sophisticated as current physics. In general, materialism usually concerns the composition of things, while naturalism is a broader outlook and is equally concerned with methodological and epistemological issues. However, materialism can also function as a synonym for naturalism.

Unlike materialism, positivism got its official start with the French sociologist and philosopher August Comte relatively recently. Comte's *Course in Positive Philosophy* was published from 1830 to 1842. Comtean positivism is famous for its assertion that human thought has evolved through three stages, from the primitive to the mature: theological, metaphysical, and the scientific stage. Comte dreamed of a day when masses of human beings could be studied like other natural masses and sociology (a term he coined) would be a kind of physics of society, used for its beneficent control and development.

In the early twentieth century a related, but different, form of positivism developed through philosophers associated with the Vienna Circle and non-Viennese thinkers such as A.J. Ayer and Ernest Nagel. The movement to promote the verifiability principle, atomism in language and metaphysics, and the fact-value distinction became known as logical positivism. The well-known Polish philosopher Leszek Kolakowski summarized this kind of positivism. He pointed out that logical positivism is "a normative attitude, regulating how we are to use such words as 'knowledge,' 'science,' 'cognition,' and 'information'" and the positivists desire to "distinguish between philosophical and scientific disputes that may profitably be pursued and those that have no chance of being settled."[48] Kolakowski discussed the tenets of positivism in terms of four rules they promulgated.

The first rule is that of phenomenalism. "This may be briefly formulated as follows: there is no real difference between 'essence' and 'phenomenon.'" Expressed differently, "[w]e are entitled to record only that which is actually manifested in experience; opinions concerning occult entities of which experienced things are supposedly the manifestations are untrustworthy."[49] So positivists reject explanations that rely on the notion of "spirit" but also ones that rely on a philosophical concept of "matter."

The second rule is nominalism. This means that "we may not assume that any insight formulated in general terms can have any real referents other than individual concrete objects."[50] Consequently, there is no referent for "the triangle" or "the good." Such universal terms are merely linguistic and mental constructs. In the world of our experience, we find only individuals, not universals.

The third rule "denies cognitive value to value judgments and normative statements." "For instance, the principle that human life is an irreplaceable value cannot be so justified: we may accept it or we may reject it, but we must be conscious of the arbitrariness of our option."[51] Why is this the case? It is a result of the previous two rules:

> For, by the phenominalist rule, we are obliged to reject the assumption of values as characteristics of the world accessible to the only kind of knowledge worthy of the name. At the same time, the rule of nominalism obliges us to reject the assumption that beyond the visible world there exists a domain of values "in themselves," with which our evaluations are correlated in some mysterious way. Consequently, we are entitled to express value judgments on the human world, but we not entitled to assume that our grounds for making them are scientific; more generally, the only grounds for making them are our own arbitrary choices.[52]

This means that moral judgments are the result of subjective affective preferences. Of course this rule would also apply to other areas of life in which normative judgments are made, such as aesthetics, law, and etiquette. Since positivism itself is a set of norms, one supposes that it, too, is an arbitrary choice and a subjective preference. As critics of both positivism and naturalism have pointed out, this self-referential incoherence undermines the rational basis for this view.

The fourth rule is the "belief in the essential unity of the scientific method." In other words, "the methods for acquiring valid knowledge, and the main stages in elaborating experience through theoretical reflection, are essentially the same in all spheres of experience."[53] So instead of using one method in physics and a different method in sociology or political science, the same method should be used in all three. We have seen this commitment to the unity of the sciences in the attempt to naturalize all aspects of life and we shall see this commitment critiqued in the section of this paper on the arguments against naturalism.

There is significant overlap between positivism and naturalism, yet the two are not identical. One can be a naturalist, of some sort, and not be a positivist. While naturalism is the predominant worldview among Anglo-American philosophers, positivism is not. According to Craig and Moreland, "in a recent retrospect of the twentieth century, Tyler Burge has remarked that 'the central event' in philosophy during the last half century has been 'the downfall of positivism and the re-opening of discussion of virtually all the traditional problems in philosophy.'"[54] This is good news for "big tent" or pluralistic naturalists and supernaturalists, including Swedenborgians.

NATURALISM, SWEDENBORG AND HIS CONTEMPORARIES

Swedenborg, being well educated at university, a voluminous reader and a well-connected traveler, knew about naturalism before his spiritual eyes were opened. Indeed, his 1734 work *The Infinite and The Final Cause of Creation* is a sustained attempt to persuade his naturalistic contemporaries to become theists. As the subtitle of the book—*Outlines of a Philosophical Argument*—shows, Swedenborg sketches the various ways that one can reason with naturalists using methods and terms acceptable to them.[55] His goal is to develop a line of reasoning to lead the human mind to acknowledge "God as infinite, and as the cause of the finite, and consequently of nature," so that "it no longer rests in the primitive substance of nature, so as to make God and primate nature one and the same; or to attribute all things to nature" (Inf 29). As we saw in the previous section, to make God and nature the same, or to attribute all things to nature, constitute forms of naturalism.

Swedenborg analyzes the reasoning of philosophers to see where their thinking leads them to mistakenly take a naturalist position: "by his own imperfect investigations and analyses, [the philosopher] becomes a worshipper, not of God, but of nature" (Inf 18). For example, some philosophers seek the Infinite in terms of space or time, and when they cannot find it there, they "secretly" conclude that "the divine essence is probably not infinite, but indefinite, and . . . that the Divine is the prime being of nature, and consequently that nature and God are in a manner one and the same" (Inf 17). Thinking in terms of space and time, and also trying to apply "geometrical conditions" or analogues of quantity also cause the mind of the philosopher to take this path (Inf 17, 30).

Other causes of naturalism include the thought that nature has such "great and vast resources, which seem to transcend both sense and perception" that it is impossible to assign any limits to it, and so it must be God (Inf 81). "On these grounds they deified the universe in its largest sense; and the more readily as their admiration for the whole was filled and illustrated by their knowledge of the astounding marvels and harmonies, of situation, figure and motion" (Inf 81). Others "deified the minimal or atomic world; from the same cause as before, viz., from admiration or ignorance of its properties" because "under the operation of reason the minimum seems more and more to approach the indefinite, or to exceed the limits of conception" (Inf 81–2). Here we see the way that eighteenth century science and mathematics were used to support naturalism instead of theism.

Swedenborg frequently shows sympathy with his interlocutors. He reflects upon the ways that people use reason, which is finite, in order to strive to comprehend God, who is infinite. Poor reason gets lost in mazes of its own making when undertaking such a Herculean task. He agrees that nature is marvelous, and if one thinks of nature as proceeding from the Infinite, it is indeed a divine work (Inf 82). Swedenborg uses the experience of wonder and awe, which he himself must have had, to persuade the naturalist to become a theist:

> For the greater adorers and worshippers of nature we are, the more we go back to the causes and primitives of nature; the more also we come to simple principles, and the more we acknowledge that all the others originate successively from the natural primitive; and the more again we are led to wonder at the state of this natural primitive [what today's physicists call the singularity] . . . . I am anxious therefore that the reasoner should center all his admiration in that first or least principle with which he supplies me; for by this means will it not all end in the cause of that principle? . . . Therefore in proportion as we worship nature, and believe in her as the origin of natural things, in the same proportion we may become worshippers of the Deity; because, out of the entirely perfect succession of things, modes, causes, contingents, we may experience *deeper wonder* over primitives, than others can do in contemplating the whole field of derivatives. (Inf 38; emphasis added)

But Swedenborg can also be very critical of naturalists. He observes that when we find a clever, well-built machine, even though we attribute a force and power to it, we don't give credit to, or congratulate, the machine itself. Instead, we praise its inventor and craftsmen. Using argument by analogy, he says that nature is like a machine, and while it too has force and power, it is finite and all praise and wonder should be given to its Infinite Maker (Inf 43).

The most trenchant criticism is the one in which he compares modern naturalists to ancient idolaters. In what has become a well-known move against the supernatural religious believer, and in anticipation of thinkers such as the Scottish Enlightenment philosopher David Hume, Swedenborg links the ignorance of natural causes and fascination with the miraculous to—not the origin of supernatural religion—but to modern naturalism, that is, the deification of nature and the universe (Inf 81). Modern philosophers, having failed to rationally grasp the nature of God, conflate God with nature and the infinite with the finite, which reason can grasp.

> And thus the source of error among the idolatrous vulgar is identical with its source among those philosophers who make an idol of nature: the only difference being what there is between the gross and the subtle, between the more and less plausible, between reason little developed and reason overdeveloped. (Inf 74)

Not only is the use of the category of idolatry an interesting foreshadowing of the revelation to come, but this accusation would have been *deeply* offensive to his contemporaries who fancied themselves, as moderns, so much wiser and better than their inferior ancestors or the "barbarous" (non-European) nations of the eighteenth century.

Regarding naturalism as a target of criticism: was Swedenborg arguing against a straw man? Not at all. According to the historian of philosophy, Aram Vartanian, many continental philosophers after Descartes attempted to solve the problems in his metaphysical dualism and advance his promotion of science by adopting some form of naturalism. For example, in 1651 the English philosopher Thomas Hobbes published *Leviathan,* a book in which he attempted to work out a philosophy consistent with the materialistic assumption that all reality is matter in motion. Ralph Cudworth (1617–1688), the Cambridge Platonist, in his 1678 work *The True Intellectual System of the Universe: wherein all the Reason and Philosophy of Atheism is confuted,* observes that theists and Christians have helped the atheistic cause by persuading people that the universe was derived from the necessary and unguided motion of small particles of matter in a vortex without the direction of any mind. This led to "the Atheists . . . laughing in their sleeves and not a little triumphing, to see the cause of Theism thus betrayed by its professed friends and assertors."[56]

Vartanian states that

> The heretical tendency of Cartesianism must, in the last quarter of the seventeenth century, have made considerable headway, for in 1692 the Jesuit Daniel's widely-read satire, *Le Voyage du Monde de Descartes,* took up at length several of the topics already discussed.[57]

Pere Daniel was convinced that it was a bad idea for Cartesians to elude theology, that this was a way of refusing to submit to its authority. If they succeeded, there would be "dangerous consequences that favored heretics, infidels, and libertines."[58] Then the Abbe Jean Meslier's 1729 *Testament* supported the idea that Cartesians believed that the whole universe and all its works could result from natural forces alone.[59]

But it was the French doctor and philosopher, Julien Offray de La Mettrie (1709–1751), author of *L'Homme machine* (Man a Machine, published 1748), who

> laid down the first and most radical materialist thesis of the period. His automatist conception, put from 1748 at the *philosophes'* disposal, soon found application in a fuller ideological context. It was mainly through La Mettrie's efforts that Cartesian mechanistic biology, together with its consequences for moral determinism, became the basis of a consistently materialistic view of man. Also contributing to the biological phase of scientific naturalism . . . were Buffon, Maupertuis, and D'Holbach. Each of these thinkers, carrying out certain implications of Descartes's philosophy of organism, participated in the special progression of ideas that terminated in the complex of evolutionary materialism best set forth by Diderot.[60]

In 1754 the French thinker Denesle wrote *Examen du materialisme,* "which contended that Descartes's' rejection of finalism could only have resulted in the type of naturalistic science, which, at the time, was steadily gaining favor everywhere."[61] The "rejection of finalism" refers to the elimination of ends, or teleological causality (purpose), from modern scientific discourse.

Vartanian's assessment of the status of naturalism in the eighteenth century reveals how science became a weapon in an ideological battle waged by naturalists in their culture war with the first Christian church:

> What scientific naturalism meant to the eighteenth century is illustrated, for example, by the description of it given in a typical (and perhaps the most successful) attack on Diderot's group: Moreau's *Nouveau memoire pour server a l'histoire des cacouacs.* The caricatural exaggeration of this diatribe reveals the salient features of the materialist ideology. The land of the "cacouacs," that is, the camp of scientific naturalism, takes as its gospel the various and latest physical or biological theories of Buffon, Diderot, Maupertuis. The author devotes many pages to recounting how the life of the "cacouacs" is built upon

the interpretation of nature thus obtained, with a ritual to match. The telling point of Moreau's satire is a portrayal of scientific naturalism as a rival of the traditional theology, indeed to the point of having taken over, by its multiple functions, the authority of established religion for its adherents.[62]

Jacob Nicholas Moreau published his book on the Cacouacs in Amsterdam in 1757, the same year that the Last Judgment took place. Swedenborg makes the same point as Moreau, namely that naturalism, while not a religion, functions like a religion for some people.

> Suppose the faith is that nature is the creator of the universe. It follows from this that the universe is what is called God, and that nature is its essence. All these consequences, and many more of the same sort, are contained in that faith that nature is the creator of the universe, and emerge from it when it is laid open.[63]

Swedenborg analyzes naturalism as a faith, as a religiosity, that is, something that functions like a religion, but is not.[64] Naturalism has become a pseudo-religion, or what a contemporary American philosopher, John E. Smith, has called a "quasi-religion."[65] The naturalists, beginning with Lucretius and re-surfacing with some Enlightenment philosophers, such as David Hume, have been eager to give a scientific explanation of religion with the hope that naturalizing religion will explain it away. Here Swedenborg, who had the idea even before he penned the Heavenly Doctrines that eighteenth century Europeans could worship nature and so be classified as modern idolaters, continues that line of analysis. As we will see, in the final work of his life *True Christian Religion*, he turns the tables on the naturalists by giving a theological explanation of naturalism, in effect spiritualizing the naturalist and his or her commitments.

THE HEAVENLY DOCTRINES AND NATURALISM

Now that we have seen that naturalism was a serious force to be reckoned with in the late seventeenth through the eighteenth centuries and that Swedenborg was aware of this prior to his enlightenment, we turn to his theological works. When Swedenborg penned them, he used forms of the neo-Latin terms for naturalism (*naturalismus, naturalismum, naturalista, naturalismo*) about seventeen times. They were used over several years: from the 1763 work *Divine Love and Wisdom* [66] to the many uses in *True Christian Religion* published in 1771. While "naturalism" is sometimes used as a synonym for "atheism," the philosophical concept is readily identified in passages that pre-date *Divine Love and Wisdom*. For instance, *Arcana Coelestia* 8944[67] and *Heaven and Hell* 353[68] discuss the learned who do not acknowledge the Lord, but instead acknowledge nature. Although the term is not used, Swedenborg clearly demonstrates an understanding of the ontological form of naturalism.

Beyond the mere use of the term, when we analyze the passages in which naturalism is discussed, we find that the various contemporary meanings or kinds of naturalism are included. Certain passages address the use of methodological naturalism. For example, in *Intercourse between the Soul and the Body* 9[69] Swedenborg observes that some people base all their reasoning on their senses. Consequently, the evidence for their beliefs is sensory. So it is no surprise that they "ascribe all rational things" to nature and "absorb naturalism as a sponge does water." In other words, having taken the epistemic position that only beliefs that can be supported by evidence from the natural sciences are justified, such a position leads one to accept naturalism as a worldview quite readily. The same position is taken by satans when they have a debate with angels in *True Christian Religion*. "What is more evident than that nature is all in all?" "Are not the bodily senses the witnesses of truth?" they rhetorically ask, appealing to evidence from the eyes, ears, nose, mouth, and skin. It is all nature. (TCR 77).

This same memorable relation in which the spiritual contest between angels and satans is recounted contains the positivistic form of naturalism also. The satans, who are in a fury, state that "God" is a word without meaning, unless nature is meant. This is the nominalism that Kolakowski gives as the second rule of positivism and its origin can be traced at least back to the Scottish Enlightenment philosopher David Hume.

Swedenborg also has an awareness of the second element of
naturalism mentioned by Craig and Moreland, namely the Grand Story
which combines the atomic theory of matter and part of evolutionary
biology, in *True Christian Religion* 20. Without an idea of God as first
substance in a human form, we tend to think of God as nature in its first
principles, or as the expanse of the universe. Moreover, people who
think in this manner also conceive of the origin of humans as a result
of the concatenation of elements fortuitously adopting a human form.
Of course the theory of evolution was developed after Swedenborg's
lifetime, but the idea that human life is the result of a fortuitous accident
can be found in ancient Epicurean philosophy which was revived
during the seventeenth and eighteenth centuries.[70] It is the denial
of Providence, not the effects of environment upon the diversity of
species, that is at issue here.

It has been said that the theory of evolution made atheism
intellectually respectable, partly because it supposedly provided, or it
could in theory provide, an explanation of how life arose by purely
natural means.[71] This idea circulated through the intelligentsia of the
eighteenth century as well as our own. The naturalist *philosoph* Denis
Diderot, who, like Swedenborg before him, wrote on the development
of the chicken in the egg, asserted that the chick developed by purely
natural means without design or purpose. In his *Dream of d'Alembert*,
(written in 1769) Diderot asserted that

> from inert matter organized in a certain way and impregnated with other inert
> matter, and given heat and motion, there results the faculty of sensation, life,
> memory, consciousness, passion, and thought.

This development "overthrows all schools of theology."[72]

The naturalistic notion that life emerged from non-life through
purely natural means is clearly rejected by Swedenborg. In the work
Divine Providence he states that naturalists think that everything is
governed by natural light and heat, or to update the statement as a
physicalist would, that everything is governed by whatever today's
physicists say are the fundamental forces and substances of nature.

Swedenborg asserts that these are dead. So he rhetorically asks: "Does not what is itself living govern what is dead? Can what is dead govern anything?" Then, directly addressing a crucial belief of the naturalist which is part of the Grand Story: "If you think that what is dead can impart life to itself you are spiritually insane, for life must come from life" (DP 182:3).

More evidence of Swedenborg's awareness of naturalism is found in *Intercourse between the Soul and the Body* 17. There he states that when thinkers are ignorant of the doctrine of degrees, they end up in a form of atomistic naturalism. This leads them to "naturalize" what is spiritual, including human rationality (they equate it with the minds of animals) and the human soul (it is a "breath of wind"). This is quite similar to today's naturalistic epistemology which seeks to dispense with the transcendental metaphysics of mind and the idea of consciousness as spiritual. Recall that in Danto's definition of naturalism from the 1960s, he repeatedly asserts that human beings are only natural objects (in points #5 and #6). Today's neurophilosophy does not even countenance the idea of a soul. In 1986 the well-known Existentialist philosopher William Barrett published *Death of the Soul: From Descartes to the Computer* and biologists and philosophers continue to practically equate human beings and animals, especially the higher primates.[73]

Usually Swedenborg uses the term "naturalism" as a synonym for atheism. For example, in *Arcana Coelestia* 8783 he writes that people who trust their own intelligence and exalt themselves above others reject the Word. This is "very evident from the fact that they who are atheists and naturalists, as they are called, are those who are learned. This the world knows, and they themselves know." Swedenborg saw the closed and darkened understandings of people in the spiritual world who had "confirmed themselves in favor of nature from the visible things of the world, until at last they became atheists" (DLW 357). Here Swedenborg asserts that a person can become a naturalist to such an extent that he or she is an atheist. So whether one is called an atheist or naturalist often amounts to the same thing.

But "naturalist" is not always strictly used as a synonym for "atheist." For example, in *True Christian Religion* the phrase "*naturalista atheus,*" that is, "naturalistic atheist," is used twice (TCR 382, 759.3).[74] This phrase implies that there are other kinds of atheists. Also, a person can be a theist outwardly by speaking about God, reading the Bible, attending church and by being well-behaved, yet inwardly be an atheist. So as far as intellect and behavior are concerned, such a person is not a naturalist. The person believes, or is willing to state publicly, that God created the world, that there is a life after death, and that one should not act in uncivil or immoral ways. Internally, however, such a person thinks that evil actions are allowable, does not shun them because they are sins against God but merely for the sake of reputation and wealth, and so does not have a conscience. Thus the person is at heart an atheist, but publicly not a naturalist and does not associate with people of that ilk. All people in the whole world, whether Christian, Muslim, or Gentile, who lived a merely externally holy life constituted "the first heaven" in the world of spirits during the Last Judgment. Such people are said to be natural, not spiritual, but not philosophical *naturalists* in public (LJ 69).

This distinction between being "natural" and not an intellectual naturalist was especially the case for Christians of the Reformed Protestant churches. Since they had an external connection with heaven, but an internal connection with hell, they "could not be torn away in a moment," so they were "detained in the world of spirits" (CLJ 18). These people underwent processes of separation during the Last Judgment (CLJ 16). However, people who were openly atheistic and at the same time openly naturalists, that is, those who "did not believe in God, who condemned the Word, and rejected from their hearts the holy things of the church" did not go through the processes of the Last Judgment. Instead, they proceeded directly into hell (CLJ 17).

Since most of the passages use the terms "naturalist" and "atheist" interchangeably, one should not make too much out of this distinction. Another reason is that there are general teachings such as this: everyone in hell worships nature (TCR 77.4). This kind of statement should guide our interpretation of the use of the terms "atheism" and "naturalism."

What can we conclude regarding naturalism and the Heavenly Doctrines? We can conclude that Swedenborg knew what naturalism was, that he repeatedly addressed it and condemned it, and that naturalistic positions and themes have changed so little over the past 250 years that the important parts of the definition of naturalism are contained in the Heavenly Doctrines. As in the eighteenth century, so also today: intellectuals and others assert that the universe created itself, that the cosmos and the human beings in it are accidents, that humans are merely complex animals, that there is no God, there are no angels, no devils nor any other supernatural beings, that natural science is our only means of acquiring knowledge of reality, that only scientific explanations are legitimate, and so on. What *has* changed since the Last Judgment is that more people, at least in the West, believe in naturalism and more people openly assert and accept naturalism. It is no longer a scandalous secret.

Let this illustration suffice to show that Western society's attitude toward naturalism is quite different now. When the French physician Julien de La Mettrie published his materialistic view of human beings in *The Natural History of the Soul* in 1745 he lost his post as medical officer of the Gardes Français and on July 9, 1746, the Parliament of Paris condemned the book to be burned by the public hangman.[75] La Metterie the atheist, the Epicurean, fled to Holland, and, after the publication of *Man A Machine* in 1748 had to seek refuge with Frederick the Great in Berlin.[76] Some two and a half centuries later, people in the West hardly raise an eyebrow at such naturalistic books, sentiments, or persons—except when they undermine political commitments to liberalism.[77]

Also, as we have seen, the terminology has changed and there are more detailed expressions of naturalism as philosophers and other intellectuals have tried to "cash out" their program and clarify their commitments, but these are variations on a theme.

THE HEAVENLY DOCTRINES
ON THE CAUSES OF NATURALISM

It is important to identify the causes of naturalism for two reasons. First, people who are committed to living a spiritual life should know what causes naturalism so that they can avoid wandering from the path that leads to heaven. Second, if we are to help the Lord actualize what we pray for every day, namely that His will be done on the earth as it is in heaven, then we must identify the causes of naturalism at work in ourselves and in society and strive to counteract them. There are several causes of naturalism, not just one.

The first and spiritually mildest cause of naturalism is ignorance. An ignorance of the sun of heaven, influx from it, the spiritual world and its state, have lead some people to think that "the spiritual is a purer natural; consequently, that the angels are in the ether or in the stars; and that the devil is either man's evil, or, if an actual existence, that he is in the air or the abyss; also that the souls of men, after death, are either in the interior of the earth, or in an undetermined somewhere till the day of judgment" (DLW 350). Ignorance of the spiritual sun as a cause of naturalism is also cited in *Intercourse between the Soul and the Body* 9. In this work Swedenborg adds that an ignorance of discrete degrees can lead people to adopt naturalism when they investigate the nature of the human soul, mind, and the life after death (ISB 16–17). The reason is that without the concept of discrete degrees, one ends up with a form of monism.

There is a second cognitive cause of naturalism: the propensity to think of everything, including spiritual and Divine matters, only in terms of space and time. Reasoning about such things from space and time "is like thinking from the thick darkness of night about those things that appear only in the light of day. From this comes naturalism" (DLW 69). To counter-act this propensity, people need to learn how to raise their minds above ideas drawn from space and time. Swedenborg claims that every person who has an understanding is able to transcend in thought the spatiotemporal plane of nature (Ibid.).

A third cause of naturalism is theological falsity, specifically the doctrine of faith alone.[78] The false doctrine of faith alone is said to be "the source of the naturalism which prevails at the present time" because it "makes no account of repentance, of the law of the Decalogue, and of works and charity" (Inv 9). Without these goods, a person remains natural and fails to become spiritual. Thus faith alone is not the cause of methodological, reductive, or some other form of philosophically sophisticated naturalism. Instead it is the source of moral naturalism which implies ontological naturalism through the person's behavior because moral naturalism (disordered love of the world and self) is the "default" setting of human nature.

Swedenborgians tend to be aware of this falsity of faith alone, and well they should. Yet attention should not be completely absorbed by this doctrine, or the falsities of the trinity of persons in the Godhead and the vicarious atonement, important as these are, to the exclusion of the other causes of naturalism. The Heavenly Doctrines do state that the growth of the hells prior to the Last Judgment and the Lord's Second Advent was due in part to "those who had falsified the Word by convincing themselves of their fictitious faith in the three Divine Persons." But the hells also grew because of "so-called Christians" who had accepted naturalism or nature-worship (TCR 121). In other words, hell was populated by people who were outwardly pious Christians, but who in fact lived selfish, materialistic lives.

This means that problems with the intellect alone, such as ignorance and false beliefs, are not the only causes of naturalism. The human will, or the affective domain of the mind, is also a source of error. Certain attitudes, which combine affections with the intellect, are identified as causes. For example, conceit and the pride of self-intelligence can cause naturalism.[79] Swedenborg says that even though people have the intellectual capacity to think what is true and see things spiritual and Divine in their own light, they sometimes do not *wish* to do so (DLW 69). Like the prisoners in Plato's cave allegory, some people do not want to elevate their thinking for fear of what they might see.[80] Even a "satan can understand truth as well as an angel when he hears it, but he does not retain it, because evil [desire] obliterates truth and substitutes falsity" (TCR 77.3). If not properly controlled, the loves of self and the world overwhelm the understanding to such a degree that people became nauseas at the mere thought of anything spiritual.

The misuse of science is another cause of naturalism,[81] but one that is not really separate from conceit and the pride of self-intelligence. This claim is an important, and for a naturalist, very contentious one. Theists assert that in the history of science there is plenty of evidence that a person can be a good scientist and also a supernaturalistic theist, such as Robert Boyle who was a seventeenth century Christian chemist, or Francis Collins, who is a contemporary theistic biologist. Theists maintain that it is not science itself that causes naturalism, but a misuse of science. As Vartanian wrote of the French Enlightenment thinkers:

> For the *philosophes*, by and large, natural science, in addition to being the means of ascertaining objectively truths of a certain category, was an effective instrument of ideology.[82]

Scientific knowledge can be used to confirm a belief in nature or a belief in God. In fact, people who believe in a

> Divine operation in all the details of nature, are able by very many things they see in nature to confirm themselves in favor of the Divine, as fully as others confirm themselves in favor of nature, yea, *more* fully. (DLW 351; emphasis added)

Science is a tool that can be used for good or for evil. Scientific knowledge is like wealth which can be used for heavenly purposes or worldly and hellish purposes. It can be used to confirm and illustrate a theistic worldview or a naturalistic worldview.

Another cause of naturalism is a life of evil (TCR 77) when it comes to general intentions, that is, the loves of self and the world (AC 5116.4, 6201, 8378). In particular, the Heavenly Doctrines link committing adultery with naturalism (AE 981.2; AC 2747, 5084; ML 464, 500). Spiritually, this seems to be the most serious and damaging cause of naturalism. It is this last cause, adultery, which would strike almost any contemporary Western philosopher as a shocking and unbelievable assertion. It deserves further investigation.

THE LINK BETWEEN NATURALISM AND ADULTERY

Why do naturalism and adultery make one?[83] And in what way do they "make one"? First, we must be clear about what the Heavenly Doctrines mean by adultery. It certainly means the physical act of sex outside of marriage. For example, when a husband has sex with the wife of another man, a widow, a virgin, or a prostitute from a loathing and aversion to marriage, these behaviors destroy marriage love. They all are instances of adultery (AE 1010.4). Another passage broadens adultery to include not only sex outside of marriage, but even within marriage if it springs from a love of adultery (AE 988.6). In *Married Love* and *True Christian Religion* various meanings and degrees of adultery are spelled out. *Married Love* states that there are four degrees of adultery, which range from mild to the most grave: adultery of ignorance, of lust, of reason (deliberate), and of the will (purposeful) (ML 478).

The discussion of adultery in *True Christian Religion* is organized around the sixth commandment.

> In the natural sense, this commandment forbids not only committing adultery [in act], but also having obscene desires and realizing them, and so indulging in lascivious thoughts and talk. (TCR 313)

"In the spiritual sense committing adultery means adulterating the various kinds of good in the Word and falsifying its truths" (TCR 314). This kind of adultery has been committed by members of both the former Jewish and Christian churches.

> In the celestial sense committing adultery means denying the holiness of the Word and profaning it. . . . The holiness of the Word is denied and profaned by those who in their hearts ridicule everything connected with the church and religion. (TCR 315)

The typical naturalist denies the holiness of the Word, indeed, he or she often emphasizes its harmfulness along with its worldly, man-made features, concluding that its origin is natural. The typical naturalist also ridicules the teachings and practices of churches and religion, calling them forms of superstition, dogma, myth, stupidity, immaturity and so on.

Next, which way does the causality run? Is it the case that being a naturalist leads one to commit adultery? Or does committing adultery make a person more likely to adopt naturalism? While the Heavenly Doctrines indicate that either one is possible, there are several passages which state that committing adultery causes a person to become a naturalist. In some places the Heavenly Doctrines categorically assert that adulterers are not Christian, in fact, they are not religious; even more, they are not spiritual, but natural (AC 2750; AC 10,175; Life 77; ML 432.2; ML 495; ML 497; AE 982.5; AE 985.4). This is especially true of the two worst degrees of adultery: purposeful adulteries arising from the will, and deliberate adulteries arising from a persuasion of the intellect (ML 495). There are three degrees of naturalistic people: the natural properly called, the sensual, and the carnal, each degree worse than the previous one. Adultery leads people into these degrees of naturalism (ML 496). This kind of naturalism can become a worldview, but the way the term "natural" is being used here, it is a naturalism of morality and character primarily. So in this case, the *cause* is immoral behavior from a defective character and the *effect* is a naturalistic outlook. This does not mean that a person who commits adultery on Saturday will not attend church on Sunday because he or she has suddenly thrown one worldview, theism, out the backdoor while ushering naturalism in through the front. Spiritually though, an adulterer has made it more likely that this shift in outlook will occur and then the behavior will take place. (AE 982.5) A person might continue to live, hypocritically, in a pious manner, especially when there are worldly benefits to be gained by doing so, but pious behavior is not the same as religion (HH 360, 535).

On the other hand a person who is, cognitively speaking, a naturalist from philosophical conviction, tends to see humans and animals as the same, or extremely similar. This view of human beings usually involves the rejection of immortality, the soul, and the internal human. Or, if the soul and the internal part of the human are not rejected, they are "naturalized," that is, seen to be parts of the brain or electro-chemical reactions and nothing more. On such a view of humans, what then is love but a kind of neural satisfaction and why live under outmoded restraints on such satisfaction when agreement between consenting adults is all that is needed to achieve satiety?

There is also a theological naturalism that supports adultery.

> Adulteries are less abhorrent with Christians than with the Gentiles, and even with some barbarous nations, for the reason that at present in the Christian world there is no a marriage of good and truth but a marriage of evil and falsity.

This passage is referring to the doctrine of salvation by faith alone to the exclusion of good works (AE 1008.2). The reason why the "chastity of marriage makes one with religion, and the lasciviousness of adultery makes one with naturalism" is "unknown at this day" is that "the church is at its end, and is devastated as to truth and as to good" (AE 981.2). When the church (as a spiritual organism, not a social one) is in such a state, people come to believe that

> adulteries are not detestable things and abominations, and thus [they] come into the belief that marriages and adulteries do not differ in their essence, but only as a matter of [civil] order. (AE 981.2)

Is there any empirical or anecdotal evidence to support this claim? Yes. Since space precludes a full treatment of this important subject, let the following illustrations suffice.

Pierre Bayle, the son of a Huguenot minister, was born in south-western France in 1647.[84] First he was a tutor, but eventually became professor of philosophy and history at a municipal academy in Rotterdam, Holland. He died in 1706. Bayle published the *Dictionnaire historique et critique* in 1697 in Rotterdam.[85] While it was very large (five volumes) and very expensive, it was also very successful.

A few statistics will serve to give some idea of Bayle's influence in the eighteenth century. The *Dictionary* was, despite its size, one of the most popular and widely read books of the time. Two editions had appeared by 1706, the date of Bayle's death. By 1750 no fewer than nine French editions of the complete work had appeared, as well as three English editions and one in German. The selections given in this volume are taken from the English translation of 1734–1738, the very edition recommended by [Thomas] Jefferson. In addition, numerous abridgments were made, including two, in 1765 and 1780, at the insistence of Frederick the Great. There is some reason to believe, indeed, that the *Dictionary* was the most popular book of the century in France.[86]

Here is an excerpt from the article on Martin, or Matthias, Knuzen in Bayle's *Dictionary* which illustrates the awful blend of naturalism and infidelity in Christendom prior to the Last Judgment. This lengthy quotation serves to give one a feeling for the mood of the times.

Knuzen (Matthias) a native of the country of Holstein, arrived to such a degree of extravagancy, as publickly to maintain Atheism, and undertook great journies to gain proselytes. He was a restless man, who discovered his impieties first at Konigsberg in Prussia. He boasted, that he had a great number of persons of his opinion in the principal towns of Europe, and even seven hundred in the single town of Jena.

[These are his words. "No one will impute it to me as a crime, if, with my companions (an infinite number of whom, at Paris, Amsterdam, Leyden, in England, at Hamburgh, Copenhagen, Stockholm, and even at Rome, and the adjacent places, agree with me in opinion) I look upon the whole Bible as a fine invented tale, with which the beasts, that is the Christians, captivating their reason, and running reason mad, are delighted." We must not imagine, that he used the stratagem of state-conspirators, who, to bring more people over to their party, always pretend they have a vast number of accomplices. It is more probable he spoke in this manner, because that he was a hare-brained fool.]

His sect was called the *Conscientiaries*, because he said, there was no other God, religion, or lawful magistracy, than conscience, which teaches all men the three precepts of justice, to do no injury, to live honestly, and give every one his due. He drew up a summary of his system, in a short letter, of which several copies were spread.

[Micraelius's continuator has reduced the contents of the letter to six articles. "I. That there is neither God, nor devil. II. That the magistrates are to be looked upon as nothing, the churches are to be despised, and the priests rejected. III. That knowledge and reason, together with conscience, which teaches to live honestly, hurt no body, and give every one his own, is in the room of magistrates and priests. IV. That there is no difference between marriage and whoring. V. That there is but one life: that after the present there is neither reward nor punishment. VI. That the Scripture contradicts itself." This system, besides its horrible impiety, is also plainly extravagant; for one must be stark mad, to believe that mankind can subsist without magistrates. It is true, they would not be necessary, if all men would follow the dictates of conscience, which this impious man exhibits to us; but are they followed even in those countries, where judges punish, with the greatest severity, the injustice done to our neighbour? I do not know but it may be said, that there is no impertinence, be it never so extravagant, but may teach us some truth or other. The follies of this German shew us, that the ideas of natural religion, in a word, the light of conscience, may subsist in the mind of man, even after the ideas of the existence of God, and the firm belief of a life to come, are extinguished in it.]

It is dated from Rome. You will find it entire in the last editions of Micraelius. He dispersed also some German writings. All this was confuted in the same tongue, by John Musaeus, a Lutheran professor.

This sect began about the year 1673.

A book was printed against Knuzen at Wittemberg in the year 1677. [The title of it is, *Exercitatioines Academicae II de Atheismo Renato des Cartes & Matthiae Knuẓen* oppositae Autore Valentino Greissingio Corona-Transsylvano Elector. Saxon. Alumno. This I have from a book of Caspar Sagittarius.][87]

Here is another illustration: this is an excerpt from a "Letter to Lady R., 1716" by Lady Mary Wortley Montagu. Lady Montagu (1689–1762) was a well-known British literary figure. This letter of advice to a young aristocrat reveals her circle's attitude toward marriage.

No woman dares appear coquette [flirt] enough to encourage two lovers at a time. And I have not seen any such prudes [a person who is overly modest or proper] as to pretend fidelity to their husbands, who are certainly the best natured set of people in the world, and look upon their wives' gallants [a stylish man who is attentive and polite to women, a lover] as favourably as men do upon their deputies, that take the troublesome part of their business off their hands. They have not however the less to do on that account: for they are generally deputies in another place themselves; in one word, 'tis the established custom for every lady to have two husbands, one that bears the name, and another that performs the duties. And these engagements are so well known, that it would be a downright affront, and publicly resented, if you invited a woman of quality to dinner, without, at the same time, inviting her two attendants of lover and husband, between whom she sits in state with great gravity. The sub-marriages generally last twenty years together, and the lady often commands the poor lover's estate, even to the utter ruin of his family.[88]

Lady Montagu adds that the woman is expected to get a pension from her lover, and the amount is as well known as their annual rents. As one scholar of English society has noted, "[e]ven pious and chaste upper-class women in the late eighteenth century turned a blind eye to their husband's infidelities, so long as only sexual passion and not deep emotional attachment was involved."[89]

Finally, consider these statements from one the *philosophes* who was a contemporary of Swedenborg's, Claude-Adrien Helvétius (1715–1771). This author of *A Treatise on Man: His Intellectual Faculties and His Education* was a materialist and hedonist. The main problem concerning happiness is the discontent that arises from a lack of new sensory stimulation. Consider Helvétius' ruminations on this problem:

> Little account is now made of Platonic love, the corporeal affection is preferred, and this in fact is not the least poignant. When the stag is inflamed by this last love, from timid he becomes brave. The faithful dog quits his master to follow his favourite female; if he be separated from her, he neglects his food, he trembles in every limb, and sends forth hideous howlings. Can Platonic love do more? No: I declare therefore for corporeal love. M. Buffon does the same, and like him I think that of all loves it is the most agreeable, except however for the idler; for him the coquette is the delicious mistress. When she enters an assembly adorned in that gallant manner, that gives all room to hope for what she grants but to very few, the idler is roused; his jealousy is inflamed; his discontent vanishes*. A coquette therefore is the mistress of an idler, and a fine girl for a man of business." Note* "The ruling passion of a coquette is to be adored. For which purpose she constantly excites the desire of men, and scarcely ever gratifies them. A woman, says the proverb, is a table well provided, that we view with a different eye before and after the repast.
> The chase after a woman, like that of game, should be different according to the time we have to employ in it. When we have only an hour or two, we go out with a gun; when we have more time than we know how to employ, and wish for long exercise, we set the dogs to rouse the game. A woman of address will afford the idler a long chase.[90]

After praising cohabitation prior to marriage, so that "if they do not agree, they part, and the girl goes to another," Helvétius argues that laws concerning marriage should be changed so that the "inconvenience of divorce will then be insignificant, and the happiness of the married parties secured."

> To conclude, if the variable and roving desires of men and women urge them sometimes to change the object of their tenderness, why should they be deprived of the pleasure of variety, if their inconstancy, by the regulation of wise laws, be not detrimental to society?[91]

While a naturalist could use some very worldly reasons to support a faithful heterosexual monogamous relationship, such as the financial well-being of his or her children, the descriptions of naturalists and their conversations in the Heavenly Doctrines as well as excerpts from their own books suggest that they view marriage as a mere social convention which can be overridden by a person's desires. Naturalists set up very external criteria for making judgments. The criteria exclude spiritual realities such as the soul, the spirit, and transcendental good and truth. From such superficial bases for judgment arises "the madness of many today, that they do not see anything evil in adulterous affairs" (ML 478).[92]

This madness is chillingly summarized by David Blankenhorn in his recent book, *The Future of Marriage*. Dorian Solot and Marshall Miller have written a book, *Unmarried to Each Other*, and founded an organization, the Alternatives to Marriage Project. They have "emerged in recent years as tireless campaigners for not-marriage."[93] Instead of marriage they are in favor of cohabitation, polyamory, and same-sex "marriage," that is, the legal recognition of same-sex couples.[94] Blankenhorn describes several people who dislike traditional marriage and advocate for a diversity of alternatives: Jonathan Rauch, Judith Stacey (a professor of sociology at NYU), Evan Wolfson, Ellen Willis (also a professor at NYU), Maria Bevacqua (women's studies professor at Minnesota State U.), David L. Chambers (law professor at University of Michigan), John Corvino (philosophy professor at Wayne State U.), queer theorist Michael Warner, Irene Javors (a therapist and community organizer) and so on.[95] After surveying the people, organizations, books, and websites, there can be no doubt that there is a movement in the U.S. to undermine traditional marriage by advocating for legal, economic, social, and moral acceptance of various forms of "diverse relationships" because, in their eyes, all relationships are the same. To these people, traditional marriage is a mere social convention, not something rooted in the nature of reality. Unless, that is, one thinks of humans as animals, but then since animals display a wide range of sexual behavior, this legitimizes just about anything humans would like to do. This merely natural attitude is expressed in popular culture through these lyrics:

> You and me baby ain't nothin' but mammals
> So let's do it like they do on the Discovery Channel
> Do it again now
> You and me baby ain't nothin' but mammals
> So let's do it like they do on the Discovery Channel[96]

The Heavenly Doctrines clearly assert that adultery is evil and that marriage (heterosexual monogamy) is good. Committing adultery breaks one of the Lord's commandments in the Decalogue, and in spirit it "is all sin against the Decalogue, for he who is in that is in all the evil of the Decalogue."[97] The love of adultery communicates with the deepest hell (DP 144.3). Indeed, adultery *is* hell (LJ post 339) and hell *is* adultery: nothing is more profane (AC 9961.4). Committing adultery closes heaven, and the influx from heaven is not received by a person again until there is actual repentance.[98]

THE EFFECTS OF NATURALISM

There are several negative effects or manifestations of naturalism mentioned in the Heavenly Doctrines. I include this list with references primarily as an aid to future research:

1) The belief that humans and animals are the same (AC 3646–47; ML 151r)
2) The belief that if humans have a soul, it is merely natural (AC 5084.4,6; ML 151r)
3) The belief that humans have no immortal soul and thus no life after death (AC 5084.5; ML 151r; TCR 178)
4) The belief that the mind, our thinking and willing, is only natural and that changes of state in the mind are the result of natural forces alone (TCR 178)
5) The belief that all delight of life consists in luxury and sensuous pleasures and the development of "life styles" based on this, in other words, an increase in the acceptance of hedonism (AC 8378, 6201)
6) The belief that supernatural, or spiritual, religion is "a tale devised by the clergy in pursuit of honors and profit," so religion is bunk and religious believers are "out of touch with reality" and "lackeys of the priests" (TCR 177)
7) The worship of nature, a rise in the practice of paganism (HH 353–54; DLW 267; AE 1220; TCR 121, 178)
8) An increase in the number of learned, or academics, trying to convince people that naturalism is true, or the learned just assuming that naturalism is true and that inferior people will follow their lead (AC 3483, 6316, 8627–28; HH 353–54; ML 500.2; Inv 27; TCR 639)
9) The breakdown of marriage and destruction of society (AE 981.2; AC 2747, 5084; ML 464, 500)
10) A rise in the practice and acceptance of beastiality (AE 1006.3)

It would be interesting to see if these effects could be empirically verified through social science research. For example, the well-known naturalist philosopher, Peter Singer, who holds a chair in ethics at Princeton University, together with Paola Cavlieri founded the movement to grant rights to the great apes. It is called the Great Ape Project (whose motto is "equality beyond humanity"). According to its website, in March 2007 the parliament of the Balearic islands of

Spain presented a resolution requesting a declaration of support for the Great Ape Project.[99] Singer also wrote a very favorable review of a book on beastiality.[100] Given Singer's metaphysical and ethical naturalism (he is a preference utilitarian, which is form of hedonism), this is not surprising. But one would need to conduct some surveys to find out if beastiality is practiced more widely than it used to be, or if it is accepted by more people because they believe that there are no morally significant differences between humans and animals.

Are there any positive effects from the growth of naturalism? Could the prominence of naturalism be useful in some way? Three admittedly speculative possibilities come to mind.

First, naturalism, particularly in its ontological form, may produce gentiles. It is sad to contemplate the slaughter and cruelty brought about by naturalistic regimes in Russia, China, North Korea and elsewhere, but this may have been a form of creative chaos in which people were disrupted from their inherited religious patterns and forced to "wipe the slate clean." *If* this is the case, perhaps naturalism has produced gentiles who will be open to new religions. While some of these people may have false beliefs from their new naturalistic environment, it is possible that the false beliefs from their old religions have either been weakened or removed by these brutal governments. In countries that have democratic governments naturalism may loosen the hold of the falsities of the old church and produce gentile states in people. As one of the promoters of the naturalistic movement has written, naturalism has benefited modern society by freeing it from "the constraints of a repressive theology."[101]

Next, by promoting science and historical critical hermeneutics, methodological naturalists have made it more difficult, if not intellectually impossible, to maintain a literal stance regarding all parts of the Bible. As Swedenborg notes in *The Last Judgment*, due to continued biblical literalism and the advancements of science, people have lost faith in a spiritual world and the things of the church. They ask within themselves, "How can the stars fall from heaven upon the earth when the stars are larger than the earth? How can bodies eaten up by worms, consumed by putrefaction, and scattered to all the winds, be collected again for their own souls?" (LJ 15) For theologians who use an allegorical approach to scripture, this movement can help them make their case. In effect, if one is going to believe in the Bible at all, one must interpret at least parts of it in an allegorical or spiritual manner. There are signs that interest in this mode of hermeneutics is reviving, even amongst Protestants.[102] (Catholics have always had this mode, so interest in it among them is not as surprising.)

Third, by ceaselessly promoting science, methodological naturalists have produced amazing discoveries about the natural world that can be used to confirm a belief in an orderly rational God. By combating superstition and magic, naturalism encourages a disenchanted view of nature. This can make believing in miracles more difficult, but it can also open people's eyes to the "everyday" miracles all around them. There is no predicting what impact scientific discoveries will have upon religion and spiritualism. The discovery of "the God gene" (or *a* God gene) could end up reinforcing the notion that humans naturally need God the way we need energy and companionship, thus making atheism (ironically) "un-natural."[103] This is another area for future research.

THE PROMINENCE OF NATURALISM
AFTER THE LAST JUDGMENT

Even though we have some understanding of the causes of naturalism, there is still the question of why naturalism has grown in strength and become so prevalent in Western society since the Last Judgment. One would think that with new freedom of thought in religious matters and new light coming through the spiritual world to enlighten people's minds that naturalism would decline and in its place spiritualism or transcendentalism would increase. There are four reasons that naturalism, rather than spiritualism, has become increasingly accepted, or at least openly accepted.

First, for things to become orderly, often there is a period of chaos. Anyone familiar with the past two hundred and fifty years, especially the last one hundred years, of world history can easily see that the human race has passed through a time of tremendous chaos. The chaos occurs so that "things that are not compatible may be separated from one another" (AC 842.3). This is part of the process of the Last Judgment itself, and I think it is a necessary phase in the reforming of society. Just as evils must be seen before they can be combated on an individual basis (in the microcosm), the same is true on the level of society (the macrocosm) (DP 278). Naturalism grew so that it could be made manifest, especially its consequences, and then judged for what it really is. This is particularly true of the naturalism that was in the first Christian church, covered up by social forms of piety, ranging from manners to institutions. We must choose either God or nature as our governor (DP 182.2). If naturalism continued to remain hidden from people's consciousness, then we would not be presented with a clear choice, thus remaining in an underdeveloped state of mind. While atheism and naturalism have long been dominant modes of thought and life in Europe, it has taken longer for America to "catch up." The relatively recent publication of several books, with titles such as *The God Delusion, Breaking the Spell: Religion as a Natural Phenomenon, God: The Failed Hypothesis, How Science Shows that God Does Not Exist*, and *God is Not Great: How Religion Poisons Everything*, and the launching of a new group called "The Brights" constitute something of a "coming-out" for naturalists.[104] But this is a continuation of a process that started quietly in the seventeenth century prior to the Last Judgment and has grown quite loud. One theist and critic of naturalism, Phillip E. Johnson, welcomes this development:

> I conclude that the new atheist crusaders are dangerous only to themselves. Once they step out of the protected haven called "science," they invite the public to examine their philosophical biases and lay themselves open to a devastating rebuttal that will readily be forthcoming. That is why I look forward to the prospect of an intellectual battle in which the evolutionary naturalists are no longer able to cloak their vulnerabilities in the manifest falsehoods of the "Inherit the Wind" mythology that they have exploited for so long.[105]

Second, in *Apocalypse Explained* 981.2 it is asserted that naturalism and adultery make a one. This logically implies that spiritualism or supernatural religion and marital fidelity make a one. In fact, this is what the work on marriage states: that true marriage love is the repository of the Christian faith and that only religious and spiritual people can come into this love (ML 57, 116, 239–40, 443). Swedenborg reports that the hell of the adulterers was growing in his day, and that it was being filled by people from the so-called Christian world (AC 824). Christians are adulterers above all others in the whole world, and the worst adulterers are so-called Christians (AC 1032.8; 2744; AC 5060.3; AC 8904.2; HH 374). In fact, Western "Christian" society is so immoral that not only is there no shame in committing adultery, but adultery is held to be honorable, and people who believe otherwise are laughed at (AC 6666.3; AE 1008.2). True married love is real, but "today is so rare that people do not know what it is like, and scarcely that it exists" (ML 57). Few Christians go to the Lord or live what the church teaches (ML 337). Once some angels called together several hundred Europeans "distinguished for their genius, learning, and wisdom," and asked them if they saw any difference between marriage and adultery. "All but ten replied that statutory law alone makes a distinction" (ML 478.2). If adultery leads to naturalism and Christian Europe was and is plagued by adulterous behavior and attitudes which tolerate or celebrate it, then it is no surprise that naturalism is so prevalent in Western society. Since America is in several ways an extension of European culture, then it is not surprising that adultery and naturalism have increased in the U.S. as well.

Speaking of the learned, a third reason for the prominence of naturalism is that a disordered love of self often includes an unjustified pride in one's own intelligence. If the group which constructs the framework for society is an intellectual elite which lacks humility, and this group engages in immoral behavior and justifies it with false ideas and specious arguments from theology, philosophy, or science, then these cultural leaders model behaviors and beliefs that other members of society are inclined to emulate. Arrogant educators and the proud in heart are atheists, for they reject Divine Providence, heaven, hell, a life after death, and the truths of faith. This leaves only nature and oneself in which to believe. Swedenborg writes that in the other life "an immense number" of the "educated of the European continent at the present day" are atheists (AC 9394). And we must remember that in the seventeenth and eighteenth centuries, "the learned" were not secular professors at public universities. There were just as many clergy, or professors who had to take holy orders, as there were *philosophes* outside of the universities, who were "the learned." During a debate between two angels and two satans over whether God or nature is ultimate reality, Swedenborg saw them surrounded by a large number of people who were famous for their learning when they lived in the natural world. This group of intellectuals was very fickle in their faith, at one moment they supported the angels, the next moment they supported the satans. They then told Swedenborg a secret:

> We looked down to earth to see those distinguished for their learning and we found six hundred out of a thousand on the side of nature, and the rest on the side of God. And those who were on God's side, because they spoke not from the understanding but only repeating what they had been told, kept saying that nature came from God. (TCR 77.5)

Swedenborg is reporting that while the learned in the spiritual world are fickle, a majority of the learned in the natural world are naturalists, and the theistic minority here hold their position not from a deep understanding of philosophical theology, but from memorization based upon someone else's authority. Thus theism is not getting much support from the spiritual world, in fact it is being undermined there, and it has a very weak foundation in the natural world. So it is no surprise that when Swedenborg conversed with angles about the future of our world after the Last Judgment, that the angels "have slender hope" for the people of Christendom, but much hope for "some nation far distant from the Christian world, and therefore removed from infesters" (LJ 74). This nation is "capable of receiving spiritual light, and of being made a celestial-spiritual man" (LJ 74). Unfortunately, the name of this nation is not given.

The fourth reason for the growth of naturalism is the influence of a very materialistic and hedonistic sphere from people in both the spiritual and natural worlds. Our thoughts are influenced by sensuous spirits, who indulge the pleasures of the body and reject thought beyond what they sense, including thought about eternal life. Again, we should remember that the people that Swedenborg met in the spiritual world were often not scientists but church leaders who had covered up their materialism with a cloak of piety. Swedenborg reports that "spirits of this kind abound in the other life at the present day, for troops of them come from the world" and the influx from them prompts people to indulge their "natural inclinations" and to live for self and the world (AC 6201). In other words, there is strong peer pressure to be a naturalist and live a hedonistic life-style, both of which make a person reject a spiritual view of human life—so much that such a person loathes the very mention of eternal life.

ARGUMENTS CONCERNING NATURALISM

In general, philosophy concerns itself with reason and the giving of reasons for one's positions and beliefs, or adopting the most reasonable of them. To philosophers, the person with the best arguments wins the contest of ideas. This means that even an argument that is very technical and contains little or no rhetorical devices, is very exciting because arguments are at the center of action. Also, in a broadly democratic culture, or one that aspires thereto, engaging in reasoned debate rather than violence to persuade others to adopt a policy or course of action is essential. So it is important to be familiar with the reasons and arguments both for and against naturalism. This is not an exhaustive treatment of all the arguments for and against naturalism, but I think there are enough to show what philosophers take to be the strengths and weaknesses of naturalism. While there is some overlap between arguments for and against naturalism, and arguments supporting theism, we will not be reviewing arguments that attempt to prove the existence of God and objections to these. This is apologetics and there are very helpful books one can consult regarding this.[106]

In the next two large sections of the paper I quote philosophers at length. The reason for this practice is that when professional philosophers write for one another, their arguments are frequently complex and very carefully worded so as to avoid becoming easy prey to objections. This makes summarization not only difficult, but can also lead to inaccuracies and misunderstanding. Reading these arguments may not be easy, but it does give the reader an accurate idea of the work that goes on in philosophy while advancing one's understanding of the intricacies of the issue. Depending upon one's cast of mind, the thrill of tracking the jousting motions of the different camps through the twists and turns of the debate may be experienced.

ARGUMENTS FOR NATURALISM

We will begin with arguments from Sidney Hook (1902–89), a professor of philosophy at New York University, student of John Dewey, and an advocate of pragmatism, naturalism, and socialism. Hook characterizes the use of any other method of knowing besides science as a "failure of nerve."[107] In the quotations that follow, note well Hook's emphasis upon the commitment to methodological naturalism, particularly through his use of the word "evidence."

> The intelligent demand for evidence need not paralyze the pioneers of truth who catch glimpses of what may until then be undreamed of. For the sciences themselves do not demand complete or exact confirmation of an hypothesis to begin with, but only enough to institute further inquiries; and the history of science is sufficient evidence that the discipline of its method, far from being a bar against the discovery of new truths, is a positive aid in acquiring them. As for decreeing what does or can exist, there is nothing in scientific method that forbids anything to exist. It concerns itself only with the responsibility of the assertions that proclaim the existence of anything. It does not jeer at the mystical swoon of rapture; it only denies the mystic's retrospective cognitive claims for which no evidence is offered except the fact of the trance.
>
> Scientific method does not entail any metaphysical theory of existence and certainly not metaphysical materialism.[108]

> Naturalism is opposed to all known forms of supernaturalism, not because it rules out a priori what may or may not exist, but because no plausible evidence has been found to warrant belief in the entities and powers to which supernatural

status has been attributed. The existence of God, immortality, disembodied spirits, cosmic purpose and design, as these have been customarily interpreted by the great institutional religions, are denied by naturalists for the same generic reasons that they deny the existence of fairies, elves, and leprechauns. There are other conceptions of God, to be sure, and provided they are not self-contradictory in meaning, the naturalist is prepared in principle to consider their claims to validity. All he asks is that the conception be sufficiently definite to make possible specific inferences of the determinate conditions—the *how*, *when*, and *where* of His operation.

So long as no self-contradictory notions are advanced, he will not rule out the abstract logical possibility that angelic creatures push the planets any more than that there exists a gingerbread castle on the other side of the moon. All he demands is the presence of sufficient precision of meaning to make it possible to test, let us say . . . the existence of extra-sensory perception. The possibility of extrasensory perception cannot be ruled out a priori. Here, as elsewhere, the naturalist must follow the preponderance of scientific evidence. He therefore welcomes those who talk about the experiential evidence for religious beliefs as distinct from those who begin with mystery and end in mystery. He only asks to be given an opportunity to examine the evidence and to evaluate it by the same general canons which have led to the great triumphs of knowledge in the past. It is natural in this case, as in the case of extrasensory perception, that he should scrutinize with great care reports which if true would lead him radically to modify some of his earlier generalizations. The unusual must clear a higher hurdle of credibility than the usual. But only on its first jump. Unfortunately, for all their talk of appeal to experience, direct or indirect, religious experientialists dare not appeal to any experience of sufficiently determinate character to permit of definite tests. There is a certain wisdom in this reluctance. For if experience can confirm a belief, it can also invalidate it. But to most supernaturalists this is an inadmissible possibility. We therefore find that the kind of experience to which reference is made is not only unique but also uniquely self-authenticating. Those who are not blessed by the experiences are regarded as blind or deaf or worse![109]

In these passages Hook tries to take the position of a completely objective inquirer, claiming that science is metaphysically neutral with regard to supernaturalism and that he might believe in supernaturalism, but by golly, there just isn't any plausible evidence. By "evidence" Hook means scientific evidence, since for him there is no other kind, at least none that is epistemically reliable. But science is not a metaphysically neutral method or set of methods. Scientists prefer to work with things that can physically observed, counted, measured, controlled in some manner, and duplicated. Not all phenomena occur under these conditions. By claiming that science is its only method, naturalism does, (contrary to Hook) rule out *a priori* various entities and our belief in them. Hook is like a man who, having discovered how helpful a microscope is when seeking knowledge of various entities, declares that microscopy is the only method that can be trusted to give us knowledge of reality *tout court*. If we don't have any microscopic evidence for the existence of something, then we don't have any evidence for it at all.

Hook's naïve realism concerning the objectivity of science has been exploded by the findings in the history and sociology of science. During the last quarter of the twentieth century, we have become increasingly aware that scientists are subject to the same sorts of cognitive, affective, economic, etc. distortions as the rest of us mere mortals. Granted, the scientific method dampens bias significantly, but bias remains nonetheless and the entire enterprise is shot through with values and value judgments. This is powerfully illustrated in the various fields of medicine.[110]

Next, consider the arguments for naturalism put forth by the American philosopher Arthur Danto along with some comments and questions of my own.

1) "[N]atural objects are the only objects about which we know directly, and it would be only with reference to their perturbations that we might secure indirect knowledge of non-natural objects, should there be any." This argument rests on the following assumptions: that we have direct knowledge of natural objects; that we have, at best, only indirect knowledge of non-natural objects; that direct knowledge is better than indirect; that one natural entity (humans) can know other natural entities entirely by natural means.

2) People everywhere seek natural explanations. "Recourse is taken to non-natural explanation only in moments of despair. But a non-natural explanation merely underscores the fact that something cannot be explained. . . . at the moment—it does not provide an

alternative kind of explanation or intelligibility." The first premise in this argument is an empirical claim. Is it true?

3) "All non-natural explanations, the result of using non-natural methods, are in principle replaceable with natural explanations." This is a very large promissory note. When will we know that it has been paid? What are the criteria for success?

4) "Non-naturalists contradict in their practice what they profess in their theories. Naturalists alone hold theories consonant with their practice." In other words, when a hail storm destroys his crops, the farmer does not attribute the storm to Divine action. Instead, the farmer blames the storm on the atmospheric conditions that brought it about, and this is a naturalistic explanation. To blame God for the hail storm is a non-natural explanation or attribution. Since we do not indulge in this practice in our daily lives, the naturalistic theory alone is the one that reflects this and is congruent with it. So theists and supernaturalists hold theories that are inconsistent with the way they live; their worldviews are not congruent.

5) "Science is naturally self-corrective if we think of it as it is, as a method to which its own doctrines are unremittingly subjected." In other words, science is the only discipline we can trust because it has self-correcting mechanisms built into it. This is a form of the "science is successful, so you should believe in naturalism" argument. The phrase "its own doctrines" must refer to specific theories, otherwise Danto puts himself in the awkward position of claiming that the fundamental assumptions of the scientific method are unremittingly critiqued by the outcomes of the scientific method, which is a circular argument and question-begging process.

6) Unlike others who merely wrangle ineffectually, "naturalists will be engaged in helpful clarifications of problems which arise in the course of human life." In other words, theists or supernaturalists are impractical and unhelpful. If you really cared about people and their problems, you'd be a naturalist.[111] One could argue that scientists are the people who are most effective at solving problems in life. Most scientists are naturalists. Therefore, it is the naturalists who are most helpful to others in this life. If one counts donations

of time and money to charitable causes as being helpful toward others, it is not the case that naturalists are most helpful. Social research shows that theists are most helpful, even when donations to ecclesiastical bodies are removed from the data.

Here are Danto's replies to the objections aimed at naturalism along with some commentary:

- "It is not the aim of naturalism to impoverish experience" by saying that "the only mode of experience which is cognitive is scientific." In other words, humans have lots of kinds of experience, aesthetic and affective for example, and naturalists don't want to be seen as excluding them and so impoverishing human life.
- "Nor is it the aim of naturalism to insist that all natural objects are really reducible to one favored *sort* of natural objects or that only the objects or descriptions of objects recognized by the natural science are *real*. All natural objects are equally real, and the descriptive vocabulary of the sciences does not exhaust the reality of nature." This reply is similar to the first one. It too is made in response to an objection that charges naturalism with impoverishing our experience of nature, or elevating the scientific description of nature above all others, say, the poetic description of nature.[112]

In his online encyclopedia entry, philosopher David Papineau rejects the suggestion that naturalism rests on "some kind of unargued commitment" which "seems to be supported by the historical contingency of naturalist doctrines."[113] Instead he asserts that "naturalist doctrines . . . are closely responsive to received scientific opinion about the range of causes that can have physical effects." In his view, naturalism rests on the

> widespread acceptance of the doctrine now known as the "causal closure" or the "causal completeness" of the physical realm, according to which all physical effects can be accounted for by basic physical causes (where "physical" can be understood as referring to some list of fundamental forces).

The widespread acceptance of the causal closure doctrine occurred by the middle of the twentieth century.

> The causal closure thesis implies that any mental and biological causes must themselves by physically constituted, if they are to produce physical effects. It thus gives rise to a particularly strong form of ontological naturalism, namely the physicalist doctrine that any state that has physical effects must itself be physical.[114]

In my opinion, the causal closure doctrine seems like an assertion of naturalism, or a part of it, not something independent of it that can be used to support it. The same seems to apply to physicalism. Also, linking the acceptance of that doctrine to the findings of science does not do away with its contingency, for the findings of science are themselves contingent, as other naturalists have asserted. Papineau's assertion ultimately rests on the "appeal to science" and its success. But he raises a very important philosophical point, namely, how are we to understand causality? The Heavenly Doctrines take a position directly opposite to the naturalists when they claim that all causes are spiritual, or are in the spiritual world (DLW 119). The New Church view of reality is also shot-through with purpose; it is a highly teleological view of nature (DLW 168, 189, 197, 241). There is much work to be done in explaining exactly what this means and how it relates to our understanding of science and the natural world. This is another opportunity to conduct some very import research in the future.

ARGUMENTS AGAINST NATURALISM

At the beginning of this paper we saw that naturalism is the reigning worldview of today's Western philosophers. This does not mean that there are no critics of naturalism. Even though naturalism is *the* position to hold, and has been for most of the twentieth century, during the past twenty-five years a number of arguments have been advanced against it. These arguments have been produced by both theistic and secular philosophers. What follows are quotations from both sets of philosophers along with my summarizing statements.

Let us first consider one of the arguments made by a Christian philosopher. As we have seen, according to the naturalists we should believe in naturalism because of science. Since this is the most frequent reason given for naturalism and typically the most powerful today, the truth or falsity of this claim is crucial to the debate between naturalists and spiritualists. In this argument, "The Incompatibility of Naturalism and Scientific Realism," Robert C. Koons attempts to drive a wedge between a certain understanding of science and ontological naturalism.[115]

> [The typical] defense of naturalism presupposes a version of scientific realism: unless science provides us with objective truth about reality, it has no authority to dictate to us the form which our philosophical ontology and metaphysics must take. Science construed as mere instrument for manipulating experience, or merely as an autonomous construction of our society, without reference to our reality, tells us nothing about what kinds of things really exist and act. (49)

Koons argues that scientific realism and naturalism are incompatible by showing that

> the following three theses are mutually inconsistent: 1. scientific realism 2. Ontological naturalism (the world of space and time is causally closed) 3. There exists a correct naturalist account of knowledge and intentionality (representational naturalism)" (49) "By scientific realism, I intend a thesis that includes both a semantic and an epistemological component. Roughly speaking, scientific realism is the conjunction of the following two claims:
> 1. Our scientific theories and models are theories and models of the real world, including its laws, as it is objectively, independent of our preferences and practices.
> 2. Scientific methods tend, in the long run, to increase our stock of real knowledge. (50)

Koons then explains that his argument requires two assumptions, which he labels PS (Preference Simplicity) and ER (Essential Reliability).

I will argue that nature is comprehensible scientifically only if nature is not a causally closed system—only if nature is shaped by supernatural forces . . . . My argument requires two critical assumptions:

PS: A preference for simplicity (elegance, symmetries, invariances) is a pervasive feature of scientific practice.

ER: Reliability is an essential component of knowledge and intentionality, on any naturalistic account of these. (50)

After giving a defense of PS and ER (50–55), Koons moves to the proof of the incompatibility of the three theses.

Proof of the incompatibility.

1. Scientific realism, representational naturalism, and epistemic reliability entail that scientific methods are reliable sources of truth about the world.

2. From practices of science it follows that simplicity is a reliable indicator of the truth about natural laws.

3. Mere correlation between simplicity and the laws of nature is not good enough: reliability requires that there be some causal mechanism connecting simplicity and the actual laws of nature.

4. Since the laws of nature pervade space and time, any such causal mechanism must exist outside spacetime. By definition, the laws and fundamental structure of nature pervade nature. Anything that causes these laws to be simple, anything that imposes a consistent aesthetic upon them, must be supernatural.

5. Consequently, ontological naturalism is false.

Hence one cannot consistently embrace naturalism and scientific realism (55–56). Koons then tests his position in the following manner:

David Papineau and Ruth Garrett Millikan are two thoroughgoing naturalists who have explicitly embraced scientific realism. If the preceding argument is correct, this inconsistency should show itself somehow in their analyses of science. This expectation is indeed fulfilled. (56)

In a recent paper [1995] Malcolm Forster and Elliot Sober offer a justification of the scientific preference for simplicity that seems to be compatible with scientific realism and yet which does not acknowledge any sense in which simplicity is a reliable indicator of the truth. (58)

A pragmatic justification of our scientific practice, when combined with representational naturalism, yields the conclusion that scientific theories must be interpreted non-representationally, either as mere instruments for generating empirical predictions, or as conventional constructs valid only for a local

culture. Pragmatism, by eschewing any commitment to the objective reliability
of scientific methods, cannot be combined with a naturalistic version of scientific
realism. (61)

In other words, a pragmatic justification of science undermines the
objectivity of scientific naturalism; it no longer has any "bite" upon
reality, instead science is a temporarily useful and interesting story that
we tell about nature. The idea that science is merely a likely story is
too Platonic for a full-blooded naturalist, and dangerously close to the
position that humans project their ideas on to reality (something theists
are routinely accused of doing) rather than discovering it. Koons
concludes:

> Philosophical naturalism, then, can draw no legitimate support from the
> deliverances of natural science, realistically construed, since scientific realism
> entails the falsity of naturalism. If scientific theories are construed non-
> realistically, it seems that the status of ontology cannot be affected by the
> successes of natural science, nor by the form that successful theories in the
> natural sciences happen to take. If scientific anti-realism is correct, then the
> "manifest image" of the scientific world-view must not be taken as authoritative.
> Instead, that image is merely a useful fiction, and metaphysics is left exactly as it
> was before the advent of science. (61–2)

Koons has developed an interesting dilemma for the naturalist,
which can be stated in this somewhat over-simplified manner: If
natural science is accurately telling us about the nature of reality,
then naturalism is false. This of course would not be acceptable to a
naturalist. On the other hand, if natural science is not accurately telling
us about the nature of reality, then naturalism can be true, but not in its
ontological form. This means that we are not justified in claiming that
only nature exists, and this leaves the door open for theism and forms
of spiritualism. So the other horn of the dilemma is not acceptable to a
naturalist either.

Another argument against naturalism, one that has received quite
a bit of attention, has been formulated by Alvin Plantinga. Plantinga
is probably the most well-known Christian philosopher in America
today. He is a professor at Notre Dame University who specializes

in epistemology and the philosophy of religion. Like the previous argument, he attempts to drive a wedge between science and naturalism by posing a dilemma. Plantinga's claims have been summarized by James Beilby.

> Not only is theistic belief rational, but one who denies the existence of a creative deity and accepts contemporary evolutionary theory is irrational in doing so. More accurately, the conjunction of metaphysical naturalism (N)—namely, the view that only natural objects, kinds, and properties are real—and evolution (E) is, according to Plantinga, self-defeating. Those who accept both N and E have a "defeater" for the belief that human cognitive faculties, so evolved, are reliable. This defeater . . . cannot itself be defeated and thereby constitutes a defeater for any belief produced by those cognitive faculties, including the beliefs which comprise N&E. Therefore, despite the fact that metaphysical naturalism and evolution are typically thought of as very closely and comfortably connected, taken together, their conjunction cannot rationally be held.[116]

Plantinga's argument should *not* be mistaken for an argument against evolutionary theory in general or, more specifically, against the claim that humans might have evolved from more primitive life forms. Rather, the purpose of his argument is to show that the denial of the existence of a creative deity is problematic. It is the conjunction of naturalism and evolution that suffers from the crippling deficiency of self-defeat, a deficiency not shared by the conjunction of *theism* and current evolutionary doctrine.

Plantinga's argument involves three steps. First, Plantinga claims that the objective conditional probability that we have reliable cognitive faculties, given naturalism and evolutionary theory, is either low or, since it is difficult to even start to specify relevant probabilities, inscrutable. Hence: (1) P (R/N&E) is either low or inscrutable [where R stand for the proposition: "Human cognitive faculties are reliable"].

According to Plantinga, the mechanisms of evolution select for adaptive behavior, not necessarily true belief, and it is not obvious that adaptive behavior guarantees, or even make probable, true belief. Evaluating the first step of Plantinga's argument involves considering the nature of evolutionary mechanisms and the nature of the relationship between belief and behavior from an evolutionary point of view.

The second step of Plantinga's argument involves the claim that one who accepts N&E and comes to realize the truth of (1) acquires a defeater for R. Hence: (2) If S accepts N&E and (1), she has a rationality defeater for her belief in R. Even the inscrutability of P (R/N&E), according to Plantinga, is sufficient to give one who accepts N&E a reason to withhold belief in R. Further, this defeater cannot itself be defeated since any prospective defeater-defeater would involve beliefs which would be subject to defeat as well.

It seems clear that if the naturalist, or anyone for that matter, came to believe that she had a defeater for R, then the third and final step of Plantinga's argument would certainly follow: (3) S has a defeater for all of her beliefs, one of which is N&E.[117]

Less rigorously, we can re-state the argument this way: Naturalism is a sealed mental box that does not allow any transcendental help when it comes to the truth of our beliefs or the reliability of our belief-generating organs. A theist can claim that even though our brains might be just complex monkey-brains, we receive epistemic assistance from God and His angels when it comes to the formation of beliefs, our rational assessment of them, and the organs used to generate them. This means that we have a transcendental basis for confidence in our ability to (eventually) know the truth. We can know some true things some of the time, because God knows all true things all of the time and He designed us to be finite knowers in His all-knowing image.

If a naturalist holds that all our beliefs are produced by evolutionary processes, and that these are governed by chance, then our beliefs are also produced by chance and we are not justified, or warranted, in placing a high degree of confidence in them. In other words, naturalism undermines the trust we have in our brains and there is no Being outside of the "box" of nature that can be used as a source of reliability to shore up the belief-generating organs and processes. So if everything, including belief, is the result of selection pressures from the environment and there is no Divine Hand designing or directing those pressures, but only chance, then we are not warranted in attributing a high degree of reliability to our beliefs or our brains. This forces the naturalist into a dilemma: one can believe in either naturalism or evolution, but not both. Yet evolutionary theory is part of the naturalist creation narrative and is what makes this position a worldview and not just boosterism for science.

Michael Ruse, a leading philosopher of biology, has replied to Plantinga's dilemma by asserting that even if we are systematically deceived in our beliefs, the theory of evolution can still account for this. Survival and reproduction are reliable touch-stones for small scale deceptions, and "if there are no good reasons to suspect deception, then it should not be assumed."[118] Moreover, even if systematic deception was the case, we could never check our condition against the "real" world postulated by metaphysics. "One simply has to pull back from a correspondence theory of truth and go with coherence at this point."[119] Ruse acknowledges the fact that Plantinga is aware of these moves and argues against them, but Ruse denies that the circularity of coherence is vicious:

> rather, as the success of science (including evolution) shows, you get an ever-bigger and better picture, as you (that is, the human race) get ever-more experiences and put them into the picture. You get a reinforcing circularity.[120]

Obviously Ruse, like other naturalists, is relying on a form of the "success of science" argument here.

Now let us turn to the arguments against naturalism made by other philosophers. There are two main arguments in "The Charm of Naturalism," which originally appeared in the American Philosophical Association's *Proceedings* because it was given by Barry Stroud as a presidential address. It was re-printed in *Naturalism in Question.*[121] The first argument against naturalism is that it is self-referentially incoherent. Stroud points out that there are sharp disagreements over what counts as "nature" and that "those disagreements are not themselves to be settled by what can be recognized as straightforwardly 'naturalist' means. So one thing that seems not to have been 'naturalized' is naturalism itself" (22). This is quite ironic. Naturalism boldly claims that everything must give way to scientific investigation and that we must bow before its results. This means that everything from axiology and epistemology to religion and worldviews must be naturalized. Yet naturalism cannot live up to its own standard, for there are disputes about what nature is and what naturalism is that cannot be settled in accordance with its own commitments. So naturalism is self-defeating.

Yet there is one sense in which one can begin to naturalize naturalism, namely by investigating the properties of the people who believe that it is true. If we confine naturalism to people who report that they are atheists, it turns out that naturalists "tend to be more educated, more affluent, and more likely to be male and unmarried than Americans with active faith," according to a study by the Barna Group.[122]

The second argument that Stroud presents is this:

> "Naturalism" seems to me in this and other respects rather like "World Peace." Almost everyone swears allegiance to it, and is willing to march under its banner. But disputes can still break out about what it is appropriate or acceptable to do in the name of that slogan. And like world peace, once you start specifying concretely exactly what it involves and how to achieve it, it becomes increasingly difficult to reach and to sustain a consistent and exclusive "naturalism." There is pressure on the one hand to include more and more within your conception of "nature," so it loses its definiteness and restrictiveness. Or, if the conception is kept fixed and restrictive, there is pressure on the other hand to distort or even deny the very phenomena that a naturalistic study—and especially a naturalist study of human beings—is supposed to explain. (22)

Stroud, like previous thinkers, has posed a dilemma. Either naturalism is inclusive or exclusive (restrictive and fixed). If naturalism is inclusive, then it is not definite; it is loose and might let in entities that are usually labeled "supernatural." If naturalism is exclusive, then it distorts or denies the very phenomena it is supposed to study. Thus naturalism is either open to the supernatural or it is not capable of giving us an accurate comprehensive account of reality, which means that there is more to reality than nature. Either horn of the dilemma seems to open the door to spiritualism, and this is precisely what the naturalist wants to either keep out, "naturalize," or ignore.

Stroud proceeds to illustrate his point by examining two large areas of philosophy that are highly problematic when exclusive or restrictive naturalism is seen as the only or best option. These two areas are morals and mathematics.

> Naturalism is widely understood to imply that no evaluative states of affair or properties are part of the world of nature. On that assumption, either evaluative thoughts and beliefs take as their "objects" something that is not to be found in

the natural world at all, or their contents are equivalent to something that is true in that world, so they are not really evaluative. (30)

This is a continuation of Stroud's dilemma. Values are not part of nature; nature is value-free or value-neutral. From this naturalistic assumption it follows that value judgments or beliefs, such as "Killing for revenge is immoral," refers to something not in nature. A naturalist cannot abide this because it opens the door to spiritualism and the idea that morals have a transcendental basis, one that might ultimately empower God or revelation as a source of moral authority. This, from their point of view, would be a disaster.

Yet as John E. Hare has argued, a modern moral theory such as Immanuel Kant's deontology, cannot be sustained without some transcendental assistance.[123] The reason is that Kant's moral theory includes a gap between the demand of the moral law for impartiality and the fact that our natural capacities are unequal to the demand. Something is needed to bridge the gap between the "ought" of the moral demand and the "can" of our human nature. Kant bridged this gap through his appeal to the idea of a holy being and supernatural assistance, but this of course is not allowed in naturalism. So Hare has analyzed three secular strategies for dealing with this problem. One is to increase the capacity of human nature to meet the demand (which would result in a dubious picture of human nature), another is to reduce the demand so that it fits our natural capacities (which results in watered-down morality). A third strategy is to find a substitute for divine assistance to bridge the gap. He analyzes the development of evolutionary ethics in this light and it turns out that it is highly problematic.

The other option, that the contents of moral judgments or evaluations are the same as something that is true in nature, say a certain electro-chemical state in one's brain, means that this judgment or belief is not prescriptive, only descriptive. This option is intolerable because it either distorts what we take morality to be, or it abolishes morality entirely, and holding a position that does this would make naturalists rather unpopular.

Like Stroud, Richard Foley has also argued that naturalism and scientific realism cannot both be true because science cannot explain the nature of justification, partly because this is an ethical matter.[124] The answer to the question, What should I believe?, cannot be given by a series of descriptions about some part of nature or about what I actually do believe. If one answers, You should believe in science, one can always ask why one should accept science as a method of inquiry. But the answer to this question cannot come from within science, otherwise it would beg the question. Ironically, this means that the epistemic imperatives promulgated by naturalists and positivists are, themselves, incapable of being justified through naturalistic means. Still, What am I to believe? "is a question we must answer if we are coherently to back our beliefs and decisions with reasons."[125]

"The same pattern," Stroud asserts, "is present in the philosophy of mathematics, where the quandary is perhaps most obvious, and has certainly been widely acknowledged" (32). One problem with naturalizing math and logic is that if they are seen as mere human conventions, or products of non-human nature, they are the results of contingent truths.

> But it could not have been otherwise than that seven plus five is twelve or that everything that is both red and round is red. No contingent truths, however important, could be adequate to express such necessities. What is more, any naturalism that takes a specifically scientific form, and says that the natural world is the world described exclusively in the terms of the natural sciences, would seem forced to accept truths of logic and mathematics anyway.
>
> It can no longer be identified as simply the world that a scientific naturalist believes in, since if he now accepts logical and mathematical propositions, they are not excluded from what he believes. If this still counts as naturalism, it will be a more open-minded or more expansive naturalism. It does not insist on, or limit itself to, a boundary fixed in advance. It will have expanded to include whatever has been found to be needed in order to make sense of everything that is so in the natural world. (33)

Again, Stroud has placed a dilemma before the naturalist. If he or she holds a restrictive view of nature and naturalism, then this leads to either the exclusion of things that we commonly use and believe in, such as mathematical entities, or it leads to a distortion of those things, which undermines the goal of naturalism to be a rigorously descriptive and objective project. On the other hand, if a naturalist holds to an unrestricted or open form of naturalism, this does not amount to anything more than promoting the scientific investigation of something, and the term naturalism might as well be dropped. If the term is not dropped, it signals that naturalism is really an ideology, which is certainly not science. The result of this dilemma, as with previous arguments, is that a wedge is driven between naturalism and science, and the two are incompatible. This is certainly the opposite of what naturalists assert and desire.

There is another interesting point in Stroud's speech which is not an argument against naturalism, but is still a problem for naturalists.

> The point is that conclusions of naturalist epistemology can be drawn only from the study of what actually goes on with human beings. If it turns out that women's knowledge differs in certain ways from men's, for instance, or poor southern black's knowledge from that of affluent urban whites, that is something that a naturalistic epistemologist should welcome, or at any rate should not resist. Studies in the sociology, economics, and politics of knowledge could also be called "naturalist epistemology" too. The lively interest in such matters these days is certainly on the whole a good thing. Not because naturalism is a good thing, but because coming to see more and more differences among things in the world—if they are actually there—is almost always a good thing. (26-7)

A tough-minded naturalist like Papineau would deny that Stroud presents a problem for him on the basis that the social sciences he lists— sociology, economics, and political science—are not really sciences, or are really extensions of the natural sciences and their findings. But I think Stroud has touched a nerve here. If we take the findings of these social sciences seriously, it means that they could uncover aspects of people's knowledge that are politically controversial if not downright dangerous. It also means that these same investigative methods and their conclusions can and should be applied to people working in the natural sciences and in philosophy. This is something that most naturalists will probably want to resist, and this for two reasons. First, the natural sciences and philosophy, being embodiments of reason, should be above the influence of things like money, race, gender, class, power and political commitments. Second, if the people in the natural sciences and philosophy are not immune to these kinds of influence, then the objectivity of their inquiries and their results is undermined and some sort of postmodern account of the sciences will be supported. But postmodernism tends to put all disciplines on an equal footing, or to exalt the study of language above the sciences (since the truth or falsity of their theories is communicated through language) and this removes the natural sciences from their privileged place in the hierarchy of knowledge.

We now consider the arguments against naturalism written by John Dupre in "The Miracle of Monism."[126] One of the reasons it is such a vigorous essay is that it applies categories of analysis and critique to naturalism, such as mythology, that are associated with supernaturalism and the "soft" disciplines, and these are anathema to most naturalists. Even the title seems to be a direct response to a book by J. L. Mackie entitled *The Miracle of Theism*. Dupre also links the acceptance of naturalism to poor healthcare practices and the domination of the "medical model" of health, to which an increasing number of people can relate and have criticized. This criticism is important because it shows that naturalism is a worldview whose ideas and attitudes have "real life" consequences, not just theoretical ones.

Dupre claims that the naturalist's commitment to both empiricism and monism is incompatible. So this version of naturalism is self-defeating. "Monism," he says, "far from being a view of reality answering to experience, is a myth. And myths are just the sort of thing that naturalism, in its core commitment to anti-supernaturalism, should reject" (39). A main bridge from naturalism to monism is through the explanatory reach of science. If this is combined with the idea that science is a continuous and homogenous activity,

> and even more specifically that its explanatory resources depend on its sole concern with the material structure of things, then we are well on the way to naturalistic monism. (30)

Monism is a myth that derives its credibility from the myth of the unity of science. Dupre analyzes attempts to construct this unity through two means: a unity of method and a unity of content.

> Paradoxically, while unity of scientific method is intuitively a far more plausible thesis than is unity of content, contemporary philosophical defenders of science generally defend the latter rather than the former. (42)

Dupre proceeds to review the reasons why the idea of unity of scientific method has declined.

> [The British philosopher of science, Sir Karl] Popper's ideas had a great deal of influence with scientists and surely had a significant effect on the kind of scientific work that was carried out. It is my impression that many scientists still consider Popper's the last word on scientific method; and no doubt this is especially true among those scientists employing quantitative or experimental methods in fields also explored by more qualitative and discursive approaches. But although there are still a few able defenders, among philosophers of science Popper's view of science has been very largely rejected. There are some serious conceptual problems that have contributed to this, most centrally a persisting worry about the great difficulty of falsifying hypotheses: given a recalcitrant observation, how does one decide whether the observation was inaccurate, some unknown factor has interfered, some unquestioned background assumption is erroneous, or finally, that a hypothesis under test is false? It seems that this variety of options always leaves it open to a scientist to rescue a hypothesis. And the work of [philosopher of science Thomas] Kuhn and others has even made it plausible that this is almost always the right thing for a scientist to do. (43)

Such a problem undermines the notion of the scientific method and suggests, instead, the notion of a less objective judgment.

Dupre concentrates on the concept of falsification that is part of Popper's philosophy of science. Popper thought that scientists do not really try to prove that a theory is true. Instead, they try to falsify it or find something that will disconfirm it. After all, it only takes one observation of a non-elliptical orbit to show that a theory which holds universally that planets have elliptical orbits is false. Yet scientists do not always reject theories when faced with counter-evidence, and the history of science has shown in some cases that the scientists were justified in pursuing a problematic theory. Dupre says that Popper's falsificationism has not illuminated

> the ways that various kinds of scientific work contribute to the growth of scientific knowledge. . . . the variety of scientific practices makes any uniform account of scientific method unlikely. Methodologies have developed in wholly different ways in response to different kinds of problems, and the methodologies we have accumulated are as diverse as those questions. (46)

Dupre is a pluralist: there are scientific methods.

Dupre then turns to the other kind of unity that shores-up the miracle of monism, the unity of content, specifically as it occurs in neurology and the philosophy of mind.

> The problem is simply that to replace mind talk with brain talk requires that the latter can serve the purposes of the former. But it is exceedingly unlikely that this is so. Even if, in some sense, we are talking about the brain when we refer to features of our mental lives, there is not the slightest reason to believe that, say, my belief that the U.S. stock market will crash soon can be identified with some well-defined part of my brain; still less that the same part of my brain will consistently correspond to just this belief; and least of all that everyone has a structurally identical part of their brain if, and only if, they believe that the U.S. stock market will crash soon. And it seems that it is this last that would be needed if there were to be some piece of brain talk with which, in principle, one could replace this bit of belief talk. (I suggest, indeed, that this is a place where the supernatural qualities of monism appear clearly. Magical powers are being attributed to brain cells on the basis of no empirical evidence, merely from metaphysical commitment.) (49)

After Dupre has discussed the two aspects of the myth of the unity of science, he offers a powerful exposé of the functions of the myth.

> Unity provides solidarity and protects the weaker brethren. (52)
> Unity, in short, distributes epistemic warrant. The claim to be scientific is not an important one for solid-state physicists or organic chemists, it is one they take for granted. But on the more controversial margins of science such claims are all-important. Economists claim to be scientific in ways that their more interpretative rivals among the social sciences cannot aspire to, and evolutionary psychologists claim to be uniting the study of humanity with science in ways

that must spell the end of more traditional exceptionalist accounts of our species [such as ones given by philosophy or theology]. The status of "science" might ... much better be used as an honorific to be bestowed on investigative practices when they have provided convincing evidence of success in their investigations. On the other hand, if there [really] is just one system of interconnected truths that constitutes science, a science moreover that ultimately, at least in principle, exhausts the truth about the world, then everything depends on establishing the claim of one's practice to belong to this totality. And if such could be done on general grounds that do not require the demonstration of actual empirical successes, the relevance of such claims will obviously be greater still. Here I suggest we see Science as a whole in its supernatural guise. Just as membership of the True Church guarantees redemption, so membership of the One True Science guarantees credibility. (53)

This last line is very damaging to the naturalist position, for Dupre has analyzed the way that the unity of science functions in human society, a kind of naturalistic explanation for naturalism, and then explained it using terminology usually reserved for religion.

The next step is to show that not just a theoretical debate about the nature of science and naturalism is occurring. Naturalism has had, and continues to have, harmful real-life consequences when it comes to medical care.

The consequences of the ideology of scientific unity are not limited to matters merely theoretical. Reductionist models of scientific unity have a particularly and potentially damaging effect on the practice of science. The ultimate goal of articulating unified science in its full glory leads naturally to a preference for seeing phenomena as depending on the internal structure of the entities that produce them rather than emphasizing the influences of the environment. Probably the most serious practical consequences of this tendency are in the human sciences, and most especially in the medical sciences. Consider, for instance, the several million American children (mostly boys) recently discovered to be suffering from Attention Deficit Disorder Syndrome but, happily, being treated with apparent success with the drug Ritalin. It is somewhat surprising that such a widespread disorder should have been unknown a few decades ago. But of course that doesn't mean that there were not numerous sufferers. (53–4)

No doubt among these millions are some seriously sick children. But I do not find it a bit surprising that many children now, and in the past, have had difficulty paying attention in schools. I do doubt whether this proves that there is something wrong with these children's heads that is appropriately treated with psychotropic (and, apparently, addictive) drugs. Schools are, after all, often boring. The fact that powerful drugs can alleviate the manifestations of the syndrome shows very little. Threats of violence may be equally effective at concentrating the minds of recalcitrant students, but this would not prove that they were suffering from corporal punishment deficiency syndrome. There are many ways of influencing behavior. It is evident that there is some kind of mismatch between the dispositions of the problem child and the social context in which that individual is placed. Such a mismatch could, on the face of it, be addressed by changes to the child, to the environment, or both. I do not deny that changes to the child brought about by the ingestion of psychotropic substances may, in the end, be the best solution in many cases. . . . My worry is that the reductionist perspective on science makes this sort of response look natural, if not inevitable. Millions of drugged children . . . are, arguably, the price we pay for action on the basis of this myth. (54)

Is Dupre's concern unfounded? No. Since the people associated with naturalism believe nothing except what physics teaches, and believe that no one else is justified in accepting the truth of propositions not founded on physics, they reject medical therapy that is not based on the "medical model." For example, an article entitled "Mystical Medical Alternativism" states that alternative forms of treatment "posit numerous forms of energy alien to physics" and the goals of "alternativism" are to "make health science a sham and to desecularize healthcare."[127] According to the naturalists, these are two of the deadliest sins—pseudoscience and religion—one can commit. The alternative treatments described in the article include Alternative 12 Steps, Bach flower therapy, homeopathy, karuna reiki, Pranic psychotherapy, stress pattern processing, and vibrational medicine. Some of these treatments might be shams designed to prey on people who are ill merely to profit from their illnesses. This is immoral and ineffective and should be exposed as such. However, I have seen both homeopathy and Bach flower treatments work on infants. I have no scientific explanation for why or how they work (the placebo effect does not apply here), but that they can work, I do not doubt. Since this is the case, I do not want naturalists controlling my access to healthcare treatments by means of federal agencies such as the Food and Drug Administration or the National Institutes for Health.

Here is Dupre's conclusion:

> Monism is surely not grounded on empiricism. For one thing, if it were, there
> would be no need of the vast amounts of work expended in the elaboration of
> eliminativist, instrumentalist, and supervenientist theses designed to explain the
> empirical failures of monism. More simply, our empirical experience of nature
> is, on its face, an experience of a huge diversity of kinds of things with an even
> huger diversity of properties and causal capacities. Some of these properties
> are open to causal inspection; others require careful . . . scientific investigation.
> Neither causal experience nor detailed investigation suggest that all these
> properties are best understood through attention to the physical stuff of which
> things are made. The advance of science does in deed lend credence to the view
> that we do not deed to appeal to supernatural things in explaining phenomena.
> One variety of supernatural things are those that are made out of non-physical
> stuff, like angels or Cartesian minds. So we may allow that naturalism commits
> us to the monism that insists that all stuff is material, even physical, stuff. The
> corollary that insight into the properties of stuff holds the key to understanding
> the properties and behavior of all those diverse things that are made of that stuff
> is another matter altogether. And this indeed is the kind of doctrine that suggests
> the attribution of supernatural powers to physical stuff in a way wholly inimical
> to naturalism. (55)

Somewhat surprisingly, Dupre's own position is a kind of
naturalism: he advocates a "pluralistic naturalism" based upon the
great diversity of kinds of things in the world and the great diversity of
the means of inquiring into them. Some of the virtues of science also
characterize the non-sciences, and while Dupre provides illustrations
of this, he states that:

> [w]hat is most valuable about this picture of diverse and overlapping projects of
> inquiry is that it makes unsurprising what seems empirically to be the case, that
> complex phenomena are far more likely to be understood if a variety of distinct
> but complementary approaches are brought to bear on them. (56)

In other words, Dupre rejects the unity of science approach to the
study of phenomena and instead encourages a variety of disciplinary
studies. This, he observes, is a more accurate reflection of our experience
with the way the world works. Dupre also rejects W.V.O. Quine's
notion that philosophy is continuous with science (57). Since he is a

pluralist when it comes to science, his question to Quine, the famous
Harvard "god-father" of late twentieth century philosophy, and his
followers is: *Which* science is philosophy supposedly continuous with?
Dupre's view is that philosophy emphasizes different epistemic virtues
and has different goals.

Finally, here are two more arguments that parallel ones that have
been raised against supernatural religion. Let us label the first one the
"fear argument."

The Fear Argument

It is irrational to believe anything based on fear.
Naturalism is based on fear.
Therefore it is irrational to believe in naturalism.

This parallels the arguments made by Lucretius, Nietzsche,
Fuerbach, and most famously, Freud. These thinkers have argued
that supernatural religion must be false due to its psychological
origin, namely, fear or some sort of wish-fulfillment. Secular, "tough-
minded" philosophers have used this line of thinking to belittle the
religiously committed for believing in God on a very subjective "soft-
minded" basis. So it is shocking, fascinating, and wonderful to have
a contemporary philosopher at the height of his career at New York
University, Thomas Nagel, admit that atheism, that is naturalism, has
the same psychological origin: "The thought that the relation between
mind and the world is something fundamental makes many people in
this day and age nervous. I believe this is one manifestation of a fear of
religion which has large and often pernicious consequences for modern
intellectual life."[128] Nagel has a fear of religion, so he *wants* atheism to
be true.

> In speaking of the fear of religion, I don't mean to refer to the entirely reasonable
> hostility toward certain established religions and religious institutions, in virtue
> of their objectionable moral doctrines, social practices, and political influence.
> Nor am I referring to the association of many religious beliefs with superstition
> and the acceptance of evident empirical falsehoods. I am talking about something

much deeper—namely, the fear of religion itself. I speak from experience, being strongly subject to this fear myself: I want atheism to be true and am made uneasy by the fact that some of the most intelligent and well-informed people I know are religious believers. It isn't just that I don't believe in God and, naturally, hope that I'm right in my belief. It's that I hope there is not God! I don't want there to be a God; I don't want the universe to be like that.[129]

The fear argument as stated above is valid, but unsound. The reason is that the truth of its first premise "It is irrational to believe anything based on fear" is dubious. This premise is open to the following sort of case that functions as a counter-example.

Suppose I live in a town in which a number of my fellow citizens fall ill and die despite receiving good medical care. (Unbeknownst to me, a strain of the Ebola virus has grown and is beginning to spread.) I come to hold the belief that I should flee from the town for my dear life and I base this belief on my fear of death. Almost no one would say that I was acting irrationally even though my belief is generated by fear. So at a minimum, for the argument to be sound, the first premise must be modified: "It is irrational to believe anything based on an *unjustified* fear." However, I think the larger point is still sound, namely, that if theistic or spiritual beliefs are based on non-rational features of the human mind and are really psychological projections, then the confession of Thomas Nagel makes it plausible that atheistic and naturalistic beliefs are also based on non-rational features of the human mind and are therefore really psychological projections. As Donald Campbell, past president of the American Psychological Association and a naturalist said, he *wanted* to do away with a supernatural transcendent authority in morality and that is why he supported the idea of evolutionary ethics.[130]

While this does not prove that spiritualism is true and naturalism false, it certain does level the playing field between the two positions and seriously undermines the exclusive association of objectivity with naturalism. As the American philosopher William James (1842–1910) pointed out in his famous exchange with William K. Clifford (1845–1879), when it comes to naturalism versus religion, psychological passion occurs on both sides, not only on the side of religion.[131]

Here is the second argument directed against naturalism. It is designed to show the social pathology of naturalism. Let us label it the "mass murder" argument.

The Mass Murder Argument

Mass murder is immoral.
If naturalism leads to mass murder, then it is immoral to be a naturalist.
Naturalism does lead to mass murder.
Therefore it is immoral to be a naturalist, or to believe in naturalism.

Both Fascism and Communism are political expressions of naturalism. Fascism is based on an interpretation of Darwinism and racial science. Giovanni Gentile, Mussolini's philosopher, completely naturalized religion by equating spirituality with the State. Marx was a vehement naturalist in the negative sense, that is, consistently decrying the horrors and superstitions of supernaturalism. In his *Towards a Critique of Hegel's Philosophy of Right,* Marx wrote that German theory is practically radical because "it starts from the decisive and *positive* abolition of religion. The criticism of religion ends with the doctrine that *man is highest being for man.*"[132] And what is man but the nexus of material forces? Communism is based on Marx's, and other theorists', dialectical materialism. Like the positivists before them, Fascists and Communists assumed the mantel of science in order to legitimize their understanding of society, especially predictions about society, and their desire to control it. The Nazis and the Soviets systematically committed genocide, murdering approximately sixty million Europeans during the first half of the twentieth century.[133] Of course this figure does not include the number of people killed by Chinese, Vietnamese, Cuban, Angolan, and Peruvian Communist regimes and the number of people killed by the Italian, Spanish, and Japanese fascists.[134]

This second argument is one that I have not encountered in recent philosophical books, although a similar one circulated in American thought during the time of the Second World War.[135] Because it is little discussed, I raise it here. Even *Reason in the Balance: The Case Against Naturalism in Science, Law, and Education* does not include this argument.[136] (However, this book does contain a good argument against some Marxist assumptions concerning human nature.) Benjamin Wiker's book, *Moral Darwinism*, links naturalism to Nazi eugenics as well as the endorsement of abortion and eugenics by the founders of Planned Parenthood and the sexual hedonist movement, but it does not advance this Mass Murder Argument or link naturalism specifically to Communist genocide.[137] While not a work of philosophy per se, but rather apologetics, Dinesh D'Souza's *What's So Great About Christianity?* does contain a chapter on the mass murders carried out by atheists and their regimes.[138]

Some might say that this is a cheap argument, or even one that is "below the belt." I disagree. Sidney Hook called it a "malicious expression" designed to show that a "naturalist or positivist cannot in principle accept the philosophy of democracy."[139] Of course during the second world war this would be the intellectual equivalent of tarring and feathering one's philosophical opponents. So it is no wonder that the naturalists were quick to remind people of their association with democracy. "Sometimes it is even charged that naturalists and positivists constitute the philosophical fifth column of Western civilization" says Hook with much exasperation.[140] While there are many things that can undermine Western civilization, naturalists and positivists are certainly two groups capable of this. While today's "war on terror" is waged, secular humanists use the same type of argument against their opponents when they charge that the religious right in America wants to establish a theocracy and that Christians must be opposed to prevent the formation of an American Taliban frame of mind.[141] If this type of argument is "cheap," then it must be so for atheists such as Christopher Hitchens as well. If it is not, then the atheists have clearly lost this round, for the historical analysis of atheistic regimes shows that the argument given above is true.

Philosophers may care very deeply about the status of non-material objects, such as numbers or concepts, the "consciousness-wars," and the role and status of science, but they are a minority of the world's population. While these are important philosophical concerns, with the exception of the status of science, these are not "bread and butter" issues for society. Most people want to live in peace and they yearn for a world free of murder and totalitarian regimes. Yes, one can say that this argument is just part of a strategy to pin the worst events of human history on the position held by one's opponents. Some philosophers of the Enlightenment, especially Voltaire, used this strategy quite successfully against the corrupt first Christian church. Many naturalists and secular humanists nowadays use the Crusades as an argument against Christianity, attempting to show by this means that Christians are prone to violence. If the argument linking naturalism as a cause to mass-murder as an effect is true, then it is naturalism, not Christianity, that is responsible for genocide on such a massive scale that the crusades pale in comparison.[142]

While American naturalists see themselves as the defenders of liberal democracy, some of them feel so strongly the desire to promote atheism, that some of their statements suggest that the end justifies any means. During the question and answer period at the end of a session at a recent conference on naturalism, the speaker wondered why Americans were still so religious compared to their European counterparts and said that where science is strong, secularism will flourish. One member of the audience said that she had a friend who lived in the former East Germany (a communist dictatorship), and that many people were indifferent to religion there, so perhaps American naturalists could learn some lessons from them about how to promote secularism.[143] Ironically, this comment was made at the end of a paper devoted to the promotion of a real, that is secular, liberal *democracy*. Yet no one in the audience publicly commented on the incongruity of the suggestion.

NATURALISM, ARGUMENTS,
AND THE HEAVENLY DOCTRINES

What can we learn about naturalism from the Heavenly Doctrines that we don't already know from the world or from the arguments already given? First, that despite the naturalists' efforts to promote themselves as having an objective position, this is not the case. Ultimate choices, such as the one that a person makes between competing worldviews, are not purely matters of the intellect. Instead, affections from the will are involved and so the basis for naturalism is the same as the basis for theism or spiritualism. It is important to exercise one's reason by studying the arguments for and against naturalism, theism, or any other worldview. But naturalism and spiritualism both rest on "some kind of un-argued commitment."[144] However much a worldview may rest on reason, it ultimately rests on a non-rational (not necessarily irrational) foundation. "Love is the life of man [humanity]. Man knows that there is such a thing as love, but he does not know what love is." A person might believe that life is nothing but "perceiving with the senses and acting" or "merely thinking," but "thought is the first effect of life, and sensation and action are the second effect of life" (DLW 1–2). It is the denial of the existential and affective basis of naturalism that in the long run contributes to its being a form of anti-humanism. Once Swedenborg met an intellectual spirit that induced coldness in him. The spirit was a cold person due to the fact that he only looked at things in a natural light (AC 8629). While this coldness can be present in forms of spurious theism, it is endemic to naturalism.

Second, a choice between worldviews or religions not only depends upon one's affections and one's will, both of which are more fundamental to human nature than reason, and so are somewhat opaque to reason's gaze, it also depends upon a person's character. This certainly includes the quality of one's will, but also one's attitudes and moral behavior. The Heavenly Doctrines assert that naturalism is rooted in a self-centered will and worldly loves and it can also be brought about by immoral behavior, especially adultery. This view of naturalism is similar to the one advocated by Benjamin Wiker. However, Wiker's analysis runs this way: naturalism is an intellectual position, a product of philosophical understanding, and it is bad because of the immoral consequences that follow from it (abortion on demand, euthanasia, and eugenics). Swedenborg's analysis is related but different. Yes, the causality can run so that a philosophical worldview is woven by the intellect and then its implications are consistently lived out, but Swedenborg asserts that it can also be the case, and frequently is, that naturalism is a justification for our desires and behaviors, the selfish and worldly desires we are committed to loving and evil actions we have already taken. So while some naturalists would like to separate the association of, say, lust and greed with the term "materialism," the Heavenly Doctrines assert that the link between the *metaphysical* meaning of materialism and the *moral* meaning of materialism is quite strong, and indeed natural. This idea helps explain why contemporary philosophers are opposed to the traditional family and the marriage at the center of it, and this despite the social scientific evidence showing that people are happiest and thrive in the traditional family.[145]

This does not mean that every self-described metaphysical materialist behaves in an overtly materialistic manner. Indeed, Harvard Professor Edward O. Wilson, a naturalist's naturalist, is described as unfailingly polite and a very sincere person. Just as there exist some infamous public examples of Christian preachers living in very naturalistic and unethical ways, so people who are scientistic materialists do not always consistently live out their beliefs by adopting radical life-styles. But with each passing secular humanist manifesto, the gap between genuine Christian morality and naturalistic morality widens.

This is what one expects given the kind of morality advocated by the naturalists of the late eighteenth and early nineteenth centuries. *A Treatise on Man*, published in 1772, a work of the *philosophe* Claude-Adrien Helvétius (1715–1771), openly states that human beings are only motivated by the love of sensual pleasure, power, and self-gratification.[146] This inspired the work of the English jurist and philosopher Jeremy Bentham (1748–1833), whose Utilitarian ethical theory promotes a hedonistic calculus of consequences, which has been frequently adopted by governments, corporations, and groups in Western countries.

The third thing we learn from comparing the Heavenly Doctrines with naturalism relates to the alleged "warfare" between science and religion. Naturalism is not merely associated with science, but claims exclusive rights to science and that science is the main reason for supporting naturalism. The battle between naturalism and spiritualism can be construed as one of science vs. religion. Some naturalists take science (especially the natural sciences) as an exemplar of reason. Thus we have the well-worn faith vs. reason controversy. All this takes us back to the old "warfare of religion against science" paradigm. Since science is generally popular and most people would like to be seen as reasonable, it is advantageous for naturalists to promote this paradigm and, at the same time, the apparently contradictory nature of religion and science. This way spiritualists can be labeled as anti-science and unreasonable. Likewise, it is advantageous for spiritualists to replace the old paradigm and emphasize, where possible, the complimentary nature of science and religion, reason and faith. This old paradigm has received sustained criticism from many sources, so I will not review them here.[147]

The Heavenly Doctrines offer quite a different perspective on this "warfare." While it is true that naturalism enslaves people to science, so that the tool becomes the master, instead of linking naturalism primarily with science, Swedenborg links it with a certain cast of mind which uses science, philosophy, and even theology as means to justify its attitudes and desires. What is really shocking to people who might be inclined to accept the old warfare of religion against science paradigm is that Swedenborg replaces it with the warfare of spiritual religion against natural religiosity,[148] and this includes the first Christian church, at least as it was constituted during the eighteenth century. Now a Protestant might accept this when it comes to Catholicism, but Swedenborg extends his critique to include Protestants, or the Reformed. The idea that naturalism is part of Reformed Christianity would, in the minds of many American evangelicals today, constitute the scandal of all scandals.[149] The center of the battle in the eighteenth century was, and still is in the twenty-first century, Christianity. What is the soul of Christianity? What does it stand for? These are still crucial questions.

But this struggle is not limited to the center, to the "church specific" or "special church." Instead, it includes the "church universal" or all of the world's religions. This is why the cultural alignments have changed. While there still are fundamentalist Christians who do not accept the theory of evolution, or even its facts, this is in my view a side show. The main battle is between people who believe in some form of spiritual worldview and really live it, against the so-called "liberal" or radical naturalists. The naturalists are not just scientists, for some scientists are religious believers. Nor are the religious believers all spiritualists, for there are quite a few in the West who advocate for a naturalized Christianity—or for a morality that is naturalistic—and this shallow morality effectively undermines an acknowledgment of God and the authority of revelation.

THE FUTURE: NATURALISM AND SPIRITUALISM

The Future of Naturalism

From the perspective of the naturalists, naturalism has a future, but one that requires an uphill battle against the spiritualistic forces of darkness. One strategy proposed by naturalist Ronald N. Giere is to promote science more thoroughly in the U.S.[150] Improved education in science will help young people see that naturalism is the most rational choice in life. More importantly, a scientifically rigorous explanation of supernatural religion will convince people that religion is not something special but really just a natural phenomenon, and that so-called "religious" needs can be met much more sensibly through secular humanism. There are several scientific theories of religion: the genetic, the evolutionary, the cognitive, the social and economic, and the psychodynamic. According to Giere this is the problem: there is no over-arching scientific explanation that takes into account all of these approaches, and the current researchers show far too much respect toward religion by not debunking its truth claims. What naturalists must do is continue the work of John Dewey and show that even though there is no cosmic purpose in life, we can still have values, meaning, and life can be very satisfying. In order to show this, values must be disconnected from idealistic spiritualism and supernaturalism. Only then, he says, will we have a sound and proper liberal democracy.

Another philosopher, Randall Dipert, agreed that the future of naturalism lay in promoting science, but criticized philosophers for not being scientific.[151] Even naturalists, he observed, do not read scientific research on teaching methods and then use them in class. If they did, they would be good models for their students to follow. Moreover, philosophers don't make important political and social decisions using science. He illustrated this charge by reviewing the way that the members of the American Philosophical Association voted to condemn the U.S.-led war in Iraq. Dipert investigated the idea of a pre-emptive war using rational choice theory and developed a computer program based on historical input to model the outcomes of pre-emptive wars. He found that such wars could lead to stability. Philosophers who specialize in ethics are still using intuitions as data points, but this is problematic in two ways. First, no moral sense theory is credible post-Darwin, and second, philosophers use their own opinions rather than conducting a careful sociological study across cultures and genders when considering people's moral intuitions. Dipert's message is that if philosophy is to have a meaningful future, it needs more science more consistently.

Not all philosophers agree with such a heavy emphasis on science and a reduction thereto. Prof. Nicholas Rescher grants that there is one sense in which naturalism is really just a euphemism for science, especially a kind of Neo-Darwinian positivism.[152] But there is another sense in which naturalism stands for the concept of nature as a developing intelligent organism in the idealistic tradition. Rescher takes it as a historical fact that the Western mind has been dualistic ever since the Pre-Socratics. Throughout the history of Western philosophy, thinking has revolved around two poles: mind and matter, or nature and grace, or matter and spirit, or phenomena and noumena, or nature and culture, or facts and values. When one pole is emphasized, science puts all else within it; when the other pole is emphasized, the humanities and social sciences place the natural sciences within them as another human endeavor. Rescher thinks that the outlook for either scientistic or idealistic naturalism by itself is bleak. So he advocates a synoptic realism that adopts both views because both are needed for our cognitive health, and this explains our intellectual past. The sort of naturalism that has the best hope for the future is open-minded, inclusive of both intelligence and mind.

So we find that naturalists will continue to face the same dilemma that Barry Stroud described, namely, the choice of a naturalism that is restrictive (or exclusive) and one that is inclusive. As we saw in the section on arguments against naturalism, Stroud showed that both types of naturalism are problematic.

From a New Church perspective, naturalism has a future, since as long as there is human freedom, there will be naturalism. People will always have a choice between God and nature, between seeing themselves as animals or angels, between relying on a sensory-based epistemology to the exclusion of revelation or relying on a combination of faith and reason. In addition, the Heavenly Doctrines state that reasoning against what is good and true can never be exhausted (AC 1820.3). Thus there will always be naturalistic groups and books.

Another (highly speculative) reason that naturalism has a future is that it contributes to an equilibrium in society. Not just insofar as an individual can choose between theistic and atheistic philosophies, but as groups who exert social pressure on one another and who use political power to advance their agendas. Such opposing forces from the extremes of the spectrum may create an equilibrium that ensures social stability. Naturalism has spread beyond the academy into other areas of culture and has changed from the provincialism of a few individuals to the institutionalization of several groups. Certainly the Council for Secular Humanism continues to take on new projects and expand its publications, library, public policy initiatives, and facilities—and not just in the U.S. but around the world. As Paul Kurtz, the chairman of the Council for Secular Humanism, has recently written: "We need alternative institutions that will support us in appreciating the majestic reality of the universe, in forging our determination to enter into nature, . . . to build a better world . . ."[153] But must naturalism retain its dominant position among Western elites, or among intellectuals? Not necessarily.

The Future of Spiritualism

While the peoples of the West, especially Europeans, are strongly naturalistic and peoples of the East, for example the Chinese and North Koreans, live under naturalistic governments, much of the world is not naturalistic. Most of the people in south and central America, Africa, India, and southeast Asia are either theists or hold some form of spiritual worldview. In fact, the center of Christianity soon will no longer be Europe or America, but it will instead shift to the "global south."[154] This coincides with a shift in population too. Most of the world's people will not live in the northern hemisphere, but in the southern. Currently the world's institutions are located in and run by people in the northern hemisphere. So while some of us toil away in parts of the globe that are strongly influenced in one way or another by naturalists, let us not forget that spiritualists are not alone and are not a minority. Most of the people in the world are either theists or spiritualists—they are not naturalists.

What about the United States specifically? It is important to consider the situation in the U.S. since it is currently the world's "superpower." This is true in a militaristic and economic sense, but also in a cultural sense. This will not always be the case, but presently what happens in American culture can have a tremendous effect on the rest of the world. On the one hand there is plenty of evidence to show that during the twentieth century the naturalists staged what Christian Smith has called a secular revolution.[155] The naturalistic elite has taken over important institutions in American public life, including public education, law, and much of the media.

On the other hand, Christians in the U.S. have woken up to the threat of naturalism and are doing something about it. Conservative Catholics, Protestants, and Jews have formed an alliance. Philosophers are producing arguments against naturalism and others are writing to appeal to general audiences. Surveys show that Americans are consistently more open to religion and spirituality than their European relatives. This is what one would expect given that the Doctrines say that a new church never, or almost never, grows among the members of the former church (AC 409, 1366, 2986). This was true of all previous churches on the earth. It took remnants of the former churches to start new ones and keep them going until they could spread to gentiles. Even though naturalists occupy some key positions in American culture, they have by no means won the day. For example, Americans are open to near death experiences today in a way that they were not sixty years ago. Evolutionism continues to be challenged in publications, on the internet, and in the courts.

People long for meaning, not just local meaning, but cosmic meaning and the naturalists are still somewhat frustrated by some people in their own camp, such as Dawkins and Dennett, who have not been subtle enough in their naturalism to make it appealing to the masses. As Philip Kitcher remarked at a conference: supernatural religion, while false, still provides genuine caring in an atomistic society through ethical community and a Grand Story that people use to make sense of their lives.[156] So to be successful, naturalism must find a way to fulfill these human needs and functions of religion. The Dawkins' response to the bleakness of Darwinian naturalism is to say, "Don't be depressed! We have the great scientific adventure." But the Kansas farmer says, "That's okay for you, but you are a participant in it. What about me?" There is the naturalism of Aristotle or Hobbes, but they don't really appeal to people either. So Kitcher has encouraged his confreres to draw up plans to make naturalism appealing through the use of the arts.

This echoes the Catholic counter-reformation strategy: seduce people into adopting naturalism as their religion rather than persuading people through the use of reason. This is a rather embarrassing position for such self-proclaimed "free thinkers" and "rationalists" to adopt. However, it is really quite consistent with the general attitude that naturalists have taken toward the great unwashed masses ever since the Enlightenment, namely, as most people are too stupid or lazy (or both) to believe what is true, they must be convinced by other means.

Research on human nature shows that people have spiritual experiences. The work of Sir Alister Hardy in his *The Spiritual Nature of Man* has been continued by David Hay.[157] Their findings show that spiritual experience is a fact of life. In Europe there is an enormous amount of social pressure to suppress one's spiritual experience.[158] European society makes people feel embarrassed about their experiences, but they continue to have them anyway. There is much anecdotal evidence too. On the other side of the Atlantic, this has been collected by Edward Hoffman in his book *Visions of Innocence: Spiritual and Inspirational Experiences of Childhood.*[159] This work is especially important because it is harder for the naturalistic critic to argue that these experiences are the result of education or other forms of socialization. There is also the evidence published by the Academy of Religion and Psychical Research in *The Journal of Religion and Psychical Research*. Then there is the *Journal of Scientific Exploration*, a publication of the Society for Scientific Exploration. Just because these books and journals exist does not prove that spiritualism is true. Persuasion rests on the quantity and quality of the evidence. Here I simply want to make the reader aware of resources for future research in spirituality.

If one is an open-ended naturalist, it seems that one of the facts that must be accounted for is spiritual experience. There is interesting research being done in the relatively new field of positive psychology. One of the founders of the field, Prof. Martin Seligman, has concluded that one of the factors in human happiness is an experience of spirituality or transcendence.[160] Believing in these things is an essential part of living an authentically happy life. What will the naturalists do about this? After all, they are committed to the findings of science and to helping people be happy, yet this research pointedly states that naturalism is not the whole truth about human nature. There are a number of moves available to the naturalist regarding these experiences, e.g., one might assert that they are abnormal brain states. Like Seligman, they could try to tie the concept of God into evolutionary theory, or they could try to explain such experiences and beliefs away as a kind of placebo or Hawthorn effect. In other words, there is no God or spiritual world, but the *belief* that there is has a positive effect anyway.

Spiritual experiences will not pound the last nail in the coffin of naturalism, but these experiences certainly constitute a large anomaly in the naturalist ontology. No one who has actually had a spiritual experience could believe that it was "really" a result of one's brain or the large pepperoni pizza consumed the night before. Consider this illustration from a book on Non-Hodgkin's lymphoma (NHL):

> About two weeks before my mom died, she dreamed that my father, who had died the year before, was calling her. When she told me, I was terribly upset— even angry with her—for being so superstitious. Recently, after my own NHL diagnosis, I also got a "call" from my Dad. He said he wanted to "come home." I interpreted that as meaning that somehow he knew I have NHL, and wants to help. (I hope he can.) I will no longer deny anyone's contact with the nonliving.[161]

Still, to guard our freedom, the naturalistic explanation will always be available, and we should anticipate that some of the means used to explain them away will be quite clever.

The Heavenly Doctrines assert that humans were designed by the Lord to have spiritual experiences:

> The human being has been created by the Lord in such a way that while living in the body he could at the same time talk to spirits and angels, as actually happened in most ancient times; for being a spirit clothed with a body he is one among them. But because, after a period of time, people have so immersed themselves in bodily and worldly interests that they hardly care about anything different, that path has therefore been closed. But as soon as bodily interests in which a person is immersed retire into the background, the path is opened, and he finds himself among spirits and shares his life with them. (AC 69, Elliot trans.)

Notice the form of naturalism, namely materialism, that is mentioned in this passage. True, this is not exactly the kind of intellect-oriented naturalism that we have in academic philosophy, specifically metaphysics and epistemology. Still, if one holds that nature is the sum total of reality and that natural science constitutes our only reliable method for acquiring knowledge, then one will of course have only bodily and worldly interests, for there is nothing else to be interested in and no legitimate transcendental way to satisfy one's interests.

"Spiritist" is a label that will, at least in certain countries, continue to haunt Swedenborg and Swendenbogian organizations. Yet there are some positive trends. First, Christians who know their Bible have to admit that spirits, angels, and devils are real beings, and they are all spiritual beings, not natural. Moreover, American Christians are becoming increasingly aware of the naturalism in society and thought. This means that naturalism is a recognized enemy and that spiritualist, or supernatural theism, is an ally. The New Church, as a form of supernatural theism, can be an ally.

Second, New Church people have become more open about their spiritual experiences and using the Heavenly Doctrines to shed light on them. Vera Glenn's book about encounters with loved ones who have departed this life, *A Dove At The Window,* is a good example of this.[162] By producing this kind of work we stand up to naturalism and we witness to not only our faith but also the reality we live. It is also a way of appealing to people who have had similar experiences. In addition, it helps show that human beings are not just sophisticated animals. The more spiritual experiences we can compile, the more these "anomalies" will undermine the explanatory power of naturalism and eventually people will not see them as anomalies but as normal parts of human life. Recall these challenging words by Sidney Hook:

> The unusual must clear a higher hurdle of credibility than the usual. But only on its first jump. Unfortunately, for all their talk of appeal to experience, direct or indirect, religious experientialists dare not appeal to any experience of sufficiently determinate character to permit of definite tests. There is a certain wisdom in this reluctance. For if experience can confirm a belief, it can also invalidate it. But to most supernaturalists this is an inadmissible possibility.[163]

Theists and other people who hold to a spiritualist worldview need to face squarely the challenge regarding the understanding of, and epistemic reliability of, experience. Ever since Immanuel Kant's dismissal of Swedenborg's experiences as "non-sense," those who have had spiritual experiences have been on the defensive. It is time take a fresh look at what is meant by "experience" and how a certain understanding of it has failed to explain what happens to people everyday across the planet.

Given the centrality of spiritual experiences in the revelation for the New Church and the importance such experiences typically have in people's lives, Bryn Athyn College should consider establishing its own Spiritual Experience Research Center. Such a center could not only collect and evaluate studies and arguments produced by others in fields such as neuroscience, psychology, theology, and philosophy, but it could also conduct original research. It could also give people a new understanding of, and appreciation for, the experiences that Swedenborg himself underwent. Studying experience in general or other people's particular experience, or even having certain experiences, such as those that accompany near-death, will not convert many naturalists into theists or spiritualists. In other words, I don't think we can use science to prove that a New Church or supernatural worldview is correct. However, such study can help people understand themselves, make sense of their lives, and it supplies an alternative view to naturalism that provides people with the freedom to choose between two robust interpretations of life. If approached with the right attitude, scientific and philosophical investigation can confirm and illustrate spiritual truth and give us a broader and deeper understanding of them (AC 2568.4–5). Factual knowledge can make a person either wise or foolish, and this depends not on the facts themselves, but on the quality and quantity of good with a person (AC 4156).

While some people are organizing themselves to abolish marriage and the traditional family, others are organizing themselves to strengthen it. Books are being written, conferences are being held, some churches are developing outreach programs, and governments are interested in this movement. In my opinion, marriage is *the* issue of Western, particularly American, culture and its outcome will determine the future of society. For as marriage goes, so goes the family, and as the family goes, so goes society. There is some agreement from the opposite point of view. At a recent conference, Prof. Laura Purdy, a naturalist, said that sexual ethics are at the core of the culture war in the U.S.[164] The intention of the Lord and His hope expressed in the book *Married Love* is that true marriage love will not be a rare occurrence on this planet but will increase in quantity and quality to the point at which it rivals the experience of the ancients. But this hope of Providence can only be realized with the cooperation of mortals.

As we have seen, naturalists have for centuries clung tightly to science. The old paradigm in which science was locked in warfare against religion has been exploded by research in the history and philosophy of science.[165] The postmodernists have deconstructed science, especially its authoritarianism, and have shown that it is a very human endeavor built through social networks and institutions. In other words, science is not an un-stoppable, monolithic, completely objective, machine of unquestionable progress. Instead, it is a very diverse set of processes organized by fallible human beings, prone to economic, governmental, and other social pressures, who establish facts through inter-subjective agreement. Apart from what may be considered the dangerous and destructive work of the postmodernists is the work of the John Templeton Foundation. The purpose of this foundation is to promote dialogue between science and religion. From a naturalist's point of view this project is bad because it gives far too much credence to religion. There is an important caveat to this otherwise positive institution: recent developments at Templeton signal a shift in the organization's engagement away from religion and theology and toward science and philosophy. This is good news for the naturalists and the National Office of the American Philosophical Association is now happy to propose that the APA pursue large grants from Templeton.[166]

Despite the fact that naturalism is the dominant worldview among professional philosophers, not all philosophers are naturalists. It is important to realize that there are many people in the world and the U.S. who care about living a spiritual life and promoting a spiritual worldview. They are monotheists, polytheists, or deists and while some have not adopted a particular church, they know that naturalism does not tell the whole story about life. There are philosophers such as Jacob Needleman and Pierre Hadot who critique the naturalist view of life and philosophy and who offer a positive spiritually-inclined alternative. The well-known philosopher Huston Smith has provided a very interesting analysis and critique of both modernism and postmodernism in his book *Beyond the Postmodern Mind*. Regarding the former mind-set, Smith asserts that it is motivated by the desire to control and dominate, which has led to the adoption of an empiricist epistemology. In turn, these led to the acceptance of naturalism as a worldview. The result has been alienation, alienation of people from nature, of people from one another, and even people from their inner selves. The logical alternative, Smith states, stems from a desire to participate, cooperate, and spiritually engage in self-transformation. This leads to an epistemology of intuitive discernment and a transcendental worldview. The result will be a deep fulfillment, not just external comforts.[167]

CONCLUSION

We began this paper with what is known logically as a disjunct: "It must be thought that either God or nature governs all things" (DP 182.3). Both naturalists and theists agree that this is the choice that human beings individually and collectively face. As we have seen, those who think that nature governs all things have developed arguments to support their position, while those who disagree with them have developed arguments to show that their position is either very problematic or false. We have also seen that, according to the Heavenly Doctrines, naturalism is false and serves the purposes of evil.

But what of our attitude toward naturalists? The Heavenly Doctrines say that there are two kinds of naturalists whom we should excuse. The first kind is someone who continues to believe in angels, the devil, souls, and the life after death but thinks of these in terms of space and time (DLW 350). For example, such a person tries to fix the location of the soul after death. The other kind of naturalist believes that God produces all things on the earth, but observes that this includes not only good things, but also evil things. So to avoid attributing evil things to God, this person conflates God and nature into one (DLW 350). These two kinds of naturalists are ignorant about the way the spiritual world works and how it interacts with the natural world and the way that God governs both. Both types of naturalists can be excused because, evidently, both have their hearts in the right place, both continue to believe in spiritual entities, such as God, angels, souls and so on. Their naturalism stems from ignorance and a lack of understanding. I think our attitude toward these kinds of naturalists should be one of understanding, patience, and a willingness to alleviate their ignorance.

Yet there is a kind of naturalist that is not excused, namely, the confirmed atheist.

> But those who have made themselves atheists by confirmations in favor of nature are not excusable, because they might have confirmed themselves in favor of the Divine. Ignorance indeed excuses, but does not remove falsity which has been confirmed, for such falsity coheres with evil, thus with hell. (DLW 350)

This kind of naturalist "separates the Divine from nature" and so regards "nothing as sin, because all sin is against the Divine" (DLW 350). Swedenborg met such people in the spiritual world. They "regarded the Lord as worthless and despised all Divine worship." "Such spirits . . . attribute everything to themselves and their own prudence, and boast that they stand in fear of none." "[T]heir intention [was] to meet those with whom they could join forces and bring others under their control" (AC 950).[168] The former kinds of naturalists seem to retain some innocence of ignorance, but the latter kind of naturalist has done away with this and has consequently shut off an interior plane of the mind into which the Lord can flow and so lead the person to Himself. This kind of naturalist rejects Divine leadership and spiritual authority. The plane of the mind receptive of the Lord is known as conscience, and people caught up in external things alone, motivated only by selfish and worldly loves, are without a conscience (HD 13–140; AC 4459). Unless "conscience" refers to wealth, worldly honors, and bodily pleasures, the merely natural person does not believe in conscience at all (AC 7217). This kind of naturalist cannot be trusted and is completely dependent upon good laws and social rules to live even an outwardly decent life. Toward such a person and toward the naturalistic tendencies in ourselves we must be as "wise as a serpents, and as innocent as doves" (Matt.10.16). ✂

NOTES

1. Emanuel Swedenborg, *Angelic Wisdom concerning the Divine Providence*. trans. W.C. Dick and E.J. Pulsford (London: Swedenborg Society, [1764] 1949), 182.3.

2. *Voltaire Selections*. Edited by Paul Edwards. (New York: Macmillan, 1989), 7.

3. Emanuel Swedenborg, *The Last Judgment* [1758] and *Continuation concerning The Last Judgment* [1763]. trans. John Whitehead in *Miscellaneous Theological Works*. (New York: Swedenborg Foundation, 1951).

4. In metaphysics, the words "spiritual" and "natural" are often used to designate two different realms or two very different qualities of something. Throughout the paper I will be using the term "spiritualism" as a term whose construction parallels "naturalism." Other terms, such as "supernaturalism," are sometimes used in this paper to designate the worldview which is the opposite of naturalism. "Supernaturalism" and "non-natural" are terms frequently used in philosophical discourse. "Supernaturalism" is used in the Heavenly Doctrines, at least twice (in AC 4063 and DP 34.3). Because "supernaturalism" literally means an intensification of naturalism, Rev. Doug Taylor suggested that I use "supra-naturalism" (that which is beyond the natural). While this is an accurate term, I think "spiritualism" better expresses the whole thrust of the Heavenly Doctrines and Swedenborg's experience. The Heavenly Doctrines are *heavenly* and full of spiritual experiences; *Arcana Coelestia* and *Apocalypse Revealed* explain the meaning of Genesis, Exodus, and Revelation by means of the spiritual sense; *Heaven and Hell* is a book about the spiritual world and what happens to one's spirit after the death of the body, and so on. True, the term "spiritualism" does run the risk of being confused with "spiritism" and spiritualism

was a movement in the nineteenth century that included communication with spirits. Indeed, today's spiritualism is organized into a Spiritualist National Union, publishes the *Two Worlds* magazine, and runs a small college (Arthur Findlay College for spirituality, healing, and psychic and mediumistic studies) in the UK. The seven principles of spiritualism as a movement are the fatherhood of God, the brotherhood of man, the communion of spirits and the ministry of angels, the continuous existence of the human soul, personal responsibility, compensation and retribution hereafter for all good and evil deeds, and eternal progress is open to every human soul. (See the website of the Spiritualist National Union: http://www.snu.org.uk) As *The Catholic Encyclopedia* states, the term "spiritism" captures the meaning of communication with spirits, whereas "spiritualism" is a doctrine which "suitably stands opposed to materialism." ("Spiritualism," by Michael Maher and Joseph Bolland, vol. XIV. New York: Robert Appleton Co., 1912. Available at http://www.newadvent.org/cathen/14229a.htm)

5. Ernest Campbell Mossner, "Deism" in *The Encyclopedia of Philosophy*. Edited by Paul Edwards. (New York: Macmillan, 1967), 2.326-7. This statement is not meant to imply that Deism is not addressed in the Heavenly Doctrines, for it most certainly is; it is not addressed by name.

6. Emanuel Swedenborg, *Apocalypse Explained*. 6 vols. trans. John Whitehead. (New York: Swedenborg Foundation, 1976), 981.2.

7. Benjamin Wiker, *Moral Darwinism: How We Became Hedonists* (Downers Grove, IL: InterVarsity Press, 2002).

8. *Naturalism in Question*. Edited by Mario de Caro and David Macarthur. (Cambridge, MA: Harvard University Press, 2004), 1-2.

9. Barry Stroud "The Charm of Naturalism" in *Naturalism in Question*, 22.

10. David Papineau, "Naturalism." *The Stanford Encyclopedia of Philosophy*. 22 Feb. 2007. http://plato.stanford.edu/entries/naturalism.

11. Charles Taliafero, "Naturalism and the Mind" in *Naturalism: A Critical Analysis*. Edited by William Lane Craig and J.P. Moreland (New York: Routledge, 2000), 134.

12. "Naturalism and Material Objects" by Michael Rea in *Naturalism: A Critical Analysis*, 110.

13. De Caro and Macarthur, 3.

14. John Dupre, "The Miracle of Monism" in *Naturalism in Question*, 39; Craig and Moreland, xi; Stroud, 22–24.

15. John Herman Randall, "The Nature of Naturalism" in *Naturalism and the Human Spirit*. Edited by Yervant H. Krikorian (New York: Columbia Press, 1944), 357.

16. Randall, 357.

17. Ibid. 358.

18. Alan Lacey, "Naturalism" in *The Oxford Companion to Philosophy*. Edited by Ted Honderich (New York: Oxford University Press, 1995), 604.

19. de Caro and Macarthur, 3.

20. Roy Bhaskar, *The Possibility of Naturalism*, third ed. (New York: Routledge, 1998), 3.

21. *Naturalism: A Critical Appraisal.* Edited by Steven J. Wagner and Richard Warner (Notre Dame: University of Notre Dame Press, 1993), 12.

22. For some fascinating untangling of the threads involved in objectivity, subjectivity, science and religion, see Mary Midgley's *Evolution as a Religion: Strange Hopes and Stranger Fears* (London: Methuen, 1985), especially chapter 12: "Mixed Antitheses."

23. Craig and Moreland, xi.

24. Michael Rea, 110.

25. Sellars's statement is based on an Ancient Greek saying attributed to the Sophist Protagoras: "A human being is the measure of all things—of things that are, that they are, and of things that are not, that they are not." See *A Presocratics Reader: Selected Fragments and Testimonia.* Edited by Patricia Curd. Translated by Richard D. McKirahan, Jr. (Indianapolis, IN: Hackett, 1995), 98.

26. De Caro and Macarthur, 4.

27. Linda Wiener and Ramsey Eric Ramsey, *Leaving Us to Wonder: An Essay on the Questions Science Can't Ask* (Buffalo, NY: SUNY Press, 2005), 15. The other authors to whom they refer are John Dupre, Neil Postman, and Simon Critchley, 142.

28. Tom Sorell, *Scientism: Philosophy and the Infatuation with Science* (New York: Routledge, 1991), 1.

29. Hilary Kornblith, "Introduction: What is Naturalistic Epistemology?" in *Naturalizing Epistemology.* Edited by Hilary Kornblith (Cambridge, MA: MIT Press, 1985), 1.

30. Ibid., 3.

31. Ibid., quoting from Quine's *Ontological Relativity and Other Essays.* (New York: Columbia University Press, 1969), 69–90, but also found in the Kornblith anthology on page 24.

32. George D. Hadzsits, *Lucretius and His Influence* (New York: Longmans Green, 1935).

33. Author's notes from Flanagan's lecture at "Reasons to Believe: An Interdisciplinary Conference on Naturalistic and Non-naturalistic Perspectives" held at Elizabethtown College, Elizabethtown, Pennsylvania, July 17, 1997, 1.

34. de Caro and Macarthur, 5.

35. Wagner and Warner, 1.

36. de Maro and Macarthur, 3.

37. Arthur Danto, "Naturalism" in *The Encyclopedia of Philosophy.* Edited by Paul Edwards. (New York: Macmillan and Free Press, 1967), 5.448–9; all emphasis is in the original article.

38. See Emanuel Swedenborg, *Angelic Wisdom concerning the Divine Love and Wisdom*, [1763] Translated by John C. Ager. (New York: Swedenborg Foundation,

1976), part three. All future references to this work will use the abbreviation DLW followed by the paragraph number.

39. "Naturalism" published Feb.22, 2007, in the online *Stanford Encyclopedia of Philosophy*.

40. Ibid.

41. Randall, 374.

42. Ibid. 375.

43. Ibid. 382; emphasis added.

44. John Dewey, *A Common Faith*. (New Haven, CT: Yale University Press, 1934), 87.

45. The modifier "secular" is important because not all humanisms are secular. In fact, if one were to count the ancient Greeks, such as Plato, as the first humanists, then humanism is certainly not naturalistic, but is more spiritual and religious. There have been, and continue to be, Christian humanists. Indeed, properly understood, Christianity is *the* humanist philosophy and secular humanism is an oxymoron. The reason is that Christianity presupposes a Divine Human from which mortals are descended and to which they can ascend whereas secular humanism presupposes nothing of the kind.

46. Paul Kurtz, "The Culture War Continues in Spite of the Recent Election" on the Council for Secular Humanism website: http://www.secularhumanism.org/index.php?section=library&page=pkurtz_election.

47. Different kinds of materialists are, for example, central-state, dialectical, eliminative, and historical.

48. Leszek Kolakowski, *The Alienation of Reason*. Translated by Norbert Guterman (Garden City, New York: Doubleday, 1968), 2–3.

49. Ibid., 3.

50. Ibid., 5.

51. Ibid., 7–8.

52. Ibid., 8.

53. Ibid.

54. Craig and Moreland, xiv. Alan Lacey, author of the article on logical positivism in *The Oxford Companion to Philosophy* agrees: "By the late 1960s it became obvious that the movement had pretty much run its course." Edited by Ted Honderich. (New York: Oxford University Press, 1995), 508.

55. Emanuel Swedenborg, *The Infinite and the Final Cause of Creation*. Translated by James John Garth Wilkinson (London: The Swedenborg Society, [1734] 1908). All future references to this work will use the abbreviation INF followed by the page number to this edition.

56. Aram Vartanian, *Diderot and Descartes: A Study of Scientific Naturalism in the Enlightenment* (Princeton: Princeton University Press, 1953), quoting Cudworth, 67.

57. Vartanian, 68.

58. Ibid. 70.

59. Ibid. 72.

60. Ibid. 203-4.

61. Ibid. 49-50.

62. Ibid. 32-3.

63. Emanuel Swedenborg, *True Christian Religion*. trans. John Chadwick (London: Swedenborg Society [1771] 1988), TCR178.

64. In order to belong to a genuine religion (*religio*), and not just a mere religiosity (*religiosum*), the following three conditions (based on HH 318–19; DP 322.4; AC 8944) must be met:1. acknowledgement of the Divine 2. living a life of mutual charity (living a good life) and some conscience (obeying rules that ought not to be broken) 3.the second condition, the living of a good life, must be the goal, or aim of the individual and community (AE 847.3). There are two basic ways that religiosity is used in Swedenborg's Writings. First, from the perspective of the New Church as the one true Christian religion, all other faiths, or systems of life, are religiosities. This includes other forms of Christian faith. It is in this sense that both forms of Christianity (such as Catholicism) and forms of other religions (such as Judaism and Islam) are called "religiosities." If we take chapter XVI of *True Christian Religion* as our guide in defining religion (apart from God, charity, and faith there is no religion), then we must conclude that Roman Catholicism and faith alone Protestantism are not religions (TCR 450–53). Second, religiosity is also used from the perspective of the universal church, or universal genuine religion. Religiosity thus employed refers to systems of life and belief that function like a genuine religion, but are not. Religiosity in this sense refers to a pseudo-religion, or an inauthentic form of religion. This use of religiosity denotes principles hatched from one's own self-intelligence, or fashioned from the human proprium (i.e., what is one's own) (AC 8941–44). From this perspective such belief systems as Marxism, secular humanism, blind forms of nationalism and capitalism, and even evolutionism are religiosities (AC 10,640–10,642). They are forms of idolatry. TCR 450 states that apart from God, charity, and faith "there is no religion." Also "religion consists in the acknowledgement of One God, and in the worship of Him from faith of charity" (*Brief Exposition*. trans. John Whitehead in *Miscellaneous Theological Works* (New York: Swedenborg Foundation, [1769], 1951), MTW 45).

65. John E. Smith, *Quasi-Religions: Humanism, Marxism, and Nationalism* (New York: St. Martin's, 1994).

66. Emanuel Swedenborg, *Angelic Wisdom concerning the Divine Love and Wisdom*. trans. John C. Ager (New York: Swedenborg Foundation, 1976).

67. Emanuel Swedenborg, *Arcana Coelestia*, trans. J.F. Potts. Revised by Acton and Buss. (London: Swedenborg Society, [1749–1756] 1978).

68. Emanuel Swedenborg, *Heaven and Its Wonders and Hell*. Translated by Doris Harley (London: Swedenborg Society, [1758] 1966). All future references to this work will use the abbreviation HH followed by the paragraph number.

69. Emanuel Swedenborg, *Intercourse Between the Soul and the Body* in *Miscellaneous Theological Works*. Translated by John Whitehead (New York: Swedenborg Foundation, [1769] 1951). All future references to this work will use the abbreviation ISB followed by the paragraph number.

70. See the introduction by Justin Leiber to Julien Offray de La Mettrie's *Man A Machine* and *Man A Plant*. Translated by Richard A. Watson and Maya Rybalka (Indianapolis, IN: Hackett, 1994), 5.

71. Richard Dawkins has said that evolution makes atheism intellectually respectable, but I suspect that this phrase was coined by someone else.

72. Norman L. Torrey, "Diderot, Denis" in *The Encyclopedia of Philosophy*. Edited by Paul Edwards. (New York, Macmillan and Free Press, 1967), 2.400.

73. William Barrett *Death of the Soul: From Descartes to the Computer* (New York: Doubleday, 1986).

74. Thanks to my colleague Scott Frazier for clarifying the Latin phrase in an email to the author dated August 13, 2007.

75. Introduction to La Mettrie's *Man A Plant* and *Man A Machine*, 2–3.

76. Ibid. 4.

77. Which is what John Gray's *Straw Dogs: Thoughts on Humans and Other Animals* did (London: Granta, 2002).

78. Emanuel Swedenborg, *Invitation to the New Church* in *Posthumous Theological Works*, vol.1. trans. John Whitehead (New York: Swedenborg Foundation, 1954), 9.

79. AC 3483, 6316, 8627–28; HH 353–54; Inv 27; TCR 639 *Married Love* (trans. N. Brue Rogers. Bryn Athyn, PA: General Church of the New Jerusalem, [1768] 1995) 500.2. Future references to this work will use the abbreviation ML followed by the paragraph number.

80. *Republic*, book VII.

81. SD 768, 2299–2301.

82. Vartanian 21.

83. An illustration of this link can be found on the naturalist Richard Dawkins' website. In the store he sells shirts with the scarlet letter A on them. For him, the scarlet letter stands for Atheist, but in literary minds this is linked to Nathaniel Hawthorn's famous story in which a woman must wear the scarlet letter A because she has committed adultery. Dawkins encourages his fellow atheists to come out of the closet and not be ashamed of their atheism. See www.richarddawkins.net/store.

84. *Selections from Bayle's Dictionary*. Edited by E.A. Beller and M. duP. Lee, Jr. (Princeton: Princeton University Press, [1734–38] 1952), viii.

85. Beller and Lee, xix, xxxiii.

86. Ibid. xx.

87. Ibid. 153-6. The brackets [ ] are in the quotation from this edition of Bayle's *Dictionary* and do not indicate material inserted by me.

88. Mary Wortley Montagu, *Works*, Vol. II (London: Richard Phillips, 1803), 57–59 in *Western Civilization: Images and Interpretations*, second edition. Edited by Dennis Sherman (New York: Knopf, 1987), 2.50–51.

89. Lawrence Stone, *The Family, Sex and Marriage in England 1500–1800*, abridged ed. (New York: Harper, 1979), 317.

90. Helvétius, Claude-Adrien, *A Treastise on Man: His Intellectual Faculties, and His Education*. Translated by W. Hooper (New York: Burt Franklin, [1777] 1969), 2.220–21. See also James F. Traer, *Marriage and the Family in Eighteenth-Century France*. (Ithaca, NY: Cornell University Press, 1980), 56.

91. Helvétius, 274.

92. Not all was madness regarding marriage during the Enlightenment. There is some evidence that the idea that people should marry primarily for love, and not for money or status, took root at this time. See James F. Traer, 71-75.

93. David Blankenhorn, *The Future of Marriage* (New York: Encounter Books, 2007), 127.

94. Blankenhorn, 128; their website is www.unmarried.org.

95. Blankenhorn, chapter 6.

96. Bloodhound Gang, "The Bad Touch" on *Hooray For Boobies* (Geffen Records, 2000).

97. Emanuel Swedenborg, *The Last Judgment Posthumous*. trans. John Whitehead in *Posthumous Theological Works*, vol.1. (New York: Swedenborg Foundation, 1954), 340.

98. But why is adultery so wrong? Also, it seems harsh to say that adultery closes heaven for a person. However, when we understand the laws of life, and the way reality works, we realize that this statement is not harsh. It is not the Lord who is shutting the door to heaven on a person. Instead, it is the adulterer, especially a purposeful one, who closes his or her mind to the influx from heaven. This is a spiritual consequence of a person's choice within the order of reality that the Lord has created for the sake of human well-being and happiness. A person cannot be heavenly unless he or she is reformed, and a person cannot be reformed when the understanding is blind. The understanding is blind when the lust of adultery is in the will (DP 144; ML 497.2). This is why heaven is closed to an adulterer. It also explains why an adulterer finds naturalism so appealing. The mind of the adulterer is sensuous and the will treats the understanding like a prostitute, that is, it uses the understanding to satisfy its desire. The naturalistic worldview is a convenient rationalization for the lust of adultery. No wonder then, that Donatien Alphonse Francois, comte (or marquis) de Sade (1740–1814) reasoned that since sexual deviation and criminal acts exist in nature, they are natural, so the infliction of pain to attain sexual pleasure is morally acceptable.

There are several additional reasons why adultery is wrong and is harmful to human beings but they will not be pursued here.

99. See http://www.greatapeproject.org/news.php.

100. Peter Singer's review, entitled "Heavy Petting," of Midas Dekkers' *Dearest Pet: On Beastiality* (London: Verso Routledge, 2000) can be found at http://www.nerve.com/opinions/singer/heavypetting.

101. Paul Kurtz, "Naturalism and the Future," *Free Inquiry* 28.1 (Dec./Jan. 2008): 4.

102. See "Recovering the Spiritual Sense of the Scriptures" an interview with Fr. Paul Quay, S.J. in *Touchstone* (1991). This can be found in the Touchstone Archives at: http://touchstonemag.com/archives/print.php.

103. Dean Hamer, *The God Gene: How Faith is Hardwired into Our Genes* (New York: Doubleday, 2004).

104. Richard Dawkins, *The God Delusion* (New York: Houghton Mifflin, 2006); Daniel C. Dennett, *Breaking the Spell: Religion as a Natural Phenomenon* (New York: Penguin, 2007); Christopher Hitchens, *God is Not Great: How Religion Poisons Everything* (New York: Twelve Books Hachette, 2007); Sam Harris, *The End of Faith: Religion, Terror and the Future of Reason*, (New York: Norton, 2005); Victor J. Stenger, *God: The Failed Hypothesis, How Science Shows that God Does Not Exist* (Amherst, NY: Prometheus, 2007). For the Brights, see their website: http://www.the-brights.net.

105. Phillip E. Johnson, "Prime Removers," *Touchstone* 20.2 (March 2007):12.

106. Peter Kreeft and Ronald K. Tacelli, *Handbook of Christian Apologetics* (Downers Grove, IL: InterVarsity Press, 1994).

107. Sidney Hook, "Naturalism and Democracy" in *Naturalism and the Human Spirit* 40–41.

108. Ibid. 42–3

109. Ibid. 46

110. See *Science and Ethics* by Bernard E. Rollin (New York: Cambridge University Press 2006), especially chapters 1, 2, 9, and 10.

111. Arthur Danto, "Naturalism" in *The Encyclopedia of Philosophy*. Edited by Paul Edwards (New York: Macmillan and Free Press, 1967), 5 and 6: 448–9.

112. Ibid.

113. David Papineau, "Naturalism" published Feb. 22, 2007, in the Stanford Encyclopedia of Philosophy online.

114. Ibid.

115. Robert C. Koons, "The Incompatibility of Naturalism and Scientific Realism" in *Naturalism: A Critical Analysis*, 49-62.

116. *Naturalism Defeated? Essays on Plantinga's Evolutionary Argument Against Naturalism*. Edited by James Beilby. (Ithaca, NY: Cornell University Press, 2002), vii.

117. Ibid. viii.

118. *Taking Darwin Seriously* (Amherst, NY: Prometheus, 1998), 296.

119. Ibid., 297.

120. Ibid.

121. Barry Stroud, "The Charm of Naturalism" in *Naturalism in Question*.

122. As reported in the article "Atheists attempting a show of strength" by Jacqueline L. Salmon. *The Philadelphia Inquirer* (Sunday Sept.23, 2007): A9.

123. John E. Hare, "Naturalism and Morality" in *Naturalism: A Critical Analysis*, Craig and Moreland eds., 189–211.

124. Richard Foley, "What Am I to Believe?" in *Naturalism: A Critical Appraisal*, Wagner and Warner eds., 147–162.

125. From the introduction by Wagner and Warner summarizing Foley's argument, 16.

126. John Dupre, "The Miracle of Monism" in *Naturalism in Question*.

127. Jack Raso, "Mystical Medical Alternativism," *Skeptical Inquirer* 15.5 (Sept.–Oct. 1995), 33.

128. Thomas Nagel, *The Last Word* (New York: Oxford University Press, 1997), 130.

129. Ibid.

130. See "Naturalism and Morality" by John E. Hare in *Naturalism: A Critical Analysis*, especially page 199 and the endnote on Campbell.

131. Clifford's "The Ethics of Belief" and James' "The Will to Believe" have been reproduced many times. Both can be found in *Philosophy of Religion: Selected Readings*, third edition. Edited by Michael Peterson, William Hasker, Bruce Reichenbach, and David Basinger (New York: Oxford University Press, 2007), 104–117.

132. *Karl Marx: Selected Writings*, edited by David McLellan (New York: Oxford University Press, 1977), 69.

133. Norman Davies, *Europe: A History* (New York: Harper, 1996), Appendix III, 1329.

134. See Stephane Courtois et al. *The Black Book of Communism* (Cambridge, MA: Harvard University Press, 1999).

135. See Sidney Hook's essay "Naturalism and Democracy" in *Naturalism and the Human Spirit*, 40–64.

136. *Reason in the Balance: The Case Against Naturalism in Science, Law, and Education* by Phillip E. Johnson (Downers Grove, IL: InterVarsity Press, 1995).

137. Benjamin Wiker, *Moral Darwinism*, 256, 261–65.

138. Dinesh D'Souza, *What's So Great About Christianity?* (Washington, D.C.: Regnery, 2007), chapter nineteen, 213–224.

139. Sidney Hook, "Naturalism and Democracy" in *Naturalism and the Human Spirit*, 44.

140. Ibid.

141. See for example *God is Not Great: How Religion Poisons Everything* by Christopher Hitchens, 32–34.

142. Again, see D'Souza, *What's So Great about Christianity?*, chapter eighteen.

143. The speaker was Ronald N. Giere, and the person who suggested that the east Germans could teach us a few lessons was Prof. Laura Purdy of Wells College (Friday, Sept. 21, 2007, 9:00am session).

144. See David Papineau's claim to the contrary regarding naturalism; here I take "un-argued" to mean beyond the scope of reason, not a commitment that has not been at all reflected upon.

145. Christina Hoff Summers "Philosophers Against the Family" in *Virtue and Vice in Everyday Life*. Edited by Christina Hoff Summers and Fred Sommers (New York: Harcourt, 1985), 804–829.

146. Claude-Adrien Helvétius *A Treatise on Man*, 1772, trans. by W. Hooper. (New York: Bart Franklin, 1969), vol. I, chap. VII, 124–140.

147. See, for example, Mary Midgley's *Evolution as a Religion* (New York: Methuen, 1985), and her *Science as Salvation: A Modern Myth and its Meaning* (New York: Routledge, 1992).

148. Or the idolization of nature and the merely natural self.

149. See James W. Sire, *The Universe Next Door*, fourth ed. (Downers Grove, IL: InterVarsity Press, 2004), 59–86.

150. Ronald N. Giere, "Naturalism and Secularism." Paper presented at *The Future of Naturalism* conference, Friday, Sept. 21, 2007.

151. Randall Dipert, "Naturalism's Unfinished Project: Making Philosophy and Philosophers More Than Superficially Scientific." Paper presented at *The Future of Naturalism* conference, Friday, Sept. 21, 2007.

152. Nicholas Rescher, "The Future of Naturalism." Paper presented at *The Future of Naturalism* conference, Friday, Sept. 21, 2007.

153. Paul Kurtz, "'Yes', to Naturalism, Secularism, and Humanism," *Free Inquiry*, 27, no.3 (April/May 2007): 7.

154. See the work done by Philip Jenkins and the book *The Desecularization of the World*, Peter L. Berger ed., (Grand Rapids, MI: Eerdmans and Ethics and Public Policy Center), 1999.

155. See *The Secular Revolution: Power, Interests, and Conflict in the Secularization of American Public Life* Christian Smith ed., (Berkely, CA: University of California Press, 2003).

156. Author's notes from the first Prometheus Prize lecture given by Philip Kitcher, entitled "Darwin and Democracy" Friday, December 29, 2006, American Philosophical Association meetings in Washington, DC.

157. Sir Alister Hardy, *The Spiritual Nature of Man* (Oxford: The Religious Experience Research Centre, 1979) and David Hay, *Something There* (Philadelphia: Templeton Foundation Press, 2006).

158. See David Hay, *Something There*, 76–89, 113–4.

159. Edward Hoffman, *Visions of Innocence: Spiritual and Inspirational Experiences of Childhood* (Boston: Shambhala, 1992).

160. Martin E.P. Seligman, *Authentic Happiness: Using the New Positive Psychology to Realize Your Potential for Lasting Fulfillment* (New York: Free Press, 2002); see especially chapters 8 and 9.

161. Lorraine Johnston, *Non-Hodgkin's Lymphoma: Making Sense of Diagnosis, Treatment and Options,* (Sebastopol: CA, O'Reilly, 1999), 423–4.

162. Vera P. Glenn, *A Dove At The Window* (Rochester, MI: Fountain Publishing, 1999).

163. Sidney Hook, "Naturalism and Democracy" in *Naturalism and the Human Spirit,* 46.

164. Prof. Laura Purdy, "What Religious Ethics Can Tell Us about Sex." Paper presented at *The Future of Naturalism* conference, Thursday, Sept. 20, 2007.

165. See *God and Nature: Historical Essays on the Encounter between Christianity and Science.* Edited by David C. Lindberg and Ronald L. Numbers (Berkely, CA: University of California Press, 1986). *Putting It All Together: Seven Patterns for Relating Science and the Christian Faith* by Richard H. Bube (Lanham, MD: University Press of America, 1995), is also useful.

166. "Proposal to Authorize Pursuit of Grant Money from Templeton" in *Proceedings and Addresses of The American Philosophical Association,* no.5, vol.81, May 2008, 61-2. The proposal contains the following quotations from a letter written by Professor Phillip Clayton: "The agenda of religious studies or theology no longer dominates the Templeton Foundation. . . . Senior Vice President, Charles Harper, a planetary scientist from Harvard, . . . saw the dead end that JTF was heading into and has dramatically switched directions."

167. Huston Smith, *Beyond the Postmodern Mind,* revised third ed. (Wheaton, IL: Quest Books, 2003), 189.

168. For an example of what appears to be this kind of naturalist, view the websites for the British biologist Richard Dawkins: www.richarddawkins.net and www.evolvefish.com.

BIBLIOGRAPHY

Barrett, William. *Death of the Soul: From Descartes to the Computer.* New York: Doubleday, 1986.

Bayle, Pierre. 1734–38. *Selections from Bayle's Dictionary.* Edited by E.A. Beller and M. DuP. Lee, Jr. Princeton: Princeton University Press, 1952.

Beilby, James, ed. *Naturalism Defeated? Essays on Plantinga's Evolutionary Argument Against Naturalism.* Ithaca, NY: Cornell University Press, 2002.

Berger, Peter L. ed. *The Desecularization of the World*. Grand Rapids, MI: Eerdmans and Ethics and Public Policy Center, 1999.

Bhaskar, Roy. *The Possibility of Naturalism*, third edition. New York: Routledge, 1998.

Blakenhorn, David. *The Future of Marriage*. New York: Encounter, 2007.

Bube, Richard H. *Putting it All Together: Seven Patterns for Relating Science and the Christian Faith*. Lanham, MD: University Press of America, 1995.

Courtois, Stephane et al. *The Black Book of Communism*. Cambridge, MA: Harvard University Press, 1999.

Craig, William Lane and J.P. Moreland, eds. *Naturalism: A Critical Analysis*. New York: Routledge, 2000.

Davies, Norman. 1996. *Europe: A History*. New York: Harper, 1996.

De Caro, Mario and David Macarthur, eds. *Naturalism in Question*. Cambridge, MA: Harvard University Press, 2004.

Dewey, John. *A Common Faith*. New Haven, CT: Yale University Press, 1934.

Dipert, Randall. "Naturalism's Unfinished Project: Making Philosophy and Philosophers More than Superficially Scientific." Paper presented at *The Future of Naturalism* conference, Amherst, NY, Friday, Sept. 21, 2007.

D'Souza, Dinesh. *What's So Great about Christianity?* Washington, D.C.: Regnery, 2007.

Edwards, Paul ed. *The Encyclopedia of Philosophy*. 8 Vols. New York: Macmillan, 1967.

Flanagan, Own. Paper presented at *Reasons to Believe: An Interdisciplinary Conference on Naturalistic and Non-naturalistic Perspectives*, Elizabethtown College, Elizabethtown, Pennsylvania, July 17, 1997.

Giere, Ronald N. "Naturalism and Secularism." Paper presented at *The Future of Naturalism* conference, Amherst, NY, Friday, Sept. 21, 2007.

Glenn, Vera P. *A Dove at the Window*. Rochester, MI: Fountain Publishing, 1999.

Hadzsits, George D. *Lucretius and His Influence.* New York: Longmans Green, 1935.

Hamer, Dean. *The God Gene: How Faith is Hardwired into Our Genes.* New York: Doubleday, 2004.

Hardy, Sir Alister. *The Spiritual Nature of Man.* Oxford: The Religious Experience Research Centre, 1979.

Hay, David. *Something There.* Philadelphia: Templeton Foundation Press, 2006.

Helvétius, Claude-Adrien. 1810. *A Treatise on Man: His Intellectual Faculties, and His Education.* 2 Vols. Translated by W. Hooper. New York: Burt Franklin, 1969.

Hitchens, Christopher. *God is not great: How religion poisons everything.* New York: Twelve Books Hachett, 2007.

Hoffman, Edward. *Visions of Innocence: Spiritual and Inspirational Experiences of Childhood.* Boston: Shmbhala, 1992.

Honderich, Ted, ed. *The Oxford Companion to Philosophy.* New York: Oxford University Press, 1995.

Israel, Jonathan I. *Radical Enlightenment: Philosophy and the Making of Modernity 1650-1750.* New York: Oxford University Press, 2001.

Johnson, Phillip E. *Reason in the Balance: The Case Against Naturalism in Science, Law, and Education.* Downers Grove, IL: InterVarsity Press, 1995.

Kolakowski, Leszek. *The Alienation of Reason.* Translated by Norbert Guterman. Garden City, NY: Doubleday, 1968.

Kornblith, Hilary. *Naturalizing Epistemology.* Cambridge, MA: MIT Press, 1985.

Krikorian, Yervant H., ed. *Naturalism and the Human Spirit.* New York: Columbia Press, 1944.

Kurtz, Paul. "Yes, to naturalism, secularism, and humanism." *Free Inquiry* 27, no.3 (April/May 2007).

Kurtz, Paul. "The Culture War Continues in Spite of the Recent Election." *Council for Secular Humanism* http://www.secularhumanism.org/index.php?section=library&page=pkurtz_election.

La Mettrie, Julien Offray de. 1751. *Man a Machine and Man a Plant*. Translated by Richard A. Watson and Maya Rybalka. Indianapolis, IN: Hackett, 1994.

Lindberg, David C. and Ronald L. Numbers, eds. *God and Nature: Historical Essays on the Encounter between Christianity and Science*. Berkely, CA: University of California Press, 1986.

Maher, Michael and Joseph Bolland. "Spiritualism" in *The Catholic Encyclopedia*, Vol. XIV. New York: Robert Appleton Co., 1912. http://www.newadvent.org/cathen/14229a.htm.

Midgley, Mary. *Evolution as a Religion: Strange Hopes and Stranger Fears*. London: Methuen, 1985.

————. *Science as Salvation: A Modern Myth and its Meaning*. New York: Routledge, 1992.

Nagel, Thomas. *The Last Word*. New York: Oxford University Press, 1997.

Papineau, David. 2007. "Naturalism." *The Stanford Encyclopedia of Philosophy*. 22 Feb. 2007. http://plato.stanford.edu/entries/naturalism

Purdy, Laura. "What Religious Ethics Can Tell Us about Sex." Paper presented at *The Future of Naturalism* conference, Amherst, NY, Thursday, Sept. 20, 2007.

Rescher, Nicholas. "The Future of Naturalism." Paper presented at *The Future of Naturalism* conference, Amherst, NY, Friday Sept. 21, 2007.

Rollin, Bernard E. *Science and ethics*. New York: Cambridge University Press, 2006.

Ruse, Michael. *Taking Darwin Seriously*. Amherst, NY: Prometheus, 1998.

Seligman, Martin E.P. *Authentic Happiness*. New York: Free Press, 2002.

Sherman, Denis, ed. *Western Civilization: Images and Interpretations*, second ed. New York: Knopf, 1987.

Sire, James W. *The Universe Next Door*, 4th ed. Downers Grove, IL: InterVarsity, 2004.

Sorell, Tom. *Scientism: Philosophy and the Infatuation with Science.* New York: Routledge, 1991.

Smith, Christian, ed. 2003. *The Secular Revolution: Power, Interests, and Conflict in the Secularization of American Public Life.* Berkely, CA: University of California Press, 2003.

Smith, Huston. *Beyond the Postmodern Mind*, revised 3rd ed. Wheaton, IL: Quest Books, 2003.

Smith, John E. *Quasi-religions: Humanism, Marxism, and Nationalism.* New York: St. Martin's, 1994.

Stone, Lawrence. *The Family, Sex and Marriage in England 1500–1800,* abridged ed. New York: Harper, 1979.

Swedenborg, Emanuel. *Angelic Wisdom concerning the Divine Love and Wisdom.* 1763. trans. John C. Ager. New York: Swedenborg Foundation, 1976.

———. 1764. *Angelic Wisdom concerning the Divine Providence.* trans. W.C. Dick and E.J. Pulsford. London: Swedenborg Society, 1949.

———. 1785–89. *Apocalypse Explained.* 6 vols. trans. John Whitehead. New York: Swedenborg Foundation, 1976.

———. 1749–56. *Arcana Coelestia.* 12 vols. trans. J. Faulkner Potts. London: Swedenborg Society, 1977.

———. 1769. *Brief Exposition.* trans. John Whitehead in Miscellaneous Theological Works. New York: Swedenborg Foundation, 1951.

———. 1763. *Continuation Concerning the Last Judgment.* trans. John Whitehead in *Miscellaneous Theological Works.* New York: Swedenborg Foundation, 1951.

———. 1758. *Heaven and Its Wonders and Hell.* trans. Doris Harley. London: Swedenborg Society, 1966.

———. 1734. *The Infinite and the Final Cause of Creation.* trans. James John Garth Wilkinson. London: Swedenborg Society, 1908.

———. 1769. *Intercourse Between the Soul and the Body.* trans. John Whitehead in *Miscellaneous Theological Works.* New York: Swedenborg Foundation, 1951.

———. *Invitation to the New Church.* trans. John Whitehead in *Posthumous Theological Works.* 2 vols. New York: Swedenborg Foundation. 1954.

———. 1758. *The Last Judgment*. trans. John Whitehead in *Miscellaneous Theological Works*. New York: Swedenborg Foundation, 1951.

———. *The Last Judgment (Posthumous)*. trans. John Whitehead in *Posthumous Theological Works*. 2 vols. New York: Swedenborg Foundation, 1954.

———. 1768. *Marriage Love*. trans. N. Bruce Rogers. Bryn Athyn, PA: General Church of the New Jerusalem, 1995.

———. 1741. *A Philosopher's Notebook*. trans. Alfred Acton. Philadelphia, PA: Swedenborg Scientific Association, 1931.

———. 1771. *True Christian Religion*. trans. John Chadwick. London: Swedenborg Society. 1988.

Traer, James F. *Marriage and Family in Eighteenth-century France*. Ithaca, NY: Cornell University Press, 1980.

Vartanian, Aram. *Diderot and Descartes: A Study of Scientific Naturalism in the Enlightenment*. Princeton: Princeton University Press, 1953.

Voltaire, Francois-Marie arouet de. *Voltaire Selections*. Edited by Paul Edwards. New York: Macmillan, 1989.

Wagner, Steven J. and Richard Warner, eds. *Naturalism: A Critical Appraisal*. Notre Dame: University of Notre Dame Press, 1993.

Wiener, Linda and Ramsey Eric Ramsey. *Leaving Us to Wonder: An Essay on the Questions Science Can't Ask*. Buffalo, NY: SUNY Press, 2005.

Wiker, Benjamin. *Moral Darwinism: How We became Hedonists*. Downers Grove, IL: InterVarsity Press, 2002.

Ideas and Consequences

STEPHEN D. COLE

In 1948, Richard Weaver published a book entitled *Ideas Have Consequences*.[1] I do not plan to discuss the content of the book, but simply wish to celebrate the assertion of its title. The proposition that ideas have consequences is dear to the heart of academics. While living, to a great extent, in the world of ideas, we take satisfaction in the belief that these ideas matter; that they have impact; that they will change the lives of the students who join us in exploring them. Our belief, put in theological terms, reflects the teaching of the *Arcana Coelestia:* "What is doctrine but that which teaches how man shall be?" (AC 1799).

In discussing the papers before us in this session, let us note that if ideas have consequences, then consequences often have ideas—that is, not only can we begin from ideas and seek out their impact, we can also look at significant developments in the world and ask what ideas may have led to them. We can trace the roots of many of the changes, shifts, or events in the twentieth century, for instance, to one fundamental shift in thinking in the nineteenth century. The weightiest idea of that century was the appearance of evolutionary thinking. The *Origin of the Species*[2] was published in 1859, and laid the groundwork for much of the naturalistic thinking that Dan Synnestvedt, in his paper, observes in our world today.

---

1. Richard M. Weaver, *Ideas Have Consequences* (Chicago and London: The University of Chicago Press, 1948).

2. Charles Darwin, *On the Origin of the Species by means of Natural Selection* (London: John Murray, 1859).

Of course the *Origin of the Species*, as original as its ideas were, did not emerge from a vacuum. Darwin himself explains some of the precursors that went into his thinking. One of the key influences was *The Principles of Geology*[3] by Darwin's friend Charles Lyell. In this work, which was published in the 1830s, Lyell popularizes the idea that has come to be known as uniformitarianism and which was first developed by James Hutton in the 1780s. Uniformitarian geology asserts that the earth is in its present condition not because of certain great catastrophes in the past but because of the slow working of processes we still see operating today. But this slow working required vast amounts of time to unfold—millions upon millions of years instead of the 6000 years which had been presumed from the Bible to be the age of the earth.

Somehow the uniformitarians were able to look at the geological strata and see, not evidence of a great flood some thousands of ago, but rather the record of age after age of geological change. Without this concept of eons of geological age, Darwin could not have made the leap from seeing the Linnaean taxonomy of plants and animals as a chart of degrees of resemblance, to seeing it as a family tree unfolding through time.

What made it possible for Hutton, Lyell, Darwin, and others to look at the same things people had been looking at for generations, only to see static relationships, and now see instead the image of gradual processes developing by stages?

One of the themes Allen Bedford develops in his paper is that the Heavenly Doctrine warns us not to look for natural consequences of the Last Judgment, but rather for spiritual consequences, especially as evidenced in a greater freedom of thought in spiritual matters. While the nineteenth century theories of geological and biological change were not, in themselves, matters of spiritual thought, the new ideas were a remarkable parallel with the new view of spiritual change revealed in the Heavenly Doctrine.

The account of salvation in the new revelation is strikingly different from that of traditional Christianity. Many fundamentalist Christians

---

3. Charles Lyell, *Principles of Geology* (London: John Murray, 1830–1833).

believe that salvation is a matter of a spiritual change that takes place in a moment, without any process before or after. Surely one of the consequences of this idea is the belief that the physical creation of the universe took place in an instantaneous way, rather than through a process containing progressive stages and requiring vast amounts of time.

The idea of spiritual change, unfolded in the *Arcana Coelestia* in the eight years leading up to the Last Judgment, was not the idea of an *event* of salvation, but rather the idea of a step by step *process*. And surely the capacity to think of other phenomena as processes rather than as mere events was one of the subtle but powerful ways in which the Last Judgment set the minds of people free, whether or not they were consciously aware of the teachings of the Heavenly Doctrine.

The perspective of seeing process where before only event was seen, is applied by the doctrines to the Last Judgment itself. Traditional Christianity had envisioned a specific and literal day of judgment when Christ would come to judge the living and the dead, a day when the visible world order would come to an end. The doctrines, however, offered a new picture of a dynamic interplay between events and process. A year is given for the judgment in the spiritual world, which year is 1757. But it is also clear that there was a process leading up to this judgment, a process during the judgment, and process in the years following the judgment.

The doctrines teach that the redemption effected by the Lord at each judgment on the human race has involved three parts: the subjugation of the hells, the re-ordering of the heavens, and the establishment of a new church (TCR 117, 640). These things follow in order, each depending on what has gone before. When we look at the judgment of 250 years ago, we see that even in the immediate proximity of the judgment there was a process. Apparently it was necessary for the *Arcana* to be published, progressively, in the years leading up to the judgment, in order that there might be preparation for the judgment. The judgment was then followed by a series of works, after the subjugation of the hells in 1757, but before the birth of the New Church in 1770, explaining the new order that was being established. And finally there was the one crowning work, *True Christian Religion*, published in 1771.

But the processes surrounding the Last Judgment were even broader; there was preparation for the judgment for many years preceding and the process resulting from the judgment is clearly, even now, still unfolding. The three papers of this session conveniently relate, each in its principal focus, to three stages: before, during, and after the Last Judgment. Andy Dibb, in his very title, notes that he is speaking about the preparation for the Last Judgment. Allen Bedford especially treats of the development of concepts in the course of the publication of the Heavenly Doctrine. And Dan Synnestvedt, although he speaks about the role of naturalism in preparation for the judgment and also Swedenborg's own reaction to naturalism, deals primarily with the growth of naturalism since the Last Judgment.

PREPARATION FOR THE LAST JUDGMENT

Andrew Dibb takes us on a delightful tour of the scientific, political, and theological ideas that had to be set in place before the Heavenly Doctrine could be written and the Last Judgment take place as a consequence. His emphasis is especially on conditions in England and most particularly on the ideas of John Locke. The attention to England makes good sense, for, as he notes, Swedenborg himself speaks favorably of the civil freedoms in England, and the New Church itself found there circumstances which nurtured its first growth.

The treatment of Locke is particularly welcome, as there has not been that much written about the parallels between Locke's and Swedenborg's thinking and the actual debt of Swedenborg to Locke's ideas. Indeed, Inge Jonsson mentions Locke largely to dismiss him as a profound influence.[4] This very point should give us pause. Dibb's essay seems to suggest that although Swedenborg was trying to bridge

---

4. Inge Jonsson, *Emanuel Swedenborg* trans. Catherine Djurklou (New York: Twane, 1971), 79.

the divide between the empiricist Locke and the rationalist school of thought, his sympathies were predominantly with Locke. But there is no direct attempt to address and evaluate the claims of Jonsson and others that the balance actually fell on the rationalist side.

A PROGRESSIVE REVELATION

The term "progressive" here is intended with a dual meaning: both "forward looking" and "developing through time." Allen Bedford's thoughtful paper portrays the Heavenly Doctrine as progressive in both these senses. He notes how the doctrine gives us a view of the Last Judgment that is both more subtle and more supple than the more superficial conceptions of former times. He also elaborates on examples of how teachings on specific subjects evolve in the course of the publication of the various works, especially as to how they are treated in the doctrine before and after the judgment itself.

An important theme of the paper is that recognizing the progressive nature of the Heavenly Doctrine can help to give us a more humble, cautious, and respectful engagement with the teachings, lest we fall into the conceit and arrogance that at some point we have arrived at the final answer or last word on any given subject.

Bedford also relates this cautious engagement with the doctrine to the theory, advanced by some in recent years, that the Heavenly Doctrine has fallacious appearances in the same way the Old and New Testaments do. The evidence for this latter does not seem compelling, nor does it seem necessary to invoke this perspective in order to maintain a non-dogmatic stance on the perceived meaning of the teachings. Is there really, as to our humility, a functional difference between thinking and acting, on the one hand, with an allowance for possibly fallacious appearances in the Heavenly Doctrine, or with an allowance for fallacies in our own understanding of truth genuinely appearing?

Either way that one approaches the text, one realizes that one is not in the possession of the final answers and that one

must attempt to be sensitive and supple in both understanding and
applying the teachings.

NATURALISM

Comprehensive and masterful are words that come to mind in
contemplating Dan Synnestvedt's treatment of naturalism. In defining
the term, useful distinctions are made between the words "naturalism,"
"materialism," "physical," "positivism," and even "atheism." There
is also careful discrimination between different uses of the term
"naturalism" itself. Particularly helpful is the distinction between
the ontological and methodological components of philosophical
naturalism.

In surveying Swedenborg's reaction, even in his pre-theological
years, to the naturalism already emerging at his day, we learn both how
sensitive he was to the philosophical currents of his time and how able
he was in marshalling the resources of reason in defense of a theistic
worldview.

The history of naturalism provides a striking illustration of what
the doctrines say about how a judgment takes place as the hidden work
of the hells becomes more openly manifest. The lurking evil is one of
the forces that brings on the judgment and the judgment itself is really
effected not by some unilateral action of God, but rather in the choices
that people are enabled to make once the true nature of the alternatives
is exposed.

Thinking in these terms, it is clear that as far as the question of
naturalism goes, we are in the midst of the turmoil of judgment in the
natural world. Judgments take on the form of battles and many in our
day see that the culture war is only getting more desperate as time
goes by.

Perhaps the most important part of the paper comes in its
unfolding of the causes of naturalism, as described by the Heavenly
Doctrine. Although naturalistic ideas can arise simply from mistaken
thinking, there are more sinister origins as well, including evils of life

and especially adultery. This, of course, leads to a vicious circle, for naturalism can lead to the undermining of the foundation for moral values and behavior.

NUNC LICET

Swedenborg reports seeing these words over the doorway of a temple representing the New Church. Many New Church people are aware that they signify that it is now permitted to enter with the understanding into the mysteries of faith. What I wish to draw attention to here is that the words are over a doorway—they are at a threshold. And despite the fact that we are 250 years past the Last Judgment, we are still, in a real sense, only at the threshold of a new age.

When one stands at this doorway, one can think of the path that has led there and the preparation through the Divine Providence of the Lord. One can appreciate how the human race as a whole and how we individually have been prepared by the insights of such thinkers as John Locke and Emanuel Swedenborg himself, in his philosophical writings.

One can look through the doorway at the challenges and adventures ahead. The teachings of the New Church have so much to offer for the new world to come. But to arrive at a happier and more harmonious future requires weathering the clash of cultures that is inaccurately regarded as a warfare between science and religion. A clearer understanding of the character of philosophical naturalism will not only help us to steer our presently small New Church craft through the storms ahead, it may also even help the New Church to become a calming voice of reason in the broader debate itself.

We are but on the threshold; we have but begun to step into an understanding of the true significance of the doctrine of the New Church. The mysteries of faith have not simply been removed or dispelled. We are invited to explore them with a humble and sensitive understanding, appreciating how the doctrine itself was gradually unfolded two and a half centuries ago, and how it will continue to unfold into the future. ⚔

Renewing the Culture

WALTER E. ORTHWEIN

No idea can be had of spiritual life except from the things that are in civil life; therefore, if the latter is set aside, the former falls to the ground, until at last it is no longer believed in. (AC 4366.2)

Because this world is an outgrowth of the spiritual world and lives every moment from it, changes in the spiritual world affect the state of things in this world. The rise and fall of civilizations, and all developments in our earthly societies, good or bad, are the result of spiritual changes—changes in what people love and how they think, inspired by influences from the spiritual world upon the human mind. Ideas have consequences and everything of any consequence comes from an idea.

The greatest change in the spiritual world since the beginning of the Christian era over two thousand years ago was the Last Judgment of 1757. It was a spiritual "earthquake" which shook the very ground of human thought and completely changed the state of the church, bringing an end to the first Christian era and clearing the way for the establishment of a new Christian Church in heaven and on earth.

And I saw a new heaven and a new earth, for the first heaven and the first earth had passed away. Then I, John, saw the holy city, New Jerusalem, coming down out of heaven from God, prepared as a bride adorned for her husband. (Rev. 21.1–2)

As an organized body, the New Church on earth is so small it might seem insignificant, but the New Church as a spiritual entity represents a whole new dispensation of the Divine, re-creating the world. Its voice may be small amidst all the tumult of the world, but the truth that voice conveys is the most powerful force on earth. It is quietly forming a new world, from the inside out; a new ground of human thought; a new way of life; a new civilization—or, as people are wont to say these days, a new culture.

It is quite evident that radical changes are taking place in the culture which was formed by the first Christian Church, and that these changes are affecting societies all over the world as well as western culture. Two apparent examples are the spread of civil freedom and the growth of modern science. These developments—characteristic of the modern age which had its beginnings in the eighteenth century— are outward manifestations of a sweeping change in the spiritual climate brought about by the Last Judgment. Knowledge of that great spiritual change is therefore essential to a deep and true understanding of the state of the world today. It is to cultivate and promulgate this knowledge that the Cole Foundation for Renewing the Culture was founded. The foundation is dedicated to applying the truths of the new revelation given by the Lord through Emanuel Swedenborg at the time of the Last Judgment to the moral and civil issues that society is wrestling with today, issues which we might call "aftershocks" of the Last Judgment. Our hope is that the Last Judgment Conference is the harbinger of many more such events.

At the end of Swedenborg's book on the Last Judgment, he tells us that the state of the world after the judgment would be outwardly similar to how it had been before, regarding civil affairs, wars, peace treaties, various church denominations, and so on. What would be quite different, however, would be the inner, spiritual condition of mankind: people would be

> in a more free state of thinking on matters of faith, thus on the spiritual things which relate to heaven, because spiritual freedom has been restored. For all things in the heavens and in the hells are now reduced into order, and all thought concerning Divine things and against the Divine inflows from thence—from the heavens all thought which is in harmony with Divine things, and from the hells all which is against Divine things. (LJ 74)

The fact that the freedom we now have is freedom to think about "spiritual things which relate to heaven" shows the importance of the new knowledge about such things. Greater freedom of thought about spiritual things presumes greater knowledge of them. And since this knowledge is meant to be applied on the natural plane of life, I think the need for greater political freedom is also implied. Greater freedom of thought requires a corresponding expansion of such civil liberties as freedom of speech.

Generally speaking, freedom means the ability to do what you wish, but spiritual freedom involves wishing for the right things— namely, things which are in harmony with the truly human order of life produced by Divine love and wisdom in heaven. True freedom is the freedom to think, will and do, not just anything, but that which is good and true (DLW 240, 264, 425). This basic principle enables us to avoid confusing freedom and license, or genuine freedom and the illusory freedom of hell, which is really slavery. What good is civil liberty if the soul remains imprisoned by "the vanity of the world and the allurement of the flesh, the pride of self-intelligence and the lust of power, sordid avarice and covetous desire"? The Last Judgment gave us freedom to follow the Lord, but also freedom to turn away from Him. If a love of self and the world cause us to turn away from Him, then the new freedom we have received has not served the purpose for which it was intended. A sense of responsibility to the One who restored our freedom is required in order to make this new freedom a reality on earth.

Just as a free market makes prosperity possible, so the new spiritual freedom ushered in by the Last Judgment will bring various natural benefits with it if the truths that can now be seen are recognized and applied. Materialism and the idea that religious and moral considerations have no place in formulating public policy are obstacles to realizing these benefits.

"Separation of church and state" is necessary for the protection of both, but banishing religious ideas from public discourse on civil affairs is a destructive modern perversion of that principle. Adhering to the truth of the Word is not contrary to civil liberty: just the opposite—

this is the truth that makes us free (John 8.32). Were not appeals to that truth a major element in the abolition movement and later in the civil rights movement? Why should religious truths now be excluded from the debate on such topics as abortion, stem cell research, euthanasia, and the definition of marriage? By "religious truths" I do not mean sectarian dogmas, but the basic Divine principles set forth in the Word, especially the Ten Commandments, along with acknowledgment of God as their Author. The small minority of people in society who do not believe in God or that He has revealed Himself and His intentions for us in His Word have a right to express their opinion along with everyone else, but not to prevent believers from expressing their opinions freely in discussions of public policy.

All logic rests upon some premise which is simply assumed as self-evident, or axiomatic. The premise is not arrived at by logic, rather, it is the starting place and foundation upon which reason and logic rest. Facts and logic can confirm a theistic premise or paradigm as well as a materialist one. So there is nothing inherently "logical" or "reasonable" about materialism and nothing illogical or irrational about the theistic paradigm.

The specter of "theocracy" has been raised, but it is a red herring. Accepting a theistic paradigm—much less even considering one along with others—is hardly theocracy. In fact, since everyone's "God" is what they value most highly, then the basis of all passionately held opinions could be said to be "religious." The god in question may be nature or human reason, but if that is what is accepted and appealed to as the highest good and source of truth, then that "god" and those who point to that god as the basis of their arguments could be said to be "imposing their religion" on society. Forcing the removal of the Ten Commandments from a courthouse wall is just as "theocratic" as placing them there in the first place was, although the "religion" that dictated their removal is a secular one.

THE CULTURE WARS

Leading up to the Last Judgment there was "war in heaven," in which "Michael and his angels fought with the dragon, and the dragon fought, and his angels" (Rev. 12.7). The war was a "spiritual war, which is of falsity against truth, and truth against falsity." The "heaven" referred to is "the former heaven which passed away" (Rev. 21). It was an imaginary heaven produced by evil spirits in the world of spirits. "Michael" stands for "those who confirm from the Word that the Lord is the God of heaven and earth." It is from such people that the New Church is formed. The "dragon" represents those who turn from the Lord to themselves, and from heaven to the world, and thus become "sensual from the corporeal" (AR 548).

The description of the "dragon" seems quite pointed when we consider the strains of extreme individualism, intellectual conceit, materialism, and hedonism in our "post-Christian" culture. In saying this I do not mean that these are the culture's only traits or that there is an absence of beneficial influences which are favorable to the establishment of the New Church. The "Michaels" of the New Church are not alone in resisting the dragon, and we should gratefully acknowledge the help provided by many others whose thought is based on the Scriptures and whose work is especially impressive because they are doing it without the visible support of the Heavenly Doctrine.

The war in the spiritual world was won by the armies of the Lord, and a new spiritual order was established. But on earth, the battle rages on. Along with thoughts inspired by new truth from heaven, we are also influenced by thoughts from hell, which are against Divine things. This is as true for New Church people as for anyone else.

Spiritual struggle, I believe, is the cause behind the so-called "culture wars" in which our society is engaged at present. What are we to make of these "culture wars"? I find myself in sympathy with many of the stands taken by Christians, but, knowing what the Writings say about the state of the former church, as well as being aware of some of the wicked things in history which were carried out in the name of Christianity, my sympathy with the "Christian" or "evangelical" position in the culture wars is not absolute. I assume that some of the Christian leaders with illuminating analysis of social trends would take a dim view of the New Church. On the other hand, there are some particulars on the agenda of religious groups responding to the extreme secularism and moral disorders of contemporary society with which I think New Church people can make common cause.

The doctrine of conjugial love—and the whole relationship of the sexes and their respective uses—has often been a focus of controversy between the New Church and the world around it and occasionally even within the New Church. The fact that this same area of life is prominent in the "culture wars" is not surprising when we consider who the central figure is in the story of the "war in heaven" (Rev. 21)— a woman about to give birth. Later in the story the New Church is compared to "a bride adorned for her husband." It is not surprising that marriage and childbirth are two of the main fronts in the culture wars.

Freedom is a property of love, and since conjugial love is the highest of all loves it brings the greatest freedom (CL 257). We can see then that the restoration of freedom and of conjugial love are closely linked. Both have been renewed in the new heaven; both are in the process of being more firmly established on earth. It is a difficult, laborious process of birth. But the Lord has provided for new and expanding freedom in this world and has also given us the promise that "conjugial love will be raised up anew by the Lord. . . . such as it was with the ancients. . . . with those who are made spiritual by Him through the Word" (CL 81e).

The New Church on earth has not been persecuted so violently as the Christian Church was in its beginning, but the challenge comes when we work to apply its doctrine to how we actually live. The challenge from our own individual contrary inclinations should be our primary concern, but the culture around us also challenges our efforts.

There are two opposite errors we must avoid. One is self-righteous accusation of others—pointing out the speck in others' eyes while ignoring the plank in our own. The other is to be so paralyzed by awareness of our own sin and unworthiness that we fail to sound a warning when we see a wolf approaching the fold. Whether evil is ignored because its harm is not seen, or because those who see it are so demoralized by awareness of their own imperfection that they fail to object, the effect is the same. We are not speaking of "casting a stone" at a sinner but simply of acknowledging that evil is indeed evil and harmful. A doctor who had (or even has) the flu is still capable of diagnosing that illness in others and prescribing remedies.

The Last Judgment culminated in the formation of a new heaven and the birth of a New Church on earth. The next step—what we need now—is a new culture, which will support and nurture the order of life the church is seeking to establish. Here is the progression: the Word comes from the Lord, the church comes from the Word, the culture comes from the church; the church, in turn, is supported by the culture. The culture that surrounds the church can be compared to the atmospheres derived from the spiritual sun, which serve to receive, store up, accommodate, and transmit the life from that sun to the heavens (DLW 174). Similarly, all aspects of a culture—the traditions, customs, mores, language, art, and entertainment—can serve to communicate the life and faith of the church from which the culture is derived. The culture diffuses the faith as the atmosphere diffuses the sun's energy.

Or, to change the analogy a little, the culture is like the natural sun in relation to the spiritual sun—that is, an "aid and support" to the spiritual sun. Thus a culture should aid and support the church in bringing the life of heaven to people on earth. The culture lives from the church, receives its goods and truths, and conveys them to society. It makes those abstract, spiritual, transcendent things real and visible and present with people; it weaves them into the fabric of their daily lives. This is why the state of the culture around us is a matter of concern for the church; and why the culture should respect and nurture the church as the source of its vitality.

One more comparison: the truths of the church are like the tea leaves that impart flavor and color to the whole cup. The "leaves" are rational truths from the tree of life in the midst of the New Jerusalem;

the "tea" is the culture that surrounds the church and gets its quality from the truths of the church.

I once read an interview by Bill Moyers with Isaac Asimov, the great science fiction writer. Asimov did not believe in God or an afterlife in which we would be judged, and he rejected the idea that human morality depended upon such belief. Human reason is enough of a basis for morality, he said, and claimed that he was a moral person. I don't doubt that he was, but I think that his morality was very much derived from religion, although indirectly. His mind was formed within a culture produced by the Judeo-Christian tradition. The ethos, character, and mental atmosphere that surrounded him was steeped in that tradition. In his mind the "tea bag" may have been removed, but the water Asimov was imbibing and swimming in retained the quality it had received from it. The moral sensibility that persists among people in a secular society is the remnant of a departed spirituality, not the product of human reason. But as the "tea" becomes increasingly diluted by secular thought, the moral influence from the former age also weakens. Just as a body continues to exist for a short while after the spirit leaves it before decomposing, so moral and civil order remain in a society after religious faith departs—but not for long.

We are told in the Writings that the angels think of God as Human and cannot think of Him in any other way. The reason is that "their thought proceeds in accordance with the form of heaven," in other words, from the culture in which they live (DLW 11). Our minds also are strongly influenced by the culture in which we live.

People whose minds are thoroughly grounded on the Word are immune, more or less, to false assumptions, attitudes and currents of opinion in society, but still, the culture should reinforce and nurture and enrich their spiritual outlook, not continually work against it. A supportive culture is especially important, however for those whose minds have not been formed by the Word, and who are thus ill equipped to order their own lives according to its truths. The culture should strengthen what is good and true in people, rather than pander to the worst inclinations of human nature and constantly try to lead people astray.

I am trying to present a general idea, which I think is true, but I am aware that it could be used to justify a stifling atmosphere of intrusive moralizing by professional scolds. This would be an abuse of the principle. Real freedom and happiness, however, can exist only with order; not an order that depends mainly upon external enforcement, but one which arises spontaneously from within people who love the end for which the order is maintained. The kind of cultural matrix I have in mind is nothing like the oppressive culture of political correctness that prevails on so many college campuses (and more and more in society at large). Rather, think of the "micro-cultures" (as we might call them) composed of people in certain professions: historians, scientists, doctors, lawyers, and educators each belong to a culture that maintains the standards of the profession. The general culture of the whole society should perform a similar use, upholding and inculcating basic human decency, including reverence for human life, and for the things of religion and marriage.

Our culture today does exert a positive influence in some areas: regarding the way we speak about people of different races, for example, abusive language that once was acceptable now is not because society simply will not tolerate it. On the other hand, taking the Lord's name in vain is now something even little children assimilate from the popular culture. The culture (and even civil law to some extent) could just as well inculcate reverence and chastity instead of blasphemy and obscenity. And this is what it ought to do (see DP 129.2 and 136.2).

The Heavenly Doctrines explain that the flowing of the spiritual into the natural depends upon favorable conditions in the natural. If spiritual truth finds an inhospitable environment in the natural, it recoils and withdraws (DLW 254). It is like when something touches a nerve in your tooth. Or like stepping out of a warm bed onto a cold floor—you want to hop right back in again. This is exactly why culture is so important. It can either invite or repel the presence of angels. Just as animals need a suitable habitat in the natural environment, so angels, and people on earth who get along with angels, need a suitable habitat in the spiritual environment. We want to establish a culture on earth in which angels can feel at home. If this sounds too idealistic, substitute the word "children" for angels: we want a culture in which children will be valued and safe and encounter good and true and beautiful things to enrich their minds and character. They need a culture that values and protects their innocence, not one that seeks continually to destroy it.

A church cannot be indifferent to the state of the society around it. Just as a culture needs a church to give it its vital essence, so a church needs a culture in which the spiritual life it seeks to convey to the world can be expressed and find a foundation. Luther said, "the world is God's enemy," and there is truth in this; a certain amount of tension between the church and the world is healthy, just as it is healthy for a person to be troubled by conscience at times. But this does not mean that it is healthy for the world to be hostile to the church, for the world depends upon the church for its spiritual life.

The Writings tell us that in the spiritual world whenever any new truth is introduced into a person's mind, some reason for doubting it also shortly arises. Doubt is a useful thing. It causes us to consider carefully what is actually true. A truth which is accepted too easily is likely to be understood shallowly, without nuance or subtlety, and with little sympathy for those who see things differently (see AC 7298). I also think this applies to society as a whole. Each new truth introduced into society is met by an opposing falsity and each new falsity by an opposing truth. This produces a combat, which the Writings compare to the chemical process of fermentation. Eventually what is false and useless is rejected, and the issue becomes clear—just as the lees sink to the bottom of the bottle as the wine ferments and becomes clear (DP 25, 284). I think this is a good way of viewing the "culture wars" going on around us in the wake of the Last Judgment and the publishing of the Heavenly Doctrine. New truth, introduced from the new heaven, is met with opposition and heated debate, but greater clarity will eventually result.

Our culture today is strong on tolerance but weak on judgment. But just as "righteous judgment" can be perverted into mean-spirited self-righteous judgment of others, so tolerance can be perverted into blind acceptance of deadly evils. Sympathetic and empathetic understanding and forgiveness of the sins of others is a virtue, but calling disorders good and pretending they are not harmful is not a virtue. "Hate the sin but love the sinner" is, despite the scorn some today heap on that old idea, a sound principle, and one that we all apply regarding ourselves. Just as it does no good for an individual to deny his own disorders, so it does society no good to deny the disorders active in it.

Judgment is the opposite of profanation, which is the mixing together of what is good and evil, true and false, so completely that the good and true cannot be distinguished and extricated from the evil and false. Getting in the habit of self-examination and clearly acknowledging the evils we discover in ourselves is the first step in getting free from them. Fulfilling the promise of the Last Judgment— spiritual freedom and the creation of a new world—requires a change in our hearts. "Create in me a clean heart, O God, and renew a steadfast spirit within me" (Ps. 51.10).

But in addition, I think the Heavenly Doctrine also challenges us to do all we can to create conditions on earth, in our culture and civil order, which will make it possible for the new spiritual freedom people have to be brought down to earth and made tangible in the way we live. We need to create a culture which will encourage, support and nurture the "better angel" in our nature. The decline of the former church as a force in the world is partly a good thing since that church embraced much that was false, but it has left a vacuum at the heart of western civilization (once known as Christendom) which the New Church must fill.

Here are four specific ideas of what we can do:

1. Identify and help those in the world around us who have similar goals. There are various groups with whom we may not agree completely but with whom we can make common cause in combating certain moral disorders.

2. Write books and articles and use the internet to spread knowledge of New Church ideas, especially in relation to cultural issues. Bryn Athyn College, as well as our theological school, are vitally needed

to prepare scholars to do this. In this age of mass communication, especially, ideas are more important than numbers. The New Church is small in numbers, but very large in terms of ideas.

3. Live our own lives in such a way as to provide an example to others of the value of our religious beliefs in forming a healthy and beautiful culture. Our worship services, schools, communities, and homes should have a distinct sphere around them that will affect others. People should be able to detect a special flavor and fragrance permeating all that we say and do.

4. We need to be very aware of how important human freedom is, on every level. We need to think carefully about the Divine source and purpose of freedom, the nature of the truth that makes freedom possible, and the kind of responsibility, self-discipline and civil order required to preserve it; and then take advantage of every opportunity to defend genuine human liberty, and oppose false ideas of freedom that make a mockery of the real thing. "When liberty becomes license, dictatorship is near." (Will Durant)

In conclusion, consider the rich meaning of the word "culture." The word "cult" in it reminds us that a culture is produced and sustained by a church. Its resemblance to the word "cultivate" reminds us that a culture is an on-going work that needs to be tended and that it is the ground in which truths can take root and grow to produce good fruits. Think of what the word "culture" means in biology and medicine: a medium in which an organism is grown. A civilization is the medium in which human beings and the church they compose can grow.

A culture is a living thing and like all living things, it receives its life from the only source of life, the One who says: "It is the spirit that gives life; the flesh profits nothing. The words that I speak to you are spirit, and they are life" (John 6.63). The One who says: "Behold, I make all things new" (Rev. 21.5). ⚕

Concluding Essay: Suggestions for the Future

MICHAEL H. HOGAN*

The studies presented in this volume focus on an array of specific topics within the broader theological context of the Last Judgment. I will refer to several specifically later in this essay. They are excellent examples of historical and analytical scholarship. It is clear, however, that the nature of the Last Judgment presents the New Church scholar with an immense methodological challenge, i.e., given that the preservation of human freedom necessitated an invisible Last Judgment, we are left with the difficult task of describing the affects of an event which was intentionally kept beyond normal human sensibility.

How do we develop a theoretical framework to meet that challenge? I propose the following program. First, we attempt to locate, in human history, a series of transformational events that occurred in the general time frame of the Last Judgment. Second, these events would need to lie in cultural locations connected to what we know occurred in the Last Judgment. Third, these events should be seen to derive in a predictable way, from influx coming from the spiritual world.

This essay attempts to present such a framework for consideration. I take as my starting point the social process known as the "industrial revolution." This revolutionary event is seen by many historians as the foundational event of the modern world. In fact, the central challenge in the social sciences for past two centuries has been to explain this "revolution" and the societal modernization which accompanies it.[1]

* The author wishes to acknowledge the technical assistance of Dr. Gregory Baker in the construction of Figures 2 and 3, as well as the assistance of Kendra Knight in the preparation of the draft of this essay.

What caused the vast changes that occurred between late medieval Europe and modern times? What accounts for the vast explosion of material wealth in eighteenth and nineteenth century Europe relative to the rest of the world? This paper uses the concept of "GDP/capita" as a measure of social wealth. The GDP is defined as the sum total of all goods and services produced by a society in a given year. The division of that amount by the society's population in that year is the "GDP/capita." Economists use this value as a rough indication of the wealth available to individuals in that society at a given point in time. To assure the comparability of these data across time and place, a fixed currency value is chosen as a constant. In this paper, that currency is the purchasing power of the 1990 U.S. dollar.

A derivative challenge has been to account for changes in tribal societies after their contact with economically advanced western nations. These problems have driven intellectual disciplines just as in the real world they have driven history. What caused this fundamental break in the nature of the world society? Figure 1 presents these questions in their clearest form.

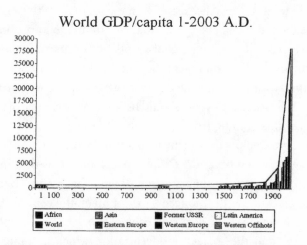

Figure 1. World GDP per Capita. Data Source: Angus Maddison. "World Population, GDP and Per Cepita GDP, 1–2003 AD" at the Groningen Growth and Development Centre. http://www.ggdc.net/, 2005. This image has been released into the public domain by its author, Ultramarine at the wikipedia project. This applies worldwide. (Y axis is in constant 1990 dollars, x axis is in years)

As Figure 1 makes clear, world per capita GDP remained constant (in the $400–450 range per year) for over 1500 years. This value held true for all areas of the world for which any data exist. The trend line for this period has no upward slope. Beginning around 1500 and continuing to 1700 the trend line for Western Europe has a slight upward slope while the rest of world remains constant. This initial increase in GDP per capita was primarily due to returns from foreign trade. This trade was made possible by ingenious shipping and navigational innovation created by the Europeans. These developments were applications of a much larger scientific revolution originating in the sixteenth and seventeenth centuries. These accomplishments were then interactively diffused throughout the continent by means of the printing press. Thus, the Europeans were able to penetrate into all the world's oceans. The riches brought back from these voyages, whether the gold and silver plundered by the Spaniards and the Portuguese or the trade goods carried by the Dutch, English, and French accounted for the gradual rise in European per capita GDP between 1500 to 1700. Angus Maddison, a leading quantitative historian of economics sums up the process as follows:

> These developments in Europe were an essential prelude to the much faster economic development that occurred in the nineteenth and twentieth centuries. [*They had no counterparts in other parts of the world.*] (emphasis added) [2]

Between 1700 and 1820 the trend line for Western Europe again increased its upward slope relative to the rest of the world. In this case, however, the increased per capita GDP does not include bullion extraction, since the Spanish colonies had already begun to decline, but rather to the growing manufacturing wealth and trade of Great Britain with her Western off-shoots (the United States, Canada, Australia, and later New Zealand). During this crucial period a fundamental change had transformed the process of wealth production. It was becoming mechanized. This process, once started, developed an increasing momentum. The slope of the growth line trends dramatically upward between 1820 and 1900. In the West, per capita GDP increased by over three times during this eighty year period. These growth rates were sustained and indeed accelerated. Unlike the growth of the Spanish Empire, which collapsed after the flow of precious metals ended, the Anglo-American world continued to expand. This expansion exploded by the end of the twentieth century as the per capita GDP in the West increased over five times what it had been in 1900. This growth spread to all areas of the world to such an extent that at present the world per capita GDP is ten times greater than it had ever been in the entire history of mankind. A world-transforming event such as this had never occurred before.

	1000	1500	1700	1820	1870	1913	1973	1998
United Kingdom	400	714	1,250	1,707	3,191	4,921	12,022	18,714
Western Europe	400	774	1,200	1,232	1,974	3,473	11,534	17,921
Western Offshoots (US+CA+ AUS+NZ)	400	400	473	1,201	2,431	5,257	16,172	26,416
Asia (excluding Japan)	450	572	571	575	543	640	1,231	2,936
Africa	416	400	400	418	444	585	1,365	1,368
World	435	565	615	667	867	1,510	4,104	5,709

Table 1: GDP Per Capita presents these data in detailed form: Adapted from: Angus Maddison, *The World Economy: a Millennial Perspective* OECD, 2001.

The apparent cause of this income growth was the mechanization of production on a large scale, i.e. industrialization. This change was readily observed by contemporary witnesses, and given the benefit of hindsight, it is clear to us today. It also seems clear that while the world was eventually affected, these events began in Great Britain during the eighteenth century and spread to the Anglo-American world and Western Europe. So decisive was this process that Eric Hobsbawm, the dean of twentieth century social historians, stated that "the British Industrial revolution was the most fundamental transformation in the history of the world recorded in written documents."[3]

There were several competing explanations put forward to account for this process. At one point in the late nineteenth and early twentieth centuries an evolutionary approach, Social Darwinism was favored. It posited that the inherent racial superiority of the Anglo-Saxon peoples accounted for their economic prosperity. Thus it became the "white man's burden" to bring civilization to other, less advanced, parts of the world. Its racial and reactionary character provoked intense conflict and it was ultimately defeated. Another contender was economic determinism, Marxism, which attempted to both predict and control society based on a complex analysis of "class relations to the means of production." This approach also provoked genocidal conflict. Other approaches emphasized a cultural evolutionary process but they too were abandoned as they appeared to justify paternalism and colonial power relations. These naturalistic approaches have failed to provide a satisfying explanation of modernization. Thus, the underlying question of the "Cause of Modern Times" remains unanswered. Today, the explanations are more modest but they remain firmly in the naturalist tradition.

Currently it is argued that the great changes in wealth, technology, and social values which we now experience had their specific origins in the industrial revolution of the eighteenth century. These economic changes were then supplemented by cultural changes which essentially derived from them. This model is the one which dominates social science discussions of development. In the brief discussion which follows I will analyze this approach, using historical data on world per capital GDP because these data are universally accepted in the development literature as the most straightforward indication of modernization. I will then use this discussion to suggest that a New Church frame of reference is more inclusive in its explanatory power and expands the scope of discussion to include a greater range of human activities.

During the 1970s and 80s several economic historians began to argue that the Industrial Revolution occurred much more gradually than had been previously thought, that it had its roots in much earlier periods, and that the impact of these changes had been overstated. They also argued that the dominant (Eurocentric) view undervalued the scientific and technical achievements of other areas of the world and accorded a privileged position to the West. Two areas of the world were particularly put forward as examples of economic and technical innovation which were slighted by the Western dominated approach i.e. Imperial China and the Islamic Middle East. This "gradualist" approach sparked an intense intellectual debate. It contended with the more traditional historians who argued that the Industrial Revolution represented a true "discontinuity" in social history. This acrimonious and politicized conflict finally resulted in the ascendancy of the "discontinuity" position.[4] The present consensus not only stresses the abruptness of this process but also located Great Britain as the primary starting point for it. Joel Mokyr, the leading modern historian of economic development states, "The historical record indicated without any doubt that European technology and institutions moved from Europe elsewhere, and that this spreading coupled to the continuing advance of the West, constitutes the central dynamic force of modern times."[5]

However, historians still divided over two major issues: 1) when the divergence between West and East began in earnest and 2) how to explain it. The first issue has been resolved in general terms. Social antecedents for the Industrial Revolution date from the 1740s and 1750s[6] while the actual mechanization of production began in the Manchester and Birmingham areas in the 1780s. Modernized production processes then found their way into Western Europe by the 1830s. It was during this period that the "divergence between West and East" became apparent. The second issue, "how to explain it," is still being hotly debated by opposing sides. These may be grouped under two headings: those who give precedence to technological/institutional explanations and those who favor cultural ones. Although these two explanations appear to differ and have generated a truly profound discussion of modernization as part of their century-old debate, there is an essential underlying assumption which unites them. That underlying assumption is naturalism.[7]

The leading proponent of the technological/institutional approach has been Simon Kuznets. He has argued consistently that "the cause of economic growth is knowledge." He places great stress on the growth of science.[8] However, this growth requires an institutional context. Science must be placed at the service of production. As C.A. Blyth explains Kuznets' argument, "High rates of growth associated with the application of new scientific knowledge and technical innovation to production problems make a shift in the structure of production likely."[9] These changes have a progressive impact. Blyth continues:

> Structural changes lead to other economic changes which *affect the political and social system and beliefs*, leading to changed conditions of work and life and their effects on demand. This process becomes on-going because the application of new knowledge to production and high rates of growth are indispensable for growth in the stock of useful knowledge and of science itself (the major permissive factor in modern economic growth). [emphasis added][10]

Without structures to put science to use, Kuznets argues, "It will not prove useful any more than it did in the ancient world." "Ancient World" in this context refers to the empires and city states which existed in southern Europe, western Asia and northern Africa from approximately 2000 BC to 650 AD. The term is primarily used by Western historians. Kuznets uses the term in this way. His statement points out the failure of the "ancient world" to generate sustainable economic growth. That world was reasonably stable, possessed vast resources, was inhabited by intelligent, organized people and had on occasion, reasonably efficient political systems. And yet during its entire length it never generated an annual GDP per capita beyond $450. The last great state of this world, Justinian's Roman Empire was finally destroyed by a fatal combination of bubonic plague and Islamic conquest in the early seventh century. This began a period of chaos and confusion which lasted for hundreds of years. It was not until the sixteenth century that Western Europe generated annual per capita GDP of approximately $700. The remainder of the world did not reach this level until the nineteenth and early twentieth century. Kuznets' analysis is quantitative and relies on institutional structures to apply science to concrete problems. As I emphasized in Blyth's quote, Kuznets sees societal and cultural changes *following* from the technological innovations. He states this progression with additional force in *Economic Growth and Structure*.

> The transformation of an underdeveloped into a developed country is not merely the mechanical addition of a stock of physical capital; it is a thoroughgoing revolution in the patterns of life and a cardinal change in the relative power and position of various groups in the population.[11]

Note that even though Kuznets mentions "mere" mechanical additions he still places them first in his causal sequence. There can be no serious doubt that Kuznets is correct to say that sustained economic development required "the extended applications of science to problems of economic development." The next questions, however, is what else did it require? Why did science not transform the "ancient world"?

An alternate group of scholars addresses this question from a cultural perspective. They see values and beliefs as fundamentally important to rapid development. A leading member of this group, Margaret C. Jacobs, provides the following analysis.

> There is such a thing as Western Culture. Its components differed from country to country at any given time, yet by the mid-eighteenth century there was one common element that would prove immensely germane to the mechanization of the manufacturing and transportation systems: the belief that science and technology could control nature and that creativity in both was desirable.[12]

Jacobs stresses the West's belief in the value, i.e., the "rightness," of controlling nature. This preceded the mechanization process and *legitimized* it. It provided a cultural foundation for it as well as a continuing justification. The boldest statement of the cultural perspective comes, ironically, from a senior historian of technology, David Landes. "If we learn anything from the history of economic development it is that culture makes all the difference . . . what counts is work, thrift, honesty, patience, tenacity"[13]. Although there is a great deal of truth in this statement, it is obviously too general to provide an explanation for a specific historical event. These character traits have existed throughout human history without producing an Industrial Revolution. The import of Landes' perspective is more fully developed in his discussion of "sustained growth."

> Sustained growth is not possible without technological progress and gains in productivity. And that, history tells us, requires sooner or later the creation or assimilation of new kinds of knowledge and organization, which in turn depends on transformations within the society. . . . Such transformations require not only the absorption and adoption of new ways, but also, in many societies, the creation and acceptance of a new ethic of personal behavior. *New ways demand and make new people.* Time consciousness must become time discipline: the organization and character of work, *the very relations of person to person, are transformed.* These changes do not come easy [emphasis added].[14]

There are two implications to Landes' commentary that deserve mention here: first, that "new ways . . . make new people" and second, that "relations of person to person are transformed." These cultural transformations are in response to "the organization and character of work." They must follow from it if modernization is to take hold. If a nation cannot make the necessary cultural changes it will fail to produce "sustained growth." On this sequence of change, both Kuznets and Landes—both the technological/institutional and the cultural positions – are in agreement. They see the process unfolding as follows: scientific innovation > alteration of organization of work > increased economic output > cultural/family adaptations > social adjustments > political transformations. The links in this causal chain are identical whether one emphasizes a technological or cultural approach. The differences between them are essentially matters of emphasis. To put it another way: they both argue that however a technical improvement in production is generated, it cannot be *sustained* unless a derivative and significant cultural change takes place to institutionalize it. In the Ancient World these cultural changes did not follow on after the production innovations. They could not overcome the entrenched interests of the existing society. Therefore, the Ancient World did not modernize. This latter point is worth emphasis. Kuznets is correct to argue that the transformation of a society to accommodate to a technical innovation is extremely difficult. Indeed, for most of human history it has proven impossible. The resistance of privileged groups, enduring cultural patterns, and social inertia have defeated innovations on a consistent basis. These are still extremely powerful in the developing world today. When production innovation confronts unified cultural resistance it will almost always fail to transform a society. In our own day it has required widespread colonial domination to bring about even limited social changes. The social costs of that process have been extraordinary. The question remains; how did western technical innovations "transform Anglo-American" and European society if they were confronted by a unified and hostile cultural environment? I do not believe that the answer can be found in either of the approaches that have been discussed thus far.

I wish to propose a different approach. Instead of assuming that the changes in the eighteenth and nineteenth centuries occurred sequentially, each following in a general causal pattern from the mechanization of production, to cultural adaptation, I propose a model which hypothesizes the simultaneous emergence of these changes within a single culture area: Western Europe and its dependencies. I propose this as a model consistent with the spiritual assumption of the Last Judgment (see my introductory essay), but also because it best fits the empirical, historical data available to us. I further propose that the social/cultural changes in the West of the period, while emerging independently, had a distinctly positive effect on per capita GDP when combined with the changes in production then occurring. I would further argue that several of these changes (e.g., value of science, religious sanction of useful knowledge, increased fertility rates, early onset of monogamous marriage, increased rural infant survival rates) actualy preceded and facilitated the transformation of production and added essential momentum to it.

By way of illustration, let us return to the graph of world per capita GDP (Figure 1) at the beginning of this essay. Note the increasing slope of the income curve from 1700 to 2003. In Figure 2 the two trend lines from Figure 1 are broken out. The first measures the aggregate world GDP while the second expresses that for the West. (Please suspend the valid methodological caution that aggregate world GDP is largely driven by contact with the West. These graphs are approximate schematics and for illustration only.)

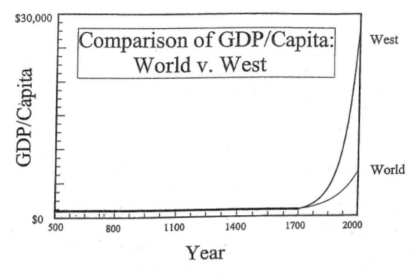

Figure 2: Comparison of GDP/Capita World v. West

As has been pointed out, the essential divergence of these lines began in the eighteenth century. I propose that the increasing slope of the West's income line is not consistent with the Landes-Kuznets hypothesis. They argue that the cultural resistance to economic innovation is a lengthy and energy consuming process. It involved profound social transformations, i.e., creating "new people." The phenomenal rise in Western GDP per capita after 1700 is not a congenial fit for this process as they describe it.

A truer fit for the Landes-Kuznets hypothesis is actually the slope of the World per capita GDP from 1700 to the present. In this instance, the changes in production processes were brought to non-Western cultures from the outside. These truly were met by strong indigenous resistance from many levels of these societies. In most instances, this resistance was led by the local elites. In reality, the history of the world for the past four centuries is largely the saga of conquest, resistance, and adaptation in the period following European contact. If these changes were occurring sequentially in the West as Landes-Kuznets would suggest, then the West's aggregated per capita GDP for the period would resemble that of the world in general rather than being several orders of magnitude greater.

In contrast, my hypothesis suggests that in the West, congenial cultural changes were occurring somewhat before or *at the same time* as the production changes and were not "caused" by them. These cultural changes seem to me to be disparate manifestations of spiritual freedom applied to various social relationships and organizations. They tended to weaken the hold of traditional society. I propose that all of these changes then entered into a synergistic relationship, within the same cultural milieu to produce "modernity" as we know it today. At this point I return to the suggestive comment made by Angus Maddison, "These [intellectual] developments [occurred] in Europe. . . . They had no counterparts in other parts of the world." The earlier essays by Dristy and Baker in this volume should be read to provide a deeper context for Maddison's remarks.[15]

If we look briefly at some of the major cultural occurrences of the seventeenth and eighteenth centuries they do not bear a consistent relationship to the emerging manufacturing economy. The movement for political freedom and reform began in the American colonies and France in the 1760s and 1780s;[16] the free labor movement (antislavery) began in Sweden in the 1770s.[17] Increased fertility and early marriage date from the English countryside of the 1740s and 1750s,[18] while women's suffrage movements gathered momentum in the rural and religious counties of western New York and Ohio in the 1820s.[19] As Jane Williams-Hogan pointed out earlier in this volume, "the songs of innocence" were heard and heeded at this time as well. This increased the *moral* value of children *before* large advances in food production increased their economic value.[20]

The list goes on and on. The essential points to keep in mind about these developments are their spatial dispersion within the cultural context of Western Christianity and their relative simultaneity with economic developments. These movements were definitely not originated to somehow aid the mechanization of production nor were they a response to it. They had altogether different aims and justified themselves on essentially religion and moral grounds.[21] What is undeniable however, is that when these movements interacted with those transforming the economic structure of society they created the most powerful engine of economic prosperity in the history of the world. The detailed explanation of how these changes became "cultural multipliers" of economic growth is an ongoing project for future New Church scholarship. However, the general direction of their impact is quite clear.

Figure 3 presents my hypothesis in schematic form:

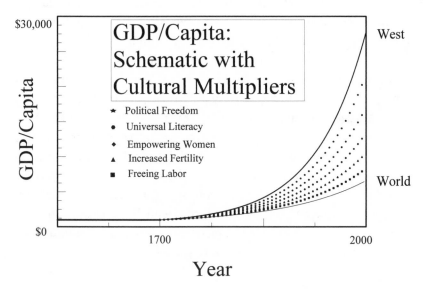

Figure 3. GDP per capita: Schematic with Cultural Multipliers

The multiplier effects depicted here are for conceptual illustration. Clearly, they are not immediately quantifiable. I suggest that cultural multipliers propelled the West's GDP per capita above the World's aggregate income level. They interacted with each other in a dynamic fashion and moved the West's income line significantly upward as history (time) progressed. I chose these particular cultural variables because of their obvious importance. They correspond to the concept of institutions in the broad sense as defined by Douglass C. North:

Institutions are the humanly devised constraints that structure political, economic and social interactions. They consist of both informal constraints (sanctions, taboos, customs, traditions, codes of conduct) and formal rules, (constitutions, law, and property rights). Throughout history institutions have been devised by human beings to create order and reduce uncertainty in exchange. Together with the standard constraints of economics they define the choice set and therefore determine the transaction costs, and hence the profitability and feasibility of engaging in economic activity.[22]

While we have cast a wide net in the topics covered in these proceedings, we have had to be selective in our coverage. Due to constraints of time and personnel we have said virtually nothing of many important cultural developments. There have been radical changes in the visual arts, literature, dance, music, fashion, medicine, urbanization and family structure occurring during this time period. These changes definitely deepened and contributed to the reality of modernity.

However, as has been pointed out in the first essay of this volume, there is a sobering truth hidden within the extraordinary change of the past three centuries. That truth is the reality of human spiritual freedom. Our ability to choose good or evil has remained constant. Our power, however, has increased exponentially. The tragic history of the twentieth century should provide a vivid incentive to anyone of good faith who seeks to penetrate the secrets of modern life with understanding.

In this concluding essay I have attempted to present a New Church model for analyzing the eighteenth and nineteenth centuries. I have emphasized that the spiritual forces of the Last Judgment brought significant energy toward progress in cultural and economic reality. My aim is to enhance our understanding of this extraordinary period by reinserting the spiritual dimension into the explanatory model. I have complete faith, based on the Writings, that changes in the spiritual world led to the world we now inhabit. I also believe that a New Church perspective presents a more efficient, congruent, and robust explanatory paradigm of these disparate events than do its naturalistic rivals. Only the inherent materialistic bias of modern culture prevents this reality from being more widely known and taught.

It is my hope that the Last Judgment Conference and these proceedings will serve as a stimulus to an expanded reach in New Church intellectual life. As the preceding essays certainly demonstrated, we possess an abundance of highly sophisticated and committed scholars. If we can encourage this group and others like it, to direct their energy to questions where a New Church perspective makes a concrete and distinctive contribution to human knowledge, we will indeed have served a great use. We will have stimulated our own intellectual traditions, but more importantly, we will have reached out to a world struggling desperately to find purpose and peace. ⚘

ENDNOTES

1. The historical sociologist who has made the most profound contribution to this question has been Max Weber (1856–1920). My indebtedness to him will be apparent to those familiar with his work. In particular, his two studies *The Protestant Ethic and the "Spirit" of Capitalism* (1905) and *Economy and Society* (1920) have had an impact on all the social sciences. They are the most important sociology texts of the twentieth century.

2. Maddison, Angus. *Growth and Interaction in the World Economy, The Roots of Modernity*. AEI Press (2001), 30.

3. Hobsbawm, E.J. *Industry and Empire*. Louisiana: Pelican Publishing, 1968, 13.

4. Berg, Maxine, and Pat Hudson. "Rehabilitating the industrial revolution." *Economic History Review* XLV, I (1992), 24–50. This is the definitive article on this controversy and presents both sides of this discussion in depth. Their conclusion is straightforward. "Evidence of radical discontinuity is reappearing at every level of analysis" (41).

5. Mokyr, Joel. "Eurocentricity Triumphant." *The American Historical Review*. 104.4 (Oct. 1999), 323.

6. Goldstone, J.A. "The Demographic revolution in England: a re-evaluation." *Population Studies*. XLI (1986), 5–33. He pays particular attention to the fertility of young marrieds.

7. Synnestvedt, Dan, "Naturalism and the Last Judgment" in *The World Transformed*.

8. Kuznets, Simon. *Economic Growth of Nations*. Cambridge: Harvard University Press, 1971, 323.

9. Blyth, C.A. Review of Kuznets' "Economic Growth of Nations: Total output and Production Structure." *Economica, New Series* 40.160 (Nov. 1973), 457–458.

10. Ibid. Note that the possibility of "social systems and beliefs" determining economic changes is not seriously considered.

11. Kuznet, Simon. *Economic Growth and Structure*. New York: Norton, 1965, 30.

12. Jacobs, Margaret C. "The Cultural Foundations of Early Industrialization" in *Technological Revolutions and Europe*. ed. Maxine Berg and Kristine Bruland. U.K.: Cheltenham, 1998, 80.

13. Landes, David S. *Why Are Some So Rich and Some So Poor* (1998), 80. Landes openly acknowledges his debt to Weber throughout this vital text.

14. Ibid. "Why are We so Rich and They So Poor." The American Economic Review 80:2 (May 1990), 11. Papers and Proceedings of the One Hundredth and Second Annual Meeting of the American Economic Association.

15. Dristy, Forrest. "The Liberation of Mathematics and the Last Judgment" in *The World Transformed* and Baker, Gregory L. "Possible Mathematical and Scientific Consequences of the Last Judgment" in *The World Transformed*.

16. Dibb, Andrew. "Preparation for the Last Judgment: John Locke and Emanuel Swedenborg" in *The World Transformed*.

17. Henderson, Brian. "From Thought to Action: the Last Judgment, Swedenborg and the Antislavery Movement" in *The World Transformed*.

18. Schofield, R.S. "English marriage patterns revisited." *Journal of Family History* 10 (1985), 34–45. I was particularly struck by Schofield's finding that after 1700 changes in fertility (increasing) and age of marriage (decreasing) "were relatively unresponsive to real

wage indices," i.e., they varied independently and were not primarily market driven.

19. Werner, Sonia. "The Last Judgment and Women In The Modern Western World" in *The World Transformed*.

20. Williams-Hogan, Jane. "A New Refrain: 'The Child and Songs of Innocence'" in *The World Transformed*.

21. Appelgren, Göran. "Possible Consequences of the Last Judgment on Society" in *The World Transformed*.

22. North, Douglass C. "Institutions," *The Journal of Economic Perspectives;* vol. 5 no. 1 (Winter 1991), 97. This seminal paper, together with his extensive research in quantitative economic analysis constitutes an extraordinary body of work. He was awarded the Nobel Prize for Economics in 1993. His work provides an extremely important pathway for New Church scholarship on the development of modernity. Unfortunately, we must defer our next steps along that pathway for a future occasion.

Index

human mind
  contiguum of successive degrees or levels   425
  liberation of the   379
Hume, David   330–331, 347, 396, 399
humility   705
Hunt, Harriot   393
Hus, Jan   391
Hutton, James   702
Huygens, Christian   551
hyperbola   473

I

Iblis   102
idealist   ix, x, xi, xii, xiii, xiv
Ideas Have Consequences   701
identity formation of ethnic groups (China)   164–171
idolatry   94, 96, 616
ijtihad   89, 110–111
illegitimate children   197
imaginary numbers   468
Imam, last true   115
immense methodological challenge   721
The Imperative to Find the Ancient Word in China: A Result of the Last Judgment   180
Imperial China   726
India   109–110, 117
individualism   255, 257, 713
industrialization, England   204
Industrial Revolution   721, 725
infancy, in Heavenly Doctrines   241
infant mortality   205, 253
infants and children in eighteenth century   368
Infant School Movement   229, 237, 265, 373
Infant School Society   241
infesters   44, 184

P